THE COLLECTED PAPERS

OF

# JOHN WESTLAKE

ON

PUBLIC INTERNATIONAL LAW

# THE COLLECTED PAPERS

OF

# JOHN WESTLAKE

ON

# PUBLIC INTERNATIONAL LAW

Edited by

L. OPPENHEIM, M.A., LL.D.

Member of the Institute of International Law
Whewell Professor of International Law in the
University of Cambridge

Cambridge:
at the University Press
1914

# CAMBRIDGE
## UNIVERSITY PRESS

University Printing House, Cambridge CB2 8BS, United Kingdom

Published in the United States of America by Cambridge University Press, New York

Cambridge University Press is part of the University of Cambridge.

It furthers the University's mission by disseminating knowledge in the pursuit of education, learning and research at the highest international levels of excellence.

www.cambridge.org
Information on this title: www.cambridge.org/9781107661868

© Cambridge University Press 1914

This publication is in copyright. Subject to statutory exception and to the provisions of relevant collective licensing agreements, no reproduction of any part may take place without the written permission of Cambridge University Press.

First published 1914
First paperback edition 2014

*A catalogue record for this publication is available from the British Library*

ISBN 978-1-107-66186-8 Paperback

Cambridge University Press has no responsibility for the persistence or accuracy of URLs for external or third-party internet websites referred to in this publication, and does not guarantee that any content on such websites is, or will remain, accurate or appropriate.

# EDITOR'S INTRODUCTION

WHEN, soon after the death of Professor Westlake, the first edition of his *Chapters on the Principles of International Law* was exhausted, the Syndics of the University Press resolved, instead of simply bringing out a second edition of this work, to publish a Collection of all the smaller contributions of Westlake to Public International Law and to embody therein a new edition of the *Chapters on the Principles of International Law*. With the consent of Mrs Westlake I undertook the task of editing the present Collection, which comprises all the English papers of Westlake on the subject, with the exception of book reviews. Westlake's French Papers on Public International Law, which for the most part have appeared in the *Revue de Droit International et de Législation Comparée* (see below, Appendix, pp. 678–686), had, for want of space, to be excluded from the present volume; they are, however, easily accessible, since the *Revue de Droit International et de Législation Comparée* is in the hands of all those interested in International Law.

Much thought has been given to the question of the order in which the Papers should be reprinted, and it was finally decided to divide the Collection into two parts, the first to consist of the *Chapters on the Principles of International Law*, and the second to comprise all the other Papers in the chronological order of their appearance. In this way the reader is enabled to follow the literary life of Westlake, in so far as Public International Law is concerned, from 1856, the date of the first Paper, to 1913, the year of his death. But Westlake's literary output was not confined to Public International Law; it extended over a much wider area. For this reason, I have, with the permission of Mrs Westlake, embodied in the present volume, as an Appendix, the list of all the writings of Westlake, printed on pp. 147–154 of the *Memories of John Westlake*, a volume which has been compiled by friends and was published by Messrs Smith, Elder and Co., London, 1914.

All the Papers are here reprinted without alterations, subject to a few misprints which had to be corrected. All the footnotes are Westlake's, with the exception of a few which are bracketed and signed L. O.

To facilitate reference to the various topics discussed, an exhaustive alphabetical index, the diligent work of Mr C. F. Pond, has been added.

I am obliged to Dr Almá Latifi, to the Editors and Proprietors of *The Law Quarterly Review*, the *Journal of the Society of Comparative Legislation*, *The Nineteenth Century and After*, the *Quarterly Review*, and *The Times*, without whose permission, readily given in every case, many Papers could not have been reprinted here.

As regards an appreciation of Westlake's life-work, I cannot write a better short account than the one I gave a few days after his death in *The Cambridge Review* (Vol. XXXIV, No. 854, April 24th,

1913). It is here reprinted by kind permission of the editor:

"By the death of Professor John Westlake, which occurred on Monday, April 14, Cambridge has lost one of her most illustrious sons. Born in 1828, Westlake entered Trinity College in 1846, and in 1850 was sixth wrangler and sixth in the first class of the Classical Tripos. In 1851 he was elected a Fellow of Trinity College. He was called to the Bar in 1854, and became Q.C. and a Bencher of Lincoln's Inn in 1874. He was Whewell Professor of International Law from 1888 to 1908, and he was one of the British members of the International Court of Arbitration at the Hague from 1900 to 1906. Up to the time he was elected Whewell Professor he practised at the Bar, and he was counsel in some memorable cases. But throughout his long life Westlake stood in the foreground as a researcher in, and writer on, International Law. His treatise on Private International Law, which first appeared in 1858, and went through five editions, the last appearing in 1911, was the first systematic exposition of this important subject published in England; it is recognised as a standard work, both in the Courts and in literature. In 1869, together with Asser, of Amsterdam, and Rolin-Jaequemyns, of Ghent, he founded the *Revue de Droit International et de Législation Comparée*, which was the first periodical devoted to International Law; and he continued to be a co-editor and very frequent contributor up to the time of his death. He was, moreover, in 1874, one of the founders of the Institute of International Law, an International Academy comprising 60 Members and 60 Associates, elected from the most prominent International jurists of the world. In 1894 he published an important volume under the title *Chapters on International Law*, which embodies a considerable amount of research concerning a number of matters of Public International Law. In 1904 and 1907 appeared his *International Law*, in two volumes, dealing with 'Peace' and 'War,' which, though it is rather a collection of monographs than a comprehensive treatise, will have great and lasting influence. A second edition of the first volume appeared in 1910, and the second edition of the second volume is now in the press. In 1912 he re-edited, adding a valuable introduction of his own, Balthazar Ayala's *De Jure et Officiis Bellicis et Disciplina Militari Libri III* in the 'Classics of International Law,' published by the Carnegie Institution of Washington, under the general editorship of James Brown Scott. But these works form only the landmarks of Westlake's literary activity; besides them he wrote innumerable papers dealing with a great many questions of Public and Private International Law for English and foreign periodicals. Moreover, the 25 volumes of the *Annuaire de l'Institut de Droit International* comprise several valuable reports on important subjects which Westlake laid before the Institute of International Law. He was a regular attendant at the meetings of the Institute, and his influence there was not surpassed by that of anyone. He was President of the Institute at its meeting in Cambridge in 1895, and he was elected permanent honorary President at its meeting in Madrid in 1910.

" Westlake was a most profound jurist and thinker, with a very wide range of interests. Generations to come will appreciate his works. International Law is, to a great extent, the product of the nineteenth century, and Westlake has assisted much in developing and shaping it. It was characteristic of him that he never evaded difficult problems, but sought them out, faced them, and, so to say, wrestled with them. It is for this reason that almost every page of his works is of importance; every writer on questions of International Law must take into account the opinion of Westlake on the subject concerned. As an authority he was recognized all over the world, and his counsel was frequently sought by the British and by foreign Governments. Especially noteworthy is the influence he exercised over the settlement of the Boundary dispute between this country and Venezuela, in which, in 1896, the United States intervened. In a letter[1] to *The Times* he proposed arbitration of the conflict on certain lines, which were virtually adopted by the Anglo-Venezuelan Arbitration Treaty of 1897.

" As regards his teaching in Cambridge, the present writer does not possess any personal knowledge, but Westlake's influence as the occupant, for 20 years, of the Whewell Chair must have been very considerable. Year after year many students of law, history, and economics went through his class-room. According to information obtained from former pupils of his, all the resources of his erudition were placed freely at their disposal; he spared no pains in directing their studies; and with unfailing courtesy and patience was always ready to aid in all their difficulties. His manner in oral exposition is said to have rendered his influence deep rather than wide,

[1] See below, pp. 414–418.

for he did not address himself to the dull or the idle. Those, however, who followed closely the workings of his powerful and acute intellect derived lasting benefit from his lectures. Most of the living international jurists of England were, at one time or another, his pupils. In a sense it may even be said that every living jurist is his pupil, for his works have been studied by every jurist, British and foreign.

"Although during the last few years of his life Westlake grew physically feeble, his powerful intellect did not show any signs of advancing age. Up to the last he was decidedly progressive in all his ideas, and was distinctly a partisan and a leader of the forward movement in the province of International Law. He belonged to the legal school of international jurists, who, in contradistinction to the members of the diplomatic school, desire International Law to develop more or less on the lines of Municipal Law; who aim at the codification of firm, decisive, unequivocal rules of International Law; who work for the establishment of International Courts for the purpose of the administration of international justice. For this reason he took a very active part in the controversy concerning the ratification of the Declaration of London. It was a great disappointment to him that in consequence of the Naval Prize Bill having been thrown out by the House of Lords in 1911, the Declaration of London could not be ratified and the proposed International Prize Court at the Hague could not be established.

"While appreciating the jurist, one must not forget the man. Westlake's was a most amiable character, and whomsoever he met he made a friend. He was a champion of the oppressed all over the world, as is shown by his work in favour of the Balkan nations and Finland. He was firm, outspoken, sincere, dispassionate ; and, above all, just. He was liberal-minded, and not insular in his ideas. He was free from national, racial, political, and religious prejudices. While he was always zealous for the rights and interests of Great Britain, he nevertheless paid due regard to the rights, and could appreciate the interests, of other countries. His assistance and advice were always at hand for those who asked for them. He was extremely generous in imparting knowledge to others from the vast store he had accumulated ; and no man was ever more ready to recognize merit in others. He was a good fighter, and could hit hard when attacking or attacked ; but there was no personal animosity in his polemics, and, therefore, he made no enemies.

"Westlake's interests were not confined to International Law. He took a leading part in the management, and even in the teaching, at the Working Men's College in London. Besides being a classical scholar, his knowledge of history and political economy was extensive. He took his share in politics, and was returned as a Liberal for the Romford Division of Essex to the Parliament of 1885. However, he disapproved of Mr Gladstone's first Home Rule Bill and seceded from the Liberal party with the other Liberal Unionists, although in all other respects he remained a strong Liberal. His Parliamentary career was short, as he failed to be re-elected in 1886.

"Westlake was of small stature ; yet the fragile

frame carried a most expressive head enlivened by a pair of radiant eyes. On his last appearance in public, on Friday, April 4, at the Historical Congress in London, his face vividly recalled to an old acquaintance of Mazzini's the picturesque lineaments of the great Italian publicist. His bearing was absolutely unassuming; yet wherever he was seen he at once attracted attention by the singularly bright expression of his features, which became particularly illuminated when he rose to speak. He was a fluent speaker with a great command of language, not only in his native tongue, but also in French. The portrait, subscribed for by friends and admirers, and painted by Charles Shannon, A.R.A., in 1910, is a very good likeness of him in his later years; it hangs in the Hall of Trinity College.

"A word must, finally, be said about the great happiness Westlake found in his married life. Mrs Westlake completely identified herself with all the interests of her husband. In the wide circle of his friends, and, in particular, in the small circle of the members of the Institute of International Law, she is as much esteemed as was Professor Westlake himself. His loss will be deeply felt all over the world; and while posterity will record his name as that of a great jurist, those who were fortunate enough to come into personal contact with him will always remember him as a most lovable man."

L. OPPENHEIM.

CAMBRIDGE, *July* 2, 1914.

# CONTENTS

|   | PAGE |
|---|---|
| EDITOR'S INTRODUCTION | v |

## PART I
### CHAPTERS ON INTERNATIONAL LAW

Preface . . . . . . . . . . xix

### CHAPTER I.
#### INTERNATIONAL LAW IN RELATION TO LAW IN GENERAL.

| | |
|---|---|
| International Law the body of Rules between States . . | 1 |
| Law and Society . . . . . . . . | 2 |
| Jural Laws and the Laws of Nature known to Science . | 4 |
| The Society of States compared with other Societies . . | 6 |
| A special point of Contact between International and National Law: Private International Law . . . | 9 |
| Another special point of Contact between International and National Law: Territory and Property: Natural Law, or the Law of Nature as a Jural Conception . . | 10 |
| Austin's Limitation of the term "Law" . . . . | 11 |
| The Moral Law . . . . . . . . | 15 |
| Rights and Wrongs . . . . . . . | 16 |

### CHAPTER II.
#### THEORY BEARING ON INTERNATIONAL LAW DOWN TO THE RENAISSANCE.

| | |
|---|---|
| Greece . . . . . . . . . . | 17 |
| Rome: Jus Gentium . . . . . . . | 18 |
| Rome: Jus Naturale . . . . . . . | 22 |
| The dissolution of the Roman empire: Isidore of Seville . | 23 |
| The Renaissance: Suarez . . . . . . | 25 |

## CHAPTER III.
### AYALA: GENTILIS: GROTIUS.

|  | PAGE |
|---|---|
| Ayala | 30 |
| Gentilis | 33 |
| Grotius | 36 |

## CHAPTER IV.

The Peace of Westphalia and Pufendorff . . . . 52

## CHAPTER V.
### BYNKERSHOEK: WOLFF: VATTEL.

| Bynkershoek | 66 |
|---|---|
| Wolff | 70 |
| Vattel | 76 |

## CHAPTER VI.

The Principles of International Law . . . . . 78

## CHAPTER VII.
### THE EQUALITY AND INDEPENDENCE OF STATES.

The Independence and Legal Equality of States, and Semi-Sovereignty . . . . . . . . 86
The Political Inequality of States, and the Great Powers of Europe . . . . . . . . . 92
The Equality of States in Civilisation, and the Protection of Subjects abroad . . . . . . . 101

## CHAPTER VIII.
### INTERNATIONAL RIGHTS OF SELF-PRESERVATION.

Self-preservation as an alleged Primary Right . . . 111
Rights of Self-preservation actually allowed by International Law . . . . . . . . . 115
The Balance of Power . . . . . . . 121
Alleged right of Self-preservation against the Contagion of Revolution . . . . . . . . 123
Self-preservation as a ground of Criminal Jurisdiction . 126

## CHAPTER IX.

### Territorial Sovereignty, especially with relation to Uncivilised Regions.

|  | PAGE |
|---|---|
| Territorial Sovereignty distinguished from Property | 131 |
| The Title to Territorial Sovereignty | 136 |
| The Position of Uncivilised Natives with regard to International Law | 139 |
| Government the International Test of Civilisation | 143 |
| Treaties with Uncivilised Tribes | 145 |
| Discovery and Occupation as International Titles | 158 |
| The Inchoate Title by Discovery or Occupation | 163 |
| The Ripening of an Inchoate Title into a Complete one | 166 |
| The Geographical Extent of International Titles in Uncivilised Regions | 169 |
| Alleged International Title by Civilising Influence exerted beyond the limits of Occupation | 177 |
| Protectorates in Uncivilised Regions | 181 |
| Spheres of Influence | 191 |

## CHAPTER X.

### The Empire of India.

| | |
|---|---|
| The East India Company and Companies in general | 194 |
| Rise of the British Empire in India, from the point of view of International Law | 197 |
| The Empire of India in relation to International Law | 216 |
| The Empire of India in relation to Constitutional Law | 224 |

## CHAPTER XI.

### War.

| | |
|---|---|
| The Rules of War considered as Laws | 237 |
| Principles relating to Particular Military Operations | 241 |
| Principles relating to the Conduct of War generally: Kriegsmanier and Kriegsraison | 243 |
| The treatment of the Peaceable Population, and of Private Property on Land and at Sea | 250 |
| Retorsion | 259 |
| The General Theory of the Relation of Subjects to a War | 264 |
| Humanity in War | 271 |
| The Improvement of the Laws of War | 274 |

# PART II

## MISCELLANEOUS PAPERS

| | | PAGE |
|---|---|---|
| I. | Relations between Public and Private International Law. 1856 | 285 |
| II. | Commercial Blockade. 1862 | 312 |
| III. | Is it desirable to Prohibit the Export of Contraband of War? 1870 | 362 |
| IV. | Introductory Lecture on International Law. 17 October, 1888 | 393 |
| V. | The Venezuelan Boundary Question. 1896 | 414 |
| VI. | The Transvaal War. 1899 | 419 |
| VII. | Continuous Voyage in relation to Contraband of War. 1899 | 461 |
| VIII. | The Nature and Extent of the title by Conquest. 1901 | 475 |
| IX. | The South African Railway Case and International Law. 1905 | 490 |
| X. | Is International Law a part of the Law of England? 1906 | 498 |
| XI. | Contraband of War. 1907 | 519 |
| XII. | The Muscat Dhows. 1907 | 523 |
| XIII. | The Hague Conferences. 1908 | 531 |
| XIV. | Holland and Venezuela. 1908 | 568 |
| XV. | Pacific Blockade. 1909 | 572 |
| XVI. | Reprisals and War. 1909 | 590 |
| XVII. | Trade Domicile in War. 1909 | 607 |
| XVIII. | Belligerent Rights at Sea. 1909 | 613 |
| XIX. | The Native States of India. 1910 | 620 |
| XX. | The Declaration of London. 1910 | 633 |
| XXI. | The Declaration of London. 1911 | 651 |
| XXII. | The Aegean Islands. 1913 | 676 |
| | Appendix: A List of the Writings of John Westlake | 678 |
| | Index | 687 |

# PART I

## CHAPTERS ON INTERNATIONAL LAW

## PREFACE

THIS book is not a detailed treatise on international law, but an attempt to stimulate and assist reflection on its principles. It is primarily intended in part performance of a professor's duty to his university, though not without hope that it may be of use to others as well. International law being the science of what a state and its subjects ought to do or may do with reference to other states and their subjects, everyone should reflect on its principles who, in however limited a sphere of influence, helps to determine the action of his country by swelling the volume of its opinion. Indeed to prepare men for the duties of citizenship is the chief justification for introducing into education a subject which, on account of its inevitable defect in precision, is less suited as a training for the mind than as an exercise for the trained mind. Again, international law is not a highly technical subject, and it would be a mistake to aim at giving it more technicality by the mode of treating it. The law of a country is bound by written enactments and recorded judicial deliverances, and the procedure for applying it is as fixed as the law and by similar means. Hence arise struggles between the letter and the spirit, and the spirit receives no effect unless means can be found of bringing it within the letter. But there is little of the letter, little of express convention or authoritative formula, to enter into the problem of determining the duty of a state towards its neighbours. If any one says that the technical duty of a state is to take or abstain from taking a certain course, but that in the given circumstances it may justifiably act otherwise, we may be pretty sure that he had no sufficient reason for laying down the technical duty in the terms which he has chosen. On more than one ground, therefore, there ought in this case to be less than the usual difficulty in combining academic and general readers.

In the first chapter the reader is invited to consider shortly the place of international law among the sciences, and in what sense it is law. This is necessary because the writers on our subject speak much of a law of nature, which has to be distinguished from the laws of nature familiar to us in what are called the natural sciences. It is also necessary because of the dominant position which certain views of John Austin have held in the English universities, as to which therefore I must ask the general reader to excuse a few sentences which will scarcely interest him. That eminent thinker rendered great service by elucidating the various elements, psychological states and states of fact, which have to be provided for by the law of a country, and the knowledge of which makes up the larger part of what in the English universities is called jurisprudence. But he prefaced his system by analysing the law of a country into commands addressed by a sovereign to subjects, including in his description of the sovereign all those who participate in the supreme authority. And the definition of the law of a country which resulted from that analysis he gave as the definition of law, so that international law, not being set by an Austinian sovereign to Austinian subjects, was in his view not law at all, but what he called positive international morality. Now this was beside the mark of what followed in his own lectures. In elucidating the elements with which the law of a country must be concerned Austin found no use for his definition of law, perhaps it was impossible to find any ; and thus we are fortunately able to retain most of the fruits of his labour, unaffected by the doubt which has at last arisen about that definition.

What is called the historical school contends that Austin's definition is not applicable to law in all states of society or under all political systems, in particular that customary law often exists in communities in which they tell us that no Austinian sovereign issuing Austinian commands can be pointed out ; and they bid us begin our study by enquiring what law has in fact been in its various forms, from the earliest times which can be traced, and from the rudest savages that can be found, to the most highly organised of modern states. Those on the other hand who demand that some clue shall be given before that labyrinth is entered are called the analytical school, and in England it has been too often assumed that no one can belong to the analytical school without accepting Austin's definitions. I am keenly sensible of the interest and value of historical and even of prehistorical investigations, informing us of institutions and states of society remote from our own. We learn from them how the different peoples whom we study usually conducted themselves with regard to family, property, or any other matter which in our actual England is regulated by law ; by what beliefs and motives, and by what commands or compulsion if any, their conduct was kept to its usual lines. And by accumulating a number of such investigations we learn how what we now know as the law of a country has arisen. But the analytical school are certainly right in maintaining that, if we give the name of law to anything which we so discover in a remote state of society before we have fixed in our minds what we mean by that name, we beg the question, and have no security that our language has any consistent, or therefore useful, sense.

It does not therefore seem to me admissible to dispense with an analytical enquiry into what we mean by law, but whatever merit Austin's analysis may have for the law of a country, his treatment of international matters appears to be inadequate, as notwithstanding his great ability it well may have been from his not having given them much attention. We may grant, though it has been disputed, that a sovereign in his sense, the commanding part or body, may always be found in a state if looked for carefully ; also, what cannot be disputed, that no commanding part or body can be found among the states of Europe and America. Still, it will not follow that there is nothing in the intercourse between those states which can be more properly classed with law than with morality. Whether that is so must be determined by observation, and observation will probably bring us back to certain very ancient conclusions. We may find that, besides approving conduct as moral or reprobating it as immoral, men distinguish the morality which they deem from that which they do not deem themselves justified in enforcing; that every society tries to express that distinction in rules suitable to the purpose for which it exists, and acts on it with more or less consistency; that the nation with its law is merely the strongest case in point; and that another case, not less real because weaker, is presented by the society of states with its international law. And we may find an incidental advantage in having cleared the foundations of our subject from Austin's nomenclature. His definition of a sovereign included that the person or body called by that name should not only be the commanding portion of the state, but should not be, himself or itself, subject to any commands, in other words, should be independent. Now sovereignty and independence are terms of international law, but at least in that science they belong to the state as a whole and not to any part of it. In the system of Europe and America a state is accepted as a unit, whatever may be its internal constitution. It is the state, and not the Austinian sovereign within it, that is sovereign and independent. Consequently an attempt to adhere to the nomenclature which we have rejected might have led to confusion, and to enquiries, irrelevant to international law, as to where in any political body the Austinian sovereignty lies.

We can now return to matters of more general interest. The international lawyer is in search of the rules existing in the international society and more or less enforced by it, but very few of those rules have been laid down by conventions between states. They must be looked for in the practice of states; but when a practice is quoted as carrying authority, it must be further shown that it has not consisted of a number of purely voluntary acts or abstentions, but that the thing has been done or abstained from in obedience to a persuasion that such was the law. Thus the appeal to practice obliges us to join with it the study of opinion, and there are cases in which we are driven to the study of opinion alone, because no practice may exist on the point in question, or because we may be called on to recognize that, through a change of opinion, an old practice has ceased to be accompanied by the general persuasion of enforceable right without which it cannot be law. We also have to examine the history of international relations for the purpose of seeing how far in different ages a real society has existed between states; from what date the society which now exists between them in Europe and America may be reckoned, so that its practice may be quoted as carrying authority; and how the development of opinion has been connected with the changes in international relations. All this forms a complicated investigation, the parts of which act and react on one another, and the historical method seems to be the best for entering upon it. Therefore in the chapters from the second to the fifth I ask the reader to accompany me from ancient Greece to the middle of the eighteenth century, confining his attention to the most important events and thinkers, for which alone there is room in so short a sketch, but to which, even in a larger work, it would be desirable to introduce him before entering into further detail on any part. It has sometimes seemed to me that the brief accounts of the older writers which are given in modern treatises have lost, in passing from hand to hand, a little of their likeness to the originals, and that the points in the originals which are selected for mention are rather those to which later systems attach the most importance than those which best represent the thought of the writers. The great work of Grotius is especially one of which it would be difficult to form either an adequate or even a correct notion from the few lines in which his opinions are usually mentioned, and some pains have here been taken to represent it as it is. The Peace of Westphalia has been dwelt on with insistence, as marking the era from which the existing international society dates, and as giving important help towards understanding its nature.

It is, or ought to be, familiar to all who have engaged in these studies that communion of thought between England and the Continent meets with a certain difficulty from the fact that *jus, droit, recht*—in Latin, French and German—combine the two meanings of law and right, which in English are so sharply distinguished that there is no word combining them. Latin, though as widely known in England as in any other country, does not make us sufficiently alive to the circumstance, because law, which to an Englishman is apt to appear the more important meaning of the two, is also the predominant meaning of *jus*. But *droit* and *recht*, when not used with a definite reference to the law of a country, seems to carry to a French or German ear a sense of which the nearest English equivalent would oftener be right than law. This does not place the continental thinker in Austin's point of view. The international right which he understands by *le droit international* is something more than that conduct which is entitled to moral approval. It is a true jural right, which, as he holds, not only ought to reign but ought to be made to reign in the conduct of states. But there is a difference between him and the English thinker. Both those who speak of international law and those who speak of *le droit international* may regard their subject as being the body of rules of a society, but the former would think primarily of the rules, and then of the right as ordinarily measured by them, the latter primarily of the right, and then of the rules as ordinarily embodying it. Both may regard the rules as to be obeyed, subject to exceptions, but the former would regard the exceptions as matter rather for casuistry than for law, while the latter would see in them the vindication of a higher jural right. The practical difference would be most felt when the change of a rule was advocated. Those whose prepossession was chiefly with law, while unable to contend that in the absence of an organised legislature law might not be changed by the same power of opinion which had established it, would be slow to admit the change. But those whose prepossession was chiefly with right would be impatient of the continued existence of any rule which they no longer believed to embody it. The prepossession with right, though not necessarily united with the notion of abstract or primary rights inherent in persons and states, is apt to lead to it: towards the end of the historical chapters I have introduced the reader to that notion in speaking of Wolff, who made it one of the foundations of his system. All the more important considerations having, it is hoped, been brought forward and received some discussion in the pages thus far referred to, I proceed in Chapter vi to the delicate task of laying down the general principles of international law in short form. My point of view is that of law, and I think that the paragraphs which I have drawn up express what is generally held in England, while the more moderate of those who set out from right will perhaps not substantially dissent from them, though for themselves they would have expressed some of them differently.

Coming now to particular principles, Chapter VII explains those concerning the legal equality of states, their political inequality, and the position and protection of the subjects of a state when in foreign countries or contracting with foreign governments. These are matters which, if we set out from the idea of primary rights, would fall under those of independence and equality. Chapter VIII deals with what, in such a system, would be placed under the primary right of self-preservation, and discusses the alleged right and the actual rules relating to the matter.

Chapter IX is devoted to the nature and acquisition of territorial sovereignty, with the allied topics of protectorates in uncivilised regions and spheres of influence, and contains much on which controversy may be expected. It is based on a sharp distinction between territorial sovereignty and property, with a consequent abandonment of those arguments relating to the former which have been derived from the Roman law as to the latter or from feudalism. This position has not been previously taken up by any English writer, and it was necessary to fill the void by a new treatment of the title to territorial sovereignty, especially in uncivilised regions, with regard to which the Roman doctrine of occupation as a natural mode of acquiring property had been made to do duty. Hence again it was necessary to consider the relation of civilised powers and their international law to uncivilised natives, and the nature and limits of the rights which such powers and their subjects can possibly derive from the natives by the treaties which have been so much in vogue in Africa. The great human interest of that question would of itself have been a sufficient motive for its introduction into this book, even had it not been required for the scientific purpose mentioned. My views as to natives and treaties with them, and on inchoate titles and the conditions for their completion, have already been published in the *Revue de Droit International*, in connection with the disputes of a few years since between England and Portugal. In dealing with protectorates in uncivilised regions, I have pointed out the radical distinction between them and protectorates over states, and have tried to put this new form of territorial aggrandisement on its proper and independent basis.

Chapter x is an attempt to make the British position in India scientifically intelligible. Here again the great interest of the subject would have justified its introduction, even did not our position, and the steps by which it has been attained, illustrate more than one of the principles that have formed the topics of the preceding chapters. The discussion which the subject here receives has been greatly facilitated by the recent publications of Mr Tupper and Mr Lee-Warner, but it had already occupied my attention.

The eleventh and last chapter of the present series treats of the principles of the laws of war as between belligerents. Attention has been drawn in it to the extreme license on the ground of necessity which has received a certain scientific sanction from one of the contributors to the important Handbook of International Law edited by the late Professor von Holtzendorff.

The title of chapters which has been chosen instead of that of essays implies a certain connection and sequence in their subjects, which the foregoing summary may show to exist. But several more chapters would have to be added in order to make this a complete work on the principles of international law. My intention in planning it included one on the principles of neutrality, and another giving examples of the growth of international law, in which one would have borne on neutrality. These have been postponed because it was found that a more elaborate treatment of that subject would be necessary than would have been in proportion to the scale of what is now published. The rights and duties of neutrals are the part of international law which has changed most since the time of Grotius, and with regard to which ideas tending to further change are still the most rife; and I hope to make a thorough examination of its principles at no distant time. Meanwhile it is trusted that the present volume may furnish students and others with matter for reflection, and assist them in attaining clear notions, on the nature of the society formed by states and on many parts of their mutual obligations.

J. WESTLAKE.

*8th September,* 1894.

# INTERNATIONAL LAW

## CHAPTER I

INTERNATIONAL LAW IN RELATION TO LAW IN GENERAL

*International Law the body of Rules between States.*

INTERNATIONAL law is the body of rules prevailing between states. It may also be described as the body of rules governing the relations of a state to all outside it, whether other states or private persons not its own subjects. These definitions are not inconsistent, because, where international law allows a state to have direct relations with a private person not its own subject, it is only by virtue of a rule prevailing between states that this is so. Any state may capture try and execute a pirate, whether its own subject or not. Any belligerent state may capture try and condemn a ship belonging to a neutral owner for violating a blockade established by it. This is so because it is a rule between states that his own state may not interfere for the protection of the pirate or the blockaderunner. If a state presumes to act directly against a private foreigner in a case in which no international rule excludes the state to which the latter belongs from protecting him, the matter becomes one between the two states: the foreigner's state is injured even though it may not seek redress.

These considerations furnish the answer to a question which is sometimes asked, whether private persons can be the subjects of international law. It would be pedantic to deny that the pirate and the blockaderunner are subjects of international law, but it is only by virtue of rules prevailing between states that they are so.

## *Law and Society.*

We have next to ask ourselves what is meant by a rule prevailing between states. It is meant that states form a society, the members of which claim from each other the observance of certain lines of conduct, capable of being expressed in general terms as rules, and hold themselves justified in mutually compelling such observance, by force if necessary; also that in such society the lines of conduct in question are observed with more or less regularity, either as the result of compulsion or in accordance with the sentiments which would support compulsion in case of need. It is an old saying, *ubi societas ibi jus est*; " where there is a society there is law." And perhaps no better account can be given of what is commonly understood by law than that it is the body of rules expressing the claims which, in a given society, are held to be enforceable and are more or less regularly observed. When a claim is urged but is not held to be enforceable, it is commonly called a moral claim as distinguished from a legal one. In order to become a legal claim it must be accompanied by the sentiment that it would be justifiable to enforce it, and that sentiment must be shared by the general mass of some society which is concerned with the matter. If in that society the claim is not with some degree of regularity either enforced or observed without the necessity of resorting to force, it will follow that the sentiment in favour of enforcing it is wanting either in width of diffusion or in strength. The claim may be in process of becoming a legal one, but as yet it is only a moral one. On the other hand, where no claims have become legal ones, there cannot be a society in any true sense. A number of men having certain concerns in common may feel no need of a particular society with laws to regulate them, because the men themselves are included in the larger society of the state, the laws of which are sufficient for their as well as for other particular purposes. But if a number of states attempted to live with no common sentiment at the back of their mutual claims sufficient to secure some regularity and impose some limits with regard to them, disorder and violence would reign unchecked by any social bond. So the maxim *ubi societas ibi jus est* correctly puts before us society and law as mutually dependent. They must have been inseparable as facts from the earliest time at which there was any intercourse between men, probably before there was any clear consciousness of the notions corresponding to the facts, and they are still inseparable in all departments of intercourse between men. Without society no law, without law no society. When we assert that there is such a thing as international law, we assert that there is a society of states: when we recognise that there is a society of states, we recognise that there is international law.

## *Jural Laws and the Laws of Nature known to Science.*

The law which belongs to society is a rule for human conduct. That the laws of nature in the modern scientific sense are different in kind from rules for human conduct may seem too obvious to need pointing out, but in fact the two senses of the word "law" have led to so much confusion that it is necessary to insist on the distinction between them at the outset of my subject. It will assist us if we speak of laws for human conduct, whether national or international, as jural laws. Laws of nature are statements of certain facts of nature, namely of certain invariable sequences of antecedents and consequents. Jural laws are directions. The formula of the one is " this is " ; the formula of the other is " do this." Consequently laws of nature are never broken : if it were found that a phenomenon contradicting an asserted law of nature had happened, the conclusion would be that the asserted law was not one. But jural laws are broken by men's disobedience to the directions which they convey, even although the lawbreaker may be punished. The only link between the two is that the uniformity with which the consequents in nature follow the antecedents suggests the uniformity with which a jural law applies or is intended to apply to a whole class of cases. On account of that meagre analogy the term " law " has been extended metaphorically from jural laws to laws of nature, and the extension has been defended on the ground that jural laws will not be beneficial, in most cases will not even obtain any wide observance, if the facts expressed by the laws of nature are not duly taken into account in framing them. That is a true remark : a wise lawgiver must take facts of all kinds into account. But to take a fact into account is not blindly to copy it, and the metaphorical extension of the term "law" has tended to conceal the truth that one of the most important functions of jural law is not to copy but to limit and correct those habits and impulses which, regarded merely as facts, are laws of nature. Thus an impulse to defend ourselves is linked to many forms of danger by a sequence of cause and effect. The various manifestations of that impulse are proper subjects of enquiry for the natural historian, and furnish him with laws of nature so far as they are found to take place in uniform courses. But the impulse is often so strong and unreflecting that its free gratification would be incompatible with any society among men. It prompts us to ward off danger from ourselves by transferring it to innocent persons, and jural law has to distinguish and punish the cases in which it is reprehensible to yield to the impulse of self-defence. This example is an instructive one with regard to international law. The word "nature" is so suggestive of praise that self-defence, being as an impulse a law of nature, has been erected into a primary right. Writers have been found to treat the right of self-defence, not as a compendious expression for summing up those rights of defending itself which on jural principles can properly be allowed to a state in various circumstances, but as a natural source from which it may be deduced that a state may justifiably do every thing necessary for its defence. Now such reasoning is not only immoral, but it leads to no definite result. The action of the licensed self-defender exposes other states to danger, and their rights of self-defence meet that of the first state in a conflict for the solution of which no principle is furnished. The only remedy is to bear well in mind the distinction between the laws of nature and jural laws.

*The Society of States compared with other Societies.*

Returning to international law as the jural law of the society of states, we have to compare that society with other forms of human association. Possessing little organisation and no officers, never indeed performing a truly collective act, the body of states might at first sight be likened to what is commonly called " society," consisting of persons interested in maintaining the rules of good breeding, or what at the time and place they consider to be such. In that loosest of all forms of association rules are maintained by the independent, though concurrent, action of individual members in shunning intercourse with those who do not observe them, and by the support which the members give to one of their number who shows resentment against a person by whom the rules have not been observed towards him. States however do not to any great extent use the shunning of intercourse as a means of enforcing international rules. The populations of different countries are too closely united by commerce, travel, intermarriage, and even by the lines of religion crossing political boundaries, for public intercourse between them through their national organs to be easily dispensed with. Permanent diplomatic intercommunion has been forced by European states on Eastern empires which were unwilling to admit it, and the withdrawal of ambassadors is either a prelude to war or a step which brings war within measurable distance, while when war ends public intercourse is restored. In this respect the society of states is closer even than a cricket club or a trades union, notwithstanding that these perform collective acts when they enforce their rules by formally expelling recalcitrant members. The exclusion of a state from the international society is scarcely more thought of than, within a state, the expulsion of a subject is thought of as a means of enforcing the law of the land. The international society answers to a want of mankind which no one is permitted to ignore. And it is far from lacking that other mode of enforcing its rules which consists in the support given by the members to one of their number who has been injured by a breach of them. Often, it is true, a justly offended state is left in the particular case to fight its own battle, but it receives a moral support from the general recognition that its resort to arms was the exercise of a right, and the interests of states meet and cross each other at so many points that there is generally, before long, some point at which the offender is made to feel the loss of sympathy which his conduct has occasioned.

If on the other hand we compare the international society with the national one which exists by virtue of the state tie, the differences which strike us most are the collective character and overwhelming strength of the power which enforces the rules of the latter, and the great variety of topics to which those rules relate. In other words, there is in a state a sovereign authority and the citizens are in general subjection to it, while in the society of states there is no sovereign authority and the life of each is touched by international law only at a few points. A third difference, that which exists in the amount of obedience paid to international and national law respectively, does not seem to deserve the prominence sometimes given to it. The truth is that much the larger part of the mutual relations of states is carried on with great regularity in accordance with the international law relating to the several matters concerned, and that the cases which have a contrary appearance are mostly those in which a rule is uncertain or in which the change of a rule is strongly advocated. For example, there is no universally received enumeration of the articles which a belligerent may treat as contraband of war when carried to his enemy by a neutral, nor any universally received principle on which the contraband character of a particular article may be determined, and even between enemies the progress of humanity is continually demanding some further restriction of the license of war. Hence have arisen many of the complaints of violating international law made by neutrals against belligerents and by belligerents against one another, but it is more correct to say that international law is an imperfect body of rules than that, so far as it is perfect, it is not obeyed. The want of international organisation chiefly makes itself felt, so far as concerns international rules, in the imperfection of the power to define and develop them. But that is a defect from which the law of the land is not always exempt in countries which have attained some considerable degree of advancement. Take for instance the laws of England in the period of Glanville and Bracton, say the reigns from Henry the Second to Henry the Third, when old local customs, new feudal principles and habits of action, and a good deal of Roman law, then lately made known in this country, were being fused together into our common law, and that by the judges, to whom but little express legislative help was given before Edward the First. While the process was going on, uncertainty reigned over as large a part of the law of England as the part of international law over which it now reigns. And if we add the private violence, which then exceeded in frequency and impunity the public violence of European states in the nineteenth century, it may safely be said that international law is now not less certain and better obeyed than was the law of England till the process referred to was fairly complete.

## A Special point of Contact between International and National Law : Private International Law.

Again, the comparison between international law and state law or the law of the land would be inadequate, if we left out of account that to some extent they have to protect the same interests and are therefore concerned with the same topics. It is one of the undoubted functions of a state to secure private rights over things within its territory, or disputed between persons who, through being established within its territory, are habitually amenable to its laws. But the performance of this function often involves the consideration of private rights over things situate in foreign countries, or arising from transactions which took place in foreign countries ; and often disputes have to be settled between parties one or both of whom are absent from the territory or only casually present in it, and such absence or casual presence of a party is again varied by his being politically a subject of the state in question or a foreigner. Hence arises the necessity of determining, at least to some extent, the limits of a state's jurisdiction and of the application of its laws in private matters. The science of those limits is called private international law or international private law. It is true that the international society leaves to the states which are its members considerable latitude with regard to that science, but not an unlimited latitude. A state might depart so widely from any accredited principles, in its claim to exercise jurisdiction or apply its laws, that a foreigner who suffered by such departure would be considered to have suffered an international wrong and his state would resent it. Therefore state rules affecting the interests of individuals are in some degree concerned with international principles, and a part of the body of law which regulates those interests is common ground to a state and to the society of states.

*Another Special point of Contact between International and National Law: Territory and Property: Natural Law, or the Law of Nature as a Jural conception.*

There is still another point of contact between national and international law, in that certain international rules dealing exclusively with public interests have been borrowed from private law. This occurred for two reasons, which it is necessary to mention here for the sake of completeness in the subject now occupying us, but which will have to be more fully treated hereafter. First, the right of a state in its territory bears a great resemblance to that of property, and the resemblance was even closer in the sixteenth and seventeenth centuries, when the doctrines of international law were assuming shape, because the feudal confusion between government and property, and between a state and its sovereign, had not then been wholly got rid of. Hence many rules of property law, which of course were sought in that of Rome, were taken over as international rules applicable to territory. Secondly, it was in the age when international law was being formed that a theory, by no means confined to that age, attained its fullest development and currency. I mean the theory of a state of nature in which men once lived or might be supposed to have lived, for it is difficult to say how far it was believed in as an historical truth, and of a natural law or law of nature proper to that state. The term so used bore a sense quite different from that of the laws of nature in modern science, which we have already considered, for the conception was a jural one, however ill founded. The theory went on to represent nations as individuals who, from their not having any common political superior, were in the same mutual relations as men in the state of nature, and who were consequently bound by this natural law. But the Roman jurists had also speculated on the same natural law, and had identified with it much of what was their own law as embodied by Justinian in its final shape. And thus a door was opened for the introduction into international law, under the name of the law of nature, of no small part of the private law of Rome on obligation as well as on property.

*Austin's limitation of the term "Law."*

At this point it becomes necessary to mention that John Austin confined the term "law" to the commands issued by a sovereign authority to persons in general subjection to it, and therefore denied its application to the rules prevailing between states which have no political superior. We shall probably feel less surprise that the revolt against that nomenclature has now become so general than that a writer of such great ability should have adopted it, and that it should have reigned so long in the legal literature of England. Without laying stress, in a question of definition, on the links which bind international to national law through its dealing with the same topics or borrowing its rules, it seems strange that a distinction can have been missed which transcends political boundaries and runs through every kind of human society, the distinction between rules which the conscience of man allows and often even requires him to enforce, and the claims, commonly called moral ones, which he asserts no such right of making good. It is possible that the distinction was not missed, but that its importance was underrated in consequence of some view about the source of the conscientious obligation which may rest on man to obey a rule. Undoubtedly the question about the authority of law may be asked in that sense, and it may not receive exactly the same answer in the case of international as in that of national law. Since a loosely organised society can give less protection than a highly organised one, and its rules are not ascertainable with equal precision, it may have less claim to the obedience of its members. But the obligation of law on the conscience is a question of ethical philosophy different from that of the objective existence of law in a society, and lying deeper. No one will contend that the obligation to obey the law of the land is absolute. There have been both Christian martyrs and political martyrs whose resistance to it was praiseworthy. But that circumstance does not affect the classification of institutions or facts, and it is with law as an institution or a fact that the legal student has to deal. Finding that in all societies the right to enforce rules is asserted and exercised, for his purpose *securus judicat orbis terrarum*, and he need not hesitate to give the name of international law to the rules of a society as necessary to human existence as the state itself.

The only alternative to doing so would be to describe those rules as international morality. But that terminology would obscure the fact that the rules in question do not exhaust the ethical duties of states, that in the forum of conscience rules which it is proper for his fellow man to enforce can no more measure the whole duty of man when he is aggregated into nations than when he acts as a private person in his own country, and that this is recognised in the intercourse of states by their from time to time advancing claims which they do not feel justified in supporting with the last degree of pressure, though the growth of opinion sometimes ripens them at a later date into legal ones. Austin indeed, proposing the term " positive international morality " as the substitute for " international law," recognised by the word " positive " some distinction among the mutual claims of states, though not connecting it clearly, if at all, with the general conviction and exercise of the right of enforcement. But unless it be recognised that the distinction rests on that basis there is danger on the one hand of checking the progress of mankind by depreciating the less ripened claims, and on the other hand of putting claims founded only in sectional or individual interests on a par with those which express the general needs of the international society.

The late Professor Mountague Bernard drew attention to the latter of these dangers when he said that "the fallacy suggested by the phrase 'international morality' is a more practically mischievous one than the fallacy suggested by the phrase 'international law,' because the temptation to overstrain legal analogies and clothe mere opinions indiscriminately in the robe of law is less dangerous than the contrary tendency to degrade fixed rules into mere opinions[1]." It is submitted that both fallacies may be avoided if we decline to treat the law of the land as the only proper kind of jural law, for then, while keeping law distinct from morality, we shall not encourage an undue attribution to international law of the characters only appropriate to the law of the land.

In the abstract science of geometry the groups, from the highest to the lowest, are equally real or equally unreal. The rectilinear figure, the triangle and the isosceles triangle are equally unreal in the sense that no objects occur possessing those exact forms, and equally real in the sense that their contemplation by the sentient mind is inevitable. Each therefore is defined in the same way, by enumerating the characters contemplated in it. But natural history deals only with external facts, and wherever these furnish for the determination of genera only such a balance of resemblances as leaves it disputable to what genus a certain species shall be referred, no good end is served by trying to establish the genus on an enumeration of arbitrary characters. Jural law, as a product of human action, is the subject of a natural science. The law that any state has jurisdiction over a pirate, and the law which punishes a

[1] *Four Lectures on Subjects connected with Diplomacy*, p. 171.

murderer with death or imprisonment, are individuals. They fall at once, as natural individuals do, into their natural species, international and national law respectively. Between these species it is submitted that enough resemblance exists to justify comprising them in one genus by the common name of law. But to preclude the enquiry into resemblance by laying down *a priori* that law must be the command of a political superior is to import into a natural science the mode of defining proper to an abstract one.

## The Moral Law.

Besides the jural laws which we have been considering, and the laws of nature in the sense of modern science at which we have glanced, "the moral law" is a term often used to express the obligations which are incumbent on men in the forum of conscience. As rules for human conduct, perpetually violated, those obligations can have no connection but that of metaphor with the laws of nature in the sense of modern science, but they have so much analogy with jural laws that the question arises whether they do not form with these last a real class of the highest or most comprehensive kind, to the whole of which the term "law" is applied with an identical meaning. In order to answer that question in the affirmative the notion of human enforcement, which accompanies all jural laws and makes by its presence the very distinction between them and rules of only moral obligation, would have to be excluded from the meaning of law in the largest extension which it can receive without going into metaphor. But the notion of enforcement by superior determination might remain, since in an enlightened conscience the test of a duty is its consonance with a moral order not to be violated without evil consequences, and such a moral order, with the consequential penalties for its breach, may be reverently regarded as imposed by a superior power. Here at last, not by arbitrary definition but by following the train of observable resemblances, we arrive at the final meaning of law.

## Rights and Wrongs.

Along with law there goes the notion of a right, that is, of a claim against the person who has violated the law to our disadvantage; and he is said to have done us a wrong, which our right serves to redress. The right and the wrong are jural or moral ones according as the law which has been violated is a jural or a moral one, but in popular language a jural right is called a legal one, so that that language is guilty of the inconsistency of opposing a legal right to a moral one at the same time that it recognises a moral law.

There is no chronological order of priority between society, law, and rights and wrongs. They must have arisen together in the earliest times. No human society can have existed a day without its law, and the breach of no law can be unaccompanied by the feelings of a wrong and a right. The maxim *ubi societas ibi jus est* must have been as true always as now, and in every age its truth is equal in both senses of *jus*: " where there is a society there is law " and " where there is a society there are rights." But the logical order is that which we have followed. Rights and wrongs presuppose laws, and laws presuppose society. Even the moral law is not adapted to man in isolation.

## CHAPTER II

THEORY BEARING ON INTERNATIONAL LAW DOWN TO THE RENAISSANCE

*Greece.*

IT is in the literature of Rome that we meet with the first serious reflection on international relations. Active as was the Greek mind in most directions it never busied itself with law, and when the law of a city received little attention except as a branch of politics it could not be expected that the law which was possible between cities should be made a subject of philosophical treatment. The Amphictyonic oath imposed the obligation not to destroy a city of the league or cut off its water supply, and among " the lawful customs of the Hellenes," " the observances to which Hellenes have a mutual claim[1]," we find mentioned the prohibition of poisoned arrows, the duty of releasing prisoners of war for ransom, and that of offering to submit disputes to arbitration before resorting to war. How small was the practical influence of these oaths and maxims the reader of Thucydides knows from the sad stories of Platæa and Melos, but at their best they aimed at little more than mitigating or preventing the horrors of war, they scarcely disclose any recognition of a justice which should govern all international relations, their root

[1] τὰ τῶν Ἑλλήνων νόμιμα, τὰ πρὸς τοὺς Ἕλληνας δίκαια.

seems to have been feeling and not reason. Therefore they were not observed, and even the feeling stopped at the limits of Greece. "With other races, with barbarians, all Greeks are eternally at war," said the Macedonian envoys at the Ætolian council[1].

## Rome : Jus Gentium.

To teach law to the world was the especial mission of the Romans. Accordingly they believed that peace and not war was the normal relation between them and other nations, and that in their conduct towards other nations there was a path of justice to be followed. They had a college of *feciales*, whose duty it was to see that at least the formal requisites of fair and hallowed dealing with foreign sovereigns and communities were observed, and one of whom solemnly claimed redress as a preliminary to a declaration of war on its refusal. And it is from the Roman lawyers that the world inherits the name and the conception of *jus gentium*, the original import of which must be explained before we can venture to translate it by the modern phrase, "the law of nations."

"If any one," says Pomponius, "assaults an ambassador of the enemy, it is considered to be a breach of the *jus gentium* because ambassadors are held to be sacred. And therefore, in a case where ambassadors were at Rome at the time when war was declared against their nation, it was determined that they remained free in accordance with the *jus gentium*[2]." But for their character as ambassadors they might have been enslaved as enemies. Disregard

[1] Cum alienigenis, cum barbaris, æternum omnibus Græcis bellum est, Livy, xxxi, 29.
[2] Pomponius, lib. xxxvii ad Quintum Mucium, in Dig. 50, 7, 17.

however this trait of barbarism, and the ideas of Pomponius are quite those we are accustomed to in the modern world. He recognises the sanctity of diplomatic intercourse, which is clearly a matter of public law between states, and he refers it to the *jus gentium*. Why should we hesitate to translate that phrase by " the law of nations " ? One reason is that, with us, "the law of nations " has come to mean exclusively the law prevailing between states, or international law, while the Roman jurists included more in their *jus gentium*. Another reason is that, to many modern minds, " the law of nations " is a law which rests on the consent of nations or states as such, while the Roman jurists regarded their *jus gentium* as resting on the consent of mankind, of the whole body of men as thinking and feeling individuals distributed among the nations. Let us see how this results from the employment of the phrase on other occasions.

The courts of law at Rome had to determine litigation between foreigners, of whom the influx was large, and between foreigners and Romans. They could not apply the law of their own city for that purpose, because the law of a city was regarded in the ancient world as the peculiar inheritance of its citizens, not lightly to be communicated to others, and because it would not have been just to apply the law of Rome to transactions which must often have been entered into without reference to it. Such a state of things must also have arisen at Athens or at any other great political and commercial centre, but the Roman genius for law could not bear to meet it unsystematically by trying to do the best in each case as it arose. It demanded rules, and they were reached through the display of another Roman tendency, that of resorting to observation rather than to reasoning *a priori*. It was noticed that in every institution, such as marriage or contract, there was a kernel of substantial importance in which the laws of all nations agreed, and a husk of forms in which they differed. Accordingly, where Roman law could not be applied, the husk was stripped off and the kernel was deemed to be sufficient. Thus a Roman stipulation had to be made by the words *dari spondes? spondeo;* " do you undertake that such or such a thing shall be given ? " " I undertake." But the *prætor peregrinus*, the judge whose business it was to administer justice where foreigners were concerned, held that by or with them a contract had been sufficiently entered into by the words *dabis? dabo;* " will you give ? " " I will give " ; or by any other words that expressed the intention of incurring an obligation[1]. In doing this he was said to administer the *jus gentium*, but the law which he applied was not one existing between nations or indeed any public law, nor as private law was the bare kernel which he applied the law of any nation, nor did it derive its force from the consent of any nation as such, except of course such consent of Rome as was involved in its application by a Roman official. It was a law embodying the elements which were proved, by comparing the laws of different nations, to have the approval of men to whatever nations they belonged. Hence the classical jurists give, as equivalents for *jus gentium*, " the common law of all men " (*commune omnium hominum jus*), " that which is equally observed among all peoples " (*id quod apud omnes populos peræque custoditur*), " the law which all nations use " (*jus gentium, quasi quo jure omnes gentes utuntur*)[2]. And in all these expressions

[1] Gaius, 3, 93.   [2] Gaius, 1, 1 ; Just. Inst. 1, 2, 1.

we shall more accurately seize the sense of the original if we remember that *jus* included the principles of legal right as well as the rules of law, although, as the English language possesses no one word comprising both, the translation must necessarily be inadequate.

Having thus arrived at the true meaning of *jus gentium* so far as concerns private law, we perceive that its meaning in public law was the same. When Pomponius relates the determination (*responsum*) that ambassadors were sacred by the *jus gentium*, he means, and the authority which he quotes meant, that they were sacred by the universally recognised principles of legal right. They were sacred because, in matters concerning nations as well as in those concerning private persons, principles which commended themselves to the conscience of all men were to be observed. The principles were plain enough in the particular instance. Ambassadors are necessary to intercourse between nations, and they had entered Rome in reliance on the public faith. But what put the stamp on those principles was the universality of their recognition by reflecting beings. This it was that made ambassadors sacred by the *jus gentium*. No special department of law in force between nations was appealed to, nor was the consent of any nation as such implied. If Pomponius had been told that some strange people claimed to enslave Roman ambassadors, or objected to the Roman prætor's holding its members bound by stipulations not couched in a prescribed form of words, he would doubtless have replied in each case that the general judgment of mankind was to be followed, and would have felt in each case that his reply rested on the same basis.

### Rome: *Jus Naturale.*

The Roman appeal to the general judgment of men, founded on observation of their wide agreement, was reinforced by Greek philosophy. The Stoics, whose system was the most accepted at Rome, taught that nature recommended certain principles of conduct, and of justice as a part of conduct. Principles so recommended were necessarily independent of state boundaries, and harmonised in their liberality with those which analytical observation detected as underlying the variety of state laws. The classical jurists therefore readily identified the natural law which the Stoic philosophy suggested—*jus naturale*, the jural as distinguished from the scientific laws of nature—with the *jus gentium*, which in the spirit of that identification came to be applied between Roman citizens as well as where foreigners were concerned. Gaius uses the former term as equivalent to the latter when he contrasts delivery, as a mode of transferring property *naturali jure*, with mancipation and other modes of transfer existing by the peculiar law of Roman citizens, *jus proprium civium Romanorum*; and he declares in general terms that the *jus gentium* is "what natural reason establishes among all men," a declaration which Justinian adopted from him[1]. One jurist however of the great age, Ulpian, noticing that some legal institutions are based on natural facts common to men with other animals, carried his love of subtlety so far as to found on that circumstance a distinction between *jus naturale* and *jus gentium*. He defined the former as "that which nature has taught all animals, and from which come the union of male and female

---
[1] Gaius, 2, 65; 1, 1. Just. Inst. 1, 2, 1.

called by us marriage, and the procreation and education of children[1]." In an age less philosophical even than that of Ulpian Justinian adopted this definition along with what he took from Gaius, but it must be condemned. It favours the notion that statements of fact about natural habits, which so far as they are true are laws of nature in the scientific sense, can be directly transmuted into jural or moral laws, without considering whether the habits in question need encouragement or check. Or if it be admitted that the legal institutions based on natural facts must be moulded by other considerations besides that of the bare facts, still it is irrelevant to those other considerations whether the basal facts are common to all animals or peculiar to man. So far as it is permissible to speak of a law of nature in a jural or moral sense, it can only be understood to comprise those precepts which, all things considered, reason establishes. And the classical Roman tradition must be followed in holding that where and so long as there is a general concurrence of civilised men in favour of certain precepts as established by reason, there and so long such precepts must be accepted for practical purposes as those of natural reason, without prejudice to the efforts of reformers to bring the world over to a different opinion, as they have often done.

*The dissolution of the Roman empire : Isidore of Seville.*

But in consequence of the refusal of Ulpian and Justinian to treat *jus naturale* and *jus gentium* as equivalent, or to distinguish them as reason propounded

[1] *Jus naturale est quod natura omnia animalia docuit...hinc descendit maris atque feminæ conjugatio, quam nos matrimonium appellamus, hinc liberorum procreatio et educatio*, Just. Inst. 1, 2.

by philosophers and reason accepted by the world, they came to be treated during a long course of ages as separate departments of law. Perhaps no one again laid much stress on the difference between fundamental facts as being common to all animals or peculiar to man, but other lines of demarcation were found. Isidore of Seville, writing early in the seventh century of the Christian era, reserves the term *jus gentium* for what we should now describe as international law, so that here for the first time we find that term fairly translatable by " law of nations[1]." All the remaining matter of the old *jus gentium*, namely the law common to all nations, *jus commune omnium nationum*, he includes in *jus naturale*. When Isidore wrote independent kingdoms had been founded by the northern races within the ancient limits of the Roman empire, and it was doubtless owing to that circumstance that the rules prevailing between states acquired importance enough to be treated as a separate branch of legal science with a name of its own. This rapid development of the scientific classification in accordance with the political changes suggests the true cause why in a more enlightened age, and with such excellent principles to start from, the Roman jurists never worked out a system of international law. It is that in their time there was hardly an international society. The Roman and

---

[1] Isidore also has a *jus militare*, among the subjects of which he mentions *belli inferendi solemnitas* and *fœderis faciendi nexus*. But by this seems to be intended only as much as a military commander need know about those subjects, for *bella*, *fœdera* and *paces* are enumerated by him among the subjects of *jus gentium*. Etymologiarum libri xx, l. 5, c. 4 to 7; quoted by Nys, *Le Droit de la Guerre et les Précurseurs de Grotius*, p. 12. Isidore died in 636, and is said to have been engaged on the Etymologia at the time of his death.

Parthian empires divided the world within which international relations on any thing like an equal footing were possible. But the society which is to give birth to law must contain a sufficient number of members for the questions which arise among them to be viewed in a general light. Between two or three individuals particular interests determine and general rules do not arise. For the rest, the earliest enumeration of the subjects of the law of nations is interesting enough to be quoted, though not of any scientific importance. *Jus gentium*, Isidore says, "is the occupation of territory, the building and fortification of cities and castles, wars, captivities, enslavements, the recovery of rights by postliminy, treaties of peace and others, truces, the scruple which protects ambassadors from violence, prohibitions of marriage between persons of different nationality[1]." The first and the last items in the list vividly reflect the land-hunger of the northern invaders, and the jealous separations which they had substituted for the unity of the Roman peace.

## *The Renaissance : Suarez.*

The definitions of Isidore of Seville were copied in the Decretal of Gratian and generally followed during the middle ages[2], but the Renaissance writers, returning to classical authority, restored to *jus gentium* a larger meaning than international law, though they did not in general reassert its equivalence to the *jus*

[1] *Jus gentium est sedium occupatio, ædificatio, munitio, bella, captivitates, servitutes, postliminia, fœdera, paces, induciæ, legatorum non violandorum religio, connubia inter alienigenas prohibita*, Isidore of Seville, u. s.

[2] Nys, u. s., p. 13.

*naturale*. On the one hand the enlightenment of the conscience by Christianity, on the other hand the experience of centuries of practical barbarism, had made it evident to the best thinkers that general consent tolerated and even approved of much which could not be fairly charged on nature in any sense in which that term implied reason. Hence *jus naturale* and *jus gentium* came to be currently distinguished, the former as those rules whether of public or of private law of which the necessity could be seen, the latter as those rules whether of public or of private law of which the necessity could not be seen, and which were to some extent though by no means altogether reprehensible. This classification, in its bearing on the mutual relations of states, is admirably given in a passage of Suarez which it is well worth while to quote at length.

" The human race, however divided into various peoples and kingdoms, has always not only its unity as a species but also a certain moral and quasi-political unity, pointed out by the natural precept of mutual love and pity which extends to all, even to foreigners of any nation. Wherefore although every perfect state, whether a republic or a kingdom, is in itself a perfect community composed of its own members, still each such state, viewed in relation to the human race, is in some measure a member of that universal unity. For those communities are never singly so self-sufficing but that they stand in need of some mutual aid society and communion, sometimes for the improvement of their condition and their greater commodity, but sometimes also for their moral necessity and need, as appears by experience. For that reason they are in need of some law by which they may be directed and rightly ordered in that kind of communion and society. And although this is to a great extent supplied by natural reason, yet it is not so supplied sufficiently and immediately for all purposes, and therefore it has been possible for particular laws to be introduced by the practice (*usu*) of those same nations. For just as custom (*consuetudo*) introduces law in a state or province, so it was possible for laws to be introduced in the whole human race by the habitual conduct (*moribus*) of nations. And that all the more because the points which belong to this law are few and approach very nearly to natural law, and being easily deduced from it are useful and agreeable to nature, so that although this law cannot be plainly deduced as being altogether necessary in itself to laudable conduct (*ad honestatem morum*), still it is very suitable to nature and such as all may accept for its own sake[1]."

In this passage Suarez, dealing with the rightful foundation of international law, does not notice the fact, to which he was certainly not blind, that custom had introduced bad rules as well as good ones. Also his reference to the human race as the source of binding international custom is too large, for no international society has ever been of that extent, even if we suppose only the civilised part of mankind to be intended. This was not long afterwards pointed out by Grotius who, after describing *jus gentium* as that law which has received its obligatory force from the will of all or of many nations, proceeds—" I have added ' many ' because scarcely any law except the

---

[1] Tractatus de Legibus et Deo Legislatore, 2, 19, 9; quoted by Nys, u. s., p. 11. This treatise passed the censure in 1611 and was published at Coimbra in 1612.

natural law, which itself is often called *jus gentium*, is found to be common to all nations[1]." Already Ayala had spoken of " laudable and ancient customs" as having " been introduced between Christians[2]." But Suarez has put on record with a master's hand the existence of a necessary human society transcending the boundaries of states, the indispensableness of rules for that society, the insufficiency of reason to provide with demonstrative force all the rules required, and the right of human society to supply the deficiency by custom enforced as law, such custom being suitable to nature.

A complete theory of international law, as of every other subject of human activity, must include both a statical and a dynamical branch, a branch dealing with the subject in a state of equilibrium and one dealing with it in a state of movement or progress. When reason and custom were recognised as the two sources of international law, the statical branch of that science had been placed on the footing on which alone it can stand. At the same time, since reason is fallible and customs change, the dynamical branch existed in germ. But the men of the Renaissance scarcely perceived this, because the boundless intellectual confidence of that spring time led them to regard the dictates of natural law as capable of clear and exhaustive enumeration, and because the material conditions on which custom so largely depends had been little altered during many ages. We however have learnt that the term " natural law," as then employed, was little more than the expression of a

---

[1] *De Jure Belli ac Pacis*, I, 1, 14.
[2] *De Jure et Officiis Bellicis et Disciplina Militari libri tres*, l. 1, c. 5, no. 19.

sentiment so strong that for the time it seemed to be a pledge of its own perpetuity. The possibility of change in the law of nations has been proved by experience. Many of its rules are now quite different from what they were two or three centuries ago. That the international society possesses no legislature, no organisation for declaring a change, puts great obstacles in the way of making and ascertaining one, and that difficulty is increased by the complicated interests which attend a high state of civilisation. But mere difficulty cannot stop a natural process, and the development of the social relations of man is a natural process. Every international rule was in its establishment a change, if not from a preceding rule at least from the absence of rule, and the causes which established international rules and justified them are in eternal operation.

# CHAPTER III

AYALA : GENTILIS : GROTIUS

## Ayala.

THE end of the sixteenth and the beginning of the seventeenth centuries saw the appearance of three works on the laws of war : Balthazar Ayala's *De Jure et Officiis Bellicis et Disciplina Militari libri tres*, the *De Jure Belli libri tres* of Albericus Gentilis, and the famous *De Jure Belli ac Pacis* of Hugo Grotius. It is not surprising that the part relating to war should have been made a distinct branch of study before any other part of international law. Even now war is by far the most striking fact in international relations, though the whole tenour of those relations has settled us in a point of view from which war seems natural. States, and not any sovereign or other persons, stand prominently out as the parties to international discussions. Those discussions generally relate to topics and are carried on by means of arguments very different from the topics which occur and the arguments which are used in private matters, and we are prepared to see them decided by methods unknown in private litigation, and in which the respective forces of the parties have free play. But as long as the feudal system prevailed, with its confusion between the notions of property and government, very many of the disputes which we should now call international were disputes between rulers or cities standing towards one another in the personal relation of lord and vassal or having the personal relation of vassals to a common lord, and claiming territory by virtue of the same rules of law by virtue of which smaller persons claimed a piece of ground before a judge. Vague notions of a supremacy in the pope, or even in the emperor beyond the acknowledged limits of the Holy Roman Empire, on which last however too much stress must not be laid, also tended, so far as they had any influence, to keep the quarrels of rulers and cities on a level with those of private individuals; and the arguments used in them, where feudal principles were not concerned, were mostly derived from Roman private law, rather because there had been little reflection on the difference of the cases than from the recognition of any bond of connection between them as different. On the whole, when we read the international controversies of the middle ages and the time of the Renaissance, we are struck by the fact that the disputants move in a sphere of private law, not as extending that sphere by analogy, but because they do not perceive that their matter carries them into a higher sphere. When such a controversy ended in war, and in war carried on with a savagery but little limited either in theory or in practice, the conclusion was felt to be more disparate from the premises than it is now easy to understand. A transition was suddenly made from a region of law less open to question than much of international law would now be asserted to be, to a mode of decision unknown to that region of law and stained by inhuman license.

Naturally therefore the first topic of international law which forced itself on the attention of thinkers was what rational account could be given of war, how it might be distinguished from the unlicensed violence of private persons towards one another, whether any principles of right could flourish on such a soil, to what extent principles of right, if applicable at all, might curb the passions which war seemed to let loose.

The first attempt to give a complete answer to these questions was made by Ayala, whose work was published at Douai in 1582. It was dedicated from the camp before Tournay, 31st October, 1581, to the prince of Parma, in whose army the author was *supremus juridicus*, judge advocate. The three books into which it is divided have no separate titles, but correspond to the three parts of the general title, *de jure bellico, de officiis bellicis*, and *de disciplina militari*. In the preface Ayala declares his intention of combating the common opinion that war is incompatible with law, and that to seek to reduce its practice to a rule of justice is as though we should seek reason in madness. He must be given great credit for this design, though he pursues it without much philosophy or method. He adopts the common view of his time, that of a natural law to which the *jus gentium* was added by general consent; but he fluctuates within a few lines, and without perceiving that it is a fluctuation, between asserting on the one hand that all men enjoyed liberty by the natural law and that the *jus gentium* has abolished that enjoyment by introducing slavery, and on the other hand that the *jus gentium* is consistent with the natural law because the latter had not prohibited slavery but only not established it[1].

[1] L. 1, c. 5, no. 16.

We need not follow him into detail. The most important point to remark is that while making the legal effects of war depend on its being *justum bellum*, he disconnects the epithet from the justice of the cause and makes it depend on the war being carried on by princes having no superior, so that it may be *justum bellum* on both sides in the sense of possessing *plenitudinem quandam*, a certain satisfaction of legal requisites, as in the phrases *justæ nuptiæ, justa ætas* and others. It is clear that, since the justice of a war is necessarily in dispute, no laws of war could be established on any other basis than this ; but Ayala puts it on the ground that it is not fitting, *non convenit*, to discuss the equity of what is done by princes who have no superior[1].

## *Gentilis.*

Albericus Gentilis, a native of San Ginesio in the March of Ancona and a doctor in the civil law of the university of Perugia, left Italy in consequence of his having adopted Protestant doctrines, and in 1588, the year of the Spanish Armada, was Regius professor of the civil law at Oxford. Already, in 1585, he had published a book *De Legationibus.* In a letter which Professor Holland has printed in the preface to his excellent edition of the *De Jure Belli libri tres* (1877) we find Gentilis inviting a friend to the Oxford Commencement of July 1588, when he was to discourse " on the laws of war, the causes of making it, the mode of carrying it on, and the rights of conquerors and conquered " ; and disputations were to be held under his presidency on the questions :—

[1] L. 1, c. 2, nos. 33—35.

"Whether a war can be just on both sides; whether the laws of diplomatic intercourse apply to civil wars; and whether a subject who differs in religion from his prince ought to bear arms against a prince of his own religion—that is," as Gentilis adds, "whether a papist is right in serving his prince in arms against the pope."

A *De Jure Belli commentatio prima*, published about October of the same year, and a second and third published in 1589, doubtless gave to the world the matter which had been thus propounded at Oxford; and the *De Jure Belli libri tres*, in which these treatises are enlarged Professor Holland says to five times their extent, appeared in 1598. But the list of subjects contained in the letter of ten years before expresses with considerable accuracy the scope of the book even in its final shape. The opportuneness of those subjects to England threatened by the Armada, when the conduct that would be pursued by the English Catholics was so important a question, is obvious. We cannot doubt that it was because of such opportuneness that Gentilis rushed into print without giving himself the time to work out his subject with the fulness he afterwards gave it, but the turn of his mind must bear the responsibility for the fact that, even in 1598, his first chapter presents his principles in a manner which I once summed up as follows, and I think without parody:

"The proper foundation to build on is natural reason, the consent of all nations (the terms are treated as convertible). *All* nations? Well, no; that is the way Donellus presses definitions, but do not let him mislead you, for the consequence is that he has to give the definitions up. And the Roman lawyers did know nearly all the world, and the unknown must be judged of by the known. Besides, if all do not agree, the major part must govern, just as with individuals in a state (remember that Gentilis came from an Italian city). And then, too, natural reason is plain in itself. It is enough to say, 'Nature teaches us,' for you know there are things that are only made darker by trying to prove them. We shall quote great authors, as in other arts and sciences, and the doings of great and good men, and Roman law, and the Bible. Go to the mathematicians for proofs: the nature of my subject only admits of persuasion. 'Come then; there is no lack of matter to ground our decisions upon, so let us begin[1].'"

Indeed the superiority of Gentilis to his predecessor lies in the completeness with which he ultimately worked out his subject, and in his conception of its unity and limits, free from the connection with tactics and military administration in which Ayala had presented it. His inferiority in principles is strikingly illustrated by his mode of dealing with the question whether a war can be *justum bellum* on both sides, so as to produce its legal effects on both sides, as in changing the property of things captured. He misses the true solution given by Ayala, and labours to reconcile the correct answer, which he cannot help seeing to be necessary, with the assumption that legal effects can only flow from the justice of the cause, and that this is implied in the phrase *justum bellum*. For that purpose he urges that there is generally a show of justice on each side; that the mean in which virtue consists is not a point but a space possessing breadth, within which room may be found for each, though the one is more just than the other; that a man may try his chance if the case is obscure, and that " when utility conflicts with honour there is no little obscurity which we ought to follow"; lastly, that it will not often happen that the injustice of one side is evident, and that laws are not to be framed to suit exceptional cases[2]. And this he finds satisfactory.

Nor was Gentilis a man from whom any assistance

[1] The Academy, 5th January, 1878, p. 2. [This is a review of Holland's edition of Gentilis' *De Jure Belli libri tres.*]
[2] L. 1, c. 6.

could be hoped in mitigating the ferocity of war. Liviano, he says, put a prisoner to death with insult, because he had been accustomed to call him a beast; and Liviano was right. It has been very common, he says, to hang persons who try to introduce supplies into besieged towns; and rightly, if they are mercenary merchants, because they are not helping their country but have been led by greed so far as to despise a power stronger than themselves. Apparently neutral merchants are intended by mercenaries. Again, Gentilis agrees that it seems very hard to kill hostages for other men's faults, but he holds it to be both just and expedient. Bodin says that the practice of killing hostages was given up because bad faith is now so common that it would have to be too often done; but I, Albericus, say that faith has ceased to be kept since its breach has ceased to be punished[1].

### *Grotius.*

Hugo Grotius was born at Delft, in Holland, in 1583. He took an active part in the political and religious dissensions of the United Provinces, was imprisoned on the defeat of the Arminian and republican party, to which he belonged, escaped by the aid of his wife, and took refuge in France. There he wrote the *De Jure Belli ac Pacis*, which appeared in 1625, dedicated to Lewis XIII. By negotiating the alliance between France and Sweden, which decisively turned the fortune of the Thirty Years' War against the emperor and the Catholic cause, he contributed to the foundation of the new Europe which

---

[1] The first two passages are in l. 2, c. 18, and the third in l. 2, c. 19: pages 220, 227, 233 of Professor Holland's edition.

was consecrated by the Peace of Westphalia ; but he died in 1645, three years before that peace was concluded.

The *Nouvelle Biographie Générale* mentions forty-eight different publications of Grotius, besides his letters. All are in Latin except " Proofs of the true religion," in Dutch verse, intended to show sailors how to convert pagans, and an introduction in Dutch to Dutch law. He begins in boyhood as a poet, soon writes sacred dramas, and continues to compose verses and dramas all his life. He translates modern mathematics and philology and Greek astronomy, the history of Procopius, the Greek anthology and the Phœnissæ of Euripides. He edits Lucan and Tacitus. He writes on the antiquities of the American Indians and of the institutions of Holland ; the history of the Dutch republic ; on law, Roman and modern Dutch. He annotates the Old and New Testaments, and pours out a flood of political and theological writings, being greatly occupied late in his life with a scheme for the reconciliation of the Protestant and Catholic Churches, as he had been earlier with the evidences of Christianity and the controversy against the Socinians. Nor is this enumeration exhaustive, but only one of his works appears to have been philosophical, and that not original but a compilation : *Philosophorum sententiæ de fato*, published posthumously in 1648. If international law could even otherwise have been overlooked by a writer with such varied interests, it was forced on his attention by the hostilities in the straits of Malacca between the Dutch East India Company and the Portuguese, and by the scruples of conscience which led the Mennonites and others in Holland to refuse their share of the booty.

Grotius, then only in his twenty-second year, vindicated the Company and its right to the booty in a treatise *De Jure Prædæ*, which contains the germ of his great work, but was never printed in full till 1868. Four years indeed after its composition, when Spain was proposing to Holland terms which included the abandonment by the republic of the commerce of the Indies, he published the twelfth chapter of the *De Jure Prædæ* under the title of *Mare Liberum*, in order to animate his countrymen to refuse such an accommodation ; and this work became famous at a somewhat later date, when Selden, in order to maintain the sovereignty of England over the narrow seas, published in answer to it the equally famous *Mare Clausum*. But the main thread of his ideas on our subject Grotius only resumed when in exile. He resumed it however so soon after acquiring that enforced leisure, and made such use of his earlier studies, that we cannot doubt his having always borne them in mind, or attach much importance to the statement that the composition of his great work was undertaken at the instance of Peyresc.

To form an idea of such a man and such a life we must imagine a leading statesman of the end of the nineteenth century who in periodical literature, daily monthly and quarterly, should pour forth a stream of contributions on all subjects, and should at the same time write for the stage and be a minor poet. To whatever subject he turned for the moment one of the thousand facets of his mind, we should expect keen remarks and more or less sagacity, but for depth of view on any of them we should look to some one who felt more need of concentration. Yet we should be unjust to Grotius if we took his measure from the comparison suggested. No department of knowledge had in his time been carried so far as to become the property of the specialist, and the future advancement of knowledge was so little foreseen that erudition was valued out of proportion to originality. He possessed a love of truth, and an unwearied industry in seeking it where it was believed that it might be found, which must command our admiration all the more because those are not the most characteristic qualities of the active politician or the universal writer.

Still less should we be just to Grotius if we forgot the goodness of his heart. The sack of Magdeburg had not taken place when the *De Jure Belli ac Pacis* appeared, but the war which was to be that of Thirty Years had already given signs that in savagery it would not fall behind those of the preceding century, and while the men most advanced in feeling and thought were asking whether some restraining principles might not be found, to no one did the horrors of the time appeal with greater force than to him. He tells us that sorrow and indignation moved him to write[1]. But his mind was too systematic to attack the subject of his primary interest without considering it in a more general light. There is therefore in the book so much both of theory and application not directly relevant to the mitigation of war, as entitles it to be considered the first fairly complete treatise on international law. The theory, as the logical rather than philosophical character of the author's mind dictated, largely takes the form of distinctions with most of which we need not trouble ourselves much, but one is so important that it must be fully explained.

[1] *De Jure Belli ac Pacis*, Prolegomena, 28; and in his letters Grotius expresses himself to a similar effect.

The distinction to which I refer is the very ancient one between expletive and distributive justice, *justitia expletrix* and *justitia attributrix*[1]. Expletive justice redresses wrongs, and the right of the party who invokes it is called in Latin *facultas*. Within a state it is administered by courts of justice. But how does any one come to have something of his own, his enjoyment of which can be interfered with, and he be thereby wronged? It is because law has given him something of his own. But law ought not to be arbitrary. Whether it proceed from a legislature or from a society of men establishing a custom among themselves, and whether that society be a national or an international one, law ought to be guided by distributive justice, which depends on a wise consideration of all the claims existing in the circumstances. The claim which any one has to such an exercise of distributive justice as shall frame the law in his favour is called in Latin *aptitudo*. When the law has been so framed, a legal right or *facultas* arises under it by expletive justice against all who do not respect the claim so recognised. Until then, and within a state, the claim ought not in English to be called a right without the epithet *moral*, to indicate that something is wanting to the power of enforcing it. But outside the state tie, Grotius held that any one might right himself to the extent measured by distributive justice operating as natural law, so that in those circumstances and to that extent the distinction between legal and moral rights disappeared for him. The measure of expletive justice is definite, namely that of the wrong to be redressed. The measure

---

[1] *De Jure Belli ac Pacis*, Pr. 9, 10; l. 1, c. 1, v—viii. The *expletrix* is Aristotle's δίκη ἐπανορθωτική, the *attributrix* his διανεμητική.

of distributive justice varies with circumstances, and it often happens that an exercise of it overrides the existing legal right, making a new distribution between the parties, which in its turn expletive justice is charged with maintaining. Thus, to take modern examples, a legislature exercises distributive and overrides what before was expletive justice when it enables a tenant to demand a reduction of rent which he could previously obtain only from the free will of his landlord, when it enables a bankrupt debtor to obtain a discharge from his liabilities or alters the conditions on which he could previously obtain it, and when it restricts the rights of the lord of a manor over a common. It is often the moral duty of a private person to regulate his dealings with others on the principles of distributive justice, as in the cases of landlords creditors and lords of commons. He may go further and act with charity or generosity. But the existence of the moral duty is the ground for legislative interference, where it is not sufficiently performed or cannot well be so without such interference.

I will now pass rapidly over Grotius's other distinctions. An enumeration of them is necessary in order that the reader may form a notion of what a famous book is like. We meet then with two kinds of law, that which enforces expletive justice, called by Grotius *jus æquatorium* because it restores a party to a position equal to that in which he was before he suffered the wrong, and that which dispenses distributive justice or at least is supposed to do so, called by Grotius *jus rectorium* because by conferring legal rights it governs[1]. The latter kind of law may

---
[1] *De Jure Belli ac Pacis*, l. 1, c. 1, iii.

either be that of nature, which at least outside the state tie is sufficient of itself to confer rights, or be imposed by some will (*jus voluntarium*); but when rights have been conferred it is natural law that their violation should be redressed, and so *jus æquatorium* is a branch of natural law. Grotius in his mature judgment very properly declines to consider any part of the latter as being common to man and animals, though in his youth he had given in to that view[1], but *jus voluntarium* falls into divine and human law. Human law is then divided into that of a state (*civile*) and that of nations (*gentium*). In his use of the latter term Grotius so far deviates from the language of the Roman jurists as to exclude all institutions belonging to state law, though common to many states[2]: his *jus gentium* only comprises institutions prevailing between states, but as to these he recognises the will of the society as having the force of obligation, of course within the limits set by reason[3]. This *jus gentium* he again divides into that which is truly and entirely law, and that which only produces a certain effect like that of the primitive law[4]. Of these two species the former is identical in substance with the law of nature, the classification only differing according as nature or the will of a society of states is considered as the source of its authority; the other rests merely on the will of that society, and includes laws good and bad, among others the bad laws of war against which Grotius fights. We have now reached the fifth stage of

---

[1] Compare *De Jure Belli ac Pacis*, l. 1, c. 1, xi, with *De Jure Prædæ*, p. 50.
[2] *De Jure Belli ac Pacis*, l. 2, c. 8, i.
[3] Ib., l. 1, c. 1, xiv.      [4] Ib., Pr., 41.

subdivision, and cannot get further in our distinctions about law. But we can start again, and enumerate those classes of rights (*facultates*) which it is necessary to distinguish in giving a detailed exposition of any body of national law[1], and we can distinguish the permissions in the Mosaic law into full and less than full (*permissio plena* and *minor plena*). Only the full permissions are to be allowed as proof that the thing permitted is not contrary to natural law, but the value of this proof does not seem to be great, for Grotius immediately admits that it is often necessary to refer to the natural law in order to judge whether a Mosaic permission is full or less than full, because the divine words do not mark the distinction[2].

The upshot of the foregoing, so far as concerns the rightfulness of dealings between states, may be thus simply stated. Certain institutions exist among all men, or at least among all the inhabitants of our international world, and are consonant with reason as applied to the conditions of man's existence in that world. They are examples of distributive justice, even if neither history nor any fair presumption to be made about prehistoric times enables us to refer their beginning to a conscious exercise of such justice. Among these are property, with binding contract as its necessary adjunct, the redress by expletive justice of wrongs done to property and the faith of contracts, and, Grotius added, the moderate punishment of the wrongdoer[3]. All such therefore are parts of natural law. States give effect to these branches of natural

---

[1] Power, property, rights of contract; private and public rights. *De Jure Belli ac Pacis*, l. 1, c. 1, v, vi.

[2] Ib., l. 1, c. 1, xvii.

[3] Ib., l. 2, c. 20, ii, iii.

law as between their members, and are charged with protecting the natural rights of their members as against outsiders. But where, as between states, there is no power supreme over both parties to a difference, each must and may protect with his own strong hand what he conscientiously believes to be his natural rights, even to the extent of inflicting due punishment on the wrongdoer. The responsibility of such a position is great, but it cannot be avoided unless, abandoning the attempt to distinguish natural law, you incur the still more serious responsibility of accepting customary law in its entirety, just and unjust, humane and barbarous. Deeply feeling his responsibility, Grotius, with an erudition and labour rarely equalled, fortified his declarations of natural law by the testimonies of men in all ages and countries, but was obliged to acknowledge the difficulty of distinguishing testimony to what was from testimony to what ought to be. By the side of natural law Grotius placed a principle which, in his elaborate classification, fell under the divine branch of law imposed by some will (*jus voluntarium divinum*). It appears in his book under a great variety of names. Sometimes it is the law of charity, or the love of one's neighbour (*proximi caritas*) " especially as enjoined by the Christian law." The natural rule is that you may do to your enemy whatever is necessary to attain the end of a just war, but this Christian principle forbids you to do more harm to an enemy than in the judgment of prudence is likely to be amply compensated by the good expected[1]. In that form it will be noticed that it approaches nearly to the greatest

---

[1] *De Jure Belli ac Pacis*, l. 3, c. 1, iv ; c. 11, ii ; c. 18, iv.

happiness doctrine of Bentham. Elsewhere it is modesty (*pudor*), or equity and human kindness (*æquitas et bonitas*), restraining us from insisting on the pound of flesh which the law of nature would give us. Again it is the respect due not merely to what is equitable and good (*æquum et bonum*), but to that which is most equitable and best (*ejus quod æquius meliusque est respectus*), or the preference of that which is best among the things allowed by nature[1]. And sometimes what the modifying principle enjoins is said to be a thing which ought to be done on moral grounds (*ex morali ratione faciendum*) as opposed to a debt of justice[2]. By whatever name the principle be designated, the contrast which Grotius makes between it and the true natural law, the *jus stricte dictum*, is one of the most characteristic points in his teaching. Although strict natural law was not in his view the final measure of duty by which a man ought to regulate his own conduct, it was in his view the measure of the conduct which a man is entitled to require from others. We are bound for ourselves both to pay the debts of justice and to do what morality further demands, yet if others fail us in the former we may do ourselves right, and even wage war for punishment as well as for restitution, but a failure in the latter is no just cause of war[3]. As little, if a state transgresses in war the limits of hostile pressure which natural law taken in combination with Christian charity would impose, does Grotius admit that third parties may properly interfere to enforce the observance of those limits or to avenge their non-

---

[1] *De Jure Belli ac Pacis*, l. 3, c. 10, i; c. 11, xvi; c. 12, viii; c. 14, i.
[2] Ib., l. 2, c. 22, xvi.    [3] Ib., l. 2, c. 22, xvi.

observance[1]. If Bentham ever noticed this point in Grotius, it must have surprised him that a principle so near to his own of greatest happiness was allowed so little scope in action.

With these general views Grotius set himself to examine the customary law of war, the current *jus gentium* of war. He found that here and there it might be salutary, as in prohibiting the employment of poison, between which and the sword natural law knew no distinction[2]. Or its greater latitude might be inevitable. For example, natural law allowed you to kill your enemy and capture his property only in a just war, and even then to capture his property only to the amount of the damage for which he was liable, with the addition of a reasonable penalty. But the customary law of nations, having no means of determining the justice of the war or the amount of the fair damages and penalty, allowed you in all wars to kill your enemy and capture his property without limit[3]. In general however the customary law of war was so savage that the great labour of Grotius was to establish, by the side of each license which it granted, some correction (*temperamentum*) which might reduce it to the measure of the natural law as modified by the principle of love to one's neighbour. How moderate were his hopes in that direction may be seen from the fact that he does not absolutely prohibit sacking cities, or enslaving prisoners in countries where slavery exists, or holding them to ransom where slavery does not exist[4]. He sometimes seems to feel about, as it were, for a milder practice than he

[1] *De Jure Belli ac Pacis*, l. 3, c. 4, iii.   [2] Ib., l. 3, c. 4, xv.
[3] Ib., l. 3, c. 6, i, ii.
[4] Ib., l. 3, c. 12, viii ; c. 14, i, ix.

enjoins[1]; and doubtless he hoped that Christian principles would one day govern conduct to a degree which he did not venture to anticipate in detail.

When we pass beyond the laws of war to other parts of our subject, we shall find that by Grotius and thenceforward much of Roman law was adopted into the substance of international law, consciously, and as a consequence of the general views entertained. As Justinian had handed the Roman law down, cleared of the forms and fictions of earlier ages, it was largely composed of that *jus gentium* which the jurists had elaborated by a comparison of the laws of different peoples and which they identified with natural law. Here then was ready at hand exactly such an embodiment of general consent—consent, not of states as such, but of the enlightened part of mankind—as was looked for to give an attestation to nature. And the vehicle which contained it commanded the highest respect. After its revival in the twelfth century, the close alliance of Roman law with the cause of monarchical power against ancient liberties and privileges had raised much opposition to it. But this had passed away as the political controversies concerned had partly been decided and partly come to be waged on other grounds, and little remained to conflict with the prepossession in its favour which the worship of the Renaissance for antiquity occasioned. The law of Rome was called written reason. Thus what it contained on the mutual relations of private persons, and especially so much of it as the Romans themselves identified with natural

---

[1] See *De Jure Belli ac Pacis*, l. 3, c. 13, iv; where Grotius suggests the poverty of the subject of an enemy state as a consideration to be entertained on the question of taking his property

law, was applied to the mutual relations of states so far as they had any analogy to those of private persons. Such an analogy was very obvious between the territorial rights of states and the proprietary rights of individual citizens, and thus, among other parts, the Roman law of property passed over almost bodily into the international law of territory. A result was produced coincident with that which would have flowed from the principles soon to be proclaimed by Hobbes and Pufendorff, that " states, when they are once instituted, assume the personal qualities of individual men," and that therefore the law of nature is identical for states and for natural individuals[1]. If Grotius did not fully make that identification, at least he had not rejected the notion of patrimonial governments, and, so far as any government was admitted to be such, the state over which it existed was merged for legal purposes in the person of its sovereign.

Thus through the labour of Grotius, crowning those of the philosophical theologians with Suarez as their chief and of the philosophical jurists down to Gentilis, a fairly complete body of international law was produced at the moment when the international society for which it was to serve was assuming the form which a little later was consecrated by the Peace of Westphalia. The coincidence was not casual. Then for the first time, through the decay of the Empire and of the coercive power of the Catholic Church, it could be seen that the society would be a purely secular one, and would be composed of such a crowd of practically independent states that only

[1] Hobbes, *De Cive*, c. xiv, 4, quoted with approval by Pufendorff, *De Jure Naturæ et Gentium*, l. 2, c. 3, § 23.

general considerations could be applied to their mutual relations. Then too, as the volume of history was being finally closed on mediæval Europe, the jealousy of Roman law also finally disappeared. I proceed to discuss one point in which the theory of international law, as we find it in Grotius, bears the marks of an age no later, as in others it bears the marks of an age no earlier, than that in which it saw the light.

Since that age great changes have taken place in the substance of international law. Neither the laws of war as between enemies, nor the laws of war as affecting the duties and rights of neutrals, nor several parts of the law for times of peace, are the same now as then. The process of change has uniformly been and could only be the conversion of moral claims into legal rights, taking the distinction between these to be what we find it in Grotius, namely the distinction between claims which the general conscience allows you to enforce and those which it allows you to urge but not to enforce. Every such change is therefore a phenomenon of the same kind as the existence of the law itself. If with Grotius we speak of distributive justice and natural law, the change is a new application of distributive justice in the international field, corresponding to a new view entertained of natural law. If with modern Germans we speak of the idea of right or of the jural conscience, the change expresses a further development of that idea or conscience, just as the old law was an assertion of them so far as they were at one time developed. Now it certainly seems that Grotius did not contemplate it as a possibility that our view of natural law should be progressively expanded. With the intellectual confidence of the men of the Renaissance to which

I have already referred, he seems to have regarded natural law, and therefore the measure of justice between states, as capable of being settled once for all by an exhaustive investigation. It would be unfair to believe that he regarded his own investigation of it as perfect, but his mental attitude may be inferred from his dealing with those corrections, *temperamenta*, of the brutality of war which it is his chief glory to have preached. He could hardly have supposed that any reform of the law of nations would ever press more urgently for adoption than these, and certainly not that any could come with a higher authority than that of Christianity which he claimed for them. Yet he did not plead for their admission as law, and he prohibited third parties from interfering in order to restrain the use of unconscientious methods in exacting a debt of justice. Such a belief in the finality of the international law of his day, and so narrow a view of the mutual interest which should unite the members of the international society, would not have been possible much later.

The amount of regulation which a society requires will be in proportion to the closeness of contact between its members and the complication of their mutual dealings. We have been made familiar with the truth that the growth of society has been a gradual transition from status to contract, but it is no less true that after a certain point contract needs regulation and society passes again under law. An active commerce requires a system of bankruptcy, sanitary laws become more necessary as population becomes more crowded, the pressure of population on the soil has been found to call for legislative interference between landlord and tenant. It is well that our sympathy should be on the side of liberty, that we should be jealous in limiting the restraints on individual action as narrowly as can be at all consistent with the welfare of the society. But the principle that closer intercourse needs more regulation remains true, though it may be abused. And the same principle has forced itself into application between states ever since the great advancement in arts and commerce, and the system established by the Peace of Westphalia under the protection of which they have flourished, has led to such intimate and constant international relations. If we think of the navigation of rivers flowing through different territories, the race for the appropriation of uncivilised regions, the extradition of criminals, the influence which the acts of neutrals may have on the fortune of a war, and many other topics, we shall see that, as population increases and intercourse extends, new causes of international friction arise and the friction from old causes is increased. The only complete remedy is the improvement of law, and the necessary condition of the improvement of law is that each individual shall not wrap himself in unconcern when a wrong done to another is unredressed or the moral claim of another is brutally ignored.

# CHAPTER IV

### THE PEACE OF WESTPHALIA AND PUFENDORFF

THE empire of Charlemagne broke into fragments amid the fluctuating arrangements of which only France and the Holy Roman Empire attained lasting distinctness, and each of those great sovereignties was further broken up into a group of feudal vassals and privileged cities. These, from the Baltic to the Tiber, continually advanced in the direction of independence, while in France an opposite tendency under the Capetian kings progressively reinvigorated the central authority at their expense. The point of disintegration in Germany and Italy, or of reintegration in France, which had been reached at any moment depended more on practical force than on constitutional doctrine, and any theory of government was additionally confused by the extravagant pretensions of the papacy to temporal power and of the so-called Holy Roman Empire to a vague primacy. Throughout France, the Low Countries, Germany and Northern Italy, power was scarcely to be found during the middle ages without a dispute as to its rightfulness or its measure.

Encircling the vast block of territory over which Charlemagne had reigned, a considerable number of states, mostly kingdoms, enjoyed some degree of internal cohesion as well as independence. Such were England and Scotland, Portugal and Castile, Naples and Venice, Hungary, Poland and the Scandinavian kingdoms : Navarre and Aragon must be reckoned with them, although Carlovingian sovereignty had extended to the lower Ebro. But these were too widely separated, having regard to the imperfect means of communication, to have, as states, the constant relations necessary for developing a body of rules.

The maritime cities of the Mediterranean belonged partly to the central and partly to the encircling sphere. Even when not fully independent, as Venice, they were so little dependent in fact as to carry on war on their own account, and they were involved in the wars of their more or less nominal sovereigns. The hostilities thus arising took place in the midst of a network of intimate and active commercial relations and jealousies, and these cities consequently reduced the rights of belligerents and neutrals at sea to a system which is recorded as already established in the Consolat del Mar, a code of maritime law drawn up at Barcelona about the fourteenth century. They formed for themselves a real international society, though limited in its scope, with the consequence that within the range of that scope they possessed well understood and enforceable rules. But the example is unique in the middle ages, and while it illustrates the dependence of international law on the existence of certain conditions, it throws a stronger light on the absence at that time in the rest of Europe of any regulated society of independent states.

Before the end of the fifteenth century it had

become clear that in any future system of Europe France would take her place as a unified and independent state and her feudatories would not be heard of, while the power of the emperor had sunk so low that an opposite result seemed probable for his nominal dominions. But the latter result was thrown back into doubt by the great accessions of strength which the Hapsburgs received from marriage with the heiresses of the Low Countries and Spain, and, when religion was added to the causes of political strife, the influence of the emperors in the Catholic part of Germany was increased by their championship of the church. The forces on the other side were, however, still stronger. The Protestant cause was linked to that of the independence of the princes and cities. France was compelled, by the pressure of the Hapsburgs on her northern eastern and southern frontiers at once, to assist in Germany the cause of her politics and not that of her faith ; and the vigour of Sweden, which was exerted on the same side in the later scenes of the contest, was of greater weight than the declining energy of Spain. The struggle could only end in the defeat and practical nullity of the imperial power, and in the recognition of the imperial princes and cities as members of the future European system.

In the meantime the struggle had powerfully assisted in creating a new sentiment of unity among the populations which were to be comprised in that system. During the middle ages a striking tale might be the diversion of the moment, wherever its scene was laid, but a steady interest in European events hardly extended beyond the merchants whose traffic might be affected by distant occurrences, and the higher nobility who acquired cosmopolitan relations by foreign marriages and the intercourse of courts. But during the hundred and thirty years between the commencement of the Reformation and the Peace of Westphalia the victory of the church would have endangered the Reformation everywhere, and Protestants and Catholics living under any government mostly sympathised with their fellow religionists under any other government. A general mutual interest in the fortunes of states arose, widely extended alliances resulted from it, and men felt with a novel force that a moral tie united them. That feeling was aided by the intimate relationship between the literatures of different countries which sprang from their enjoyment of a common Renaissance, and from the identity of the problems which were occupying the minds of all. It was further aided towards the end of the period by a natural revulsion from the horrors with which war had come to be waged, and the growth of commerce which followed the discovery of America and of the passage round the Cape of Good Hope was not without a similar effect. When the plenipotentiaries at Munster and Osnabruck signed the Peace of Westphalia in 1648 the ground had been well prepared for an international society, such a society had indeed been gradually emerging, and we must now look at the shape in which it was completed and consecrated by their work.

First, no questions that had ever before received a diplomatic settlement had been of such far reaching import, or had been settled with the concurrence of so many powers. The questions concerned all Western Christendom either by their political or by their religious bearings, and the representatives of nearly all Western Christendom were assembled to determine them. The very meeting of such a congress was not only the first affirmation, but by its scale a striking affirmation, of the existence of a body of states which their various interests, whether agreeing or clashing, did not permit to be strangers to one another. Such a body, the discussions arising between any of which are matters of general interest to all, has ever since existed in our portion of the globe, and its limits have been extended as occasion has arisen. Early in the eighteenth century Russia entered it as a consequence of her increased strength and civilisation, and the necessity arising from her geographical situation led to Turkey being formally admitted to the European system by the treaty of Paris in 1856. It is true that, since 1648 as well as before, two or more of the powers comprised in that system have often altered the map of Europe by settling their differences without others intervening. It is one of the consequences of the absence of international organisation that the right of intervention in the general interest is not held to be accompanied by a corresponding duty, and the system is therefore a very imperfect protection of the weak against the strong. But the right of intervention in the general interest has not been denied, and the proceedings at Vienna in 1814 and 1815, the participation of Sardinia in the Crimean war though not directly concerned, and the congress of Berlin in 1878, are examples of its exercise.

Secondly, the society of states was definitively established in 1648 as a secular one. The Protestant states in Germany were admitted on an equal footing with the Catholic ones, and the claim of the papacy to a supreme temporal authority was already obsolete.

Thirdly, the right of the princes and cities comprised within the Holy Roman Empire to contract diplomatic engagements with each other and with states outside the empire was formally acknowledged, subject only to the condition that their engagements should not be prejudicial to the empire or the emperor. But the imperial diet was so hampered by its constitution in determining whether such prejudice existed, and so ill provided with the means of enforcing its determinations, that the princes and cities thenceforth acted and were received as unquestioned members of the European society. They became real states in the international sense, and if one of them so acted as to incur the formal hostility of the empire, the practical case was merely that it had an enemy the more, and not a formidable one.

Fourthly, the fact that the princes and cities of the empire were admitted as members of the international society had its influence on the nature and rules of that society, which became a crowd of individual members, many of them petty, instead of being composed of a few powers all more or less considerable. The situation was the extreme opposite of that which had existed when Rome and Parthia confronted one another, and although the discussion of international law from general points of view might have been sufficiently secured with a much smaller number of states, the tendency to base it on abstract principles was promoted by the inclusion of so many for which there could be little safety if grounds of principle were abandoned. To some extent however this tendency was balanced at first by the circumstance that the members of the Holy Roman Empire brought with them into the international society rules which can hardly otherwise be accounted for. Thus, when private war was a general evil within most mediæval monarchies, a vassal who did not oppose the march of another vassal across his fief to attack a third was not deemed to offend against the latter: the assailant was merely using the public ways of the monarchy. So when private war, put down elsewhere, became in Germany public war, it was not there deemed the duty of a neutral to prevent the passage of belligerent forces across his territory; and that rule, opposed as it was to principle, found its way into international law and long maintained itself in it[1]. In no part of the development of our subject since the Peace of Westphalia has the influence of principle, in combination with the natural interest of weak states, been more visible than in that part which concerns the laws of neutrality.

Fifthly, the recognitions of the independence of the United Netherlands and Switzerland, the former of which had been conceded by Spain a few months before, put the seal on successful insurrection. Modern international society was stamped from its origin with the principle that states alone are regarded in it, not governments or sovereigns for their own sakes. That principle indeed has not reigned without opposition. That it should have been violated in practice is only what must happen from time to time to every principle in so loosely constituted a society as that of

---

[1] Grotius teaches the equal grant of passage to each belligerent when the justice of the war is doubtful between them: *De Jure Belli ac Pacis*, l. 3, c. 17, § 3.

nations. But even in the nineteenth century the combination of absolute powers popularly, though not quite correctly, known as the Holy Alliance attempted to base international relations on a contrary principle of legitimacy, which would have justified working them for the benefit of established governments. The attempt however failed, we may hope finally, and we can see that its success would have given rise to widely different kinds of international society and law from those which in the long run have existed ever since 1648.

Sixthly, the practice by which each state is permanently represented at the capitals of other states by resident ambassadors or ministers of inferior rank, previously an exception, dates as a general one from the Peace of Westphalia. That practice is an outward and visible sign of the common interest which is presumed to bind together even the remotest members of the European society, and is a useful means for the interchange of views in due time on all questions that may affect that interest. If the discussion of such questions was left to special embassies, their despatch would often be delayed till passion and accident had greatly increased the difficulty of an amicable settlement, and the states less directly interested would often lose the opportunity of making their sentiments heard.

Such from the international point of view did Western Christendom emerge from the long contest between Protestant and Catholic, between the kings of Spain and the Dutch people, and, although this branch of the contest was not yet finally disposed of, between the house of France and the house of Austria. There was now a society, and the maxim *ubi societas ibi jus est* vindicated itself. International law was born. There was, first, a general conviction that, besides the friendly offices demanded by good neighbourhood or moral perfection, there were duties for the slighting of which a nation might take its redress into its own hands : secondly, there was a general agreement as to where the rules defining those duties were to be looked for : thirdly, the international society was sufficiently intimate and large to justify an injured member in expecting that his vindication of its rules would meet with some appreciable support, direct or indirect, as the result of the general approval. Of these three points, the combination of which amounted to law, the important one for the lawyer is the second. He can only deal with rules so far as they are ascertainable. Now general opinion at the era which we are considering sought the matter of international rules in two quarters, both of which were equally recognised in the broad philosophy of Suarez and in the painstaking system of Grotius. One was the natural law dictated by reason, about the contents of which the confident spirit of the men of that age did not apprehend much doubt, and which really was much clearer to them than might otherwise be supposed, because it was generally admitted to include that large part of Roman law which the classical jurists had attributed to a natural source. In case of doubt it was to be proved as Grotius had proved it, by testimonies culled from writers and statesmen of all nations, and therefore establishing that kind of consent which the Roman jurists had relied on for the *jus gentium* which they identified with it, a consent of mankind and not of nations as such. The other quarter in which international law was looked for was the *jus gentium* as that term was then commonly used, the rules by which the natural law had been supplemented through the custom of nations as such, provided that the rules of this class were at least not repugnant to natural reason. The authority of reason and of custom so limited appeared to be an unquestionable necessity of human intercourse.

The greatest practical difficulty which attended these views was that, when the custom of nations as such was purged from those remains of savagery which Grotius had taken the lead in denouncing, there was not much left of it for which a custom could be quoted coextensive, or nearly so, with the society for which rules were needed. Take for instance that important chapter of the laws of maritime war which affects the rights of neutrals. The Mediterranean rules embodied in the Consolat del Mar allowed neutral property to pass free on board enemy's ships, and confiscated enemy's property on board neutral ships. These rules had received no inconsiderable amount of recognition in the Atlantic also. Edward III of England had adopted them in treaties which he concluded with the seaports of Biscay Castile and Portugal, the Hollanders had acted on them in a war with the Hanse towns in 1438, and they appear in the Black Book of the British admiralty. But the rule of France was *robe d'ennemi confisque robe d'ami*: the enemy's ship infected the neutral goods on board and the enemy's goods infected the neutral ship which carried them, and all were condemned. And the northern powers, strong at sea, did not really allow to neutral commerce the freedom which the Mediterranean cities, more equally matched, were obliged to tolerate. England

Denmark Sweden and the Hanse towns laboured to put down neutral commerce with their enemies by treaties, by solicitations to neutral sovereigns, and even by arbitrary prohibitions. The close of the sixteenth and the beginning of the seventeenth centuries were marked by the Dutch invention of blockade and by a greater readiness to limit general prohibitions to articles distinguished as contraband of war, and the doctrines of the Consolat thus began to stand out more clearly, in the practice of the powers which professed them, as applicable to neutral commerce in all cases except those of blockade and contraband. But they were still confronted by the French rule, and in the middle of the seventeenth century the Dutch, in view of their interest as neutral carriers, made efforts which were widely successful to introduce by treaty the rule "free ships free goods, enemy ships enemy goods." Evidently then there was no custom of nations on the subject.

With this state of things Grotius dealt feebly. He did not mention contraband of war; he subjected blockade to a condition not dreamed of by his countrymen, that a speedy surrender of the blockaded place should be expected; he suggested a baseless presumption that the goods on board an enemy's ship would be enemy's, in order to justify the infection of neutral goods by the enemy character of the ship; and he would have made the infection of a neutral ship by the enemy character of the goods on board depend on whether the shipowner had consented to carry them. Indeed the book of Grotius obtained an instant and wide currency as expressing the milder sentiments of the age which was coming in, and as containing, in spite of all its gaps, the most complete code to be found of the law which was wanted. But it must from the first have been felt to be wanting with regard to the questions for which, because they were those of the day, erudition could do the least. It is not surprising that Pufendorff, the next theorist on international law, entirely eliminated from his sources of it the custom of nations which had given so little of useful result.

The boundary between the natural law and the superadded custom of nations had been difficult to trace in those points of established usage of which the justification by reason was so simple that they might just as well be regarded as necessary deductions from reason. Pufendorff elected to refer such points to the natural law, and for all the rest he denied that the custom of nations had any binding force on the conscience. Thus Grotius had included the rules relating to diplomatic intercourse (*jus legationum*) in the *jus gentium*, but Pufendorff referred the immunities of ambassadors to the natural law so far as he regarded them as necessary for legitimate purposes, while, so far as they covered the residence of ambassadors more for the purpose of spying than of treating, he held that any state might refuse them if it was ready to have its own ambassadors dealt with in the same way[1]. His point of view was that of the theologian and the moralist and not that of the lawyer. His interest lay rather in determining the limits which conscience might allow to the action of an individual man or state in conceivable circumstances, than in determining the rules which ought to control such action in the main. Hence, while insisting much on the social nature of man as the source of his duties,

[1] *De Jure Naturæ et Gentium*, l. 2, c. 3, § 23. This work appeared in 1672 at Lund in Sweden, where Pufendorff was then a professor, but he was a native of Chemnitz in Saxony.

he missed the essential facts that, if society is to exist, it must establish rules free from such undefinable elements as the principal purpose of an ambassador's residence, and those rules must be acquiesced in by the members of the society. He missed what Suarez, casuist as he too was, had been able to see. But even Pufendorff could hardly have missed it if in his time the custom of nations had furnished a body of rules more adequate to their intercourse and more imposing by its comprehensiveness.

The passage in which Pufendorff sums up his international principles is worth giving in his own words. "Lastly," he says, "we must consider whether there is any peculiar and positive *jus gentium* contrasted with natural law, for the learned are not agreed on the question. Many regard the law of nature and the *jus gentium* as being one and the same, differing only in name. So Hobbes (*De Cive*, c. xiv. 4. 5) divides natural law 'into the natural law of men and the natural law of states commonly called *jus gentium*. The precepts of both,' he adds, 'are the same, but because states when once they have been established put on the characters belonging to the persons of men, the law which we call natural when speaking of the duty of individual men is called *jus gentium* when applied to entire states or nations.' To which opinion we fully subscribe, nor do we deem that there is any other voluntary or positive *jus gentium*, at least with the force of law properly so called, binding nations as proceeding from a superior[1]." Thus Hobbes and Pufendorff discarded from their understanding of the phrase *jus gentium* all reference to the authority on which that law was based, whether the conscience of mankind or the custom

[1] U. S.

of nations, and employed it in the sense of the law existing between nations, as in Isidore of Seville and the Decretal. Among the writers who copied them in identifying it in that sense with the law of nature, " the law of nature and of nations," the title which Pufendorff gave his book, became a standard phrase. Startling results flowed from the absolute parity so asserted between the technical individual formed by the state and the natural man. Thus, since between natural individuals a contract extorted by force is not binding, those for whom the law of nature and of nations was one and the same could not hold that a treaty of peace was binding between states, if one of the belligerents had so completely gained the upper hand in the war that the other had no choice but to accept the terms proposed. Pufendorff did not shrink from that conclusion. If a state rushes into war without first trying all pacific means of settling the dispute, he considers it to be under a kind of contract to abide by the event. But if it is unjustly attacked, and after having vainly appealed to pacific means is driven to conclude an unfair peace, it may try to repair the injustice done it when opportunity offers[1]. For the rest, Pufendorff contributes nothing to fill the void which his elimination of the customary law of nations tended to leave. He passes without notice those great topics, such as the laws of maritime war, on which the need of positive rules was the greatest want of his time in international law. The identity of the law of nature for private persons and for states could lead to no rules for the guidance of states in situations in which private persons are not and cannot be placed.

[1] U. S., l. 8, c. 8, § 1.

# CHAPTER V

### BYNKERSHOEK : WOLFF : VATTEL

*Bynkershoek.*

FROM the Peace of Westphalia to the present day the great desideratum of international law has been the union of reason and custom in a satisfactory body of rules, satisfactory in the sense in which alone the term can be applied to arrangements made or accepted by man, as supplying a system capable of being put in practice under actual conditions, and fairly meeting the needs which arise from them, without excluding improvement, or modification to suit changed conditions. That desideratum can never be fully attained till the society of states has been provided with some organisation, but to aid in realising it ought to be the aim of every writer on the subject and of every statesman who is concerned with international affairs. Writers and statesmen however will naturally address themselves to the task with different prepossessions. The former, so far as they are impelled by ideas to write, will magnify the part of reason ; the latter will find their way smoothed by adherence to custom. Even writers are grouped by personal or national characteristics into schools leaning more to the one or the other element, and within the first half of the eighteenth century that difference may already be traced between Cornelius van Bynkershoek, the Dutch lawyer and president of the high council of Holland, and the German professor Christian von Wolff.

The principal work of Bynkershoek on our subject is the *Quæstionum Juris Publici libri duo*, published in 1737. He had previously published a *Dissertatio de Dominio maris*, and *De foro Legatorum tam in causa civili quam criminali liber singularis*. He uses the term *jus gentium* in the sense of the law between states which Hobbes and Pufendorff had stamped on it. To whatever extent later theorists might differ from those authorities by admitting an element of custom into the mutual obligations of states, they did not recur in their language either to the Roman meaning of *jus gentium* as the law in which mankind agrees, or to its meaning in Grotius as a branch of voluntary human law. A term which had implied a certain source or a certain part of international law, having been extended to the whole of it through the view that it had but one source in the law of nature, remained identified with the whole, and any distinction had to be made by other words. Henceforth *jus gentium* and the terms that literally translate it—*le droit des gens, das Völkerrecht*, the law of nations—mean simply international law.

Bynkershoek's general views are expressed in the few pages which, under the title *ad lectorem*, he prefixed to the *Quæstiones Juris Publici*. "In the law of nations no human authority can prevail against reason, but where reason is doubtful, as is often the case, that law must be judged of by nearly constant practice (*ex perpetuo fere usu*). But many things were once a part of the law of nations which are not so now; for example, treaties are not now valid without ratification, though the negotiators who concluded them held full powers from their governments, which formerly was otherwise. And therefore the examples and treaties which I here use I take rather from recent than from older times, desiring that what I write shall be practically useful." The authority of custom is thinly veiled by representing reason as doubtful whenever custom is allowed to prevail over it, or is admitted to have changed. And in the body of the work the veil is scarcely maintained. The right of putting captive enemies to death, for instance, is stoutly maintained by reasoning, but it is immediately admitted that it has become obsolete, and that the right of enslaving captive enemies, which succeeded to it, has become obsolete in its turn[1]. And in speaking of contraband of war Bynkershoek roundly says: " the common law of nations on this matter can only be learnt from reason and custom[2]."

But what Bynkershoek has become most famous for is his use of treaties as evidence of custom. " I do not deny that authority may add weight to reason, but I prefer to seek it in a constant custom of concluding treaties in one sense or another, and in examples that have occurred in one country or another, rather than from the testimony of any poet or orator, Greek or Roman: verily they are the worst teachers of public law. They serve more to display erudition than to furnish authority. The

[1] *Quæstiones juris publici*, l. 1, c. 3.
[2] U. S., l. 1, c. 10.

authority of those who transact affairs in the sight of all men, and who have learnt wisdom from what has happened before, weighs more with me. They are in the habit of concluding treaties on the footing of the practice of nations. Not that I would pay deference even to their authority without reason, but that, where reason is on the same side, I value them more than a pack of poets and orators[1]." It will be observed that in this declaration of principles, as well as in the previous quotation from the *ad lectorem*, the appeal is made to statesmen and to examples without a limitation to treaties, although treaties are mentioned with emphasis. And accordingly we find that in the body of the book great use is also made of the unilateral acts of states. The chapter on blockade, for instance, would have little left if the Dutch proclamations were taken out of it[2]. But in building on foundations of that character Bynkershoek was at one with Selden, Zouch, and the whole of the English school, who applied the doctrines of the English admiralty to the sovereignty of the narrow seas and the legal position of neutral commerce. Treaties however had been too much employed in introducing the rule " free ships free goods," in opposition to the Consolat del Mar and the doctrines of the English admiralty, to be regarded in the same quarter with equal favour. The English school drew from a treaty, at least presumptively, the inference that the rule which it adopted was not that which existed in the absence of treaty ; else what necessity was there for a stipulation on the subject ? Bynkershoek was on the same side as to the particular

---

[1] U. S., *ad lectorem*.   [2] U. S., l. 1, c. 11.

question of " free ships free goods[1]," but he would have contended that, when treaties of a certain purport become numerous enough, the question is no longer what is the rule in the absence of treaty, but whether the rule they adopt is not, now at least, to be deemed the most consonant to reason. That mode of looking at treaties is of course approved by those whose devotion to reason as the only source of the law of nations is less qualified than was Bynkershoek's, and he is justly credited with its authorship.

Lastly, what is the reason which is of so much account even in the system of Bynkershoek? If men differ about it, what common ground is there for disputants? Hardly any but the Roman law, to which an appeal is frankly made[2]. Outside this we find arguments drawn from a state of nature believed or feigned to have preceded human institutions, but about which there could be no certain knowledge, or from any other consideration thought appropriate to the matter for the moment in hand. Evidently the school which leans to reason will try to find some better foundation than those which have contented the school which leans to custom.

## Wolff.

Few names which have been great in their day have sunk deeper into oblivion than that of Wolff, whose philosophy reigned in Germany during the

---

[1] U. S., l. 1, c. 14. "One or two treaties differing from custom do not change the law of nations": u. s., l. 1, c. 10.

[2] *Non quod in iis quæ sola ratio commendat a jure Romano ad jus gentium non tuta sit collectio, sed quod Paulus agat de magistro qui &c.*: u. s., l. 1, c. 14.

interval between Leibnitz and Kant, yet he has left a mark on international law. Having already written on natural law, he published in 1749 a ponderous treatise entitled *Jus Gentium methodo scientifica pertractatum, in quo jus gentium naturale ab eo quod voluntarii pactitii et consuetudinarii est accurate distinguitur*. He starts from the principles that by association in a state all its citizens are obliged in conscience to promote the common good and the sufficiency tranquillity and security of the life of each; that this duty further obliges them to maintain their association in the state, without which it cannot be fulfilled; and that it is consequently the duty of a state to preserve itself as an association of its citizens, to perfect itself in all things necessary to its end, and to avoid every thing tending to its destruction or imperfection (§§ 28—31, 33, 35, 36). Next he invokes the principle, which he considers himself to have proved in his previous writings, that the law of nature gives men a right to those things without which they cannot satisfy their obligations of duty; and it follows at once that states have a right to those things by means of which they may avert their destruction and what tends to it, or without which they cannot perfect themselves or avoid what tends to their imperfection (§§ 32, 34, 37). The legacy of Wolff to international law is this doctrine of abstract rights, or of rights to things inherent in persons and states and determining their mutual relations in respect to those things, put in place of the doctrine that rights flow from the disposition made of things by law. The meeting point of the two doctrines is in the admission which every one must make, that there is a distributive justice by which law ought to be guided[1]; but to set up inherent rights as the measure of distributive justice is to invite conflict, for what two men or what two states require in order to avert their destruction or to promote their perfection may be incompatible.

Wolff appears to accentuate the conflict when he treats nations as members of a *civitas maxima* (§§ 9, 10), and as bound to one another by duties equal in extent to those which they owe themselves, only differing in the priority which he grants to the latter (§§ 156, 206). But he tries to part the litigants. " Since," he says, " every nation owes to every other nation what it owes to itself, so far as the latter does not possess it and the former can furnish it without neglect of its duty to itself, and every nation is free and by virtue of natural liberty every one must be allowed to be the judge of his own actions, it follows that every nation must be the judge of what it can furnish without neglect of duty to itself, and any other nation must put up with a denial of what it asks for; in other words, the right of a nation to what other nations naturally owe it is an imperfect one" (§ 157), and cannot be enforced (§ 158). Thus inherent rights are confronted by the maxim *beati possidentes*, a barrier so ineffectual in fact that it is scarcely needful to discuss its sufficiency in theory.

No nation ought to hurt another, and the notion of hurt is in natural law much wider than in civil law, and extends to every thing which impairs the perfection of another nation or of its condition (§§ 173, 645). Every nation has a perfect, that is an enforceable, right not to suffer hurt from another

---

[1] See above, pp. 40—41.

(§§ 252, 253) : this is called the right of security, and arises even when the hurt is only intended (§ 254).

Christian Thomasius, with whose writings I am not acquainted at first hand, is said to have introduced in 1705 the nomenclature of perfect and imperfect duties for those of which the fulfilment can and cannot be enforced consistently with justice, in connection with the principle that the only duties of the former kind are those which arise from the maxim " do not to others what you would not wish them to do to you," in other words, that negative duties alone belong to justice, affirmative ones being permanently relegated to the domain of morals[1]. That principle is practically identical with Kant's, whose system on this subject was based on liberty, to be enjoyed by each so far as compatible with the equal liberty of all, so that the only perfect and enforceable obligation is not to interfere with the liberty of your neighbour.

But neither in the form given to it by Thomasius nor in that given to it by Kant has such a limitation of the province of law received any great amount of favour, except in periods of reaction against over-legislation. It does not in the long run satisfy the exigencies of human affairs, nor does it atone by clearness for what it lacks in sufficiency. Even so illustrious an attempt as that made by the younger Mill to extract a definite limit to legislation from the notion of liberty serves for little except to give a wholesome bias to the mind, when considering the multitudinous claims to the intervention of law which assail it. Nor are we on surer ground if, with Wolff, we dangle inherent rights more largely

[1] See Professor Lorimer's *Institutes of Law*, book 1, chap. xi.

conceived before the eyes, and fancy that we shall baulk the expectations we have raised by making men or nations judges in their own cause, as against those who would realise the rights by active measures. The distributive justice at which humanity aims will always defy set bounds, it will consent to be nothing less than Leibnitz's "charity of the wise," the best feelings coupled with the greatest wisdom to which the race has attained[1]. As that charity is developed the limit between perfect and imperfect rights will be placed at different points. The range of the former will not always be enlarged, the improvement of men may make it safe to extend the range of liberty. But the limit will not be an abstract one, settled *a priori*. It will never be possible to determine from the nature of a right alone whether it ought to be enforceable.

In connection with the international application of Wolff's doctrine a point remains to be mentioned which seems to have escaped him. For the full enjoyment of a right under the sanction of law it is often not enough that it should be recognised by the legislator, he must regulate it. Within a state, the regulation will accompany the recognition. The right will be recognised in certain circumstances and on certain conditions. Between states, the circumstances and conditions will in many cases bear no settlement by doctrine, none but by express agreement. Take the extradition of criminals for instance. Doctrine may lay down that extradition ought to be

[1] *Justitiam igitur, quæ virtus est hujus affectus rectrix quem φιλανθρωπίαν Græci vocant, commodissime ni fallor definiemus caritatem sapientis, hoc est, sequentem sapientiæ dictata.* Leibnitz, quoted by Lorimer, u. s.

granted only for grave crimes, but it cannot determine precisely for what crimes. It may lay down that a *prima facie* case ought to be made out against the person accused, but not precisely what evidence not satisfying the usual requirements of the court ought to be received from abroad for that purpose. Or take the navigation of what are called international rivers, that is, rivers flowing through the territories of more than one state. Doctrine may lay down that a state ought not to bar the peaceful passage across its territory along such a river, or hamper it by customs duties, but it cannot determine the measure in which those who use the passage ought to contribute to the cost of maintaining the navigation, or the regulations to which they ought to be subject for the security of the state across which they pass. Therefore extradition and the peaceful navigation of international rivers must be imperfect rights in the sense that conventions are indispensable to their due enjoyment. But it does not follow that there is in them no element of law or of perfect right. If a state persistently refused either to conclude proper conventions for extradition or to surrender fugitive criminals without them, it is not to be supposed that other states would feel themselves bound to put up for ever with its being an Alsatia, rendering the due repression of crime within their own limits impossible. Nor is it to be supposed that states desiring commerce with one other, which might well be what Wolff would have described as necessary to the perfection of their condition, would feel themselves bound to forego it for ever because a state across the territory of which it was necessary to pass along a navigable river was persistently churlish. Consequently between nations three degrees of right have to be admitted. Besides the claims to the enforcement of which by compulsion the general opinion of the civilised world would give no approbation, and those which it considers to be enforceable as they stand, there are claims which that opinion would certainly not be content to leave to the caprice of the states on which they exist, and which yet are not as a general rule enforceable until they have been embodied in conventions. The first are only moral rights, the second are legal. The third have a legal basis, generally left without notice, but which in rare cases obtrudes itself on the attention and may justify action. Perhaps it would be convenient to reserve the term " imperfect rights " for the last, although Thomasius introduced it for moral rights.

## *Vattel.*

Vattel was a native of the principality of Neuchâtel, then belonging to the king of Prussia, but served the elector-king, elector of Saxony and king of Poland, successively as *conseiller d'ambassade*, minister in Switzerland, and *conseiller privé du cabinet*. His famous work was published in 1758, under the title of *Le Droit des Gens, ou principes de la loi naturelle appliqués à la conduite et aux affaires des nations et des souverains*. Its philosophical principles are those of Wolff, of whom Vattel was a great though not a servile admirer, but its chief merit is on the practical side. It presents the law of nations as it then stood with a fulness of which there had been no previous example, including the topics which had grown up since the time of Grotius or on which Grotius had not dwelt, and on which Wolff had had little or nothing to say; and it does so from the point of view of a man versed in affairs, familiar with the customs which had been taking shape since the Peace of Westphalia, and duly appreciating their value. Its reputation was therefore as well deserved as it was immediate, and it must remain of lasting importance in the study of international law, as the focus in which the schools of reason and custom were first brought together, and from which the succeeding divergences may be traced.

It is not necessary to pursue our historical sketch further. Indeed, if carried further, it could only display the operation, with regard to particular questions, of those general tendencies and principles of which we have seen the origin. Such operation can best be studied in relation to each question as it offers itself, but we may first spend a little time in fixing our own point of view.

# CHAPTER VI

#### THE PRINCIPLES OF INTERNATIONAL LAW

1. THE society of states, having European civilisation, or the international society, is the most comprehensive form of society among men, but it is among men that it exists. States are its immediate, men its ultimate members. The duties and rights of states are only the duties and rights of the men who compose them.

2. The consent of the international society to the rules prevailing in it is the consent of the men who are the ultimate members of that society. When one of those rules is invoked against a state, it is not necessary to show that the state in question has assented to the rule either diplomatically or by having acted on it, though it is a strong argument if you can do so. It is enough to show that the general *consensus* of opinion within the limits of European civilisation is in favour of the rule.

3. The consent of the international society, defined as in the last paragraph, and given to a rule as an enforceable rule of law, is normally binding on the consciences of men in matters arising within the society and transcending the state tie, as state law is normally binding on the conscience within that tie. Such consent therefore normally determines the

mutual duties and rights of the states in which men are grouped. This is so because the international society is not a voluntary but a necessary one, and the general *consensus* of opinion among its members is the only authority that can make rules for it. The men who compose any state derive benefits from that society, and therefore cannot at their pleasure adhere to it in part and not altogether. The existence, in geographical proximity to the international society, of a state which was not bound by its rules, would be a source of intolerable inconvenience and danger to the members of the society. The social nature of man lies at the bottom of these reasons.

4. International rules ought to be made with due care that they shall not restrict liberty more than is necessary, that they shall be suited to the cases which most commonly arise, and that reciprocity in their application shall be possible. It is no reason for not applying a rule that a different one would have been better suited to the particular case.

5. In matters transcending the state tie, and so far as a rule founded on the consent of a society is wanting, the men who guide the action of states have only to obey their consciences. The want of a rule to define the action allowable does not exclude all action. The largest field for the application of this principle is in dealings with states or populations not having the civilisation necessary for forming part of the international society, but the principle is sometimes applicable between states included in that society.

6. When a state has to act although a rule is wanting, it ought as far as possible so to act that a rule might be framed on the precedent.

7. The obligation of international rules on the conscience, even when they have once been founded on a general *consensus*, is subject to exception, as is the obligation of state law on the conscience. And in the former department the conscience will have a somewhat greater latitude than within a state, because there is no international legislature, and diplomatic agreements for the change of a rule can with difficulty be made to comprise so large a number of states as to prove that the general opinion has been changed ; wherefore an international rule can rarely be changed otherwise than by its ceasing to be followed and general approval being given to such change of practice, of which some state must set the example. Hence it is not a conclusive, though a strong, argument against a state that it has itself applied the rule of which it resists the application. It would be contrary to the moral nature of man that he should be fettered, absolutely and permanently, by any external rule.

8. When a state is confronted by a rule which it deems to be bad, either originally or because it has become bad through a change of circumstances, it ought to take into account the greater or less evil which always results from violating known rules, and, if it decides to violate the rule in question, it ought as far as possible so to act that a better rule may be framed on the precedent. Neither in violating a rule nor in acting where a rule is wanting, is a state at liberty to consider only its particular case, without reference to the conduct which would be best suited to the cases which most commonly arise.

9. No law, national or international, will be durable unless it is fairly well adapted to the

character and circumstances of the men who are to observe it. Hence the social nature of man, and his material and moral surroundings in the regions and at the time in question, are the ultimate source of international law, in the sense that they are the cause why any rules of international law exist, and that they furnish a test with which any particular rules of that law must comply on pain of not being durable rules. And consent is the immediate source of international law, in the sense that the social nature of man and his material and moral surroundings may furnish principles of action, but only the consent of a society can establish rules.

10. The international society to which we belong, and of which what we know as international law is the body of rules, comprises—*First*, all European states. These, as explained in speaking of the Peace of Westphalia, form a system intimately bound together by the interests of its members[1]. Concert is another word used to express a system in this sense. The French text of the treaty of Paris, 1856, Art. 7, says that the Sublime Porte is admitted to participate in the advantages *du droit public et du concert Européens*, for which the English version has " of the public law and system (concert) of Europe." *Secondly*, all American states. These, on becoming independent, inherited the international law of Europe, as will be seen in the next paragraph, and they are as necessary parties as the European states for its further development. That they do not form part politically of the European system is due to the fact that, on account of their geographical situation, they

---

[1] See above, pp. 55, 56.

do not desire to do so. *Thirdly*, a few Christian states in other parts of the world, as the Hawaiian Islands, Liberia and the Orange Free State. The same cannot be said of all Christian states, not for instance of Abyssinia.

11. No new state, arising from the dismemberment of an old one within the geographical limits of our international society, has the option of giving or refusing its consent to the international law of that society. Since all obligations are ultimately those of men, the men who compose the new state were bound by that law as members of their former state, and they cannot by a unilateral act change the footing on which their intercourse with the other members of the international society is based.

12. Our international society exercises the right of admitting outside states to parts of its international law without necessarily admitting them to the whole of it. Thus a large part of the relations between the European and American states on the one hand, and China and Japan on the other hand, is conducted on the footing of ordinary international law; but the former enjoy in the latter a consular jurisdiction, substituted for the rules of jurisdiction belonging to ordinary international law. By a singular anomaly a similar consular jurisdiction is still enjoyed by the other European and American states in the Turkish empire, although that empire has been admitted not only to the public law of Europe but even to the European political system. This is an instance of the way in which all human institutions, being free and not mechanical products, shade off from one to another.

13. There are claims between states to things

the normal enjoyment of which requires definition and regulation not obtainable, in the absence of an international legislature, otherwise than by express convention, but with regard to which general opinion does not leave it free to states to enter into reasonable conventions or to refuse them. Such claims are imperfect legal rights, and must be distinguished from the merely moral claims which a state is considered to be free to refuse. The extradition of criminals and the peaceful navigation of rivers flowing through the territories of more than one state are examples. These imperfect legal rights are analogous to the claims to which, within a state, effect can only be given by the legislature, but to which the sense of distributive justice prevailing in the state requires the legislature to give effect[1].

14. The best evidence of the consent which makes international law is the practice of states appearing in their actions, in the treaties they conclude, and in the judgments of their prize and other courts, so far as in all these ways they have proceeded on general principles and not with a view to particular circumstances, and so far as their actions and the judgments of their courts have not been encountered by resistance or protest from other states. Even protest and resistance may be too feeble to prevent general consent being concluded from a widely extended practice.

15. The arguments adduced by statesmen in despatches and other public utterances are very important as showing what were the principles proceeded on, especially in the case of treaties, which

---

[1] See above, pp. 74—76.

are so often concluded with a view to particular circumstances that great care must be taken in using them as evidences of international law.

16. Special authority is often claimed for the practice of those states which are most concerned with a particular branch of international law, as for that of the chief maritime powers with regard to the laws of maritime war. There is a good foundation for such a claim in the fact that the powers most concerned with a subject must understand it best, and be best able to distinguish good from bad reasoning about it. On the other hand, special knowledge is often accompanied by the bias of special interest. But when the states most concerned with a subject in turn apply the same rules and suffer their application, that bias may be supposed to be eliminated, and the agreement which those concerned in the vast majority of cases find suitable must count for a general agreement in spite of much comparatively speculative criticism from other quarters.

17. The opinions of private writers must of course be counted towards the general consent of men, especially when the writer's reputation proves that he represents many persons besides himself. Moreover, for much of international law, which is so well observed that discussions about it between states are not easily quoted, its admission into accredited text-books is valuable testimony to its being observed as law, and not from any option still remaining free to states. And when a rule is disputed, or there is a question whether an old rule ought to be changed or a new one introduced, it is only through public discussion that reason can be made to appear and prevail.

18. Time cannot supply the want of general agreement, but where the agreement in favour of an altered or added rule is sufficiently general, it is an element in determining the limit of the forbearance to be shown to a state which persists in resisting the change or the addition. When reasoning has stood the test of time, it can no longer be urged that it resulted from caprice, or from the undue consideration of a transitory interest.

## CHAPTER VII

### THE EQUALITY AND INDEPENDENCE OF STATES

*The Independence and Legal Equality of States, and Semi-Sovereignty.*

IN Wolff, and through him in Vattel, the doctrine of the equality of nations appears in the following form. Being regarded as persons living in a state of nature, nations are naturally equal as men are naturally equal; a small nation is as much a nation as a large one, just as a dwarf is as much a man as a giant; it is therefore natural or necessary that all nations have the same rights and the same obligations, as much and no more being allowed to one nation as to another[1]. If we leave out the attempt at deduction contained in this, it amounts to no more than a statement of the fact that international law is a body of general rules. But besides that fact there is another. The general rules of international law apply in their fulness only to sovereign states like France or the United Kingdom, and to natural persons brought into relation with sovereign states, as is the case of pirates and blockade-runners. Between sovereign states and natural persons international

[1] Wolff, *Jus Gentium*, §§ 16, 17, 18; Vattel, *Le Droit des Gens*, §§ 18, 19 of the *Préliminaires*.

law recognises groups of the latter not on an equality with the former, of which Bulgaria may be taken as an example[1], and which may be classed together as semi-sovereign though they may and do differ in their particular condition and rights. When this second fact is taken into account, it results that the equality of states cannot usefully or even intelligibly be presented as a deduction unless the deduction also furnishes a test showing to what states it applies. Let us look at the truth as it stands.

Independence, like every negative, does not admit of degrees. A group of men dependent in any degree on another group is not independent, but has relations with that other group which as between the two are constitutional relations. Sovereignty is partible. A group of men is fully sovereign when it has no constitutional relations making it in any degree dependent on any other group: if it has such relations, so much of sovereignty as they leave it is a kind or degree of semi-sovereignty, though the constitution may not call it by that name. Thus the independence and the full sovereignty of a state are identical, but it would be an abuse of language to speak of semi-sovereignty as partial independence.

The constitutional relations between a semi-sovereign state and the state on which it is dependent

[1] By Art. 1 of the treaty of Berlin, 1878, "Bulgaria is constituted an autonomous and tributary principality under the suzerainty of His Imperial Majesty the Sultan." And, by Art. 10, Bulgaria takes the place of the Imperial Ottoman Government in its railway obligations, as well pecuniary as with regard to the working of the railways, and both towards the companies and towards Austria-Hungary; and "the conventions necessary for the settlement of these questions shall be concluded between Austria-Hungary, the Porte, Servia and the principality of Bulgaria immediately after the conclusion of the peace."

may exclude the former from any public intercourse with foreign states, as in the case of the United States of America and the so-called sovereign states comprised in the union. Or they may permit such intercourse within certain limits, and with the difference that the whole may not be able to compel the parts to observe those limits, as in the case of the Holy Roman Empire which was dissolved in 1806, or may enjoy enough both of material strength and of popular good will to make obedience to its constitution practically secure, which is doubtless the case of the present German empire[1]. And there may be this other difference, that foreign states may be parties to the constitutional arrangements by which a semi-sovereign state is allowed to have a limited public intercourse with them, as in the case of the Holy Roman Empire by the Peace of Westphalia, and in that of Bulgaria by the treaty of Berlin, or those arrangements may have been made without the concurrence of any foreign power, as in the case of the present German empire.

The result of the foregoing is that the states between which the rules of international law prevail in their fulness are, *First*, those which are sovereign and independent constitutionally as well as internationally, such as France and the United Kingdom;

---

[1] See above, pp. 57, 58, as to the Holy Roman Empire. The constitution of the present German empire reserves to the imperial authority all treaties of peace, of alliance or for any other political objects, all commercial or postal treaties, and all treaties relating to copyright, extradition, domicile, emigration or the administration of civil or criminal law. But diplomatic relations between foreign powers and the states of the empire are not entirely excluded, and England has ministers resident or *chargés d'affaires* at many of the German capitals.

*Secondly*, those which other states accept in their dealings with them as being sovereign and independent, although they may be nominally hampered by a weak constitutional tie. Of the latter class there is perhaps no example at present, but the states of the Holy Roman Empire were formerly examples of it. The states of both classes, as far as they exist or have existed, deal with one another on the footing of equality in the sense of Wolff and Vattel, that is, they admit the identity of rights and obligations for all, which is merely to say that the international law which they recognise is a body of general rules and not of particular solutions.

Thus the duties of neutrality are the same for a weak state as for a powerful one, though they may be burdensome to the one and easy to the other. The weak state must endure the burden as long as it clings to its independence. And this equality, as it is not necessarily connected with any constitutional or other antecedent character in the states enjoying it, but is essentially attached to independence in fact, cannot be deduced by reasoning from any higher source than the fact. The states which do not enjoy it while at the same time possessing certain foreign relations, because the constitutional tie which limits their sovereignty is internationally respected, are semi-sovereign internationally as well as constitutionally, and the dealings between them and foreign states which their constitutional limitation permits are conducted on the basis of ordinary international law so far as applicable. Where on the other hand, as in the case of the United States, the component parts of an independent state are effectually precluded from having any foreign relations, not only can the constitutional condition of those parts not really exceed semi-sovereignty, by whatever name it may be graced, but internationally they are not even semi-sovereign, they have no international existence at all.

The word "suzerainty" is used in the treaty of Berlin to express the relation of the Sublime Porte to the principality of Bulgaria, which it created. That, in the middle ages, was the proper term for the relation of a feudal superior to his vassal, while "sovereignty" was more properly superiority in jurisdiction, the highest court in a territory which was distinct for judicial purposes being called a *cour souveraine*. The queen is our sovereign because she is "over all persons and in all causes within her dominions supreme." Consequently a modern description of a state as subject to a suzerainty does not by itself shut it out from any of the rights that were enjoyed by the states of the Holy Roman Empire, which were internationally accepted as sovereign states, and were so called, while they recognised the empire as their suzerain power. How many of those rights it is intended that the state in question shall enjoy must be ascertained from the more detailed provisions of its constitution.

Questions sometimes arise whether a certain whole is a federal state or a federation of states, and whether a certain union of monarchies is real or personal. The notions of full and partial sovereignty appear sufficient to cover the former question and to guide to an analogous solution of the latter. If *de facto* the whole of the union confronts all foreign powers as the exclusive representative of its territory and population, it is internationally a federal state or a real union. If *de facto* the several portions entertain any relations with foreign powers, then for the international lawyer the whole in strictness of language can only be a federation of states or a personal union, although it might be pedantic to insist on such strictness where the foreign relations possessed by the several portions were of trifling importance. Thus I should not propose to call the present German empire anything but a federal state, so long as the justification for giving it that name is ·distinctly understood. From these principles of nomenclature, if they are accepted, it seems to follow that a personal union may grow into a real one by habit, without any change of constitution. Thus, when James the Sixth of Scotland became James the First of England, the union between the two countries was only personal. James remained at peace with Spain as king of Scotland, but was at war with Spain as king of England until the war which existed at his accession was closed by a treaty of peace. But it would surely be pedantic to say that in the international sense the union was still only personal under William the Third, and under queen Anne at the date of the battle of Blenheim. No British or foreign statesman then dreamt of different treaties or different terms for England and Scotland as being possible, nor were England and Scotland represented by different negotiators. The case of Hanover was not the same as that of Scotland, rather because the king negotiated for that country through his Hanoverian ministers than because the Salic law might carry the crown of Hanover to a different sovereign, as it ultimately did. The dominions which had been personally united in the Hapsburgs came to be regarded internationally as one state long before a constitutional tie had been established between them, or the Pragmatic Sanction had obviated the danger that a female succession might carry Hungary to a different line from Austria.

### *The Political Inequality of States, and the Great Powers of Europe.*

When a matter arises, and the states which are agreed as to the mode of dealing with it carry their plan into effect as far as it is possible to do so by their own action, without directly compelling a state which does not agree with them to join in their action and without directly affecting that state, they do not violate its independence. But their action may indirectly compel that state to join in it, or to endure without opposition a conduct which it deems to affect it injuriously though indirectly, or of which it disapproves in the general interest of the European system. In that case a political victory has been gained over the state in question. And a state may be so weak that it is not much or at all consulted by other powers, and that little attention is paid to its opinion if given. In that case it is in a situation of political inferiority, and many states of the European system are permanently in such a situation towards what are called the great powers, yet their legal equality is not necessarily infringed thereby. It is true that politics are not law, but an adequate motion of a body of law cannot be gained without understanding the society in and for which it exists, and it is therefore necessary for the student of international law to appreciate the actual position of the great powers of Europe.

At no time and in no quarter of the globe can small states ever have been admitted by large ones to political equality with themselves, and the eighteenth century in Europe was certainly no exception to that rule. But in that century the balance of power was the chief study in international politics, and the great powers were usually divided into two nearly equal bodies. These were not always composed of the same members: Austria, for instance, was allied with England in the war of the Austrian succession and with France in the Seven Years' War. Yet, in whatever direction a minor sovereign deemed that his interest pointed, there was a strong body to which he could bring an assistance by no means to be despised in a contest against another body of nearly equal strength. In no war of the age was the division of Europe so unequal as in that of the American revolution, in which England stood alone while the larger part of the Continent was arrayed against her either in hostility or in unfriendly neutrality. But then some of the smaller powers, whose importance at sea was far greater than by land, were brought into prominence by the maritime character of the struggle. What was wanted in order to bring the contrast between the great powers and the lesser ones into a strong light was a crisis on the main aspect of which all or nearly all Europe should be united, while its management should raise questions of some though only minor importance. Then it would be seen how far the great powers would assume the management of such a crisis to themselves, even in points deeply interesting to the smaller ones. The opportunity was afforded by the fall of Napoleon and the arrangements which became necessary in consequence of it.

The war which led to the first fall of Napoleon and the restoration of Louis XVIII was ended by what is called the treaty of Paris, but which was in reality four treaties concluded 30th May, 1814, in the same terms, between the restored king of France on the one hand and England, Austria, Prussia and Russia respectively on the other hand. It was of course a foregone conclusion that France should be deprived of the immense conquests she had made, and accordingly by Art. 3 of the treaties the new boundary of France was fixed and she renounced all that lay beyond it, without saying to whom. Then Art. 32 provided that all the powers which had taken part in the war should send their plenipotentiaries to Vienna, " to settle in a general congress the arrangements which are to complete the dispositions of the present treaty." To those treaties the three other powers which had been allied with the four in the war against Napoleon, Spain Portugal and Sweden, acceded. But each of the treaties with the four great powers contained secret articles, of which the first ran thus : " The disposition to be made of the territories which His Most Christian Majesty renounces by the 3rd Article of the public treaty, and the relations from which a system or real and lasting equilibrium in Europe is to result, shall be settled at the congress on the bases determined by the allied powers among themselves, and in accordance with the several dispositions contained in the following articles." Then followed an outline sketch of the mode in which Europe was to be reconstituted, leaving however much matter of the highest importance to be filled in.

Thus the congress which the public treaty charged with making the new arrangements was to be composed of all the powers which had taken part in the war, a description that primarily included France and her seven allied antagonists, known collectively at the congress as the eight powers. Strictly the description would also have included the sovereigns who, as the wave of reconquest passed westward, had abandoned the fortunes of Napoleon or been restored before the close of the war on the principle of legitimacy; and in fact all Europe was represented at Vienna except Turkey and the principalities dependent on her, but although the other states had to sign the particular arrangements which concerned them, the general act of the congress was prepared for signature only by the eight and was signed only by seven of them. By the secret articles however the five great powers, including France, pledged the congress in advance of its meeting to a large part of the settlement; and when the plenipotentiaries were assembled, it appeared that the four great powers other than France understood that they alone, as the allied powers mentioned in the first secret article, were to decree the rest of the settlement. With what skill Talleyrand gained the admission of France to the inner conclave belongs to the general history of Europe and to the particular history of the principle of legitimacy. He did not carry his point without appealing to the powers of the second order, but when it was carried " the committee of the five great powers " formally constituted itself, and meetings of the eight powers were recognised, but no general meeting of the congress ever took place. A "German committee" was also recognised, consisting of Austria Prussia Bavaria Wurtemberg and Hanover, and having for its province the organisation of a Germanic confederation. But when Wurtemberg declared in it that she could not bind herself about the constitution of such a confederation till it was known what the possessions of each member of it would be, Metternich replied for Austria and Prussia that all which related to what he called the political question, by which he meant territorial arrangements, was outside the competence of the committee, the great powers having reserved to themselves to pronounce on such matters, and that enough was known about them in a general way for settling the act of confederation. The king of Wurtemberg was not satisfied with this answer, and reasonably, for the fate of Saxony was still undecided, and the "German committee" ceased to meet. Afterwards the five great powers agreed among themselves that the king of Saxony should be deprived of two-fifths of his dominions in favour of Prussia, and his consent to cede them was compelled by restraining his personal liberty till he had given it, which must be considered to have vitiated any title derived from such consent. But that circumstance was unimportant, for the king had been faithful to Napoleon to the last, and his dominions might therefore have been disposed of by right of conquest, and indeed England Russia and Prussia had been willing to carry out the arrangement on that basis, and dispense with an enforced signature.

This was the state of things when Napoleon returned from Elba, except that the king of Saxony had not then agreed to the dismemberment of his dominions, though the five great powers had determined on it. In face of the danger caused by Napoleon's easy recovery of his throne, the great German powers showed a more conciliatory spirit towards the smaller ones, the negotiations for the establishment of the Germanic confederation were hastened and completed by signature on 8th June, 1815, and on the following day the general act of the congress was signed by the eight powers except Spain, Talleyrand and his colleagues being permitted to sign on behalf of Louis XVIII though he was an exile at Ghent, and a few remaining questions being handed over to the states directly concerned in them for settlement between themselves. The reasons given by Spain for refusing her signature were " (1) that the act included a stipulation contrary to the immediate and complete restitution of the three duchies of Parma, Placentia and Guastalla ; (2) that the plenipotentiaries of Austria Russia Great Britain France and Prussia had no power to determine the destiny of Tuscany and Parma without the concurrence of the Spanish plenipotentiary ; and (3) that the act included many articles which had not been reported at the meetings of the plenipotentiaries of the eight powers." Meanwhile a new European alliance against Napoleon had been formed, Sweden not joining because she was too much occupied in her peninsula by the present of Norway which had been made her against the will of the Norwegian people, and Spain refusing her accession because " the dignity of her crown and the importance of the services which her subjects had rendered to the European cause did not permit her to accede to a treaty of alliance if she was not considered to be a principal party in it ; if the accession which was proposed to her was understood in that sense, the king was ready to give it ; otherwise he would act in concert with the other powers so far as concerned military operations, but when it came to treating he would treat in his own name, and would not consider himself to be comprised in what the plenipotentiaries of the other powers might stipulate."

Short as was the campaign of Waterloo, several of the smaller powers had taken part in it and all had moved troops or at least incurred expense. Accordingly they claimed admission to the conferences for settling the terms of peace. The four great allies however informed them on 10th August 1815 that they did not think fit to comply with their desire, and that they would communicate nothing until they had agreed among themselves on the principles which were to govern their relations with France and on the conditions to be exacted from her. The treaty of peace concluded on 20th November by France with Austria Russia Prussia and England placed the territorial renunciations of France at the disposal of the other contracting parties, and stipulated that the pecuniary indemnity which France agreed to furnish should be paid to them. They, in advance of the treaty, had determined the disposition of the ceded districts by a protocol of 3rd November, and that of the pecuniary indemnity by one of 6th November ; and the smaller states submissively took the shares of territory and money which were thus assigned to them.

Such was the commencement of what during a long succeeding period was described as the moral pentarchy of Europe, pentarchy because France was readmitted to it at the Congress of Aix-la-Chapelle in 1818. It has been necessary to dwell on it in some detail because the origin of a movement is usually its most instructive part, and especially is that so when we are tracing an authority the exercise of which is veiled under legal forms, the necessary signatures being usually obtained in the end without always leaving an official trace of how they were obtained. In that respect the authority of the great powers in Europe may be likened to that of the house of commons in the British constitution: how much of real independence is implied by the concurrence of the crown and the house of lords can only be known from the history of earlier struggles: machinery is apt to work smoothly when the power of its different parts to resist has been tested and is known. For a time the pentarchy was worked with great effect in the interest of the principle of legitimacy[1], but common action in that direction was broken up through the change made in the policy of England by Canning, that made in the policy of Russia by the Greek insurrection, and that made in the policy of France by the same insurrection and the revolution of 1830. Still, in spite of dissensions between the great powers which at times brought them to the verge of mutual war, the skill of statesmen was able to preserve enough of common action to impose on Holland and Belgium the terms of their separation, and to deal with several phases of the Eastern question. From 1848 the pentarchy must be said to have altogether ceased to exist, but the causes which determine the mutual relations of large states and small ones within

[1] See above, p. 59.

the same political system lie deep in the nature of things, and while Berlin in 1878 reproduced on a smaller scale Vienna in 1814 and 1815, it was able to do so with less friction because the controlling authority of the great powers in congress was no longer novel, but had sunk so far into European habits as to carry moral as well as material weight. There can be little doubt that for that reason it was easier for Russia to submit to the treaty of San Stefano being cut down to the treaty of Berlin, but our present subject is more concerned with the attitude of the congress towards the smaller states. Servia and Roumania had been semi-sovereign, with the power of entering into limited foreign relations: their independence was recognised. Montenegro had already been recognised as independent by all the great powers except England and Turkey: those powers also recognised its independence. The boundaries of all three were modified, Servia and Montenegro being enlarged and Roumania compelled to submit to an exchange of territory, and in all three it was provided that religion should be free and should be no cause of incapacity. Greece was an independent state of half a century's standing: an enlargement of her territory at the expense of Turkey was recommended to the latter by the other six great powers[1]. Yet neither Roumania Servia Montenegro nor Greece was a party to the treaty of Berlin, nor was Greece a party to the protocol of the congress recommending the enlargement of her territory, nor was she a party to the convention of 24th May 1881 by which the seven great powers, Turkey being this

[1] Six, because Italy had been added since the days of the pentarchy: Germany had taken the place of Prussia.

time a party, fixed the limits of the enlargement which she was to receive. No doubt all these arrangements were subsequently accepted by the states concerned, and what was treated as an acceptance of her new limits had been obtained from Greece before the convention of 24th May 1881 was signed, but was not recited in the convention. Still, when no such acceptances were thought to be even formally necessary to a declaration of the will of Europe on the several matters, we can appreciate what political inequality is compatible in the European system with legal equality. The fact is not one to be condemned. It may prove to be a step towards the establishment of a European government, and in no society can peace and order be permanently enjoyed without a government. But the fact is one which the student of international law is bound to note, whatever development may await it.

*The Equality of States in Civilisation, and the Protection of Subjects abroad.*

Throughout Europe and America, if we except Turkey, habits occupations and ideas are very similar. Family life, and social life in the narrower sense of that term, are based on monogamous marriage and respect for women. The same arts and sciences are taught and pursued, the same avocations and interests are protected by similar laws, civil and criminal, the administration of which is directed by a similar sense of justice. The same dangers are seen to threaten the fabric of society, similar measures are taken or discussed with the object of eluding them, and the same hopes are entertained that improvement will continue to be realised. The literature which is occupied with the life and destiny of man, which entertains him and expresses his most intimate feelings, is read everywhere from whatever country it emanates. There are differences of detail, but no one who has had a liberal education feels himself a stranger in the houses, schools, law courts, theatres, scarcely even in the churches, of another country. Not only is there a great circulation of people regardless of territorial boundaries, but the native subjects of one state travelling or resident in another do not form a class apart; they mix freely with the population, and usually feel themselves safe under the local administration of justice. All this is summed up by saying that Europe and America have a common civilisation.

Turkey and Persia, China, Japan[1], Siam and some other countries have civilisations differing from the European, and so far as they are not Mahometan from those of one another. The Europeans or Americans in them form classes apart, and would not feel safe under the local administration of justice which, even were they assured of its integrity, could not have the machinery necessary for giving adequate protection to the unfamiliar interests arising out of a foreign civilisation. They are therefore placed under the jurisdiction of the consuls of their respective states, pursuant to conventions entered into by the latter with the local governments. The consuls are allowed to dispose of small forces, but the maintenance of their jurisdiction must depend in the long

[1] I write of facts as they stand, without expressing any opinion on the desire felt in Japan to be freed from the consular jurisdiction as having become unnecessary there.

run on the support which the local governments give them pursuant to the conventions. But the latter could not furnish that support if each of the countries in question did not possess an old and stable order of its own, with organised force at the back of it, and complex enough for the leading minds of the country to be able to appreciate the necessities of an order different from theirs. Such countries therefore must be recognised as being civilised, though with other civilisations than ours.

The international law with which we are concerned having arisen among the former of the two classes of populations here contrasted, it is based on the possession by states of a common and in that sense an equal civilisation. The case of Turkey must in this part of our subject be left out of sight, because of the anomalous position of that empire, included on account of its geographical situation in the political system of Europe, but belonging in other respects rather to the second group of contrasted populations. She may benefit by European international law so far as it can be extended to her without ignoring plain facts, but her admission to that benefit cannot react on the statement of the law, which is what it is because it is the law of the European peoples. The common civilisation then, explained as it has here been explained, contains the principle that the institutions, whether of government or of justice, which the inhabitants of a state find suitable to themselves, must normally be accepted as sufficient for the protection of foreigners among them. Those foreigners are subject to the local courts and authorities, and not to separate jurisdictions, and their own governments will not, normally, interfere for their protection so long as they enjoy equal treatment with natives.

Van Bokkelen, a citizen of the United States, was imprisoned for debt in Hayti, and if he had been a Haytian could have obtained his release by making an assignment of his property in favour of his creditors (*cessio bonorum*). There appears to have been something in the laws of Hayti, I do not clearly gather what, which probably laid him under no express incapacity to do this, but at least made it impossible for him as a foreigner to do it. The United States interfered and obtained his release from prison, Mr Bayard, secretary of state, writing that " to close to an alien litigant some given channel of recourse open to a native, without leaving open some equivalent recourse, is a denial of justice[1]." Reference was also made to a treaty, but it was not clear on the point: any one who questioned the principle of international law would also have questioned the interpretation of the treaty. The principle however is clear: there must be no unfair discrimination against a foreigner.

The example also illustrates how, in spite of the common civilisation, cases arise in which unfair discrimination is attempted, or in which other circumstances arise to prevent the normal rule of non-interference applying. The civilisation has grown up by degrees, and populations have become included in it among whom it did not originate. It may not everywhere have adequately permeated institutions and habits of action. Even where its normal reign is assured, political religious or other

[1] Wharton's *Digest of the International Law of the United States*, § 230, vol. 2, p. 643.

excitements may rouse the passions to break through the crust which has been formed over them. If, from whatever cause, the security promised by the common civilisation is flagrantly wanting, the fact must override the presumption. " Justice," Vattel says, " is denied, 1°, by refusing to hear your complaints or those of your subjects, or to admit the latter to establish their right before the ordinary courts; 2°, by interposing delays for which no good reasons can be given, and which are equivalent to a denial or still more ruinous; 3°, by a manifestly unjust and partial judgment. But the injustice must be very evident and palpable[1]." It must be evident and palpable to the general *consensus* of the part of the world which possesses European civilisation, and not turn on the omission of some security to an accused person or a litigant, such as trial by jury, which does not enter into the common law of that part of the world.

When the law of a country, such as it is, is violated towards foreigners, there is in ordinary circumstances a right of interference on their behalf. The principle of equality of treatment with natives can scarcely operate, because, if the law of the land were violated towards all alike, there would not exist anything that could claim to be recognised as a civilised government. But in any country disturbances may arise so serious as to make it necessary for the government to strain the law with a view to restore order, either in pursuance of some constitutional power vested in it, or in reliance on a legislative indemnity to be procured when possible. What is to be said if in

---

[1] *Le Droit des Gens*, liv. 2, ch. 18, § 350.

such a case the law is violated towards foreigners just as towards natives, without greater harshness than in most countries of European civilisation the emergency would be held to warrant, not imprisoning any one without reasonable ground of suspicion, and not punishing any one without reasonable proof of guilt ? This question was much discussed at the time of the civil war in the United States, in connection with the suspension of the *habeas corpus* by president Lincoln as a measure applicable equally to citizens and to foreigners ; and it was complicated by the further discussion, in the United States themselves, whether that suspension under the so-called war power was within the constitutional right of the president. Earl Russell, then British secretary of state for foreign affairs, ultimately acquiesced in the suspension as regarded British subjects, having regard to the quantity of opinion which there was in the States in favour of its being constitutional, and being unable to say that the detentions under it were without reasonable grounds of suspicion. The strongest case was perhaps that of Rahming, in whose favour the Supreme Court issued an attachment against the military commandant who, under orders from the executive, refused to obey the writ of *habeas corpus*. Mr Hall says of the case that " a sovereign, if bound to abandon his subjects to any moderately reasonable law, however hardly it may press on them, is not bound to allow them to be treated in defiance of law, even though they may be so treated in common with all the other inhabitants of the territory in which they are. In the particular case the authority of the Supreme Court " [as to the law] " was undoubtedly superior to that of the executive[1]." With great deference, I think that in the circumstances England had nothing to do with the constitutional question. An emergency had arisen which in most European and American countries would be met by an assumption of power if no reserve of constitutional power existed with which to meet it, and it therefore seems impossible that there should be any general *consensus* of the international society condemning that mode of meeting it. And the mode would be condemned, very probably to the extent of frustrating its employment, if its application to foreigners in the country gave their governments any other right than to see that they were treated on an equality with natives, without undue harshness, and with reasonable grounds in the case of each person. In the instance furnished by the American civil war, the assumption of power by president Lincoln was approved by whatever in the northern states could claim to represent those states towards England, and it was scarcely our right to inquire whether that approval was the approval of the majority, or whether it arose from a conviction of the constitutionality or of the necessity of the course adopted. If the Supreme Court was correct, the result would be that the president, at the worst, was in the position of a successful striker of a *coup d'état*, and international recognition is not denied to the acts of strikers of *coups d'état* whose power is *de facto* established.

A very important question is whether the normal rule of non-interference for the protection of subjects in foreign countries applies to the protection of the interests which they have under contracts with

[1] *Treatise on International Law*, § 87, 3rd edn., p. 277.

foreign governments. Here a distinction seems to exist between the case of bonds forming part of a public loan on the one hand, and private contracts, such as those for concessions or for the execution of works, on the other hand. Interests of the latter kind usually enjoy regular protection by law, notwithstanding that the government is the defendant against whom relief is to be sought. There is a petition of right, a court of claims, or an appropriate administrative tribunal before which to come. The case is not essentially different from any other arising between man and man. The foreigner who has contracted with the government has not elected to place himself at its mercy, and the normal rule of equal treatment with natives requires that he shall have the full benefit of the established procedure, while if in a rare instance there is no such established procedure, or it proves to be a mockery, the exceptional rule of protecting subjects against a flagrant denial of justice also comes in. But public loans are contracted by acts of a legislative nature, and when their terms are afterwards modified to the disadvantage of the bondholders this is done by other acts of a legislative nature, which are not questionable by any proceeding in the country. If therefore the normal rule of equal treatment with natives be looked to, the foreign bondholder has no case unless he is discriminated against. And if the exceptional rule of protecting subjects against a flagrant denial of justice be looked to, the reduction of interest or capital is always put on the ground of the inability of the country to pay more—a foreign government is scarcely able to determine whether or how far that plea is true—supposing it to be true, the provisions which all legislations contain for the relief of insolvent debtors prove that honest inability to pay is generally regarded as a title to some consideration—and the holder of a bond, which in case of default was never otherwise enforceable than through the intervention of his government, is trying, when he seeks that intervention, to exercise a different right from that of a person whose complaint is the gross defect of a remedial process which by general understanding ought to exist and be effective. The one would make his government his debt-collector, the other stops far short of that point. Hence the propriety of intervention is not questioned when justice is denied by a government on its private contracts; it is treated as a matter of expediency whether in a particular case the intervention should be granted to the claimant. But the common practice is to refuse intervention to the sufferers by defaults on public loans, unless the defaulting government presumes to treat its internal and external debts on terms of inequality unfavourable to the latter. It must however be mentioned that Mr Hall, in opposition to the doctrines here supported, sees no difference in principle between the private contracts and public loans of a government, though he admits the difference in practice relating to them. And he quotes Lord Palmerston and Lord Salisbury as maintaining the view that the right of intervention on behalf of bondholders is unquestionable, and that its exercise ought to depend on the balance of considerations, the amount of loss in the particular instance being weighed against the general expediency of discountenancing hazardous loans[1]. On the other hand, the

[1] *Treatise on International Law*, § 87, 3rd edn., pp. 277—280.

accepted principles of the United States seem to be in accordance with the doctrines here supported[1].

[1] "What the United States demand is that in all cases where their citizens have entered into contracts with the proper Nicaraguan authorities, and questions have arisen or shall arise respecting the fidelity of their execution, no declaration of forfeiture, either past or to come, shall possess any binding force unless pronounced in conformity with the provisions of the contract, if there are any ; or if there is no provision for that purpose, then unless there has been a fair and impartial investigation in such a manner as to satisfy the United States that the proceeding has been just and that the decision ought to be submitted to. Without some security of this kind, this government will consider itself warranted, whenever a proper case arises, in interposing such means as it may think justifiable in behalf of its citizens who may have been or who may be injured by such unjust assumption of power." Mr Cass, secretary of state, 25th July 1858 ; in Wharton's *Digest of the International Law of the United States*, § 232, vol. 2, p. 661. "There have been instances however in which our ministers have received instructions of the character proposed [to collect foreign bonds (*Wharton*)] to the extent of permitting them to accept payment from a foreign government on account of the principal or interest of its obligations. Such permission however was preceded by the assumption that the foreign government was ready and willing either to make the payment or to negotiate with its creditor in such connection, and where the intervention of a consular or diplomatic agent of the creditor's country was a convenience to both." Mr Frelinghuysen, secretary of state, 12th January 1884 ; ib. p. 662.

# CHAPTER VIII

### INTERNATIONAL RIGHTS OF SELF-PRESERVATION

*Self-preservation as an alleged Primary Right.*

WHEN a fully sovereign state employs force in its own territory, or on the high seas on board a ship which carries its flag as belonging to itself or to its subjects, or when by its laws it threatens its subjects with punishment on their return for their acts committed abroad, its independence is internationally its sufficient warrant. For the sovereignty of a state extends over its subjects, over its territory, and over the ships which carry its flag on the high seas; and full sovereignty is independence[1]. But when a state employs force in the territory of another state, or on the high seas on board a ship which carries the flag of another state as belonging to it or to its subjects—or when it attempts by threats to restrain the freedom of action of another state within the territory of the latter, or that of the subjects of another state elsewhere than within its own territory or on the high seas under its own flag—the state so acting or threatening must find its justification in some other principle.

[1] See above, p. 87.

The principle commonly put forward on such occasions is that of self-preservation, which writers on international law often class among their fundamental, primitive, primary or absolute rights. It is no doubt a primitive instinct, and an absolute instinct so far as it has not been tamed by reason and law, but one great function of law is to tame it[1]. Accordingly law does not permit us to ward off danger from ourselves by transferring it to an innocent person. When a shipwrecked crew is in danger of starvation, it is not lawful for them to kill and eat one of their number, however pressing the necessity[2]. Liability to suffer hurt, whether in person, in property or in rights, and whether by sentence of law or by private action which the law permits, presupposes a duty violated by the person who is to suffer it. When a small injury is inflicted in obedience to an almost irresistible impulse, the law may overlook it, but in principle we may not hurt another or infringe his rights, even for our self-preservation, when he has not failed in any duty towards us.

It is easily seen that this must be so between states as well as between natural persons. That conclusion is necessary for those who regard states as technical persons for whom and for natural persons legal principles are identical, while if we look at the substantial difference between a state

---

[1] See above, p. 5.
[2] *Queen* v. *Dudley and Stephens*, 14 Q. B. D. 273, decided unanimously by Lord Chief Justice Coleridge, Justices Grove and Denman, and Barons Pollock and Huddleston. Their lordships also stated that they had Justice Stephen's authority for repudiating an inference in favour of the contrary opinion which had been drawn from some passages in his writings; p. 286.

and a natural person, we shall find that the case of the former is at least not more favourable than that of the latter for pushing self-preservation to an extreme. In the case of a state it would be difficult to say more in support of the right than what Wolff said, that a state ought to preserve and perfect itself as an association of its citizens in order to promote their common good[1]. But although it is certainly indispensable for the welfare of men that they should be associated in some state tie, it does not follow that their welfare imperatively requires the maintenance in its actual limits, and with resources entirely unimpaired, of the particular state tie in which they happen to be engaged. Nor can the international society be quoted as having consented to an absolute right of self-preservation. A society can only consent to rules: the principles in which their justification is sought must be left to appreciation by individual men. But since the cases in which the right of self-preservation is alleged are precisely those in which it would clash with the right of independence, which is equally asserted by the advocates of abstract rights, it follows that no rules, but confusion, must result from recognising either right as absolute.

Nevertheless the view which adopts primary rights as the foundation of law has struck such deep root during the last century and a half, that the tendency has prevailed more and more to understand *droit* or *jus*, when not expressing a particular right, as expressing a body of rights rather than a body of law. So while the predominant meaning of *le droit naturel* or *jus naturale*, down to the end of the seventeenth century, seems to have been what we call in

[1] See above, p. 71.

English natural law, that is a body of rules at one time believed to be ascertainable and primary, those terms seem now to have acquired for their predominant meaning that of a body of rights believed to exist by nature, and to secure which is supposed to be the primary function of law. In the same spirit M. Pillet, in a remarkable recent article, contends that the rules prevailing between states, so far as they are founded on certain primary rights which he regards as extending beyond the international society, are treated only by a defect of method as belonging to *le droit des gens* or *le droit international*, and that what they really belong to is *le droit commun de l'humanité*[1]. Those who have followed me thus far will be aware that I maintain the definite line which in England has always been drawn round the notion of law. The considerations in which the notion of primary rights is founded cannot indeed be ignored, but their proper place is in that distributive justice which ought to govern in questions, whether national or international, *de lege ferenda*. Such rights are only moral till the law recognises them, and between moral and legal rights there is a grave practical difference. And when a term, be it *droit* or *jus*, which is the only one available for describing a body of law[2], becomes mixed up with the notion

[1] *Le Droit International Public. Ses éléments constitutifs, son domaine, son objet.* In the *Revue Générale de Droit International Public*, no. 1.

[2] The *législation* of a country is a term often used to describe the whole body of its law, whether arising from express legislation or not, but there is always a danger of its being confounded with express legislation, and it is not used to describe the whole body of international law. When a body of law is codified it stands out unmistakably as positive law, clear of the notion of right. And the want in French of a term appropriated to positive law irrespective of the form in

of rights, it is especially international relations that suffer, because they do not present facilities for ascertaining the true or positive law equal to those which exist within a state. We will therefore build nothing on a primary right of self-preservation, but inquire what are the limits which, for the better security of states all round, our international society has set to the inviolability of each. Thus we shall learn the actual international rights of self-preservation.

### *Rights of Self-preservation actually allowed by International Law.*

A state may not attack another, threaten to attack another, or make preparations from which an intention to attack another may be reasonably inferred. The same prohibitions extend to the subjects of a state. These indeed can seldom undertake any thing against another state as a whole, although filibustering expeditions directed against weak states are not unknown, but the interference of foreigners is common where a state is divided by faction, and it always bears in law the character of an attack on the state as represented by the government which the interfering persons' own state recognises.

So far as a state attacked or threatened cannot defend itself by measures taken within the physical limits of its sovereignty, namely its territory and the ships carrying its flag, its normal duty is to seek redress from the state at fault or the subjects of which are at fault; and such redress may include

which it exists, and at the same time clear of the notion of right, powerfully aids the mistaken view that a body of law cannot be fixed without codification.

reparation for the past as well as security against the repetition of the offence. But it often happens that the injury or the danger will not admit of the delay which the normal course of action would involve. If within a state it is a matter of daily necessity that a citizen should repel an actual or avert a threatened attack by his own force, because the police cannot be present everywhere, much more must a corresponding necessity be liable to arise between states, an international police being wholly wanting. In such cases a state may take its defence into its own hands, even to the extent of employing force within the territory of another state, on condition of limiting its abnormal action to what the emergency requires.

Whatever right of action outside the physical limits of its own sovereignty is allowed to a state by these rules may be described as a right of self-preservation. And whatever right of action within the physical limits of its own sovereignty is left to a state by the same rules may be described as the measure of the uses which, internationally, it may make of its independence. Its independence is not itself thereby defeated, because the prohibition against attacking or threatening another state does not place it in a position of dependence on any other state in particular, and the international society is too ill organized for subjection to its rules to be described as dependence on the society at large.

To illustrate these rules two cases may be quoted, one where the right of self-preservation given by them was exercised within foreign territory, the other where the action was taken on board a ship flying a foreign flag on the high seas. The first " happened during the Canadian rebellion of 1838." I use Mr Hall's excellent summary of the facts. " A body of insurgents collected to the number of several hundreds in American territory, and after obtaining small arms and twelve guns by force from American arsenals seized an island at Niagara within the American frontier, from which shots were fired into Canada, and where preparations were made to cross into British territory by means of a steamer called the Caroline. To prevent the crossing from being effected, the Caroline was boarded by an English force while at her moorings within American waters, and was sent adrift down the falls of Niagara...There was no choice of means, because there was no time for application to the American government ; it had already shown itself to be powerless, and a regiment of militia was actually looking on at the moment without attempting to check the measures of the insurgents[1]." The United States complained of the violation of territory, and declared that it lay on England " to show a necessity of self-defence, instant, overwhelming, leaving no choice of means and no moment for deliberation...also that the local authorities of Canada, even supposing the necessity of the moment authorised them to enter the territories of the United States at all, did nothing unreasonable or excessive, since the act justified by the necessity of self-defence must be limited by that necessity and kept clearly within it." This was a correct statement of the law, except so far as concerns the emergency's leaving no moment for deliberation, which is an unnecessary condition if the emergency is such that deliberation

---

[1] *Treatise on International Law*, 3rd edn., p. 267.

can only confirm the propriety of the act of self-preservation. But the case was within the substance of the conditions laid down, and the incident was allowed to drop. Mr Hall well remarks that " the government of the United States must have felt that it would have been placed in a position of extreme gravity if the English authorities had allowed things to take their course, and had then held it responsible for consequences to the production of which long continued negligence on its part would have been largely contributory." The observation points out the advantage which accrues, even to the state of which the territory is violated, from the permission of proper acts of self-preservation. But the threatened attack on Canada by citizens of the United States, for whom their country was responsible, was sufficient, even had there been no negligence on the part of their government, to constitute the fault which, in conjunction with the emergency, justified the act.

The other case is that of the Virginius, a ship belonging to Cuban insurgents but which had obtained a United States register from the proper authority by a fraudulent affidavit. She was captured by the Spaniards on the high seas, while on her way under the American flag to assist an insurrection then on foot in Cuba. Many of those on board, including certain American citizens and some Englishmen who formed part of the crew, were tried by court martial and put to death. The United States asserted that the Virginius had a right to the American character against all the world except themselves, but having regard to the fraud in obtaining their register they accepted her surrender without any salute to their flag by way of reparation for her capture, Spain however undertaking to proceed against the persons who had offended their sovereignty. It does not seem to have been discussed between the two governments whether, even admitting the American character of the Virginius, her capture was not authorised on the ground of self-preservation; and perhaps the distance outside Spanish territorial waters at which she was taken would have made it difficult to sustain that plea. But I cannot doubt that such a plea may be good in a proper case, for the mischief might be irremediable otherwise, and a ship on the high seas can surely enjoy no greater immunity than national territory itself. Shooting the Americans and Englishmen could not be justified if the Virginius was to be regarded as American, for in that case they had not come within Spanish jurisdiction, whatever offence they may have committed. If the capture of the ship was justifiable, and they had been killed in resisting it, it would have been a different matter and they must have taken their chance; but as soon as they were prisoners they were incapable of further mischief, and the emergency was at an end so far as they were concerned. And although Spanish jurisdiction over persons on board a Spanish ship cannot be denied, the Virginius could scarcely be regarded as a Spanish ship as against any sailors who might have taken service in her without a knowledge of her true ownership, or at least such jurisdiction ought in that case to have been exercised with the greatest moderation. The British government did not complain of the seizure of the Virginius or of the detention of her crew, but said that " it was the duty of the Spanish authorities to prosecute the offenders in proper form of law, and to have instituted regular proceedings on a definite charge before the execution of the prisoners." The United States obtained pecuniary reparation for the families of their executed citizens[1].

The rule as it has been here stated requires attack, the threat of attack, or preparations from which an attack may be reasonably inferred, before a right of self-preservation arises. But what if the absence of all these be admitted, and yet a state will manifestly be unable of itself to prevent a hostile use being made of its territory or of its resources? May not the state against which such hostile use is manifestly impending transgress the foreign boundary in order to avert the consequence it foresees? Probably no one will doubt that it may. Suppose two strong powers to be at war, and a weak power bordering on them both to be neutral. And suppose that one of the belligerents has sure information that a corps of the other, quite beyond the ability of the neutral to resist, is on march to obtain a strategic advantage by violating the territory of the latter. It can hardly be said that the belligerent against whom the blow is aimed may not anticipate it on the neutral's territory. Not that even in such a case we ought to admit a right of self-preservation without fault on the part of the state of which the rights are infringed. By that admission we should abandon all jural foothold. But the case really comes within the doctrine laid down, by virtue of the jural principle

---

[1] See Wharton's *Digest of the International Law of the United States*, § 327, and Hall's *Treatise on International Law*, 3rd edn., pp. 271—5.

that every one must be presumed to intend the necessary consequences of his actions. When a state is unable of itself to prevent a hostile use being made of its territory or its resources, it must either be deemed to allow proper measures of self-preservation to be taken by the state against which such a use is manifestly impending, or it must be deemed to intend the hostile use as being the necessary consequence of refusing the permission. This principle covers the seizure of the Danish fleet by England after the treaty of Tilsit in 1807, when there was irresistible reason for believing that Napoleon and Alexander would have compelled, by force if necessary, its addition to the naval armaments arrayed against them. The act of self-preservation must in this as in all other cases be limited to what is strictly imposed by the emergency, and in the instance cited England offered to Denmark the most solemn pledge that, on the conclusion of a general peace, the fleet of which the surrender was asked should be restored in the same condition and state of equipment as when received.

## *The Balance of Power.*

In order to bring out fully the scope of the above rules it is necessary to draw attention to what they do not include as well as to their affirmative contents. A state has no right to security against mere fear. It has no right to prevent another state's acquiring power of which it can only be said that it may be used to the injury of neighbours, when there is neither an express threat so to use it nor any conduct from which an intention so to use it can be reasonably inferred, and when the power which causes the fear merely results from the growing population and wealth of the state in question. The apprehensions which may be excited by the annexation of territory do not fall within the subject which we are now considering. Every rearrangement of the map of Europe is regarded as of general interest to all the members of the European political system, and any of them may claim to have a voice in it. And on similar principles general opinion in the United States claims a voice in American arrangements beyond the limits of the great republic. But putting the case of territorial aggrandisement aside, the law may be taken to be that the natural growth of a state in power, and even the increase of its armaments in a fair proportion to its population and wealth and to the interests which it has to defend, gives no special rights of self-preservation to its neighbours so long as an intention to misuse its power cannot be imputed to it on sufficient evidence. The uses of independence can be restricted only for the fault of the state which suffers the restriction, or of those for whom it is answerable as being its subjects.

The place which the doctrine of the balance of power has held in the international relations of European states, and which has been accorded to it by accredited writers on international law, may occasion a doubt whether the law on the subject has always since the Peace of Westphalia been such as it now is. But the legal significance of that doctrine must not be hastily judged. The times are not remote when international practice was so bad that an intention to abuse power might correctly be inferred on slighter evidence than would now be necessary. Again, when international politics were largely the personal and family affairs of monarchs, the combination of the power of two states by marriage, without either state being merged in the other or its frontiers enlarged, presented a question of general interest not altogether out of comparison with that which was presented by a case of territorial aggrandisement. And when the merger of crowns arises by marriage or inheritance, the resulting territorial aggrandisement may be of as serious consequence to the European political system as if it arose from conquest, and it would probably be thought even now that rules suited to the descent of property cannot oust the authority of that system over the rearrangement of its map. It is not meant to justify all the wars which have been waged for maintaining the balance of power, or all the terms in which that balance has been expressed as a principle of international law, but it may well be doubted whether it was ever held that any special right of self-preservation accrued to a state from the internal growth of its neighbour, without the fault of the latter in act or intention.

### *Alleged right of Self-preservation against the Contagion of Revolution.*

While pointing out what the rules concerning self-preservation do not permit, a caution must be given against another doctrine of a more insidious character than any misconception about the right to a balance of power, the doctrine that the government of a state, on its own account or as representing its constitution, has any right of self-preservation against the consequences which may follow from the principles of government asserted in another state, when no attack is made threatened or intended on the state itself or on its internal freedom of action.

The international society to which we belong is not one for the mutual insurance of established governments, though from time to time attempts have been made to work it as such[1]. The most memorable of those attempts is that which during a few years after the Congress of Vienna was made by the pentarchy to rule Europe in accordance with the principle of legitimacy. In the circular despatch which on the occasion of the insurrection at Naples the courts of Austria Russia and Prussia dated from Troppau, 8th December 1820, they said that " the powers have exercised an incontestable right in occupying themselves with taking in common measures of security against states in which the overthrow of the government by a revolt, even could it be considered only as a dangerous example, must have for its consequence a hostile attitude against all constitutions and legitimate governments. The exercise of that right was still more urgently necessary when those who had placed themselves in that situation sought to extend to their neighbours the misfortune which they had brought on themselves, and to propagate revolt and confusion around them. Such a position and conduct is an evident infraction of the pact which guarantees to all European governments, besides the inviolability of their territory, the enjoyment of peaceable relations excluding all encroachment on the rights of one another."

[1] See above, p. 59.

Lord Castlereagh's answer was dated 19th January 1821. He repudiated the interpretation which converted the treaties between the powers into a pact between their governments, and he refused to connect England with the intervention in Naples on which Austria had decided. But he added: "it should be clearly understood that no government can be more prepared than the British government is to uphold the right of any state or states to interfere, where their own immediate security or essential interests are seriously endangered by the internal transactions of another state. But as they regard the assumption of such right as only to be justified by the strongest necessity, and to be limited and regulated thereby, they cannot admit that this right can receive a general and indiscriminate application to all revolutionary movements, without reference to their immediate bearing upon some particular state or states, or be made prospectively the basis of an alliance. They regard its exercise as an exception to general principles of the greatest value and importance, and as one that only properly grows out of the circumstances of the special case; but they at the same time consider that exceptions of this description never can, without the utmost danger, be so far reduced to rule as to be incorporated into the ordinary diplomacy of states, or into the institutes of the law of nations[1]."

This language altogether failed to repudiate intervention for self-preservation against the mere contagion of principles. The true ground was taken by Canning on the occasion of the French intervention against the government which had been established

[1] *Annual Register*, vol. 62, part 2, p. 738.

by insurrection in Spain. In his despatch of 31st March 1823 to the British ambassador at Paris Canning wrote: "No proof was produced to his majesty's plenipotentiary of the existence of any design on the part of the Spanish government to invade the territory of France, of any attempt to introduce disaffection among her soldiery, or of any project to undermine her political institutions; and so long as the struggles and disturbances of Spain should be confined within the circle of her own territory, they could not be admitted by the British government to afford any plea for foreign interference. If the end of the last and the beginning of the present century saw all Europe combined against France, it was not on account of the internal changes which France thought necessary for her own political and civil reformation, but because she attempted to propagate first her principles, and afterwards her dominion, by the sword[1]." The right of intervention in a foreign state, with the motive of self-preservation against the effects of its internal troubles, was here put on its true basis and with its true limits. Those limits have not always been since observed, but at last they are generally admitted.

### Self-preservation as a ground of Criminal Jurisdiction.

The independence of a state within its territory appears to carry with it the exclusive authority over the actions of all persons within its territory, the exclusive decision of what they shall be free or not free to do there. This refers to the criminal law,

[1] *Annual Register*, vol. 65, p. 141*.

and has little bearing on that civil branch which is called private international law[1]. There we mostly deal with what men do in the exercise of that liberty which is left to them through the absence of interference by the criminal law of the place where they are, as in marrying, contracting, making a will and otherwise; and we deduce the consequences of such acts with reference to the civil laws of the countries which they concern. For example, a marriage is valid everywhere if celebrated in the form required by the law of the place of celebration, and if the parties are capable of contracting it according to the law of the state to which they are subject, or of their domicile, the latter being a point on which there is not as yet a full agreement. Sometimes, even in private international law, the civil consequences have to be considered which flow from a criminal act, as, for example, where an act is both a crime and a civil wrong giving a right to damages. But what we are here concerned with is only the criminal side of acts, and the independence of a state with regard to its territory would seem to be violated if a foreign power presumed to restrict the liberty of men on its soil by denouncing penalties for acts done there with the license of the local law, even if the enforcement of such penalties was postponed till the persons to be affected by them came within the territorial limits of the foreign authority.

On the other hand, a state is a society of men over whom as well as over its territory its sovereignty extends; the acts of its subjects, wherever done, may affect the population with which they have a continuing tie and among which they are likely to return;

[1] See above, p. 9.

and the independence of the state with regard to its subjects would seem to be violated if a foreign power stood in the way of its control over their acts, even though done abroad, when the penalties by which such control was to be made effectual were only to be enforced in their home.

The latter principle is allowed to prevail. Foreigners in a country are subject to two sovereignties, each of which may restrict their liberty by the provisions of its criminal law. They are subject to the local criminal law just as native citizens are, and they are subject to such criminal enactments as the law of their own country may apply to its people abroad, on condition that no attempt is made to enforce the latter until they come within the physical limits of their home sovereignty, its territory and its ships. England has acted on this doctrine by legislation which began as early as the reign of Henry the eighth, and British subjects are now punishable in the British dominions for many grave offences committed in foreign countries.

But most countries other than England and the United States apply more or less of their criminal legislation not only to the acts of their subjects but also to those of foreigners in foreign countries, always under the condition that its enforcement can only take place within the physical limits of their respective sovereignties. The Institute of International Law adopted at Brussels in 1879 by 19 votes against 7, and reaffirmed at Munich in 1883 by a large majority, a resolution containing a principle on which this may be supported. " Every state has the right to punish acts committed even out of its territory, and by foreigners, in violation of its penal laws, when those acts attack (*constituent une atteinte à*) the social existence of the state in question and endanger its security, and are not provided against by the penal law of the country on the territory of which they have taken place[1]." The principle thus invoked is that of self-preservation, but not as an abstract and absolute right. A right of self-preservation is allowed by the resolution where the penal law of the *locus delicti* does not prohibit the noxious act, but, where such prohibition is forthcoming, the state which is threatened is not allowed to supplement a sanction which it may deem insufficient. I opposed even this moderate resolution, observing that in criminal matters territorial competence and personal competence are justified by the duty of knowing the laws of the country where you act or to which you belong, but that no one is bound to know the laws of a foreign country, yet the doctrine maintained would impose on writers and speakers the necessity of knowing those of all the countries which their words may have reached and which they may afterwards visit. The peace of the world would be better preserved by resorting to diplomatic redress for attacks made on a state by foreigners abroad, than by legislation of so irritating a character. And Mr Hall has said of the resolution in question that under it " precisely the class of acts remains subject to exceptional jurisdiction which there is most danger in abandoning to it. Probably as between civilised states political acts are the only acts, satisfying the description, which would not be punishable by the law of the state where they are committed. The question presents

[1] *Annuaire de l'Institut du Droit International*, vol. 3, pp. 276—281; vol. 7, pp. 151—157. *Tableau Général*, 1873—1892, p. 100.

itself therefore whether self-preservation is really involved to so serious an extent as to override the rights of sovereignty. It would be rash to say that it never is so deeply involved, but it is not rash to say that the occasions are rare, and that it is doubtful whether it would be possible to allow such exceptional crimes to be dealt with without in practice permitting ordinary political acts to be also struck at[1]." But continental legislation takes no account of the condition that the acts to be penal when committed by foreigners abroad shall not be penal in the *locus delicti*. And while in France and several other countries the penalty in question is confined to offences against the safety of the state or against its currency, in others it is applied to offences against subjects. Self-preservation seems especially in the last case to be stretched to an unwarrantable extent.

[1] *Treatise on International Law*, 3rd edn., p. 210, note.

## CHAPTER IX

### TERRITORIAL SOVEREIGNTY, ESPECIALLY WITH RELATION TO UNCIVILISED REGIONS

*Territorial Sovereignty distinguished from Property.*

THE civilised world, and so much of the uncivilised world as nations of the European race have assumed to themselves in sovereignty, is mapped out among them as the territory of one state or another. Each state has a sovereignty in and over its territory which presents some points of resemblance to property in land, but more important points of difference. The resemblance chiefly consists in exclusiveness and in being alienable. A state may exclude other states from doing acts of sovereignty in its territory, as a landed proprietor may exclude other persons from acting as proprietors on his land; and a state may alienate its sovereignty subject to the rules of the society of states, one of which, as we have seen, makes every alteration of the map of Europe a matter of common interest to that quarter of the globe, as a landed proprietor may alienate his property subject to the laws of his country. But property and sovereignty play widely different parts in the system of acts and purposes which makes up civilised life, and sometimes they are contrasted with one another in circumstances which would make it very inconvenient to say that a state has the property in its territory. For instance, when a state cedes a province it cedes the territorial sovereignty over the whole, and the property in those parts which belonged to it as property, such as fortresses and public buildings, but the property in all other parts remains unaffected. If the state which receives the cession desires to erect a new fortress or enlarge an old one, it must acquire the necessary site from the proprietors by purchase or expropriation according to law. The power of expropriation for public purposes is one of those powers of the state subject to which all property is enjoyed, and which are collectively described as eminent domain; and in this another reason has been found for treating territorial sovereignty as a kind of property. The alienation of territory has been regarded as an exercise of the right of eminent domain, and that right again has been regarded as a reserved portion of the property, so that the alienation of territory would be the exercise of a proprietary right. But objection may be taken to that reasoning. The right of eminent domain as it exists within a state rather limits, and when exercised affects, property, than is a reserved portion of it; but the cession of territory, as we have seen, does not affect any property except what is included in the cession because it happens to belong to the state and is therefore alienated in exercise of the ordinary rights of property[1].

[1] A government may assume the power to cede land to a foreign state in property as well as in sovereignty, taking on itself the burden of expropriating the private owners; and the state receiving the

Again, the principle of the feudal system by which all land was ultimately held of the crown has a superficial resemblance to eminent domain, but only a superficial one. That all land was ultimately held of the crown gave the latter a right of escheat in default of heirs which was really a reserved part of the property, as much so as the landlord's reversion on a lease; but it never put the crown in a position to exercise those rights of interference with property for public purposes which constitute eminent domain. For those rights a clear thinker must seek another source than tenure, under the feudal system as well as under any other. On every ground then I shall treat territorial sovereignty as distinct from property, and shall avoid describing it as eminent domain.

But besides the notion of tenure, carried up to the king as the ultimate proprietor of whom all others held, feudalism contained—nay, as a practical system was even based on—a confusion between the notions of property and government. It belonged to the lord to govern his manor as it belonged to the king to govern his kingdom, and it belonged to the king to govern his kingdom as it belonged to the lord to govern his manor. The kingdoms and principalities which had this view of things as their principle were the patrimonial kingdoms and principalities of which we read in Grotius and other writers of the sixteenth and seventeenth centuries, when they began to be felt strange. They were the property of their kings

cession would not in that case be bound to enquire whether the government contracting with it had exceeded its constitutional power, for a government may be accepted internationally as representing not only its state but its subjects and all rights of whatever kind existing in relation to its territory. But this does not alter the effect of a mere cession of territory.

or princes, and capable of passing by marriage, bequest or inheritance in accordance with the rules of property. Often indeed the notion of a state, dimly perceived even in the middle ages across the prevailing view of things, interposed some limitation of the power of bequest, or some rule for the case of marriage or inheritance not quite the same as for private property; but it was of continual occurrence that the operation of rules of property transferred, united or separated populations without regard to their interests or wishes. There was therefore then no clear distinction between property and territorial sovereignty, and the great geographical discoveries of the period which succeeded the middle ages helped to continue the confusion, because they directed the attention of thinkers to the title by which territory may be acquired in new countries, and so let in the theories about original modes of acquisition in a state of nature, which state, such as it was imagined, hardly admitted a sharp contrast between property and government. In short, as Holtzendorff says, " without the historical and juristic aid of the idea of property, and its application to the territory of a state, it would not have been possible for the old theorists to discover the principle of political sovereignty[1]."

The distinction however was clearly perceived by Grotius, and indeed, whatever obscurity might be thrown over it by the misapplication of Roman speculations about natural modes of acquiring property, it could hardly fail to make its way when Roman law as a practical system, and the Latin

[1] *Handbuch des Völkerrechts*, vol. 2, p. 228.

language, came to be more accurately studied[1]. *Imperium* is the Latin for sovereignty, expressing primarily an authority over persons, but extended to the relation which a state bears to its territory, so that, when international law is discussed in Latin, it is the proper word for sovereignty in both its aspects. The Latin for property is *dominium*, whether a piece of land belongs to a private person or, as in the case of a fortress, to the state in the character of property. And eminent domain, *dominium eminens*, as it exists within a state, is a result of sovereignty, so that there would be an inversion of the true order if we explained the latter, with its accompanying power of alienation, by reference to the former. It may safely be said that the confusion between territorial sovereignty and property is not now made by any one in substance, and it is fast disappearing even from the language of international law, though we may sometimes remark a regrettable persistence in ancient modes of speaking and reasoning[2].

[1] *Imperium duas solet habere materias sibi subjacentes, primariam personas,....et secundariam locum qui territorium dicitur. Quanquam autem uno actu quæri solent imperium et dominium, sunt tamen distincta : ideoque dominium non in cives tantum sed et in extraneos transit, manente penes quem fuit imperio.* Grotius, *De Jure Belli ac Pacis*, l. 2, c. 3, § 4. The *quanquam uno actu quæri solent* refers to acquisition in new countries by the so-called natural modes.

[2] Besides von Holtzendorff, Pasquale Fiore rejects the expression "right of international property" : *Trattato di Diritto Internazionale Pubblico*, 3rd ed., § 863, vol. 2, p. 109. Professor Guido Fusinato writes : "The introduction into public law, for territorial cessions, of the methods and considerations of private law, in the forms too which are usual in private law for declaring the will of a party, was intelligible in former times when the idea of the patrimonial state prevailed, and public law was confounded with private, sovereignty with property." Article *Annessione* in the *Enciclopedia Giuridica*, note

*The Title to Territorial Sovereignty.*

Let us consider the old civilised world, including not only the international society of European origin but those Asiatic and other countries which we have noticed as possessing different civilisations from ours[1]. All the states in it hold their territory by the same kind of title by which their subjects hold their property in land, that is by a series of human dealings—as cession or conquest in the one case, conveyance *inter vivos* or will in the other—deduced from a root assumed as presenting an irreducible situation of fact. But that situation was itself a local distribution of territory or property, of the same nature as the one which results for the present time from the deduction of title. You have got no nearer to an origin of territorial sovereignty or of property. You may discuss the origin of either by way of philosophical or prehistorical speculation, but with no relevancy to international or to national law. You may discuss the motives for maintaining either, with some relevancy to international or national legislation, but with no other relevancy to law. Thus, the title to territorial sovereignty in old countries not

---

on p. 6 of the separate print. Professor F. de Martens writes: " It is to the territorial sovereignty that belongs the exclusive rule in all the extent of its possessions. Placing one's self at that point of view, and considering only the international situation of the state, one may say that it is the owner of its territory. In fact it alone can dispose of it, and it does not admit the interference of other powers. As to the private properties situate within its limits, it exercises with regard to them all public rights, that is to say the supreme right to protect them and dispose of them, but they no way belong to it according to the principles of private law (*dominium*)." *Traité de Droit International*, translated from Russian into French by Léo, vol. 1. p. 452.

[1] See above, p. 102.

being capable of discussion apart from the several dealings, as cession or conquest, which transfer it, we must turn to new countries.

When a new country is formed by a civilised state into a colony, the title to land in it may sometimes be deduced by the proprietors from a situation of fact which existed before the civilised government was established, and which that government has accepted and clothed with its sanction. This will be the case where the colony was formed among natives of some advancement, or where its formation was preceded by the settlement of pioneers of civilisation. But in general the title to land in a colony is traced from a grant by the state, and the authority of the state to make the grant resulted from its territorial sovereignty. Or you may say if you please that, at the moment of acquiring the sovereignty, the state assumed to itself the property in so much of the land as it was not morally compelled to acknowledge as belonging to natives or to the pioneers, and that subsequent grants by the state were carried out of the property so assumed. Either way you carry back the property granted to an origin in sovereignty, but the origin of the latter is still to be considered.

But here again all that can really be considered is the extension of territorial sovereignty over new areas. In other words, the question is what facts are necessary and sufficient in order that an uncivilised region may be internationally recognised as appropriated in sovereignty to a particular state? Whatever the answer may be, the international institutions of the old civilised world cannot have arisen in exactly the same manner, for the appropriation with which we are dealing supposes that territorial sovereignty is already known. The states of the old world may have arisen from the settlement of wandering tribes in regions only occupied, if at all, by tribes on a still lower plane of advancement, and that mode of origin would present great similarity to the extension of an existing state over a new locality. Or the states of the old world may have arisen quite differently. In any case the truth will bear repetition that, whatever light philology or archaeology may throw on the early history of mankind, an impassable barrier separates their researches, in spite of the great interest that must be felt in them, from the subjects with which international law has to do.

The form which has been given to the question, namely *what facts are necessary and sufficient in order that an uncivilised region may be internationally appropriated in sovereignty to a particular state ?* implies that it is only the recognition of such sovereignty by the members of the international society which concerns us, that of uncivilised natives international law takes no account. This is true, and it does not mean that all rights are denied to such natives, but that the appreciation of their rights is left to the conscience of the state within whose recognised territorial sovereignty they are comprised, the rules of the international society existing only for the purpose of regulating the mutual conduct of its members. Seen from that point of view the proposition, which at first is startling, becomes almost axiomatic. A strongly organised society may enact rules for the protection of those who are not its members, as is seen in the case of a state which legislates for the protection of foreigners, or against cruelty to animals. But this is scarcely possible for a society so weakly organised as the international one, in which, for want of a central power, the enforcement of rules must be left in the main to the mutual action of the members as independent states. In such a society rules intended for the benefit of outsiders would either fall into desuetude and oblivion, or be made pretexts for the more specious promotion of selfish interests. The subject, however, must be treated at greater length.

*The Position of Uncivilised Natives with regard to International Law.*

No theorist on law who is pleased to imagine a state of nature independent of human institutions can introduce into his picture a difference between civilised and uncivilised man, because it is just in the presence or absence of certain institutions, or in their greater or less perfection, that that difference consists for the lawyer. But in the early times of international law, when the appropriation of a newly discovered region was referred to the principles which were held to govern the so-called natural modes of acquisition, the occupation by uncivilised tribes of a tract, of which according to our habits a small part ought to have sufficed for them, was not felt to interpose a serious obstacle to the right of the first civilised occupant. The region was scarcely distinguished from a *res nullius*. When again men like Victoria, Soto and Covarruvias maintained the cause of the American and African natives against the kings and peoples of Spain and Portugal, they were not so much impugning the title of their country as trying to influence its conduct, they were the worthy predecessors of those who now make among us the honourable claim to be " friends of the aborigines." Then and now such men occupy a field to which international law may be said to invite them by keeping itself within its own limits. Even those who, in accordance with the modern tendency, make rights instead of law their starting point, can hardly avoid admitting that the rights which are common to civilised and uncivilised humanity are not among those which it is the special function of international right to develop and protect[1]. But when the African conference of Berlin was laying down the rules for the appropriation of territory on the coasts of that continent, Mr Kasson, the plenipotentiary of the United States, expressed himself thus :

"Whilst approving the two paragraphs of this declaration as a first step, well directed though short, it is my duty to add two observations to the protocol.

" (1) Modern international law follows closely a line which leads to the recognition of the right of native tribes to dispose freely of themselves and of their hereditary territory. In conformity with this principle my government would gladly adhere to a more extended rule, to be based on a principle which should aim at the voluntary consent of the natives whose country is taken possession of, in all cases where they had not provoked the aggression. (2) I have no doubt as to the conference being agreed in regard to the signification of the preamble. It only points out the minimum of the conditions which must necessarily be fulfilled in order that the recognition of an occupation may be demanded. It is always possible that an occupation may be rendered effective by acts of violence which are foreign to the principles of justice, as well as to national and even international law. Consequently it should be well understood that it is reserved for the respective signatory powers to determine all the other conditions from the point of view of right as well as of fact which must be fulfilled before an occupation can be recognised as valid[2]."

---

[1] See above, pp. 113, 114.

[2] Protocol of 31st January, 1885. Parliamentary Paper c. 4361, p. 209. The two paragraphs referred to by Mr Kasson are those which form Arts. 34 and 35 of the General Act.

Herr Busch, German under-secretary of state for foreign affairs, was presiding, and

"remarked that the first portion of the declaration of Mr Kasson touched on delicate questions, upon which the conference hesitated to express an opinion. It would suffice to reproduce in the protocol the views put forward by the plenipotentiary of the United States of America. The second portion of the declaration of Mr Kasson reverted to the explanations exchanged in the commission, from which it resulted that, in the unanimous opinion of the plenipotentiaries, the declaration drawn up by the conference did not limit the right which the powers possessed of causing the recognition of the occupations which might be notified to them to be preceded by such an examination as they might consider necessary."

No more was said on the subject, and the result is that when an accession of territory on the coast of Africa is notified to the powers they will have the opportunity of objecting. It cannot be doubted that if the aggrandisement was made at the expense of a civilised population without its consent, or was attended with proceedings of great inhumanity to an uncivilised population, this would be a good ground of objection on the part of any power that pleased to take up the cause[1]. But it would be going much further, and to a length to which the conference declined to go, if we were to say that, except in the case of unprovoked aggression justifying conquest, an uncivilised population has rights which make its free consent necessary to the establishment over it of a government possessing international validity. Any such principle, had it been adopted, would have tended to defeat one of the chief objects of the conference, namely to avoid collisions between its members by regulating more clearly their mutual position

---

[1] See what has been said above, p. 79, no. 5: "the want of a rule to define the action allowable does not exclude all action."

on the African coast. For on that system a power might have fulfilled the conditions of notification and establishment of authority which the conference laid down as necessary for making a new acquisition, but it would have still been exposed to see the validity of its acquisition disputed by another power, under the sanction of the conference itself, on the ground of some native title which it might be pretended had not been duly ceded to it. Is any territorial cession permitted by the ideas of the tribe? What is the authority—chief, elders, body of fighting men—if there is one, which those ideas point out as empowered to make the cession? With what formalities do they require it to be made, if they allow it to be made at all? These questions are too obscure among uncivilised populations, or, if they are clear to them, too obscure for the whites who are in contact with them, for the latter to find much difficulty in picking a hole, when desired, in a cession alleged to have been made by a tribe. And then there would be the controversies whether the irregular violence to which savages are prone amounted to aggression justifying conquest. All these are questions for which, in the general interest, the civilised powers do well not to give occasion in their mutual arrangements, so long as they are unprovided with the means of deciding them in the particular cases which may arise. Those arrangements are not to be construed as denying, because they do not affirm them, the rights of any who are not stipulating parties to the conventions by which they are made. The moral rights of all outside the international society against the several members of that society remain intact, though they have not and scarcely could have been converted into legal rights.

Becoming subjects of the power which possesses the international title to the country in which they live, natives have on their governors more than the common claim of the governed, they have the claim of the ignorant and helpless on the enlightened and strong; and that claim is the more likely to receive justice, the freer is the position of the governors from insecurity and vexation.

## *Government the International Test of Civilisation.*

Civilisation is a term which has often occurred during the last few pages, and we must try to give ourselves an account of what for the present purpose we mean by it. We have nothing here to do with the mental or moral characters which distinguish the civilised from the uncivilised individual, nor even with the domestic or social habits, taking social in a narrow sense, which a traveller may remark. When people of European race come into contact with American or African tribes, the prime necessity is a government under the protection of which the former may carry on the complex life to which they have been accustomed in their homes, which may prevent that life from being disturbed by contests between different European powers for supremacy on the same soil, and which may protect the natives in the enjoyment of a security and well-being at least not less than they enjoyed before the arrival of the strangers. Can the natives furnish such a government, or can it be looked for from the Europeans alone? In the answer to that question lies, for international law, the difference between civilisation and the want of it. If even the natives could furnish such a government after the manner of the Asiatic empires, that would be sufficient. Those empires are formed of populations leading complex lives of their own, so far differing from that of Europe in important particulars, as in the family relations or in the criminal law and its administration, that it is necessary to allow to Europeans among them a system more or less separate under their consuls; but whatever may be the influence which the foreign powers derive from the force which they are known to possess though they do not habitually exercise it, it is the local force of the empire which on all ordinary occasions maintains order and protects each class of inhabitants in the enjoyment of the legal system allowed it. Whereever a population furnishes such a government as this, the law of our own international society has to take account of it. The states which are members of our international society conclude treaties with it as to the special position to be allowed to their subjects in its territory, as to custom duties and the regulation of trade, as to postal and other administrative arrangements. When at war with it, they observe the laws of war as among themselves, and expect those laws to be observed by it towards them; and they make peace with it by treaties as among themselves. And, what is more particularly to the purpose of the present chapter, they regard its territory as held by a title of the same kind as that by which their own is held, so that the territorial sovereignty of the government in question is a root from which title may be derived to themselves by conquest or cession, and which excludes all modes of acquiring it, whether by discovery occupation or otherwise, which are or pretend to be original modes going back to the inception of sovereignty[1]. But wherever the native inhabitants can furnish no government capable of fulfilling the purposes fulfilled by the Asiatic empires, which is the case of most of the populations with whom Europeans have come into contact in America and Africa, the first necessity is that a government should be furnished. The inflow of the white race cannot be stopped where there is land to cultivate, ore to be mined, commerce to be developed, sport to enjoy, curiosity to be satisfied. If any fanatical admirer of savage life argued that the whites ought to be kept out, he would only be driven to the same conclusion by another route, for a government on the spot would be necessary to keep them out. Accordingly international law has to treat such natives as uncivilised. It regulates, for the mutual benefit of civilised states, the claims which they make to sovereignty over the region, and leaves the treatment of the natives to the conscience of the state to which the sovereignty is awarded, rather than sanction their interest being made an excuse the more for war between civilised claimants, devastating the region and the cause of suffering to the natives themselves.

## Treaties with Uncivilised Tribes.

Let us suppose that the officers or private subjects of a European state, or of one of European origin, advance into a region where they find no native government capable of controlling white men or under which white civilisation can exist, and where also no state has yet acquired the sovereignty under the rules

---

[1] See above, p. 82, no. 12, and p. 102.

which are internationally recognised between white men. We find that one of their first proceedings is to conclude treaties with such chiefs or other authorities as they can discover : and very properly, for no men are so savage as to be incapable of coming to some understanding with other men, and wherever contact has been established between men, some understanding, however incomplete it may be, is a better basis for their mutual relations than force. But what is the scope which it is reasonably possible to give to treaties in such a case, and what the effect which may be reasonably attributed to them ?

We have seen that natives in the rudimentary condition supposed take no rights under international law, but that even the fulfilment of the conditions laid down by Art. 34 of the Final Act of Berlin does not preclude the possibility that objection may be made to an appropriation of territory which one civilised state notifies to another. Hence it follows that no document in which such natives are made to cede the sovereignty over any territory can be exhibited as an international title, although an arrangement with them, giving evidence that they have been treated with humanity and consideration, may be valuable as obviating possible objections to what would otherwise be a good international title to sovereignty. And this is reasonable. A stream cannot rise higher than its source, and the right to establish the full system of civilised government, which in these cases is the essence of sovereignty, cannot be based on the consent of those who at the utmost know but a few of the needs which such a government is intended to meet.

Uncivilised tribes partake in various degrees of

those elements out of which the full system of civilised society is built up. Settled agricultural populations know property in land, either as belonging to individuals or to families, or, if as belonging in full measure only to the tribe, at least with such rights of a proprietary nature vested in individuals or in families as are necessary for cultivation. Hunting and nomad tribes may have so slight a connection with any land in particular as to share but little, if at all, the ideas which we connect with property in the soil. Both classes may possess, and a settled population can scarcely fail to possess, the practice of trade, by way of barter if not for money, to such an extent as to be familiar with its regulation by the authority which they recognise. To whatever point natives may have advanced, the principle must hold that a cession by them, made in accordance with their ruling customs, may confer a moral title to such property or power as they understand while they cede it, but that no form of cession by them can confer any title to what they do not understand. Hence, while the sovereignty of a European state over an uncivilised region must find its justification, as it easily will, not in treaties with natives but in the nature of the case and compliance with conditions recognised by the civilised world, it is possible that a right of property may be derived from treaties with natives, and this even before any European sovereignty has begun to exist over the spot. In that case the state which afterwards becomes sovereign will be bound to respect such right and give effect to it by its legislation, morally bound if only its own subjects are concerned, but if the previous right of property existed in a subject of another state, there can be no doubt but that respect to it would constitute an international claim as legally valid as any claim between states can be. On the coasts of Africa it would fall within " the obligation to insure the establishment of authority sufficient to protect existing rights," which is recognised in Art. 35 of the Final Act of Berlin.

The principles which I have here sought to lay down have been expressed by the Portuguese statesman J. B. de Martens Ferrão, in a passage which I am the more glad to quote because in their application, and on some further points, England and Portugal have differed.

"It is clear," he writes, "that in savage tribes as Lubbock describes them we must recognise all natural rights. Natural rights are born with man; they constitute his personality, which the want of cultivation does not extinguish. But international rights cannot be recognised in those tribes, for want of the capacity for government (*capacité dirigeante*). Being nomads or nearly such, they have no international character. For the same reason they have no constituted sovereignty, that being no doubt a political right derived from civilisation, and therefore having civilisation as its base and the condition of its existence. Modern international law is a result of civilisation. On this ground I do not consider successive cessions of sovereignty, made by native chiefs, half or wholly savage, to the chance comer who gives them the most, without any valid sanction of right, as a reasonable base, sufficient to affect rights founded on the facts just mentioned. And all the less can I so consider them because civil property is not their subject, but is left by the negotiators to the possessor of it if there be one. Such cessions of sovereignty can furnish no juridical argument to oppose to the facts which were recognised as lawful titles by the public law in force at the time in question[1]."

These principles again do not differ from those on which the European states dealt with the native in-

[1] *L'Afrique: la question soulevée dernièrement entre l'Angleterre et le Portugal considérée au point de vue du droit international*, par J. B. de Martens Ferrão: Lisbonne, 1890, p. 6. The passage is on p. 10 of the pamphlet as issued, without the author's name, from a press at Rome.

habitants of the American continent north of Mexico, although their enunciation in that connection has often been less clear than it can now be made, partly because of the old confusion between territorial sovereignty and property, and partly because the natives concerned were hunters and only to a limited extent cultivators, not possessing so well developed a notion of property in the soil as is possessed by the settled populations of Africa. With Mexico and Peru we have nothing here to do. Those countries had attained a degree of advancement ranking them rather as states than as uncivilised tribes. The history and methods of the British conquest in the more northern parts of the continent were well described by Chief Justice Marshall, in delivering the opinion of the Supreme Court of the United States in the case of *Johnson v. McIntosh* in the year 1823[1]. He observes that

"The potentates of the old world found no difficulty in convincing themselves that they made ample compensation to the inhabitants of the new, by bestowing on them civilisation and Christianity in exchange for unlimited independence. But as they were all in pursuit of nearly the same object, it was necessary, in order to avoid conflicting settlements and consequent war with each other, to establish a principle which all should acknowledge as the law by which the right of acquisition which they all asserted should be regulated as between themselves. This principle was that discovery gave title to the government by whose subjects or by whose authority it was made against all other European governments, which title might be consummated by possession. The exclusion of all other Europeans necessarily gave to the nation making the discovery the sole right of acquiring the soil from the natives and establishing settlements upon it. It was a right with which no Europeans could interfere. It was a right which all asserted for themselves, and to the assertion of which by others all assented. Those relations which were to exist between the discoverer and the natives were to be regulated by themselves.

[1] 8 Wheaton's Supreme Court Reports (21 U. S.), p. 543.

The rights thus acquired being exclusive, no other power could interpose between them.  In the establishment of these relations the rights of the original inhabitants were in no instance entirely disregarded, but were necessarily to a considerable extent impaired.  They were admitted to be the rightful occupants of the soil, with a legal as well as just claim to retain possession of it and to use it according to their own discretion ; but their rights to complete sovereignty as independent nations were necessarily diminished, and their power to dispose of the soil at their own will to whomsoever they pleased was denied by the original fundamental principle that discovery gave exclusive title to those who made it [1]."

It will be observed that while the Indians passed under political subjection without its being deemed necessary to ask their consent, the right in the soil which they were held to preserve is described as that of occupants, and occupancy is the term used for it in this and all other judgments of the Supreme Court which deal with the question.  That it was not a greater right was not due to any incompatibility between a greater civil right of property and political subjection, but to the fact that the Indian hunters knew no greater right among themselves.  Such as it was, they could admit a white individual to it, but could not expand it into full property, even in his favour.

" Admitting," says Chief Justice Marshall, " their power to change their laws or usages so far as to allow an individual to separate a portion of their lands from the common stock and hold it in severalty, still it is a part of their territory and is held under them by a title dependent on their laws.  The grant derives its efficacy from their will, and if they choose to resume it and make a different disposition of the land, the courts of the United States cannot interpose for the protection of the title.  The person who purchases lands from the Indians within their territory incorporates himself with them so far as respects the property purchased, holds their title under their protection and subject to their laws[2]."

[1] 8 Wheaton's Supreme Court Reports (21 U. S.), pp. 573, 574.
[2] Ib., p. 593.

The Indian occupancy, though in them and their grantees it cannot rise higher, is yet so firmly vested in them that even the United States cannot extinguish it otherwise than by a treaty with them. But when the tribe surrenders it by such a treaty, whatever share they may have carved out of it even for a white is surrendered also, unless the Indians reserve or regrant his rights under the sanction of the commissioners with whom the treaty is negotiated. In the absence of such a reservation or regrant it is presumed that any conveyance which the tribe may appear to have previously made to him, and under which he, even though a citizen of the United States, may afterwards claim, was considered by the Indians as invalid[1]. But grants by the British crown passed the full property, and even when they were made before the Indian right of occupancy had been extinguished by treaty, they passed the property subject to that right[2].

We have here a clear apprehension of the principle that an uncivilised tribe can grant by treaty such rights as it understands and exercises, but nothing more. On the practical aspect of the case as affecting the Indians within the territory of the United States it may be remarked that, although they are precluded from converting their right of occupancy into one of property by their own power, whatever aptitude they may show for imitating the civilisation which is closing in on them, yet tribes which show

---

[1] 8 Wheaton's Supreme Court Reports (21 U. S.), pp. 593, 4, 7, 8.
[2] Ib., pp. 579, 596. "The soil" is an expression often used in this case for the property, as distinguished from the Indian occupancy on the one hand, and from the sovereignty, often called the jurisdiction or the dominion, on the other hand.

such an aptitude have been admitted as citizens, not to mention the facilities given for individual Indians to be naturalised as citizens in proper cases. It may also be remarked that the Act of Congress of 3rd March 1871[1], which transfers the relations with the Indians from the treaty-making to the legislative power of the United States, is by no means inconsistent with a practical observance of the principle that their right of occupancy cannot be extinguished without their free consent. But it would be beside our purpose to enquire into the conduct of Indian affairs either by the United States or by the British government, or even whether the original assumption that the redskins were only hunters, incapable of a larger right than one of occupation, was justified in the case of all the tribes.

In Africa, notwithstanding the caution with which Mr Kasson's ideas were received at the conference of Berlin, an importance has sometimes been attached to treaties with uncivilised tribes, and a development has sometimes been given to them, which are more calculated to excite laughter than argument. A turn so different from that which things have taken in America is due to several causes. First, the uncivilised populations of Africa are mostly settled agriculturists or cattle-breeders, in a stage of advancement higher than that of the redskins, though still short of that which would relieve the white races, on their arrival among them, from the duty of furnishing a government. Secondly, the climate being less suitable for European settlement, the populations in question long continued to be less known, and hence it was possible, as in the case of Monomotapa, to

[1] Revised Statutes, § 2079.

exploit their names by vaunting as empires, comparable to those of Asia, what were certainly nothing more than transient agglomerations effected by savage Napoleons. Thirdly, the adventurers—I use the term in no derogatory sense—who in recent times have led the way to the partition of Africa, have had a sufficient tincture of the forms and language of international law to hope for an advantage over European competitors through what have really been travesties of them. Lastly, it may be trusted that some part has been played by a real desire to respect the just, though not well understood, claims of the natives. I am not aware of any national bias in expressing these opinions. During the recent discussions between England and Portugal, if the latter built unsoundly on cessions by the "emperor" of Monomotapa in 1607 and 1629, the former built with as little reason on a treaty by which Lobengula, in 1888, accepted British protection for a region over which he and his father and his people had never been any thing but cruel raiders. If the antiquity of the Portuguese treaties exposed them to the answer that, whatever they had been in the beginning, they had lapsed into desuetude at least for the larger part of the territory alleged to be comprised in them, it was all the more difficult to treat the British one seriously, just because the facts relating to what it comprised were so modern and transparent. Leaving instances which have contributed to international dissension rather than to enlightenment, the present section may be brought to a close by two instructive examples of what a treaty with an uncivilised chief should and should not be.

A treaty which exemplifies what one with natives

ought not to be is that which Mr Colquhoun, as "representative of the British South Africa Company," concluded on 14th September 1890 with Umtasa or Mutassa, dignified as "king or chief of Manika." In the "kingdom" of this savage, for so he may be described without disrespect to the much more advanced though still uncivilised natives found elsewhere in Africa, who was such a drunkard as to be subject to *delirium tremens*, adventurers had been prospecting for gold under a Portuguese title; and Mr Colquhoun, on 21st September, thus described his behaviour in the circumstances. "With regard to the result of the mining, Umtasa says he has till now been 'sitting watching'; while the Portuguese have ignored Umtasa, the latter on his part has ignored the presence of the white men in his country[1]." And during the events of this and the following months, which saw the English and the Portuguese forces alternately at his kraal, fearing only for his skin, he pursued the policy of granting every demand of those who were present, and excusing himself, or even denying what he had done, to those who were absent. Such a pattern adept in all the branches of civilised administration was made to grant to the company:

"The sole absolute and entire perpetual right and power to do the following acts over the whole or any portion of the territory of the said [his] nation or any future extension thereof, including all subject and dependent territories.

(*a*) To search, prospect, exploit, dig for and keep all metals and minerals.

(*b*) To construct, improve, equip, work, manage and control public works and conveniences of all kinds, including railways and tramways, docks, harbours, roads, bridges, piers, wharves, canals,

[1] Parliamentary Paper c. 6495, p. 26.

reservoirs, waterworks, embankments, viaducts, irrigations, reclamation, improvement, sewage, drainage, sanitary water, gas electric or any other mode of light, telephonic and telegraphic power supply, and all other works and conveniences of general or public utility.

(c) To carry on the business of miners, quarry owners, metallurgists, mechanical engineers, ironfounders, builders and contractors, shipowners, shipbuilders, brickmakers, warehousemen, merchants, importers, exporters; and to buy, sell and deal in goods or property of all kinds.

(d) To carry on the business of banking in all branches.

(e) To buy, sell, refine, manipulate, mint and deal in bullion, specie, coin and precious metals.

(f) To manufacture and import arms and ammunition of all kinds.

(g) To do all such things as are incidental or conducive to the exercise, attainment or protection of all or any of the rights, powers and concessions hereby granted[1]."

And the company agreed :

" That it will, under the King's supervision and authority, aid and assist in the establishment and propagation of the Christian religion and the education and civilisation of the native subjects of the King, by the establishment, maintenance and endowment of such churches, schools and trading stations as may be from time to time mutually agreed upon by the King and the Resident hereinbefore mentioned, and by the extension and equipment of telegraphs and of regular services of postal and transport communications[1]."

It would be superfluous to quote the political stipulations which the treaty also contained. Taken alone they might not have been beyond Umtasa's understanding, but when they were mixed with a farrago which must have been mere jargon to him, the whole must be dismissed as something which could not have received his intelligent consent.

It is pleasant to be able to quote an example to be followed from a British source also. On 26th September 1889 the following treaty was signed with Mr Buchanan, " Her Majesty's acting Consul for

---

[1] Parliamentary Paper c. 6495, p. 28.

Nyassa," by the chiefs of a nation which for intelligence and character ranks very high among those which must still be called uncivilised.

"We the undersigned Makololo chiefs (sons of the late Chiputula) do, in the presence of headmen and people assembled at this place, hereby promise:

1. That there shall be peace between the subjects of the queen of England and our subjects.

2. That British subjects shall have free access to all parts of our territory (country), and shall have the right to build houses and possess property according to the laws in force in this country; that they shall have full liberty to carry on such trade or manufacture as may be approved by Her Majesty; and should any difference arise between the aforesaid British subjects and us the said Makololo chiefs, as to the duties or customs to be paid to us the said Makololo chiefs or the headmen of the towns in our country by such British subjects, or as to any other matter, that the dispute shall be referred to a duly authorised representative of Her Majesty, whose decision in the matter shall be binding and final.

3. That we the said Makololo chiefs will at no time whatever cede any of our territory to any other power, or enter into any agreement treaty or arrangement with any foreign government except through and with the consent of the government of Her Majesty the queen of England, &c.[1]."

Here we observe that there is nothing beyond the comprehension of the Makololo chiefs; that there is no cession of territorial sovereignty by them, or any pretence of founding on their consent the right which the queen may one day come to exercise of founding a regular government in their country in the character of territorial sovereign, such right being tacitly left to be developed in the progress of events, and in accordance with the rules of international law as between Her Majesty and other European powers; that in the

[1] Parliamentary Paper c. 5904, p. 156. The final "&c." is so given in the paper, but the matter it covers was probably only ceremonial. On p. 155 is a similar treaty entered into by Mlauli with Mr Buchanan, and the form was probably supplied by authority as a common one to be used.

mean time the Makololo are recognised as a nation under their chiefs, capable of entering as such into relations with the queen's government in matters within their comprehension, and acknowledging the final supremacy of the queen's government in such matters, the same government having immediate authority over the white settlers in matters belonging specially to civilisation, as trade and manufacture; that property in land is recognised as among the matters within the comprehension of the chiefs and people, so that white settlers may acquire title to it under native law; and that the exclusion of other powers is stipulated, so far as such exclusion may depend on the Makololo. Every foundation is therefore laid, to the extent admitted by the nature of the case, for the future development of territorial sovereignty in the civilised and international sense, and for the permanence under it of such rights as the Makololo already possessed. To use an expression employed in the United States Supreme Court for the position of the Red Indians, the Makololo are admitted as a " domestic dependent nation[1]," but, as became their condition, with rights beyond that of mere occupancy allowed in the territory of the United States to the tribes of hunters.

---

[1] See *Cherokee Nation v. State of Georgia*, decided in 1831, 5 Peters's Supreme Court Reports (30 U. S.), p. 1: Chief Justice Marshall said, p. 17, that "they [the Indians] may more correctly perhaps be denominated domestic dependent nations. They occupy a territory to which we assert a title independent of their will, which must take effect in point of possession when their right of possession ceases. Meanwhile they are in a state of pupilage. Their relation to the United States resembles that of a ward to his guardian."

*Discovery and Occupation as International Titles.*

The position of uncivilised natives having now been fully discussed, the ground is clear for a discussion of the titles to territorial sovereignty in uncivilised regions which states belonging to the society of international law invoke against one another.

Discovery and occupation or settlement have often been opposed to one another as rival titles, discovery being regarded with more favour by the old law of nations and especially forming the base of the Spanish and Portuguese claims, while experience and good sense led to greater stress being laid on occupation or settlement, which thus formed the base of the claims maintained in more recent times. It cannot be denied that there is some truth in this contrast, although it does not present itself in history with quite such sharp lines. That original discovery not followed by any act of possession should create a right for all time, would be too bold an assertion for a practical diplomat to think of formulating it. He would naturally seek to fortify his position by drawing every possible advantage from any occupation of the region in dispute, however illusory, which he could claim that his country had enjoyed. On the other hand, that a state should try by a hasty occupation to anticipate another state in reaping the fruit of its discoveries would be so unfriendly a proceeding that a diplomat, even while in the main resting his case on occupation, would not fail to put forward every plausible claim of discovery which he might be able to make on his side. Yet, if we take a general view of the international controversies on the subject, we shall find that certain doctrinal lines correspond more or less accurately to the conditions of certain nations and certain periods. It is here as in many philosophical controversies. At first sight there appear to be irreconcilable theses. A nearer examination discloses a remarkable agreement among the greatest minds. But the third and last review shows that after all there are differences[1].

The titles which Portugal and Spain first claimed over the eastern and western worlds were not founded on discovery, but on papal grants. In 1454 pope Nicholas V granted Guinea to king Alfonso V of Portugal, and in 1493 pope Alexander VI granted to Ferdinand and Isabella, and to their successors kings of Castile and Leon, all lands situate further west than a line drawn from north to south a hundred leagues west of the Azores. In 1494 the sovereigns of Spain and Portugal modified their boundary by the treaty of Tordesillas, extending the right of Portugal to a line drawn 370 leagues west of the Cape Verde Islands; and in 1506 pope Julius II confirmed that treaty. But the title so obtained could not be successfully pleaded against protestant states, and when Mendoza, Philip II's ambassador,

---

[1] It has been objected to English writers on our subject that they argue too much from practical considerations, and show a weakness in principle which again is attributed to a want of systematic study of the literary sources of law, especially the Roman law. If however there is principle in considering how men would settle the proportional weight that would be given to discovery and to occupation in a supposed state of nature to which the international society is assimilated, and then laying down that, because of that assimilation, the members of the international society must accept the law of nature so arrived at, it may be thought that there is as much principle and more certainty in going direct to the way in which nations have settled for themselves the proportional weight to be given to discovery and to occupation.

complained of the expedition of Drake, he based his claim on discovery, to which Elizabeth replied that

"as she did not acknowledge the Spaniards to have any title by donation of the bishop of Rome, so she knew no right they had to any places other than those they were in actual possession of; for that their having touched only here and there upon a coast, and given names to a few rivers or capes, were such insignificant things as could in no ways entitle them to a propriety further than in the parts where they actually settled and continued to inhabit[1]."

Evidently a controversy of this kind could not be long maintained on the ground of abstract and contradictory principles, neither of which could be entirely ignored by those who invoked the other. So both theoretical writers and official documents, so far as they are concerned with the title which civilised powers may claim to the sovereignty over savage countries, generally try to blend discovery with possession or occupation and not to determine clearly the several parts which belong to them. Vattel for instance writes as follows :

"Thus navigators, being on voyages of discovery with commissions from their sovereigns, and meeting with islands or other desert countries, have taken possession of them in the names of their nations; and that title has generally been respected if it has been closely followed by a real possession[2]."

Similarly, in the declaration of 4th June 1790 signed by the Count de Florida Blanca and sent to all the courts of Europe during the Nootka Sound controversy, the king of Spain limited his claim in the Pacific to "the continent islands and seas which belong to His Majesty, so far as discoveries have been made and secured to him by treaties and immemorial possession, and uniformly acquiesced in,

[1] Camden's Annals, year 1580. Translated as in Twiss, *Oregon Question*, p. 161.
[2] Book I, chap. 18, § 207.

notwithstanding some infringements by individuals who have been punished upon knowledge of their offences[1]."

In the application of this doctrine to particular cases, it is natural that the element of discovery which it contains should have been oftener appealed to by the Spaniards and Portuguese, whose energies were so rapidly enfeebled that they failed to occupy the vast regions which they had been the first to discover, and that the element of possession should have been oftener appealed to by the English and the other nations which entered on the field later. But there is no state which has not insisted in its turn on that part of the doctrine which best suited its convenience at the moment, or which has maintained a perfectly uniform attitude on the questions of detail into which the general doctrine resolves itself.

In considering those questions of detail I shall admit that discovery can only confer what has been called an inchoate title, to be completed by occupation within a reasonable time. But I shall also admit that it confers such an inchoate title by no virtue proper to discovery, but because another state, if it seized on the newly discovered country too soon, would be guilty of a proceeding so unfriendly that international rules are justified in regarding it as an act of hostility. Also we cannot help being struck by the fact that titles having their source as well as their completion in occupation or possession, which for a considerable time past must have been the case of those in Africa, now the chief field for the application of the doctrine, present much resemblance

[1] Twiss, *The Oregon Question Examined*, pp. 109, 163.

to those having their source in discovery, as was the case with the older titles both in that continent and in America. For occupation as well as discovery has its duties, which must be fulfilled before a solid title can result from it, and which can seldom be completely fulfilled at the moment at which occupation begins. Those duties consist in establishing in the country occupied an authority which may protect the natives with whom contact has become inevitable, and under which the civil rights essential to European or American life can be enjoyed in tranquillity. This is in effect what Art. 35 of the general act of the conference of Berlin lays down for the coasts of Africa[1]. Accordingly the sufficiency of the occupation must be measured by the fulfilment of the obligation attaching to it. If a state claiming sovereignty by occupation should fail to establish the necessary authority, no other state can be bound to overlook the injury that may be thereby caused to its own subjects penetrating into the country, or the inhumanity to the natives which must inevitably result. But occupation commonly begins through private enterprise, recognised and supported by the state to which the adventurers belong, but not organised in the form of an expedition sent by the state itself, so that the development of public authority in the occupied region can only be gradual. Therefore the title which originates in occupation will usually, like that which originates in discovery,

[1] " The signatory powers of the present act recognise the obligation to insure the establishment of authority in the regions occupied by them on the coasts of the African continent, sufficient to protect existing rights and, as the case may be, freedom of trade and of transit under the conditions agreed upon."

present an interval during which the fulfilment of the conditions for the ultimate acquisition of sovereignty will be more or less in suspense. But for the close analogy thus arising between the two titles, there would be little use in dwelling on the questions relating to discovery, now that the world has been so fully discovered.

*The Inchoate Title by Discovery or Occupation.*

The first of the questions of detail which have been alluded to is *under what conditions did discovery formerly, or does a commencement of occupation now, confer an inchoate title to territorial sovereignty—that is, the right of occupying or completing the occupation within a reasonable time, and of subjecting or expelling the settlements which other civilised powers or their subjects may have made in the interval?* The most important condition is that the state claiming the inchoate title shall make known its intention of deriving the full benefit from the discovery made or occupation commenced by itself or its subjects, or at least that there shall be no reasonable doubt about the intention in the circumstances. Were this not the case, another state or its subjects might enter the country under a reasonable belief that it had not been appropriated by a foreign power, and might justifiably complain if an inchoate title claiming precedence over theirs was afterwards sprung on them. Accordingly it has always been usual for the state which intends to claim an inchoate title to make its intention known from the beginning. " In newly discovered countries," Lord Stowell said, " where a title is meant to be established for the first time, some act of possession is usually done and proclaimed as a notification of the fact[1]." Here notification is to be understood in the general sense of making known, and not in the special sense of an express communication to other powers, in which it is used in Art. 34 of the general act of the Conference of Berlin :

"Any power which henceforth takes possession of a tract of land on the coasts of the African continent outside of its present possessions, or which being hitherto without such possessions shall acquire them, as well as the power which assumes a protectorate there, shall accompany the respective act with a notification thereof addressed to the other signatory powers of the present act, in order to enable them if need be to make good any claims of their own."

What has been deemed sufficient to make known the intention of appropriating the sovereignty has naturally varied with the circumstances of different times. It never was thought that a discovery might be kept secret and the benefit of it retained. But when all the powers were so eager to extend their colonial possessions that discovery by them without that motive could hardly be imagined, a discovery made by the public ships of a state might be followed by a merely formal act of possession, as planting a flag : the public expedition was notice enough of the intention to appropriate its results, whether or not the formal act was expressly mentioned in the report of those results which ran round the world. But the same conclusion did not follow from a private discovery. There was always some burden attached to extending the territory of a state, were it only the defence of its subjects who settled or acquired interests in the new acquisition, and it was never thought

[1] In the *Fama*, 5 C. Robinson 115.

that a state could be saddled with the burden without its own consent. Consequently it would seem that the intention of a state to appropriate a country discovered by its subjects, or which its subjects have made a commencement of occupying, ought to be quickly signified in some unmistakable mode, if it is to be availed of against foreign interests which have grown up in the country and have led to its being claimed by another state. And this may be regarded as the doctrine generally accepted. It will be observed that Vattel, in the passage which has been quoted from him, only speaks of discoveries made by navigators commissioned by their sovereigns[1]. But in the Oregon dispute the United States rejected the distinction between public and private discoveries, and founded their claim on the discovery of the mouth of the Columbia river by a private adventurer, Captain Gray, followed by an establishment which one of their private citizens made on the Columbia at Astoria, although up to the time when that establishment was sold to the British Northwest Company their government had not adopted the discovery, and had returned no answer to the letter by which Mr Astor had requested it to authorize his proceedings. The British negotiators did not admit the claim, and the region was divided by the convention of 1846. Holtzendorff is so far from attaching importance to the acts of private persons that he does not consider even a discovery by a commissioned officer as founding a title, unless the intention of his government to acquire the territorial sovereignty is proved and made known to the world in general by a public taking possession. And he

[1] See above, p. 160.

adds that when an expedition is organised by a government with the avowed object of scientific research, that object excludes the presumption of the *animus rem sibi habendi*, and the discoveries made by the expedition found no title[1]. In these circumstances it must be admitted that the Conference of Berlin took no great step in advance so far as concerns the principle of publicity, though it acted wisely for the certainty which is so important in international titles, when, as above quoted, it required an express notification for the assumption of territorial sovereignty on the coasts of Africa.

### The Ripening of an Inchoate Title into a Complete one.

The second practical question is, *how long a duration may be allowed to an inchoate title by discovery or occupation—that is, after what time will effective occupation come too late to complete the title as against settlements made in the interval by other states or their subjects?* For titles originating in a commencement of possession on the coasts of Africa notified under Art. 34 of Berlin, the analogous question will be, *how long a time must be allowed for fulfilling the obligation recognised by Art. 35, namely to establish authority sufficient to protect existing rights and, as the case may be, freedom of trade and of transit under the conditions agreed upon in that general act?* Practically the last question amounts to this: *how long a time must be allowed for organising the country with sufficient solidity to secure the common rights of civilised life?*

---

[1] *Handbuch des Völkerrechts*, vol. 2, p. 258.

Professor Pasquale Fiore has proposed twenty-five years as the term to be fixed " within which the country discovered must be really occupied, or within which acts suitable and sufficient must be done for determining the extent of territory which the occupying state is to retain in its real possession[1]." Mr Dudley Field, whom he cites, had already proposed the rule that " the right of possession is deemed abandoned if the intent to exercise it is not manifested within twenty-five years after the discovery[2]." It is needless to say that no definite term has been fixed, and with all deference to the authorities quoted it may be said that much would not be gained by fixing one unless the still more difficult question, what extent of country is affected by the discovery or occupation of one or more points, were settled at the same time. To refer to a constructive abandonment the loss of the inchoate title of which the accompanying conditions have not been fulfilled would be inconsistent with the principles thus far maintained, well as I am aware that that language has often been used. It would imply that the title by discovery or the commencement of occupation was more than inchoate, and, though not followed by effective occupation, need not have been lost if not abandoned ; unless it is intended that the abandonment is to be a presumption *juris et de jure*, in which case it seems better to keep the facts in view than fictions. The truth is that the doctrine of constructive abandonment suited certain bygone conveniences. It tended to save the dignity of sovereigns when they were less accustomed to hear

---

[1] *Trattato di Diritto Internazionale Pubblico*, 3rd ed., vol. 2, § 882, (c). The citation of Mr Dudley Field is at § 875.

[2] *Outlines of an International Code*, 2nd ed., Art. 76.

of the rules of a society, and of the duties which attended their claims. It squared with fashionable theory, comparing the acquisition of uncivilised regions to the acts of men living without government in a supposed state of nature, in which state, if it existed, the relation concerned would be property, the moral duties of which are not so strongly marked as those of sovereignty. Where the right of sovereignty has been fully acquired it may be abandoned, as has more than once happened to the island of Tobago; but that is another matter. For our present purpose, without further dwelling on a definite term of years for the loss of an inchoate title or on its presumptive abandonment, we must observe that since enterprise and necessity have drawn civilised man towards new regions with accelerated speed, less time than before can be allowed for establishing effective occupation and a reasonable measure of authority and order.

We should certainly be going too far if we said that authority must always be present when its action is required. Even in old countries the means of restoring order and punishing its breach are by no means always ready on the spot where a crime has been committed or a right has been violated; and the rights conferred by an inchoate title would be reduced to very small proportions if other states were allowed to enter the region and set up their own sovereignty at every point where their traders may have suffered a momentary injury. Common sense points out that much must depend on the nature and rapidity of the stream of emigration or of enterprise which is directed to the region. The crowds which flock to new gold-diggings must be speedily provided with a government, if it is wished to maintain the pretension to the sovereignty of the country. Pastoral settlements scattered over a vast area may be followed more slowly by a regular administration. What is above all necessary both for the theorist and the statesman is to bear well in mind that no title can prevail against the substantial non-fulfilment of the duties attached to it, not even if the notification required by the Conference of Berlin has been made and has not met with any objection from the powers which have received it. Dr Geffcken has said:

"It is a very doubtful question whether the Congo state can rightfully claim the sovereignty over a territory of more than 2,000,000 square kilometres with 40,000,000 inhabitants, extending in part over regions entirely unexplored and certainly not yet reduced into possession, even though its right to those limits has been acknowledged by other states. These regions will only become the territory of the Congo state in proportion as they are occupied by it[1]."

I am disposed to adhere to that opinion.

## The Geographical Extent of International Titles in Uncivilised Regions.

The questions which may be put with relation to territorial sovereignty in uncivilised regions are so intimately connected with one another that already, when considering how inchoate titles are ripened, we have been obliged to refer to the question what extent of territory is affected by the discovery or occupation of one or more points, and to indicate the

[1] Heffter's *Europäisches Völkerrecht der Gegenwart*, 8th edn., by Geffcken, p. 159.

principle on which it must be solved so far as complete title is concerned, namely, as Holtzendorff writes :

"No state can appropriate more territory through an act of occupation than it can regularly govern in time of peace with its effective means on the spot[1]."

An establishment at one or more points may complete the title to sovereignty over an extent of country within their reach, but it cannot on any geographical considerations be accepted as a substitute for effective authority at points not within their reach.

But our principle does not solve the question which formerly arose when one or more points had been discovered and formal possession taken of them, and which may conceivably now arise on real possession being taken of one or more points on the coast of Africa and all necessary notifications being given in pursuance of Art. 34 of Berlin ; namely, *over what geographical extent was or is an inchoate title acquired, to be completed by real possession within a reasonable time?*

In the law of property it is not necessary to perambulate the whole of an estate of which seisin is meant to be taken, when the seisin taken at one point can be referred to some unity otherwise known, as by deeds or records. But in an uncivilised region, as sovereignty in the European sense has no existence prior to the seisin taken, there is no unity which stands in any relation to it ; and hence the difficulty which besets the problem. There might have been some convenience, especially to the natives, in allowing the inchoate title to comprise one or more entire tribes, in order that their chiefs might not be exposed to conflicting claims from different states. But such

[1] *Handbuch des Völkerrechts*, vol. 2, p. 263.

an arrangement could hardly have been made in the case of unsettled hunters, and even in that of agriculturists it has not been much thought of. Thus the final settlement between England and Portugal divided the tribe and country of Umtasa, who we have seen had been judged capable of understanding the finance of the City and the language of Lincoln's Inn and Exeter Hall[1]. For acquisitions of territory on the coasts of Africa the question, though left theoretically possible, was deprived of almost all practical importance by the fact that the commission at Berlin reported on the draft articles which, as amended, became Arts. 34 and 35, that " it remained understood that the notification was inseparable from a certain determination of limits, and that the powers interested could always demand such supplementary information as might appear to them indispensable for the protection of their rights and interests[2]." Independently then of the partition of Africa which has since taken place, it was in effect settled from 1885 that the limits of inchoate titles would have to be determined at their commencement. All that remains is therefore the historical interest attaching to the various topics of argument which were invoked while much of the world was still undiscovered or unexplored, and of these we will take a summary view. When in old writers those arguments are employed with regard to titles by discovery and formal taking possession, not expressly qualified as to their finality, it must be remembered that the doctrine of presumptive abandonment to which allusion has already been made reduced those titles

[1] See above, pp. 154–155.
[2] Annex 1 to Protocol No. 8.

to a position not much better than that here attributed to inchoate ones[1].

(1) The most extravagant of the claims now in question was that to the back country (*hinterland* in German) to an indefinite extent behind the coast of which discoverers had taken some kind of possession. In the charter which James I granted in 1609 for "the first colony in Virginia," the limits were stated to be along the coast 200 miles northward and the same distance southward from Cape Comfort, "and all that space and circuit of land lying from the seacoast of the precinct aforesaid, up into the land throughout from the sea, west and north-west." The grants of Carolina and Pennsylvania were similar in principle, and the Georgia charter of 1732 granted "all the lands and territories from the most northern stream of the Savannah river all along the sea-coast southward unto the most southern stream of the Alatamaha river, and westward from the heads of the said rivers respectively in direct lines to the South Seas, and all that space circuit and precinct of land lying within the said boundaries[2]."

(2) This claim to back country was represented by the United States during the Oregon controversy as falling under a more general principle of claim by continuity or contiguity, by virtue of which they maintained that the possession of Louisiana gave them the right to the country as far west as the Pacific, and so far north as to include the region disputed with England. But some attempt was

[1] See above, p. 167.
[2] The Virginia charter is quoted in the report of *Johnson v. McIntosh*, 21 U. S. 544. The Georgia charter is quoted and those of Carolina and Pennsylvania referred to by Twiss, *Oregon Question*, p. 282.

made to limit the principle. " It will not be denied," Mr Gallatin wrote, " that the extent of contiguous territory to which an actual settlement gives a prior right must depend in a considerable degree on the magnitude and population of that settlement, and on the facility with which the vacant adjoining land may within a short time be occupied, settled and cultivated by such population, as compared with the probability of its being thus occupied and settled from another quarter[1]." This limitation however leaves the pseudo-scientific principle of contiguity in a position of near equivalence to the "manifest destiny" of rhetoricians.

(3) More scientifically precise than indefinite back country or manifest destiny is the "claim to all the inland territory as far as the line of watershed, founded on the discovery and occupation of an extent of sea-coast, about which position of law," Sir Travers Twiss writes, " there is no dispute amongst nations[2]." A claim falling within these terms may be made in two different cases. We may suppose that two nations establish settlements at the mouths of two rivers which are next to one another on the same coast, and it may then be claimed that their land boundary should follow the watershed of those rivers, notwithstanding that this would give to one of them

[1] Twiss, *Oregon Question*, p. 311 : see also p. 301. Mr Calhoun, writing to Mr Pakenham on 3rd September, 1844, spoke of continuity, and represented the claim to the disputed region not as an incident to the possession of Louisiana, but as belonging to the ancient right of the English colonies to extend from ocean to ocean, which he considered, so far as concerned the country west of the Mississippi, to have been ceded to France in 1763, and to have passed from France to the United States as a part of Louisiana. Wharton's *Digest of the International Law of the United States*, vol. 1. pp. 6, 7.

[2] *Law of Nations, Peace*, 2nd ed., p. 209.

a tract forming the back country to the settlement of the other. Or we may suppose that the claim is made by a nation ascending a river from its mouth, not as against nations desiring to occupy on its right or left hand, but as against discoverers descending the river, after having reached from the other side its innermost watershed, to which the ascending nation claims to extend by virtue of its occupation of the mouth. In the latter form this was another of the arguments used by the United States on the Oregon question, when they founded on the proceedings of Captain Gray and Mr Astor at the mouth of the Columbia as against those of British adventurers on the head waters of that river[1]. And since Sir Travers Twiss repels the argument so used, it may be inferred that his own statement of the doctrine of watershed was meant to apply only to the case first mentioned. If that doctrine were adopted in its fullest extent it would lead to the conclusion that France, while she held Canada and Louisiana, was entitled to all the basins of the St Lawrence and Mississippi, except such portions of the former as were comprised within the settled area of the English colonies, and such portions of the latter as were well understood to belong to Mexico. But during the negotiations with England in 1761 France repudiated any such claim, and proposed that the Indians " between Canada and Louisiana as also between Virginia and Louisiana should be considered as neutral nations, independent of the sovereignty of the two crowns, and serve as a barrier between them[2]."

[1] See as to the latter proceedings Twiss, *Oregon Question*, pp. 13, 14.
[2] Ib., p. 307.

(4) The doctrine of middle distance is thus stated by Sir Travers Twiss: "in cases where there is intermediate vacant land contiguous to the settlements of two nations, each nation has an equal title to extend its settlement over the intermediate vacant land, and thus it happens that the middle distance satisfies the juridical title, whilst it is the nearest approximation to a natural boundary and the most convenient to determine[1]."

(5) Another consideration is mentioned by the same authority as follows. "When a nation has discovered a country and notified its discovery, it is presumed to intend to take possession of the whole country within those natural boundaries which are essential to the independence and security of its settlement[2]." And, "where the control of a district left unoccupied is necessary for the security of a state, and not essential to that of another, the principle of *vicinitas* would be overruled by higher considerations, as it would interfere with the perfect enjoyment of existing rights of established domain[3]." But the principle of security can hardly be relied on as governing the distribution of territory except for very small areas contiguous to real settlements. To that extent however it would seem that the title conferred by it should be complete and not merely inchoate.

(6) "Although considerations based on economic and administrative interests, or on political convenience, may throw light on the advantage or disadvantage of a solution conformable to the views

---

[1] *Law of Nations, Peace*, 2nd ed., p. 216.
[2] Ib., p. 205.
[3] *Oregon Question*, p. 174.

of one or other party, such reasons cannot stand in place of a mode of acquisition recognised by international law[1]." This was said by the Baron Lambermont, in his award between the respective British and German companies, on the farm of the customs and administration of the island of Lamu, dated 17th August 1889. The case was not one of discovery or occupation, but of the effect in the circumstances of the acts and engagements of the Sultan of Zanzibar and his predecessor. The doctrine of the eminent arbitrator however is worth noticing here, especially since it shows that the principle of security mentioned in the preceding paragraph must be strictly construed.

(7) Islands may be so near a coast and so intimately connected with it that the title to them may follow that to the coast, but in one instance this claim was not only made but admitted to an extravagant extent. The Falkland Islands are considered to have been discovered under Spanish auspices by Amerigo Vespucci in 1502, but were first occupied by the French company of St Malo, whence their French name of Malouines, in 1764. Spain claimed them as "a dependence of the South American continent," and Louis XV, probably less from a sense of justice than on account of the political and family connection of the two courts, surrendered them on the payment by Spain of an indemnity to the company. It is said that Lord Anson, when First Lord of the Admiralty in 1754, had contemplated occupying the islands, but that the British government abandoned the scheme in

---

[1] 22 *Revue de Droit International*, p. 353.

deference to Spanish objection[1]. In the protocol relative to the Sulu Archipelago which was signed at Madrid by England, Germany and Spain on 7th March 1885, the two former powers recognised Spanish sovereignty over the archipelago, including " the places effectively occupied as well as those places not yet occupied " ; and Holtzendorff regards this as a recognition of the principle of effective possession[2]. The arrangement included the renunciation by Spain, " as far as regards the British government," of all claims of sovereignty over any parts of Borneo which belonged or had belonged to the Sultan of Sulu ; and that concession may justify such an interpretation, if it be taken as the price of the recognition of Spanish sovereignty over the unoccupied parts of the islands. There were also commercial stipulations on each side.

*Alleged International Title by Civilising Influence exerted beyond the limits of Occupation.*

During the recent dissensions between England and Portugal with regard to their mutual limits in Africa, a claim was put forward on behalf of the latter which must be stated in the words of M. Martens Ferrão.

" Portugal has possessed for centuries in Western and Eastern Africa vast colonies governed by Portuguese authorities, in which she exercises *dominium* and *imperium* :

She possesses states in *vassalage* according to the system established in Africa by all colonising nations :

She has also countries with which she has established *rudimentary relations*, founded on the right of first discovery, never abandoned and

[1] Calvo, *Le Droit International Théorique et Pratique*, vol. I., § 218.

[2] Parliamentary Paper c. 4390 ; *Handbuch des Völkerrechts*, vol. 2, p. 266, note 12.

preserved in this manner. With all these tribes Portugal has always maintained relations by the *rudimentary commerce* of which these peoples are barely capable.

I consider these three formulas to be fundamental ones for determining the relations of colonial right in the mysterious dark continent. These typical forms have even been enlarged by England.

The last is recognised by public law, and will long continue to be so, in the great and uncertain enterprise of calling to civilisation tribes which at present are still either in the lowest state of decadence of the species or in the most rudimentary infancy.

That form, as just and well founded as the others, and not demanding less sacrifice, has been recognised as legitimate, and will always be so as long as true civilisation shall not take its place, an event which is still beyond the range of the most penetrating vision[1]."

The first of the forms thus enumerated needs no remark. It is that of a colony in which a civilised government is in operation under the direct authority of individuals of European race. In the second form the eminent writer appears to contemplate the immediate authority being exercised by the chiefs or other heads of the vassal state, subject to the control of the suzerain state. That is a situation with which we are familiar in the case of a protectorate exercised by a civilised state over another state possessing a civilisation of the same or of a different kind, but it may be doubted whether it is a possible situation where the people dignified with the name of a vassal state is uncivilised. M. Martens Ferrão may have framed his second formula on examples of the former class, such as those of Tunis and Zanzibar; and the traditions of such so-called empires as that of Monomotapa, handed down from the magniloquence of early explorers, may have affected his view of the possibility that natives like those with whom the Portuguese were in contact

[1] Pamphlet quoted above, p. 148, at p. 9 of the copies with the imprint of Rome. The italics are those of M. Martens Ferrão.

IX]     TITLE BY CIVILISING INFLUENCE     179

might be placed in relations similar to those of Tunis or Zanzibar. The third form is that with which we are now concerned, and it contemplates a title to territory having its roots in discovery and kept alive, not by occupation, for in that case it would have been superfluous to mention anything more than the occupation, but by rudimentary relations commercial or other, entertained with tribes whom it is desired gradually to civilise at the cost of some sacrifice to the state maintaining the relations.

There is grave objection to basing an international title on any efforts for the civilisation of native races, because the value and efficacy of such efforts are sure to be differently appreciated by the power which builds on them and by the power against which the title built on them is invoked. The use of an international title is to decide controversies, and to have that effect it ought to be based on facts to which, if I may use the expression, a yard measure can be applied. If the civilising agency of the state to which the discovery belongs is founded on a real occupation of the country accompanied by the establishment of authority in it, the yard measure is found in such occupation. When this is not the case, the civilising agency can mean little, if anything, more than either the work of religious missionaries or the indirect effect of commerce carried on by the natives with the discoverers and their successors. But commerce finds its recompense in itself, and will not justify the proposition that the third form of colonial expansion contemplated by the Portuguese statesman demands not less sacrifice than the other two, each of which involves the burden of government or of control. The profit which a state derives from trade cannot confer any right to exclude other states from the region in which it is carried on.

If on the other hand the civilising agency takes the form of missionary enterprise—which M. Martens Ferrão does not mention, and cannot be supposed to have intended—it is now generally acknowledged that to erect proselytism into an international title to aggrandisement would be highly injurious to sound religion and to peace and goodwill among men. Alluding to the dispute between Spain and Germany which was adjusted by the mediation of the Pope in 1885, Holtzendorff says: " even the sending of missionaries to convert the natives, on which the Spanish government founded in the controversy about the Caroline Islands, can no longer be considered as an act of occupation because it was the church that sent them[1]."

It is conceivable that the native population of an unoccupied country may be so permeated by influence proceeding in one way or another from a people of European race that they may have gone far towards adopting its distinctive form of civilisation and religion. There is perhaps no instance in which an uncivilised population has made so great an advance without the training and discipline which results from European government or control, but the supposition may be made. In that case it might be morally wrong for another European nation to step in and check or divert so admirable a development. But the state which lost the prospective benefit of colonial expansion over the natives in

[1] *Handbuch des Völkerrechts*, vol. 2, pp. 258, 9.

question would only have to blame itself for not having asserted in good time, over such promising neighbours, an authority which in the supposed circumstances could scarcely have been other than welcome.

On no ground then does it seem possible to admit that an international title to territory can be acquired through civilising influence exerted beyond the limits of occupation.

## *Protectorates in Uncivilised Regions.*

In the civilised world a protectorate has long been familiar as a relation existing between two states, of which the protected one is controlled or even wholly represented in its foreign affairs by the protecting one, while the latter has such authority in the internal affairs of the former, if any, as the arrangements between them provide for. The protected state is therefore not independent, but neither does it altogether lose an international existence, for its foreign affairs are distinctly its own, even when wholly managed for it by the protecting state. Thus the republic of the Ionian Islands, which was under the protection of the United Kingdom, was not a party to the Crimean war, waged by Turkey, England, France and Sardinia against Russia, because England did not make it such a party although she might have done so. Consequently the international position of a protected state falls under the general head of semi-sovereignty. On the other hand the relations between the protected and protecting states, whether in respect of the authority which the latter has over the foreign affairs of the former or of that which may be allowed to the latter in the internal affairs of the former, are constitutional relations. The two constitute a single system, possessing and exercising all the powers which belong to civilised government, and not subject to the interference of any third state as to the distribution of those powers but regulating that distribution for themselves[1]. An example lying wholly within Europe is still presented by the protectorate of the kingdom of Italy over the republic of San Marino, but the commonest case by far is now that of a protectorate exercised by a state of European civilisation over one of other civilisation, as that which France exercises over Tunis and that which England exercises over Zanzibar.

Where there is no state, that is to say in an uncivilised region, there can be no protected state, and therefore no such protectorate as has been described in the last paragraph. But in recent times a practice has arisen by which in such regions civilised powers assume and exercise certain rights in more or less well defined districts, to which rights and districts, for the term is used to express both the one and the other, the name of a protectorate is given by analogy. The distinctive characters of those rights are, first, that they are contrasted with territorial sovereignty, for, as far as such sovereignty extends, there is the state itself which has acquired it and not a protectorate exercised by that state; secondly, that the protectorate first established excludes all other states from exercising any authority within the district either by way of territorial sovereignty or of a protectorate—that is to say, while it lasts, for the question remains whether a

[1] See above, pp. 87—90.

protectorate, like an inchoate title to territorial sovereignty, is not subject to conditions and liable to forfeiture on their non-fulfilment; thirdly, that the state enjoying the protectorate represents and protects the district and its population, native or civilised, in everything which relates to other powers. The analogy to the protectorates exercised over states is plainly seen in the last two characters, exclusiveness and representation with protection. It is less visible in the first character, for, where there is a protected state, the territorial sovereignty is divided between it and the protecting state according to the arrangements existing in the particular case, while in an uncivilised protectorate it is in suspense. But on the whole the analogy is sufficient to account for the extension of the old term to the new case, although to account for is not necessarily to justify, and perhaps it might have been better had a new term been used.

The classical passage as to the international status of protectorates in uncivilised regions is the sixth chapter of the general act of the African conference of Berlin, of which the heading is: "*Declaration relative to the essential conditions to be observed in order that new occupations on the coasts of the African continent may be effective*, and which consists of the two articles nos. 34 and 35, of which the texts have been already given[1]. It will be observed that the first of these articles expressly subjects the assumption of a protectorate to the same condition of notification, carrying the same opportunity for objection to be made to it by any power receiving the notification, to which the acquisition of a possession,

[1] See Art. 34, above, p. 164, and Art. 35, above, p. 162, note.

that is of territorial sovereignty, is subjected. And it will further be observed that the second of those articles expressly mentions neither a possession nor a protectorate, but defines the obligation to establish authority which is incumbent in the case of a new *occupation*, that being the term which alone is also used in the heading of the chapter. On this it has been argued that protectorates as well as possessions are included in the occupations mentioned in the heading and by Art. 35, but that conclusion may be questioned. The heading of a chapter must be brief, and cannot always name every subject treated of in it. And the first draft of Art. 35 mentioned protectorates, but their mention was struck out on the proposal of the British ambassador, and M. Busch, the German under-secretary of state, in accepting its omission, described the omitted words, not as superfluous, but as those " which subject protected territories to the same conditions as occupied territories[1]." The point may not be without importance, because occupation is a well understood term in international law, and if it was applied at Berlin to protectorates it would be difficult to resist the conclusion that at least a commencement of occupation was thought necessary for the establishment of a protectorate. But in fact such protectorates as we are considering have been established in Africa without even a commencement of occupation, or at least with no such commencement of which the legal effect could reasonably be extended over the great areas over which they have been established. The caution of the British ambassador in objecting to the inclusion of protectorates in Art. 35 may be

[1] Annex 1 to Protocol 8 of the Berlin Conference.

justified on that ground, and on the further ground that the article as drafted did not distinguish protectorates in uncivilised regions from those over states, which are subject to very different considerations. The authority necessary for the purposes of civilised life already exists in a state, so that the obligation of the protecting state is not to ensure its establishment but to see to its proper working where foreigners are concerned.

But I am at one with Mr Hall in the opinion expressed in the very valuable work lately published by him, to the effect that a protectorate on the coast of Africa carries an obligation of establishing authority equal to that laid down in Art. 35, although that opinion for me is not based on the article but on the nature of the case. And while he considers that the obligation which he finds to be stipulated for the coast implies even for an inland protectorate a consent to civil and criminal jurisdiction over foreigners, as being necessary for the establishment of the authority, it seems to me that that consent also is carried by a protectorate over any uncivilised region, and again from the nature of the case[1]. A protectorate which was not exclusive would not make for peace, and was certainly never intended. But when the exclusive character of a protectorate is admitted, surely it follows that the government required by the conditions of the region must be supplied by the state which excludes all others from supplying it, and that that state is armed by all others which recognise its protectorate with their consent to its exercise of jurisdiction, indispensable for the purpose, over their subjects within the

[1] *Foreign Powers and Jurisdiction of the British Crown*, p. 214.

recognised area. It is true that in inland places there may be a greater difficulty of maintaining effective jurisdiction than on the coast, but then correspondingly there will be less need for it, or the form of authority necessary for efficacy will be less elaborate. As communications are opened and improved, settlement and the means of government will advance with parallel steps.

"It is believed," Mr Hall says, "that all the states represented at the Berlin conference of 1884—5, with the exception of Great Britain, maintained that a protectorate includes the right of administering justice over the subjects of other civilised states; and by the first article of the general act of the Brussels conference of July 1890 the powers, in this instance inclusive of Great Britain, declared ' that the most effective means for counteracting the slave trade in the interior of Africa are the following :—(1) progressive organisation of the administrative, judicial, religious and military services in the African territories placed under the sovereignty or protectorate of civilised nations ' ; in the second to the seventh paragraphs are prescribed the establishment of occupied stations, roads, railways, inland steam navigation, telegraph lines, and the maintenance of restrictions on the importation of firearms and ammunition. Evidently on the one hand acts of the nature contemplated and prescribed compel extensive interference with the internal sovereignty of a community[1], and involve a commensurate assumption of sovereignty by the protecting state; on the other, the objects aimed at can hardly, if at all, be attained compatibly with the exemption of European traders and adventurers from the local civilised jurisdiction[2]."

We are thus led to the conclusion that the third distinctive character above attributed to a protectorate over an uncivilised district—namely that the state which enjoys it represents and protects the district and its population, native or civilised, in every thing which relates to other powers—might have been put higher. It would be true to say that

[1] It is needless to repeat that the system advocated in this book does not permit us to speak of the sovereignty of African savages.
[2] *Foreign Powers and Jurisdiction of the British Crown*, p. 207

the state which enjoys it possesses the full powers of sovereignty over the district and its population, perhaps with the exception that a protectorate, being comparable to the personal relation of guardianship, may not be alienable by cession as territorial sovereignty is. And we are led to answer the question suggested above in connection with the second distinctive character attributed to these protectorates, namely their exclusiveness, by saying that in no case can the powers of territorial sovereignty be retained in spite of a persistent non-fulfilment of the duties attaching to them, and that consequently these protectorates stand on the same provisional footing as the inchoate title to territorial sovereignty. It will be asked why, this being so, it was found necessary to establish this class of protectorates at all; why a country assuming such a protectorate might not equally well notify that it had acquired a new possession, subject to the obligation of the establishment of authority incident to new occupations? The answer to be given is rather a practical than a theoretical one. Over an area far transcending any attempt even at a commencement of occupation, a protectorate will be more easily admitted by other powers than either an inchoate title to possession or, to use the old language, a title by discovery and formal possession to be lost by presumed abandonment on failure to take real possession. The three theoretical forms may be nearly equivalent, but the power of names is great. Even the state which assumes the protectorate feels itself less committed. If it wearies of its task, it can abandon a protectorate with less loss of self-respect than a possession, even though the latter be held only by a title admittedly inchoate. Practically then the institution of protectorates over uncivilised regions has given greater freedom to the initial steps towards their acquisition.

It remains to notice the question how far British legislation has entrusted British courts with the jurisdiction, especially over the subjects of foreign powers, which is necessary to the performance of the international duties attached to British protectorates in uncivilised regions, and which we have seen is generally admitted by foreign powers to belong internationally to such protectorates. This is indeed not a question of international law, but the branch of it which relates to the power of the crown to supply such legislation by order in council involves questions which it may be useful to consider. The Foreign Jurisdiction Act 1890, s. 1, declared that the queen may exercise any jurisdiction which she then had or at any time thereafter might have within a foreign country. A protectorate is a foreign country, the rights held over it being still distinguished from territorial sovereignty, by however thin a line. And jurisdiction over persons of all nationalities, which is attached by the general understanding of states to a protectorate itself recognised by them, must surely fall within the description of jurisdiction which the queen has. But it has been suggested that the meaning of the section must be cut down by reference to the recital that " by treaty, capitulation, grant, usage, sufferance and other lawful means, Her Majesty the queen has jurisdiction within divers foreign countries" —combined with the fact that the act is a consolidating one, and that at the dates of the acts consolidated, or at least at that of the original act of 1843, the queen had no jurisdiction through protectorates. I cannot adopt that suggestion. It seems to me incorrect to say that " the act of 1843 referred only to certain wholly independent states, in which a limited jurisdiction over British subjects had been obtained in the various ways specified in the recital." Such jurisdiction may have been all that there then was to fall within the section, but the section referred to all that might fall within its terms. It will hardly be said that the section cannot be applied to jurisdiction acquired since 1843, or even since 1890, within independent states, by any of the means specifically mentioned in the recital. And if the section is not to be confined to jurisdiction existing in 1843, as little I think can the words " other lawful means " be confined to means which were lawful in 1843, so as to exclude jurisdiction acquired by a class of protectorates which has since become internationally lawful. I conclude that the section in question empowers Her Majesty to grant to her courts in protectorates the jurisdiction over all persons there which is necessary for maintaining order and enforcing rights. No argument to the contrary can be drawn from the s. 2 of the Foreign Jurisdiction Act 1890, which gives the queen jurisdiction, but only over her own subjects, in " a foreign country not subject to any government from whom Her Majesty might obtain jurisdiction in the manner recited." The countries so described would be those outside both states and protectorates; and such description of them involves the assertion, insisted on in this chapter, that the uncivilised natives who inhabit them are not sources by cession from whom the queen can obtain the powers of civilised government. A country over which the civilised world has so far asserted its authority as to recognise the establishment of a protectorate over it is not one in which the acquisition of jurisdiction is impossible.

Mr Hall, who takes the limited view of the operation of the Foreign Jurisdiction Act, argues that " in assuming a protectorate the crown takes to itself powers which, so far as they go, are identical with those that it would have in a conquered country. It can prescribe laws until parliament chooses to legislate, and it can subject to its administration all persons upon the protected soil[1]." This seems to be sound. The power which the crown has in a conquered country is that which is conferred on the state by international law, and which is deposited in the crown because the constitution of the United Kingdom has made no provision for its being deposited elsewhere. In the same way the power which international law confers on the state in the case of a protectorate is deposited in the crown till parliament may provide for its being deposited elsewhere. Perhaps it may be said that this reasoning is inconsistent with the decision in *The Queen v. Keyn*[2]. But that decision, whether it was right or wrong, was that the jurisdiction of English courts could not be enlarged by the development of an international doctrine that the sea within the three-miles limit was territorial. And it does not follow that the crown is unable to accept for the benefit of the state an authority given by the development of an international doctrine about

---

[1] U. S., p. 225.  [2] L. R., 2 Exch. 63.

protectorates, when such acceptance does not affect the jurisdiction of an English court or anything else internal to the realm of England. Whether therefore under the Foreign Jurisdiction Act or by the analogy to conquest, we may fairly conclude that the queen, by order in council, can confer jurisdiction over foreigners on her courts in her protectorates in uncivilised regions.

On the question whether she has done so it will be sufficient to refer to Mr Hall's able discussion in the work mentioned. He sums up as follows.

"It is clear that in the less developed instances Great Britain has assumed smaller powers than might reasonably have been taken, and that in some cases, as for example on the Somali coast, enough power has certainly not been appropriated to meet the demands which may rightly be made by foreign states, or to prevent the continuance or establishment of foreign extraterritorial jurisdictions, the existence of which may be productive of grave embarrassment in the future. On the other hand, in the protectorates where she has invested herself with fuller powers, while refraining from any undue invasion of internal sovereignty, she has secured to herself sufficient authority to meet all contingencies[1]."

## Spheres of Influence.

Spheres of influence result from mutual agreements of abstention made by two or more powers. An example may be taken from the declaration of 6th April 1886, by which England and Germany defined their respective spheres of influence in the Western Pacific. The reciprocal engagement was in these terms.

[1] *Foreign Powers and Jurisdiction of the British Crown*, p. 220. With reference to what is said about an undue invasion of internal sovereignty, it must be remarked that, in the chapter quoted from, protectorates over states are treated of as well as protectorates over uncivilised regions.

"Germany [Great Britain] engages not to make acquisitions of territory, accept protectorates, or interfere with the extension of British [German] influence, and to give up any acquisitions of territory or protectorates already established, in that part of the Western Pacific lying to the east south-east or south [west north-west or north] of the said conventional line."

This was accompanied by certain collateral stipulations, as may always be the case; but the essence lies in the promise by each contracting party to abstain from every form of aggrandisement on the other side of the boundary agreed on. On its own side of the boundary each must pursue its aggrandisement, if at all, by the methods and subject to the conditions applicable in other cases to the acquisition of possessions or protectorates. A sphere of influence is not in itself a recognised form of aggrandisement, and if either power, within the sphere reserved to it, meets with a third power not a party to the agreement, the rights of such third power are intact. The agreement is *res inter alios acta*, and cannot be quoted against it.

A very remarkable incident in connection with this subject is the agreement of 12th May 1894, by which England granted to the Congo state a lease of certain territories in which England herself had no other right than that arising from agreements made by her with Germany and Italy, by which those powers respectively delimited with her their spheres of influence in such manner as to leave the territories in question in the British sphere. If it be admitted that sovereignty is an apt subject for a lease, still that admission would not cover the case. No one can lease more than he has, and here all England had was the right to the abstention of Germany and Italy; while those powers might well say that an agreement for abstention is of a personal nature, in other words that state (A), which has made such an agreement in favour of state (B), cannot be forced, either by lease or by an attempt at permanent transfer, to treat it as binding in favour of state (C), which it might think a less desirable neighbour. In fact neither Germany nor Italy has objected, though Germany objected to another clause of the same agreement with such effect that it was cancelled by the parties. By that clause the Congo state had leased a part of its territory to England, thereby bringing the latter into a geographical situation to which Germany had refused to consent when delimiting her own sphere of influence with her. It was therefore natural that Germany should desire to object to the same effect being produced by an arrangement made between England and the Congo state, even for the duration of a lease. But that she could do so proves that the principle established with regard to the map of Europe, that any alteration in it is matter of common interest to all the European powers, and can be objected to by any of them which may think the case requires it, is beginning to be recognised for the map of Africa also. Nor is it at all surprising that this should be so, now that the European powers have acquired such important interests in conterminous parts of that continent.

## CHAPTER X

### THE EMPIRE OF INDIA

*The East India Company and Companies in general.*

WE have seen in what relation states stand to international law, whether they are the fully sovereign states of the white society whose rules are that law, or semi-sovereign, oriental or protected states[1]. We have also seen how the uncivilised part of the world is related to international law, by what means states appropriate portions of it as their possessions, how beyond the limits of their territorial sovereignty they exercise over other portions of it protectorates not to be confounded with those exercised over states, and how, in regions still less advanced, they agree to leave each other free scope within limits which as between the contracting parties mark out their spheres of influence. India presents no further kind of international relation to be added to these: indeed it would be difficult to imagine any kind which would not fall within one or other of the foregoing. But the modern history and present political arrangement of India, apart from the great interest they must offer to Englishmen, furnish to the student

[1] See above, as to semi-sovereign states, pp. 87—90; as to oriental states, pp. 82, no. 12, and 102, 103; as to protected states, pp. 181, 182.

of international relations a remarkable example of the rapidity and ease with which such relations may shift in substance while remaining unchanged in form, so that even instructed observers have sometimes been bewildered as to their true classification in their successive phases.

It may have occurred to some that, in saying that India presents no kind of international relation which has not already been touched on, it must have been intended to refer to the system under which she is now governed, and not to a history which includes that of the East India Company. But the statement was meant to refer to the history as well as to the present political conditions of India. An incorporated company is the creature of the state to the law or to the government of which it owes its corporate existence and powers, and if it is incorporated for an object which brings it into relations with foreign states, the state which has created it cannot escape responsibility for the acts of its creature. The relations into which the company was empowered to enter, or into which it has in fact entered without being restrained by its parent state, are those of the parent state, of which for all such purposes the company is as much an organ as the department of its government ostensibly entrusted with the conduct of its foreign affairs, or as the commanders of the forces which the state employs in its own name. In framing the constitution of the company care may or may not have been taken that its members or its directors shall be subjects of the state which grants the incorporation, but that does not matter. The company, as a technical person having an existence in law, is a technical subject of the state which has called it from nothingness into that mode of being. Such was the case of the East India Company, and such is now the case of the Imperial British East Africa Company, the British South Africa Company, and others. If any of these companies acquires territory, the territory and the international sovereignty over it belong to the British crown, though they may be held mediately by the company, as the Earls of Derby were at one time mediately kings of the Isle of Man. If the company, in its character of a mediate territorial sovereign or in any other character, suffers wrong from a foreign state, or from a company similarly created by a foreign state, as the Dutch East India Company or the Mozambique Company of Portugal, the British Crown can treat the wrong as done to itself or its subjects. If the company does wrong to a foreign state or company, the British Crown is responsible to the same extent as if the wrong were done by a natural person being a British subject, and so far further as the commission of the wrong may have been made possible or facilitated by the incorporation of the company or the powers granted to it. If the company is engaged in hostilities with a foreign state or a company created by a foreign state, there is war *de facto* between England and the state in question, and it is at the choice of either to treat it avowedly as an international war if it pleases. Consequently we shall consider as international lawyers that the part which the East India Company has played was played by England. Any distinction which might be drawn between the times before and after the assumption of direct rule in India by parliament and the Crown, as it would relate only to the organ by which the British state was pleased to act, must belong not to international but to constitutional history.

That whatever the East' India Company held it held mediately as an organ of the state, was implied by parliamentary interference with the company from its commencement in 1773, and was expressed in the subsequent renewals of the company's charter. The act of 1793 confirmed the title of the company to its territorial acquisitions " without prejudice to the claims of the public." The act of 1813 declared that its provisions were without prejudice to " the undoubted sovereignty of the crown of the United Kingdom of Great Britain and Ireland in and over the said territorial acquisitions." The act of 1833 declared the company to be " trustees for the crown of the United Kingdom," and by the act of 1858 the trusteeship was terminated and the sovereignty of the state, which had never been doubtful to the discerning eye, was unveiled to every one.

*Rise of the British Empire in India, from the point of view of International Law.*

Bombay was acquired by England in full sovereignty, by cession from Portugal, as a part of the dower of Catherine of Braganza. With that exception, the condition of India and the position which the East India Company held there in the eighteenth century may best be understood by the analogy of the Holy Roman Empire between the Peace of Westphalia in 1648 and its extinction in 1806. The states of that empire acknowledged the emperor as their suzerain, but they were formally empowered to enter into foreign relations of great importance on their own account and in their own names, and the emperor and the imperial diet were quite unable to enforce the formal limitation of their foreign relations. Therefore, following fact and not constitutional theory, the states of the empire were not treated by the other powers as semi-sovereign but as full members of the European international society[1]. The Mogul empire had fallen into a similar decrepitude, and its provincial governors, as the Nizam of the Deccan and the Nawab Wazir of Oude, asserted a practical independence similar to that of the German states, but, again similarly, without wholly ignoring the nominal sovereign of India. The confusion into which India fell was increased by the apparition of merely insurgent powers, as the Marhattas, and became beyond comparison greater than any confusion which existed in Europe, so that the British company was compelled to provide for its own defence. In doing so it became an Indian power enjoying the same practical independence as the other rulers who had risen on the ruins of the Moguls. It treated those rulers as internationally sovereign, and made alliances, wars and peace with them, just as England and France acted with regard to the elector of Brandenburg or of Bavaria. But like the Nizam and the rest it bowed, in compliment only, to Mogul supremacy, again as England and France, Brandenburg and Bavaria, all admitted on paper that the Holy Roman Emperor was the head of Germany.

Thus, when the company obtained from the emperor of Delhi the confirmation of the grants of

[1] See above, pp. 57, 58, 81.

certain districts which they had already received from the Nizam of the Deccan and the Nawab of the Carnatic—or when it obtained from him a grant of the *dewannee*, or administration and enjoyment of the revenue, of Bengal, Behar and Orissa, of which provinces it was already in secure possession through the victory of Buxar, gained by Major Munro over the forces of Mir Kasim of Bengal and the Nawab Wazir of Oude—this was very similar to what occurred when Francis II, in his capacity of Holy Roman Emperor, ceded to France at Lunéville in 1801 territory including what she had already obtained from Prussia by the treaty of Basle in 1795[1]. At least in each case there was the acceptance of a paper title to confirm what had been acquired by cession or conquest from the real predecessor, the difference being that the paper title which Clive deemed it convenient to seek maintained the paper supremacy of the Great Mogul, while the First Consul used the authority of the Holy Roman Emperor for its own extinction in the territory in question.

The emperor of India had become a puppet in the hands of the Marhattas when the great campaign, memorable for the victories of Wellesley (Wellington) at Assaye and Argaon and of Lake at Delhi and Laswari, was terminated by the treaty of Sarje Arjengaon, concluded 30th December 1803 with Sindhia, the Marhatta ruler of Gwalior. By that treaty Delhi was left in British hands, and the Marhattas ceased to pull the strings of the puppet, but England declined the farce of pulling them in her turn. The time had come for her to

[1] The analogy is not affected by the emperor's want of constitutional power to make that cession without the concurrence of the diet.

assume a position more nearly in accordance with her real power. The *modus vivendi* which was established between the Company and the politically effete representative of the Moguls is thus described by Mr Tupper :

"The emperor sought the protection of the British government, and it was arranged that certain territories near Delhi should be assigned as part of the provision for the maintenance of the royal family; that these lands should remain under the charge of the resident at Delhi; that the revenue should be collected and justice administered in the name of Shah Alam under regulations fixed by the British government; that the king should appoint a dewán and other officers; and that two courts should be established for the administration of the Muhammadan law to the inhabitants of the city of Delhi and of the assigned territory, death sentences however being subject to confirmation by the king[1]."

An honourable position, commensurate with the splendour of their former estate, was thus made for the Mogul family within a narrow area, subject to British control even there. But outside that area no use was any more made of the imperial name to cloak the independence of the British power.

"In describing these arrangements on June 2, 1805, Lord Wellesley wrote : 'It has never been in the contemplation of this government to derive from the charge of protecting and supporting His Majesty the privilege of employing the royal prerogative as an instrument of establishing any control or ascendancy over the states and chieftains of India, or of asserting on the part of His Majesty any of the claims which in his capacity of emperor of Hindustan His Majesty may be considered to possess upon the provinces originally composing the Mogul empire.' The benefits claimed were the preclusion of hostile projects, which might be founded on the restoration of the authority of the emperor under the direction of agents of France, and the confidence and good feeling amongst states and people which the British government could secure by becoming the lenient protector of the representative of the house of Timur. The Delhi emperor was not to be a Nawab of Arcot or a Nawab of Murshidabad, for the purpose of consolidating British dominion throughout the continent;

[1] *Our Indian Protectorate*, by Charles Lewis Tupper, p. 38.

for indeed the days when it was necessary to proceed under the countenance of some native power had passed away[1]."

Thus it was but an empty form that for nearly forty years more, till Lord Ellenborough stopped the practice, bags of gold were offered to the Great Mogul by officers representing the British government. Such tribute, if it can be so called, had no greater significance than the presents which down even to our own times Burma and Siam have sent to the court of Pekin. All that can be said is that a nation less conservative of old usages than the English would have sooner discontinued the practice[2]. Certainly, from 1803, in order to find a European analogy for the relations of England to the princes whom she encountered in India, it would no longer be correct to refer to the Holy Roman Empire. But it must not be supposed that this made a substantial difference in the situation, any more than the fall of the Holy Roman Empire made a difference to the real relations between the German states and other European powers, or between the German states themselves. And in connection with the history both before and after 1803 we must next note a circumstance bearing on the rules of international law as applicable in India, and not on the formal footing on which the powers

[1] *Our Indian Protectorate*, by Charles Lewis Tupper, p. 39.

[2] It was a bad practice, all the same. When the emperor of Delhi was tried and sentenced for joining the mutineers in 1857, it might have been pleaded, at least in mitigation, that only some fifteen years before his dynasty had been still led to believe that England was its tributary. We fight against an evil as long as we deem it to be formidable, and as soon as we think we have overcome it we appear to take a delight in preserving the symbols of it. That is all very well for ourselves, if such is our pleasure, but allowance ought to be made for its effect on the minds of others.

stood between whom those rules were to be observed.

If the reader will refer to what has been said on the *Rights of Self-preservation actually allowed by International Law*, and on the *Alleged right of Self-preservation against the Contagion of Revolution*[1], he will see that no provision is there contained for the case of a country's falling into a condition of chronic misgovernment and anarchy, constituting in itself a standing danger to neighbouring countries, apart from any threat of attack on them or unlawful propaganda of political principles, and from any preparations leading reasonably to the inference that such attack or propaganda is intended. Such a case was not contemplated in the sections mentioned because it does not occur and can scarcely be imagined as occurring in the international society of the white race, and therefore it cannot be expected that the law of that society shall provide for it[2]. But it is unhappily a case by no means unknown among those states of other civilisations with which the white race is compelled to be in contact, and this is one of the causes why the primary rules of international law cannot be extended without limitation to the intercourse resulting from such contact[3]. It is

[1] Above, pp. 115—121, 123—126.

[2] It will be remembered that chronic anarchy constituting a standing danger to neighbours was the pretext for the successive partitions and ultimate suppression of Poland, but the case, even as it stood, was far from being as bad as was represented, and the neighbours, with cruel foresight, had systematically thwarted all the attempts at reform which were not wanting in Poland. The example has met with general reprobation, and is a warning against inscribing any such principle in the body of rules to be applied between ordinary European and American states.

[3] See above, p. 82, no. 12, and pp. 102—104.

eminently an occasion for applying the principle that the want of a rule to define the action allowable does not exclude all action, which has been noticed as having a large field in dealings between members of the international society and outsiders to that society[1]. The existence of such a case in Turkey in 1821 was revealed by the Greek insurrection, and a majority of the great powers had at last to recognise the fact and act on it, although that result was delayed by the obstinate attempt of Austria to extend her then favourite principle of legitimacy even to the Ottoman empire, an attempt which Russia for a time unavailingly combated on the ground of religion instead of that of misgovernment. In India England could not be long in perceiving that the internal anarchy of the states beyond her borders was one of the chief causes which had compelled her to advance, and that, unless it was checked, it would continue to compel her to advance. Lord Cornwallis hoped that the policy of non-intervention would lead to its being checked, by permitting the growth of strong organisations outside British India through what would now be called the survival of the fittest[2]. It is not for us to study here how that expectation was disappointed, for we have to do with history only in its bearing on international law. But our purpose obliges us to notice how Lord Wellesley in 1801, impelled by the necessity which arose from the condition of Oude, "annexed more than half the country and endeavoured, without success, to provide for the better government of the

---

[1] Above, p. 79, no. 5.
[2] Lee-Warner, *The Protected Princes of India*, p. 91.

residue[1]." Lord Cornwallis's system, even had Lord Wellesley been inclined to adopt it, would not have been applicable to Oude, the geographical and other circumstances of which hardly permitted its being absorbed without danger to us in any strong extra-British organisation. In the result, in spite of numerous threats, the successive kings of Oude refused to conduct themselves better in the territory which remained to them, and in 1855 it was recognised that the situation had become intolerable, and annexation was determined on. In the minute written on that occasion by him as a member of council, Sir J. P. Grant placed our right, among other grounds, on our having succeeded to the empire of the Mogul, and to his duty of terminating incorrigible misgovernment in his dominions. Lord Dalhousie, in his minute, rejected that ground, but in his dealings with Sattara he had claimed that the British government was "the successor of the emperors of Delhi[2]." These however, on one side or the other, were the reasonings of individual statesmen. In no public act did the British government claim any political power as deduced to it from the pageant dynasty which it maintained at Delhi, and even in 1801 Lord Wellesley dealt with Oude as an independent state, regardless of constitutional memories which had ceased to have any correspondence with fact. The intervention on the ground of misgovernment to which he had recourse was not founded on any question about Oude's possessing that character, but on the principles of

---

[1] Tupper, *Our Indian Protectorate*, p. 65.
[2] Ibid., pp. 76, 78, 87.

international law which it was necessary to apply to independent states in India.

The native states have since lost the character of independence, not through any epoch-making declaration of British sovereignty, but by a gradual change in the policy pursued towards them by the British government. Encountering the ambition of some of its neighbours and the internal anarchy of others, and the efforts of France or of French adventurers to build on those elements a power rivalling its own, that government was early led to see that its only security, even within the limits which it had from time to time attained, was to make for itself among the states of India such a preponderant position as Charles V, Louis XIV and Napoleon had essayed or were essaying with less justification to make for themselves among the states of Europe. This, and little more, was its purpose until ten years after the time when the Great Mogul ceased to be a mysterious fountain from which his strongest neighbour might pretend to draw authority.

" With respect to the French, supposing the present questions in Europe not to lead to an immediate rupture, we are now certain that the whole course of their policy has for its object the subversion of the British empire in India, and that at no distant period of time they will put their plans in execution. It is absolutely necessary for the defeat of those designs that no native state should be left to exist in India which is not upheld by the British power, or the political conduct of which is not under its absolute control." Sir George Barlow, on the policy of the treaty of Bassein (31st December 1802), 12th July 1803 : Tupper, *Our Indian Protectorate*, p. 33.

" The fundamental principle of His Excellency the governor-general's " [Lord Wellesley's] " policy in establishing subsidiary alliances with the principal states of India is to place those states in such a degree of dependence on the British power as may deprive them of the means of prosecuting any measures or of forming any confederacy hazardous to the security of the British empire, and may enable us to preserve the tranquillity of India by exercising a general control over those states, calculated to prevent the operation of that restless spirit of ambition and violence which is the characteristic of every Asiatic government, and which from the earliest period of Eastern history has rendered the peninsula of India the scene of perpetual warfare, turbulence and disorder. The irremediable principles of Asiatic policy, and the varieties and oppositions of character, habits and religions which distinguish the inhabitants of this quarter of the globe, are adverse to the establishment of such a balance of power among the several states of India as would effectually restrain the views of aggrandisement and ambition and promote general tranquillity. This object can alone be accomplished by the operation of a general control over the principal states of India established in the hands of a superior power, and exercised with equity and moderation through the medium of alliances contracted with those states on the basis of the security and protection of their respective rights." Despatch from the Indian government to the resident at Hyderabad, 4th February 1804: Tupper, *Our Indian Protectorate*, p. 40.

" The picture above drawn of the state of politics among Asiatic powers proves that no permanent system can be adopted which will preserve the weak against the strong, and will keep all for any length of time in their relative situations and the whole in peace, excepting there should be one power which, either by the superiority of its strength, its military system or its resources, shall preponderate and be able to protect all." Reply of General Wellesley (Wellington) to Lord Castlereagh's strictures on the treaty of Bassein, probably written in November 1804 : Ibid., p. 36.

The chief place among the alliances referred to in the second of the preceding extracts was held by those known in Indian history as subsidiary alliances. These attained under Lord Wellesley, though they did not originate under him, a developed form which, with more or less variation in particular cases, may be described as follows. They established friendship between the contracting parties, who employed towards one another all the complimentary language befitting independent powers, and British interference in the internal affairs of the native state was excluded. The native prince bound himself to have no negotiations with any other power without giving previous notice to the company's government and entering into mutual consultation with it, and to submit his differences with third parties to the company, which was to aid him if it failed to adjust the difference on reasonable terms ; and he on his part was to help the company in case of attack on it with forces fully proportioned to his means. The company was to supply a certain subsidiary force, not to be employed on trifling occasions or in collecting the prince's revenue, but to execute services of importance, such as the care of the prince's person, the protection of his country from invasion, and the suppression of rebellion against him ; and the cost of that force was borne by the prince, either in periodical payments or, as was oftener the case, by the cession of territory deemed equivalent. And there might or might not be a stipulation for another force, called a contingent, to be maintained by the prince for general service with the British troops pursuant to his obligations, and to be commanded by British officers.

A European power, at the close of an unsuccessful war, has often had to submit to terms little less onerous, and the condition thus made for a state did not cause it to drop out of international existence. The native states subjected to the system were commonly described as protected, and this was an accurate description, but the kind of protectorate intended by it must be carefully considered. Of course it was not that kind of veiled or suspended sovereignty which occurs in the case of a protectorate over an uncivilised region : it was a relation existing towards a state, though one enjoying what I have called another civilisation than ours. Neither was it a case in which the protected state was *represented* in its foreign affairs by the protecting one, for negotiations between the protected state and third ones were not excluded, but the protecting state was to have an opportunity of controlling them, and the protected state was not to carry them to the point of war without submitting itself to the company's decision. The two did not stand before the international society of India as forming one system, the parts of which might have different international relations, but to one alone of which it was admissible for third states to address themselves in matters concerning the international relations of either. It was a case in which the protected state was *controlled* in its foreign affairs by the protecting one[1]. And Lord Cornwallis, who in his second governor-generalship succeeded Lord Wellesley, was anxiously desirous to remove all fear that the tie might be drawn closer by interference in the internal concerns of the protected states, beyond what might be imperatively demanded for the security of the company's own dominions.

But even this system failed to establish throughout the peninsula the *pax Britannica* which was indispensable for the secure enjoyment of quiet by the company's possessions. The next steps in advance which were taken in treaties and grants were to exclude the prince dealt with from having any connection or engagement with other chiefs or states, and even to make the sanction of the British government necessary for his having any communication with them, sometimes but not always with the exception of amicable correspondence between friends and relations—thus transforming the protectorate

[1] See above, pp. 181, 182.

into one in which England became the sole representative of the native state in all external intercourse—and to bind the prince to "act in subordinate cooperation with the British Government," sometimes also to "be guided in all matters by the advice of the British agent." These steps mark the governor-generalship of Lord Hastings, which extended from October 1813 to the first day of 1823[1]. By virtue of them that administration may be singled out as the turning point in the course of shifting the affairs of India from an international to an imperial basis, although that course neither began with it nor was completed by it. The isolation of the native states was the negation of an international society, and subordinate cooperation in maintaining the *pax Britannica* implied that the peace to be maintained was the peace of the imperial state to which the cooperation was subordinate. "In 1819," Mr Lee-Warner says, Lord Hastings "raised the Wazir of Oude to the dignity of king, thus announcing not merely that the ruler of Oude no longer held his title from the emperor of Delhi, but that the British government, which had pensioned the emperor and suppressed the sovereignty of the Peshwa, could bestow a kingly title[2]." True: and the difference is obvious between such a bestowal and the assumption of a higher title by a European prince, notified by him to his fellow sovereigns, and then employed by them in their correspondence with him.

The princes whose treaties or grants dated from an earlier period were not called on, in the absence

[1] Lee-Warner, *The Protected Princes of India*, ch. iv. and ch. ix.; and see Tupper, *Our Indian Protectorate*, ch. ii. and ch. iii.

[2] u. s., p. 115.

of other circumstances requiring it, to enter into new treaties or to accept new grants expressing isolation and subordination. The British government preferred to adopt on its own responsibility the principle that it was not only preponderant in India but paramount, not merely the strongest power but the rightful superior, and that all treaties and grants of whatever date were to be construed as reserving the exercise of that superiority when needed for certain beneficent purposes. There was a very large number of princes, mostly with small possessions, who enjoyed British protection without any treaty or grant; and the paramount position was equally claimed over them. Although this far-reaching principle was not inscribed in any proclamation or other public formula, its adoption can scarcely be called tacit, for it was avowed by statesmen on occasions calling for its application.

" ' We have by degrees,' said Sir Charles Metcalfe—I quote here from Marshman, vol. ii. p. 408—' become the paramount state in India. In 1817 it became the established principle of our policy to maintain tranquillity among the states of India ;...and we cannot be indifferent spectators of anarchy therein without ultimately giving up India again to the pillage and confusion from which we then rescued her.... We are bound, not by any positive engagement to the Bhurtpur state, but by our duty as supreme guardians of tranquillity, law and right, to maintain the legal succession of Balwant Singh..... Our supremacy has been violated or slighted under the impression that we were prevented by entanglement elsewhere from sufficiently resenting the indignity.... A display and vigorous exercise of our power, if rendered necessary, would be likely to bring back men's minds in that quarter to a proper tone ; and the capture of Bhurtpur, if effected in a glorious manner, would do us more honour throughout India, by the removal of the hitherto unfaded impressions caused by our former failure, than can be conceived.' This advice was accepted and acted on. Lord Lake had been baffled before Bhurtpur in 1805. It was quickly taken in 1826 by Lord Combermere." Tupper, *Our Indian Protectorate*, p. 55.

The treaty of Umritsur, 16th March 1846, guaranteed the independent possession of Kashmir to the Maharaja Golab Sing. On 7th January 1848 Lord Hardinge, who had himself made that treaty, found himself under the necessity of stating to the Maharaja that "the British government are bound by no obligation to force the people to submit to a ruler who has deprived himself of their allegiance by his misconduct." And he supported that statement by saying: "Your highness is aware of the principle by which the British government is guided in its treaties with Eastern princes." That is, he construed a treaty not by its bare words, but as necessarily reserving the right of the paramount power to follow its known principles of action. The doctrine has been well put as follows: "There *is* a paramount power in the British Crown, of which the extent is wisely left undefined. There *is* a subordination in the native states, which is understood but not explained. The paramount power intervenes only on grounds of general policy, where the interests of the Indian people or the safety of the British power are at stake. Irrespective of those features of sovereign right which native states have for the most part ceded or circumscribed by treaty, there are certainly some of which they have been silently but effectually deprived." And the latest expounder of our Indian system, who is also one of the most authorised, teaches that the treaties and grants held by the protected princes, and the precedents of our dealings with them and with the protected princes who hold no treaties or grants, must be read as a whole, like the decisions of English courts of justice, so that the principles most recently laid down are to be applied to all, and those relating to any department of conduct, as military affairs or the duties of humanity, are to be ascertained for all from the document in which that department is most fully worked out for any one—a doctrine which evidently presupposes the enjoyment of a very thorough superiority by the power to the unilateral acts of which such an effect is ascribed[1].

A paramount power such as this is defined by being, wisely or not, left undefined. That to which no limits are set is unlimited. It is a power in India like that of the parliament in the United Kingdom, restrained in exercise by considerations of morality and expediency, but not bounded by another political power meeting it at any frontier line, whether of territories or of affairs. It is in fact the power of the government and parliament of the United Kingdom themselves, and the protected Indian states may rely on its exercise towards them being confined within limits not more vaguely understood than those within which an Englishman relies that its exercise towards him will be confined. But it exists, it constitutes the British empire in India, and it is incompatible with international relations between the princes which are subject to it, or between them and the empire. No precise date can be named for its establishment, for several reasons. Its immediate historical origin being that of a doctrine become a habit, and the habit of command being insufficient to establish a political condition without the habit of obedience, there is twice the usual uncertainty which attends the question of when a habit became fixed. And the subject is further veiled by what inevitably

[1] Lee-Warner, *The Protected Princes of India*, pp. 37—40.

accompanied gradual development, namely that the forms and language befitting international relations continued to be used in many cases after such relations had really ceased. But limiting dates may be named. The empire in a strict sense, as now understood, is a distinct advance on the treaties concluded by Lord Hastings, though the rhetorical employment of the name may be found earlier. He probably foresaw the advance, for he recorded his opinion that the right of bestowing titles should be exercised direct by the British government, as an " essential and peculiar attribute of sovereign rule[1]"; but certainly the double habit referred to had not been formed in his time. On the other hand, British statesmen must have firmly held the imperial doctrine for themselves, and perhaps also have been convinced that already before the mutiny it had acquired a strong hold on native opinion, when in January 1858 they placed the so-called king of Delhi on his trial for " that he, being a subject of the British government in India, and not regarding the duty of his allegiance, did at Delhi, on May 11, 1857, or thereabouts, as a false traitor against the state, proclaim and declare himself the reigning king and sovereign of India, and did then and there traitorously seize and take unlawful possession of the city of Delhi, &c." And after the suppression of the mutiny not even the native princes or their subjects can have felt much doubt that the imperial doctrine had acquired practical reality. Thus the forty years from 1818 to 1858 are all, or more than all, that can be allowed for the growth and establishment of the imperial idea.

[1] u. s., p. 308.

Lastly, it may be asked by which of all possible international titles England holds the sovereignty or *imperium* of India. It is not by occupation, for India possessed a civilisation placing her as far as Europe beyond the reach of any such title. It is by cession or conquest, so far as concerns the territories under direct British government; but so far as concerns those under the immediate government of the protected princes it is not by cession, for with many of them there are no treaties, and we have seen that the imperial right is claimed as overriding the letter of the treaties which there are. Neither does the right over the protected states present an ordinary case of conquest, for conquest usually operates either by the suppression of the conquered state, as in the case of Poland, or by cession when the defeated state is left in existence to make it. The imperial right over the protected states appears to present a peculiar case of conquest, operating by assumption and acquiescence.

We have now followed in outline the public relations which England has entered into in India or has assumed there. To put the case with strict accuracy, it would be necessary to describe the phases of those relations which have been traced as being the most advanced ones that at each successive time have existed between England and any Indian states. To complete the picture of the rise of the empire, we should have also to follow the geographical advance from the forts of Bombay, Madras and Calcutta to the Suliman, Karakoram and Himalaya mountains and the frontier of Siam. If this were done we should find a system of two limits early established, and each limit thereafter constantly receding. The narrower at any date would bound the territory absolutely acquired by England, and outside the wider would be the states with which relations on a footing of equality were still entertained by her. Between the two, we should see at first forms of relation in which her preponderant power stood confessed, but these would give way to forms which acknowledged her paramount but not undefined authority, and those in turn would be replaced, or modified in their effect, by her assumption of an imperial position. The narrower limit now includes about three-fifths of the area, and a still larger proportion of the population, comprised between the Suliman range and Siam: the wider limit includes the whole, except Nepal, Bhutan, and the almost imperceptible possessions of France and Portugal. Between the two limits, more than six hundred native princes acknowledge the queen of England as empress of India; and even Nepal and Bhutan, although their relations with England are conducted on international principles, cannot be regarded as standing towards her on the same footing of political equality on which the great powers of Europe stand towards one another[1].

But to complete in this manner the sketch which has been given would be to write history in the light of international law, and not to illustrate the

[1] See political equality distinguished from legal, above, p. 92. The treaty of 1816 " excluded the intervention of Nepal in the affairs of Sikkim, and precluded the employment or retention of British, or foreign European, or American subjects in the service of the Gurkha government without the consent of the Company ": Lee-Warner, *Protected Princes of India*, p. 98. Thus the political inferiority of Nepal to England is more marked than that of the smaller European powers, as such, to the greater. But there is no doubt that she is not included in the empire: she made her own peace with Tibet in 1856.

theory of international relations by history. What remains for us to do with regard to the empire of India is in the first place fully to exhibit its international unity, obscured as that sometimes is by the use of language which has descended from earlier stages of its existence, and in the second place, in order that the true character of the imperial power may not be misunderstood, to indicate the boundaries which it has set to itself in dealing with the subordinate members.

### *The Empire of India in relation to International Law.*

The empire may be said to comprise all the Gangetic peninsula except Nepal and Bhutan, and the western part of the Transgangetic peninsula. The six hundred subordinate members which are found within those limits are called in British law princes or states in alliance with Her Majesty, and the population of their dominions is described as their subjects, while the remainder of the total area is described as British India or the Indian territories under the dominion of Her Majesty, and its population as British subjects or subjects of Her Majesty. What is the real significance of these appellations we shall have to consider, but they are so carefully maintained that a subject of a native prince is capable of the same process of nationalisation which is applicable to a Frenchman or a German, and, without it, does not even in British India possess the rights of a British subject.

The most important characteristic of the political condition of the native states is thus expressed in the preamble of the act of parliament which applies to them the British Indian legislation against the slave trade, st. 39 and 40 Vict., c. 46:

"And whereas the several princes and states in India in alliance with Her Majesty have no connections, engagements or communications with foreign powers, and the subjects of such princes and states are, when residing or being in the places hereinafter referred to, entitled to the protection of the British government, and receive such protection equally with the subjects of Her Majesty."

The places referred to are the high seas, or any part of Asia or Africa which the queen may specify by order in council, but this is only because the act relates to the slave trade. What is said is equally true of any part of the world, and must be so, because the power which cuts off the native princes from the communications that would be involved in self-help cannot do less than undertake the protection for which self-help is consequently wanting. With that enlargement the parliamentary recital is true at the present day of all the six hundred subordinate members of the empire, from the smallest to the greatest, whether they hold treaties or grants or depend for their position entirely on precedent or understanding, and whether or not any treaties or grants which they may hold express their position fully and correctly according to the present understanding. They have no official intercourse either with one another or with any power outside the empire. They cannot even send representatives to Calcutta, but must communicate with the British government through the British representatives at their courts. When it is necessary to establish a course of extradition or of any other dealing between two of them, each has to make an agreement with the British government to that effect, or, according to the practice now preferred, the British government frames rules to which both the native princes are invited to consent, and for the execution of those rules each of them pledges himself to comply with the demands of the other when intimated through the resident at his court. They cannot unite in any representation to the government of India, even when having identical interests on any question, but each must approach it separately. Not only can they not receive for themselves even the commercial agents of foreign states, but they have no direct communication with the consuls or commercial agents accredited by foreign states to the government of India. They are precluded from receiving foreign decorations or even academic distinctions except through the British government, and from conferring any honours or privileges on any persons but their own subjects. They cannot employ Europeans or Americans in their service without the consent of the British government.

The particulars thus far mentioned would not be incompatible with international relations which might be represented as an extreme case of a protectorate exercised by one state over others. The native states of India might have had with foreign powers relations of their own, distinct from those of the protecting state, although entirely managed for them by the latter, as the Ionian Islands were capable of being at peace with Russia while England, which was their protector and managed their foreign affairs, was at war with that power. It is true that consuls, though not diplomatic envoys, were accredited to the Ionian Islands, which therefore were in a position of less complete dependence than the native Indian princes would have held even had there been no more to say; but the extreme dependence of the latter would not have amounted to complete international effacement. There is however more. Not only are separate relations between England and the respective allied states substituted for any international society within the empire, but it is the settled policy of England, in negotiation with foreign powers, to treat the empire as a whole, and not to admit distinct relations of such powers to its several parts. Even the limited meaning, with which for internal purposes the term "British subjects" is employed, is occasionally relaxed for external purposes. Thus the Sultan of Muskat, by the treaty of 1873, agreed that in all treaties between him and England the words "British subjects" should include subjects of native Indian states. If this is not done, still, as in the treaty of 1874 with Yarkand, the subjects of the native states are placed on the same footing with British subjects, as a part of the agreement made with England. Foreign powers are permitted to know the native states exactly as far as the United States of America permit them to know the several states of the union, and no further. The names of either may occur among the facts with which a negotiation deals, but nothing can be concluded with them or in their name. It would be understating the case to say that the Empire of India is an international unit. The true international unit, for peace or war, neutrality or negotiation, is the United Kingdom and its dependencies, of which the empire of India is one. If a commercial or other treaty between England and some foreign power is not made to extend to India, that is only as it might be made not to extend to New South Wales; and this, in either case, would be only as a treaty might stipulate rules to be observed by shipping as far as a certain cape and no further.

Hence the native princes who acknowledge the imperial majesty of the United Kingdom have no international existence. That their dominions are contrasted with the dominions of the queen, and that their subjects are contrasted with the subjects of the queen, are niceties of speech handed down from other days and now devoid of international significance, though their preservation may be convenient for purposes internal to the empire, in other words for constitutional purposes. So too the term " protectorate " as applied to the empire in its relation to those princes, and the description of their subjects, when abroad, as persons entitled to British protection, are etymologically correct, but they do not bear the technical meaning which belongs to the protection of the republic of San Marino and its citizens by the kingdom of Italy, or that other technical meaning which belongs to a protectorate in Central Africa. They are etymologically correct because every state is the protector of its own people, and the United Kingdom has, for international purposes, absorbed the Indian princes and their subjects into itself. And the government of India was fully justified in the notification which it published in its official gazette, No. 1700 E, 21st August 1891 : " The principles of international law have no bearing upon the relations between the government of India as representing the queen-empress on the one hand, and the native states under the suzerainty of Her Majesty on the other. The paramount supremacy of the former presupposes and implies the subordination of the latter[1]."

The Indian government itself has admitted and acted on the existence of a personal tie between the queen-empress on the one hand and the native princes and their subjects on the other hand, which might not only be described with etymological accuracy as the subjection of the latter to the former, but which is the very tie that in political language is described as the relation of sovereign to subject, whenever the history of its origin does not furnish a motive for abstaining from the use of those terms. Loyalty and allegiance as expressing the duty to the queen-empress, treason and rebellion as expressing the breach of that duty, are terms familiar in Indian official language. We have seen what were the charges on which the last of the Moguls was tried, emphatically marking as they do that the transition from an international to an imperial system in India was complete[2]. In 1875 the Gaekwar of Baroda was tried for an attempt to poison the British representative at his court, under a proclamation of 13th January 1875 in which it was said: "whereas to instigate such attempt would be a high crime against Her Majesty the queen, and a breach of the condition of loyalty to the crown under which Mulhar Rao Gaekwar is recognised as ruler of the Baroda state, and moreover such an attempt would be an act of hostility against the British government." Now there was no treaty with Baroda or grant to the Gaekwar in which the condition so referred to was

[1] Lee-Warner, *The Protected Princes of India*, p. 373.
[2] Above, p. 213.

laid down. The Gaekwar was deemed to be subject to it only by virtue of the imperial doctrine that the position of all the native princes is to be ascertained from the principles latest adopted in dealing with any of them, as the position of all vendors and purchasers of property, or of all drawers and endorsers of bills of exchange, is to be ascertained from the latest decisions with regard to any of them. The grants (*sanads*) by which the native princes were secured in the perpetuity of their dynasties had long run in a form adopted by Lord Canning in 1858.

" Her Majesty being desirous that the governments of the several princes and chiefs of India who now govern their own territories should be perpetuated, and that the representation and dignity of their houses should be continued, I hereby in fulfilment of this desire convey to you the assurance that, on failure of natural heirs, [the adoption, by yourself and future rulers of your state, of a successor according to Hindoo law and the customs of your race will be recognised and confirmed.] Be assured that nothing shall disturb the engagement just made to you, so long as your house is loyal to the crown and faithful to the conditions of the treaties, grants and engagements which record its obligations to the British government."

For Mahomedan princes the words in square brackets were replaced by :

" any succession to the government of your state which may be legitimate according to Mahomedan law will be upheld."

Still, it might have been argued that the condition of loyalty, with the accompanying liability to punishment in case of its breach, applied only to the prince and not to his subjects; just as in the feudal system, as it existed on the continent of Europe before men's ideas of the royal power were enlarged by its beneficent operation under kings like St Louis and by the revived study of the Roman law, the vassal of a vassal owed allegiance only to his immediate and not to his ultimate superior. But in the case of Manipur the principle which William the Conqueror established for the feudal system in England, that the whole population owes allegiance to the king in addition to the ties which may bind individuals to mesne lords, was seen in operation for the empire of India. In that case, in 1891, trial and punishment for breach of the conditions of loyalty were extended to subjects of a native state, one of whom had indeed usurped the throne but had not been recognised on it by the Indian government; and that government officially enjoined " the subjects of the Manipur state to take warning by the punishments inflicted on the persons guilty of rebellion and murder."

Mr Austin made his definition of law depend on the existence in a state of a subject part, habitually obeying the general commands issued by another part which he called the sovereign[1]. The question of ascertaining the sovereign part in the empire of India, and the more difficult one what importance should be attached to the solution if it could be discovered, may have at times perplexed the men who with high education and great practical ability have moulded that empire. But neither question was relevant externally, and internally both have in effect been happily ignored. To international law a state is sovereign which demeans itself as independent; a state is semi-sovereign to the extent of the foreign relations which the degree of its practical dependence allows it; and is non-existent if no foreign relations are allowed it. This, whatever may be the constitutional theories relating to them

[1] Of course a man may individually be an Austinian subject, at the same time that he is a member of a corporate Austinian sovereign.

respectively. And the empire of India has been moulded in its constitutional substance by no deduction from assumed principles of sovereignty, but by the essential conditions of peace and order in the circumstances, complied with so far as those great interests of man demanded, yet on the whole with a prudent and tender reverence for such native institutions of government as were compatible with them, and for the sentiments which accompanied those institutions and their names.

### *The Empire of India in relation to Constitutional Law.*

I must ask the reader to bear with me if I pursue the subject of India a little further than may properly belong to a series of chapters on international law. There are some points forming a natural sequel to the line of thought which has been here pursued; constitutional points, in the sense in which that term has already been employed in this book. Wherever a body presents itself externally as a unit—whether outsiders pay an entire regard to its unity, as they do to that of France or the United States of America, or to that of the German empire so far as that empire presents itself externally as a unit, or whether they pay as little regard for the unity claimed by the body as was paid to that claimed by the Holy Roman empire during the last period of its existence—in every such case the term "constitutional" may fairly be used to express whatever political relations, possessing any degree of fixity, exist between the smaller bodies or the individual men that constitute the unit. Those relations may be guarded by definite rules applied by the regular action of public force, or they may be guarded only by understood habits of action. Some part of them, and not always the same or a corresponding part, may be distinguished as constitutional in a narrower sense. Thus what is called the constitution of the United States is no less a set of definite rules applied by the regular action of public force than is any statute passed by congress; while in England it is understood habits of action that are usually called constitutional, in contrast to such rules. The term is used in another narrower sense when government by an absolute monarch is called unconstitutional, even although the monarchy follows understood habits of action, while government by a parliament is called constitutional, without reference to whether the parliament follows understood habits of action. But experience teaches that no term can secure for itself a settled and permanent meaning, in matters so complicated and variable as are the political institutions of men. Perhaps, in such matters, no more can be expected of a writer than that the distinctions he tries to express shall be real and important, that the terms which he selects to express them shall not violently shock current usage, and that he shall employ them consistently. On those conditions he may be read with advantage, although his terms may never become fixed in the senses which he gives them, nor does he intend that they should. A student of international relations as they are, and not as an attempt may be made to mould our conception of them by *a priori* definitions, can hardly avoid grouping together, in contrast to them, all other political relations which possess any degree of fixity; and an extension of the term "constitutional" to meet that purpose seems not to be a forced one, while any writer on the internal affairs of an empire will none the less be free to use it in his own manner.

The first point to be noticed in this section is almost forced on us even as international lawyers, in order that we may comply with the law of thought which makes it necessary to supply a true notion in order to drive an untrue one out. We have seen that the Indian "states in alliance with Her Majesty" are not states in any international sense: what then is the constitutional sense in which they are states? In Indian political language the test which distinguishes a native state from British territory is that the former is not subject to legislation by the governor-general in council or by the legislative councils of the presidencies, or to the jurisdiction of the ordinary British courts of law. Thus, with regard to treaties in which the Company had agreed to have " no manner of concern with the Maharaja's subjects,"

"It was explained," Mr Lee-Warner says, " that the Company had guaranteed the states against the intrusion of its own courts of law, or against any extension of its ordinary jurisdiction beyond the territorial limits of the Company's possessions. But where interference and the intrusion of British jurisdiction were absolutely called for, as the only means of avoiding annexation "—because the power which protected the princes and maintained them on the throne could not be deaf to the cries which from time to time arose against their misgovernment—" the courts which were created for its exercise were established by the government in its executive capacity, and not by the legislative authorities of British India. This cardinal distinction may appear subtle, but it has been the cornerstone of the judicial system introduced into the Indian states[1]."

[1] *The Protected Princes of India*, p. 13.

And with regard to certain states which were tributary to the Gaekwar of Baroda, and were taken over from him by the Bombay government, and subjected to a special system on account, not of any abuses, but of their extreme smallness, Mr Lee-Warner writes:

> "The rest of the once semi-sovereign communities are grouped under one or more political divisions called *thana* circles, over each of which a thanadar with magisterial and judicial powers presides. All of the descendants of the original chiefs conduct the revenue administration of their patches of territory on their own system, and are treated as beyond the jurisdiction of British India. But their jurisdictory powers vest for them, and by their tacit assent, in the political officers of government. The thanadars, and the British agent who supervises them, are subject to the orders of the British government but not to the jurisdiction of the High Court. The native state thus subsists, and is not converted into the British province; and the remedy applied avoids the precedent set by Rome of annexation under the plea of misrule. That which has happened in the Mahi Kanta has occurred also in Kathiawar and in the Rewa Kanta, where many talukdars who have lost their jurisdiction retain the status of native chiefs[1]."

Here also, as in the former extract, the jurisdiction of the political officers was conferred on them by British executive acts of state, and not by acts of the Indian legislatures. So too the various trials of native princes, and that of the Manipurees, have been by special commissions instituted by executive acts. But the British parliament is supreme throughout the empire, and although it does not in fact make laws to be carried into effect within the dominions of the native princes, yet the Act 39 and

---

[1] *The Protected Princes of India*, pp. 35, 36; and see pp. 109—112. The reader will notice the use of the term "political" established in India, meaning what relates to foreign affairs or to those of the native states. It furnishes another example of the endless variety with which we must always expect that terms relating to the doings of men will be employed.

40 Vict., c. 46, contains a remarkable assertion of its supreme authority. The object of that act was to extend the British Indian legislation against the slave trade to the subjects of the native princes, commensurately, as was just, with the protection received by them abroad from the British crown. And it provided that if they should contravene that legislation "upon the high seas or in any part of Asia or Africa which Her Majesty may from time to time think fit to specify by any order in council," they may be dealt with as if the offence had been committed by them at any place in British India where they may be found. We have seen that while most countries apply more or less of their criminal legislation to acts committed by foreigners in foreign countries, always under the condition that it can only be enforced within the physical limits of their own sovereignties, England has hitherto refrained from doing so[1]. When therefore the enactment in question is read in the light of English ideas, it will be seen to rest on the principle that the subjects of the native Indian princes are British subjects.

This being so, the constitutional position of a native Indian state (so-called) appears to be that of a separate part of the dominions of the queen-empress, as New South Wales and British India are other such separate parts—having its local government, vested in its native prince—that local government subject both to the sovereign as executive head of the state formed by all her dominions, and to the parliament of the United Kingdom of Great Britain and Ireland as the legislative head of the same state—the authority of the sovereign as

[1] See above, pp. 128–130.

executive head applied to it through the British Indian government and the controlling department in England, both acting in that respect distinctly from their functions with regard to British India, and not limited in theory by the principles which, being carried out with them by settlers from the United Kingdom, limit that authority in colonies founded by settlement—but both the authority of the sovereign as executive head and that of parliament limited in practice by considerations pointing to the past and to the future, respect for the long and splendid history of the princes and their peoples, and belief that under British superintendence they can be the most useful instruments of their own advancement. It is a position which, in the degree of dependence, is intermediate to those of a self-governing colony and of a crown colony. The name of sovereign is still attached to it, but really it is a position of constitutional, though not of international, semi-sovereignty[1].

In the constitutional situation thus presented British India and the native states stand in a quasi-foreign relation to one another, and we are prepared to find the legislature of the former making laws, enforceable within its limits, for observance by its proper subjects in the latter, or even outside the empire altogether. Accordingly we find the governor-general in council progressively receiving from parliament power to make laws " for all servants of the Company within the dominions of princes and states in alliance with the Company " (st. 3 and 4 Wm. 4, c. 85); " for all British subjects of Her Majesty within the dominions of princes and states in India

[1] See above, p. 89.

in alliance with Her Majesty, whether in the service of the government of India or otherwise " (st. 28 and 29 Vict., c. 17); and " for native Indian subjects of Her Majesty without and beyond British India " (st. 32 and 33 Vict., c. 98). But with this there comes into combination the fact that, as expressed in the preamble to the Indian Act XXI of 1879, " by treaty, capitulation, agreement, grant, usage, sufferance and other lawful means, the governor-general of India in council "—this time not representing the special government of British India, but as the executive organ for applying the imperial supremacy—" has power and jurisdiction within divers places beyond the limits of British India." The authority thus exercisable by the governor-general within native states, so far as it is in the form of jurisdiction, is in some of its branches defined by certain localities, and consequently includes a jurisdiction over all persons in such localities. Examples are furnished by the houses and grounds occupied by the residents and political agents in native states (not accredited to the princes as though these were international entities)—by railways having through communication and some parts of canals—and by certain stations at which imperial jurisdiction is desirable on account of British trade, European residents, or imperial administration—so far in all these cases as the localities have not been made parts of British India, but, as is now the practice, have been left as parts of native states subject to special imperial rights. In other branches the imperial jurisdiction in question is over persons within native states, irrespective of any particular locality within them. Examples are furnished by

European British subjects, who are not as a rule left to native justice, though they may be so in special circumstances, especially if they have entered the service of a native prince—by servants of the British government or of the political agent, or of any officer of the British government officially employed within the state—and by some cases in which an imperial jurisdiction, called " residuary," is exercised over certain subjects of the native states within their boundaries. In all the other cases mentioned in this paragraph the imperial jurisdiction is described as " delegated," while again the term " residuary " includes the extraordinary jurisdiction which we have already noticed as being exercised over native princes and their subjects for rebellion, and that which is sometimes exercised over disputes between a native prince and one of his own subjects[1]. The great amount of imperial jurisdiction within the native states necessitates the appointment by the governor-general in council of justices of the peace to act within them, and thus a means is supplied by which even the British Indian legislation for its proper subjects is enforced within those states, although nothing corresponding to such enforcement would be possible in the mutual relations of two self-governing colonies. It speaks for itself that, since the machinery for the enforcement is furnished by an act of state, independent of the judicial system

[1] This difference of terms does not correspond to any difference in the modes by which the imperial jurisdiction was established, for both delegated and residuary jurisdictions, so called, may be found which were established by agreement with the native states, and both may be found which were established by usage. " Substituted " jurisdiction is still another term employed, and expresses the temporary administration of justice in a native state by imperial officers on account of the minority or misgovernment of the prince.

of British India, there can be no appeal to the courts of that system when the law offended against is British Indian, any more than when the imperial act of state introduces the law as well as the jurisdiction.

It would be quite beyond the scope of the present work to pursue in further detail the rules and practices which make up what may be called the constitutional *modus vivendi* between native Indian states on the one hand, and on the other hand the central unity and the remaining portions of the British empire. What has been said with regard to legislation and jurisdiction, though far from being exhaustive even on those topics, will serve to illustrate the distinctions relating to them which, as we have seen, are made in our public language the test of a native state as opposed to a British province in India. But it may be said generally of the *modus vivendi* that its growth has been gradual, like that of the Indian empire itself; that its particulars have in the same manner been imperceptibly shifted from an international to an imperial basis; and that the process has been veiled by the prudence of statesmen, the conservatism of lawyers, and the prevalence of certain theories about sovereignty. Veiled, but neither prevented nor retarded. The courses followed have not been devious, though the attempts to explain them have sometimes perhaps been needlessly intricate, and their now fairly complete result is consistent enough in the light of their true idea.

Has that idea been a righteous one? The point which raises the most doubt about it is the position which treaties and grants have been made to assume. Speaking of the subsidiary alliances concluded by Lord Wellesley and the terms of isolated and subordinate cooperation which were imposed by Lord Hastings, the highly authorised expounder to whom I have so often referred says with truth that " when they were fresh minted they represented different policies and different periods," but that " the action of time and of customary law has worn them down to a common value." He adds that " the same contrast is to be observed in the title-deeds creating new sovereignties which were issued in the two periods of treaty-making." And he has added in effect elsewhere that the common value to which the treaties and title-deeds of both periods have been worn down is below the face value of either[1]. It is no justification to construe a stipulation, that " the jurisdiction of the British government shall not in any manner be introduced into the principality," as referring only to " the ordinary judicial system of British India created by the legislative authority of British India," a construction which certainly could not at the time have been in the mind at least of one of the parties. Nor is it a justification to appeal to "the effect of parliamentary legislation," the foundation for which is in question. We touch more solid ground when we read that by the treaty referred to Bhopal had undertaken, in Lord Hastings's terms, to " act in subordinate cooperation with the British government[2]." Even in 1818 the ruler of Bhopal might have known that the task in which England demanded cooperation was to maintain the peace of India, within and as against attacks from without; for that purpose, to prevent gross misgovernment;

[1] Lee-Warner, *The Protected Princes of India*, p. 119; and above, pp. 211, 212.

[2] See the reply given to the Maharanee of Bhopal, as stated by Mr Lee-Warner, u.s., pp. 331, 332.

to enforce toleration between Hindoo, Mahometan and Christian; to put down infanticide, suttee and other inhuman practices; and generally to raise the standard of enlightenment and civilisation. If the cooperation by which that task was to be pursued was to be a subordinate one, much was thereby left to the determination of England, in enlargement of views and choice of means. But could it be understood that the latitude allowed her reached to restricting her obligations under other clauses of the same document, or extending her empire over what was still a distinct state? It is possible that Lord Hastings foresaw that result, it is scarcely possible that he intended the treaty as furnishing a legal basis for it, and it is impossible that a native prince should at the time have so considered the treaty.

On the other side we may ask whether the treaties and grants—for the latter were in the nature of treaties so long as they were deemed to create states not subject to the empire—would have been likely to fare better if the complications, in which their strict interpretation would have resulted between European and Asiatic governments in juxtaposition, had been left to be worked out on an international basis. No part of international law has been more discussed or with less result than the limits to the obligation of treaties. No human arrangements can escape from decay. In all states the legislative power sets aside the obligation of contracts, either in regular course as by bankrupt laws, or by occasional interference when public interests call for it. Since between nations no superior authority exists to perform that function, the very conclusion of a treaty has been considered to be subject to the tacit reservation *rebus sic stantibus*, the true extent of which has hitherto defied definition. And the doctrine is taught by international lawyers no less than practised by statesmen, that although war can justifiably be commenced only for legal reasons, it may be continued in order to place the relations of the belligerents on an improved footing, which may diminish the danger of its recurrence. In no part of history has the inherent want of permanence in human arrangements been more strikingly illustrated than in that which relates the contact between European and Asiatic peoples. The methods of dealing with that contact which were tried by England, down to the imposition on the native states of the system of isolation and subordinate cooperation, were successively defeated by outbreaks of disorder. That system did not put an end to such outbreaks, nor did experience warrant the expectation that any remedy could be complete that was not thorough in its scope and uniform in its application to the whole body of states dealt with. This must be the justification of England for securing thoroughness and uniformity by the establishment of an imperial principle, and it may be supported by experience other than her own. Russia, having the same necessities and the same aims, the peace of a continent and the elevation of its inhabitants, has been similarly led to bring all northern Asia within her empire.

In truth, the treaties and grants themselves are safer under a constitutional system than under an international one. They are no longer subject to the chance of war, from which, when it happens, the shape in which the relations of the parties may issue can scarcely be forecast. They are no longer mined by jealousy of foreigners. They are placed under the guardianship of the fellow feeling which already exists, and may be expected to increase, between all who acknowledge the supremacy of the queen-empress, and of the good faith and dislike to unnecessary innovation which in the long run mark all great nations, because without them they could not have been great. The sense in which England understands the task which has been set to her in India is at least as fixed as that in which she understands the duty of the state in her own islands, a practice now of many years' standing has settled with much certainty the restrictions which that task places on written terms, and subject to those restrictions the treaties and grants are sacred. If such a situation leaves much to precedent and constitutional tact, the princes and people of the native Indian states may reflect that England relies on precedent and constitutional tact for her own liberty and good government. The question whether we might not with advantage make more use of written political rules has already been pointed out by leading statesmen as worthy of consideration, but thus far the just rights of all component parts of the queen's dominions, down to those of individual men, have been fairly well maintained, and it need not be feared that those of states once independent and still honoured, now that the empire has come to include them, will be less secure[1].

[1] [When, in 1910, Sir William Lee-Warner published a second edition of his work under the altered title *The Native States of India*, Westlake published, in the *Law Quarterly Review*, vol. XXVI, a paper under the same title which is reprinted *infra*, Part II, No. 19. L. O.]

# CHAPTER XI

## WAR

*The Rules of War considered as Laws.*

ALL such rules or principles of action as exist among nations with regard to the conduct of war fall into two great divisions, that which relates to the action of the belligerents against one another and that which relates to the action of a belligerent with regard to neutrals. The latter of these divisions surpasses every other part of international law in the clearness with which it presents all civilised states to us as members of a society. In no other branch have the rules composing it been hammered into their present shape by so general or active a cooperation of the members of the society. Most of the international disputes which do not end in war are settled by the states between which they arise without the intervention of third parties, and though seldom without some expression of opinion by the thinking part of the world, yet often without an indication of any opinion by any government not directly concerned. But let war break out between two powers, and the whole non-belligerent world is at once related to that war as neutral, its political and commercial interests are affected by the views entertained about the mutual rights and duties of neutrals and belligerents, incidents occur which oblige even the remotest state to act on some view about those rights and duties, and a general vigilance is aroused not only as to the observance but even as to the shaping of the rules on the subject. For us therefore, who take for our very idea of jural law that it is the body of rules of a society, it follows that among all generalisations that are possible on international matters the rules of neutrality are preeminently law.

But as to the mutual rights and duties of belligerents the case is very different. When third powers intervene in a war, or make their pressure felt in settling the terms of peace, they do so for political reasons concerned with the result to be attained, and not with any violation of rules of which one belligerent may have been guilty towards the other. Hence, for the rules of this class, settlement and enforcement by a society exist in a lesser degree than for any other part of international law. In treating the laws of war between belligerents as being law at all, we have little else on which to ground ourselves than that the general opinion of the international society assists in shaping the rules, and allows each party to enforce their observance towards himself if he is able to do so. But again we are met by the fact that here, of all parts of international law, the opportunities for giving a definite expression to opinion, and for a party's doing himself that right which opinion demands, are at the lowest. A belligerent may complain that his enemy has violated the laws of war, he may use measures of retorsion, but the discussion which so

XI] THE RULES OF WAR CONSIDERED AS LAWS 239

arises is seldom brought to any clear decision. The victory of one party, or such balance of power as may be reached between the parties, brings to a single comprehensive close the war and everything connected with it, the disputes which led to the war, the ulterior aims which have been developed in its course, and the recriminations to which its incidents have given rise. In drawing up the treaty of peace what is thought of is the new departure in the relations of the parties, and that departure is determined by the sword. Resentment at an act which he deems to have been a violation of the laws of war may swell the indemnity demanded by the conqueror, but the amount added on that score cannot be distinguished, the vanquished pay the indemnity without admitting the violation, and if they condemn the conduct of the war by the conqueror, their remonstrances remain wholly without effect. When in a subsequent war the temptation arises to repeat an act the lawfulness of which has been questioned in a previous war, the records of the latter furnish no pronouncement on its lawfulness which can be appealed to.

On the other hand, if we are thus thrown back on general opinion, it is fortunate that there is no part of international law which so deeply interests the majority of men, or on which therefore public discussion contributes so actively to form the general opinion of the international society, as the laws of war between belligerents. They are connected with the most striking incidents that vary the generally even current of civilised life. Those incidents excite our sympathies with the most penetrating force. Subject as so large a part of Europe is to compulsory military service, there are few men whose training does not enable them to realise more or less vividly the scenes among which they take place, and still fewer persons of either sex to whom the questions about them do not carry a personal interest, bearing on what they may themselves have to do or to suffer, as combatants or as inhabitants of an invaded country. It may be doubted whether, latterly, the popular feeling thus stirred has always operated in the direction of humanity. In proportion as really national wars have taken the place of wars of dynastic or personal ambition, there has tended to grow up, on the conquering side in any struggle, a public impatience of all laws which might impose restraints on the fullest measure of success, which was not felt by subjects on behalf of the schemes of their rulers. But governments have in recent times done much to guide opinion in this matter. They have abstained from modes of damaging their enemies which might have been of military value, they have framed regulations for their commanders and have blamed them for excesses, they have concluded the Geneva and St Petersburg conventions, and in the conference at Brussels they have taken an important step towards the preparation of an international military code. Thus, in one way or another, laws of war between belligerents are maintained and ameliorated. In the sixteenth century almost everything was permitted against an enemy, and hardly any attempt was made to distinguish the degrees in which combatants and non-combatants partake of the hostile character. Since then, limitation after limitation has been imposed on the right of armed strength, and the improvement will be seen if we contrast the modes of conducting war at successive intervals of a century. On many points the opinion of the civilised world has become fixed, and warrants belligerents in using the means available to them for securing a practice in conformity with it.

*Principles relating to Particular Military Operations.*

With regard to modes of fighting and to conduct immediately connected with fighting—in a word, with regard to military operations—it is agreed that everything is prohibited which is not of a nature to contribute to success in the operation concerned. Such is the use of projectiles which make death certain and painful, without increasing the number of men disabled by a shot; as glass, or explosive bullets of less weight than 400 grammes, in the last of which cases the convention of St Petersburg has added express prohibition to the general opinion condemning such bullets. Other examples are killing men already disabled and the sack of places taken by storm. A great progress may here be noted, for cities taken by storm have been sacked within the nineteenth century, probably not with the consent of the victorious commander in any case so recent, but because it was impossible to hold a soldiery in hand which had not yet learnt to relinquish the traditional reward of the labours of a siege.

Some things are prohibited as too inhuman by a universal agreement which cannot be entirely referred to the foregoing principle, because in certain circumstances they might possibly contribute to success in a military operation, and yet the prohibition admits of no exception. Such are the employment of poison, which was held to be unlawful even in the ancient world, and killing prisoners or refusing quarter when the fight is over, although the victorious army may be seriously hampered by the necessity of guarding a large number of able men.

It is further agreed that even where a thing does not fall under any absolute prohibition, it may only be done in the circumstances and in the measure in which it may reasonably be expected to contribute to the success of the operation concerned. Examples are devastating a tract of country in order to prevent the enemy's occupying it or crossing it, and bombarding the parts of fortified cities which are inhabited by the civil population. It is in this connection that the employment of red-hot shot ought to be mentioned, though some theoretical writers set it down as absolutely prohibited. Red-hot shot saved Gibraltar by setting the Spanish floating batteries on fire, and it is impossible to say that it can never again be of real use. The military commander is the judge of the circumstances and the measure for things which are conditionally permitted, at the risk of being accused of inhumanity if general opinion is not satisfied with his decision.

But suppose it to be clear that the employment of a certain means is likely to contribute to the success of a military operation. Can we go further, and say that there must be a reasonable proportion between the destruction or suffering to be caused and the military advantage to be expected? This is a question which hitherto it has scarcely been necessary to ask, but which the fearful destructiveness of the most modern weapons may force on the attention. A ram or a torpedo may by one blow sink a ship with hundreds of men on board, perhaps thousands if she is a transport, and although this may have been done in a fair fight, and there must always be some military advantage in reducing the number of the enemy, still the circumstances may be such that she might have been captured instead of sunk with no great delay or damage to the operation in hand, or that even her escape would not have been likely to lead to any serious consequences. It can hardly be maintained that such a wholesale slaughter for no adequate purpose would be justifiable. We may hope that a public opinion will be formed which, while by no means interdicting the newest methods of warfare, will recognise that a duty of self-restraint is imposed on combatants in their use.

*Principles relating to the Conduct of War generally: Kriegsmanier and Kriegsraison.*

We pass now to measures not belonging to any particular military operation, but which may have an effect on the war generally. Such are the bombardment of unfortified places, and the devastation of tracts of country with no special strategical purpose, the motive of either being to weaken the enemy through the loss occasioned to him, or to bring him to terms through the fear of further acts of the same kind. In order to discuss the questions thus raised it is necessary to notice a distinction often made between the ordinary rules of war (*kriegsmanier, les lois de la guerre*) and what is exceptionally permitted (*kriegsraison* or *kriegsräson, raison de guerre*), both being included in the law of war (*kriegsrecht, le droit de la guerre*)[1]. Since the distinction has not made its way into English thought, I will give it, for information and by way of caution against certain tendencies, as it has been fully worked out by Professor Lueder.

"*Kriegsraison* embraces those cases in which, by way of exception, the laws of war ought to be left without observance. This can only happen in two cases, one that of extreme necessity, when the object of the war can only be attained by their non-observance and would be defeated by their observance, the other that of retorsion, as a retaliation for an unjustifiable non-observance of the laws of war by the other side...

"The right not to observe the laws of war exists in the case of retorsion because, according to known maxims, non-fulfilment by one party deprives that party of the right to claim fulfilment by the other. At least this may be the case in war, where, if the violations of the laws of war by the enemy were passed without retaliation, a belligerent would be at a disadvantage and worse off than his enemy who was guilty of the violations, with reference to the end which has to be striven for by all means, namely breaking down the determination of the other side and gaining the victory.

"As little can the justifiableness of *kriegsraison* be denied on occasions of extreme necessity. If the necessity of individuals is recognised as exempting them from punishment for things never so injurious done by them from that necessity, this must be still more the case in war, since so much more is at stake. When therefore the circumstances are such that the attainment of the object of the war and the escape from extreme danger would be hindered by observing the limitations imposed by the laws of war, and can only be accomplished by breaking through those limitations, the latter is what ought to happen. It ought to happen because it must happen, that is, because the course of no war will in such extreme cases be hindered and allow itself to end in defeat, perhaps in ruin, in order not to violate formal law. No prohibition can in such a case effect any thing, or present a claim to recognition and validity; and it would be idle to formulate one, for from what commander or from what state could such heroism of meekness and renunciation be expected?

"Of course such a conflict can only be of exceptional occurrence, for the laws of war are so framed by ordinary custom and well weighed

[1] Rivier, in his *Lehrbuch des Völkerrechts*, uses *kriegsrecht* in the sense of *kriegsmanier*, but does not exclude the exceptional law. He says "*kriegsräson geht vor kriegsrecht*": p. 376.

conventions that ordinarily it is possible to follow them. They are built on those relations of fact which are usually met with, just as are the rules of public national law (*staatsrecht*) and private law, and in the one case as in the other only specially exceptional conditions can make it impossible to follow them. How should the laws of war, which have been laid down in order to the protection of helpless civilians, wounded and disabled soldiers, private property, flags of truce, and the maintenance of conventions which have been concluded for the protection of an occupied territory against unnecessary oppression, devastation and plundering—how should such laws be lightly unobservable ? That they should be so, and that a conflict should arise between what the laws of war prescribe and what the necessity of war demands, is inconceivable except in quite extraordinary cases of exception and stress. It is therefore entirely out of the question that *kriegsraison* should be applied frequently, lightly and at pleasure, and come to be considered as standing in its practical use on the same line with the laws of war. Much rather are we dealing only with something quite exceptionally happening, and for that reason the admission of *kriegsraison* certainly appears not to be too questionable. When however the exception happens, it excludes the rule, as its nature is to do, and *kriegsraison* takes precedence of the laws of war.

"The regular normal validity of the law of war (*kriegsrecht*) is preserved by the introduction of *kriegsraison*, possible as it is only exceptionally. If this admissibleness of *kriegsraison* in extraordinary cases of necessity and exception, an admissibleness which at any rate has to be fully and decisively acknowledged, should lead one to think that there was at bottom no binding law of war, by reason of its not having to be observed in the critical cases of conflict with the demands of warfare, and that instead of a law of war there was only a usage of war in the sense condemned above (§ 52)—that would be to shoot far beyond the mark, and to ignore the final and inner cause of every law and legal institution. *Kriegsraison* is related to the law of war as necessity to criminal law, and it might be said with the same right and supported by the same argument that there was no criminal law, because its rules have not to be observed in cases of necessity. The misapprehension above referred to would lead to the one conclusion as well as to the other. Thus by the full recognition of a *kriegsraison* exceptionally justified the doctrine which has been set forth above, that there really exists a law of war and not merely a usage of war to be observed at pleasure, is not in the least altered ; and as little can there be on that account any question of the right, asserted by Grotius and Pufendorff but above confuted, to free one's self from the law of war by a declaration to that effect. Even the ordinary rules of war cannot be denounced at pleasure, but only disregarded exceptionally on a few well-defined grounds. If however *kriegsraison* were considered as something outside law (*unrechtlich*) and as a breach of the law of war (*kriegsrecht*), even then the non-existence of a law of war could not follow, though such law would be liable to possible violation. For from this point of view also the state of things would be the same as in other departments of law, in all of which violations likewise occur, and indeed in some cases violations which are unatoned for and cannot be made good[1]."

Another extract from the same writer will show the principles maintained in the last extract in their application to such methods of war as those referred to at the commencement of this section.

" That ravage, burning and devastation, even on a large scale, as of whole neighbourhoods and tracts of country, may be practised where it is not a question of any particular determinate result or strategical operation, but only of more general measures, as in order to make the further advance of the enemy impossible, or even to show him what war is in earnest when he persists in carrying it on without serious hope (*frivol*) and so compel him to make peace—this cannot be denied in cases of real necessity, as of a well-grounded *kriegsraison*. But it is only in such cases that it cannot be denied, and if measures of that kind are taken otherwise than under the most extreme compulsion, they are great and inhuman offences against international law[2]."

I am unable to approve of the distinction between *kriegsmanier* and *kriegsraison*. It is not wanted to justify retorsion, and must therefore be considered with reference to the ground of necessity alone. Now those who make the distinction allow the employment of every means in some circumstances, except so far as an absolute prohibition has been adopted by express convention, or rests on an ancient horror felt by mankind, as in the case of poison, to which if they were consistent their argument would equally apply. On the other hand, even the mildest means

[1] In Holtzendorff's *Handbuch des Völkerrechts*, vol. 4, §§ 65 and 66, pp. 254—256.
[2] In Holtzendorff's *Handbuch des Völkerrechts*, vol. 4, § 114, p. 484.

employed in war are based on some necessity, for war itself has no other rightful foundation. Little or nothing therefore seems to be gained by making two classes of measures, distinguished not really by necessity but by so vague a test as the degree of necessity, while much may be lost by the opposition in which such a system inevitably stands to any extension of the list of absolute prohibitions beyond those already existing. The two sources from which it seems possible to hope for an amelioration of the practice of war are such an extension, and a better recognition by public opinion of the duty of weighing scrupulously the degree of necessity or the amount of advantage under or for the sake of which recourse is had even to permitted measures. The immediate responsibility in the case of particular military operations, as with regard to the use of rams and torpedoes, lies chiefly with commanders: in the case of the wider questions relating to the conduct of a war it lies chiefly with governments. It is probable that both will be as humane as the excitement of a people feeling that a war is its own war will allow them to be, and it need not be greatly feared that Professor Lueder's own government will ever give effect to his doctrine by ordering the devastation of a whole region as an act of terrorism. That the extension of the list of absolute prohibitions need not be despaired of may be inferred from the labours of the military delegates assembled in conference at Brussels on land war in 1874. A draft declaration was adopted there, unfortunately not yet ratified by the governments represented, of which Art. 15 runs that " towns, agglomerations of houses, or villages, which are open and undefended, cannot be attacked or bombarded." Similarly Art. 32 (*c*) of the *Manual of the Laws of Land War*, adopted by the Institute of International Law at Oxford in 1880, lays down that " it is forbidden to attack and bombard localities which are not defended." The principle must equally prohibit the bombardment of open and undefended coast towns by ships, and we may fairly hope that any violation of it, either in land or in naval war, would meet with general reprobation. But a French admiral has advocated the bombardment of undefended coast towns in the British Isles in the event of a war between England and France, as a generally permissible means of exhausting the resources and weakening the spirit of an enemy, without limitation by such a condition of necessity as we have seen Professor Lueder imposing on operations of that class. The gallant officer was probably unaware of the support which his advice might receive up to a certain point by learned theories of *raison de guerre*, and a Frenchman might well hesitate to take a line of action against England which could not be justified by any argument that would not expose his own country and Germany, if at war with one another, to the risk of mutual devastation not of a military but of a political character. That the advice should have been given illustrates the fact that there remain in the world many relics of a less advanced moral condition, and the danger of teaching that everything is permitted to an undefinable necessity of which the party interested is the sole judge.

But however desirable may be the extension of the list of absolute prohibitions in war, care must be taken not to infer that a certain means is prohibited from the mere fact that it is not employed, when there is no reason to believe that it has been abstained from in obedience to a sentiment of right or a persuasion of law. Abstention is in itself ambiguous. An act may not have been done because the circumstances promised no advantage from doing it, or no advantage corresponding in its importance to the odium which attaches to acting harshly, even when the harshness does not exceed the limits of what is permitted. And abstention for that reason may run through a long series of years, during which the conditions of war have not been such as to tempt to the act, or during which the states which were able to do it have not been placed in circumstances which tempted to it. A change in the conditions of war then takes place by which the advantage to be obtained from the act is much increased, or the states which are able to do the act are brought by a change of circumstances within the temptation to do it. If still it is not done, the abstention can only be attributed to a governing sentiment, and the existence of the prohibiting rule may be inferred. But what if the act is now done? There will of course be protest from the enemy, and we must see whether that protest is echoed by public opinion in third countries, and whether opinion, if adverse, is strong enough to prevent repetitions of the act when the occasion for it recurs. If it is so, the existence of a rule is established: if it is not, there is no rule, only opposing principles, which may lead to the act being sometimes done, and at other times abstained from even under strong temptation.

An illustration may be drawn from the question

whether the coast fisheries of a belligerent state enjoy exemption from interference by the enemy. It has not been usual to capture the boats or men engaged in such fisheries, though no exemption has ever been claimed for deep-sea fisheries. But during the wars of the French revolution and empire the danger of invasion under which England lay was deemed to require that no means should be spared of crippling the enemy at sea, both in respect of fighting power and of transport, and accordingly the boats and men belonging to the French coast fisheries were captured. Protest followed on the part of France, as might have been expected, and continental writers generally lay down that coast fisheries are exempted from interference by the enemy, and inveigh against the non-observance of this supposed rule by England. Those writers are certainly free to advocate such principles of action as seem to them fit, but in the circumstances mentioned they cannot assert with truth the existence of a prohibitory rule.

*The Treatment of the Peaceable Population, and of Private Property on Land and at Sea.*

After the operations which a belligerent may undertake and the weapons which he may use, we come to the conduct which he must observe towards persons not taking part in the fighting. These may be prevented from assisting the enemy, as by giving him information or attempting to leave their abodes in order to swell his ranks. For the purpose of preventing such assistance being rendered, an invader may threaten and inflict penalties of the severity which may be necessary, but those penalties must not be connected in our minds with any notion that a crime is committed by those who, without acting treacherously, are led by patriotism to incur them. Subject to due severity being taken for their not assisting the enemy, the peaceable population of an invaded district are entitled to protection for their life, honour, family rights and religion; also for their liberty, with the exception of being compelled to serve as guides and to execute works which the invader deems necessary for his purposes; they must not however be compelled to take a more direct part in operations against their own country. As regards their property, they are entitled to immunity from pillage, but they must submit to its appropriation by an invading force, both in the form of goods, under the name of requisitions, and in that of money, under the name of contributions. Requisitions are intended for supplying specifically the wants of the invaders, as clothing, boots, provisions and forage. Contributions are described in Art. 41 of the draft declaration adopted at the Brussels conference as " equivalents for taxes, or for payments which should be made in kind, or fines." And what fines may cover is illustrated by Professor Lueder's mentioning, in perfect consistency. with recent practice, persistence in a war without serious hope (*frivol*) and "irrecusable requirements of policy," as reasons for justly levying contributions[1].

The traffic of a belligerent country by road, railway or canal is practically stopped so far as it comes in contact with its enemy, by the indirect

---

[1] In Holtzendorff's *Handbuch des Völkerrechts*, vol. 4, § 117, p. 505.

effect of the communications being crowded by troops and supplies, and of the measures taken on each side to prevent such traffic being of assistance to the other side. To this however an exception must be made for the internal traffic of an occupied district, and for that between an occupied district and other countries, which continue as well as they can under the difficulties of the case, and subject to regulation by the invader.

So far all authorities are agreed, except as to the motives and occasions for levying contributions. And with regard to them the latitude allowed to an invader turns perhaps less on national differences than on the personal idiosyncrasies of the governments or commanders concerned, or of the writers who discuss the question, although the leaning of writers in England and the United States is towards greater mildness than seems to prevail on the continent of Europe, as is certainly the case with the practice of England and the United States with regard both to requisitions and to contributions.

But at sea the differences are more important. Notwithstanding the protests of a large number of writers and the example set by Austria and Italy in their war of 1866, the principal maritime powers continue to prohibit all commerce of their enemies so far as it is not placed out of their reach by being carried on in neutral bottoms, to appropriate the enemy's ships and their cargoes so far as they are the enemy's property, and to detain the seamen as prisoners. If this practice be regarded as based on a desire to weaken the enemy by impairing his resources, it is an example of a hostile measure taken with a view to success in the war as a whole, and not to success in any particular military operation. Individuals suffer, but so do the individuals from whom contributions are levied—what is a locality but a number of individuals?—and it does not seem that the practice can be consistently objected to in principle by any government which has levied contributions as " an irrecusable requirement of policy," or by any writer who has approved of contributions so levied. If again the captures by the maritime powers be regarded as intended to deprive the enemy of seamen who might serve in his military navy or in his transports, they are on the same lines as the measures which an invader employs to prevent his enemy's forces being augmented by any recruits whom he can reach. Of course the question remains whether the practice of capturing the enemy's merchant-ships is worth retaining in any case but those of breach of blockade and carriage of contraband of war, in which cases a belligerent could not expect to fare better than a neutral. Every mitigation of war of which it can be proved that it would not be dangerous to our national safety ought to be promoted, but not by means of unsound comparisons between war as carried on by land and by sea.

With reference to the course which England ought to take about the capture of an enemy's merchant shipping, otherwise than for breach of blockade or carrying contraband, the following considerations may be submitted.

First, if policy requires England to maintain the capture, there is nothing in law to oppose her doing so. As long as the principal maritime powers uphold the claim, no rule of the international society of Europe and America can exist against it[1]. Nor is the argument against the claim more advanced if *le droit international, das völkerrecht*, be understood, not as international *law*, but as a body of *rights* believed to exist internationally *a priori*[2]. The surrender of the claim would place belligerent property at sea in a better position than it holds on land, whether we look at war as it is practised or at the doctrines of continental writers on requisitions and contributions. And the claim is not inconsistent with the relation which exists for international purposes between individuals and the states to which they belong, unless the theory of that relation be taken from the *Contrat Social* of Rousseau, in despite of the saner statements of other thinkers and of the facts of international life. But this theory cannot be discussed till some further points which bear on it have been mentioned[3].

Secondly, merchant vessels can be used as transports, and the sailors who navigate them can navigate regular transports, even if they are not fit for service in the more active part of the military navy; and in certain countries all sailors have received some training for the military navy, and are held liable to serve in it. Circumstances may therefore well arise in which not merely the maintenance of England's supremacy at sea, which is so necessary for the support of her population, but even her safety from invasion, may require that an enemy's ships and sailors, of whatever descriptions respectively,

---

[1] See what has been said of the special authority of the states most concerned with a particular branch of international law, above, p. 84, no. 16.

[2] See above, pp. 113—115.   [3] See below, p. 264.

should be captured and detained. It is not to be supposed that the advocates of *kriegsraison* would deny to England, under imminent danger of invasion, the right of capturing and detaining the enemy's sailors and his ships which might be used as transports: the ships and cargoes, they would probably say, ought to be released, with the men, on the conclusion of peace. The question for us is whether it is better to hold our right on its present footing, or to receive back a part of it, to be used only in our extreme need, and on the terms of accepting, along with the part, a theory hitherto strange to us, which practically reduces to narrow limits the protection given by any laws of war. I venture to think that it is better to hold our right on its present footing, even without reference to the pecuniary value of the ships and cargoes: for one reason, because when the danger of invasion was imminent it would be too late to parry it by capturing ships and men already collected in harbours ready for use; and for another, because humanity will be safer if war is governed by laws which are meant to be kept so far as prohibitive, and to be used with due self-restraint so far as permissive, than if laws of fairer seeming are laid down for it together with a licence to disregard them on the plea of necessity.

Thirdly, we have to consider whether the present right of capture agrees with the true policy of England in other respects than that of national defence. Let us imagine that she is opposed to a power or to a combination of powers at all considerable at sea, and try to form an idea of what would then happen. Many persons appear to suppose that there would immediately be a wholesale transfer of British mercantile shipping to neutral flags, and that under the cover of these the supply of England with food and the raw materials of our manufactures would proceed much as before, only we should have lost our carrying trade. That view certainly errs by not taking sufficient account of the immense aggregate of the prices which would have to be paid for wholesale *bona fide* transfers of British ships, an aggregate far exceeding what neutral buyers could supply on short notice—of the fact that transfers which were not *bona fide* would not be valid as against a belligerent—and of the necessary consequence from those two premises, namely that an enemy would bring in the transferred ships wholesale, for inquiry by his prize courts into the circumstances of the transfers. A great rush to transfer would be followed by the discovery that war rates of insurance were heavy even under the neutral flag. And since it must be easier to convoy fleets of merchantmen kept together by the general use of steam power than it used to be to convoy fleets scattered by unequal rates of sailing, it is probable that after a little experience the British flag would still be flying over the greater part of our shipping, even were there nothing else in the case than what has yet been mentioned. It is however very possible that if England were at war with a considerable sea power, the interference with her commerce undertaken by the latter would to a large extent take place under cover of the law of blockade. It is not indeed likely that a blockade of any port in the British Isles could be made really effective, except for a short time by a rare combination of circumstances. But the power of a steam navy to maintain a blockade is much greater than used to be that of sailing ships in the old wars between England and France—both the common law of nations and the declaration of Paris are very vague in what they require for the effectiveness of a blockade—one of the most recent blockades in history was also one of the most ineffective, that of the Confederate coast during the first year of the American civil war (for afterwards it became really effective), and yet all neutral states respected it—the respect which they paid to it was highly commendable, considering what were the issues at stake in that war, but all the same it goes to show how much more the behaviour of neutrals towards an ineffective blockade depends on political than on legal considerations—and to declare a blockade of British ports, if neutrals could in any way be induced to respect it, would have the advantage of attacking our supplies under the neutral flag as well as under our own. I have little doubt therefore that the attempt would be made, and that the behaviour of neutrals towards it would depend mainly on their political sympathies; or at least that, if it was not made, it would be because the superiority of England at sea was so overwhelming that our commerce had little to fear in any state of the law. But such an employment—abuse, if you like—of blockade would seriously weaken the motive for transferring ships to the neutral flag; and this is, to me, an additional reason for hesitating to believe in the ruin which we are told that our next great war will bring to British commerce if the existing law is maintained.

On the other hand, I do not believe at all in the capture of traders at sea as a means of breaking either the resources or the spirit of a great land power. It was not such capture, even when reinforced by blockades admirably maintained, that brought the Napoleonic and Confederate wars to an end, but the advance of the allies to Paris and Toulouse, and that of the United States' armies to Richmond and Savannah. And the multiplication of railways makes continental states less than ever dependent on the sea for supplies. I submit then that we need neither be driven by the stress of apprehension to one solution of the question before us, nor be led by the prospect of advantage to the opposite solution. We are free to consider calmly the painful losses caused to individuals by belligerent captures—losses which it is not possible wholly to provide against by insurance, because they may ruin a trade that will not bear the insurance, and which ought not to be inflicted without adequate justification. We may also consider that capture on no other legal ground but that of enemy's property is in fact, whether consistently or not, condemned as unjust throughout a large part of Europe and America; and that England incurs on its account an unpopularity which the continental nations do not seem to incur with one another by any severity in the exaction of requisitions and contributions— perhaps because they have all acted alike in that respect, or may hope to do so, while they cannot hope to rival England in the power of capturing at sea. And the true conclusion appears to be that a real cause, when such may exist, for desiring the detention of the enemy's sailors and ships in order to prevent invasion or the loss of our naval supremacy, is the only adequate motive for maintaining the present practice ; and that at the commencement of a war England should offer to her enemy to enter with him into a convention, determinable by either side on short notice, for mutual abstention from maritime capture except under the heads of blockade and contraband.

## *Retorsion.*

Retorsion in war is the action of a belligerent against whom a law has been broken, and who retorts by breaking the same or some other law, in order to compensate himself for the damage which he has suffered and to deter his enemy from continuing or repeating the offence. Where the same law is broken the proper term is retaliation, but there is no difference of principle between the cases, and the term retorsion covers both. The principle is justified by the analogy of national law. We have seen Professor Lueder saying: " according to known maxims, non-fulfilment by one party deprives that party of the right to claim fulfilment by the other[1]." In England a party to a contract cannot enforce its performance by the other party if he has himself failed in some performance which, either by the express terms of the contract or by what can be collected to have been the intention, was made a condition precedent to performance by the other party. A similar result is reached by Art. 1184 of the Code Napoléon, which runs that " in bilateral contracts a condition is always understood by which the contract is dissolved if one of the parties does not fulfil his engagement.... The dissolution must be sued for, and time can be given the defendant

[1] See above, p. 244.

according to circumstances." The practice is that in an action under that article the court appreciates the circumstances, and only grants the dissolution in cases in which an English court would arrive at the conclusion that the defendant's performance was intended to be a condition precedent to the plaintiff's. Thus a principle of relativeness is acknowledged by national law even in contracts in which it is not expressed, and although the mutual duties of enemies cannot be considered as arising from contract, yet the student of ethics will admit that there is scarcely any duty which is not more or less relative. Whether then we regard the laws of war between belligerents as merely moral laws or as the laws of an international society, we must admit for them in either character a relativeness within proper limits. A state having a claim which it believes itself to be justified in prosecuting by force of arms—which is the case of every belligerent—cannot reasonably be expected to observe every rule of the game, at the risk of its own defeat or of leaving its soldiers and subjects exposed to avoidable suffering, when its antagonist has added to his original wrong by breaking the rules of the game. Nor can it be supposed that any society has adopted a law to that effect.

But the immediate sufferers from retorsion are hardly ever the persons who were guilty of the offence which called for it. This will be illustrated by an example which is worth citing, since it illustrates much else besides. During the war of 1870–1 the French detained as prisoners the crews of the German merchantmen which they captured, but the German government, in a note addressed to that of France, besides alleging illtreatment of the prisoners, objected in principle to their detention and threatened to resort to retorsion if they were not liberated. It was urged in the note that the only object of detaining seamen of the mercantile marine was to diminish the number of sailors from whom privateers could be manned, and that therefore, since France was a party to the declaration of Paris by which privateering was abolished, it must be supposed that she had sanctioned the enjoyment thenceforth by such seamen of an immunity from detention. The Count de Chaudordy, who was minister of foreign affairs in the " government of national defence," rebutted the inference drawn from the declaration of Paris by pointing out the services which merchant seamen are still capable of rendering in war at a moment's notice, and that the reasons for their detention were of double force as against Germany, in which all seafaring men are subject to conscription for the navy of the state. The German government, in execution of its threat, sent forty notables from Dijon, Gray and Vesoul as prisoners to Bremen. The war closed without either of the conflicting claims being withdrawn, and the seamen and the notables were released in consequence of the peace. Subsequent German writers, as Geffcken and Lueder[1], uphold the rule propounded by their government, that mercantile seamen cannot be detained as prisoners, while the writers of other nationalities generally maintain the old rule that they can be so detained.

This incident strikingly exemplifies the want of

[1] Geffcken, note 8 to § 126 of Heffter's *Europäische Völkerrecht der Gegenwart*, 8th edition, p. 279: Lueder, in Holtzendorff's *Handbuch des Völkerrechts*, vol. 4, § 113, note 6, p. 479.

definition which, as already remarked, the laws of war between belligerents suffer in consequence of the usual absence of any clear pronouncement on alleged breaches of them. With regard to the reasoning employed by the German government, since the detention of merchant seamen was admitted to be lawful before the declaration of Paris[1], those who think of laws as the rules of a society cannot hold that it became unlawful by a mere inference from that declaration unless the international society was in some way committed to the legitimacy of the inference. It might have been so committed by the general opinion of writers, expressing that of European and American men, only in the case before us the inference was supported by no such general opinion, and was not likely to be so[2]. And if it were common for governments to act on inferences or opinions not heard of until propounded for use on the occasion, and then disputed, it would be absurd to speak of any laws of war at all as between belligerents. What Selden said of the English system of equity while it was in process of development, that it was as if you were to take the measure of length from the chancellor's foot, might be applied to any assertion that could be made about the lawful conduct of war. And lastly we remark the lesson for which the incident was cited, that the notables of Dijon, Gray and Vesoul suffered by retorsion for an offence which, if it was one, was not theirs. On that score however no reasonable objection can be made, and we must see why.

[1] This is not admitted by those who adopt Rousseau's theory of the relation of individuals to war, as to which see below, p. 265.
[2] See above, p. 84, no. 17.

That it should be deemed just for an individual to suffer by retorsion for the offence of his government implies that for the purposes of war he is held to be identified with his state. Retorsion may even imply a double process of identifying an individual with his state, for it may be employed or threatened in reply to something which has not been done by the enemy's government, and which that government may have been unable to prevent. In that case the responsibility is first carried up to the state by the identification with it of the individual who has done the wrong, and then the suffering for the wrong is brought down to another individual by identifying him in turn with his state. In no other way can the relative character of the laws of war be made to support the practice of retorsion. No analogy that can be drawn either from ethics or from national law will warrant any one's being deliberately made to suffer for the fault of another from whom he is regarded as distinct. There can be only one reason why the notables of Dijon, Gray and Vesoul could justly lose their claim to the fulfilment by an invader of his duties towards the peaceable population, because France had failed to release German prisoners, supposing that she was bound to release them. It is that all claims of Germany against France were claims against the notables of Dijon, Gray and Vesoul among other French citizens, not indeed to be pressed against those individuals without adequate occasion, but giving a relative character to their claim to a certain treatment by the invader, and therefore superseding the latter claim on adequate occasion arising.

The same result will follow if retorsion be placed

on the ground of necessity. We have seen that Professor Lueder, justifying *kriegsraison* on that ground, says that "the necessity of individuals is recognised as exempting them from punishment for things never so injurious done by them from that necessity[1]." That statement goes too far, both for ethics and at least for English law. It is true that homicide is excused by the necessity of defending yourself against an attack by the person killed, but it is not justifiable to kill some one who has not attacked you, in order to throw on him, rather than bear yourself, the consequences of a fatality in which neither was at fault[2]. If therefore the analogy be truly weighed, it will appear that the admission of necessity as a ground for retorsion presupposes that those on whom the burden is made to fall are regarded by international law as sharing the faults of their state. And the same is true of all the burdens which the laws of war allow to fall on individuals. Neither requisitions nor the exaction of the most moderate contributions can be explained unless the subjects of the enemy state be in some way identified with their state.

*The General Theory of the Relation of Subjects to a War.*

The way has now been cleared for considering from a general point of view the relation of subjects to a war carried on by their state. Are they parties to the war? are they simply strangers to it? or in what intermediate relation to it are they placed? In the middle ages the answer did not seem doubtful:

---

[1] Above, p. 244.  [2] See above, p. 112.

the subjects were parties to the war, and not only were they enemies of the state with which it was waged, but the subjects of the two states were enemies one of another as individuals. If the state was a feudal one, the tie of personal allegiance had for its consequence that all the quarrels of its lord were also the quarrels of his men : those who had defied the lord or whom he had defied—put out of faith—were thereby out of faith with the homage. If it was an Italian or other republic, the citizens felt that they were themselves the state ; it had not occurred to them that from the personality and relations of the latter their own personality and relations were to be distinguished. This view of war led to great savagery. The life and property of every individual member of each belligerent state was legally exposed to be taken or pillaged by every individual member of the other belligerent state, and on a declaration of war it was usual to incite all subjects by proclamation to attack and spoil the enemy by every means in their power (*courir sus aux ennemis*).

In the middle of the eighteenth century, when a great improvement had already been made in the practice of war, an attempt was made to place its theory at the opposite extreme by a sudden transition. Rousseau wrote, in his famous *Contrat Social* :

"War is not a relation of man to man but of state to state, in which individuals are enemies only accidentally, not as men nor even as citizens but as soldiers, not as members of their country but as its defenders. Lastly, a state can only have other states for enemies and not men, seeing that no true relation can be established between things of different natures[1]."

[1] *Contrat Social*, bk I. ch. 4.

The levity of mind displayed by such a passage is extraordinary, even for a man of Rousseau's character. If no true relation can be established between states and men, it must be impossible for men not only to be the enemies, but also to be the citizens or members of a state, which in the same passage they are described as being. And if it is only as soldiers that men are enemies even accidentally, every measure employed in war with reference to the civil population, including the most moderate requisitions, contributions and interferences with their liberty, must be unlawful. That legal situation would make war almost impossible, a result which Rousseau would probably not have regretted, but if he had intended it he would have mentioned it: he had thought so little about what he was writing that he did not see it. As little had he reflected that the power of creating corporations with limited liability may well be granted to individuals by states, which can impose the conditions and exercise the control necessary to prevent injustice, but that ethical principle must condemn the claim that men, acting in groups not subject to regulation by a superior, can repudiate their personal responsibility, and leave outsiders to seek their only satisfaction from the means with which they have chosen to clothe the group.

In 1801 M. Portalis, in his discourse on the opening of the French prize court, made the more moderate pronouncement that " war is a relation of state to state and not of individual to individual." It will be observed that this expressly negatives only the doctrine that the subjects of two belligerent states are enemies one of another as individuals. It leaves open the question whether the subjects of each state are not responsible to the other, and therefore in war its enemies ; in other words, whether the theory of war does not require that for its purposes the subjects of a state shall be identified with it, as I have put it in speaking of the principles of retorsion and necessity. Consequently the pronouncement of M. Portalis, while justly incompatible with pillage, is not incompatible with any of the practices that in the nineteenth century are still usual. But the arbitrary assertions of Rousseau continued to exercise the fascination which extreme doctrines seem to possess, especially when an end is to be served by them ; and Napoleon prefaced as follows a decree of 18th November, 1804 : " considering that England does not admit the law of nations universally followed by all civilised peoples, that she reputes as an enemy every individual belonging to the enemy state, and consequently makes the crews of merchant ships prisoners of war." Thus the emperor bettered the philosopher by asserting for their views a universal agreement, both in theory and in practice, with the single exception which to so many minds seems to carry a comforting assurance of their own superiority. We have seen however that when Bismarck reproached the French for doing the same thing which Napoleon considered to take the English out of the list of civilised peoples (*peuples policés*), he used neither the authority nor the same argument, but practically repudiated both by basing his claim on the later declaration of Paris[1].

The general view which Professor Lueder takes of the relation of subjects to a war is in accordance

[1] Above, p. 261.

with that which has here been intimated. He quotes Portalis with approval, and says that " in war only states and not private persons are opposed to one another as enemies," a maxim which is equivalent to that of Portalis and leaves the same point open[1]. And that he perceived and intended the lacuna in the maxim, whether Portalis did so or not, may be seen from another passage in which he fills it as follows.

" The commencement of war and the entry of the law of war on the scene introduce for the subjects of the belligerent states the condition of war (*kriegstand*), that is, the special relation which in consequence of the outbreak of war arises between them and the opposite party. All the subjects of the states which are at war are under that condition, though not in the same degree, notwithstanding that the rule holds that peaceable private persons belonging to the belligerent states are not mutually enemies. For even those who take no part in the operations of war have to bear, in the measure of what has above been established in general and in the following pages will be carried out in detail, certain burdens, restrictions, sacrifices, disadvantages, in one word duties towards the hostile state, which war naturally brings with it[2]."

And a few lines further on the same writer describes the peaceable population as being " enemies in the passive sense[3]."

The notion of duties towards an occupying invader which is thus adopted by the learned professor, and not by him alone, appears to be open to grave objection. It brands as criminal acts done by the invaded population, or by individual members of it, which are only deserving of praise as patriotic, whatever may be the right of the invader to repress them in his own interest, or even in that of the quiet of the occupied district. The limit of what

---

[1] In Holtzendorff's *Handbuch des Völkerrechts*, vol. 4, § 69, p. 265, with note 5 on p. 267.
[2] *Handbuch des Völkerrechts*, vol. 4, § 90, p. 371.    [3] *Ib.* p. 372.

patriotism may justifiably attempt in such cases is not the quiet of the occupied district in particular, but the real good of the country at large, and humanity will be better respected if the necessary repression is exercised with a regretful consciousness of the interest in which that is done, than if the invader tries to cover his interest by the pharisaical assumption that he is punishing guilt. The steps which must be taken against the peaceable population can properly be put only on the ground of their being enemies, as Professor Lueder calls them after all, though with evident reluctance. And so the *a priori* school seems to have arrived at last at the same point which we have reached inductively, by enquiring what view of the relation of subjects to a war is implied by retorsion and necessity as admitted principles of action. To sum up:

First, war is undoubtedly a relation of state to state, whatever else it may be as well.

Secondly, war establishes between each of the states which are parties to it and the subjects of the enemy state a relation which entitles the former to treat them as identified with their state, in other words as enemies, so far as the necessities of war require, under the limitations which are recognised as being imposed by humanity. This measure is different for combatants and for the peaceable population, as the necessities and limitations referred to are different for them, but the difference does not arise from any absence in the one case of a relation existing in the other. The men who form a state are not allowed to disclaim their part in the offences alleged against it, whether those on account of which the war was begun or those charged as having been committed by it in the course of the war, or therefore to claim that hostile action shall not be directed against their state through them in their respective measures. And this is just. Whatever is done or omitted by a state is done or omitted by the men who are grouped in it, or at least the deed or the omission is sanctioned by them. That must be so, because a state is not a self-acting machine. The impulse which its wheels receive can only be a human impulse, its rulers can employ only human agency, and that agency must at least tacitly consent to be so employed. But if we look more closely at the facts we shall probably find that in the foreign affairs of a state the rulers oftener act under the impulse of the mass than by its tacit permission, and that tacit permission is seldom conceded by the mass except to those who embody and represent the national character.

Thirdly, war establishes no direct relation between the members of the respective belligerent states, and in that sense it is true that war is not a relation of individual to individual. The personalities of a state and of its subjects are distinct; the duties, engagements and liabilities of the former are not the duties, engagements and liabilities of the latter; but the latter are responsible for those of the former. To use the analogy of private law, a state may be described as a corporation or technical person, though not as one with limited liability. The limitation by the laws of war of the hostile action which may be taken against an individual is analogous, not to any limitation in private law of a shareholder's liability for the debts of the incorporated company in which his shares are held, but to the joint effect in private law of the principle that the incorporated company must be the primary object of attack, the shareholders' liability even though unlimited being only subsidiary to that of the company, and of whatever limitation the law may have imposed for the sake of humanity on the execution to be obtained against a debtor in any case. So much protection as a subject derives in war from the distinction of personalities between him and his state is an advance on the views practically entertained in the middle ages, and it includes the prohibition of pillage and of all fighting not directed by public authority.

## Humanity in War.

It is often said that where in war the principle of necessity conflicts with that of humanity, the former must prevail, or, as Professor Lueder puts it, that humanity must be considered only so far as the nature and end of war permit[1]. That maxim is not intended to impair the absolute prohibitions which are among the laws of war, as that of employing poison. Its purport is to warn governments and commanders that, with regard to acts of which the admissibleness depends on occasion and measure, they must for the sake of humanity itself let necessity go before it in judging of occasion and measure. And it may, in cases of retorsion, require that severities shall be exercised against persons who, being already in the power of their enemy, would by the laws of war be exempt from severities otherwise than in consequence of their own conduct. It has been said that such severities may even go to the length of

[1] In Holtzendorff's *Handbuch des Völkerrechts*, vol. 4, § 71, p. 276.

death, regardless of the absolute prohibition which in this age the laws of war pronounce against killing prisoners; and the instance has been cited of the commander of insurgents, morally entitled by their strength and organisation to be treated as belligerents, threatening to execute a prisoner for every one of his own men who should be executed for treason. That case however is, by the hypothesis, one in which the laws of war, whether rightly or wrongly, have not been admitted to apply. It is not within the scope of the present book to discuss what insurgents may do in order to force their entrance within the protection of regular war, but in dealing with regular war it behoves us not to weaken, by any exception whatever, the few absolute prohibitions which its laws contain.

With regard to things which are permitted when due respect is paid to occasion and measure, it is alleged in justification of the maxim which we are considering that true humanity is to bring the war to the speediest conclusion, and that this is best done by the sternest interpretation of the license given by necessity. If it were put forward as a benefit for mankind that all wars should be decided by the first year or the first campaign, much might be said against such an opinion. The premium on preparation would be enormous, and suffering not beneath comparison with that caused by war would be caused by the grinding taxation necessary for the preparation which every state would be compelled to maintain. The most aggressive powers, and therefore those the least entitled to succeed, would generally be the best prepared and therefore the likeliest to succeed. Even perfect readiness would scarcely be thought to give sufficient security without alliances, and alliances by which large parts of the world are divided into opposing camps are apt to lead to war though intended for defence. But such general considerations can have no effect on the conduct of a particular war. Once engaged in a war, all governments and commanders must feel it a duty to their own people to bring it as soon as possible to a successful conclusion, and for that purpose they will certainly give necessity precedence over humanity in all things permitted. It is as much as can be expected if they abstain from causing very great suffering by acts of which the effect on the fate of the war can be but small. The best hope for the mitigation of war lies in fencing as far as possible by a prohibition every point at which the temptation to inhumanity is excessive.

There is one class of rules which it seems particularly important to lay down in a manner admitting of no exception, namely those which relate to the rights of persons engaged in fighting or in contact with it, whether as combatants or in the service of the sick and wounded. To permit exceptions is to create uncertainty, and amid scenes of carnage and devastation all uncertainty of personal position tends strongly to brutalise those who are exposed to it. Let the conditions to be satisfied for the admission of irregulars to the rights of soldiers, or for the enjoyment of immunities by those who render philanthropic services, be made as stringent as real military necessity may require, but when the conditions are satisfied let the rights and the immunities be absolutely inviolable.

## The Improvement of the Laws of War.

It is almost a truism to say that the mitigation of war must depend on the parties to it feeling that they belong to a larger whole than their respective tribes or states, a whole in which the enemy too is comprised, so that duties arising out of that larger citizenship are owed even to him. This sentiment has never been wholly wanting in Europe since the commencement of historical times, but there have been great variations in the nature and extent of the whole to which the wider attachment was felt. It was felt in a Greek city for the Amphictyons, and ultimately for the Hellenic race. In the later days of the Roman republic and the earlier ones of the empire, the Stoic philosophy made the commonwealth of mankind an object of reverence to men of cultivation. Then Christianity, by which I do not mean what its founder taught but the system which existed, substituted the Holy Catholic Church as the all-embracing community which chiefly occupied the thoughts of the faithful, though the claims of mankind were not denied; and if it practically narrowed the circle of interest, it made a compensation by the greater force of the motives which it called into play. In our own time there is a cosmopolitan sentiment, a belief in a commonwealth of mankind similar to that of the Stoics, but stronger because the soil has been prepared by Christianity, and by the mutual respect which great states tolerably equal in power and similar in civilisation cannot help feeling for one another.

We might have expected that, in each of the forms which it has assumed, the feeling of a larger citizenship would have had more effect in mitigating the practice of war than it would seem to have had. Especially we should have expected that the introduction of a new form by philosophy or religion would have marked an era in that practice. We find on the contrary that the progress of war from utter savagery to its present quasi-civilised condition has been slow and gradual. The first energies of a philosophy or a religion, from the ardour of which much might have been hoped, have spent themselves in obtaining its general acceptance; it was not in a position to determine the action of rulers and armies until it had been absorbed to a large extent in the steady current of human motives. That current, purified and deepened by the contributions which philosophy and religion have from time to time poured into it, has gone on raising by imperceptible degrees the standard of action in war as well as in peace. There have been periods during which the level has fallen, and one such period it belongs to our subject to notice. The wars of religion which followed the Reformation were among the most terrible in which the beast in man ever broke loose, and yet they occurred in an age of comparative enlightenment. Zeal for a cause, however worthy the cause may be, is one of the strongest and most dangerous irritants to which human passion is subject; and the tie of Protestant to Protestant and of Catholic to Catholic, cutting across the state tie instead of embracing it unweakened in a more comprehensive one, enfeebled the ordinary checks to passion when they were most wanted. Such a degradation of war would tend to recur if socialism attained the consistency and power of a militant creed, and met the present idea of the state on the field of battle. It is possible that we might then see in war a license equal to that which anarchism shows us in peace.

It is more agreeable to dwell on two periods of history during which the mitigation of war has advanced by unusual strides. One is the age of chivalry, when a number of influences, which it would be beyond our purpose to trace, combined to raise the warrior's regard for his personal character and moral dignity. The result was a temperament largely coloured by pride and self-respect, and most conspicuously developed in the knights and squires, but not wanting in the fighting men of other ranks. They gloried in its possession, and were determined to preserve it from contamination by anything which they deemed to be mean or derogatory. Often indeed their standard was capricious, as when the English thought that even strategy was beneath military honour, and complained that the French would not meet them at a set place and time. But to chivalry much is due in the improved treatment of prisoners which it brought about, and in the deep root taken by the idea of fair fighting, as in not covering yourself by using the enemy's flag or uniform in combat. It needs no proof that some tincture of the chivalrous temperament has been at all times the good side of the warrior's character, or that it is likely to be produced by the habit of confronting danger, especially when combined with the habit of command. It seems however that the enjoyment of a classical age is necessary in order that a virtue, attaining its full power and recognition, may afterwards take its place in the due proportion of things;

and it is remarkable that the same age was classical in Europe, through the early friars for Christian humility, and through the knights for the lofty scorn of chivalry. But what is excessive may be trusted to perish, and it was probably very much due to the impulse given by chivalry that, notwithstanding the savagery of the wars of religion, the directing classes in Europe were so prepared that Grotius could propound his corrections (*temperamenta*) for the laws of war with a chance of being listened to[1].

The lesson which we may derive is that the best hope for the further mitigation of war lies in a high standard of character being maintained among soldiers. In peace considerations of law and justice may be acted on by nations, and the action taken on such grounds will in its turn help to mould the character. In war the stress is such that no considerations can be relied on for determining action but those which are already incorporated in the character. The determination of action in war lies practically with two classes, commanders by land and sea and statesmen: the people, once excited enough for war to have broken out, will approve of any measures which their commanders and statesmen recommend for carrying it on. And of those two classes the commanders are much the more important for our present purpose, because their opinion of what necessity requires will influence the statesmen. The best chance that interference with an enemy's commerce at sea, except in the cases of blockade and contraband, should be limited to what may be strictly necessary for national defence, is that

[1] See above, p. 46.

English and French naval captains should come to think interference with it beyond that limit derogatory, not that argument should be more successful than it has been in making out a difference in principle between that and other methods of carrying on war. And those are mistaken friends of humanity who, by decrying the military and naval professions, do their best to keep good men out of them, and thereby to lower the standard of their character.

The second period during which the mitigation of war has advanced with unusual rapidity is that in which we live. Within the nineteenth century cities taken by storm have been rescued from pillage and outrage; the treatment of invaded countries, severe as it still is, has become mild in comparison with what it was during the Napoleonic wars; privateering has been abolished over by far the larger part of the world, and the rest of the world is prepared to accede to its abolition if the declaration of Paris should be extended by placing private belligerent property at sea on the same footing as that of neutrals; Austria and Italy, in their war of 1866, have set the example of that extension, in concurrence, it must be admitted, with plain self-interest, and no necessity of national defence opposing; the Geneva convention has protected those engaged in the care of the sick and wounded, and the convention of St Petersburg has prohibited a certain class of cruel explosives. The cause of this rapid career of improvement must be something more than the renewed belief in a commonwealth of mankind which has been mentioned above as marking our time. If that belief had stood alone, it might have done no more for the mitigation of war than was done by it when it was first introduced by the Stoic philosophy. But along with the renewal of that belief there has come a remarkable development of the sentiment of pity, of an enthusiasm of humanity which has caused a wider and keener sympathy with suffering than has perhaps ever before been known. As in the case of chivalry, I do not enter into the difficult enquiry as to the influences to which the phenomenon is due : it is sufficient for students of international law to note the fact. No doubt the enthusiasm of humanity and the recognition of a human brotherhood are closely allied. They are indeed the emotional and intellectual aspects of the same psychological attitude, but history proves that they may be developed in different degrees, and the latter is of course the weaker of the two for any operative purpose. Thus, to take our examples only from the nineteenth century, the intellectual recognition of a duty to mankind has failed to establish prohibitive rules where there has been no great suffering by individuals to excite pity. To destroy a harbour which a belligerent has not the means of effectually blockading has been represented with justice as a crime against the world, but the protests of opinion have not prevented the attempt from being made in the American war of secession and by Russia at the mouth of the Danube in her last Turkish war.

And now there are ominous signs that pity, as an operative force in the mitigation of war, has nearly reached its limit. The Geneva convention is probably secure, so far as concerns the protection afforded by it to the enemy, including the peaceable subjects of the enemy, in tending their own sick and wounded. But so far as concerns the Red Cross societies which flock from neutral countries to perform works of mercy on the field of battle, since their tendency is to assist the weaker party by relieving him from the necessity of attending to his own sick and wounded, it is impossible for those who hear what soldiers say about them to feel sure that the stronger party in a war will always allow them free course. Theoretical writers have been found to preach what at one time they had been unanimous in denouncing, the devastation of whole tracts of country for sheer terror, or in vengeance for stubborn resistance by the enemy. And the bombardment of undefended coast towns has been advocated by professional sailors, without restriction to the case of their containing important magazines, which forty years ago was felt to be the only justification for the bombardment of Odessa, and was not universally admitted as a justification. The pity which is effectual to work great changes is that which, in running at once through millions of men, is intensified by the enthusiasm which masses engender. But pity for suffering in war is liable in democratic times to encounter other feelings of equal extent and opposite tendency, the consciousness that the war in which the nation is engaged has been willed by it, and the national determination to triumph at any cost.

What has been said in this section may be useful to the student of international law by leading him to reflect on the conditions under which he has to work for its amendment, especially with regard to war, but it is not meant to discourage him from that work. That international law is less certain than national law is often made a reproach to it, necessarily as that consequence flows from there being no legislature to enact it and no judicature to declare it. The student of international law may to some extent console himself with the reflection that legislatures and judicatures, by the very fact of their fixing the law, are sometimes a hindrance to its improvement. In their hands, if they are too conservative, the process of development may be arrested; the living tissue of the law may become ossified; while if a branch of law is still free to develop itself under the influence of public opinion, the student has the power, and with it the responsibility and the privilege, of assisting in its evolution. Two objects to be attained have been already indicated: as to law, the extension of the list of absolute prohibitions, so that methods of warfare which are still approved or faintly condemned may gradually be brought under a ban along with poisoned weapons and explosives weighing less than 400 grammes; as to practice, an increased sensitiveness to the guilt of using even a permitted method when the suffering that must result is out of any reasonable proportion to the military advantage promised. Obviously also, in cases of the latter kind, a step is gained whenever it is found possible to reinforce the sensitiveness of conscience by a better definition of the occasion and measure on and in which alone a certain method is permitted. But in this there must always be extreme difficulty, as may be seen in the little success which has attended the attempts to limit requisitions and contributions. And where the problem cannot be satisfactorily solved, it is safer in my judgment to abstain from laying down a rule, and to appeal as strongly as the case admits to the highest principles of action, than to proclaim a rule and permit necessity to be pleaded for breaking it. The plea of necessity, even when justified, has a dangerous tendency to corrupt and degrade those who urge it ; and when it has sapped the foundations of one fence, no other fence into the construction of which it has been introduced can be greatly relied on.

# PART II

## MISCELLANEOUS PAPERS

# I

## RELATIONS BETWEEN PUBLIC AND PRIVATE INTERNATIONAL LAW. 1856.

[Reprinted from the *Transactions of the Juridical Society*, vol. 1855-58, pp. 173-192.]

PRIVATE international law is " the jurisprudence arising from the conflict of the laws of different nations, in their actual application to modern commerce and intercourse[1]." In the validity, obligation, and dissolution of contracts, in the modifications and transfer of property, in successions by will or on intestacy, in questions of the capacity or status of persons, in delicts, and in many cases not easily classed, this conflict arises from the claim of a party to the benefit of some law other than that commonly administered by the Court in which he stands. There are many and conflicting treatises and decisions on this description of cases, but two assumptions run through them : that for every such case there exists its proper law, and that in the discovery of that law the Judge must obey " some common principles adopted by all nations in this regard," without which " there would be an utter confusion of all rights and remedies[2]." Baffled by this assumed agreement and actual contrariety, we naturally turn for light to the text-writers on the public law of nations. Within their province fall all questions

[1] *Story on the Conflict of Laws*, § 4.     [2] Id. § 4.

arising between persons or bodies having no common superior ; and it is between those who, as members of different states, stand towards one another in such absence of political relation, that the class of cases described most commonly arises. It will serve to clear the subject, if I state at once the amount of help to be derived from the chief of these text-writers.

Grotius rested his international theory on the position that rights originate in the law natural, and are anterior to political society ; that states are formed by individuals relinquishing portions of these rights, and that from the sovereignty so created flows in its turn the institution of positive law. But then, since it could not be said that individuals ever relinquished rights except mutually, each in favour of his fellow-citizens, it seemed to follow that private rights against the members of foreign societies depend still on the law of nature, precisely as those of independent governments, between which positive law has no place. The generality, however, of this conclusion was restrained by the territorial character of political society. In certain modes pointed out by the law of nature, nations have acquired *dominium* and *imperium*, the property in and the rule over the tracts of land they occupy ; whence it is *natural*[1] that within those tracts their respective laws should be observed. Nay, more : it is not natural that any others should be there observed. For the law of nature does not enjoin, but permits, what are called the natural modes of acquiring property, so that they may be abrogated by the positive laws enacted in virtue

[1] Grotius, *De Jure Belli ac Pacis*, l. 2, c. 11, § 5.

PUBLIC AND PRIVATE INTERNATIONAL LAW 287

of territorial *imperium*[1]; and that men have designed so to abrogate them appears from the fact of their disuse. The Roman jurists indeed and their modern copyists enumerate some natural modes of acquisition as still in force between individuals, but they are not really such. They have been introduced by custom, and, simple as they are, the truly natural modes are simpler still[2]. Wherever therefore civil government exists, men do, both by right and in fact, contract with reference and in subjection to the positive law of the place of contract; and every jural question which can arise out of their contract, including expressly the capacity of parties, must be decided by that law. Only in places yet unoccupied, as at sea, or in newly discovered countries, or when two persons who happen at the moment to be in different territories contract by letter, can their dealings be now regulated by the law of nature; but in those cases they are still governed by that law alone[3].

As a practical system of private international law, this theory of Grotius labours under great defects. First, all those innumerable transactions of commerce, in which all the parties do not happen to be at the critical moment within the same jurisdiction, are resigned by it to the sway of a vague law natural, which can amount in practice to little else than the judge's private opinion of what is equitable. Secondly, even in those cases which it submits to positive law, it dismisses summarily many considerations—the allegiance or domicile of the parties, the place of execution of the contract,

[1] Grotius, l. 2, c. 3, § 5.  [2] Grotius, l. 2, c. 8.
[3] Grotius, l. 2, c. 11, § 5.

the situation of the thing dealt with—to some or all of which the tribunals of every country have attached more or less importance, often allowing them to override that single point of the actual place of contract to which all is attributed by Grotius. This system deviates indeed so widely from what has been current in the practice of courts, moulded as that has been by contact with men and business, that one cannot but suspect its simplicity to have been purchased at the cost of more solid advantages.

Burlamaqui, who through an entire paragraph is here copied verbatim by Vattel, gave some attention to the question of the proper tribunal by which each cause should be heard. Swiss both, they commend to universal reception the practice which between the Swiss cantons had been established by express convention, that the defendant in personal actions should be sued before his own judge; the property in immovables—Vattel adds elsewhere in corporeal chattels also—is to be decided by the judge of their situation[1]. Nothing, however, which they have said betrays a suspicion that, when the tribunal is selected, a difficulty may yet remain in choosing the law. They appear to have assumed that no court would use any but its own law; but even if this be granted, their simple rules of jurisdiction are obscured by the admission that in a sudden difficulty the defendant's judge is not that of his domicile, but of the place where he may be when it arises—an admission which should have been, but is not, accompanied by a definition of a sudden difficulty. This system, were its vague

[1] Burlamaqui, *Droit de la Nature et des Gens*, ptie 3, c. 5, § 8: Vattel, *Droit des Gens*, l. 2, § 103; l. 4, § 113.

outlines filled in, would be preferable to that of Grotius in supplying a positive law for the determination of every case, but open to similar objections on the score of rejecting considerations which have been very influential in practice.

But it is not more in their conclusions than in the extent which this subject occupies in their view, that the publicists differ from the masters of private law. While the latter have produced bulky volumes exclusively devoted to the conflict of laws, the former have furnished but a few scattered hints, more meagre and informal even than might be supposed from the slight, though systematised, sketches which I have presented. And yet it was peculiarly a part of their science. For they have maintained the doctrine that a denial of justice by the tribunals or government of one State to any member of another may furnish to that other a just cause for reprisals, and ultimately for war. It is true that this position has not passed without question, yet in the strictest theory it appears to be unassailable.

It may not be that the property and interests of citizens are, as against foreigners, those of their state; but a similar consequence follows from the narrower ground, that they are entitled to protection as though they were those of their state[1]. Nor, if the clearest compact between sovereigns could settle the law and the forum for every litigation, would it be unnecessary to reserve for great emergencies the right of enforcing its observance. Thus

See, on this subject, Wolff, *Jus Gentium*, § 289, 290; Vattel, l. 2, § 81, 82, with the note of M. Pinheiro-Ferreira; Bentham, *Principles of International Law*, in *Works*, vol. II. p. 544.

for the position of Grotius, that the authority of a judge is not the same against foreigners as against citizens[1], there must ever remain sufficient foundation; nor do I believe that in the most remarkable recent instance in which a private injury has been made the ground of hostile action, the difference between England and Greece in 1850, the theory, as abstracted from its application, was disputed even by the English opposition. Now as there are three heads under which a government may complain of the decision of a foreign tribunal —either that the law applied in such decision was erroneously selected—or that, being rightly selected according to the rules for such cases, it was so barbarous a law that civilised communities cannot admit its application to their members—or that, being the right law and a reasonable law, it was corruptly distorted in its bearing on the matter in hand—we must wonder that the first of these heads has not been more carefully attended to by writers on the law of nations. For though it be very unlikely that one or even a few erroneous decisions should give serious national umbrage, yet it is possible for a commercial country to adopt such principles on the conflict of laws as may systematically damage the interests of foreign merchants.

But in the history of the subject we may find an explanation of the different treatment which it has experienced as a department of private and of public law. When the Roman praetor under the republic judged between citizens of those states which it gradually absorbed, he aimed at extracting that supposed essence of all law in which their various

[1] Grotius, l. 3, c. 2, § 5.

codes agreed, and the result was a *jus gentium*, afterwards supposed to be identical with the *jus naturæ*. But when the conquest of Rome by the barbarians, and still more the mutual conquest of the barbarians by one another, had filled every country with a new diversity of laws, no second attempt of that kind was made, although in one respect the soil was more fitted than before for their fusion, inasmuch as a common Christianity had destroyed or impaired the religious sanction of ancestral institutions. To the German, the place of heathen religion was supplied by his personal pride, and by the invincible centrifugal force which has ever prevented or dissipated the union of his race. To the Roman, his law was the symbol of civilisation, necessary for the preservation of its yet subsisting relics, and to the transaction of his daily affairs. Nor, had there been a disposition towards a fusion of laws, did any tribunal exist which possessed at once the knowledge and the jurisdiction necessary to effect it. The German disdained to be sued in the court of the vanquished race, and his own judges knew nothing of the texts to which the Roman plaintiff might have appealed. Thus within each of the new kingdoms there arose a system of personal laws, the mode of administering which, as well as their mutual claims, were necessarily regulated by the positive institutions of the victors. The general rule was, that the law of the defendant governed; but it is not with this as a rule that I am now concerned, but with the fact that there was such a rule at all: that to the ancient idea of extracting a residuum of agreement from conflicting laws, there had succeeded the idea of choosing one of them. Thus marriage was to be celebrated by the law of the husband; and so strictly was this rule adhered to, that wives who had been married by *their* law were dismissed at caprice, a practice to which, in the year 895, the council of Tribur could oppose none but religious sanctions[1]. A thousand years before, the Roman praetor would have separated the intention in which the laws agreed from the rites in which they differed, and would have held the marriage valid by the *jus gentium*.

Nor could the principle be confined to the collision of laws within any one of the barbarian kingdoms. The German stranger who passed from one to another of them, if he did not belong to any of the races whose laws were recognised in his new abode, was aggregated to the victor people: theirs was the prior claim to what in German ideas was the benefit of the new partner. The Roman stranger brought his own law with him, for it existed everywhere; and his too was the common law of all those classes who, from the exercise of any trade or industry, were likely to have dealings creating the tie of legal obligation between subjects of different kingdoms. Thus, in the dismemberment of the Roman empire, the habit of appealing to some positive law in all possible private disputes descended unbroken from the days when the world obeyed but one master and knew but one jurisprudence.

Nor was that habit shaken when the scattered atoms of society crystallised around the civic bench and the courts of the feudal lords, and local statutes

---

[1] Mansi, t. 18, col. 151. I have been directed to this example by Savigny (*Gesch. d. Römisches Rechts i. Mitt.*, vol. 1. § 46), to whom I may refer generally as my authority in this part.

and territorial customs took the place of personal laws. The feudal customs had indeed much in their favour. They were supported by a feeling of local attachment, newly restored to Europe after a lapse of many ages, in which men embraced each other as they recognised a common home, and shook off the long and disuniting tyranny of the sentiment of race. Yet to this very circumstance, that the sympathies to which they owed their origin tended forcibly to a still closer connection between mankind, it was partly due that the feudal potentates could never establish in fact, and still less in opinion, their separation from a common European system of which they were but subordinate members. They and the customs which they protected were looked upon in a strange light. The familiar form of the imperial jurisprudence of Rome had accustomed men to see in law the footprints of supreme authority. The reception of that jurisprudence as the rule for cases not enumerated in the *coutumier* bore witness against the lords that they were still members of the Roman people, subjects, in a degree, of the emperor[1]. How then could they enact laws? Their customs were but usages, to which, under appropriate circumstances, men might be presumed to conform, so that their binding force was not their own, but derived from the intention to which they afforded a clue. In the sixteenth century, when the balance had turned, though the fight was still hot between the crown of France and its feudatories, this tendency reached its climax in the great extension given by du Moulin to the doctrine of implied contract;

[1] See particularly an important passage of Bartolus, on the Dig. 49. 15. 24, quoted in Savigny, vol. III. § 33.

but it had long before borne its share in that complex of ideas, very different from the territorial sovereignty of Grotius, by which was generated the principle of the *lex loci contractus*.

The other cause which aided this result is to be found in the *corpus juris* itself. The case of the imperial cities was not quite the same with that of the feudal lords. The jurists who professed in their chairs, and felt for them a patriotic affection, could not altogether repudiate their statutes, although they were even more difficult to justify than the *coutumiers*, because the Italian and German towns still recognised the emperor as their master. The name of *statutes* was rigidly adhered to, since no one could conceive of that as *law* which did not come by positive enactment from the highest authority. But various shifts were resorted to that the statutes might have the force of law. The name of Venice calls up the proudest thoughts of independence. But the Venetians made their wills with only two witnesses, and some of us may be surprised to hear that for this it was trusted that they had received some forgotten dispensation from the successors of Justinian ; while another argued that since by the Roman law a parent could with two witnesses divide his property between his children, a city, which was the parent of her subjects, might authorise them to distribute their substance with no more elaborate formality[1]. The queenly rival of emperors would probably have disdained the apology, at least in the age when it was made ; but if it was thus that the Lombard and Tuscan doctors defended *her*, the society will judge that they placed their

[1] Bartolus, ad Cod. 1. 1. 1.

own municipalities on no higher ground. But if the cities formed a part of the empire, their statutes fell directly under those provisions on the force of local observances which were contained in the code and the pandects. Scanty indeed were these, since, after the extension of Roman citizenship to the whole world, those differences of law rapidly became obsolete which had given an interest to the *edictum provinciale* and the treatises upon it. Yet some fragments Tribonian had still thought it worth while to incorporate, and in them, insufficient as they may seem to us, the dialectic of the schools found an ample basis for a multitude of minute, though often jarring, determinations on the conflict of laws. The *lex loci contractus* had more textual authority than any other part of these systems, but it is not their particulars which I wish to remark, so much as the fact that the selection between conflicting laws was conceived to be made in obedience to a positive law of authority superior to them all, and that no one, whether in the chair or on the bench, dreamed of deciding otherwise than by positive law any case whatever between natives of any part of the European world.

But national demarcations became clearer, as the fences of the larger circles were strengthened, while those of the narrower were thrown down. Some jural differences were abolished, or sank undisputed to the level of usages, while others were ripened into positive national laws. Yet in reference to the latter, when their claims conflicted, the idea that some positive law must be applicable to every case, which from imperial Rome had descended through the common law of mediaeval Europe, was strengthened by the facts of judicial institutions. For the magistrate was conscious that his authority was not his own, and that he could not, more than the suitor who stood before him, enforce a private conception of what was just, or decide otherwise than by the code of that sovereign from whom he held his commission. Some statute must be selected from the conflicting statutes by rules which must have the express or implied approval of his own sovereign; but reason taught him that those rules must be common, and education to seek them in those of which I have indicated the origin and growth.

Very different were the thoughts of those who, when the lawlessness of men was at its height, started from a *jus naturæ* to deduce the mutual relations of persons having no common superior. Perhaps, but for what had been already written on the subject from the side of private jurisprudence, they never would have entertained at all the notion that the litigation of members of different states could be governed by positive law. Grotius's deduction of the principle of the *lex loci contractus*, limited to exclude contracts *inter absentes* by letter, is hardly satisfactory even within those limits. Burlamaqui, whose opinions on judicial proceedings between members of different states I have already mentioned, says that if they refer their difference to arbitration, the law of nature is the only rule the arbitrator can follow[1]. When the publicists thought of the subjects of different sovereigns, the field of view was preoccupied by abstract justice and moral

---

[1] Burlamaqui, ptie 4, c. 17, § 8.

claims, as we should call them, by what they styled the dictates of the law natural.

Yet, without the help of public international law, the problem of private international law cannot be solved. For if we admit that such questions are not to be left to the unstable equity of tribunals, which at the command or with the support of their governments may read the law of nature by the light of prejudice and interest, then must the idea of their solution contain two things: the selection on common principles of some positive law by which the rights of parties are to be determined in their inception, and the universal recognition of rights which have once sprung from the appropriate law. But the true selection of principles can only be firmly settled with reference to the nature of law itself, and the limits of the authority which enacts it. Now of the three elements at which we thus ultimately arrive, the nature of law is a question for philosophy, while the limits of the respective national authorities which enact laws, and any validity conceded in one country to the rights which have arisen by the law of another, must depend on the express or tacit agreement of nations. The philosophical question need not detain us long. For whatever laws there may be which are not commands, and in whatever sense the name of law may belong to them, no one can doubt that, in this age, in which the judicial and legislative powers are distinct, it is only with such laws as are commands that forensic practice is concerned. In what follows, I propose briefly to inquire how far the current principles on the conflict of laws can be connected with the views now generally received on the limits of national authority, premising that in forming a practical system of private international law, any principles will have to be carried out in no intractable spirit of pure theory, but with a careful adaptation to the thousand circumstances which so richly diversify our modern life[1].

First then, the commands of law are addressed generally to the people, but the particular command on which any action is founded must have been addressed to the defendant. If I sue on a promise, I assert in effect that, whereas the law imposed on the defendant the duty of keeping his promise, he has not kept it: if on a trespass, that he has not abstained from an act productive of damage to me, from which nevertheless the law bade him to abstain: and so on.

Now the received international system confides to each sovereign an exclusive authority to command those who, whether permanently or temporarily, may be found within certain geographical limits. Thus we all know that, if we travel, our actions are subject to be directed by the police of the countries through which we pass; and if to these, then must they be equally subject to any other directions of the local government. Nor does the proposition at all interfere with that allegiance which subjects, wherever they may be, owe to their sovereign. The uninterrupted continuance of the home citizenship,

[1] The intimate connection between public and private international law was pointed out by Bentham. "Among the causes of offences *de bonne foi* and of wars," he mentions "uncertainty with respect to limits, whether actual or ideal. The object of these limits may be to keep separate either goods, or persons, or causes." And among the "means of prevention" corresponding to "disputes respecting boundaries," he gives "perfecting of the style of the laws: regulation." *Principles of International Law*, u. s. pp. 539, 544.

concurrently with the acquisition of a temporary citizenship in the countries through which we pass, has been especially dwelt on by the baron von Wolff[1]; but as the great difficulty of this subject consists in the confusion between permanent and transitory authority to command, I will enter more fully into their distinction.

Sovereignty gives no present authority to command the absent subject. Neither the French emperor, nor any agent of his, could without committing a breach of the Queen's peace attempt to enforce here the personal obedience of a Frenchman. The sovereign body in France, whatever it may be, might confiscate the French property of a Frenchman who was in England, provided he did not return to his home by a given time : it might threaten that, if it should again get him within its power, it would punish him physically for his actions here, a threat which all states continually hold out to such of their members as commit treason against them abroad, or adhere to their enemies : but only from the moment that he again set foot on French soil would the French government regain its right to the present direction of his personal conduct. In the technical sense in which a duty is called perfect when enforced by a legal sanction, the perfect duty of present obedience depends on momentary place. The allegiance of an absent subject may impose the imperfect duty of obeying his native sovereign. It is indeed a case in which, as an exception to the general rule of casuistry, the imperfect duty may *in foro conscientiæ* be of higher obligation than the perfect. The government

[1] *Jus Gentium*, § 299 et seq.

which has the temporary command of the person may give just cause of complaint by thwarting its performance, while it receives no just cause of complaint from its indirect enforcement by such means as before alluded to, and which, so far as they were used, would add an inferior degree of perfection to the duty. But it would be mere violence or kidnapping, were the subject's own sovereign to enforce the moral duties flowing from allegiance by measures taken directly against his person abroad.

My obligations flow from commands given to me. The authority to command me is in the sovereign of the place where I am. It is evident that we have here the germ of the principle of the *lex loci*. But, to become more than a germ, it needs some farther explanations. The local sovereign can command the actions of those persons only who at the time of the command are within his dominions, and he can command to them those actions only which are to be there performed. For his power is limited by that of all other sovereigns, of which, since to forbid is itself to command, one element is that every sovereign can prohibit all men everywhere from doing anything within his dominions. It is from this last proposition, the universal extent of negative commands, that the rule of the *lex situs* follows in questions of property. For the commands which create property are negative and universal. They consist in the prohibition of all such acts as would interfere with the proprietor's enjoyment of those privileges which the law attributes to him; and this prohibition is extended to all mankind, without distinction of their nationality or temporary situation, because the act of interference, if committed at all, must from its nature take place where the thing which is the subject of property is. It must therefore rest with the territorial sovereign to declare both the modes of property, and how title shall be made to it. The modes of property, that is, what privileges the owner shall enjoy, and how long he shall enjoy them, for this depends on the interferences *he* chooses to prohibit, and the term during which he will prohibit them. The title to property, that is, when, to whom, and how, the privileges shall be transferred, for the real question is the transfer of the prohibitions. Nor is there anything in theory which can, for these purposes, distinguish movables from immovables. But here we fall on one of those cases in which expediency, real or supposed, struggles hard with theory. The simple requisites which, after the abolition of the form of mancipation, the Roman law demanded for a transfer of the dominion in all things alike—the rarity and early disuse of the special forms imposed in the dark ages on the sale of chattels—led naturally to the result that the notion of conveyance was lost in that of the contract of sale, and that the view of that contract as binding the thing was absorbed in the view of it as affecting the person. Hence it was generally taken for granted that the property in movables depends on the law of the place of the contract of sale, although, from a somewhat strained interpretation of the rule *mobilia sequuntur personam*, it was held equally permissible to follow in its conveyance the law of the vendor's domicile. An opinion exists, perhaps from habit, that any attempt to subject movables to the law of the *situs* would be injurious to the freedom of commerce. Yet that attempt has been made by the great commercial state of Louisiana, which, relying on the fact that its own law recognises no title to a chattel without actual tradition, refuses to allow any preference under a foreign contract to avail against a possession taken at New Orleans[1]. That port is crowded with ships, and its warehouses are filled with goods, the property of foreign merchants indebted to Louisiana creditors, and of which a large part is deposited there for the express purpose of sale. It was therefore with an avowed view to her own convenience that her judges adopted the rule of the *lex situs* as governing the transfer of chattels. But they also enunciated the pertinent truth that what the law protects it has a right to regulate. And we shall perhaps admit that their doctrine is consonant with the strictest international theory.

As the international question of property is among the simplest in principle, I have allowed myself to mention it in a digression, from which it is now time to return to obligations. The command to keep my promise is also a command to do that which I have promised to do. Now if in England I promise to do in England a certain thing, the case is simple, for the sovereign who at the time I promise has the general authority to command me has also authority to enjoin the performance of the promised act. But if I in England promise to perform an act in France, it may be asked—how can either the sovereign of France command me

[1] See particularly *Olivier* v. *Townes*, 2 Mar. N. S. 93.

here to keep my promise, or the sovereign of England command me to do in France that which I have promised? The truth is that every promise is primarily to do the thing stipulated, and, subordinate to this, contains the alternative of compensating the promisee for the omission. That the former element is the necessary ground of the latter appears from the maxim *lex non cogit ad impossibilia*, which forbids an action to be sustained on a promise to do that which was at the time of the promise impossible, not merely with reference to the contractor's ability, but absolutely. If ever we use such language as that every promise is susceptible of a legal valuation, this must be understood as a prior condition. We are bound to compensate him whom we have disappointed, but we have not disappointed him who was not justified in reckoning on our performance. If then I in England make a promise to be fulfilled in any part of the world, let that fulfilment be possible, and an obligation by the English law is the immediate consequence of my promise. Not that the sovereign body in this country can command me to perform beyond its limits the act contracted for, but because it can impose on me the obligation—potential before the omission, actual after it—of remedying the damage my omission to execute the contract may occasion. But if I in England promise to do that in France which the law of France does not suffer there to be done, then the respect which independent nations are bound to pay to each other's sovereignty forbids the law of England to contemplate a performance which the ruler of France has, by the law of nations, authority to prevent. Thus then the *locus contractus* branches out into two divisions. There is the actual place of contract, the *locus ubi verba proferuntur*, or *celebrati contractus*, and the place of execution. In considering the mere fact of obligation, to the former belongs its positive existence, since that sovereign alone can lay me under a duty who commands my person, and to his law must therefore be referred the requisites, whether external or internal, which he demands to the perfection of a contract; to the latter, the negative power of pronouncing it illegal, on account of the nature of the thing stipulated. Nor when we consider the *vinculum juris*, or what the obligation includes, is the distinction less important. If the act be contemplated as done or to be done, its consequences must follow according to the law of the place of performance, as the parties who chose that place must be presumed to have chosen it with all its results; but whatever consequences may follow from the contract regarded in its other aspect—that is, from the duty of compensation for non-performance—must depend on the law of the *locus celebrati contractus*, which alone imposes that duty.

The society will recognise in this sketch an outline of the principles by which in practice the rule of the *lex loci contractus* is applied. Their detailed carrying out presents some of the most difficult, though most interesting, problems in jurisprudence. I will here mention but one, which I will select rather from the few cases in which the English doctrine is supposed to be adverse, than from the many in which it certainly corresponds with the theory. I allude to a foreign marriage between persons domiciled in England, whose relationship is here within the prohibited degrees. The matrimonial domicile must have a great influence on the pecuniary rights of the spouses, since the dotal stipulations which accompany the matrimonial contract suppose and refer to an execution in that place. But in the marriage contract itself, no place of execution is covenanted or even supposed. The intention to return is beside its provisions, express or implied; it may be abandoned or deferred. On what ground then could the English law interpose to forbid the contract?

Having discussed the origin of obligations, their universal validity comes next before us. But here I have only to recall what I said in the early part of the paper. For the idea that all private international rights depend on some positive law, to be selected for each case on general principles common to all nations, may be translated into this—that a right, which by the appropriate positive law has once arisen, shall thenceforward be respected and enforced by all tribunals which by the recognised rules of jurisdiction may have cognisance of the matter. And is not this the idea of modern international intercourse, commercial or social? It is not a vague comity, but the force of reason, which bids us recognise foreign laws and the rights which they originate. If I contract in London with a Frenchman to do something at New York, we know our mutual obligations at that moment, and they must be the same at all future moments. If the contract come to be enforced in London, at Paris, at New York, or perhaps at Vienna, the system of procedure used at any of those places may be adopted without inconveniencing us much. But we and all those who deal with us will be seriously inconvenienced if it be not enforced at all, or if that which is enforced be liable to vary as it may emerge in this country or in that. Perhaps, if we discussed this subject with a merchant, we should find that the universal validity of a right which has once accrued was his leading idea of it, as, in spite of manifold lapses in its application, it certainly has been the leading idea of courts of justice. This element we must take from them, and from public law, which tells us what sovereignty is and how it is limited, we must ascertain who in each case has the authority to originate a right by giving a command : and a system of private international law would then result, in which nothing would be left to a vague equity or disputable law of nature, and which would have a similar basis in the agreement of states and the facts of human society to that on which the received law of nations itself reposes.

This agreement must always be coextensive with the facts which make it possible. The possession of common ideas in those critical respects which mark the stage and character of a civilisation, though developed into particular laws sometimes perhaps widely divergent, tests the possibility of usefully enforcing in one country rights drawn from the jurisprudence of another. For from common ideas laws diverge through the local variations of circumstance. But the variations of circumstance are supported with ease, while from strange ideas men recoil with an invincible dislike. In submission to a rule of the general expediency of which we are satisfied, we can bear the loss of money with more or less of complacency. But we could never enforce in Christendom claims arising out of the Mahometan or Hindoo law of marriage, and indeed their differences on consanguinity and divorce present no small obstacle to the complete jural intercommunion even of Christian states. But in general the requisite community of ideas exists throughout Christendom, and so far it is strictly true, in theory at least, that its tribunals are open to every claim of right, wherever it may have arisen.

Laws may be in conflict upon any one of the innumerable points comprised within the vast circle of jurisprudence. In so wide a field I can to-night mention, in the most cursory manner, only those topics which tend most directly to illustrate the connection of the subject, through the idea of sovereignty, with the public law of nations. Yet upon two such topics it remains still to say a few words, since one of them may seem to be beside my theory, and the other to be even opposed to it. It may be asked, by what theory as to the nature of positive law the sovereign of a deceased person's domicile can claim to aggregate into one mass all his corporeal chattels and lucrative obligations, wherever existing or whencesoever due, and to decide upon their future destination, whether they pass by will or *ab intestato*? The truth is that as in the public law of nations there are chapters, called the voluntary part of that law, which cannot be deduced *a priori*, but rest on acquiescence and adoption, so in the private, a community of juridical ideas is, when supported by convenience, a sufficient foundation for rules. I do not know that I could justify the law of the domicile, as the rule of testaments and successions, to one who did not admit the conception of a continuation of the person of the defunct. The history of European law contains nothing more beautiful than the evolution of the idea of the person from that of the family, and the mysterious perpetuity which clings to the former as a memory of its source. It is indeed by what concerns the family, that, more than by any other thing, it is European law and not oriental. Now, this conception once admitted, the rest follows. The nations between whom a jural intercommunion is possible, do all, as a fact, treat the rights and duties of the defunct, or the larger part of them, as a *juris universitas*, to be transferred to a representative of the person. Then it is clear that the rule must be taken from that spot to which the deceased had his most intimate and permanent attachment, where is the seat of that family from whose unbroken continuance the idea of his own representation is derived.

Again, the principles as yet considered contemplate transactions between persons clearly *sui juris*, against whose competency to contract, convey, make a will, or generally to act, no objection can be raised on the ground of any law. A new element of doubt is introduced when any of the parties is pronounced by some law incapable. Now it may be said that the common rule has been that *status* depends on the law of the domicile, and yet that the law of the place of contract has been asserted in a manner which excludes any sovereign from affecting the validity of the contract, on the ground that the *promisor* owes him allegiance. The objection does not touch the English doctrine, which differs from that of most foreign jurists in measuring capacity by the law of the place of contract. But perhaps on this point it will not be entirely satisfactory to pursue any one law throughout. If a Frenchman marry without consent in England at the age of twenty-one, I reprobate that article of the French code which claims to invalidate his marriage, because at home he would, till twenty-five, have needed the consent of his father. That his own sovereign imposes no duty upon him is not to the purpose, when the only sovereign who has at the time the command of his person enjoins him to perform his contract. But what shall we say, if one who at home became of age at twenty contract at that age in England? Must it not be taken that our law intends to validate all contracts made by persons whose reason has actually been matured, and that the law of the domicile is the best possible evidence to establish such maturity? It may be replied, that the same law has been rejected as evidence of immaturity. It must be so rejected, because he who in his own country deals with a foreigner cannot be required to know the foreign law. To him the inquiry would be burdensome, difficult, and perhaps impossible. The foreigner should ascertain the law of the country which he enters, because he easily can ; and if he repudiate a disadvantageous bargain on the ground of his own omission to perform this duty, he convicts himself of having simulated a contract by words which he at all events knew to be idle. The analogy of the criminal law may show that there is no hardship in holding men bound by fraud at an earlier age than that at which they attain a ripe discretion ;

nor, when this is considered, does any country place the full age so early that inconvenience would result from its application to strangers. If then the case of an anticipated majority be essentially different from that of one deferred, why may not the law of the domicile be taken in favour of capacity, not as a law, but as furnishing that evidence of ripeness on which the law of the place of contract will impose the obligation ? This principle, which from the conflicting laws of the domicile and the place of contract would select that which most favoured capacity, has been acted on in Louisiana, and approved in England by Mr Burge. It is also consecrated in the Prussian and Austrian codes.

I have been led to sketch some of the reasoning which, in the middle ages, was applied to what we now call the conflict of laws. If to the topics I then mentioned we add the sacramental power of words to cause qualities in persons and things, and the inseparable inherence in them of those qualities when caused, we shall have a complete picture of the way in which the subject was then treated. Such a statute was, by refined implication, a part of the contract of the parties, or the *corpus juris* decided for it, or at some previous moment it had infixed in the subject or in the object a quality which thenceforward could not be effaced. In the fashion of a succeeding age and of a commercial country, comity, limited by utility, was supposed to be the ground of the reception of foreign laws. But if the schools were unsatisfactory in principle, this doctrine of Huber is vague and uncertain in its results. It is remarkable that in England and America, where his authority has met with a respect which it has not elsewhere enjoyed out of the Netherlands, the name of Huber is now invoked to condemn, on the ground of utility, the conclusions which he pronounced to be useful. The nature and limits of law have seldom been introduced into the discussion, and when they have, the immediate duty to obey has been too often confounded with allegiance, or law has been treated as a command to the judge instead of a command to the party. Yet perhaps it is in the nature and limits of law, as ascertained by that science which legislates for the republic of nations, that the surest foundations of private international jurisprudence can be laid. It is to this possibility that I have wished to draw attention to-night.

## II

### COMMERCIAL BLOCKADE. 1862.

[Reprinted from the *Transactions*[1] *of the Juridical Society*, vol. 1858–63, pp. 681–721.]

THE question of abolishing commercial blockades has been presented under circumstances which at least demand for it an attentive consideration.

At the Paris Congress of 1856, the great European powers mutually stipulated the abolition of privateering. The government of President Pierce declined to bring the United States into that agreement, unless the private property of belligerent subjects was declared free from capture on the seas, except in the cases of breach of blockade and carriage of goods contraband of war. This proposal, which is commonly identified with the name of Mr Marcy, the Secretary of State through whom it was made, not having been immediately accepted by the European powers, time was given for the government of President Buchanan to add to it, in 1859, the farther condition of the abolition of commercial blockades. Mr Cass, the new Secretary of State, announced this condition in his instructions to the ministers of the United States, which were read by them to the foreign ministers at the courts where they resided, and contained the following passage:

[1] [The pamphlet published by Westlake under the title *Commercial Blockade*, London (Ridgway), 1862, embodies in substance the paper published in the *Transactions of the Juridical Society*. L. O.]

"The blockade of an enemy's coast, in order to prevent all intercourse with neutral powers even for the most peaceful purpose, is a claim which gains no additional strength by an investigation into the foundation on which it rests, and the evils which have accompanied its exercise call for an efficient remedy. The investment of a place by sea and land with a view to its reduction, preventing it from receiving supplies of men and material necessary for its defence, is a legitimate mode of prosecuting hostilities, which cannot be objected to so long as war is required as an arbiter of national disputes. But the blockade of a coast, or of commercial positions along it, without any regard to ulterior military operations, and with the real design of carrying on a war against trade, and from its very nature against the trade of peaceful and friendly powers, instead of a war against armed men, is a proceeding which it is difficult to reconcile with reason or with the opinions of modern times. To watch every creek, and river, and harbour upon an ocean frontier, in order to seize and confiscate every vessel, with its cargo, attempting to enter or go out, without any direct effect upon the true objects of war, is a mode of conducting hostilities which would find few advocates if now first presented for consideration."

The fearful evils which the country is now suffering from the commercial blockade of the coast of the insurgent states in America, have extended to the public the interest which Mr Cass's proposition alone would have been sufficient to excite among students of international law.

I have been obliged to come to the conclusion

that commercial blockades ought to be abolished, from motives both of justice and policy : not, indeed, that we can suddenly repudiate our ancient doctrines at the moment when we begin to feel ourselves the evils which we have long inflicted on others ; but our duty is to turn the present lesson to account, and use it at the first legitimate opportunity.

Under the present law of nations, neutral commerce is subject to interference from belligerents in two classes of cases only : the carriage of goods contraband of war, with those cases, as the conveyance of troops, which are analogous to contraband, and blockade. The two classes are quite distinct, both from each other and from the mutual interference to which the commerce of belligerents is subject. The abolition of commercial blockades would in no way impair the power of excluding contraband from an enemy's ports, for the vessels which carry it might be arrested under that law by the same squadron, or by the same cruisers, which now arrest them under the law of blockade, only that squadron or those cruisers would not be paid in part by the capture of neutral vessels, engaged in what I hope to show is an intrinsically neutral trade : nor would the freedom of neutral commerce in any way involve the immunity of a single belligerent vessel, were she public property or private. And the questions of contraband and blockade, which concern neutrals, are as distinct from the third question in the arguments applicable to them as they are in their substance. The chief argument on the former must be that of justice, if not as measuring what belligerents will be disposed to inflict, yet as measuring what neutrals will ultimately submit to. The chief argument for the immunity of private belligerent property must be humanity. Policy will, of course, have to be considered on all the questions ; but as none of them can be decided but by the general consent of nations, the motives of policy which specially affect a single country are likely to be less influential in their decision than the citizens of powerful countries are sometimes willing to believe. I am therefore convinced that whoever would have any one of the three topics usefully discussed must present it on its own basis, as I do in this paper for that of blockade, or that, if there be any natural priority between them, the amendment which is proposed in the name of justice must take precedence of that which is proposed in the name of humanity, and still more of any which its advocates may rest mainly on British policy, real or supposed.

I propose to treat the subject under the following arrangement :

 I. The history of blockade.
 II. The rules of blockade between which we must choose.
 III. The rules of blockade considered on the ground of justice.
 IV. Commercial blockades considered on the ground of general international policy.
 V. Commercial blockades considered on the ground of special British policy.

## I. THE HISTORY OF BLOCKADE

Little is found in ancient times on the rights and duties of neutrals. Belligerents must always have desired to convert neutrals into allies, and when the full attainment of that object seemed hopeless, they must always have desired that neutrals should at least so far take part against the enemy as to discontinue their commerce with him. Nor need we doubt that, when this lesser aid has been refused to sympathy, strong belligerents in all ages have pressed for it as due to justice : similar arguments reproduce themselves under similar circumstances. But there is no trace that the ancient lawyers or philosophers ever theorised on the cases in which it could reasonably be demanded of a neutral that he should discontinue his commerce with the enemy. Such discontinuance is sometimes almost necessarily caused by military operations. Few neutrals, for instance, would, as a mercantile speculation, run the risk of attempting to supply a place actively besieged, though a wish to relieve it might prompt to attempts of the kind, which the besiegers again would summarily repress to the utmost of their power. These cases, therefore, might well be left to take care of themselves ; but where no military operations were otherwise on foot which would naturally impede neutral commerce, the right to undertake operations directed, like the capture of contraband or a commercial blockade, expressly and solely against neutral commerce, could only exist under a positive rule ; and the fact that in the extensive remains of classical literature no such rule appears, to govern claims which, from the permanence of human nature, can hardly have failed to be made, is sufficient of itself to indicate the judgment which the ancient thinkers passed on those claims. The discontinuance by a neutral of intercourse with either belligerent, where not an effect of the operations taking place between the belligerents, must have seemed to them so plain a form of alliance with, or subservience to, the other belligerent, that they did not dream of taking it out of the category of political acts, to rank it with those which were to be argued on grounds of law or ethics.

These views are strongly confirmed by the most remarkable ancient instance that bears on what we now call the duties of neutrality. Immediately after the close of the first Punic war, Carthage was assailed by a formidable insurrection of her African subjects, who for a great length of time besieged the city itself by land. She was aided by Hiero, whom Polybius praises for his policy in upholding Carthage as a rival to Rome : " not," says he, " but that the Romans too kept their treaty, and omitted no point of friendly conduct. At first, indeed, some discussion arose between them and the Carthaginians—for when traders sailed from Italy with supplies for the enemies of the Carthaginians in Africa, and the latter captured and took them into Carthage, till nearly five hundred of them were there in prison at once, the Romans made a complaint on the subject. But afterwards, when this affair had been settled diplomatically, and the Romans had received back all the men as the result of the negotiation, they showed so good a feeling towards the Carthaginians as immediately to make them a present in return of the prisoners that remained from the war in Sicily." Under the treaty, the Romans were not bound to release these prisoners without ransom. " And from that time," proceeds Polybius, " they acceded readily and handsomely to all the demands made upon them, so as even to allow their traders to export continually to the Carthaginians what they wanted, while preventing such export to the enemies of Carthage."—*Polyb.* i. 83.

It may, perhaps, be suggested that the concession thus ultimately made by the Romans was in obedience to some acknowledged rule, and that the position they first took up had reference to the right of enforcing that rule, just as it has been proposed in modern times that neutral governments should undertake the duty of preventing traffic by their subjects in contraband, as a substitute for the interference of the belligerents with them. But it must be observed that the presumption of a rule is displaced by the fact that the Romans acceded to other demands of the Carthaginians as well; and that Polybius does not state of what nature were the supplies furnished to the African insurgents, nor whether the Carthaginians had established a blockade of the insurgents' coast, omissions which such a writer could not have made if rules of contraband and blockade had existed. The conclusion therefore is, that the Carthaginians, as a political act, tried to stop altogether the trade of neutrals with the enemy; and that the Romans, having vindicated their independence by maintaining altogether their trade with either belligerent, voluntarily, by another political act, prohibited to their citizens and subjects the trade with the Africans.

The question seems to have remained, during a large part of the middle ages, on much the same footing as in ancient times. It has indeed been said that a new element was introduced into it by the Mediterranean cities assuming to apply to their mutual quarrels the Roman laws against commerce with the enemies of Rome, and the decrees of the popes against commerce with infidels. But I find it difficult to believe that so palpable a confusion can have been made: that Venice, for example, at war with Genoa, should invoke against Barcelona laws made by emperors or popes for their subjects, [which] could never have been regarded in any other light than as a direct and absurd claim of sovereignty over the neutral. It is more reasonable to suppose that belligerent interference with neutral commerce was justified on political rather than on legal grounds, whenever, at least, in those times of irregular violence, it was thought needful to justify it at all. Accordingly, we find that if a neutral was too strong to be forced into alliance or subservience, and not so placed that his consent to an active alliance was probable, a request that he would at least discontinue his trade with the enemy was thought not unreasonable. Thus, in 1338, Edward III requested the king of Castile to prohibit commerce between his subjects and the Flemings, with whom England was at war; but, unlike the Romans on the occasion I have referred to, the Castilian declined to comply.

It was probably indeed about this time, and under the combined influences of chivalry and extending commerce, that the modern sentiment against a partial or unfair neutrality began to take root. A state must always be at liberty to renounce its neutrality and become an ally in the war, and it may be difficult to show that this greater right does not include the lesser one of aiding either belligerent by any means, and particularly by withdrawing intercourse from the other belligerent. But a salutary responsibility is established for nations, when it is ruled that they shall not inflict on other nations any part of the evils of war, without exposing themselves in return to the chances of war by a declaration of it. Such a declaration is a grave step, and less likely to be resorted to from humour or vague political sympathy, which may easily dictate an unfair neutrality, scarcely less hurtful to the peaceful interests of men than war itself. And the name of amity, unaccompanied by its substance, offends against that spirit of truth and candour, which, however imperfectly developed as yet, marks by its mere presence the greatest ethical superiority of modern over ancient times. Therefore the belief has grown, and ought to be promoted, that neutrality is dishonoured by subservience to, or covert alliance with, either belligerent ; and from the first appearance of that belief, contemporaneously with the wide expansion of commerce, which a just neutrality protects from the ravages of war, it has been a subject of great interest to jurists and statesmen to ascertain the limits of the compliance which belligerents may fairly expect from those who have not become parties to the war.

The first rules which were laid down on this subject prohibited to neutrals only the carriage of troops and contraband, and the introducing into besieged places, besides the ordinary kinds of contraband, supplies of a nature calculated to protract resistance by obviating famine. The latter prohibition must have always amounted in effect to the general interdiction of commerce with besieged places, since places so circumstanced would be very unlikely markets to seek with articles not of some immediate utility for the defence ; but that it was not formally put as a general interdiction appears both from a passage of Grotius presently to be quoted, and from the oldest treaties on the point, which enumerate " men, grain, and provisions" as the articles not to be carried into invested towns. But the practice of blockade, through which belligerents extend the prohibition in question to places besieged only in a figure of speech, is of later introduction, and its history can be traced from the commencement.

The importance of that history lies in the fact that it registers the nature and limits of the consent which each nation has given to the practice, and that by such consent alone can any nation be bound. There are indeed parts of international law, as the rights of embassy, of which the outlines have existed from time immemorial, and which are therefore the common rights of man, like the institutions of property or marriage. It is not necessary to shew the specific consent of any nation to these. There are other parts of international law of which it is possible to assign the origin, but an origin prior to that of modern nations, as the rules concerning the title to national territory may be traced to the private law of Rome. Neither to these is it necessary that the specific consent of any nation should be shewn, for none can be permitted, in matters affecting others, capriciously to withdraw itself from an order of ideas which all have alike inherited. These parts are to international law what the common law is to that of England; but an institution not three centuries old is analogous to our statute law, and the statute law of nations is not enacted by majorities, nor are the writings of private jurists of any authority for it. It is the more necessary to insist on these principles, because the writings of private jurists are apt to carry on these questions a weight to which they have no claim. The men who practically deal with international law are busy statesmen immersed in affairs, and lawyers who, to advise statesmen, snatch a moment from still more engrossing professions. Bynkershoek and Hautefeuille, Grotius and Vattel, lie at hand, and well indexed, but leisure and pains are needed to ascertain the consent of nations from history and treaties. And yet more deceptive is the halo thrown in any country around a writer by the respect which is paid him in its prize courts, though his selection for that respect may have been due merely to his maintaining what were supposed to be the interests of that country. Thus a recent English writer of great ability, who has poured on Hautefeuille the contempt of which he is a master, has exposed himself to a rejoinder, in which it is not necessary to imitate his own style, by elevating Bynkershoek to that popedom of international law which he denies to his later rival. I need not disclaim the worship of Hautefeuille in a paper so opposed as this is to his principles. Yet some tribute is here due to the learning and general accuracy with which he has illustrated the history of neutral rights, and, by placing within every one's hands the means of knowing what obligations each nation has incurred with regard to them, has rendered for the future inexcusable all sciolistic talk about a universally recognised law of blockade, with Bynkershoek and Lord Stowell for its chief expositors. Of what in this kind is due to Hautefeuille, only those can judge who have attempted to go over any part of the same ground. But here my tribute stops. Whether it be the pompously announced primary law of Hautefeuille, or the all-justifying necessity of the Anglo-Dutch school, the adulation of authorities on either side leads to no conclusion. Let reforms be discussed; but, pending their express adoption, you have nothing to oppose to the pretensions, either of a neutral or a belligerent, but his own treaties or his own practice.

I have shewn that up to a certain time the interference of belligerents with neutral commerce, and the submission of neutrals to such interference, were either directed by the political motives arising on each case, or remained mingled with the other lawless incidents of a state of general violence; that at that time these classes of facts began to emerge into a condition of regularity, in which an attempt should be made to govern them in a uniform, general, and legal, and no longer in a desultory, individual, and political manner; and that the first rules sketched out were the prohibition of the carriage of troops and contraband, and of the introduction of supplies into besieged places. This period in the history of the subject is represented by Grotius, who, after mentioning articles so essentially of warlike use that they are always contraband, and those so essentially of pacific use that they are never contraband, proceeds thus:

"In the third class, objects of ambiguous use, there is a distinction to be founded on the state of the war. For if I cannot defend myself without intercepting what is sent, necessity, as we have elsewhere explained, will give me the right to intercept it, but under the obligation of restitution, unless there be further cause to the contrary. If the introduction of the supplies impeded me in the pursuit of my right, and this was open to the knowledge of the person who introduced them, as if I was keeping a town invested or ports closed, and a surrender or peace was already looked for, he will be bound to repay me for the damage occasioned by his fault, like one who has liberated my debtor from prison, or has assisted the flight of my debtor, to my injury ; and to the extent of the damage I may take his goods, and acquire the property therein, for the recovery of what is due to me. If he has not yet caused damage, but has tried to cause it, I shall have the right to compel him, through the retention of his goods, to give security for the future by hostages, by pledges, or in some other way. But if, besides, the injustice of my enemy towards me be very evident, and the introducer of the supplies strengthen my enemy by such introduction in a most iniquitous war, he will no longer be liable to me civilly only, as for damages, but criminally also, like one who rescues a person manifestly guilty from the very hands of the judge ; and on that ground it will be lawful to punish him according to his offence, measured on the principles which we laid down concerning punishments, for which reason he may to that extent be even subjected to spoliation" (*De Jure Belli ac Pacis*).

This results in prohibiting to neutrals, under penalty of confiscation, all commerce with places besieged and in danger of reduction ; for, as I have observed, there could be no practical mitigation in limiting the prohibition to things of essentially warlike, or of ambiguous, use. That the prohibition should be grounded on the evident injustice and iniquity of the besieged, followed from the principles of the author. From the fact that there is no human arbiter to decide on the righteousness of a war, Grotius drew the conclusion, not that no argument can be addressed to neutrals which assumes the righteousness of either belligerent, but—and this must be borne in mind in appreciating his doctrine of necessity—that neutrals must assume the righteousness of whichever belligerent they have for the time being to deal with. Now a merchant caught in attempting to trade with a besieged place has to deal with the besiegers, and therefore the solution which Grotius gives to the question was required by his method.

The treatise of Grotius was published in 1624 : it was in 1584 that an event occurred which has been described as the invention of blockade, and with justice, since it appears to have been the first attempt at prohibiting to neutrals, as of right, the commerce with places not actually besieged. The Dutch government issued in that year a placard, as its proclamations were called, by which it declared all the ports of Flanders then remaining in the power of Spain to be blockaded, that is, according to the then meaning of the word, besieged. These ports were not many, they must have been at that time all more or less strongly fortified, and the naval power of the Dutch was already considerable. It is, consequently, not impossible that a real attack on all the Flemish ports may have been intended, or at least such an intention professed ; and we may presume that, on this first occasion, it was not yet imagined that the notion of blockade could be disconnected from that of siege, and that the innovation consisted in making the public notification of a siege equivalent, as against neutrals, to one actually laid. In this way it is intelligible that Grotius never uses the word blockade, which would be very strange had it become technical, and technical it must have become as soon as it had ceased to convey exclusively its primary meaning of actual hostile investment; and we understand the motive with which he adds the impending reduction of the besieged place as a condition for the exclusion of neutral commerce, a condition which would be absurd if interpreted of degrees of probability in the success of the attack, and must have been intended to secure the reality of the attack against fictitious sieges laid only by placard.

In 1630 the States General again contemplated interdicting neutrals from commerce with Flanders. But the circumstances were so changed that an actual siege of all the Flemish ports at once could not even be pretended. Ostend had passed into the hands of the Spaniards, making a great addition to the importance of the places from which neutrals were to be excluded, while England from a co-belligerent had become a neutral power. Before risking the step, cases for opinion were laid before the Admiralty of Amsterdam, and also, as is believed, before private lawyers. What perplexity these learned persons must have felt, with the book of Grotius under their eyes and only six years old, we may realise from Bynkershoek's naive account of the perplexity which, even in the following century, it could cause him. "Siege," says he, "is the only cause why it is unlawful to convey supplies to the besieged without reference to the question whether they are contraband or not, for besieged persons are compelled to surrender, not by force alone, but by hunger and the want of various things.... Thus far I agree with Grotius, but I wish he had not added the condition that a surrender or peace is already looked for" (*Quæst. jur. pub.*, i. 11). By some means or other, however, the Admiralty and counsel were enabled to come to the conclusion which Bynkershoek also reaches at the end of the discussion from which I have quoted :—" the rule which obtains in the case of towns, which are properly said to be besieged, and which has with good reason been applied to camps, which are as it were besieged, extends also to the enemy's ports, which, when invested by ships, are deemed to be besieged." On the strength of the opinion given, the States General, by the placard of 9th July, 1630, not only declared that the whole coast of Flanders should be deemed under blockade, but announced their intention to confiscate neutral ships caught at any distance sailing for Flanders, as also those which, having broken the blockade, should be caught at any time before the completion of the voyage. This was the full blown modern institution, the official investment substituted for the real siege. But the opinion on which the States acted demanded at least the simulation of an investment, and they released neutral vessels taken when a sufficient naval force for this purpose was not present, with those parts of their cargoes which were not contraband.

This blockade did not prove to be of long duration, and on the next occasion when the Dutch decreed a blockade of Flanders, in 1645, the placard of 1630 was not renewed. The reason of this omission is not stated, but it may be conjectured that the rights claimed by that placard had excited remonstrance from France : certainly at this time a series of treaties commences, to which France was a party, and in which the rules are stated in the old and strict manner. Thus, in 1646, there is a Franco-Dutch treaty, denouncing confiscation of ship and cargo "against those who shall have succoured, or thrown men, grain, or provisions into, a place attacked by his majesty's armies": in 1655, there is an Anglo-French treaty with mutual stipulations translated from those last mentioned, only the word "succoured" being omitted, probably as having been found too vague, for in the interval there had taken place the greatest extension of the claim of blockade ever up to that date attempted by the Dutch: and in 1659, at which time the Spaniards, copying the example of the Dutch, were professing to blockade Portugal, the Franco-Spanish treaty of the Pyrenees, while prohibiting commerce with "towns and places besieged, blockaded, or invested," added an express prohibition of commerce with Portugal, as being a revolted province of Spain, apparently with the object of shewing that the words "besieged, blockaded, or invested" were still regarded by the French as synonymous, and would not have been held to include by their proper force a blockade of Portugal, which the French king might yet, from political motives, be willing to respect. These treaties are in Dumont, t. 6, pt. i, p. 342, & pt. ii, pp. 121 & 264.

During this period, and that which followed down to the English revolution, the conduct of the Dutch was marked by the widest renunciation of the right to interfere with neutral commerce, the widest actual interference with it when opportunity offered, and the absolute refusal to recognise a similar interference with it by others.

In 1652, being at war with the English Commonwealth, they placarded that blockade of all the coasts of the British Isles, to which I have already alluded as having probably suggested the omission of the word "succour" from the Anglo-French treaty of 1655 : for it is undeniable that all neutral commerce whatever does in fact succour a belligerent, and the only question is as to the cases in which such succour may be repressed as amounting to a participation by the neutral in the war. Next, the Dutch refused to recognise the Spanish blockade of Portugal ; and then, as if to justify this last step in their policy, they even for some years outran all other nations in their zeal, on paper, for the old and strict rules which they had been repeatedly violating ever since 1584. Treating with Algiers in 1662, and with Sweden in 1667, they confined the prohibition of commerce with besieged places to contraband, and articles which might tend to the convenience or assistance of the enemy : and these treaties, which will be found in Dumont, t. 6, pt. ii, p. 445, & t. 7, pt. i, p. 37, are remarkable as the last which observe the ancient form, never, as I have before pointed out, of any practical importance, exempting articles of essentially pacific use from the prohibition. The treaty of the Pyrenees, and the Anglo-Swedish one of 1661 (Dumont, t. 6, pt. ii, p. 384), had already made the prohibition general, in respect of the nature of the articles to be introduced into besieged places, though in the latter treaty the right of capture had been restricted to cases of contraband : if, it was said, goods not contraband should be carried by either party to ports or places besieged by the other, they might either be sold to the besiegers or carried away freely to ports not besieged. But besides the formality of exempting articles of essentially pacific use from the restrictions of blockade, the Dutch on these occasions took the utmost pains to confine blockades to cases of siege. The Algerine treaty prohibited the commerce with "towns actually besieged in regular form (*obsidione justa realiter cinctis*) either by sea or land, and by no means in any other case": and the Swedish treaty prohibited it with "fortresses, towns, or places having military garrisons, so long as it shall happen that they are under siege or attack by an armed force, with the intention of reducing them into the power of such force, and, in respect of places situate on the coast, by land as well as by sea." On this followed an Anglo-Dutch treaty in 1674, and another Dutch-Swedish one in 1679, in both of which commerce in articles not contraband is declared to be free, "except with towns or places besieged, shut in, or invested (*obsidione cinctis, circumseptis, vel investitis*)"; to which the English treaty adds "*Gallice, blocquées ou investies*," as if to put on record that, diplomatically as well as etymologically, blockaded meant besieged. And the Franco-Dutch treaty of 1678 is to an effect precisely similar. (Dumont, t. 7, pt. i, pp. 282, 437, 357.)

Only ten years from the date of the last of these treaties with Sweden, the rights of that neutral state were violated in the most flagrant manner by the allied English and Dutch, who concluded between themselves, and notified to all the European powers, the famous convention of 1689, by which they not only prohibited all neutral commerce with the whole coast of France and with all French possessions in every part of the world, but also, applying to the case the rule of the placard of 1630, announced their intention of seizing on the high seas, at any distance from France, any ship which might be found sailing for her ports. But if the treaties were unable to prevent the thing from being done, they seem at least to have influenced the manner of doing it. The convention (Dumont, t. 7, pt. ii, p. 238) does not use the word blockade. It scarcely professes to exercise a belligerent right against neutrals so much as it professes to forbid neutrality. The general preamble, it is true, dwells on the necessity of destroying the commerce of France in order to prevent a great effusion of blood ; but the allies, as if conscious that that plea was insufficient, added a separate preamble to the article containing the principal invasion of neutral rights, in which they recite that many sovereigns have prohibited trade with France and that others will soon prohibit it, wherefore, much in the manner of Lewis the XIV, who revoked the edict of ·Nantes because he said that the conversion of the heretics had rendered it unnecessary, they prohibit trade with France themselves. By a separate article, the allies promised to aid each other in suppressing the resistance which they expected the step would excite. The blockade just begun is generally said to have lasted nearly four years, and to have been then abandoned in consequence of the combined resistance offered by Sweden and Denmark, which gave on this occasion the first example of an armed neutrality. But the naval and diplomatic history of this war is very obscure, and there are reasons, into which it is not necessary now to enter, for thinking that the blockade was not attempted to be enforced for more than some months, and that the armed neutrality of 1693 was caused by other infractions of maritime law.

However this may be, the blockade of 1689 is of great historical importance. It was the first appearance of England on the scene as a blockading power, except in cases of siege : unless we think it necessary to reckon the unlucky attempt of Spain to blockade Portugal, it would seem to have been the first appearance in that character of any power other than the United Netherlands. It is probable that to the alliance of England with the Dutch on this occasion we owe her adoption of the placard of 1630 as the basis of her prize-law on the subject : " the received law of nations," to which reference is continually made in the reports of the English Admiralty and United States' Supreme Courts, means that placard, if it means anything. Lastly, the blockade of 1689 terminates a distinct period, that of the divorce between theory and practice, in which the same powers, when negotiating, attempted to limit, sometimes in an impracticable manner, the belligerent right of restricting neutral commerce, and, when belligerents, restricted that commerce without any other limit than that of what they could venture on, and, apparently, with a complete absence of shame. In the authors and stipulations of that period, the advocates of neutral rights may find more than all they desire : in its practice, belligerents may find precedents for treating neutrals as enemies bound not to retaliate. That which one chiefly misses is the blockade according to what we are now told is " the received law of nations," the application of the state of siege to coasts watched by cruisers in sufficient number to create what the captor's prize courts regard as great danger, but limited to coasts so watched, and accompanied by capture for intended and accomplished breaches, but limited to the same voyage. This blockade, if I mistake not, they will find neither in the authors nor in the stipulations of the period, but only in the placard of 1630. Nor will they find it in the practice of the period, farther than as that and some other blockades of Flanders may have answered the description ; and then only by accident, since on the one hand the Dutch did not hesitate on other occasions to placard the blockade of coasts which they had not cruisers enough to watch, while on the other hand Grotius and the treaties make it clear that even such blockades as those which there may have been of Flanders were not generally regarded as rightful.

It was certain that the divorce between theory and practice would not long be tolerated when, with the preponderating power at sea, the interest in maintaining blockades had been transferred from Holland to England, not yet a manufacturing country. In spite of all that has been written on " the perfidy of Albion," neither our statesmen nor our lawyers have ever been of that class who can systematically say one thing and do another. Subjects of a state whose liberties are held by law, they have never felt easy in the reckless violation of acknowledged rule ; and the worst that can be charged against them in these matters is the haughtiness with which they have tried to impose on others the rules which suited themselves, and the ready ear which they have lent to every allegation of " a received law of nations " in their favour.

Accordingly, so great was the force now brought to bear in support of the doctrine of blockade, as it has since become traditional in the English Court of Admiralty, that the liberty of neutral commerce in all cases but those of siege and contraband, after being once more feebly asserted in the treaty of 1701 between Holland and Denmark (Dumont, t. 8, pt. i, p. 32), was laid at rest for above a century, when it was revived by Napoleon's Berlin decree. In the language already quoted from Bynkershoek, who made himself about this time the first and greatest interpreter of the new rules, the law applicable to besieged places was extended to places "as it were besieged," and to those "deemed to be besieged." So completely technical did the word blockade become that its original meaning of siege by investment was forgotten. Blockades of coast lines just limited enough to be watched by cruisers with some show of efficiency, and capture under the rules of 1630 before and after actual breach, became familiar in every war down to the fall of the first French empire. And the continental powers began to aim only at establishing some rule which should prevent ineffective, and therefore partial and inequitable, blockades.

Great Britain admitted this pretension, but the question remained how an effective blockade was to be defined. Her prize courts, as well as those of the United States, which have adopted her rules, seem to have held, and to hold, that the blockade is effective if, by all the means employed to enforce it—that is, before breach, through capture by cruisers on the plea of intended breach; upon attempted breach, through capture by the blockading squadron;

and after breach, by cruisers till completion of the voyage—if, I say, it is on the whole very much more probable than not that a neutral engaged in the business of blockade-running will get caught in some one or other of these ways. But the continental governments, Holland herself included after her decline reduced her below the rank of a blockading power, have uniformly maintained, since they have ceased to require an actual siege, that the blockade is only effective if there be manifest danger in entering the blockaded port, from the cannon either of ships, stationary and sufficiently near one another, or of works on land. This, for example, is laid down, with more or less variety of expression, in the treaty of 1742 between France and Denmark, in that of 1753 between Holland and the Two Sicilies, in the declarations and treaties of armed neutrality in 1780, in the various adhesions of the other continental states to that armed neutrality or its rules, and in the declarations and treaties of armed neutrality in 1800; and though when Russia, by a change of policy consequent on the death of the Emperor Paul, abandoned the armed neutrality of 1800, her treaty of 1801 with England required for a blockade the presence only of ships stationary *or*, instead of *and*, sufficiently near to create an evident danger in entering, yet in 1823 she assured the United States that she no longer held herself bound by that engagement (Wheaton's *Elements of Int. Law*, edition of 1863 by Lawrence, editor's note 235). In several of these pieces the place to be blockaded is described as attacked: yet, except in the treaty of 1787 between France and Russia, in which the rule of the armed neutrality of 1780 is reproduced with a variation requiring an attack by a number of ships proportioned to the strength of the place, the word is not amplified and enforced by such detailed expressions as occur in the treaties of the 17th century; and it must be admitted that the word was at this time used only from habit, or at least without any intention of any longer requiring a real attack by way of siege. Napoleon, indeed, by the preamble of the Berlin decree in 1806, complained "that Great Britain extends the law of blockade to unfortified towns and commercial ports, to harbours and the mouths of rivers, though, according to right reason and the usage of all civilised nations, it is only applicable to strong places." But this reassertion of the old rule was not made in season, and met at the time with very little support even from the continental publicists.

Such is the present state of international law as to the conditions of a lawful blockade, for the treaty of Paris in 1856 did little to elucidate the difficulty. "Blockades," it said, "to be binding, must be effective, that is, maintained by a force sufficient really to prohibit access to the coast of the enemy": an ambiguous phrase, which seems rather to lean towards the continental view, without, however, positively excluding the Anglo-American. France has, by her acts on numerous occasions, as in the blockades of Mexico, Buenos Ayres, and those during the Russian war, still farther precluded herself from impugning commercial blockades. The continental interpretation of an effective blockade is absolutely inconsistent with the Anglo-American claim to capture at a distance, for intended breach;

and it is a subject of dispute how far it is reconcilable with capture for past breach, during the remainder of the voyage. For the rest, one traditional observance, handed down from the time when blockade meant siege, has been respected by all nations alike : it is that a blockade cannot be established by privateers. Even the Anglo-American rule, which admitted privateers to enforce blockades, required at least a single ship of war to establish one.

*Etymology of blockade.*—I present my note on the etymology of the word blockade rather as an appendix to, than as a portion of, the historical part of this paper, in order to avoid the least appearance of treating it as in any sense or degree an authority for the narrative. I should do injustice to a narrative which rests on documents, and to a meaning, that of close investment, which it is otherwise abundantly certain that the word bore, by letting either seem to repose on so fertile a source of dispute as an etymology.

The word *blocus*, or *blockade*, is neither to be found in Du Cange, nor in the vocabulary of barbarous Latinity appended to *Facciolati*. *Bloc*, in the language of the Walloon country, signified a high mound ; whence persons who had died under sentence of excommunication, and whom it was not lawful to bury beneath the soil, were said to be *imblocati*, because the earth was heaped over their bodies as they lay on the surface (Du Cange, *v*. Imblocatus). We are brought still nearer to the root by *bloche*, which, in the dialect of Champagne, signified a clod of earth (Du Cange, *v*. Blesta) ; and *blocage* even now denotes in French the rubblework often used to fill up the interior of walls, or a rough wall itself, when entirely composed of such work. Our own *block* is obviously allied, though we do not use it of stones or nodules so small as to serve for rubblework. Thus, a stone, nodule, clod, or mass, smaller or larger; a funereal barrow, a dyke or mound, themselves large blocks or masses, and piled up of smaller clods and rubble; even, if occasion serves, a rough and ready wall, built with the unwrought materials obtainable on the spot; lastly, a circumvallation: such is the series of ideas presented to us by the words of this family. It is interesting to observe that the word itself, as well as its juristic extension to the cruising of a few ships off a port or a coast, comes to us from the great battlefield of Europe, the Walloon and Flemish country, of which the soil has been turned by the spade of the foreign soldier as often as by that of the native peasant.

II. THE RULES OF BLOCKADE BETWEEN WHICH WE MUST CHOOSE

RULE A.—*That blockade is only lawful in cases of siege.*

The best expression of this rule is that derivable from the Dutch-Swedish treaty of 1667. Lawful blockade is only of "fortresses, towns, or places having military garrisons, so long as it shall happen that they are under siege or attack by an armed force, with the intention of reducing them into the power of such force; and in respect of places situate on the coast, by land as well as by sea."

I have shewn that a rule agreeing in the main

with this was adopted in the treaties on the subject down to the beginning of the eighteenth century. The difference is that the treaty just quoted is the only one which expresses the condition of an attack by land as well as by sea, except so far as that condition may be implied by the word "invested," as applied to blockaded places; and I do not suppose that that word was meant to apply to it. On the other hand, Mr Cass, who mentions "investment by sea and land," appears, if his words be strictly pressed, to have proposed a form of the rule even more stringent than adopted in the treaty of 1667. Thus the siege of Sebastopol would have fallen within the latter rule, but not within Mr Cass's, for the place was attacked by land as well as by sea, and with a very effective intention of reducing it, but was never completely invested by land. A complete investment by land appears to me an unnecessary condition; while on the other hand, if an attack by sea were declared sufficient, it would be difficult to secure the reality of the attack, as a fleet might lie off a port under pretext of preparing for an attack, or while needlessly protracting the operations.

But, under any of the modifications above mentioned, this rule would amount to prohibiting the blockade of merely commercial ports; for such a port, being undefended, must be occupied as soon as attacked, and therefore the only alternative which the rule would leave would be to occupy it or withdraw from it, but not to blockade it. The rule would also prohibit the merely commercial blockade of ports at once military and commercial, for the alternative would be to proceed with a real attack or to withdraw. Nor is it easy, or perhaps even possible, to frame any rule which shall successfully compass these objects without proceeding on the principle of requiring an actual siege or attack.

Of course the capture or occupation of ports might produce some of the effects which flow from blockades. Thus, if in the Russian war the allies had landed troops and occupied Odessa instead of blockading it, no more grain would have reached it from the interior, and the export of grain from that port would therefore have been stopped as effectually as by the blockade. But the occupation of commercial ports would not, on the whole, produce results at all comparable in magnitude with those of blockades, because the process would be a much more costly one, and could not be so extensively applied.

RULE B.—*The continental rule that blockades must be effective.*

This is the rule which we have seen that the powers of the European continent have generally adopted in the treaties on the subject since the beginning of the eighteenth century. The modes of expression are various, differing particularly in completeness. They all, however, mean that there must be manifest danger in entering the blockaded port, from the cannon either of ships, stationary and sufficiently near one another, or of works on land. Such also is the apparent sense of the treaty of Paris in 1856, which runs thus :—
" blockades, to be binding, must be effective, that is, maintained by a force really sufficient to prohibit

access to the coast of the enemy." This rule permits the blockade of commercial ports.

RULE C.—*The rule of the sea powers that blockades must be effective.*

No treaty has been concluded on the footing of this rule, unless that of Paris in 1856, and those between England and the Baltic States in 1801, can be so interpreted. The rule must therefore be chiefly collected from the decisions of prize courts, and cannot be stated with full certainty. Perhaps, however, the following attempt does not do it injustice. "You may capture neutrals at any distance from the blockaded port or coast, either for the offence of being bound for it, or for that of having made their way out, provided in the latter case it be during the same voyage; and you may capture them on the spot, in the fact of trying to break the blockade: if by all of these means together the chances are very great that an offender against your law will be caught, the blockade is effective." Capture during any part of the same voyage, for having come out of a blockaded port, is generally, but not always, sanctioned by the supporters of Rule B also.

This is the rule maintained in theory by England, but in numerous wars, and notably in that of 1803–1814, exceeded by her in practice. We have seen that similar language might formerly have been used of Holland, but, since she has declined below the rank of a blockading power, she has supported the continental Rule B. The United States inherited Rule C from the Anglo-Dutch jurists and precedents, but have recently concluded many treaties to the effect of B, and are not enforcing the present blockade at a distance from the spot. Except in the ambiguous case of 1801, the Baltic States have ranged themselves, in the matter of blockade, with the continental and not with the sea powers.

The consequences of this rule are, commercial blockades in their worst form, not limited to particular ports, for the rule does not require the danger to be incurred from stationary ships, but extending over entire coast lines, for any number of leagues over which cruisers can exercise any moderately efficient surveillance; for, observe, the prize courts which must judge whether the blockade can be brought within this elastic rule are those of the captor's country. Also, general disturbance of neutral commerce in all seas.

### III. THE RULES OF BLOCKADE CONSIDERED ON THE GROUND OF JUSTICE

RULE A.—A neutral cannot be touched by a belligerent unless he has in some way identified himself with the enemy. Actual mixing in the hostilities is such an identification, and to relieve a place which is the actual object of attack at the time, whether such attack be conducted only by sea, or by land also, is actually to mix in the hostilities; therefore blockade in the case of siege is justifiable. To ship a cargo to or from a country with which the shipper is at peace, that cargo being neither contraband nor destined for the supply of a besieged place, is neither an actual mixing in the hostilities, nor in any way an identification of the shipper with the enemy; therefore blockade except in the case of siege is unjustifiable.

These maxims I hold to be clear, and they justify Rule A as well in what it permits as in what it forbids, except that they leave the condition of an attack by land as a trifling concession of principle made to neutrals for the sake of having a better rule. The objections to these maxims will be best considered under the other form which they assume, as attempted justifications of Rule C, the supporters of which are obliged to take the most opposite view to mine of what is implied in neutral and unneutral conduct.

RULE B.—The theory of neutral and unneutral conduct, contained in the above justification of Rule A, is often admitted by continental writers, who nevertheless proceed to justify Rule B on technical grounds, which have no connection with neutrality.

They say that a blockading squadron effects an actual conquest of that portion of the sea which is comprised within the crossing fires of its broadsides, assisted, it may be, by that of batteries on land, and may therefore lawfully refuse to any vessels the right of passage through or across that portion of the sea, just as it might refuse the right of passage through or across any part of its territory on land. This theory exactly covers the extent of Rule B, as understood without the right of subsequent capture for a successfully completed breach of blockade. So far as their fires cross, and no farther, can stationary ships cause manifest danger to a vessel entering a port. And, since a territorial sovereign may dictate laws and enforce them within his territorial limits, but cannot pursue and punish beyond those limits for an offence committed within them, therefore the breach of blockade can, on this theory, be only punished by capture on the spot, and not by capture on the high seas for intended or past breach. But the theory does not lead to any distinction between commercial and military blockades, for the sea off one port must be as liable to conquest by ships stationed in it as that off another. Consequently, it is argued, blockades maintained by stationary ships are lawful, whatever the character of the place blockaded, and whether or not any attempt be made to reduce it into the possession of the blockading force.

But, I answer, the sea is not the subject of property or dominion except as appurtenant to the land, to the owner of which it belongs to the extent of cannon range from it. Admitting, therefore, that the portion which the blockading squadron is said to have conquered lies within cannon range of the shore, and would therefore be transferred by a transfer of the dominion of the shore, I still cannot find any principle on which a claim to dominion over it can be sustained by persons who, by the hypothesis, have not yet conquered the shore. Again, the sea, within the limits mentioned, remains within cannon range of the shore, at the same time that the fires of the blockading squadron cross over its surface. How, then, as a matter of fact, is its conquest complete? and how can it be made out, on the theory in question, though the defenders of that theory are obliged to admit it, that a neutral vessel is not in her right if she chooses to brave the blockader's fire, and run in under cover of the shore batteries? Thirdly, as a matter of fact again, the shore batteries have usually so complete a command of all that part of the sea which is reckoned to be territorial, that blockading squadrons in general lie just outside it. M. Hautefeuille, upon this, is driven to maintain that ships of war conquer even those portions of the high seas which lie within range of their guns; a tenet which I find to be altogether inadmissible. Lastly, it is an established rule, that when a territorial sea forms the highway to the dominions of another sovereign, the right of passage through it cannot be refused. Consequently, even if we suppose a blockading squadron to have conquered the territorial sea outside a port, I submit that the question is no farther advanced. The shore still belongs to another sovereign, and you are therefore still thrown back on the previous question whether the passage, which a neutral intends to make through your territorial sea to the dominions of that other sovereign, is consistent with the duties of neutrality. If it is, you can no more forbid it than Turkey can close the Dardanelles against trading vessels bound for the Russian ports and the Black Sea.

I adhere therefore to the theory of neutral and unneutral conduct, above developed, as the only just foundation of the law of blockade.

RULE C.—It has been said in support of this rule that it is an unneutral act to carry on any trade with a belligerent, because the belligerent is thereby strengthened; and that the other belligerent is consequently entitled to prohibit all such trade by means of a blockade. This is as much as to say that my baker is guilty of unjustifiable presumption if he employs my tailor, with whom I have a law-suit. But, to treat the argument seriously, if commerce with the enemy, other than contraband, is in itself neutral, it needs no blockade to make it unlawful, and a belligerent may stop it without even the slender formalities required by Rule C: at the same time he will be bound, in fairness, himself also to forego the advantage of commerce with neutrals. Such are the inevitable results, extravagant on the one hand, absurd on the other, of this doctrine. But if such commerce be not in itself unneutral, the blockade cannot make it unneutral, because the right to establish the blockade must depend on the intrinsic character of the commerce. Plainly the belligerent cannot treat an act as injurious, or infringing on his rights, merely because he finds it detrimental to his interests, considered without reference to the moral or legal relations in which his interests stand to those of third parties. Putting the war out of the question, the neutral has an incontestable right to traffic with either belligerent : the war, to which he becomes a party so far only as he interferes in its operations, cannot affect that right while he abstains from such interference. If the neutral traffic happens to be more advantageous to one belligerent than to the other, that must be reckoned among the natural conditions of the struggle, just as the comparative resources and geographical situations of the belligerents.

Again, it has been asserted that a neutral is

bound to assume the justice of the war, and may therefore be treated by a belligerent as one who wilfully impedes the prosecution of a right of which he cannot affect ignorance. In some minds this notion has arisen from misunderstanding the principle that, as against neutrals, every war is a *justum bellum*, that is, not a *just*, but a *lawful* war. The neutral must admit the legality of the state of war as between the belligerents, and therefore bear in silence the mischiefs which may indirectly follow to him from the measures which they aim directly at one another. But with the justice of the cause of war he has nothing to do, and passes no opinion on it either way : nor can he possibly be bound to assume the justice of both sides at once, as he must be if he is bound to assume that of either. In the mind of Grotius, the assumption which he always tacitly makes, that the neutral must assume the justice of the belligerent with whom he has for the time to deal, arose of course in a more subtle manner. He only asked himself what belligerents might do. If it had occurred to him to ask what neutrals are bound to suffer, the necessity of drawing an answer from principles which the neutrals must admit would have presented the whole subject to him under a different aspect.

It is a principle that, as just intimated, war must be carried on directly against the enemy, and may be so carried on with the utmost vigour. If the neutral places himself where, when you strike the enemy, the blow reaches him through the enemy, he cannot complain of the vigour with which you have struck ; but you may not strike the enemy through him. Now whom does a commercial blockade directly strike? You fire into a neutral, board him, put him in irons if he resists, sell his ship and cargo, and appropriate the price; other neutral ships are deterred by the example from sailing for the same port, neutral workshops are closed, and neutral subjects starve in consequence of these acts in which no enemy's presence is discoverable. Yet men have been found to say that all this is aimed directly against the enemy's commerce, as if the smart which the neutral feels arose from an occult sympathy with some enemy on whom your blows immediately fell! One is led to ask whether for such reasoners there are any facts, or whether everything is not regarded by them as the sport of rhetoric.

Sometimes, again, resort is had to the doctrine of necessity in order to justify blockades to the extent of Rule C. Nations, which have no common political superior, are compared to persons living in a state of nature; and there are attributed to them those rights of self-preservation which such persons would possess. If a nation, it is argued, cannot defend itself without destroying neutral commerce, then it may destroy neutral commerce. Now the first remark which occurs on this is that nations seldom have to fight for self-preservation, but generally fight to gain or preserve advantages in the mode of their existence, and that we seek for reasons applicable to all wars, and not to some only.

But, farther, if even we suppose a war really waged for the preservation of national existence, such a war does not necessarily create rights against third parties. What a man may do against his fellow, prior to, or independent of, the institution of society, does not depend on the mere fact that there is no third person to set limits to his actions : it must flow from his nature. That is indeed confessed, as soon as natural rights are treated as capable of enumeration, and self-preservation is named as one of them : for if the mere absence of a political superior were sufficient to create a right, everything would be rightful in a state of nature. Therefore, in order to vindicate for a nation the same natural right of self-preservation which belongs to individuals, it is not sufficient to remark that nations have no common political superior, but the nature of their life must be analysed and it must be shown to present those qualities on which the right in question is founded. Now national life and the want of it differ only as more or less favourable conditions under which the several members of the body pass their individual lives. The extinction of national life is in truth the modification of some millions of individual existences, a modification often so unfavourable to all moral and material wellbeing that very large rights arise for the sake of preventing it, though never, even then, without reference to the guilt of those who have endangered so valuable a national existence. But it is not true that all national life confers rights for its preservation. To take an extreme case as an example, a nation may be imagined composed of fragments differing in blood, language, and history, held together by the brute force of an army, and presenting a constant focus of disorder to the surrounding regions of the earth, through the natural tendency of the parts to separate from each other, and unite with neighbouring bodies for which they possess affinity. Is it meant to say that that nation, in other words, that that army, by the mere fact of the supremacy which it has grasped, gains rights against third parties who do not mix themselves in any way with its proceedings ? But to return to general considerations, the moment it is realised that national life is but a form, governing the individual lives of the aggregate mass of citizens, it must be perceived that in order to claim for a nation, as against neutrals, the same rights of self-preservation which belong to individuals in a state of nature, as against unoffending persons, it is necessary to claim for individuals the right to inflict on unoffending persons, for the sake of preserving what they deem to be some more favourable condition of existence, all that they might inflict on them for the sake of preserving existence itself.

In conscience, no man can inflict a mischief on an unoffending person, in order to avoid a not greater mischief to himself. Thus, A cannot, in conscience, kill B in order to avoid being killed by C. But farther, the right as against the third party, or the third party's duty of submitting to the exercise of the right, does not depend merely on its conscientious assertion. If A and C fight, the fact that A is in danger, and, even conscientiously, seeks to inflict a lesser mischief on B in order to escape the danger, is not conclusive as to B's duty of submitting to the infliction. B may, in all good conscience, claim to exercise his own judgment on the quarrel ; and, if he finds A to be in the wrong, he may close against him the desired means of escape, except on condition of his doing towards C that which he, B, erroneously or not is immaterial so long as it be conscientiously, believes to be just. Without this right of the third party, which in very many cases is also a duty, civil society itself would be an injustice. B is rated to the police in order that A may not be robbed by C. B, in this, suffers a lesser mischief in order that A may avoid a greater; but B has, in return, the right of seeing that A does not call in the police to gratify his own malice against C.

If we apply these principles to international relations, the result is obvious. It is darkening knowledge by words without understanding, to talk of what a belligerent may do against a neutral by natural right, and yet refuse the neutral his right to judge of the merits of the cause, which is a right equally natural if he is to suffer for the cause. The nations of the earth are not yet prepared for an universal system of arbitration. Granted, and the consequence is, that they are not yet in a position in which belligerents can justly claim to inflict sufferings on neutrals. If a belligerent attempts to meddle with the commerce of a neighbour who strictly observes all the duties of neutrality, and at the same time haughtily prohibits that neighbour from expressing an opinion on the justice of the war, then, however conscientious the belligerent may be, the neutral has a clear right to refuse submission; and the sooner neutrals make it a rule to refuse submission in such cases, the more they will help forward the advent of arbitration as a substitute for war.

I conclude then that the attempted justification of commercial blockades by the doctrine of necessity will not bear criticism, and that their justice must turn on the question of neutral or unneutral conduct, in which balance we have already tried them and found them wanting.

### IV. COMMERCIAL BLOCKADES CONSIDERED ON THE GROUND OF GENERAL INTERNATIONAL POLICY

There has been much discussion lately on the proposal of Mr Marcy to exempt private belligerent property from capture on the seas, the cases of blockade and contraband excepted. In that discussion the argument has been used, that wars are made rarer and shorter by being made more terrible to belligerents. Whether the fact be as alleged it will be well worth enquiring, on the proper occasion, by the light both of reason and history; in the meantime the assertion wears a certain appearance of plausibility. But an echo of that argument has been allowed to find its way into the discussion of the present question, for it has been said that wars are made shorter by being made more terrible to neutrals, who are thereby goaded into interfering and putting an end to them. I must confess that this assertion would have seemed to me devoid of plausibility, had it not been prominently put forward as the statesman's view, and the opposite view stigmatised as the narrow and commercial one.

The patient acquiescence of the European states for two years and a half, reckoning to the publication of this paper, in that blockade which, of all those recorded, has occasioned the widest and deepest suffering among their population, ought now at length to dispel the dream that blockades shorten wars by provoking to intervention. If intervention should come in the present instance after all, is it from England or France that it may be expected? In other words, will the blockade have been the motive, or the desire of obtaining a friendly neighbour for the remodelled state of Mexico? But, if intervention should in another case be more speedily and surely provoked by a blockade, yet, being the mere effect of the smart, it must necessarily be of a nature adverse to the blockading power, and the arrangement by which it may patch up the quarrel must fail to be based on that calm appreciation of the causes of discord from which alone a permanent settlement can be expected. No man more desires than I do that arbitration may be wisely and effectively employed to compose the differences between nations. But to regard that object as attainable, without raising the arbitrator above the passing interests created by the conflict, is one of those errors which are only made in defending established abuses.

Another argument which has been used against the proposed change, and this too by a statesman, is, that it would tend to prolong wars by equalising the resources of the belligerents. The dreaded consequence of equalisation must be admitted to be in most cases true in fact; it is the stronger belligerent who is most likely to profit by the system of commercial blockades, and exclude the weaker from the legitimate benefit of neutral commerce. But is equalisation to be dreaded? For several centuries we have been in the habit of going to war to preserve the balance of power. Lately we have been accustomed to hear that our fears were often vain, and that the balance of power did not need such elaborate and costly righting. Still it is rather surprising to hear a system recommended just because it tends to destroy the balance of power. The argument may be valuable as a proof of the extent to which old ideas are losing their hold even on the minds of statesmen. But surely it cannot be seriously meant to say that, to make the liberties of every country depend on its preparation to stand the shock of a first campaign, is henceforth the great object of international law? Let those who have avowed that they admire commercial blockades because they tend to make the scale which is momentarily lighter kick the beam, ask themselves whether, if a war was to break out between Italy and Austria, their only, or their first, wish would be that it should be short, unconditionally short, without reference to any other consideration? Would they even express that wish of a war, if any most unhappily should arise, between England and France, remembering what has been the usual fortune of the first years of such wars?

Except that extreme inequality of preparation which lays a country open to be struck decisively in one campaign, there is no circumstance, between powers tolerably matched in resources, which has any influence, either in inviting to war or in prolonging it, that is worth naming in comparison with the moral and political interests at stake in their differences. I attach therefore but small importance to the argument that this or that rule concerning belligerent rights tends to promote peace. But to those who think fit to enter into such considerations, I would suggest that at least no arrangement can be devised which might more effectually deter any maritime state from war, than one by which, while its own commerce should remain in that event exposed to the mischiefs it had provoked, the commerce of neutrals should be exempted from them. Commercial blockades have been chiefly valuable to belligerents, by enabling them to restrain neutrals from using the mercantile opportunities created by their neighbours' madness. Under the arrangement alluded to, if a mercantile nation went to war, it would do so at the risk of its commerce.

## V. Commercial Blockades considered on the ground of Special British Policy

I shall take the liberty of introducing this part of my subject in the words of Mr Cobden : I could not claim an equal authority for the result of any independent researches I might make into the statistics, but the truth of the case, as Mr Cobden has presented it, must commend itself to the common sense of every one.

"One-third of the inhabitants of these islands, a number equal to the whole population of Great Britain at the commencement of this century, subsist on imported food. No other country contains half as many people as the United Kingdom dependent for subsistence on the produce of foreign lands. The grain of all kinds imported into England in 1861 exceeded in value the whole amount of our imports sixty years ago : and the greater portion of this supply is brought from the two great maritime states, Russia and America, to whom, if to any countries, the belligerent right of blockade must have for us a valuable application. If left to the free operation of nature's laws, this world-wide dependence offers not only the best safeguard against scarcity, but the surest guarantee for regularity of supply; but a people so circumstanced is, beyond all others, interested in removing every human regulation which interferes with the free circulation of the necessaries of life, whether in time of peace or war,—for a state of war increases the necessity for insuring the means of feeding and employing the people.

" This is, however, a very inadequate view of the subject. For the raw materials of our industry, which are in other words the daily bread of a large portion of our population, we are still more dependent on foreign countries...It may be alleged of nearly all articles of food or raw materials, transported over sea, that more than one half is destined for these islands. It follows that were we, in the exercise of the belligerent right of blockade, to prevent the exportation of those commodities, we should inflict greater injury on ourselves than on all the rest of the world, not excepting the country with which we were at war : for if we could effectually close the ports of one or more of these countries against both exports and imports, we should be merely intercepting the supply of comparative luxuries to them, while we arrested the flow of the necessaries of life to ourselves; and for every cultivator of the soil, engaged in the production of cotton or other raw materials, thereby doomed to idleness, three or four persons would be deprived of employment in the distribution and manufacture of those commodities.

" These facts are an answer to those who maintain that it is necessary to reserve in our hands the right of blockade, as an instrument of coercion in case of war. Against such countries as France, Germany, Holland, Belgium, &c., blockades have lost their force, owing to the extension of the railway system throughout the continent of Europe. In cases where a blow may still be struck at the commerce of a nation,—of what use, I would ask, is a weapon of offence which recoils with double force on ourselves? It would be but a poor consolation to our population, who were subjected to the evils of enforced idleness and starvation, to be told that the food and raw materials destined for their subsistence and employment were rotting in the granaries of ruined cultivators in Russia or America.

" These considerations have always led us, practically, to violate our own theory of a commercial blockade, whenever the power to do so has remained in our hands, even when the exigencies of our situation as a manufacturing people were far less pressing than they are at present. If we consult the experience of our past wars, we shall find that, as a belligerent, we have invariably abstained from taking effectual measures for preventing the productions of our enemies from reaching our shores. It is true we have maintained, for our navy, the traditional right and duty of a blockade, whilst (I beg your attention to the distinction) we have invariably connived at its evasion.

" A fair deduction from these facts and premises leads us to a very grave national dilemma We persist in upholding a belligerent right, which we have always shrunk from enforcing, and shall never rigorously apply, by which we place in the hands of other belligerents the power, at any moment, of depriving a large part of our population of the supply of the raw materials of their industry, and of the necessaries of life. In this respect the question of blockade is essentially different from that of the capture of private property at sea. In the latter case we are only liable to injury when we choose to become belligerents, whereas, in the former, we are exposed to serious calamities as neutrals; and England, by proclaiming the policy of non-intervention, has recently constituted herself the great neutral power."—*Letter from Mr Cobden, M.P., to Henry Ashworth, Esq.; Alex. Ireland & Co.*, 1862.

The chief argument from special British policy which is advanced against this cogent reasoning is, that " the last shred of our naval supremacy " would be surrendered with commercial blockades. I give the words which have been so often used, because the romantic appeal they make to our feelings constitutes their only strength. Nothing has in fact endangered our naval supremacy so much as these blockades. They have produced three armed neutralities, in 1693, 1780, and 1800, from the last of which we were delivered by the death of the Emperor Paul; and in the great war with the French empire they would have produced an armed neutrality more formidable than any previous one, but for the sympathy which Europe felt with us against the imperial conqueror. In any war of ours towards which two or three of the great maritime powers shall really feel as neutrals, our naval existence, not to speak of supremacy, will depend on our not calling down the indignation of those powers on our heads by undertaking commercial blockades of any importance. Let no one imagine that in such a case the United States will respect our blockade as we are now respecting theirs. They would not be bound to do so if, as on previous occasions, we trafficked in licences for the breach of our blockade, or in any other way connived at the productions of the blockaded country reaching our ports. And unless we were prepared so to connive, we should never be fatuous enough to establish a great blockade.

There is, however, another argument which must not be passed without notice. It is that we should lose the means which we have so often lately employed, and sometimes in conjunction with France, for the coercion of small powers, as Greece and Buenos Ayres. But the loss need not be regretted. When such coercion becomes a necessity, the end may as easily be attained by war : the ten years' blockade of Buenos Ayres, to which a few regiments landed would have dictated terms in a week, would lead one to say, much more easily. And war, in these cases, is the fairest plan. The belligerent, for in truth he always is such, does not then evade the responsibility of his acts. Even the fear that in case of a declaration of war, the weaker power will commission privateers, which was probably a leading motive for pacific blockades, now no longer exists. Nor was it ever a course worthy of great nations, unhappily involved in differences with small ones, to snap, in the mode of proceeding, at advantages which could not have been obtained against a state powerful enough to meet the blockade by declaring war itself.

I have now given the reasons why it seems to me that both practical English statesmen, and the theoretical students of international law, ought to subscribe to the proposition which has been made to abolish commercial blockades. It is, unhappily, much too late to apply the amendment, even if now adopted, to the present war. The evil example set from this side of the Atlantic must bear its fruit. But the fruit it is bearing may suggest to the nations of the earth whether the division of labour, which it has been justly said is the essence of free trade, can be carried out with safety, if commercial blockades are to continue lawful. In all other ways we help forward the time when every climate and soil shall be devoted to the produce for which it is best adapted, and every description of natural power shall be applied to work up that produce, wherever nature has made its application cheapest. Can the increasing millions of the human race be fed and clothed, taught and elevated, on any other terms? Yet, can any nation trust itself to those terms, if the machinery of so delicate a system can be thrown out of gear at a moment's notice, not by its own madness alone—the ruinous consequences may help to restrain it from that—but by the madness of any other people, over whom it has no control at all till after the fact, and a control, even then, of the most imperfect kind, and not exercisable without lending a powerful support to one or other of the belligerents, whose policy the neutral may, perhaps, abhor, though a stupid system of international law has made him interested, almost for life or death, in the ill success of the blockade which the opponent of that policy enforces?

The answers to be given to these queries are not more clear than the remedy proposed is simple and easy. And I close this paper with the expression of a full confidence that before long the rule for which I have been pleading will be established as that of future wars.

# III

## IS IT DESIRABLE TO PROHIBIT THE EXPORT OF CONTRABAND OF WAR? 1870.

[Reprinted from the *Transactions of the Social Science Association*, 1870, pp. 109–125.]

I. THE members of this Association must be well aware of the circumstances which have given occasion to the present discussion. Weapons and munitions of war were said to have been largely exported, and have been to some extent exported, from England to France since the outbreak of the present contest; and not only does the German press vehemently denounce this as a breach of neutrality on the part of England, but even the North German Government has made remonstrances to the British Government on the subject. The latter has declined to take action on those remonstrances, and the anger against neutrals which, on one ground or another, war hardly ever fails to excite, and even to leave behind, in the minds of belligerents, seems likely, as between Germany and England, to be placed for some time to come on this ground. On the other hand, the English press has on this occasion been far from showing the unanimity with which it generally repels all foreign demands for special British legislation, and several of our newspapers, including some which generally represent the more advanced schools of thought, have advocated the passing of an Act of Parliament to make the export of contraband illegal. It is the propriety of such an enactment that we are now to discuss.

II. The first step in the discussion will be to come to a clear understanding as to the existing state of International Law on the subject. There is happily no difficulty in doing so, the rule being simple, and all nations being agreed about it. I will express it in the words of one of the latest authors, Professor Bernard of Oxford, who, in his *Historical Account of the Neutrality of Great Britain during the American Civil War*, published during the present year, writes thus (pp. 332, 333)—
" Articles of military use, when transported oversea to the ports of either belligerent in neutral ships, are during the transit designated contraband, and may be captured under the neutral flag, the neutral carrier suffering the loss of his freight, and getting no compensation for the interruption of his voyage and the breaking up of the cargo.... International Law, when it prohibits (as the phrase is) the carriage of contraband, declares in effect that the belligerent importer shall not, by having the goods conveyed to him under a neutral flag, escape the risk of having them captured at sea; and that the neutral who chooses to undertake the conveyance must hazard all the losses which may attend on such an adventure. Russia, if she be at war with France, cannot be prevented from getting guns from private manufacturers at Berlin across the Russian frontier. But if she gets them from England, French cruisers may seize them anywhere on the high seas, whether under the Russian or under the English flag. The English shipowner must run the risk of that, and,

if he be the owner of both ship and goods, he may lose his ship into the bargain." But, says the professor (p. 391), " it has not hitherto been judged reasonable or expedient that neutral governments should be held bound to restrain their subjects from trafficking with belligerents in munitions of war, or from eluding blockades. The usage of nations leaves the belligerent free to take advantage of these enterprises so far as they serve his turn, and to repress them as well as he can, so far as they assist his enemy, arming him for this purpose, at the expense of the neutral, with two important powers, the power of visit and search on the high seas, and that of capture and condemnation. The circumstances of a particular war may render such adventures very difficult, or very easy—exceptionally serviceable to one belligerent, peculiarly troublesome to another; but it does not, on any of these accounts, become the duty of the neutral sovereign to stop them, nor is he chargeable with unfriendliness or negligence for not attempting to do so." To the same effect President Pierce, in his message of December, 1854, to the United States Congress :—" The laws of the United States do not forbid their citizens to sell to either of the belligerent powers articles contraband of war, or to take munitions of war or soldiers on board their private ships for transportation ; and although in so doing the individual citizen exposes his property to some of the hazards of war, his acts do not involve any breach of national neutrality, nor of themselves implicate the Government." So, too, Chief Justice Chase, in giving judgment in the Supreme Court of the United States, on the case of the *Bermuda* :—

" Neutrals, in their own country, may sell to belligerents whatever belligerents choose to buy. The principal exceptions to this rule are that neutrals must not sell to one belligerent what they refuse to sell to the other ; and must not furnish soldiers or sailors to either, nor prepare, nor even suffer to be prepared, armed ships or military or naval expeditions against either." The rule thus expressed is not merely a matter of opinion, on the part whether of publicists or of statesmen, but the liberty allowed by it to neutrals has been constantly used.

During the Crimean War large quantities of arms and military stores were supplied to Russia by the manufacturers and merchants of Belgium and Prussia ; and as their transport took place entirely by land, the Anglo-French belligerents had no opportunity to protect themselves against such traffic by any exercise of the right of capturing contraband at sea. The view which was taken of this trade by the Governments concerned, and the communications which passed between them on the subject, are thus stated in Lord Granville's note to Count Bernstorff, of September 15th instant. " During the whole of the war arms and other contraband of war were copiously supplied to Russia by the States of the Zollverein ; regular agents for traffic were established at Berlin, Magdeburg, Thorn, Konigsberg, Posen, Bromberg, and other places, and no restraint was put upon their operations. But, besides this, although a decree was published in March, 1854, prohibiting the transit of arms from other countries, and a further decree in March, 1855, prohibiting also the transit of other contraband of war, the transit trade of Belgium continued in full activity throughout the war. The Prussian Government, when this state of things was brought to their notice, affirmed, not that it was justified in permitting these exports on the principle of 'benevolent neutrality' [of which more hereafter], but that it could not interfere with the course of trade—an answer which would seem to have been based rather on the principle that the first duty of Prussia as a neutral was to consider the interests of her own subjects, not those of the subjects of a country which had engaged itself in a war with which Prussia had no concern.... On ascertaining that the Prussian Government did not mean to restrict the export of arms or contraband of war of native origin, but intended to prohibit the transit of such articles, Her Majesty's Government consulted the legal advisers of the Crown as to the extent to which they would be justified in making representations founded on their rights as belligerents. The answer was clear—that Her Majesty's Government would be entitled to remonstrate only in the event of violation of Prussian law; and it will be found, on reference to the correspondence, that though the large direct exportations from the States of the Zollverein certainly formed occasionally the subject of representations and discussions, the strong remonstrances to which your Excellency alludes were, with few exceptions, made on the subject of the continuous violation of the injunctions of the decrees forbidding the transit of arms, which violation was so systematic that, in only one case, of the stoppage at Aix-la-Chapelle of some revolvers concealed in bales of cotton, were the Customs authorities successful in interposing a check on it.

It is true that remonstrances were made on the receipt of a report, to which a full and complete contradiction was given, that rifles belonging to the Prussian Government had been sold to Russia, and of a report that waggons loaded with gunpowder had been escorted to the frontier by Prussian police ; but the distinction is obvious between these cases, and cases affecting private individuals."

During the same war both sides drew military advantages from the trade of the United States. The passage which I have already quoted from President Pierce's message of December, 1854, had reference to this, and he proceeded in the following lines :—" Thus, during the progress of the present war in Europe, our citizens have without national responsibility therefor sold gunpowder and arms to all buyers, regardless of the destination of those articles. Our merchantmen have been, and still continue to be, largely employed by Great Britain and France in transporting troops, provisions, and munitions of war to the principal seat of military operations, and in bringing home the sick and wounded soldiers ; but such use of our mercantile marine is not interdicted either by the international or by our municipal law, and therefore does not compromise our neutral relations with Russia." It may be remarked that the use made by Great Britain and France of American merchantmen as transports, though it would certainly have rendered those merchantmen liable to capture if Russia had possessed sufficient power at sea, never interrupted that cordiality of relations between the great Republic and the great Empire, which is one of the most curious phenomena of modern politics.

Both the parties to the American civil war availed themselves largely of the British market, but the Northerners much the most. The total value of arms and munitions of war shipped from this country to the United States during the five years, 1861–5, exceeded by 1,286,000*l*. that which it would have been at the average rate of 1860 and 1866, the years immediately preceding and following the war ; and in the value of those shipped during the same five years to the British West Indian Islands there was a similar excess of 704,000*l*.[1] A very small part of the arms and munitions shipped to the United States may have been sent direct from England to southern ports not effectively blockaded, but the mass of the blockade running was done from British West Indian ports, and is represented by the excess in the exports to them. Notwithstanding the greater extent to which the Federals benefited by the English market, much irritation was produced among them by the benefit which the Confederates derived from it, but so far as that irritation has found its way into any official document, or public utterance of any American statesman, it has always been in connection with the circumstance that their war was a civil one, and with a line of argument based on the assumption that the duties of neutrals are in some degree different where one belligerent party calls the other rebels. Certainly the American Government has never committed itself, in any part of the tangled mass of negotiations commonly described from one of their chief elements as the Alabama question, to any repudiation of its old doctrine as to the legality

[1] Bernard on Neutrality, &c , p. 332.

of the export of contraband during an ordinary international war.

The next instance is that supplied by the present war, and, in order to do full justice to the Prussian claim, I will read at length the memorandum communicated by Count Bernstorff to Earl Granville on the 1st of September instant :—" It would be waste of time at the present crisis to enter upon an exhaustive juridical examination of the existing neutrality laws and their ultimate bearing and scope. It is not too late, however, to glance in a practical manner at a question which every hour may cause fresh and momentous complications, especially as affecting national susceptibilities. In the first instance there is no question but France has wantonly made war on Germany. The verdict of the world and especially the verdict of the statesmen as well as of the public of England, has unanimously pronounced the Emperor of the French guilty of a most flagitious breach of the peace. Germany, on the other hand, entered into the contest with the consciousness of a good cause. She was therefore led to expect that the neutrality of Great Britain, her former ally against Napoleonic aggression, however strict in form, would at least be benevolent in spirit to Germany, for it is impossible for the human mind not to side with one or the other party in a conflict like the present one. What is the use of being right or wrong in the eyes of the world, if the public remains insensible to the merits of a cause? Those who deny the necessity of such a distinction forego the appeal to public opinion, which we are daily taught to consider as the foremost of the great powers. In examining from this point of view whether the neutrality of Great Britain has been practically benevolent as regards Germany it is best to reverse the question, and to put it in this shape :—If Germany had been the aggressor, and consequently condemned by public opinion, in what way could the Government and the people of the United Kingdom have been able to avoid taking an active part in the struggle, and, at the same time, to prove to France their benevolent intentions? Being short of coal, the French would have been allowed to find here all they needed for their naval expeditions. Their preparations for war not being so far advanced, and not so complete as they first thought, the French would have found the manufacturers of arms and ammunition in this country ready to supply them with, and the British Government willing not to prevent their obtaining here, all the material they wanted. This, we think, would have been the utmost aid which Great Britain could have granted to France, without transgressing the letter of the existing neutrality laws, had the parts of aggressor and attacked, of right and wrong, been the reverse of the present condition. In the face of the continuous exports of arms, ammunition, coal, and other war material from this country to France; in the face of facts openly made a boast of by the French Minister of War, and not denied by the British Government, it is not necessary to prove that the neutrality of Great Britain, far from being impartial towards that party which has been pronounced to be in the right, is, on the contrary, such as it might possibly have been if that party had been wrong in the eyes of the British people and Government.

"When defending the new Foreign Enlistment Act in Parliament, the representatives of the Government declared that the law empowered the executive to prevent the export of contraband of war, but that in order to make it effectual towards the belligerents it ought to be generally enforced, and would thus even affect the commerce of this country with other neutrals. This statement, however, cannot be admitted, for there is no necessity to hamper the trade with neutral countries by preventing the exportation of contraband of war to the belligerents. Had the Government declared such exportation to the belligerents to be illegal, it would have remained an exception, subject to penalty if detected. The *bona-fide* trade with neutrals would not in the least have been affected thereby. But the Government, far from doing this, refused even to accept such propositions as might have prevented direct or clandestine exportation of contraband of war to France; besides, it cannot be admitted that such prohibitive measures could in reality damage the regular and lawful trade of the English people at large. They would merely prevent some rapacious individuals from disregarding the verdict of the nation, and realising enormous profits, which never would have legitimately been made under ordinary circumstances. The rapid increase of the private fortunes of a few tradesmen by such ventures could not appreciably add to the national wealth of the country. But, on the other hand, the nation will be held morally responsible for the blood which is being shed through the agency of those individuals. It will be said that the war would have ended sooner, and that less German soldiers would have been killed and wounded, had not the people and Government of England permitted such abuses. It hardly could be seriously meant to say that the Germans are at liberty to bring each case before their prize courts, for it would be out of place thus to taunt Germany with not being mistress of the seas. The question is whether England may escape the just reproach on the part of Germany of having greatly increased the advantage France already possesses at sea, by fitting out her navy with the requisite material to attack the seaboards of Germany, and annihilate its commerce, as well as by arming the French Garde Mobile with English breech-loaders, to be used against the German soldiers in the field. England will thus be accused of feeding a war which would have ended sooner had France been left dependent on her own resources. Hence the policy of the British Government, notwithstanding the verdict of public opinion in this country in favour of the German cause, is, if not intentionally, at least practically, benevolent to France, without there being any real foundation for the excuse that the commercial interests of this country would be seriously affected by a different course.

"There is still another reason put forward by the British Government in reference to their line of action. It is the allusion to Prussian neutrality during the Crimean war. Germany is told to consider that, at that time, ' arms and ammunition were freely exported from Prussia to Russia ; and arms of Belgian manufacture found their way to the same quarter through Prussian territory, in spite of a decree issued by the Prussian Government, prohibiting the transport of arms coming from foreign States.' Lord Granville says, in his circular of the 11th inst., ' that reflection upon these points may make the German nation inclined to take a juster view of the position now occupied by Her Majesty's Government.' All who recollect the political aspect of that time will admit that there is no analogy between the two cases. At the period alluded to public opinion in Germany was very doubtful as to the wisdom of helping a Napoleon to become once more the arbiter of Europe. Besides, it was not a struggle for life and death between two nations equally matched, but it was a war waged in remote regions for remote interests by four powers against one, without the national existence of England being the least endangered. Had England alone been the enemy of Russia, the comparison of the two cases would be less wanting in point. However, it will be remembered how strongly Great Britain remonstrated at the time against the alleged wrong of Prussia. There is but one possible alternative. Either the complaints of the British Government were founded, or they were not. If they really were, how can it be maintained at present that the complaints of Germany are unfounded, should even the great difference of the two cases be entirely disregarded? By declaring the present grievances of Germany devoid of foundation, the British Government disavow implicitly the bitter charges they preferred at the time, and condemn the ill-feeling created by them and partly entertained ever since in this country against Prussia. It is absolutely impossible to conciliate with any show of reason and logic, defending the justice of those charges on one side, and refusing on the other to acknowledge the present grievances of Germany to be well founded. This being true, there is but one motive which might be alleged as an excuse for the present policy of the British Government towards Germany. That is to apply the principle of retaliation for an alleged wrong done a long time ago under circumstances completely different from the present situation in every possible respect. To establish in our times such a principle as a rule for the policy of a great nation would be too inconsistent with the general feeling and moral disposition of this country to admit of its being the intention of the British Government. Should the position now occupied by the British Government in regard to Germany, notwithstanding the admitted justice of her cause, continue to be maintained, it would be difficult even for the staunchest advocate of friendship between England and Germany to persuade the German nation that they have been fairly dealt by.—Prussia House, August 30, 1870."

Thus far Count Bernstorff. His memorandum, the statements in which as to the English remonstrances during the Crimean war have been already corrected, completes the chain of proof that no rule prohibiting to neutrals the export of contraband forms a recognised part of the law of nations, for throughout his earnest pleading to have that export prohibited in the present case he appeals to no such rule. He assumes that the cause of Germany is just, that the public opinion, and even the statesmen of England, have recognised its justice, and that therefore we should furnish, not a strict neutrality, but one which should be calculated to give effective expression to our real or supposed sentiments in favour of his country. And when we remember that these arguments are addressed to a power which in Germany has incurred obloquy, and even contempt, for its policy of standing aloof from continental quarrels, so that the first elements of the art of persuasion, which teach the speaker to shape his arguments according to the presumed tendency of the hearer, would have dictated to Count Bernstorff the wisdom of preferring his claim in the name of a strict neutrality rather than in that of a neutrality benevolent to one of the belligerents, the evidence that in Prussian opinion no such claim could be preferred in the name of a strict neutrality becomes as conclusive as it possibly can be.

III. I have finished my exposition of the law as it is, and in the course of it I have furnished you with the materials for judging of the mode in which the question before us now arises for discussion. The phenomenon presented is that of a growing disposition to treat strict neutrality as an unrighteous thing, which either belligerent, who has the power, may justly resent. This appears, though veiled, in the reclamations of the United States with regard to our conduct during the civil war, partly based as they have been on their calling it, and having a right to call it, a rebellion; for on the theory of strict neutrality, there can be no more reason why a neutral should take cognisance of the justice of the cause of an established government as against one struggling for establishment, than in any other case of belligerency. But the same repudiation is altogether unveiled in Count Bernstorff's memorandum, for he justifies the conduct of Prussia during the Crimean War on such grounds as that that war was waged by four powers against one, and that the public opinion of Germany questioned its wisdom on the part of the four. In fact, any one whose knowledge of international law was derived only from this memorandum, would necessarily suppose that the position of a neutral, merely as such, was wholly undefined, and even unrecognised by that law.

Now I believe that the phenomenon of a growing tendency to resent and disallow strict neutrality has a real foundation in the exigencies of the time, as indeed most other moral tendencies which in any age affect large masses of men. " The parliament of war, the federation of the world," does not appear to us so near to realisation as during the long European peace under which that vision was seen by our poet. But we all feel that he, and those who preceded him in the vision, were the prophets who saw the promised land from the hill-tops, and that we must be marching towards it, though for a time we miss its sight, because the road lies over lower ground. Now, no spirit can be more opposed to the realisation of such a vision than that which, when war breaks out between any two powers, would lead all others to ransack the doctrines of strict neutrality, in order to see how far it was possible for them to hold on their accustomed course, without reference to the war raging near them. If you had been in California or Australia when the gold discoveries collected populous settlements beyond the limits of established law, you would have seen that lynch law was often mistaken and often harsh, but you would have said that the determination of neighbours to interfere for the prevention or punishment of wrong was the only element out of which a better law could be organised. Seeing it present, you would have known that the day of a better law was coming : had it been absent, you would have known that the state of society was hopeless. It cannot be otherwise among nations. The interference of third powers, to prevent or redress wrong threatened or done by one power to another, is their lynch law. If the tendency to that interference died out, if even it did not increase, all hope would be at an end that a regular international tribunal could ever be established, which might submit disputes to its judgments and reduce war to an affair of police against a recalcitrant disputant. Diplomacy, like legislation, cannot found—it can but organise. The principles, and to some considerable extent even the habits which flow from them, must first be there. For this reason I rejoiced when Mr Gladstone said lately in the House of Commons, that he did not put the obligation of England to defend the independence of Belgium so much on the treaty we had signed, as on the ground that if Belgium were attacked, and allowed to perish without defence, there would be an end of public law in Europe.

Neutrality must not be pushed so far as to ignore or neglect the duties which are incumbent on every member of what, by a happy anticipation, is called the commonwealth of nations ; and I give both Americans and Germans full credit for feeling this, when they have claimed that our neutrality ought to be so regulated as to be favourable to them. But I must beg you particularly to observe that this, the regulation of our neutrality so that it may be favourable to a particular belligerent, and not a stricter interpretation of neutrality as such, is the demand diplomatically made. It is true that that portion of the British press which has supported the German demand has only done so on the ground of that interpretation, and that Lord Granville, in his answer to Count Bernstorff, has said that "Her Majesty's Government would be prepared to enter into consultation with other nations as to the possibility of adopting in common a stricter rule; although their expectations of a practical result, in the sense indicated by the North German Government, are not sanguine." But I ear that in the present temper of foreign governments to advocate a stricter, but really impartial, rule of neutrality, or to make the offer of entering into consultation as to the possibility of adopting such a rule, will be considered as the offer of a stone when bread was asked for. At least, whether or not such a consultation may follow the conclusion of the present war, it must be allowed that to change an existing rule to the prejudice of one belligerent during the war, and that in compliance with the express request of the other belligerent that our neutrality should be made favourable to him, would be a clear breach of neutrality, even although there might be the most excellent reasons for giving a general preference to the new rule on future occasions.

IV. Such being the mode in which the question is now brought under discussion, let us assume that the present war is over, and that the powers are met in such a consultation as offered by Lord Granville; and let us consider the arguments for the stricter rule proposed. They are of two kinds, the theoretical, in which the sale of contraband to belligerents is represented as logically inconsistent with the idea of neutrality, and the practical, in which the presumable consequences of the change of the rule are considered. There are also certain commonplaces about the inconsistency of furnishing arms with one hand and medicines for the wounded with the other, and about the greed of the persons who deal in the weapons and munitions of war, which are merely rhetorical amplifications of the argument that the sale of contraband is inconsistent with the idea of neutrality. If that inconsistency be proved, then it is quite proper to denounce those who make a profit out of it, and to show how it turns our charity into mockery, with all the force that rhetoric—which has its good as well as its evil use—can supply. But if to sell a rifle be no more participating in the war than to sell the cloth with which the rifleman, or the manufacturer of rifles in the belligerent country, is clothed, or to buy the wine, the price of which furnishes to the belligerent the money which has been justly called the sinews of war; then the seller of the rifle is no more to be charged with greed than the seller of the cloth or the buyer of the wine, and the sale of the rifle no more makes the gift of the medicine a mockery than the sale of the cloth or the purchase of the wine.

It is incumbent on those who maintain that the sale of the rifle is essentially a participation in the war, or what I will call an unneutral act, to draw some valid line of distinction between it and the acts which are to be permitted. Such a line might be so drawn as to prohibit only the weapons and materials immediately employed in wounding, as swords, guns, bullets, and powder. But to draw it there would be to show an attachment to the brute material form, worthy only of children or savages; and no one does propose to draw it there. The list of contraband, as recognised for the purpose of permitting its capture when conveyed by sea in neutral ships, includes all articles of exclusively warlike use, such as military accoutrements, and all such articles capable of use both in peace and in war, as coal and articles of food, as the prize courts of either belligerent may decide to be under the circumstances peculiarly helpful to the other belligerent in the operations of war, subject to the right of neutral Governments to resist any such decisions which they may think outrageous; and those who would prohibit the export of contraband do not and cannot advocate a more limited prohibition. But no principle can turn on the degree of utility of the article sold, or on the degree of proximity in which its employment contributes to the physical act of killing or wounding. International law, as it stands, recognises that no principle can turn on such questions. The right of blockading commercial ports so as to intercept all neutral trade with them recognises the truth that all neutral trade swells the resources of the belligerent, and that to put a stop to it is one means of hastening the conclusion of the war, distinct and separate from any military operations. Why then is it not lawful for belligerents to put a stop to it, except under the conditions which determine the character of contraband and the effectiveness of a blockade? Simply because those conditions have been found by experience to be the measure of the interference which neutrals will bear; for no one will pretend to say that a neutral ship and cargo going into the Elbe since the French blockade of that river has been raised swell the resources of Germany less than their entry during that blockade would have swelled them, or that their capture in the one case would be more advantageous to the French, or have more connection with any military operation carried on by the French, than in the other case; the only difference is that neutrals will suffer the capture in the one case and not in the other, because the one case is less frequent than the other and admits of previous warning. But once admit that the neutral has a duty not to do that which may indirectly assist a belligerent, and it follows that that duty cannot be measured by the number of ships which the other belligerent has stationed off a particular port, and the existence of a duty is itself a warning to fulfil it. If then the acts which it is the right of belligerents to prevent are essentially infractions of neutrality, and not merely by convention, so that the logical deduction from the idea of neutrality is that the neutral Government ought to endeavour to prevent its own subjects from doing them, then that duty, on any view which permits commercial blockades, cannot stop at preventing the export of contraband to belligerents, but must extend to preventing the sailing of ships with intent to break a blockade, and even to the sailing of all merchant vessels destined to trade with the belligerent.

It appears to me that if it were determined to fix the duties of neutrals on a strictly logical basis, the only view which would admit of being consistently worked out would be that neutrality resided in not departing during war from the habits contracted during peace. If it was the established custom during peace that country A should sell coal or rifles, then, if country B, which drew sufficient supplies of those articles from its own soil and manufactories, went to war with C, which could not do so, it would be bound to recognise the markets of the world as facts in the conditions of the case, like any geographical facts through which C was rendered less easily assailable; but the opening by A of a new trade during war might consistently be prohibited. I think that this is the view which we should take of neutrality as between individuals. Let us return to the illustration of the gold diggings, before the establishment of regular law in them, and let us suppose an armed person attacking an unarmed one before the door of an armourer's shop. If the armourer, while selling arms to others, would neither sell a weapon to the unarmed person till the fight was over nor himself help him against his assailant, I think that, being an armourer, he would be said not to be neutral, more especially if, five minutes before, he had sold to the other combatant the weapon with which the attack was made. But if we substitute the shop of a baker and suppose him to supply a weapon to the unarmed person, I think we should say that the baker had taken a part, though probably with justice. But I am far from supposing that the legal conditions of neutrality among nations can be settled on such a footing. Such speculations are allowable as an answer to those who would regulate the duties of nations by a theory as to the essential nature of neutrality, but whose theory of that essential nature is convicted of error by its own inconsistency.

I have shown elsewhere that at the commencement of the modern period of history no settled theory of neutrality existed, but that neutrals claimed to be free from all interference by blockade beyond the actual scene of military operations, while belligerents practically claimed to prohibit to neutrals all traffic with the enemy. Much of the same uncertainty rested on the subject of contraband; and it is the historical fact that the conventions on the subjects of blockade and contraband which now exist have been arrived at simply through ascertaining by experience the points at which the exactions of belligerents and the resistance of neutrals are in equilibrium. It is possible that the changes which time has wrought in the conditions of the problem may have changed the points of equilibrium, so that the future peace of the world may best be consulted by extending or diminishing the rights of belligerents. The consideration whether this be so leads me to the practical arguments for prohibiting the export of contraband.

V. The first of these is derived from the offence which is given to belligerents by the export of contraband, and the probability that through such offence the neutral will become involved in the war, thereby damaging both his own particular interest and the general interest that the area of the war should be restricted. It is obvious to remark, in answer to this, that belligerents have for a very long period put up with the rule permitting the export of contraband, without avenging the supposed injury by war, and that some reason must be assigned for holding it probable that they will be less disposed to do so in future. I am not aware that any other reason can be assigned by the advocates of the prohibition, but the recent complaints of the United States and Prussia; and since these have not been based on any alleged breach of the duties of strict neutrality, but avowedly on the circumstance that a power from which friendliness was expected has not shown a favourable neutrality, they do not afford the proof required. So far, indeed, from affording a proof, they do not even furnish a presumption that if the stricter rule contended for had been in existence, and England had been faithfully observing it by preventing the export of arms and coal, the converse remonstrances would not have been made if prompted by the necessities of the belligerent. On the contrary, if words go for anything, it must be supposed that, in the case put, the United States would have complained that the existence of a rebellion should have closed the British ports against an export of arms, of which, as the statistics I have quoted show, the larger portion would fall to their share; and that Germany, if during any future war, or at any future stage of the present war, her navy should be superior to that of France, and the public opinion should still be favourable to her, would complain of the refusal to sell coal to her as an unfriendly neutrality persisted in despite of public opinion. The importance of considering the mode in which a question arises is thus seen. The section of the English press which has denounced the export of contraband has looked at the matter from its own point of view alone, a point of view dictated by a horror of war almost amounting to a religion, and which prevents their judging calmly any act which can, on the most superficial view, be represented as a participation in war; they have forgotten that the particular call is made on us, not because our actions show partiality, but because they do not show a partiality proportioned to our real or presumed opinion on the justice of the quarrel; and they thus attribute to the rule they advocate a general consequence in soothing the feelings of belligerents, which, in the actual state of feeling on the subject abroad, there is no reason to think would follow.

But what is more remarkable still is that the expected consequence of soothing the feelings of belligerents does not, at the utmost, take into account the feelings of more than one belligerent. The prohibition of export may in many cases satisfy the belligerent in whose favour it operates, but will it ever satisfy the one to whose prejudice it operates? And, if it does not, and he happens to be the stronger, can a new conventional rule, incapable, as I have shown, of being based on any principle, have for him the same sanctity as the time-honoured compromise which now exists? In short, can the stricter rule proposed be relied on for protecting the neutral from war, at the hands of the belligerent against whom it may operate, with a certainty at all equal to that with which the present rule has protected him from attack by the other belligerent? Again, I have already referred to the list of articles of contraband as containing a variable number of articles of occasional contraband, or contraband of circumstance, being those which the prize courts of either belligerent, usually acting pursuant to the declarations of their Government, may, in each particular war, decide to be such. The importance of these may be judged of by coal being one of them, no fixed rule as to that product having been established. Now, if it were recognised as a neutral duty to prohibit the export of contraband, what authority should take the place of the prize courts in settling from time to time the list of occasional contraband? Clearly any article to the export of which either belligerent Government for the time being objects must be put on that list, or the object of the prohibition, the avoidance of offence, will not be attained. But what will the other belligerent say to the prohibition under those circumstances? If the prize courts of one party decide that to be contraband which the other party desires to import, and neutrals acquiesce, no offence is given by them, because they are merely passive. But it can hardly be imagined that a belligerent would be equally forbearing towards a neutral who, himself, at the dictate of the enemy, took the active step of preventing the export of an important article, which the first-named belligerent did not regard as properly within the prohibited category. Here is another respect in which the advocates of the prohibition have looked to the effect on one only of the belligerents, and in which the prohibition might expose the neutral to greater danger of war from the belligerent they have overlooked than he would have incurred without it from the one they have thought of. The only escape from this difficulty would be to fix the list of contraband articles by general agreement, concurrently with the adoption of the rule of prohibition. But there are few things in which past experience leads us to hope less for agreement than the list of contraband. We may be sure that a list, if any could be agreed on for the object now under discussion—an object of extending instead of limiting the obligations in respect of contraband—would be of the most extensive and onerous kind. Nor would it be possible that any list, even if agreed on, should be accepted as final, so as to exclude new products, or old ones on their being turned to new uses.

I now come to the greatest of all the practical difficulties attending the proposed rule, the impossibility of enforcing with any approach to completeness any law which the neutral might pass against the export of contraband, and the handle which the neutral who passed such a law would consequently give to belligerents, to complain of the laxity of its execution. The difficulties attending the execution cannot better be described than in the words of Lord Granville, in his answer to Count Bernstorff before cited. "Exportations, if prohibited, would be entirely clandestine; the nature of a cargo and the destination of a vessel would be entirely concealed. It would be necessary to alter the present system of exportation under which (except in the port of London) cargoes, in order to insure rapidity of shipment, are not examined by the Customs authorities, who receive the account of them from the shippers, generally after the ship has sailed. It would require the establishment of an expensive, intricate, and inquisitorial Customs system, under which all suspicious packages, no matter what their assumed destination, would be opened and examined. Finally, though it might certainly diminish the profits of certain merchants with whose proceedings Her Majesty's Government, in common with your Excellency, have no sympathy, it would also cause infinite delay and obstruction to innocent trade. Your Excellency would not interfere with the trade to neutral countries; but how would it be possible to avoid this? A ship carrying prohibited articles would invariably have a colourable destination. How is this to be detected without interfering with the trade with neutrals, if even then? During the Crimean war Prussia had no such difficulty. There could be no doubt of the destination of goods arriving on the Russian frontier; and yet the Customs authorities were practically powerless. But Great Britain has no frontier; a ship leaving her ports may shape her course where she pleases. Your Excellency has suggested the exaction of a bond from shippers; but such a measure would be most onerous to the mercantile community, would be easily evaded, and at the best would be no security against ultimate destination. It would be necessary, too, to take these bonds, not only from foreign-bound ships, but from coasting vessels, which are at present subject to little or no Customs supervision; for what could hinder a coasting vessel from crossing the Channel and delivering her cargo at a French port?"

But, say my opponents, the law being a municipal one, that is, one internal to the country passing it, would only be an assistance to that country in maintaining its neutrality, and would give no room to belligerents to insist on its complete execution. One gentleman, who read a paper here yesterday, went so far as to say that an Act of Parliament might be passed with a clause expressing that it was without prejudice to our neutral rights. But this line of argument gives up at once the idea of adopting the new rule in an International Congress, the resolution of which would of course give mutual rights to the parties to it—it even abandons the passing of the Act as one of a set of similar laws to be passed by the principal States without express agreement, for such a body of concurrent legislation would amount to a general declaration of opinion having the force of an international rule. I am, indeed, at a loss to know what the line of argument I refer to does contemplate. An isolated law, enacted by this country alone, after the complaints of the North German Confederation, would too obviously be an admission of a duty lying on us, for that Confederation, or indeed for any other power whom it suited, to hesitate one moment about claiming its execution as the mere fulfilment of international obligations, whatever flimsy veil of a without-prejudice clause we might try to throw over it. But the argument involves a deeper error still, for the custom of nations does not warrant the assertion that a foreign government cannot claim the execution of a mere municipal law. We are here concluded by our own precedent, for, as I have already mentioned, we claimed of Prussia, during the Crimean war, the execution of the decree by which she prohibited the transport of arms and munitions through her territory from Belgium to Russia, although admitting that she need not have issued that decree, and that we were not entitled to object to the export to Russia of arms of Prussian manufacture, no prohibitory decree having been issued with regard to them. I take the fact to be that the assertion I am refuting contains just so much truth as to make it fallacious. A mere municipal law may not confer a complete right on a foreign State, so that a failure in its due execution would be recognised as in itself sufficient ground for a demand of indemnity; but a failure to execute it to the best ability of the government would be one of the strongest proofs of unfriendliness, and as long as international relations are guided rather by policy than by law, the tension of those relations, due to an unfriendliness pointedly testified, will continue to be a much surer road to war than one of the minor breaches of International Law, which might be overlooked or atoned for. It is therefore idle to suppose that we could escape from the necessity of executing to the best of our ability any law which we might enact prohibiting the export of contraband.

Opinions have differed as to whether our Foreign Enlistment Act goes beyond the minimum of our international obligations. I believe that it does not, and that it is aimed against something the inconsistency of which with neutrality is plain, and rests on a ground wholly absent from any sale in the market or export in the way of trade, namely, using the neutral territory as the base of hostile expeditions. But no sane person can doubt that, whether the Foreign Enlistment Act goes beyond our international obligations or not, and on whatever ground the obligation to enforce it be put, we must practically answer, in such cases as those of the Alabama, for the execution of that Act to its full extent, so far as such execution is fairly within the power of the Government ; and so it would be with an act prohibiting the export of contraband. Now such a responsibility is a very serious thing for a Government like this to undertake, possessing fewer means of inquisitorial investigation into what passes within its territory than perhaps any other Government in the world, conducting the affairs of a people more jealous than perhaps any other of the extension of inquisitorial powers, and yet of such enterprise as to baffle all but inquisitorial powers, and ruling over a territory which, being surrounded by sea, affords peculiar facilities to the export of goods to concealed destinations. We may venture to say that if a rule prohibiting the export of contraband were generally adopted, this would be the country in which, with the best intentions and greatest activity on the part of the Government, such a rule would be the worst observed, and which would suffer most from the international difficulties to which the breach of it would give rise ; and I cannot but think it the duty of this Government to avoid entangling the country in such a predicament, without the clearest proof of some great countervailing advantage. Such advantage I have not seen pointed out as likely to result either to England or to the world at large.

One disadvantage of no ordinary magnitude I can indeed plainly see. The manifest tendency of all rules, which interfere with a belligerent's power to recruit his resources in the markets of the world, is to give the victory in war to the belligerent who is best prepared at the outset; therefore, to make it necessary for States to be in a constant condition of preparation for war; therefore to make war more probable. Another disadvantage attending all rules which increase the irksomeness of neutrality, is that they diminish the inducements to neutrals to keep out of the war, and at the same time tend to make them take a side not dictated by a just judgment on the quarrel, but by some petty scrape into which they have got about their neutrality. It is not the little rules which lead to these difficulties that constitute the truest duties of neutrals, but to preserve amid the changing phases of the strife a judgment unclouded by its passions and incidents, and to make their weight felt—it may be at the beginning of the war, at the middle, or at the end—but to make it felt at the critical moment, for securing a peace based on just and permanent principles.

# IV

## INTRODUCTORY LECTURE[1] ON INTERNATIONAL LAW. 17 OCTOBER, 1888.

[Cambridge University Press.]

THE subject of International Law—I suspend for the moment the question how far it can be considered a science—comprises, as commonly understood, all that can be said with some degree of generality about human action not internal to a political body. Let it be the mutual action of political bodies, let it be action between one political body and one or more members of another, or let it be the action of a political body towards barbarians or savages not grouped in any such body—wherever such action can give rise to any general statement or judgment, there we have matter for International Law. Of this subject the department which stands lowest in philosophical order is descriptive, presenting a picture of facts which might be called geographical in a large sense of that term. It comprises a knowledge of the actual distribution of the world into states, with their boundaries, the statistics of their material strength and, so far as such can be obtained, of their moral strength, and their mutual relations as being either wholly independent or more or less subordinate one to another. Even when they fall within the class of independent states, the description is not complete till we have added

[1] [This is the first lecture delivered by Westlake as Whewell Professor of International Law in the University of Cambridge. L. O.]

a knowledge of the treaties which exist between them, such as those of alliance or neutrality, those which pledge them to take or abstain from taking any particular course of action in given contingencies, or those which establish on the territory of one an easement or servitude in favour of another. These are ideal boundaries, comparable to physical ones, and transgressed with equal ease, perhaps with less inconvenience when it is considered how unwisely they are often laid down. Outside the system of states, the various uncivilized or half-civilized races have to be taken into account, with the several degrees in which they approach to having regular governments, and there would then be completed what might be called a Domesday Book of the world. It would be a very natural question to ask about such a book, supposing it to lie before us, whether its contents can possess any of that quality of generality which is required for placing them among International Law, even in the wide definition of that subject which I have given. Should we not be looking only at a mass of individual facts, constituting indeed a necessary apparatus of preliminary knowledge, but being the introduction to International Law, not a part of it? I answer that the facts include in themselves generalities which any proper description of them will bring out. They present us with our first general notions, and disclose to us certain widely spread habits of action. Thus, the international idea of a state has to be abstracted from the facts about more or less independent political existence, and the comparative study of treaties throws light of the highest importance on the ways in which states tend by their nature to act. The descriptive part of International Law has therefore a real claim to be a true part of our subject.

Above the descriptive rises the more purely philosophical part of International Law. This may be said to consist of the rules of conduct which states deem themselves entitled to claim the observance of from outsiders, and entitled or bound to observe for themselves towards outsiders, whether, as before intimated, the latter are foreign states, individual foreigners, or races not possessing fully developed state organization. I do not say, the rules of conduct which states deem themselves entitled or bound to observe, or to claim the observance of, in the absence of treaty, because among the rules of conduct to be considered are those which determine or limit the binding force of treaties. And the rules of conduct which thus present themselves as matters of claim have to be considered from three points of view—from one point of view, as an existing body of more or less authoritative doctrine: from another, as a body of doctrine manifestly imperfect, and giving rise to interesting and difficult questions about the nature of the amendments that may be desirable, and about the methods to be pursued for attaining such amendments: from a third, as a body of doctrine having a history, the study of which is at once gratifying to a liberal curiosity, and necessary for understanding the doctrine itself and for appreciating the possibilities of amending it.

Such is the subject which I have been called to the responsibility of professing. Evidently it does not possess the unity of mathematics or of a natural science. It does not develop the consequences of any principles so simple and clear as time and space, or as chemical or electrical laws. But it has a unity of its own, in its reference to a great department of human action. If International Law had been regarded in the way in which I have presented it at an earlier stage in the history of our language, when what is now called political science was commonly spoken of as the art of government, the practical rather than theoretical nature of its unity would probably have caused our subject to be described as an art and not as a science. At that time however the view taken of international relations was profoundly tinctured by notions about a law of nature, which, if they could be sustained, would make the theory of those relations a science in the strictest sense. And now, while the law of nature has retired into the background of English speculation, the name of science has come to be used so much more widely and loosely that I will venture to claim it for International Law, even in that comprehensive and popular acceptation of it which I have put forward.

But if the title of science is conceded, that of law may still be disputed. In a country in which legal theory has been so deeply tinctured by the writings of John Austin, and in a university in which those writings are recommended to students, it will be expected that I should declare how I stand with regard to his classification of my subject as belonging not to law but to morality. Sir Henry Maine has already protested on historical grounds against the restricted meaning to which Mr Austin wished to confine the word "law." I will take up the question on analytical grounds, and with a similar result so far as our present subject is concerned, for on those grounds also I see no sufficient reason for preferring the name of positive international morality, proposed by Mr Austin, to that of international law.

Let us consider what are the essential characters of a rule of conduct. First, there is the character of generality, which consists in its applying to a whole class of particular actions. Secondly, there is the character of precision, which consists in its being possible to state the rule so clearly that there can be no mistake about the actions to which it applies, or at the utmost so that mistake is possible only with a regard to a few cases lying on the limits of the class. Thirdly, there is the character of observance, which consists in the rule being habitually followed in practice. I say habitually, and not invariably, because invariable observance is not attained by the laws of the best ordered state. They are often broken, though their breach may be punished or redressed, and breach, even followed by punishment, is not observance. Fourthly, there is the character of recognition ; which on the part of those who according to its terms ought to observe the rule, consists in their recognizing it as not leaving them much choice in the matter, and on the part of those towards whom according to its terms it ought to be observed, consists in their fully expecting its observance. Where these four characters are present, it seems to be admitted on all hands that we have a positive rule. That admission is made in the very name of positive international morality which Mr Austin gives to so much of my subject as is composed of rules of this kind. Perhaps we may say that the characters of generality and precision make a rule, and that those of observance and recognition make it a positive rule. And the general sense of those who have framed and employed our technical phraseology on this subject has been that a positive rule of conduct may be called a law, as is seen not only in the term International Law but also in the much older term Law of Nations.

Why then does Mr Austin confine the name of law to the law of the land? Why does he insist that such rules as those, for example, which govern diplomatic intercourse, rules as general, as precise, as well observed and as fully recognized as the laws of this or of any other country against theft—why, I ask, does he insist that these are not to be called laws? We all know that it is because they are not laid down, or as he likes to call it set, by a sovereign political authority. That is a distinction, no doubt, but it appears to be one of which it is easy to overrate the importance. A rule set by a sovereign political authority is contained in a statute-book, or in writings or traditions which are authoritative in the eyes of a judge, whose decisions will in their turn be carried into effect by the executive department. A rule which forms part of International Law is contained in writings, traditions or sentiments which are authoritative in the eyes of civilized men, whose judgment on its breach will receive a pretty effective execution by the force, or at least by the disapprobation, of the states concerned. These are differences affecting the evidence which is to be given of the existence of a rule, the authority which imposes it, to a certain extent also the motives of those who observe it, for though in both cases the motive for observance is a sense of right supplemented by a fear of consequences, yet the consequences of breaking a national law and an international one are apprehended from different quarters. But surely, in a formal classification of rules irrespective of their contents, the broadest distinction between them lies neither in the evidence for them, nor in the authority which imposes them, nor in the motives of those who observe them; it lies not in how they come to be rules, but in their operation as rules, in the uniformity of their observance and of the expectation which attends it; in short, in their being or not being positive rules. It may be objected that few rules will attain any very solid character of precision or of observance where there are neither judges to pronounce on them nor a political executive to enforce them, and it cannot be denied that there is much truth in this. But if it be the fact that a large part of our subject is not likely to acquire a good title to the name of law till international relations have been more strictly organized, that is no reason for denying the name to such parts of it as already present the fully formed character of positive rules.

Again, Mr Austin's classification does not possess, and indeed he did not claim for it, the merit of bringing the use of the term law in the jural or moral sciences into any nearer accord with its use in the exact or in the natural sciences. There is a barrier of meaning, for ever impassable, between the laws of the exact or of the natural sciences and jural or moral laws. The formula of the one is " this is "; the formula of the other is " thou shalt." The one point of resemblance between the two lies in the matter of uniformity. The statement both of a rule of conduct and of a law of the exact or natural sciences applies with generality to all the cases which fall within the terms used ; and if it be a mathematical law, or one of the natural sciences, its observance is no less uniform than its statement is general—a breach, if one could be proved, would only lead to the conclusion that what had been thought to be a law was not a law. A rule of conduct, on the contrary, let it be enforced by never so great and absolute a political power, is from time to time broken, though under penalties ; but unless there were a near approach to uniformity in its observance, it would not be reckoned as a positive rule. But whether we look at generality in the comprehension of cases within the terms used, or at uniformity in the truth of the statement as applied to the cases so comprehended, it can hardly be doubted that it was their resemblance in the matters of generality and uniformity which in some way or other led to the rules of nature and the positive rules of conduct being equally called laws. What that way was, whether it was the same in the history of all languages which possess words having the same or an analogous extent of meaning to that of the word " law " in English, whether in any language the law of conduct or the law of nature was the first entitled to the common name, how far in the case of any language the notion of a lawgiver accompanied that of a law in the minds of those who first used the common name for either kind of law : these are highly interesting questions of philology and psychology. But, however they are answered, the fact remains that if the several senses of our word " law " be regarded independently of what they may connote in the minds of different persons, the one common point in their denotation is that at which they touch the notions of generality and uniformity. And when all positive rules of conduct are held to partake of the nature of law, this clue of meaning is more faithfully followed out than if we impose on positive rules of conduct, before we call them law, the additional condition of their being set by a sovereign political authority.

It will have been seen that I do not claim the name of law for any international rule, taken separately, of which the precision and the observance are insufficient to rank it as a positive rule. But no other rule could enter into the positive international morality of Mr Austin, and therefore, as against his classification, the foregoing vindication of the name of International Law covers the necessary ground. It may still however be objected to the name of International Law, as applied in its ordinary extension, that the international rules which, taken separately, can make good their title to be law are too few in number to justify us in regarding them as the dominant parts of the science, and allowing them in that character to determine the appellation of the whole. My answer to this is—first, that the real unity of the entire subject as a department of human action is such that a comprehensive name for it is indispensable: secondly, that the most extensive part of a subject is not necessarily the best entitled to give that name, but a claim of no lesser value may be urged in favour of that part which is the most perfect in scientific form: thirdly, that in the gradual improvement of international relations the precision and observance of rules is constantly on the increase, and that therefore those international rules which may already be ranked as law are typical of the subject, in that they are the completest outcome of a tendency which pervades the whole. I shall then, with some confidence, employ the name of International Law for the entirety of the wide and varied department of knowledge which I have indicated, nor can there be any doubt that the revered founder of this chair intended the name in no narrower sense. He specially directed the attention of his professors to the establishment of such rules and the suggestion of such measures as might tend to the extinguishment of war, and thereby showed that he looked down the stream of time to the day when the domain of law should be ampler and better fortified, and embraced under the name of International Law all that the straining eye can distinguish with any degree of clearness on this side of the unknown horizon.

I pass with pleasure from a controversy on a name to the question whether any principles can be found that may guide us in discussing the rules of International Law: principles by which we may accord those rules our praise or our blame where their positive existence is clear, by which we may choose among them where their positive character rests on disputable evidence, and by which we may determine the amendments or enlargements of them that ought to be advocated. Before we try to answer this question, it is necessary to come to an understanding as to the sort of principles of which we are in search. First then, they must not be in contradiction to the principles of morality, but they cannot be identical with those principles.

We are dealing with rules either enforceable, or which it is proposed to make enforceable, by human authority more or less organized and regular in its action, while, by universal acknowledgment, a large part of morality is only suitable for being left to the individual conscience, corrected at the utmost by the irregular and often ineffectual censures of opinion. Secondly, the principles which we seek, as marking the boundary between the morally right and the enforceable, must bear the same relation to the rules of International Law which what Bentham called the principles of legislation bear to national law. Each may be described as the sum total of the considerations which it is deemed proper to invoke upon a question of maintaining or altering the positive law, so far as those considerations can be reduced to a general form. It may be well, before going further, to fix our ideas by quoting concrete examples, in each department, of the cases which arise for the application of such principles. Take first the department of national law, or internal law, to use the term which Bentham proposed as correlative to international. It depends on principles of legislation what extent shall be given to the jural notion of fràud, for instance, as to the fulness of the disclosure which a vendor shall be required to make to a purchaser. In discussing the sale of alcoholic drinks, it depends on principles of this class what balance the law shall strike between sobriety and liberty. In discussing the expropriation of property for a public purpose, it depends on principles of this class whether the owner shall be paid as an unwilling vendor, as a willing vendor, or even not at all, on the ground that other property of his will be so benefited by the public purpose concerned that on the whole he will not be a loser. You see how such questions involve the extent to which candour, temperance, public spirit, are not merely moral duties but are proper to be humanly enforced ; and if no answers possessing the quality of generality in a sufficient degree can be given to them, there may be carefully considered legislation, there may be good legislation, but in the proper sense of the term there can be no principles of legislation. So, to give examples in the department of International Law, there may be questions about the responsibility of a state for the acts of its subjects, or the responsibility of subjects for the acts of their states ; about the balance to be struck between the right of self-preservation attributed to a state and the duties which would be incumbent on it if no right of self-preservation could be opposed to them ; about the force or fraud which may vitiate a treaty in its origin, or the alteration of circumstances which may authorize the plea that it is no longer applicable. Here too, in the last analysis, we have to do with the limitations to which the actions of men ought to be subjected at the hands of their fellow men, and if no answers possessing the quality of generality in a sufficient degree can be given to such questions as these, there may be carefully considered International Law, there may be good International Law, but there can in the strict sense of the term be no principles of international legislation.

The search after principles of this kind, jural as distinguished from ethical principles, has engaged many minds, but it cannot be said that either in the internal or in the international department it has been crowned with generally acknowledged success. On the other hand, the existence of a sentiment of jural right, distinct from the sentiment of ethical right, is one of the most persistent facts in human nature. If the principles could be found, they would explain that fact to the understanding. Whether they are found or not, the sentiment exists, call it jural right, justice, political justice, or what you will ; and in most of the great languages it is difficult to speak of law without implying that it is the embodiment of such a sentiment. Thus a particular rule may be a *lex* in Latin, a *loi* in French, a *gesetz* in German, but law in general is *jus, droit, recht*, words in which, whatever may be their etymology, the notion of a rule is only admitted along with that of jural right. To put it otherwise, such words as *jus, droit, recht*, if they are used of rules, imply also, in the average apprehension of the men who use them, a standard of right by their conformity to which the rules must be judged. To a Frenchman, German or Italian, *le droit anglais*, or the corresponding term in the languages of the others, carries the sense not merely of the law of England, but of the English embodiment, more or less adapted to the circumstances of England, possibly more or less mistaken in such adaptation, of a general standard. *Le droit international*, or the corresponding term in the other languages, carries the sense not merely of International Law, but of the embodiment existing among states, and possibly the more or less mistaken embodiment, of a general standard. The simple meaning which we attach to the word "law" can only be got by a qualification, *le droit positif, das positive recht*.

That our word "law" does not carry this connotation of "right" is, of course, immediately due to the fact that "law" and "right" are, with us, two distinct words, while *jus, droit, diritto, recht*, each mean both. But why have we at present this distinction of words, which it is well known did not exist in the older stages of our language? I cannot help thinking that the fact is due, at least in part, to the independent position which the law of England early assumed by the side of the Roman law, which must inevitably have made Englishmen less prone than others to assume the universality of any discoverable jural principles, more inclined therefore to emphasize the distinction between law as a positive institution and jural right as an ideal. But, however it arose, the emphasis which our language has long placed on that distinction has had, internally, the beneficial effect that the duty of respect for law has been placed on its proper grounds, and has been the less liable to be undermined by the discovery, which in every country must be sometimes made, that the law is at variance with the sentiment of right. Internationally however, both the statesmen and the theoretical writers of England have been too apt to forget that half the reasons for respecting law as a positive institution rest upon the existence of a legislature to correct it, and of a government to enforce its reciprocal observance till corrected. Where these are absent, other means must be taken to prevent the law from falling too far behind the sentiment of right, growing as that sentiment does in correspondence with the growth of society. This is the justification of revolution, when a country is cursed with a system incapable of being legally reformed; and this, as between states, makes it the duty of governments to cooperate in bringing the positive rules of International Law into accordance with the standard set by the best jural ideal of the time. Sooner or later, that ideal will vindicate itself against all opposition. It will not in the long run be argued with practical success that, because a rule has been once acknowledged, it continues to bind until it has been changed by the unanimous consent of the states concerned. If, to us, International Law is a body of rules once acknowledged and not formally repealed, we must not forget that, to most others, *le droit international* is only binding so far as it is a tolerable approximation to an embodiment of international right. And I would point out the rights and duties of neutrals in war as one of the fields in which it may be necessary for Englishmen to bear this in mind more carefully than perhaps they have always done.

I spoke just now of the growth of society. Let me ask you to consider what that means, and how it is connected with our subject. The very notion of a jural right as distinct from a moral one, that is, of a right which men will enforce as distinct from one which they will feel but not enforce, implies a society between the members of which it serves as a *modus vivendi*. Before men can consciously possess such a notion, they must have lived together in bonds which are not only valuable to their interests but which have moulded their sentiments, bonds to preserve which they will concede much to each other. But such bonds are not created aforethought. Men did not construct society, nor do they now modify it, with a preconceived idea of the rights they shall have under it. Its construction and modification are the results of an inconceivable number of individual actions, performed in obedience to individual impulses. Men live their lives, they marry and rear their children, buy and sell, are generous and selfish, fight and make peace. They do all this within the limits of their political organization, if one exists, and outside any such limits. All the while, by the very force of doing so, they are building up organizations that realize the average ways in which their mutual friction and limitation have led them to look at their mutual relations. They may be compared to bees or coral insects, so far as they produce harmonious results which they did not contemplate. But their action as individuals differs through a much wider range, so that the general result, if it be a total, partakes also of the nature of an average. Still further are they unlike bees and coral insects, in that they possess the power of looking from the outside at their accomplished work, and recognizing in it the aims towards which they were blindly struggling. And further still it is the prerogative of man that no accomplished work of his has yet been final. When the jural idea comes into sight in the social structure, national or international, so far as it has been realized, it is seen at once to have reference to the past rather than to the future, because the stirrings of a new formation are already felt beneath. To take one example among a thousand, slavery was not erased from the laws of Western Europe till the slaves had been freed by private charity, and as soon as it was erased the question of the poor took its place. Or to take an example in which the old idea is not simply built on but threatened with modification, no sooner is the independence of states vindicated from an Austrian or a French world empire, than the question begins to loom among thinkers, how far and in what manner it may be necessary to limit that independence by a parliament of the world, and statesmen begin practically to limit it by European pentarchies and congresses. Hence that contrast to which I have already alluded, between the perennial nature of the jural sentiment and the fruitlessness of the search for universal principles of legislation.

Comparing international with internal relations, there is an obvious reason why in the former the jural sentiment should be weaker than in the latter, and its embodiment in jural principle much less clearly apprehended, even with reference to the degree of advancement already realized in international society. Through all the gradations of the family, the municipality and the state, the social feeling is developed and strengthened by the habit of action in common for common ends. As soon as the boundaries of the state are passed, common action ceases, or is limited to rare occasions, like those of active alliances, or to matters conducted by officials, like international posts and telegraphs. The very existence of foreign nations is chiefly brought home to the mass of mankind by some opposition of policy or rivalry of interest, it is well if it be not by war. Would it not be wonderful if the jural idea were not weak and obscure in proportion to the weakness and obscurity of the social bond to which it corresponds? I must caution you, then, not to expect too much from my subject. Surely, in international principle, we have cause to be thankful if we can see but a little way.

To see our way at all in such a subject, a certain philosophical temper and a certain practical temper appear to be required. The philosophical temper I will venture to call the inductive one, for in this home of the inductive sciences we have perhaps the right to affirm that from their study has flowed a habit of mind, the application and usefulness of which reach far beyond the possibility of employing any process which can be formally described as inductive logic. This habit of mind may be recognized by its being more disposed to take measures from facts than to bring ready made measures to them. It is the critical temper in philology and literature, and the historical temper in jural and political investigations. Not indeed historical in the narrow sense that would measure what ought to be by what has been, for together with the external fact the tendency, which is no less a fact, has to be taken into account, and what has been and has ceased to be is presumably what it was fit should cease. The tendency indicates a need, but the external fact which has existed is not necessarily, or even presumably, the mode of satisfying that need which is best for us at the present day.

The practical temper that I would inculcate is that which will result if each one of us tries always to bear in mind his own personal responsibility in international affairs. The strong insistence with which most writers on the subject have dwelt on the artificial entity of the state, the sharp contrast which, of late more especially, they have drawn between a state and its subjects, may easily have an evil influence on a student of International Law, and on the public so far as it is affected by the tone of thought among such students. It may weaken the sense that the action of a state is the action of those within it who help to guide it, whether in a public capacity or even by merely expressing an opinion; nay, that in a lesser degree it is also the action of those who suffer the others to guide it. The influence of the same tone of thought will again be evil if it allows us to forget that not only is the action of our state that of ourselves, but that those towards whom it is taken are also men like ourselves, though they may be veiled from our eyes by the interposition of another artificial entity. I do not say this in the interest only of those improvements in International Law which the future may have in store, although the condition of their being worked out is that we shall think more of what is human in the matter and less of what is technical. Nor do I wish only to hold up to your eyes the physical and moral suffering caused by war to individuals, though these are important enough. I deprecate the ignoring of personal responsibility quite as much with a view to the effect which the conduct of a great state may have on the destinies of other populations, especially of those which, as possessing less power or a lower civilization, are exposed to be most seriously affected by our action or our abstinence from action, while least able to help themselves. There can neither be sound International Law nor sound international politics, nor sound treatment of inferior races, without a sense of duty; and a sense of duty will not be roused towards abstractions, nor by looking at abstractions. Hence I have not chosen to define International Law as the science of the rules prevailing between states, and to treat as subsidiary the questions of how far those rules are applicable to semi-sovereign states or to half-civilized or uncivilized populations. I have chosen to put in the front the idea of action, which carries with it the ideas of duty and responsibility, and to define International Law as dealing with all human action not internal to a political body. From this point of view the subject is seen to have a real unity, though the rules of action will naturally differ with the circumstances.

Now a final word on the position of this study in the university. No one will imagine that a study, from which it has been necessary to caution you not to expect too much, is one of those that can be recommended with the object of training the mind. It is rather one which demands a mind already to some extent trained. But while most of the subjects which make that demand belong to special instruction and not to a liberal education, I venture to think that International Law ought not to be considered as belonging to specialists. To what class of specialists indeed should it belong? To professional lawyers? But the parts of it which come before courts of justice, as the law of maritime prizes during war, bear no large proportion to the whole. Or does it belong to lawyers, as being conversant with the interpretation of contracts, and with the rules of national law which are borrowed in International Law? But this very borrowing requires to be controlled by a larger view than belongs to the professional lawyer as such, which his predilection for the rules of which the application is discussed may sometimes be an obstacle to his attaining. Or are the privileged specialists of the subject to be found in the Foreign Office, including the potential Foreign Office of the opposition, and in the writers who watch and criticize their proceedings ? When we have got as far as this, and have included, as we shall logically be bound to do, the public who ought to follow the writers with intelligent appreciation, we shall see that International Law is no more a subject for specialists than home politics are, nor can it be if the duty of the citizen is concerned with international action. And while, as a subject for study at the university, it differs favourably from home politics in its being comparatively independent of party spirit, the very fact that party motives do not bring it so continually under popular discussion makes it the more necessary for the university to draw attention to it. We have here the men of whom a large part will become, and all ought to become, interested participators in the international career and tasks which lie before the United Kingdom. It would be matter for regret if a too exclusive attention to the general training of their intellects permitted them to leave us without having been invited to reflect on the principles which may make that participation useful.

# V

## THE VENEZUELAN BOUNDARY QUESTION. 1896.

[A letter reprinted, with permission, from *The Times*, 6th January, 1896.]

To the Editor of *The Times*.

SIR,—The President's Message had first to be met in this country by an assertion of our own dignity and independence. That has been done, and it is now time for everyone to contribute what he can towards discovering an amicable solution of the question. I have seen with pleasure Mr Schurz's suggestion and the friendly manner in which you treat it, while pointing out the difficulties in its way. If it can be worked into a useful shape, by all means let it be so, but in the meantime I will ask permission to put forward another idea.

It is that of arbitration, with a restriction presently to be mentioned, combined with mediation. An arbitrator can only pronounce a judgment; he cannot make a recommendation as a mediator can. When England and the United States referred the boundary between Canada and Maine to the arbitration of the King of the Netherlands, that Sovereign did not adjudicate on the respective lines proposed by the parties, but proposed an intermediate one as a compromise, which the United States were not bound to accept and did not accept. Now in the present case it is more than probable that an arbitrator would find legal grounds enough for ruling out the *maximum* claims on both sides, even if he were not prevented from entertaining them by the restriction presently to be suggested. But it is also probable that for some part of the intermediate region he might be unable to find any legal grounds of decision, and that all he could do would be to propose a line of his own. Then, if the parties had from the beginning accepted him in the character of mediator as well as in that of arbitrator, they would not indeed be bound to accept a line which he did not declare to be one of legal obligation, but his proposal, made as it would be after hearing all that could be said on that branch of the subject, would carry such weight that no party desirous of peace would refuse to accept it.

The restriction which has been referred to should be that neither England nor Venezuela should be disturbed in the possession of actual settlements. Wherever people are cultivating or mining under the authority and with the protection of either Government, they should be left to that Government. So much of the disputed territory should be placed outside both the arbitration and the mediation, and the *status quo* with regard to it should be legalized by the agreement of reference. Such a restriction would probably secure the real intention of the British Government in declining to go to arbitration for the region within the second Schomburgk line. The extent to which British settlements have advanced is perhaps the point on which we are the least informed by anything that has been published. I will not, therefore, hazard a conjecture how far their actual limit differs from the second Schomburgk line, but, whether the difference be great or small, it can scarcely have been meant by our successive Foreign Secretaries that they would decline arbitration as to the tracts of untrodden forest lying between the most advanced settlements on either side. Their object must have been to secure that those who have relied on our protection shall not be disappointed, and we must allow for a similar feeling on the part of the Venezuelans, some of whose settlements are included within the British *maximum* claim. Such a feeling is reasonable on each side, and the restriction proposed ought to satisfy it for both.

Now, as to the arbitrator and mediator, there is none which, under other circumstances, we need have preferred to the United States themselves; but that selection is now impossible. I should suggest the King of the Belgians, or the President of the Swiss Confederation. Either would find in his country an abundance of well-qualified advisers, and might, if he chose, call in advisers from other countries, and neither could be suspected of partiality. The parties to the reference would necessarily be England and Venezuela, since it is between them that the contest lies. The United States would be able, as voluntary advisers of Venezuela, to give to their Monroe policy all the effect which they may consider the occasion requires. It is an inevitable incident of international disputes that a third party, deeming itself concerned, shall volunteer advice to one of the disputants. But we may be sure that the United States would not advise Venezuela to disobey an award for which, within the restriction suggested, the arbitrator might find legal ground, or to reject a compromise which, within the same restriction, he might recommend, as mediator, for the region as to which he could not find legal ground.

So far as the public will be interested, I might probably stop here, but it may be well to add a few questions for the consideration of those who combine a knowledge of international law with a study of the facts so far as published. Is there any legal ground whatever on which Venezuela can claim up to the Essequibo river over settlements which have been Dutch or English for centuries? On the other hand, can the British *maximum* claim be put on any legal ground? If it went up to the watershed of the Cuyuni basin there would be a ground, though not one universally admitted; but it stops a little short of that watershed, and I have not seen any legal reasons stated for the line thus actually selected. If both *maximum* claims are ruled out, is there any legal ground for drawing an intermediate line except possession, subject to the usual conditions for a title by possession? Having regard to what is known of the facts, is there any reason to believe that either England or Venezuela, by admitting the validity of the actual settlements of the other, would abandon anything which it could possibly maintain in the most unrestricted arbitration? But could arbitration on a question which includes settlements centuries old be honourably accepted without such a reciprocal admission? And, with it, is not all the area for which legal ground exists at the same time cut out, so that the practical settlement of all the rest of the case can only be looked for from mediation, although the arbitrator and mediator ought to be empowered to adopt a legal ground if he can find one?

I am, Sir, your obedient servant,
J. WESTLAKE.

CHELSEA, *Jan.* 4.

## VI

### THE TRANSVAAL WAR[1]. 1899.

[Cambridge University Press.]

IF a Greek or Roman writer had to tell the story of a war, he usually took some opportunity at its commencement to throw the views and motives of the parties into the form of set speeches, supposed to have been delivered by their statesmen or generals. No better occasion of the kind was ever invented than that which in sober fact presented itself in the last days of May and the first days of June this year, when Sir Alfred Milner, the Queen's High Commissioner for South Africa, and Mr Kruger, the President of the South African Republic, met in conference at Bloemfontein. You know in a general way that at that time there were great complaints of grievances suffered by Uitlanders, or foreigners, in the South African Republic, of whom the larger proportion were British subjects, and that those grievances, which I shall mention more particularly later, had their foundation in the steady resolve of the Dutch government of that republic to maintain the Dutch language and the Dutch social and political system, including their methods of treating the natives. Now at the commencement of that conference Sir Alfred Milner said that he asked for the franchise, that is the

[1] [This is a lecture delivered by Westlake on Nov. 9, 1899, in the University of Cambridge. L. O.]

power of voting for the election of the volksraad or parliament, for the Uitlanders, together with such an increase to the number of seats enjoyed by the Rand, the district where the gold mines are situated, as would give the Uitlanders a substantial representation in the volksraad. And he asked that distinctly not as a claim of right; he put it as a friendly suggestion, which would cut the root of the grievances complained of by giving the Uitlanders the power of looking out for themselves in the volksraad. It was a short way out of a great difficulty, that of dealing with all the particular cases of grievance in detail. Sir Alfred Milner tried to induce President Kruger to agree to his demand by pointing out to him that it would secure the independence of his country, because any motives for attack upon that independence which might exist would cease. President Kruger was equally clear in the manner in which he met that suggestion. He said that the effect would be to swamp the Dutch population. I should have said that Sir Alfred Milner put forward his suggestion not as though the numerical majority, which at present is with the Uitlanders, should immediately have a corresponding majority in the volksraad, but that they should at once have a substantial representation, and then, being able to fight their own battles, the increase of their number in the volksraad would follow in the natural course of things, just as we find in our own country the increase of representation of any class in parliament grows with the growth of its numbers and importance in the country. President Kruger went at once to the ultimate result. It was indifferent to him that the change was to be introduced gradually: he fixed and clung to the fact that it would only end, and in fact was meant to end, in the swamping of the Dutch population by Uitlanders. He said "we might just as well throw up the republic,"... it "would be worse than annexation." Independence preserved in that manner he regarded as "independence lost." He showed plainly that what he was contending for was not the mere independence of the South African Republic as a certain territory outlined by a coloured border on the map, within which no outside power was to interfere; what he valued under the name of its independence was the preservation of its peculiar language and social and political system. Sir Alfred Milner was firm in his demand. In answer to certain hints which had been thrown out about the possibility of compensation, he said "I cannot agree to buy with something else that just settlement which would be in your interest as well as mine." And he went on to say in words, the plainest ever used in diplomacy and plainer than are often used in diplomacy, that the failure of an agreement upon the point which he had submitted "would lead to an open breach between the two governments....There is no other way out except war." President Kruger clung to the possibility of a bargain, and the point upon which at that time it was in his mind that the bargain might turn was that of arbitration, the establishment of a system of arbitration between the Queen's government and that of his republic. But if I understand rightly the previous despatches to which he referred, he did not so much mean arbitration upon the particular differences which might from time to time arise between the two governments as arbitration on the general interpretation of their relations, by means of which he hoped to get an award which would say that his state did not exist in that condition of dependence on the United Kingdom which it was contended on the British side characterized it. That was the last point. In the position I have stated they separated, and during the months which followed until the outbreak of war the parties, although the negotiators were no longer Sir Alfred Milner and President Kruger, but Mr Chamberlain and President Kruger, never came nearer to an agreement. The negotiations dragged on, and I think I am not wrong in saying that war was declared by the South African Republic as soon as by the spring rains and the growth of grass on the veldt it became possible for them to move their forces over it[1].

Now it is often said that this is a war between two races. I would rather say that it is a war between two ideals, of which only one is a racial ideal. On one side you have the English ideal of a fair field for every race and every language, accompanied by a humane treatment of the native races. That ideal, no doubt, makes for the English language and for English institutions. We see how under it the English language and institutions are taking possession of a large part of the world, as being those which most successfully compete in that fair field; but although that may be the result it is not the object of the English ideal, neither

[1] The quotations are from the translation of the Transvaal green book containing the full minutes of the conference, published in the *Times* of 18th July from the Johannesburg *Star* of 24th June.

is it in all cases the only possible result. In proof of that one need only point to Canada, where the French language and French laws, and even, so far as is compatible with the existence of a province which forms only part of a great dominion, French institutions generally, are preserved in loyal subjection to the Queen. But the other ideal, the Transvaal ideal, is racial, not only in its result if it should succeed, but in its object. It is founded, as was practically admitted at the Bloemfontein Conference, on the desire to maintain the Dutch language, the Dutch social and political system, and its mode of treatment of the natives. We must not at once condemn an ideal because it is a racial one. The larger part of the world at present is governed by racial ideals. We see how in Russia a persistent effort is made to Russify the Finns in Finland, the Poles in Poland, and all the other subjects of the Russian Empire. We see in Germany the same eager desire to exterminate by severe pressure the Polish language and the Danish language in the parts which have been annexed from the Polish and Danish kingdoms. We see how in Austria racial ideals threaten the very integrity of the country; it seems to have great difficulty in holding together. We are, then, in a minority in having an ideal which is not a racial one, and we must look at least with respect, if not with approval, upon ideals which present themselves to the larger part of civilized mankind. Neither, again, should we look on the Transvaal ideal with contempt on account of the mixed motives with which it may be maintained. Human motives are always mixed. Certainly as long as the great revenues derivable from the gold mines are enjoyed by a small governing class, there must be large gains to be made out of them even without imputing corruption to those men. But, as I say, motives are always mixed, and we cannot condemn a great body of men on account of the motives which may actuate some of them, even the leaders of them. And if there be anything at all sordid in the motives of the oligarchy on one side, that may well pair off with the motives which exist on the other side, the desire to free the mines of the Rand from excessive taxation, and thereby to increase, I will not say only the gains of the capitalists but the gains of those interested in the mines generally, because no doubt if the taxation were reduced there would be a better field for the employment of labour, and labour as well as capital would gain. These motives may pair off.

Before leaving this comparison of the two ideals, I would point out to you two circumstances connected with any ideal. One is that ideals are always propagandist. No ideal seriously and heartily conceived was ever contented to remain entirely within its own limits, and that is true whether the ideal itself is a religious, a political, or a social one. I need not recall the Crusades to your mind. I need hardly recall the revolutionary propagandism of France at the time of her great Revolution, or the absolutist propagandism of the Holy Alliance which followed its overthrow. You may take it as a lesson of history that ideals are always propagandist, and there is another circumstance to be mentioned about them, that they admit of no compromise. There may be a compromise between different measures proposed to be carried out, but between two ideals there is none. The franchise and representation asked for the Uitlanders by Sir Alfred Milner could not be otherwise than a death-blow to the Boer ideal. Now we may think, and I have no doubt that most of us do think, that the English ideal is the better of the two, but that will not give us a right to enter upon a crusade for its propagation. If we allow propagandism to be a cause for war the result will be anarchy throughout the world. And who are we that we should take upon ourselves to say that our own ideals are not only the best, but so much the best as to make it worth while to propagate them in spite of the horrors caused by the sword ? I must say that sometimes I have a feeling, which perhaps not many of you share, when I see the extent to which the English language and institutions are spreading over the world, that even if that spreading is brought about solely by pacific and fair means, there is the possibility that that danger may be incurred which the poet has expressed when he wrote " Lest one good custom should corrupt the world." I am therefore by no means inclined to hurry the extension even of our own ideal. We must then all of us ask what is the justification for that demand which Sir Alfred Milner made at the Bloemfontein Conference and which has since been maintained, that the English ideal should be adopted in the Transvaal Republic or war should follow, as it has followed. In considering whether there exists justification, and, if so, what it is, I shall have to go to some extent through the recent history of South Africa, but I will at once, as a thread to guide you while you follow me in that history, say the result to which I hope to come. I think that the demand on our part was not founded on any legal right, but that it may have been justified, probably was justified, by one of those situations that occur in the mutual relations of nations, soluble by no canons of legal right but for which a higher justice must be appealed to, that larger justice which in this country is exercized not by courts of justice applying the law as it is but by parliament altering the law, and which is sometimes necessary between nations, bringing into operation demands not founded merely upon a legal position but upon the intolerable character which a certain situation has assumed.

In 1652 the Dutch founded the Colony of the Cape of Good Hope. That colony was reinforced about the end of the seventeenth century by Huguenot refugees from France, and then at once the Dutch began to show that worship of their own system and that tenacity in clinging to it which they have shown ever since. The French language was only allowed to the French emigrants; it became compulsory for the next generation to adopt Dutch. The colony was occupied by England during the great wars at the end of the last and the commencement of the present century, when Holland, having been overrun and annexed by France, was an enemy in our war with France. We occupied that colony in amity with the family of the Prince of Orange, which had been the ruling family in Holland, but was in exile on account of the country having become French. At the peace in 1814 the colony was left in British hands. It was ceded by the restored dynasty of Holland. Its position had become of vital importance to England as a halfway house on the road to India, and at once our difficulties with the Dutch began. In 1815, the very year after the Colony had been ceded at the peace, a Dutchman called Bezuidenhout was summoned to answer for his conduct towards a native, quite proper according to the ideas of his own people, but inhuman according to ours. He refused to appear before the court and soldiers were sent to arrest him. He fired on those soldiers and, the soldiers firing in return, he was killed. The result was a Dutch rising in revenge for his death, and five of the leaders of that rising were hanged. That incident is remembered to this day with the bitterest feeling by the Dutch. The place where it occurred is called Slagter's Nek, and it still plays a considerable part in Dutch invective against England. The feeling was brought to a head by the emancipation of the slaves in 1833, when parliament voted £20,000,000 to compensate the slave holders. The Dutch in the Cape Colony were exceedingly angry at the emancipation of the slaves taking place at all, and the compensation which was allotted to them was insufficient, I believe about two-thirds of the real value—not that they got an unfair share of the £20,000,000, but that the £20,000,000 was insufficient—and there was an undue delay in paying it. The consequence was that there commenced the great trek, as it is called in Dutch, or emigration, of the Dutch farmers from the colony into the interior, in order to shake off the dust from their feet against us. The trek commenced in 1835, and went on through several successive years.

The emigrants issued a manifesto in which they denounced the " vexatious laws " passed in the interests of the slaves, and complained of the loss thereby inflicted upon them. They also complained of " the continual system of plunder which " they said they had " endured from the Kaffirs and other coloured classes," and of the " unjustifiable odium " cast upon them by " interested and dishonest persons under the cloak of religion," by which they meant missionaries. At the end of the manifesto they said, " we quit this colony under the full assurance that the English government has nothing more to require of us, and will allow us to govern ourselves without interference in the future."

They moved from Cape Town eastward into Natal, in the south-eastern part of Africa, and northward into the interior, first across the Orange river and then across the Vaal river. They founded republics in all these districts, and the British followed them. Our claim to follow them was based on the doctrine of perpetual allegiance, by which they could not shake off their British allegiance, and, as a consequence, whatever they acquired was acquired by the British crown. That was the legal basis, and the basis of policy was the fear lest the high-handed dealings of the Boers with the natives should provoke a general native rising which might be of the greatest danger to the colony itself. That fear had been entertained by the Dutch government even in the seventeenth century, and had led to stringent regulations by it against emigration into the interior. The result was that Natal, which was one of the earliest settlements of the trekking farmers, was annexed and became a British colony in 1843, and it has remained so ever since. Not many of the Boers remained there. The Boers who had been in Natal pushed still further into the interior, where they joined others who had gone direct to the Orange and Vaal rivers, and the present population of Natal, although to a small extent Dutch, is to a much larger extent of British blood. In the interior two more lasting republics were founded, that of the Orange Free State, between the Orange and the Vaal rivers, and still further north that of the Transvaal beyond the Vaal river. Those two republics were recognized by this country—the Transvaal in 1852[1] and the Orange Free State in 1854. There has been a great deal of fog in some minds as to the effect of this recognition; I mean that some persons have not clearly realized the difference between recognizing the republics as separate states, which was undoubtedly done, and recognizing them, which was not done, as part of the British dominions enjoying a certain amount of self-government. The conventions which were entered into with the two states were not express on the subject, but that they were recognized as separate states is beyond all question from the fact that they were intended to have, and from that time down to the present have had distinct foreign relations. A part of the British dominions, no matter what freedom it enjoys with regard to its internal affairs, can have no foreign relations distinct from those of the United Kingdom. Thus they became

[1] The official name of the Transvaal was at first the Dutch African Republic, and was changed in 1858 to the South African Republic.

separate, or what in recent controversies has been called international, states, and not only that but sovereign international states, because the foreign relations allowed them were uncontrolled ; they were at their sole option. There were in the conventions which recognized them certain stipulations as to their conduct towards the natives, but these were only treaty matters. The stipulations were such as we might have in a treaty with any other power ; they were no vestiges of supremacy.

With regard to the Orange Free State matters have continued upon that footing ever since. With regard to the Transvaal matters continued upon that footing until 1877. In that year the Boers of the Transvaal suffered a severe defeat from a native chief, Sekokuni, on the west of them, whom they had attacked, and they were also in great danger from another native chief, Cetewayo, on the east, who, it was feared, would attack them. Their treasury was absolutely empty ; there were no means of paying the officials, of making or repairing roads, or even of carrying on a postal service ; and in those circumstances Sir Bartle Frere, who was then High Commissioner of the Cape, sent Sir Theophilus Shepstone, an official experienced in dealing with natives, into the country with the view of seeing whether an annexation might be arranged, on the one hand for the purpose of promoting a sort of lofty Christian imperialism which characterized Sir Bartle Frere, and on the other hand of warding off the great danger to the British colonies lest a mass of victorious natives should invade them. Sir Theophilus Shepstone shortly after his arrival in the Transvaal issued a proclamation annexing it. Unfortunately the people of the country were never consulted about that annexation. He had collected a certain amount of approval from the dwellers in the few towns in which the most civilized part of the community lived, and where they felt most the stress to which the country had been brought. The larger part of the population, the farmers living in the country, were exceedingly confident. They believed, although few else believed it, that they could beat the two chiefs. They never read or received letters, and did not care if there was no money for carrying on the postal service. They never used roads. That there were no funds for paying officials was of no consequence to them; the officials lived in the towns, and rendered services which they regarded as being of no value. Shepstone got the signatures of only 2500 out of 8000 voters to memorials in favour of annexation, but he annexed the country.

The leaders of the national party, among them Mr Kruger, never ceased to protest against that annexation, and very shortly the money brought into the country by the English government, and the victory gained by British arms over Cetewayo, had completely removed all the causes for annexation, and even the dwellers in the towns ceased to be in favour of it. The whole country became united in the hope of recovering its independence. Mr Kruger visited England to try and induce Lord Carnarvon to give back their independence, and he brought with him a memorial signed by 6591 out of 8000 voters in what had been the republic. Lord Carnarvon stood absolutely firm about undoing the annexation. In the following year, 1879, occurred the famous outbreak of Liberal feeling, which many of you will remember, against the policy of Lord Beaconsfield with regard to the Russo-Turkish war and Afghanistan. The feeling had broken out before, but in 1879, the term of parliament having nearly expired, expression was given to it in Mr Gladstone's memorable Mid-Lothian campaign. What effect that Mid-Lothian campaign had on British politics we are not here to consider, but one of the indictments Mr Gladstone brought against Lord Beaconsfield's policy was about this matter. Coupling the Transvaal with Cyprus, he said, "If those acquisitions were as valuable as they are valueless, I would repudiate them because they are obtained by means dishonourable to the character of our country." The general election took place early in 1880, and immediately the Boers reminded Mr Gladstone, by a letter written by their leaders, of his expression " I would repudiate them," and the answer which he gave—of course he had to take the opinion of his cabinet—the answer which the cabinet telegraphed was " under no circumstances can the Queen's authority in the Transvaal be relinquished." You may easily suppose that such a frustration of the hopes which they had been induced to hold, in a population which had immense confidence in themselves, brought about nearly unanimously the Transvaal insurrection at the end of 1880 ; and in the war so caused there occurred those successive defeats of the British forces at Laing's Nek and on Majuba Hill, after which— we must not say because of which—the British cabinet surrendered the country to its inhabitants.

That surrender was made by the Pretoria Convention, which took its name from Pretoria, the capital of the Transvaal, in 1881. That convention again set up the republic as a separate state, though under the name of the Transvaal State. There has been some fog about that as there was about the convention which originally recognized the republic, and certainly it is a pity that it did not more expressly exclude the supposition that it might only be intended to erect a self-governing part of the Queen's dominions. But still, if you examine the matter impartially, there is no real doubt about its meaning. The Transvaal was to have distinct foreign relations, and that was provided for by the convention itself, only those foreign relations were to be conducted for it by the Queen's government. Consequently it would be a separate state, and, being a separate state, of course its inhabitants had a distinct national character. They were citizens, or as they call it burghers, of that republic, and not subjects of the Queen. You could not combine both characters any more than you can combine the characters of Englishman and Frenchman. Of course, although a separate state, it was to be under a suzerainty, because that is a fact for which, as you know well, the convention provided. The mere circumstance that its foreign relations, although distinct, were to be made for it—its treaties concluded for it— by the Queen, was enough to place it in the position of a dependent state, not an independent one, with the Queen as suzerain or paramount. Besides that, the suzerainty was mentioned in express terms in the preamble of the convention. But it was not to be an indefinite suzerainty: it was expressed in the preamble to be on the terms of the ensuing articles[1]. And indeed the convention, with its long array of articles, would have been a mere sham if any indefinite suzerainty outside those articles had been intended to be reserved.

That lasted for three years, until 1884. Then, in deference to the agitation which the Boer leaders had never ceased to keep up, it was superseded by the Convention of London, which gave to the state a larger amount of freedom. Its foreign relations were no longer to be conducted by the Queen; it was to conduct them itself, subject to the Queen's approval. The necessity of that approval still left it not fully sovereign but semi-sovereign, although a separate and international state. You may say, if you like, that it was still under a suzerainty, but the position of the republic depended upon the terms of the convention itself. Those terms were much more liberal to it than those of the previous convention. Not only was it to conduct its own foreign relations subject to the Queen's approval, but there was no longer to be a British resident at Pretoria with the power to interfere and exercize a surveillance over native affairs either within or without the republic, and there were, as before, certain stipulations as to the treatment of natives, religious liberty, and other matters which are generally included in commercial treaties between two independent states. But the scope of those stipulations was to be measured by the terms of the convention itself and not by any vague

[1] "Complete self-government, subject to the suzerainty of Her Majesty her heirs and successors, will be accorded to the inhabitants of the Transvaal territory, upon the following terms and conditions, and subject to the following restrictions and limitations."

reservations outside it[1]. At the same time its old official name, the South African Republic, was restored to the Transvaal, which from that day to this has occupied the legal position so created.

Such has been the history down to the Convention of London, and now I will take first the claims which are supposed to have a legal foundation under that convention and the subordinate position of the South African Republic, and afterwards the considerations arising in a more general way out of the use which the Republic has from 1884 made of that degree of liberty which it possesses. There has been a certain class of claims not made on behalf of individuals, but in which the British government charged the Transvaal government with having violated the convention. There was a law passed by it to regulate the admission of aliens, for the purpose of excluding pauper aliens from its territory, which was said to be contrary to the right of immigration secured by the Convention of London. There was a law on the expulsion of aliens, by which the Boer government received the power of expelling aliens without its being judicially proved against them that they had broken

[1] It has been attempted to introduce a suzerainty controlling the interpretation and operation of the Convention of London, in place of the simple one which results from and is defined by it, by the hair-splitting argument, more appropriate to legal documents at home than to the broad manner in which international documents are usually drawn and construed, that the articles of London are expressed to be substituted for the articles of Pretoria, and not the convention for the convention. But we have seen that even in the preamble of 1881, which it is desired thus to preserve, the self-government subject to suzerainty is stated to be on the terms of the articles. And the consideration that any other suzerainty, a word undefined in international law, would reduce any and every convention to a sham is decisive.

any laws of the state. That was supposed also to be contrary to the right of residence stipulated by the Convention of London. There was a monopoly granted by the Transvaal government to a dynamite company, the effect of which monopoly was very largely to increase the cost of dynamite, and thereby the cost of working the mines. That was said to be contrary to the convention; I never could see how. There is a great deal to be said in the other two cases, but as the convention says nothing of monopolies I never could see how one could be a breach of it. Then the Transvaal government, in the exercize of that right which the second convention gave it of conducting its own foreign affairs, systematically delayed to submit the treaties which it had concluded to the Queen for approval until so late a stage that to disapprove them might cause her government to incur considerable unpleasantness with the country with which the Transvaal was negotiating. In the particular instances there was no danger of such unpleasantness arising, but by omitting to present treaties for the Queen's sanction until after they had been ratified by the government with which they had been made, which the Transvaal claimed the right to do, it might happen that in less harmless cases that other government might be seriously offended by the refusal of her sanction. Upon all or most of the matters I have mentioned the Transvaal government got abundant opinions from international lawyers that what they were doing was not a breach of the convention. On the other hand the British government was sustained by the opinion of its own lawyers in maintaining that the convention had been broken.

My opinion on one or more of the cases in which I was consulted professionally was that the Transvaal government was right, and in one of them I thought it was wrong. But they were all cases which might have been remedied without war as they turned upon the interpretation of the convention, and if it was thought that there was a wrong the course might have been adopted which the Transvaal government suggested and the question submitted to arbitration[1].

Then there were the claims of grievances to individuals. That leads me to enter into a little detail as to the extreme severity with which the Transvaal government carried out their ideal, because it was out of that severity that these grievances to individuals arose. In the first place with regard to the language. There was until quite recently no education provided for by public funds except that which was carried on in the Dutch language. There has been in the last year or two a little concession : some of the elementary schools are open

[1] The great question as to the aliens admission and expulsion laws turns on whether the scanty words in Art. 14 of the Convention of London are to be considered to deal exhaustively with their subject, or whether they must be interpreted by the usage of nations and the general policy which they appear to have been intended to secure, like the similar and no less scantily expressed stipulations in numerous commercial treaties between independent states, that similarity being itself an element in the case. Among the continental international lawyers consulted by the South African Republic there was a general concurrence of opinion in its favour as to both laws. My opinion, for what it was worth, accepted the larger principle of interpretation, but was in favour of the republic only on the admission law, against it on the expulsion law. In the dynamite case the British argument appears to rest on twisting a stipulation for equality between burghers and aliens into the prohibition of a monopoly bearing with equal hardness on both.

to education given in English up to the fourth standard. After that all must go on in Dutch. That no doubt is an extreme hardship to a population the majority of which do not speak Dutch but English. But there was nothing about education in the convention, and when we treat that as a matter which might arise with any perfectly independent country, it would be absurd to suppose that a foreigner can have a claim to have his language used in schools supported by public money. How long is it in this country that a parent has had a right to have his child taught with public money?

Then, again, with regard to the administration of justice, no doubt the conduct of the Transvaal government has been very bad. No one but a burgher can be employed as a juryman, or is employed as a policeman. That prevented foreigners from serving as jurymen in cases where other Uitlanders might be concerned, and it left the police of the great mining city of Johannesburg in the hands of Dutch-speaking burghers, mostly from the country districts, who neither knew the language of the people nor the requirements of a city population. Out of these abuses with regard to the police and juries there arose complaints that individuals had been subjected to hardships for which, it is said, we should be able to claim redress if it had been a perfectly independent country in which those hardships had been suffered. In many cases no doubt that was true. But then again why were not these grievances in particular cases made a subject for arbitration between the two governments? As to the general evil from which they arose, the extremely narrow policy with regard to the police and justice, that was something which if the country had been Germany or Russia we could not complain of, neither did the convention give us any right to complain of it in the Transvaal. And so with regard to other grievances. The real remedy for any grievances which individuals might complain of, therefore, was arbitration[1].

Then there was the claim of the franchise. Of course in no country are foreigners admitted to it. The claim of the franchise presupposed that there should be easy admission to naturalization because, the republics being states separate from the

[1] It seems desirable to draw attention to the difference between such arbitrations as I recommend here and on p. 437, on the one hand, and on the other hand an arbitration on the general relations between two states, such as I understand the Transvaal government to have been aiming at, as stated on p. 421. Art. 16 of the convention on mediation and arbitration drawn up this year [1899] at the Hague expresses that "in questions of a legal nature, and especially in the interpretation or application of international conventions, arbitration is recognized by the signatory powers as the most effective, and at the same time the most equitable, means of settling disputes which diplomacy has failed to settle." The Russian draft had been limited in the same way: see its Art. 7. And the memorandum accompanying that draft, which is a remarkably able state paper, had dwelt on the difference between international questions of law and of policy, with respect to the applicability of arbitration to them. See the Bluebook c. 9534, pp. 20, 42–45, 305. The question whether killing Mr Edgar could be justified, and even, though that example goes to the limit, the question up to what stage the Transvaal government could omit to present a treaty to the Queen for her approval without violating the Convention of London, are legal ones, to the fair determination of which either way this country might submit. But since our policy in South Africa comprized as an essential element the dependent character of the South African Republic, we could not accept a decision by an arbitrator that such was not its character. I pointed out the distinction between legal and political differences with reference to international arbitration in an article which appeared in the *International Journal of Ethics* for October, 1896.

Queen's dominions, the characters of British subject and Transvaaler or Orange Free Stater could not be combined. No doubt the policy of the Transvaal government was most illiberal. After the discovery of gold was made and the Uitlanders began to flow in it passed laws the result of which was that, whereas at the date of the London Convention a person could obtain naturalization and the franchise together after five years' residence, under the new laws he could not get the latter in less than fourteen years, and then only if individually named in a resolution of the volksraad. No such length of residence is required in any other country that I know of. But, again, in the convention there was nothing about the franchise. An attempt has been made to found that demand of the franchise on a promise said to have been made in 1881, before the Convention of Pretoria. At that time there were commissioners engaged in treating with the Boer leaders as to the terms on which the restoration of the country should take place. At one meeting of those commissioners the chairman, Sir Hercules Robinson, now Lord Rosmead, asked : " Had British subjects free trade throughout the Transvaal before the annexation ? " Mr Kruger replied : " They were on the same footing as the burghers. There was not the slightest difference, in compliance with the provisions of Sand River," that is, of the convention by which the republic was acknowledged in 1852. " The chairman : I think you will have no objection to allowing that to continue so ? Mr Kruger : No, there will be equal protection for every one. Sir E. Wood : And equal privileges ? Mr Kruger : We make no distinction in so far as burgher rights are concerned. There might perhaps be some small difference in the case of a young person who has just come into the country." And on a later day Dr Jorissen, the state attorney, explained that Mr Kruger meant a new arrival when he spoke of a young person, and referred to the fact that before the annexation a year's residence was required for naturalization. There, you see, the conversation arose not about political rights at all, but on a query about free trade, which does not involve naturalization, and its scope is further shown by the reference to the Sand River convention. Mr Kruger indeed in his answer went a little beyond the question and spoke of burgher rights, yet it is a familiar principle at least in English law that when you enter upon a written agreement after the discussion of its terms you do not go behind it, and if any terms mentioned in the discussion are not included in the agreement, they are supposed not to have been thought of sufficient importance to be so included, and what the parties are bound by is that which appears in the agreement[1].

[1] Some further observations must be made on this. (1) Even if the scope of the conversation be taken from Mr Kruger's answers and not from Sir Hercules Robinson's questions, the answers gave notice that some term of residence would be required for naturalization. (2) The term was lengthened to five years in 1882, so that, if this had been thought to be a breach of an engagement that things should remain as they were in respect of naturalization or the franchise, there was ample opportunity by the Convention of London to rectify the omission of that engagement from the Convention of Pretoria and to provide for the future. That this was not done, nor is there any trace that the subject was mentioned in the negotiation of the later convention, is proof enough that no importance was attached to the conversation at that time. (3) It is only during the last two or three years that, so far as I am aware, the conversation has turned up in the discussions on the subject of the

I sum up that neither the different claims that the convention has been broken by the Transvaal government, nor the claims to redress for grievances to individuals, have been such as could be made a cause of war. They have either been such as we could not make at all against a stronger foreign country in which the same circumstances occurred, or they have been claims for which, the facts as regards them being disputed, the true remedy would have been arbitration. And before I leave that part of the subject, I will say that I think the attempt to find for these various claims a justification on the ground of the conventions, or of the conversation of 1881, has seriously damaged our case. It has led to untenable arguments being used, and to the introduction of the principle, a perfectly untenable principle, that the conventions themselves have not to be interpreted according to their language but under the assumption of a vague suzerainty. The kind of argumentation which has been used, the introduction of this vague suzerainty, has, I think, contributed to that suspicion of our motives, to that suspicion of our being unwilling to abide by any written agreement, which no doubt has been one of the causes of this war. But I think we may pass them by in consideration of the vastly more important matters which arise out of the general policy of the Transvaal state since it was established on its present footing by the convention of 1884. It does seem to me that there is

franchise. It was therefore with amazement that I read in the Queen's speech, at the dissolution of parliament on 9th August last: "The position of my subjects in the South African Republic is inconsistent with the promises of equal treatment on which my grant of internal independence to that republic was founded."

very great reason for contending that it has systematically acted in such a manner as to constitute a grave danger, which entitled this country to throw the letter of the convention aside and to demand relief from a situation which had become intolerable[1].

At the time of the Convention of London there was no European power in South Africa except England and Portugal, a power so weak that it might be left out of account, on the east coast. England had a vague idea of claiming the tract on the west coast north of the Orange River which now on the map is coloured German. It was then not German, neither was it British, but there was a vague notion that some day it might be made British. It was in 1883 that the attention of Germany was first directed to that part of Africa. There was a great deal of shilly-shallying on the part of our government; it procrastinated and gave inconclusive answers to Prince Bismarck's question whether England was prepared to protect German settlers in that region. Finally the German flag was hoisted at Angra Pequeña on 7th August 1884, and our government acquiesced in its being so hoisted. They could not do otherwise in the pass to which they had brought the matter. Germany then was established on the west coast of Africa

---

[1] I believe that the bad and mischievous argumentation to which I refer has had a root in one of our national qualities which is entitled to high respect when kept within due bounds, namely our passion for legality. It is no new thing in our public life to strain legal arguments to the uttermost and beyond the uttermost, rather than admit that the time has arrived when help must be found outside the law, or in what the non-existence of a legislature makes difficult in international matters, a change in the law.

in the very year in which the Convention of London was concluded. Between Germany and the Transvaal republic there was Bechuanaland, the strip of country which is now coloured red, but at that time the British dominions did not stretch so far north.

The government of the Transvaal republic immediately jumped at the prospect of getting into contact with Germany on the west coast, and violated openly the obligation which it had undertaken in that very year by Art. 2 of the convention of 1884, copied from Art. 19 of that of 1881, that it would " strictly adhere to the boundaries defined in the 1st article of this convention, and do its utmost to prevent any of its inhabitants from making any encroachments upon lands beyond the said state." Freebooters from the republic overran much of Bechuanaland, and the republican government, so far from holding to its engagement to restrain any such incursions, supported them and entered into a direct conflict with the British government for the supremacy over the country. Early in 1884 the Queen proclaimed her protectorate over Bechuanaland, and in May her protection was formally declared to apply to the chief Montsioa, whom the freebooters were attacking, but in September President Kruger issued a proclamation taking Montsioa and Moshette, with their subjects and rights, under the protection and jurisdiction of the South African Republic. You will observe the dates. Mr Kruger tolerated the British supremacy over Bechuanaland till August, but one month after the hoisting of the German flag at Angra Pequeña he set it at nought. An unmistakable announcement of determination however brought Mr Kruger to his senses. He withdrew his proclamation. Parliament voted £675,000—the ultimate cost was much larger—for the expedition which was sent out under Sir Charles Warren, and that expedition succeeded in finally bringing all Bechuanaland under British control[1]. But that was not the end of Mr Kruger's .attempt to coquet with Germany. As the Uitlanders in the Transvaal increased in numbers and naturally became less willing to bear the Dutch mode of government, they formed associations for reform and thereby incurred the displeasure of President Kruger. That is expressed in a speech of his, part of which I will read to you, made on 27th January 1895, the birthday of the German emperor, nearly a year before the Jameson raid.

[1] The Transvaal government or leaders had before this attempted more than once to establish political relations with Germany, notably, it is believed, in 1874, 1878 and 1883. But I pass over what may be attributed to the desire to undo the British annexation of 1877, or to obtain better terms than those granted at Pretoria in 1881. The important point is how the legal situation has been worked which existed between the United Kingdom and the South African Republic at the outbreak of the war. It is not necessary to suggest that either in 1884 or since there has been any agreement between Germany and the republic. It is sufficient to show the Transvaal moving as it were on parallel lines with Germany, so as to take up a position from which an agreement was likely to result as soon as England might be in a difficulty anywhere. As to the breaches of the conventions, Transvaal freebooters had been in Bechuanaland from 1881 in spite of the Convention of Pretoria, and had established there the two republics of Stellaland and the Land of Goshen, which the British Government had of course not recognized. The territories of these republics were divided between the British protectorate and the Transvaal by the enlarged boundary which the Convention of London gave to the latter, but the Goshenites refused to acquiesce, and they were allowed publicly to advertize in the republic an expedition against Montsioa.

"It is the spirit of loyalty which I admire in the Germans. They are under the laws, they work under the laws, they obey the laws, and they fell in the Kaffir war under the laws. All our subjects are not so minded. The English, for instance, although they behave themselves properly and are loyal to the state, always fall back upon England when it suits their purpose. Therefore I shall ever promote the interests of Germany, though it be but with the resources of a child, such as my land is considered. This child is now being trodden upon by one great power, and the natural consequence is that it seeks protection from another. The time has come to knit ties of the closest friendship between Germany and the South African Republic, ties such as are natural between father and child[1]."

You see that was said at a time when there was no raid, no attempt at a revolution, only complaints of the hardship of the laws and the formation of associations with a view of reforming them; and when the only complaint which he could make against England was that England insisted upon interpretations of the convention which did not agree with his own interpretations. The British government appealed direct to the German government in consequence of that speech. The German government repudiated any desire to occupy the position with regard to South Africa and the Transvaal state which Mr Kruger had clearly intimated that he wished it to occupy. But it said that it objected to any alteration of the *status quo*, that is of the existing state of things in South Africa, and that even a purely commercial federation of the South African colonies and states would be an alteration of the *status quo* to which Germany would object.

In October of the same year, 1895, still before the Jameson raid, there took place the incident of the closing of the drifts or ferries over the Vaal River into the Transvaal state. Those ferries were

[1] *Edinburgh Review*, vol. 183, p. 294.

closed with a view of forcing the traffic to take the course by Delagoa Bay, in Portuguese territory, to which the Transvaalers had made a railway, instead of that by the Cape. That desire, no doubt, was partly in the interests of the railway itself, but it was not wholly a commercial or a financial desire. It was to a great extent a political desire to bring their country into a closer connection with Portuguese and German influences, and to get it out of the region of British South Africa. In connection with the closing of the drifts, President Kruger used some of that unguarded language which marks him. He did not put it only on the ground of getting traffic for the railway to Delagoa Bay; he said "it was his intention to build a wall and construct a barbed wire fence for the exclusion of goods coming from the Cape Colony[1]." The closing of the drifts was a direct breach of the convention of 1884, and our government succeeded in getting them opened again, but by nothing short of a direct threat of war.

Then followed the Jameson raid at the end of 1895, and during all this time, even before the raid, you must bear in mind that powerful forts were being built to command Johannesburg, and that the country was being armed to the very teeth[2].

[1] Report of Mr Schreiner, Cape Attorney-General, in the Bluebook c. 8474, p. 4.

[2] In how serious a situation that stupid as well as lawless raid would have placed England if it had enjoyed only a few days' success may be inferred from the anxiety of the German government to march fifty marines from the Seeadler into the Transvaal from Delagoa Bay, "for the protection of the lives and properties of Germans." The request for permission was still pressed on the Portuguese government after news had been received, not only that the British government had taken the course which its duty

Is it possible to suppose that the armament was not directed against England? Since then England and Germany have happily come to be on much better terms. There had always been until about two years ago a desire on the part of Germany to get hold of Delagoa Bay, and therefore you see that in attempting to force the traffic to that direction, President Kruger—and not only he, but many others—thought it might before long bring him into connection with German influence. About two years ago an agreement was come to between England and Germany, not yet published, but by which it is believed to have been arranged that in case Portugal should be disposed to part with Delagoa Bay to any one, it should be to England and not to Germany. If the agreement is such, it is a final renunciation by Germany of any designs upon South Africa beyond her actual limits there, and at any rate the agreement has inaugurated that better understanding which now exists between England and Germany. Since then it has been of course perfectly useless for President Kruger to attempt to get into direct contact with Germany or to avail himself of her against England.

But that was not the last of the propagandism which attends upon all ideals, and there has been another design in pursuance of which the nominally defensive alliance between the Orange Free State and the South African Republic was concluded some two years since. It is the design to unite the whole of South Africa in a big South African Republic from which England should be entirely

pointed out, but that Dr Jameson had been defeated and that foreigners were in no danger.

excluded, except so far as she might receive permission to remain at Cape Town for a time, because for a time, until the republic became strong enough to protect itself, it would be to their interest to have protection; and as England itself would cling to Cape Town as a halfway house on the road to India—it is rather a wild, chimerical design—it seems to have been thought that it might be possible to arrange terms with England to remain there, partly for her own protection, and partly for the protection of the South African Republic. It was chimerical, but there is no doubt whatever that that design—and more especially within the last two or three years—has been in the minds of the Dutch in the republics, and that an attempt has been made to instil it into the Dutch population of Cape Colony. It has been advocated largely in the press of both republics, the Orange Free State and the Transvaal. That that is not only an English opinion at the Cape I will give you this proof. Sir James Sivewright, who is a member of the party which now holds office, the party most favourable to the Dutch, and who was at that time a member of the Ministry of Sir John Gordon Sprigg, complained vehemently of the line taken by the press in the two republics, and of a republican propaganda and emissaries to support it which he said were actively at work in the districts of Worcester, Wellington and Paarl in the colony, therefore very near Cape Town itself. He made that complaint on 20th January 1897, in a public speech of which President Steyn of the Orange Free State took notice and attempted to refute it. But Sir James Sivewright in reply instanced " the writing of the republican press, notably the *Express* of Bloemfontein and the *Volksstem* of Pretoria, as taken over by the newspapers of the colony," adding " with the knowledge which from experience I have gained of the power and position of the writer in at least one of the papers named[1]." No notice was taken of the speech in the Transvaal so far as I am aware, and indeed it would have been difficult for the Transvaal government to exculpate itself, because by the press law which they enacted in 1896 the president has the power, on the advice and with the consent of the executive, to prohibit the circulation of printed or published matter being in his judgment against good morals, or dangerous to peace and order in the republic. A country which has press laws of that kind, whether it be a republic or an autocracy like Russia, must take the responsibility with the right; it cannot exculpate itself when it permits a propaganda of that kind to take place in the columns of its press.

I have given you reasons for characterizing the policy pursued by the Transvaal government since 1884, and I am quite prepared to think that the time had arrived at which it was necessary to take some serious step. Because if what I have said is correct, if the policy of the two republics is really what it has been represented as being, then the state of things was this: there were upon our borders in South Africa two states of great military power—because although their population is not great, yet the whole of that population, as we see, is trained to arms and fights very well—

[1] See for this incident the Bluebook c. 8423, pp. 91, 110–112, 125–128.

and those two military powers were engaged in a propaganda among our own people for the ultimate absorption of nearly the whole of our colonies in a big South African Republic from which England was to be excluded. It is perfectly unnecessary to say that that propaganda had already had considerable effect among the Cape Dutch. It may or may not, but what we do know is that even if it had not, such a propaganda if allowed to continue could hardly fail to have an effect sooner or later, because the fact of its not being checked would be taken as a proof of weakness on the part of this country. It is equally unavailing to say that no steps have been taken by the governments of the two republics actually to carry out the scheme of that propaganda. It is not likely, not having the support of Germany, that they would take any steps in peaceful times. But if it is the fact that there are considerable military powers on our frontiers which have that propaganda at heart, then I think it would be folly to ignore it. We must expect as reasonable men that an attempt by arms would be carried out when England was in difficulty, and the only way to deal with it was to deal with it at a time when England was not in difficulties. I know well that friends of the Boers deny the existence of the propaganda itself, or at least that it is of serious importance; they deny the existence of the designs imputed to them. I do not give what I have told you as conclusive proof, but as sufficient proof to create reasonable suspicion in cautious minds, and as reason enough for us to believe Sir Alfred Milner, a very eminent man, when he says that this is the case, at any rate not to put our own individual opinions against those of a man so placed. Now then it was expressly upon this ground that Sir Alfred Milner, not in speaking to Mr Kruger at the Bloemfontein conference—he did not wish to embitter that conference by referring to any such ground as that which I am now dealing with, a ground of course which Mr Kruger would dispute, a propaganda which of course he would disclaim—it was not in the conference but in the famous despatch which preceded the conference[1] that he, to Mr Chamberlain, expressly put the line he intended to take upon that ground. He says :

"South Africa can prosper under two, three or six governments, but not under two absolutely conflicting social and political systems, perfect equality for Dutch and British in the British colonies side by side with permanent subjection of British to Dutch in one of the republics. It is idle to talk of peace and unity under such a state of affairs. It is this which makes the internal condition of the Transvaal republic a matter of vital interest to Her Majesty's government. No merely local question affects so deeply the welfare and peace of her own South African possessions.... A certain section of the press, not in the Transvaal only, preaches openly and constantly the doctrine of a republic embracing all South Africa, and supports it by menacing references to the armaments of the Transvaal, its alliance with the Orange Free State, and the active sympathy which in case of war it would receive from a section of Her Majesty's subjects. I regret to say that this doctrine, supported as it is by a ceaseless stream of malignant lies about the intentions of the British government, is producing a great effect upon a large number of our Dutch fellow colonists. Language is frequently used which seems to imply that the Dutch have some superior right even in this colony to their fellow citizens of British birth. Thousands of men peaceably disposed, and if left alone perfectly satisfied with their position as British subjects, are being drawn into disaffection, and there is a corresponding exasperation on the side of the British."

I don't think it was very wise of Mr Chamberlain to publish that. It would have been far better,

[1] The telegram of 4th May 1899.

if it be true that the propaganda has already produced a considerable amount of disaffection among the Cape Dutch, to have kept that private. But there you have Sir Alfred Milner's statement. Mr Chamberlain sanctioned his policy on the same ground[1], and the result was that demand of the franchise with substantial representation which he put forward at the Bloemfontein conference and which Mr Kruger refused.

From the Bloemfontein conference to the outbreak of war there was no variation in the positions taken up by the two sides. Without going through the negotiations step by step, I may summarize them as consisting, first, of an attempt on the part of the Transvaal government to elude Sir Alfred Milner's demand by an inadequate franchise law, which proposed to give the franchise at the end of seven years, but which was fenced with so many conditions that, according to the opinion of those best entitled to judge, it would really have had no effect; and then, when they found that our government would not accept an inadequate franchise law, the rest of the negotiations consisted in offering a five years' franchise law without hampering conditions, but only upon other conditions which they knew that this government would not accept. Finally, the position of the Transvaal government

[1] "...Her Majesty's government are entitled to make representations with a view to securing redress. This ordinary right of all governments is strengthened in the present case by the peculiar relations established by the conventions between this country and the Transvaal, and also by the fact that the peace and prosperity of the whole of South Africa, including Her Majesty's possessions, may be seriously affected by any circumstances which are calculated to produce discontent and unrest in the South African Republic." Despatch of 10th May 1899.

is contained in their notes of 19th and 21st August, in which they offer seemingly most favourable terms, terms which if they had been offered without conditions would have been most favourable. They offered a five years' franchise, retrospective, eight new seats for the Rand, and not only a vote for the volksraad but also for the elections of the President and Commander-in-Chief, and they expressed a willingness to receive and to consider friendly suggestions as to the franchise law to be passed. Now come to the conditions. One of them was that the British government should promise in future never to interfere in their internal affairs, that this should be a final interference once and for all ; secondly, not to insist further on the existence of a suzerainty, and, thirdly, to agree to arbitration on particular matters. Mr Chamberlain's answer to that expressed satisfaction with the terms themselves, apart from the conditions. With regard to the condition not to insist further on the existence of a suzerainty, he referred to the previous correspondence in which, while insisting—theoretically insisting—upon a vague suzerainty, he had said that since the republic was prepared to abide by the convention of 1884 there was no controversy as to the essential point[1]. As to the condition

[1] In a despatch of 16th October 1897 Mr Chamberlain had refused to agree to a proposal of arbitration, which I understand to have included an arbitration on the general relations between the United Kingdom and the South African Republic, as being improper where there was a suzerainty. On 16th April 1898 Dr Leyds, the state secretary of the republic, replied that the suzerainty reserved by the preamble of the convention of 1881 no longer existed, and that it would be no reason against arbitration if it did. On 15th December 1898 Mr Chamberlain argued that the suzerainty of the preamble of 1881 still existed, but added : " Her Majesty's

to agree to arbitration on particular matters, he accepted that also. The one condition upon which

government have taken note of the assurance, once more repeated at the commencement of Dr Leyds's note, that the government of the South African Republic are prepared in every respect to abide by the stipulations of the convention of 1884. These stipulations undoubtedly include ' reservations with reference to certain specified matters.' There is thus no controversy as to the essential point in the relations between the two governments, which gives to Great Britain a position of superiority." On 9th May 1899 Mr Reitz, the new secretary of state of the republic, wrote in support of Dr Leyds's view. And on 13th July 1899 Mr Chamberlain wrote: " Her Majesty's government.... have no intention of continuing to discuss this question with the government of the republic, whose contention that the South African Republic is a sovereign international state is not in their opinion warranted either by law or history, and is wholly inadmissible." And he quoted Lord Kimberley's instructions to Sir Hercules Robinson preparatory to the convention of 1881, in which it was stated that " entire freedom of action will be accorded to the Transvaal government, so far as is not inconsistent with the rights *expressly* reserved to the suzerain power. The term suzerainty has been chosen as most conveniently describing superiority over a state possessing independent rights of government, subject to reservations with reference *to certain specified matters* " (the italics are mine). It was to this despatch of 13th July that Mr Chamberlain referred in his answer of 28th August to the terms offered by the Transvaal government on 19th and 21st August, but that reference must bring in the despatch of 15th December 1898 as a part of the connected correspondence. So far from claiming too much for the British government in saying that it expressed itself satisfied for essential purposes with the express conventional terms, it may be questioned whether, even on the despatch of 13th July alone, it is quite fair to the British government to say that it was theoretically insisting on a vague suzerainty.... The Transvaal condition as to arbitration was accepted in the despatch of 28th August subject to " a discussion of the form and scope of a tribunal of arbitration from which foreigners and foreign influence are excluded." And the reply to the general condition against future interference was expressed in a manner apparently intended to soften the rejection. " First, as regards intervention, Her Majesty's government hope that the fulfilment of the promises made, and the just treatment of the Uitlanders in future, will render unnecessary any further intervention on their behalf, but Her Majesty's government cannot there was nothing like an acceptance, but a clear and firm rejection, was the promise in future not to interfere again in the internal affairs of the republic. That promise, of course, it was impossible to give, after all the experience we have had, which teaches us at least to say that we can place no faith in the Transvaal government. The answer of the republic to that despatch was to declare that the terms were offered only subject to the conditions, that a refusal to consent to the conditions upon which they were offered was equivalent to a refusal of the terms themselves. Nothing further took place before the outbreak of war except this, that Mr Chamberlain at the last moment added a new demand. He demanded, if the franchise was settled, that the new members who represented the Uitlanders in the volksraad should be allowed to speak English. Of course, as they would not be able to speak Dutch, their presence in the volksraad would be useless without that permission. There is no objection made to the French Canadians speaking French in the parliament of Canada. But that demand the Transvaal government refused absolutely.

And then, when the grass on the veldt was grown enough to afford forage for the horses, they declared war with an ultimatum which demanded that we should remove at once all our troops from the borders of the republic, that we should remove from South Africa all troops landed there since the 1st of June, and that the troops then at sea should

of course debar themselves from their rights under the conventions, nor divest themselves of the ordinary obligations of a civilized power to protect its subjects in a foreign country from injustice."

not be landed in South Africa. The ultimatum came at a time when negotiations had never been broken off, when it was still possible for either party to make fresh proposals. It demanded too that we should leave ourselves disarmed, with nothing but our usual small garrison, in the presence of two armed republics, and it is no wonder that such an ultimatum as that was instantly refused[1].

If we are asked what it is we are at war about, I would put the final points at issue shortly thus. The British demand is for the franchise to be obtained after five years' residence, also by those who have already resided five years in the republic, together with a substantial number of new seats for the Rand. That is refused unless we give a promise, which we decline to give, of never again on any ground interfering with the affairs of the republic. That the promise so demanded was meant to include intervention on grounds of general international law is evident from the circumstance that the question of the suzerainty was made the subject of a separate condition in the terms proposed on 19th and 21st August. Then there is the other British demand of the free use of either language in the volksraad, which is refused absolutely. There is the Transvaal demand that we should submit not only particular questions but the general relations of the two countries to arbitration, which would be equivalent to referring it to an arbitrator to make a new convention[2], and that we should disarm our colonies

[1] The fact that it was so framed lights up the uncertainty that might possibly have still rested on the policy of the two republics, and exhibits them insisting on a position of military superiority in South Africa.

[2] The form in which this demand was made in the ultimatum

in the face of their armaments. These are the short issues on which we are now at war. The Transvaal ultimatum was more than an ultimatum; it was a conditional declaration of war. It declared that if its terms were not accepted by the time named a state of war would exist. The terms were not accepted by the time named, and we instantly became as much at war in the regular international sense as if the Queen had herself made a declaration of war by the usual proclamation. Thereupon the Orange Free State issued a declaration of war against England on the ground of the Transvaal republic being, as they said, unjustly attacked, so that the *casus fœderis* of a defensive alliance had arisen.

We are then internationally at war. The idea which is often expressed in a part of the press that it is not an international war, but that it is possible to treat the enemy as insurgents, is perfectly absurd. No serious person who knows anything of the case would maintain it for a moment. But although we are now internationally at war it will by no means follow that the war will conclude by our becoming internationally at peace. It may be, the war having now broken off the previous relations between the governments, that those relations may never be re-established; it may be that the only remedy for the evil will be the annexation of these

was "that all points of mutual difference shall be regulated by the friendly course of arbitration, or by whatever other amicable way may be agreed upon by this government with Her Majesty's government." This could be worked as a peremptory demand for arbitration, simply by not agreeing to any other amicable way that might be proposed. The correspondence extending over years must be examined in order to appreciate the scope of the desired arbitration.

two republics. It is now rather early to speak of that, but if that should be the remedy, if in the end there should be no negotiations, no terms of peace, no recognition of the republics as still continuing to exist but simply a proclamation of annexation, then we must remember what President Kruger said at the Bloemfontein conference, that independence on the footing of having the Dutch swamped by Uitlanders governing the country according to the English and not according to the Dutch ideal would be worse than annexation[1].

[1] The exercise of the extreme right of conquest by the annexation of the Orange Free State and the South African Republic to the British dominions would not prevent any powers of self-government which might be thought fit being given to the territories which now compose them. The empire includes examples shading off in that respect from the dominion of Canada to the rock of Gibraltar. Nor would annexation prevent the separation, if approved, of the goldmining districts in which the non-Boers greatly preponderate from the more purely Boer districts, so that in the latter the Dutch population might in some degree have the satisfaction of living their own life, under due provisions for the benefit of all other inhabitants of the same parts. Only the constitutional authority of the crown or of parliament would be supreme, and any necessary modifications of the arrangements might be made by that authority from time to time. There would be no more place for the fog which has been noticed in the lecture (pp. 429, 433) as clouding some minds about the existence of the republics as separate states.

That fog appears to have reached its climax in the Queen's speech proroguing parliament on 27th October, in which Her Majesty, after acknowledging the liberal provision made for the expense of military operations in South Africa, was made to say, " I trust that the divine blessing may rest upon your efforts and those of my gallant army to restore peace and good government to that portion of my empire." To include the two republics in the empire was to deny them a separate existence in any sense known in Europe or among people of European descent. It is just possible that the intention was to anticipate conquest as the result of the war, but I rather believe that the expression was the consequence of looking at the subject from an Indian point of view. It is well known that the relations between the United Kingdom and the native states in India cannot be expressed without contradiction in terms of international law, but that does not matter, for it has been officially notified in the Indian government gazette that "the principles of international law have no bearing upon the relations between the government of India as representing the Queen-Empress on the one hand, and the native states under the suzerainty of Her Majesty on the other ": No. 1700 E, 21st August 1891. It has suited our convenience to build up a system of our own, such as might have existed in Europe if the history of Europe had been different but does not in fact exist there. If minds preoccupied by that system cannot work one of paramount and dependent states connected by written documents such as are known among Europeans, that is another reason for annexation when a just occasion for it has been given. In that case, if there is to be no more misapprehension in the future, the proclamation of annexation must come first, whatever means be afterwards taken to ascertain what arrangements will best suit the part of the Boer population which may be willing to live as inoffensive British subjects. It is therefore gratifying to find that in the newspapers of 15th November Lord Salisbury corrects the representation given by Lord Edmond Fitzmaurice of what he had said at the Mansionhouse on the 9th, a representation into which Lord Edmond had, no doubt inadvertently, introduced a mention of " terms of peace."

# VII

## CONTINUOUS VOYAGE IN RELATION TO CONTRABAND OF WAR. 1899.

[Reprinted, with permission, from the *Law Quarterly Review*, vol. xv. (1899), pp. 24-32.]

IN the article on " the application of International Law during the Chino-Japanese war" which appeared in the last number of this *Review*, Professor Takahashi mentioned his forthcoming work on that subject. In one of the notes which I have contributed to that work I have taken occasion, from an incident concerning the *Gaelic*, to give to the doctrine of continuous voyages in relation to contraband of war a fuller discussion than I think it has yet received in England. By the kindness of Professor Takahashi I am allowed to reproduce this note here. It is as follows.

The *Gaelic* was a mail steamer which called at Yokohama in Japan in the regular course of her voyage from the United States port of San Francisco to the British port of Hong Kong. Before her arrival at Yokohama the Japanese government had received information that there were on board of her as passengers three persons of the description of contraband or analogues of contraband, seeking Chinese service and carrying to China some material intended to destroy Japanese ships. At Yokohama the Japanese government caused the *Gaelic* to be searched for the persons and material. Before the search was finished it was discovered that the persons had left the ship. In fact, notwithstanding that at San Francisco they had taken passages by the *Gaelic* for Hong Kong, they proceeded from Japan in another vessel to the Chinese port of Shanghai. But the search was continued, on the supposition that they might have left some of the material behind.

The British authorities in Japan objected to this proceeding on the ground that the *Gaelic* had no hostile destination, Nagasaki in Japan being the only port at which she would call in the regular course between Yokohama and Hong Kong: it was true that the vessels of the company to which she belonged often call at the Chinese port of Amoy, but there was no proof of any intention to do so on that voyage. And they contended that the neutral destination of the ship precluded search, it being immaterial whether anything on board her had a hostile destination ulterior to that of the ship. On the other hand, the correctness of the proceedings was maintained, on the ground both of the probability that the *Gaelic* might call at Amoy, and of the doctrine of continuous voyages as applicable in case contraband persons or goods on board her were destined for China even by way of Hong Kong. These opposing arguments call first for an examination of the doctrine of continuous voyages as affecting (1) goods contraband of war, (2) persons contraband of war, or analogues of such contraband, and afterwards for an examination of the question from another point of view which will appear.

## I. *The doctrine of continuous voyages as affecting goods.*

Goods on board a ship destined to a neutral port may be consigned to purchasers in that port or to agents who are to offer them for sale there, in either of which cases what further becomes of them will depend on the consignee purchasers or on the purchasers from the agents. Such goods before arriving at the neutral port have only a neutral destination; on arriving there they are, in Lord Stowell's language, imported into the common stock of the country; if they ultimately find their way to a belligerent port or to a belligerent army or navy it will be in consequence of a new destination given them, and this notwithstanding that the neutral port may be a well-known market for the belligerent in question to seek supplies in, and that the goods may notoriously have been attracted to it by the existence of such a market. The consignors of the goods to the neutral port may have had an expectation that they would reach the belligerent but not an intention to that effect, for a person can form an intention only about his own acts, and a belligerent destination was to be impressed on the goods, if at all, by other persons.

On the other hand goods on board a ship destined to a neutral port may be under orders from their owners to be forwarded thence to a belligerent port, army or navy, either by a further voyage of the same ship, or by transhipment, or even by land carriage. Such goods are to reach the belligerent without the intervention of a new commercial transaction, in pursuance of the intention formed with regard to them by the persons who are their owners during the voyage to the neutral port. Therefore even during that voyage they have a belligerent destination, although the ship which carries them may have only a neutral one.

In the case first put it is agreed that the goods, though of the nature of contraband of war, and the ship knowingly carrying them, are not subject to capture during the voyage to the neutral port. In the case secondly put the doctrine of continuous voyages is that the goods and the knowingly guilty ship are capturable during that voyage. That doctrine regards goods as being contraband of war when an enemy destination is combined with the necessary character of the goods, and it regards the offence of carrying contraband of war as being committed by a ship which is knowingly engaged in any part of the carriage of the goods to their belligerent destination. Those who deny the doctrine of continuous voyages can still hold that even in the second case the goods and the knowingly guilty ship are liable before reaching the neutral port if that port is only to be a port of call, the ultimate destination of the ship as well as of the goods being a belligerent one, but they deny that a further intended carriage by transhipment or by land can be united with the voyage to the neutral port so as to form one carriage to a belligerent destination, and make the goods and the knowingly guilty ship liable during the first part of it. They require a belligerent destination both of the goods and of the ship carrying them.

The doctrine of continuous voyages does not apply to breach of blockade. In contraband of war the root of the offence is in the nature of the aid supplied to a belligerent, that is in the goods, and the connexion of the ship with the offence must be proved. In breach of blockade the root of the offence is in the attempt to enter into prohibited communication with a belligerent coast, that is in the ship, and the connexion of the goods with the offence must be proved. The ship indeed, according to British and United States principles, commits the offence as soon as she sails on a blockade-running expedition, notwithstanding that it may be intended to interpose a neutral port of call before she reaches the blockaded coast which is her ultimate destination ; but a ship of which the only destination is to a neutral port cannot be connected with the blockade-runner into which her cargo is transhipped in that port. The cargo cannot be a source of infection before an offence of blockade-running from which its own guilt may be derived is committed. If, according to the French practice, the offence is committed only by the attempt to cross the very line of blockade, or by proceeding in order to do so after receiving a notification from a belligerent cruiser, the doctrine of continuous voyages cannot so much as be suggested in connexion with the case.

It was in connexion with the so-called rule of the war of 1756, namely that neutrals will not be allowed to engage in time of war in the trade between the enemy and his colonies from which they are excluded in time of peace, that Sir William Scott and Sir William Grant had occasion to establish the doctrine that goods must be considered as undergoing a continuous carriage from port A to port C, notwithstanding a call at port B where, for the sake of an appearance of importation, they are landed, duty is paid on them, and they are reshipped: the *Maria*, 5 C. Rob. 368; the *William*, 5 C. Rob. 385. The former judge is sometimes quoted as if in the case of the *Imina* he had condemned the application of a corresponding principle to the carriage of contraband of war. What however he said, namely that the contraband goods must be taken "in the actual prosecution" of a voyage to the enemy's port, was said with reference to the point that the proceeds cannot be taken on the return voyage, and he was not thinking of the exact circumstances in which an enemy destination will be held to have been actual: 3 C. Rob. 168. That he did not regard a neutral destination of the ship as conclusive against a condemnation of contraband goods on board her appears in the *Rapid*, Edwards 228, which was the case of a ship carrying a despatch addressed to a hostile minister. "It is to be observed," remarked Sir W. Scott, "that where the commencement of the voyage is in a neutral country and it is to terminate at a neutral port, or as in this instance at a port to which though not neutral an open trade is allowed, in such a case there is less to excite his (the master's) vigilance, and therefore it may be proper to make some allowance for any imposition which may be practised upon him." This distinctly gave it to be understood that the carriage of despatches, which is at least analogous to that of contraband goods if the despatches, being things and not persons, do not fall simply within the description of goods, would not necessarily be held to be innocent because the voyage of the ship was to terminate at a neutral port. In the case of the *Ocean*, 3 C. Rob. 297, Sir W. Scott held that communication by sea with a port not blockaded is not made guilty by internal communication between that port and a blockaded one, by land or inland navigation. But since we have seen that the doctrine of continuous voyages does not apply to breach of blockade, that decision does not tell against its validity with regard to the carriage of contraband.

The doctrine of continuous voyages sprang into importance and was maintained during the Civil War in the United States, but, unfortunately from the point of view of science, the carriage of contraband was then generally connected with blockade-running, and consequently the judgments in the cases of the *Stephen Hart*, the *Springbok* and the *Peterhoff* fail to distinguish between the two sets of conditions with the desirable clearness. However, in the case of the *Peterhoff* blockade, according to Sir W. Scott's doctrine in the *Ocean*, was out of the question, because the ship's destination was to the Mexican port of Matamoras, from which the communication with the Confederate territory was to be made by land or inland navigation. And here the Supreme Court on appeal, while not expressly disapproving the expressions pointing to an application of the doctrine to blockade which had been used in the district court, put the matter as to contraband in words which deserve to be quoted. "It is true that these goods if really intended for sale in the market of Matamoras would be free of liability, for contraband may be transported by neutrals to a neutral port if intended to make part of its general stock in trade. But there is nothing in the case which tends to convince us that such was their real destination, while all the circumstances indicate that these articles were destined for the use of the rebel forces then occupying Brownsville and other places in the vicinity" (5 Wallace 59).

The case of the *Peterhoff* had to be more or less considered by the English Court of Common Pleas in *Hobbs* v. *Henning,* an action brought by the owners of the condemned goods against the underwriters, the judgment in which has been represented, I think erroneously, as repudiating the doctrine of continuous voyages. In pronouncing on the demurrer to the seventh plea the Court held that the allegation that the goods were shipped "for the purpose of being sent to and imported into a port in a state engaged in hostilities with the United States" was consistent with the supposition, which we know was not in fact made by the American judges, that the plaintiff shipped the goods for sale at Matamoras, expecting to find there persons who would buy them on behalf of the Confederate States. And cases were quoted on the distinction between the expectation that goods will be applied to an illegal use and participation in an attempt to apply them to such use. What was the object of this, if it was thought that the condemnation would have been wrong even supposing that the goods were not intended for sale at Matamoras but for further transit to the Confederates? It is true that Sir W. Scott's language in the *Imina* was quoted as proving that the voyage must be to an enemy's port, but the true mind of that judge has been shown above both from the context of the *Imina* and from his language in the *Rapid.*

See 17 C. B., N. S., pp. 819, 820. The eighth plea was the United States sentence, and was disallowed for the reasons that the ground of condemnation did not sufficiently appear, and that the sentence would bear the interpretation that the *Peterhoff* "was bound to Matamoras, not for the purpose of commerce with the inhabitants thereof, but for the purpose of such *a sale* (the italics are mine) or transfer there as that the Confederates should get the use of the cargo." "We have no jurisdiction," the Court said, "to enquire into, nor are we at all considering, the validity of the legal grounds of the judgment": p. 825. On the whole then no positive opinion is to be found in *Hobbs* v. *Henning* on the doctrine of continuous voyages, and the tendency of the Court's observations is not unfavourable to it.

Among the rules on contraband of war adopted by the Institute of International Law at its Venice meeting in 1896 is one which recognizes the doctrine of continuous voyages as here laid down. " La destination pour l'ennemi est présumée lorsque le transport va à l'un de ses ports, ou bien à un port neutre qui, d'après des preuves évidentes et de fait incontestable, n'est qu'une étape pour l'ennemi comme but final de la même opération commerciale" : *Annuaire de l'Institut de Droit International*, vol. xv. p. 231[1].

[1] " A destination for the enemy is presumed when the carriage of the goods is directed towards one of his ports, or towards a neutral port which, by evident proofs arising from incontestable facts, is only a stage in a carriage to the enemy as the final object of the same commercial transaction."

## II. *Whether the doctrine of continuous voyages affects persons.*

When a person whose character would stamp him as contraband or an analogue of contraband is a passenger on board a ship bound for a neutral port and having no ulterior destination, but intends on arriving there to proceed to a belligerent port, there can be no closer connexion between the two parts of his journey than that he should hold a through ticket to the belligerent port, issued under a system of through booking by the owners of the ship in which he is. Even in that case however there is this difference between a person and goods or despatches, that the person cannot be forwarded like a thing. The through ticket is a facility given him for continuing his journey, but it must depend on him whether he will use it: he may change his intention and either continue his journey in some other way not having any unlawful connexion with the first part of it, or not continue it at all. Even therefore in the case of his holding a through ticket, and *a fortiori* where the passenger is only booked to a neutral port, he cannot be constructively bound for a belligerent destination until he is actually bound for one. There must for such destination be a determination of his own which during the first part of his journey inevitably remains contingent, and which is therefore analogous to the new determination which may be given in the neutral port as to the employment of goods which have found a market there. In the mean time the owners of the first ship may have an expectation as to his acts, analogous to that which they may have as to the ultimate destination of goods seeking a market in the neutral port, but they can have no intention as to his acts, that is no state of mind analogous to that of the owner of goods who ships them for an immediate neutral destination in order that they may be forwarded thence to a belligerent destination.

If the above view be correct it will follow that the doctrine of continuous voyages cannot be applied to the carriage of persons, and such is the conclusion to which I come. No objection to that view can be founded on cases of which the type is the *Orozembo*, 6 C. Rob. 430, where the persons are not taken on board in the ordinary course as passengers, but in pursuance of a special contact placing or virtually placing the ship in belligerent service. It may well be that in a case of that class the ship is only to convey the persons as far as a neutral port from which an ulterior carriage of them is to commence. She will not be the less capturable on her voyage to that port, not however on account of the ulterior carriage contemplated but on account of the service in which she is held to be actually engaged.

On the ground here taken up the famous international difficulty which arose out of the incident of the *Trent* receives a short and as I submit a satisfactory solution. It becomes unnecessary to discuss whether the character of Messieurs Mason and Slidell ranked them with contraband, whether they could be taken out of the ship without bringing the ship in for condemnation, or whether a destination to a neutral port precludes all further question in the case of contraband goods. It is not even necessary to point out that at St Thomas, for which the *Trent* was bound, Messieurs Mason and Slidell were to tranship for another neutral destination, England. That the *Trent's* own destination, St Thomas, was neutral, and that a neutral destination of the ship is conclusive in the case of passengers taken on board her in the regular course, as were Messieurs Mason and Slidell, is enough to close the controversy. I do not deny that if the *Trent's* own destination had been to England, merely calling at St Thomas, it would have been the neutrality of England and not that of St Thomas which would have been conclusive as to passengers on board her with tickets for England.

### III. *Application to the case of the* Gaelic.

On the principles here adopted the search of the *Gaelic* by the Japanese authorities at Yokohama cannot be justified by the doctrine relating to contraband of war. The ship was not constructively in hostile service like the *Orozembo*. Her destination was the neutral one of Hong Kong, and the passengers who might be considered as contraband were not booked beyond Hong Kong, if that would have been material. It may be admitted that packages containing explosives or machinery for causing explosion, if carried by them as part of their personal luggage and therefore not appearing separately in the ship's manifest, must be regarded for the purpose of belligerent rights as in course of carriage by the ship to the destination for which the passengers were booked. If that destination had been hostile, the luggage of passengers might on proper grounds of suspicion have been searched for such contraband articles, as well after it had been left behind as while its owners were in the ship with it, and the ship might on proper grounds of suspicion have been searched in order to ascertain whether any such luggage had been left behind. But these reasons did not apply in the case of the *Gaelic's* passengers, because there could be no ground for attributing to their personal luggage any destination ulterior to their own. The defence, if any, of the Japanese proceeding must be sought elsewhere than in the rights of belligerents against neutrals on the high seas.

It appears to me that a sufficient defence is not far to seek. The *Gaelic* was not searched on the high seas but in the waters of the belligerent who searched her. Passengers by her on their way to the enemy with proposals for destroying Japanese ships and means for giving effect to those proposals were self-constituted enemies, although their nationality was neutral. A state has the right to protect itself on its own soil and in its own waters against all enemies, whether they are such by their nationality or by their free choice, and it would be absurd to contend that any other state can make the nationality of its ships or of its subjects a ground for interfering with the exercise of that right.

Lastly, the right of self-protection must cover all reasonable measures taken for that end in circumstances of reasonable suspicion. I think therefore that the search of the *Gaelic*, and the continuance of that search after the suspected persons had left her in order to ascertain whether they had left materials or machinery for destructive explosions behind them, were justifiable against every foreign power as war measures. It is another question whether they were justifiable under Japanese law as affecting persons and things within Japanese territory or territorial waters. Even if they were not so, there is probably no government which would hesitate to supply by its own action an evident gap in the domestic legislation, and to seek an indemnity from the legislature in due course. But with that point a foreign power would have no concern.

# VIII

## THE NATURE AND EXTENT OF THE TITLE BY CONQUEST. 1901.

[Reprinted, with permission, from the *Law Quarterly Review*, vol. XVII. (1901), pp. 392–401.]

A STATE of international law may cease to exist with its own consent, expressed in some form of cession, as when the independent State of Texas merged itself in the United States of America, becoming what is called a State of that body, but which is not a State of international law. Or a State of international law may cease to exist without its own consent, by conquest, as in the case of the annexation of the South African Republic and the Orange Free State by Great Britain. In such cases the conquering State acquires a title, the nature and extent of which presents some interesting problems. Thus, with regard to the extent of the title, it may be asked:

(1) Does the conquest comprise the allegiance of persons, so that the nationals of the conquered State become subjects of the conquering State, or have they an option? And does the answer depend on whether they are resident in the former at the time of the conquest?

(2) Does the conquest comprise the corporeal property of the conquered State outside its territory,

and its rights of action in foreign courts of law whether against its own nationals or others ?

(3) Does the conquest of the capital, or of the principal part of the territory, give a title extending to the whole of the territory, as against a third power occupying the remainder of it ? As against the enemy State that question would not arise, because there would be no conquest till that State was suppressed in every part of the territory.

On such questions there are certain obvious prima facie arguments. On one side it may be said that since conquest excludes cession, the title it confers is a *de facto* one, and cannot extend further than the fact. Therefore it may be argued that conquest cannot affect the national character of persons who are not in the physical power of the conqueror, that it cannot comprise either corporeal property or rights of action existing outside the conquered territory, and that the conquest of a part of the territory, however important, can give no title against a third power occupying the remainder. On the other side it may be said that conquest, in its jural aspect, is a succession of State to State, in which succession are included all the rights of the State which has ceased to exist. The fact, it may be argued, is only important as setting up the succession, and the fact necessary and sufficient for that purpose is that the conquered State should cease to exist. That some persons, property, or rights of action that belonged to it should be outside the territory is too trifling a matter to affect the investitive fact, even if the necessary connexion in international law of a State with its territory did not make the conquest of the latter a sufficient investitive fact. Only where the complete suppression of a State is due to the action of different powers on different parts of its territory is there room for doubt, and there you have a question of degree. One part may or may not be so important as to carry the title to the other part with it.

On these prima facie arguments it may first be noticed that the one on the *de facto* side cannot escape from some recognition of the succession of State to State as an institution of international law. *De facto* conquest is merely a physical fact, and except as an investitive one it cannot explain the transfer of incorporeal rights even within the territory.

Next, let the reader think of succession on death as an institution of private law, bringing under one head a number of relations of property and obligation, and applying to them rules not found elsewhere, but arising from the point of view peculiar to the institution. And let him contrast this with a simple rule such as one requiring certain contracts to be in writing. He will then understand that the succession of State to State, with the occasions on which it is set up, the rights it brings together, the rules it applies to them, and possibly the varieties of which it is susceptible, is something different from a simple rule fixing a certain number of miles from the shore as the limit of marine dominion. And he will probably perceive that when the law of any country recognizes such an institution of international law, reasons on it and applies it, it pays to international law as a science a homage different and superior to that which is implied in recognizing an isolated rule derived from it.

The authorities on the law of England appear to be prepared to pay that homage to international law. We may refer to what was said by Vice-Chancellor Lord Cranworth in *King of the Two Sicilies* v. *Willcox,* 1 Sim. N. S. 327–9, and by Vice-Chancellor Wood in *United States of America* v. *Prioleau,* 2 H. & M. 563; and to the generality of the proposition laid down by Vice-Chancellor James in *United States of America* v. *McRae,* L. R. 8 Eq. 75. "I apprehend it," he said, "to be the clear public universal law that any government which *de facto* succeeds to any other government, whether by revolution or restoration, conquest or reconquest, succeeds to all the public property, to everything in the nature of public property, and to all rights in respect of the public property, of the displaced power, whatever may be the nature or origin of the title of such displaced power." And the recent Transvaal Concessions Commission, having to deal with more complicated cases than those before the Vice-Chancellors, namely with rights of a mixed public and private nature, said in their report (Cd. 623, p. 7): "In considering what the attitude of a conqueror should be towards such concessions, we are unable to perceive any sound distinction between a case where a State acquires part of another by cession and a case where it acquires the whole by annexation." Thus they recognized the succession of State to State as a far-reaching institution, capable of being set up on other occasions besides that of conquest. It is on the *rationale* of that institution that a lawyer must ground himself, if he wishes to find a satisfactory answer to the questions put in the beginning of this article, and so the inquiry into the extent of the title by conquest becomes one into the nature as well as the extent of that title.

Before, however, we proceed with that inquiry, it will be well to notice another sentence of the report which we have quoted. "It is clear," say the Commissioners, "that a State which has annexed another is not legally bound by any contracts made by the State which has ceased to exist, and that no court of law has jurisdiction to enforce such contracts if the annexing State refuse to recognize them." For those propositions the Commissioners refer to *Cook* v. *Sprigg* [1899] A. C. 572; and apparently they intended to refer particularly to the following passage in the judgment of the Privy Council, p. 578:

> "It is no answer to say that, by the ordinary principles of international law, private property is respected by the sovereign which accepts the cession, and assumes the duties and legal obligations of the former sovereign with respect to such private property within the ceded territory. All that can be properly meant by such a proposition is that, according to the well understood rules of international law, a change of sovereignty by cession ought not to affect private property, but no municipal tribunal has authority to enforce such an obligation. And if there is either an express or a well understood bargain, between the ceding potentate and the government to which the cession is made, that private property shall be respected, that is only a bargain which can be enforced by sovereign against sovereign in the ordinary course of diplomatic pressure."

Of course the courts of law in any country are subject to the sovereign power, and if that power, by the terms of a cession which it accepts, or by a plain expression of its will on a conquest, declares that the private property existing in the territory in which it succeeds is not to be respected, the judges can only leave its conduct to the indignation of mankind. But that where the very contrary is contained in "an express or a well understood bargain that private property shall be respected," "no municipal tribunal has authority to enforce such an obligation," but its enforcement must be left to "the ordinary course of diplomatic pressure," is one of those "things which one would rather have said otherwise." That the statement was for a moment possible was probably due partly to inadvertence, and partly to the baneful effects of Austin's narrow definition of law, effects which also appear in the opinion of the Transvaal Concessions Commissioners, quoted above, that "a State which has annexed another is not legally bound by any contracts made by the State which has ceased to exist." In each case the remarkable utterance was superfluous for the object. In *Cook* v. *Sprigg* the plaintiffs' claim was for "certain railway, mineral, township, land, forest, trading and other rights in Eastern Pondoland, granted to them by Sigcan, paramount chief of Pondoland, under and by virtue of certain four concessions." And it is stated in the judgment as proved that "the appellants never in fact obtained possession of the lands, or exercised the rights, which these documents purported to convey." The subject of claim therefore had from the beginning been of a mixed public and private nature, and consequently fell under different considerations from those which apply to purely private claims, and nothing had taken place through which any offshoot of the original claim might have come to exist in the form of purely private property. In those circumstances we must not be understood to suggest any doubt as to the correctness of the decision. And the Transvaal concessions which were before the Commissioners also, in their own language, " presented examples of mixed public and private rights," so that they were travelling beyond the record when they denied all continuing legal effect to any contracts made by the State which has ceased to exist.

Proceeding to examine the nature of the succession of State to State as an institution of international law, we first turn to Rivier, who brought to that science both vast learning and one of the acutest and soundest juristic minds that have ever been applied to it. We find him, like a host of others, laying down the general rule as well on its active side, or that of the assets, which was alone dealt with in the passage we have quoted from Vice-Chancellor James, as on the passive side, or that of the obligations : *bona non intelliguntur nisi deducto aere alieno*, and *res transit cum suo onere*. But he unites with this the caution that the analogy to the universal succession on death of private law must not be exaggerated[1]. The only remark, however, in which that caution seems to be carried out is that the domination of a conqueror over the territories and populations of the subjected State rests on its own unilateral will, and that therefore the principles of the succession of State to State are not, properly speaking, obligatory for him ; but third powers have their acquired rights, for which they will claim respect, and his own interest will therefore engage him to let them consider

[1] *Principes du Droit des Gens*, par Alphonse Rivier, 1896, tome 1, p. 70.

him as the true successor of the State which he has dispossessed[1].

Here Rivier goes on to speak of the treaties concluded by the suppressed State. Such a context shows that he was not thinking of the succession to the patrimonial condition and relations of that State, but in the former passage he may perhaps have had in his mind the circumstance that the succession on death of private law has nothing closely analogous to the questions about mixed public and private rights, where the successor, as such, is the disposer of public policy.

The difference here pointed to between succession as an institution of civil law and the succession of State to State has been brought into full light by Huber in the following passages, the doctrine of which we venture to adopt :

"§ 23. The notion of succession is a general one in law, and belongs exclusively neither to private nor to public law. Succession is substitution *plus* continuation. The successor steps into the place of the predecessor and continues his rights and obligations ; so far the successions of private and public law agree. But we now have to distinguish between those kinds of succession. A civil successor who steps into the place of his predecessor steps into his rights and obligations as though he were himself the predecessor. That is the universal succession of private law in the Roman sense, at least according to the prevailing doctrine. But the successor of international law steps into the rights and obligations of his predecessor as though they were his own. Although this distinction seems at first sight to be playing with words, we shall find in the course of our investigation that it is not so.

"§ 24. While a person of private law can in law represent more persons than one, and so an heir can continue the personality of the deceased, that is impossible between States. A State is indivisible. Either there are two or more real States or there is only one : one cannot represent another only for a certain part of its

[1] *Principes du Droit des Gens*, par Alphonse Rivier, 1896, tome 2, pp. 437, 438.

dominion. Where a State acquires dominion, it comes in with its own power as a State and does not succeed to that of its predecessor: its legal personality is extended to its new dominion. It might be otherwise if the notion of a State were a patrimonial one, if the power of the State were a piece of private property in which there could be succession; but that notion is quite obsolete in modern international law[1]."

Thus the succession of a State to its predecessor is qualified by the circumstance that it is the public law and policy of the successor which are to prevail in the future, as being inseparable from his person, which remains his own while he steps into the other's position. And this is worked out by Huber in the following paragraphs:

"§ 94. Rights which are a mixture of private and public rights perish so far as they are public, in case the successor[2] State does not possess a corresponding institution. If it possesses rules which apply to the case they will in the future govern, as for example in the cases of fiefs, knightly property (*Rittergüter*), guilds with compulsory powers, compulsion to grind at a certain mill, monopolies of sale, rights of patronage, schools, salable appointments, mintage and postal rights enjoyed by private persons, exemptions from military service, &c.

"§ 95. All subjective private rights are maintained in favour of all individuals and corporations, and the personality and property of institutions are secured to them, so far as no rule of the public

[1] Max Huber, *Die Staatensuccession*, Leipzig, 1898, pp. 18, 19. In the notes on the passage here quoted, Huber refers to Grotius, l. 2, c. 9, § 12: *Heredis personam, quoad dominii tam publici quam privati continuationem, pro eadem censeri cum defuncti persona, certi est juris.* And he recognizes that Cocceji's point of view was the same as his own, when in his commentary on Grotius he wrote: *Negamus in successionibus regnorum successoris personam pro eadem censeri cum persona defuncti.*

[2] Huber says, here and in the next paragraph, "the State which receives the cession." But his view is the same as that of the Transvaal Concessions Commissioners, who say: "In considering what the attitude of a conqueror should be towards such concessions, we are unable to perceive any sound distinction between a case where a State acquires part of another by cession and a case where it acquires the whole by annexation," *Report*, p. 7. This is also the general view.

31—2

law of the successor State prevents it. If such a corporation is to be extinguished, the new sovereign must proceed as though it had already existed in his country and he was now legislating for its suppression[1]."

Though we are not here particularly concerned with the concessions granted by a suppressed State, it is worth while to notice the bearing of the above on those with which the Transvaal Concessions Commission had to deal. Their continued existence must depend on their not being in conflict with the public law and policy of the annexing State, but if they are cancelled the persons interested will be entitled to such compensation as that State grants on cancelling a concession of its own. This doctrine of Huber we understand to be in substantial agreement with the view of the Commissioners, although their language, tinged with Austinism, has the air of denying legality to claims about the validity of which we should be loth to think that they intimated any doubt. The legality of a claim, in any but a misleading sense, does not depend on the particular method that ought to be taken in order to enforce it. Where a contract of the South African Republic or of the Orange Free State can be treated as taken over by the British State, we presume that a petition of right would lie, as on any other contract of the Crown. Where the mixture of a public element calls into play the difference between private and State successions, the impossibility of treating the annexing State as having become party to a contract having no place in its system, or which would unduly fetter its freedom of legislation, will not prevent the obligations

[1] u. s. p. 60.

resulting from the private element from passing over on that State. And the Crown would cease to be the fountain of justice if those obligations could not in some way be brought before it as matter not of grace but of right. Of course the reservations with which the Commissioners found it necessary to guard their general views are not here in question.

Without pursuing further any question about the obligations incumbent on an annexing State, we may now say that the title by conquest, as indeed any other concession of State to State, is differentiated from universal succession in private law by the circumstance that the successor steps into the position of the predecessor without changing his person, and therefore only so far as the position does not wholly depend on the person, while, so far as he steps into it, the successor is free to deal with the position, not in violation of justice, but in accordance with the maxims of his own public system. But since conquest is an institution of international law, the title by it is further subject to the general principles of the science. One of these may be illustrated by observing that within certain limits a State is free to take its own time before recognizing the international existence of a new State, although when the latter fulfils the necessary conditions of that existence its recognition cannot practically be indefinitely delayed. Evidently the underlying principle of this is that changes in the international society, though arising from facts which cannot be long ignored without offence to those in whose favour they occur, yet cannot be hastily forced on the acceptance of other members of that society whom they may affect. These must have a reasonable time to appreciate the facts alleged, and to study them in connexion with their own rights and interests, which may require some safeguard or acknowledgement on the occasion. Such a principle must find its application when a State is suppressed, or the boundaries of States are changed by a partial cession of territory, no less than when a new State comes into being. In all these cases a judgment is required to be passed which belongs to the political organs of a government. If a case were brought before our courts of law which depended on an alleged change in the international condition of a certain piece of territory, whether by the acquisition or suppression of State existence or by partial cession, probably no one will doubt that no evidence, however cogent, could dispense the courts from seeking the decision of the Foreign Office whether the alleged change had taken place, and being bound by that decision.

With the light now gained we may attack the problems stated in the beginning of this article.

(1) On the question whether conquest comprises the allegiance of persons, so that the nationals become subjects of the conquering State without a right of option, the decisive consideration appears to us to be that allegiance is a purely personal tie, and that therefore the conqueror, not being able to claim that his person is to be identified with that of the conquered State, but stepping into the position of that State only so far as such position does not wholly depend on the person, cannot demand the allegiance of its subjects. If they continue to reside in the territory, which they must have a free option to do or not, or if, not being within

it at the time when its conquest is *de facto* completed, they return to it for any but a temporary purpose, they become the conqueror's subjects by accepting his rule and protection. But if, being outside the territory at the date of its complete conquest, they remain outside it, they cannot be considered as comprised in the succession. If they do not naturalize themselves anywhere, they can have only the legal position which the State in which they reside grants to resident aliens, and such an international position as depends on residence. That *deminutio capitis* will be unavoidable for them, but it would be monstrous to suppose that the government or a court of law of the Netherlands could be required to treat ex-President Kruger as a British subject, or would be justified in doing so. And there is no difference essential to the point between an ex-President and any other citizen of the suppressed State.

In this I regret to find myself at variance with Rivier, who says:

" Les régnicoles du pays conquis deviennent régnicoles de l'État conquérant. Comme l'État subjugué n'existe plus, et qu'il n'y a pas de traité, il n'est pas question d'un droit d'option, non plus que d'un droit conventionnel d'émigration. La stricte application du principe[1] doit même avoir cette conséquence-ci : les régnicoles de l'État subjugué qui émigrent sans autorisation et sans s'être fait dégager du lien de sujétion, restent sujets de l'État conquérant ; et même s'ils acquièrent une autre nationalité, le conquérant reste libre de continuer à les traiter comme ses sujets, tant qu'il ne les a pas dégagés de la sienne. Mais cette rigueur, pratiquée autrefois dans toute sa plénitude, ainsi par la France sous la première république et le premier empire, et récemment encore par la Prusse, paraît peu conciliable avec les tendances actuelles qui affranchissent de plus en plus l'homme du sol ; tendances manifestées entre autres

[1] The principle here referred to is that which Rivier has expressed, tome 1, p. 204 : *Le changement de souveraineté territoriale entraîne de plein droit le changement de nationalité de la population régnicole.*

par la liberté générale d'émigrer, et par l'introduction constante de la clause d'option dans les cessions de territoire[1]."

We venture to think that custom cannot be invoked, to give a conquering State any claim to the allegiance of those who neither expressly nor tacitly accept the new order set up in their country. We are not among those who would wish to detract from the authority of custom as between States, but that authority can only be derived from the will, expressed in the custom, of the society of States in which it flourishes. Between a State and individuals there is not society but sovereignty on the one side and subjection on the other. Where that relation exists, there is national law. Where the question is whether the relation has been set up between a State and an individual between whom it admittedly did not exist, to quote the national law of either would be a *petitio principii*. International law has no capacity to dispose of the individual, it is between other parties, and can at the utmost preclude a third State from interfering for the individual's protection. What is sometimes called general public law remains, but that is no real law; it is not the expression of the will of any society with regard to its members, but a collection of maxims drawn partly from international law and partly from various national laws. Between the conquering State and the individuals of the conquered, reason alone is there to be appealed to.

[1] *Principes du Droit des Gens*, par Alphonse Rivier, 1896, tome 2, pp. 438, 439. The recent practice of Prussia referred to is that on her annexations in 1866. Rivier concludes: *En somme, sur ce point, le droit des gens n'est pas encore fixé, et la politique décide.* Huber expressly passes by the question of man as an object of State succession, saying that its importance calls for a separate exposition: *Die Staatensuccession*, § 50, p. 41.

(2) On the question whether the conquest comprises the property of the conquered State outside the territory, and its rights of action in foreign courts of law, whether against its own nationals or others, there seems to be no reason for making an exception to the universality of the succession. The ships of war of the conquered State in foreign harbours, and its money lodged in foreign countries or brought to them, must pass to the conqueror in common with all the other elements of its material existence.

(3) The question whether the conquest of the capital, or of the principal part of the territory, gives a title to the whole of the territory, as against a third power occupying the remainder of it, has so far as we know been raised by only one case. The last partition of Poland in 1795 is not that case, though it is perhaps the first which occurs to the mind, for the three partitioning powers acted in concert. The occasion to which we refer is the destruction of the power of the Khalifa by the British and Egyptians at Omdurman, while France occupied a part of his territory at Fashoda, and even that occasion only falls within our subject so far as the British title was put forward against the French as separate from and additional to the Egyptian. It is not surprising that international law should contain no positive rule for so rare a situation, and that in the particular instance the discussion should have been terminated in such a manner as to furnish no precedent. The Egyptian title is the one which has since been practically relied on, and the case is noted here only for the sake of completeness. There would be little interest in arguing it on principle until, if ever, a similar situation may recur.

# IX

## THE SOUTH AFRICAN RAILWAY CASE AND INTERNATIONAL LAW. 1905.

[Reprinted, with permission, from the *Law Quarterly Review*, vol. XXI. (1905), pp. 335-339.]

IN the last number of this *Review* Sir Thomas Barclay impugns the British dealing with the shareholders of the Netherlands South African Railway Company by an argument resting on two positions. One is that the " agreement as to terms of surrender," which the representatives of the British Government made on 31st May 1902 with the acting authorities, civil and military, of the two Dutch republics, amounted to an acknowledgment of the existence of those republics as having continued to that date. The other is that it was the international duty of the government which displaced those republics to assume without exception all the obligations which bound them at the last moment when it acknowledged their existence. Given these positions, the inference follows that since the persons who were shareholders of the railway on 31st May 1902 could not have been expropriated by the South African Republic except on the terms provided for that purpose by their concession, and that republic could not have objected to that conduct of theirs by which it has been contended that they forfeited all claim on the British government, the latter could not exclude from compensation the holders of shares which at the outbreak of the war were the property of the republic or of managers or agents of the company. Both the positions however appear to be very questionable.

The first of them leads us to consider the conditions under which a state is extinguished by conquest. These are commonly understood to be its complete destruction as an organized body performing the functions of a state. It may have lost its capital and the larger part of its territory, but if it continues to carry on state life in any corner of its territory it is not yet extinguished, the legal succession to it is not yet open, and there has not been conquest. This was certainly the case of the Dutch republics on 1st September 1900, when the annexation of their territories to the dominions of Queen Victoria was proclaimed; but, as I have said elsewhere[1], large tracts of those territories were then in British occupation in which the ordinary functions of government had to be provided for, all Transvaal or Free State authorities having left them; and since the resolve of conquest had been declared and its ultimate execution was not doubtful, it would have been idle to establish an administration for the occupied parts in any name but that of the Queen. The proclamation therefore may be justified as an administrative measure, although it would have been improper to apply the penalties of rebellion to resistance persisted in outside the British lines.

But I believe that by 31st May 1902 all this had been changed, and that nothing which can properly be called state life was at that time being

[1] *International Law*, Peace, p. 65.

carried on under the auspices of the two republican governments, which were merely leading a hunted and hopeless existence under the immediate protection of such military force as still remained in the field. At any rate this view was practically taken by all those who claimed authority, civil or military, in the republics, and their surrender was the consequence. To spare further suffering by a surrender on the best terms that can be obtained must always be the duty of leaders so placed, but it would be an impossible duty, because no conqueror would permit it, if, by mercifully agreeing to join in formulating the terms granted, he were held to abandon his own position, to turn conquest into international treaty, and to make what is done on the ground that state life has been extinguished into an acknowledgment that it had not been extinguished. If state life had not been extinguished in the republics the leaders would have had no authority to extinguish it. To destroy the commonwealth is beyond the attributions of any functionaries under any constitution. When they see that the commonwealth has *de facto* been destroyed, their power becomes merely that of acting on behalf of the individuals into which it has been dissolved, as being from their position the most capable of them. And this character was distinctly given to the Boer leaders by the text of the agreement of surrender. Each set of them is described as "acting as the government" of the respective republic, and they make the agreement, not on behalf of those republics or their governments, but "on behalf of their respective burghers desirous to determine the present hostilities." It is illogical and unreasonable to regard such an instrument as fixing a date for the international purposes connected with state succession.

With regard to Sir Thomas Barclay's second position, his statement that "the government which displaces another government assumes its obligations" seems to need some qualification. If taken in the widest sense which it will bear, it would involve the conclusion that the successor government must maintain the concessions of a public, or mixed public and private, character granted by the predecessor, except so far as the latter would have been entitled to recall them. And I am not sure that Sir Thomas, in applying his argument not to the expropriation of the railway but to the compensation due to the shareholders, was not solely determined by the fact that a right of expropriation was reserved by the South African Republic in the concession. For myself, I do not need that reservation as a defence of the expropriation, holding that the successor government may deal with the concessions of the predecessor on the principles of its own policy, and therefore that the British notice of 8th September 1900 was justified in claiming the right "to decline to recognize or to modify any concession...which may appear to affect prejudicially the interests of the public," that is, of the new public created by the conquest[1]. On the other hand, addressing myself to the question of the compensation necessary in connexion with the expropriation, I cannot agree with the Transvaal Concessions Commissioners, "that the shareholders were responsible for the belligerent acts of the servants of the company,

[1] See an article by me in this *Review*, vol. XVII. p. 392, and *International Law*, Peace, pp. 82, 83.

and were therefore not entitled to compensation for the loss of their property in the railway[1]."

But in public and in private international law the question of the nationality of companies is obscure. Let us first suppose that the Netherlands South African Railway Company was of Transvaal nationality by reason of the situation of its railway and of the government from which it held its concession. Then it was its duty, and that of its shareholders who on the supposition now made were Transvaalers *qua* shareholders, not only not to hinder the Transvaal government in making use of the railway, but also to assist that government by every possible employment of the means at the corporate disposal. No one will doubt that such would be the duty of the South Eastern and Chatham railways and their shareholders if England were invaded. And neither the company nor the shareholders could by doing their duty disentitle themselves to compensation from a conqueror. But now let us suppose that the company was of Netherlands nationality by reason of its incorporation in Holland and the seat of its direction there. There can still be no question of its duty not to hinder the Transvaal government in making use of its railway, which it had accepted to hold under the sovereignty of that state, but it may be said, as the Transvaal Concessions Commissioners said, that by actively assisting in the war, by all the means in the power of its servants, it had forfeited the character of a neutral company and become an enemy one.

---

[1] These are Sir T. Barclay's words, and I believe represent the Commissioners' view correctly, but I am writing in the country and cannot quote the Commissioners at first hand.

But what then ? We have just seen that, if it had been intrinsically an enemy company, it would not by the same conduct have disentitled itself to compensation : how can it fare worse for being a self-constituted, a constructive, enemy ? Grant that the company and its shareholders put on an enemy character : the enemy character does not hurt them for the present purpose. True, a neutral ship which enters the enemy's service is subject to capture and condemnation as an enemy ship (*Orozembo* case and others). But that is because the enemy character hurts private property at sea while it does not hurt it on land.

I conclude that the British government did no more than justice required, when it declined to listen to the voice which told it that it might subject the shares of the Netherlands South African Railway Company to a wholesale confiscation, but it remains that such of those shares as belonged to the Transvaal government became the property of its successor the British government, and so no question of compensation could arise about them, while as to others particular considerations may be urged. Here therefore I meet my friend Sir Thomas Barclay on the question whether it was right to except from compensation shares which at the outbreak of the war did not belong to private persons other than managers or agents of the company. So far as the managers and agents of the company are concerned, the argument which I have used as to the company itself and the body of its shareholders obliges me to admit that they are no more subject to the penalty of confiscation than the rest of the shareholders. The Germans would not have been justified in confiscating the interest of a neutral part-owner and manager of neutral property in Alsace-Lorraine, because he had allowed the property to be used, and added his active exertions in connexion with it, on behalf of France during the war of 1870–1.

But what as to the dates at which any shares may have passed from the ownership of the Transvaal government to private ownership? Sir Thomas's unqualified assertion of the duty of a successor government to assume the obligations of its conquered predecessor can only be brought into accordance with received opinion, if the obligations for money lent for the purpose of the war or of the struggle preceding it be excepted. Thus neither the United States nor Cuba has recognized the loans which Spain had charged on the island for the cost of repressing the Cubans during the long and intermittent struggle of which their emancipation was the close. And they can quote the eminent authority of Professor von Bar in support of their refusal[1]. If then the Transvaal government transferred, during the war and as security for loans made to it, shares which it held at the outbreak of the war, there would seem to be sufficient reason for refusing compensation to the transferees, without entering on any disquisition as to the date when that government ceased to enjoy the general international right to dispose of its property. Nor would it be easy to believe that a transfer of Transvaal government shares during the war was taken as an investment and not as part of a financial transaction. Those who meddle with the finance of a state at war

[1] See my *International Law*, Peace, p. 79.

must bear in mind that common-sense prevents international law from giving to that state the right to bolster up its finance by pledging the security of its enemy in addition to its own, in case of its being conquered and annexed.

# X

## IS INTERNATIONAL LAW A PART OF THE LAW OF ENGLAND? 1906.

[Reprinted, with permission, from the *Law Quarterly Review*, vol. XXII. (1906), pp. 14–26.]

THE case of *West Rand Central Gold Mining Company* v. *Rex* was a petition of right, seeking the performance by the Crown, as successor to the South African Republic, of an obligation alleged to have rested on that republic for the repayment of the value of gold commandeered by it shortly before the commencement of the late war: [1905] 2 K.B. 391. The Attorney-General demurred and the demurrer was allowed. Among the points taken for the petitioners by Lord Robert Cecil, K.C., was this: "Secondly, international law is part of the law of England." The Court, composed of Lord Alverstone C.J., and Wills and Kennedy JJ., gave to that maxim an adhesion modified as follows: "Any doctrine so invoked must," they said, "be one really accepted as binding between nations, and the international law sought to be applied must, like everything else, be proved by satisfactory evidence, which must show either that the particular proposition put forward has been recognized and acted upon by our own country, or that it is of such a nature, and has been so widely and generally accepted, that it can hardly be supposed that any civilized state would repudiate it"; p. 407. I now propose to examine further the nature and extent of the connexion between international law and the law of England, and, since *dolus latet in generalibus*, I must do it with what I hope may not prove wearisome detail.

At first sight it might be thought that no such connexion was possible. The law of England, in the sense in which it is contrasted with international law, consists of rules to be applied between the private parties who are suitors in the king's courts, including foreign states when they appear as plaintiffs claiming such rights as a private person might have, or between the king and the private parties who are amenable to his courts. International law consists of rules to be applied between states. How can a rule expressing rights and duties of states *inter se* be a part of a body of rules expressing rights and duties of private parties, whether *inter se* or between them and the king? The law of England is the law of the king's courts: a state is not amenable to those courts and is not commonly a suitor in them. If it is a suitor in them it thereby submits to their law, and, since the opposite party is always a private one, how can any rule only existing between states find a place? Before attempting to bridge the chasm it will be well to clear away some considerations which are alien to the subject.

In the United Kingdom, possibly subject to exceptions which will be noticed in due place, a treaty has no effect on private rights: if the Crown concludes a treaty which is intended to divest or modify private rights, it must obtain an act of parliament to give it that operation. In the

United States it is otherwise, for the sixth article of the constitution provides that "all treaties made or which shall be made under the authority of the United States shall be the supreme law of the land, and the judges in every state shall be bound thereby, any thing in the constitution or laws of any state to the contrary notwithstanding." Hence, when the ninth article of the Jay treaty in 1794 enabled the subjects of either country to hold lands in the other, and to sell and devise them as if they were natives, this stipulation at once took effect in the United States in favour of British subjects, repealing of itself so much either of common or of statute law on the disabilities of aliens as stood in its way, while on our side of the Atlantic an Act of 37 George III had to be and was passed in order to give effect to the stipulation in favour of citizens of the United States. This difference might seem to imply that the rule of international law requiring that treaties shall be observed was incorporated with the law of the United States though not with the law of England. But it is not so. The difference is merely that the executive possesses in the United States a power of making law by treaty not paralleled in England. That the faith of treaties is treated in the same way in the two countries is proved by the fact that as the treaties of the United States repeal their common law and their previous legislative acts, so they are in their turn repealed by subsequent acts of Congress, and the question whether such repeal was contrary to international good faith and law will not be entertained; a position firmly established by the decisions of the Supreme Court on claims to the benefit of customs conventions in spite of acts of Congress fixing duties. See *Whitney* v. *Robertson,* 124 U. S. 190, and Scott's Cases on International Law, 422, with the note on p. 426.

Again, in the case of the death caused within three miles of the English coast by the negligent navigation of the German ship *Franconia* (*Reg.* v. *Keyn,* 1876, 2 Ex. D. 63), it was discussed whether the definition by international law of the territorial extent of sovereignty could, of itself, give to the king's courts jurisdiction over the extent so defined; and there was a difference of opinion on the point. Among the majority, who gave judgment for the defendant, Sir Alexander Cockburn C.J. held that not only was there no international law awarding sovereignty over the sea within the three-mile limit, but that, even if there had been, jurisdiction would not have been thereby given to the court, but an act of parliament would have been needed for the purpose. And Lush J. made that hypothetical case the actual one, holding that as between nation and nation the waters in question were British territory, but that for want of an act of parliament the court had no jurisdiction over them. On the other hand, Lord Coleridge C.J. held that the waters were part of the realm by the agreement of civilized nations, and that therefore British law had to be administered for them by some tribunal, which for the reasons he gave could only be the Central Criminal Court. The objection to international law as giving territorial jurisdiction to the king's courts prevailed in the case, and was got rid of for the future by the Territorial Waters Jurisdiction Act, 1878, which in substance gives to the king's courts jurisdiction over so much of the littoral sea "as is deemed by international law to be within the territorial sovereignty of" the Crown, the same not being less than one marine league from low-water mark. But neither the denial nor the assertion of territorial jurisdiction as resulting from international law, nor again the conferring it by Parliament to the extent of international law, has any direct bearing on the question whether the king's courts, where their jurisdiction is admitted, must or can apply rules of international law to the decision of the matter before them.

The chasm which separates international law from the law of England or of any other country— in other words, rules to be applied between states from rules to be applied between or to private parties, including a foreign state when plaintiff— begins to be bridged when a situation exists between states which is regulated as between them by international law, and thereby state $A$ has against state $B$ a right not practically realizable without the assistance of the courts of the latter, such right belonging to $A$ either for its collective benefit or as trustee for or protector of its subjects who are to enjoy it. The simplest case will be that where the right is such that state $A$ can itself sue for it, and then the courts of $B$ must either give judgment on the question of international law under which the right is claimed, as being at least *pro hac vice* a question of the law of their land, or declare themselves incompetent to apply the international law, and thereby probably expose their sovereign to much diplomatic inconvenience. But more commonly private persons are so concerned in the situation that the court has to apply its law, whatever that may be, between or to them. Such cases are presented by diplomatic immunities, where the action of a private party may infringe an immunity which the state represented has the right to claim for its servants from the state in which it is represented ; by the neutrality of its territory which a neutral state owes to a belligerent one, but which may be infringed by the conduct of a private party within the territory ; by rights belonging to a state for the benefit of its subjects, in the enjoyment of which it may protect them when they are infringed by the state against which they exist ; and so forth, for the enumeration is not pretended to be exhaustive. In all such cases, if the rights or conduct of a private party were judged by the king's courts without reference to the international rule brought into play between him and a foreign state, the sovereign would be without the means of covering his responsibility to that foreign state.

This principle was recognized in England as early as the reign of Queen Anne, when the persons concerned in the arrest of the Tsar's ambassador, which led to the well-known Act of Parliament, were tried for a misdemeanour, on an information filed by the Attorney-General, "as infractors of the law of nations": the expression is Lord Mansfield's, in *Triquet* v. *Bath*, 3 Burr. 1480. They were found guilty, but never brought up for judgment, because, as Lord Mansfield said, "such a sentence as the court could have given he [the Tsar] might have thought a fresh insult." It was recognized again in *Barbuit's* case (sometimes referred to as *Buvot* v. *Barbut*) in Hilary Term, 1737 ; reported in Forrester's Cases temp. Talbot, 281, and a further account of it given by Lord Mansfield, who was counsel in it, in *Triquet* v. *Bath,* u.s. The point was whether a person officially described as "agent of commerce from the King of Prussia in Great Britain," an employment which Lord Talbot pronounced to be in the nature of that of a consul, was entitled to diplomatic immunities. "Lord Talbot," says Lord Mansfield, "declared a clear opinion ' that the law of nations, in its full extent, was part of the law of England,' and ' that the law of nations was to be collected from the practice of different nations and the authority of writers.' Accordingly he argued and determined from such instances and the authority of Grotius, Barbeyrac, Bynkershoek, Wicquefort, &c., there being no English writer of eminence upon the subject[1]." Now what is remarkable in this case is that although Talbot declined to discharge the agent of commerce, who had been attached for non-payment of what had been found due from him in a chancery suit, the British Government paid the amount and so obtained his discharge. Such a compliance may be attributed in part to a desire to maintain good relations with the King of Prussia, but that the case was not then thought to be clear on the law of nations, although now it would be so, results as well from the Prussian demand as at least in some degree also from the British compliance. Therefore it was not possible for Lord Talbot to limit his view

---

[1] See also *Heathfield* v. *Clinton* (1767) 4 Burr. 2015, in which Lord Mansfield said : " The privileges of public ministers and their retinue depend upon the law of nations, which is part of the common law of England."

of the law of nations to what had been "really accepted as binding between nations," or even to what had been "so widely and generally accepted that it could hardly be supposed that any civilized state would repudiate it." As chancellor, he was the principal constitutional adviser of the king in council as to the line which the king could justly maintain in such matters as against a fellow sovereign, and at the same time the head of the law, bound so to interpret the law of the land as to give the king all needful support in maintaining that line. And this he was to do in face of an actual international difference, therefore without ignoring contemporary opinion. That Lord Talbot so understood his duty appears from his quoting Barbeyrac and Bynkershoek, names clothed to us with a venerable antiquity, but of whom Bynkershoek was still living, and Barbeyrac had died in middle age scarcely eight years before. So too, in *Viveash* v. *Becker*, 1814, 3 M. & S. 284, 15 R. R. 488—where the point whether a consul is entitled to diplomatic immunities again came up, with the further question whether, in case of the affirmative, such immunities extend to a subject of the state in which he is appointed to act—Lord Ellenborough relied on Vattel, from the publication of whose great work fewer years separated him than separate us from the treatise on the Law of Domicile of Sir Robert Phillimore, whom we have scarcely ceased to regard as a contemporary.

How the principle may be called into play in questions relating to neutrality is illustrated by *Gideon Henfield's* case; Wharton's *State Trials of the United States*, p. 49. He was a citizen of the United States who had accepted a French commission in a privateer, herself equipped and commissioned in violation of American neutrality, and had taken part under it in the capture of a British ship. He was indicted in 1793 in the Federal Circuit Court, and acquitted, probably as the result of political feeling; an occurrence which led to the enactment of the first of the United States neutrality laws. It became a subject of much discussion whether the federal jurisdiction was the right one in which to try him, having regard to the fact that no act of Congress had up to that time declared it to be so, but no doubt has been expressed about the law. Both Chief Justice Jay, who delivered to the grand jury of the district of Virginia a charge carefully prepared as an introduction to the class of cases in question, and Wilson J., who presided at the trial of the particular case in the district of Pennsylvania, were clearly of opinion that conduct which Great Britain might justly resent as a breach of the peace towards her was an infraction of the common law. And it must be noted that the fact of infraction depended on the duties of neutrals, a part of international law which has been the subject of great development, probably not even yet complete, so that the international responsibility of a government for the breach of neutral duties by its subjects would not be covered by the judgments of its courts if they did not take account of the law of neutrality in its latest form.

The third class of cases, mentioned above as presenting a situation existing between states in which private parties are concerned, was that in which a state holds rights for the benefit of its subjects, and therefore has the duty of protecting them in the enjoyment of those rights. An example is furnished by a right of fishery in territorial waters conceded by treaty to a foreign power. Often rights so conceded cannot be enjoyed without divesting or modifying private rights previously existing, and then the general rule of the British constitution already noticed, that only an act of parliament can give that effect to a treaty, will apply. Thus in *Walker* v. *Baird* [1892] A. C. 491, the Attorney-General, as counsel for the appellants, admitted that the Crown cannot sanction an invasion of the rights of private persons by its officers *whenever* (the italics are mine) it is necessary in order to compel obedience to a treaty, and the Judicial Committee did not think that the occasion arose for considering the exceptions proposed, namely treaties of peace or treaties terminating such international differences as to be in the nature of treaties of peace. When the general constitutional rule applies the king's courts cannot act on the treaty till Parliament intervenes in support of it, and the king will usually have limited his liability under the treaty to doing his best to obtain such intervention. When it may not apply, either by virtue of an exception or because those in trust for whom a right is held by a foreign state can enjoy it without infringing any previous right, the king's courts are certainly bound to cover his responsibility by deciding that what such parties are entitled to under international law they are equally entitled to under the law of England.

The class of cases now under consideration

may include rights held by a state for the benefit of its subjects under a rule of international law as well as those so held under a treaty; and here we come to close quarters with the question whether the Crown, as successor to the South African Republic, is under an obligation, enforceable by petition of right, to fulfil the liability of that republic for the value of gold commandeered by it. When it is asked with reference to that question whether international law is part of the law of England, it is assumed that the international obligation exists; in other words, that a foreign state can claim from the British Crown the repayment of any part of the gold which may have belonged to one of its subjects. Assuming then, for the present, that this is so, it seems reasonable that British subjects, seeking the fulfilment of that obligation by petition of right, should not be worse off than aliens having a state to undertake their case. The answer made is that a petition of right will not lie, because the annexation by which it is contended that the Crown became successor to the conquered government was an act of state, and acts of state cannot be inquired into either by judicial or quasi-judicial proceedings. That answer does not preclude the Crown from examining the alleged succession by the light of other advisers than the judges, and it may be presumed that if such an examination led to the conclusion that the international obligation existed, the Crown would feel itself bound in conscience to do the same justice to British subjects which in that event it would have to do to a foreigner who claimed it. The answer, however, is irrelevant to the question whether international law is a part of the law of England. It merely sets up a constitutional rule by which the law of the land, whether including international law or not, is excluded, even in the mild form of a petition of right, from having a voice with regard to certain matters described as acts of state. Here then we might leave this branch of our subject, so far as the question which stands at the head of this article is concerned; but the importance of it may warrant some remarks on acts of state.

It is one thing to question the validity of an act of state, and another thing to admit its validity and draw its consequences. An annexation is an act of state, and if it be unattended by any further manifestation of the will of the Crown it will remain open, barring such a constitutional rule as has been asserted, to consider whether, and within what limits, the Crown is made by force of it the successor to the obligations as well as to the rights of the displaced government. Such consideration will not call the annexation in question. But the Crown may manifest its will, either by declaration or in some other unmistakable manner, that it will not recognize any or some of the obligations of the displaced government; and this will be a second, although perhaps contemporaneous, act of state, distinct from the annexation. If it does so, the Crown must face any international consequences of its action; but as far as the English judges are concerned, even when sitting only on a petition of right, no constitutional lawyer can doubt that they will be bound by it. The Crown is the supreme organ for international affairs, and the judges can no more question its action in them than they can question the action of Parliament in matters of legislation[1]. But the reported cases on the respect due to acts of state have not always taken note of the distinctions which may be drawn on them. In *Nabob of the Carnatic* v. *East India Company*, 1 Ves. Jun. 371 (Thurlow L.C.) and 2 Ves. Jun. 56 (Lord Commissioner Eyre), the bill was for an account of transactions which took place under agreements between an Indian sovereign and the East India Company, the latter in its political character as was ultimately held. The final agreement of the Nabob, the Lord Commissioner said, " was entered into with them [the company], not as subjects, but as a neighbouring independent state, and is the same as if it was a treaty between two sovereigns, and consequently is not a subject of private municipal jurisdiction." That, as between

[1] This is the doctrine laid down by Lord Mansfield in *Campbell* v. *Hall*, 1 Cowp. 204, at p. 209, in language quoted by their lordships in *West Rand Central Gold Mining Company* v. *Rex*, at p. 406. " It is left by the constitution to the king's authority to grant or refuse a capitulation.... If he receives the inhabitants under his protection and grants them their property, he has a power to fix such terms and conditions as he thinks proper. He is entrusted with making the treaty of peace; he may yield up the conquest or retain it on what terms he pleases. These powers no man ever disputed, neither has it hitherto been controverted that the king might change part of the whole of the law or political form of government of a conquered dominion." But their lordships were scarcely correct when they said that that language was inconsistent with the opinions of Huber and some other writers on the international law of conquest, for Lord Mansfield limited himself to the constitutional question, expressing on the international one no opinion, and therefore none inconsistent with any opinion of any one. The dispute was whether the laws of a conquered country could be altered by "the king without the concurrence of parliament." Mansfield decided that they could, and said, in words governing the interpretation of the passage quoted, " when I say ' the king,' I always mean ' the king without the concurrence of parliament.' "

the two sovereigns, is beyond controversy. To deny it would involve the consequence that if a treaty of peace stipulated the payment of a sum of money by one sovereign to another, the latter might sue the former for the amount in a court of justice—*quod est absurdum.* In *Secretary of State* v. *Kamachee*, 13 Moo. P. C. 22, the facts were that the company, acting as a sovereign power, had seized the raj of Tanjore and the property of the deceased rajah, as an escheat; and the action was brought by one who claimed that a part of what was so seized was private property of the deceased and ought to descend to his private heirs. But by a series of public acts the competent British executive authority had manifested in the clearest manner its determination to reserve the decision on that point to itself. There were thus what must be distinguished as two acts of state, one the simple annexation of the raj, the other the dealing with the question of property; and the Judicial Committee, in their judgment dismissing the action, which was delivered by Lord Kingsdown, based themselves on the latter. "If the company," they said, "in the exercise of their sovereign power, have thought fit to seize the whole property of the late rajah, private as well as public, does that circumstance give any jurisdiction over their acts to the court at Madras?" Thus the case gave an instance of obeying the constitutional rule that a British act of state cannot be questioned by a British court, but no instance of refusing, as between the government and a private party, to draw from an act of state the consequences left open by it. *Doss* v. *Secretary of State*, L. R. 19 Eq. 509, was a bill claiming a charge on the revenue of the territory of Oude, which had been annexed by the East India Company, for the amount of the debts due from the dethroned king of Oude to the plaintiffs. It came before Malins V.C., and it will probably be thought that the grounds which he gave for sustaining the demurrer, other than the one which concerns us here, were sufficient. He did, however, treat the reply of "act of state" as being fatal to the bill, and since it does not appear that there had been any act of state in the case other than the simple annexation, we here meet for the first time with a refusal by a court to draw the consequences of an act of state. As regards the international point, Lord Derby, then Lord Stanley and President of the Board of Control, stated in the House of Commons on July 5, 1858, "that the transfer of the revenues of the kingdom of Oude to Great Britain did carry with it a liability for such debts of the former government as were fairly and justly contracted": quoted by Malins V.C., L. R. 19 Eq., p. 531. The law laid down by Vice-Chancellor Malins was applied by the Judicial Committee, their judgment being delivered by Lord Chancellor Halsbury, in *Cook v. Sprigg* [1899] A. C. 572. There it was sought to enforce concessions granted by Sigcan, described as paramount chief of Pondoland, before the annexation of that country; but the doctrine in question was again far from being a necessary basis for the refusal, since, besides that it would be a joke to apply principles of international law to the concessions which white men wheedle or extort from uncivilized chiefs, it must be remarked that some of the rights said to have been conceded were of that public nature which an annexing state is always held free to deal with on its own and not on its predecessor's principles of policy. And now we have the judges in *West Rand Central Gold Mining Company* v. *Rex* holding "that matters which fall properly to be determined by the Crown by treaty or as an act of state are not subject to the jurisdiction of the municipal courts, and that rights supposed to be acquired thereunder cannot be enforced by such courts[1]." This being treated by them as a sufficient ground for allowing the demurrer, when nothing beyond the simple annexation of the Transvaal appeared as having been done on the part of the Crown, the law of England must be admitted, in the present state of the authorities, to deny the right of the judges, even on a petition of right, to draw out against the Crown the consequences of an act of state.

It needs scarcely be said that in the United States no such difficulty as that which we have been considering occurs. The constitutional position

[1] This ([1905] 2 K. B. 409) is the language in which their lordships sum up the previous authorities, and they clearly adopt it. One of the cases which they quote is that of *Rustomjee* v. *Reg.* 1 Q. B. D. 487 and 2 Q. B. D. 69, where the British government had received from the Chinese government a sum of money in respect of claims made on the latter by certain persons, of whom one presented a petition of right in order to enforce payment of his claim out of the sum so received. Lord Coleridge said that "as in making the treaty, so in performing the treaty, the Queen is beyond the control of municipal law." It must be observed that the circumstances of a treaty may contain in themselves sufficient proof that the sovereign intended to reserve his own discretion in executing it. For instance, if every such claimant as the petitioner in *Rustomjee* v. *Reg.* could succeed separately, the total awarded might possibly exceed the amount received by the Crown. Justice would require an administration of the fund, for which the law as to petitions of right makes no provision.

of the Supreme Court, and the very purpose for which it exists, on the one hand prevent it from questioning any act of state performed by the executive within its lawful powers, and on the other hand require it to draw out the consequences of any such act of state and apply them to the cases before it. When therefore a conquest made by the United States or a cession made to them is presented to the consideration of that court, it is free to apply any rule of international law which it finds relating to the situation, and it applies such rule not only between private parties but also between a private party and the republic, so far as the republic has not decided the matter by the constitutional action of its executive. In *United States* v. *Percheman,* 7 Peters 51, one of a series of cases arising out of the acquisition of Florida and Louisiana by cession, Chief Justice Marshall said (p. 86):

"It is very unusual even in cases of conquest for the conqueror to do more than to displace the sovereign and assume dominion over the country. The modern usage of nations which has become law would be violated, that sense of justice and of right which is acknowledged and felt by the whole civilized world would be outraged, if private property should be generally confiscated and private rights annulled."

Particular attention must be drawn to the last words, because the Court in *West Rand Central Gold Mining Co.* v. *Rex,* adverting to the fact that in the series of cases mentioned the rules of international law had only been enforced with regard to property locally situated in an annexed country, observed that the language used in them must be construed solely with reference to that contingency. It is no doubt true that the language which falls from many judges must be construed solely with reference to the cases before them, but the words selected by a man like Chief Justice Marshall for the purpose of expressing the principle on which he acted cannot be so treated, and his mention of conquest as not annulling either private property or private rights must be understood in all the breadth he gave to it[1].

[1] Although the judges in *West Rand Central Gold Mining Company* v. *Rex* held that their decision was made necessary by a British rule excluding any rule of international law, they attacked the rule of the latter kind which was alleged, and to discuss it would not be within the scope of this article. It can be appropriate here only to mention the two grounds on which their lordships relied in denying it. One was connected with the limitation attempted to be placed on Chief Justice Marshall's enunciation of principle. "It must not be forgotten," they said (p. 411), "that the obligations of conquering states with regard to private property of private individuals, particularly land as to which the title had already been perfected before the conquest or annexation, are altogether different from the obligations which arise in respect of personal rights by contract." What is the authority for this? The other was that the rule which makes a conqueror succeed to the obligations of his predecessor is not presented by international lawyers as being without exception, which their lordships seemed to think an objection in itself; and they also seemed to think that, even when the exceptions admit of being stated, a national court would be incapable of applying them to the facts of cases. The truth is that often the rules of international law resemble those of the common law in making their first appearance in a very general and crude form, which practice and discussion elaborate and fence; and where national courts deal seriously with international rules as necessary to their decision—take for instance the dealings of the Supreme Court of the United States with the principles of neutrality, and those of Lord Stowell with the laws of maritime war—they have shown themselves as capable of assisting in the process of definition and application as they have shown themselves to be in matters of the common law. If there were a greater difficulty in the former case than in the latter, it would speak ill for the prospects of a permanent court of international arbitration.—The other point in *West Rand Central Gold Mining Company* v. *Rex*, namely that if the obligation by international law existed it would not be a contractual one and therefore not available under a petition of right, is analogous to the point

Still another example of a situation existing between two states at peace with one another, and regulated as between them by a rule of international law, being brought before a national court through a private person's being concerned in it, is furnished by the operation of prize courts as between belligerents and neutrals. Those courts sit under national authority and must obey the determinations of the constitutional national authority. Whether or not, for instance, Lord Stowell considered the Orders in Council during the Napoleonic wars to be justifiable as measures of retorsion against the Continental System, the Orders were acts of state and he had no choice but to apply them. Consequently, for the purpose of the inquiry how far international law is a part of the law of England, a British prize court stands on the same footing as the High Court or the judges to whom a petition of right is referred; and that international law is its law, in the absence of express interference by constitutional authority, is an elementary fact. Here again, as in the preceding cases, it is the current international law which enters into the law of England, although the court performs an important and responsible function in helping to shape that law. To the admiralty judges who laid down "the rule of the war of 1756" it would have been no answer to say that that rule was not to be found in the Consolat del Mar or in Grotius; and if it should come up for decision whether the Declaration of Paris is enforceable against a subject of a state

in *Queen* v. *Keyn*, that the court would have been without jurisdiction even if England possessed the right of jurisdiction under international law.

which has not adhered to it, it will be for the judges before whom the question is brought to decide whether the process necessary for the growth of international law has been completed in that instance.

Lastly, war, even as between the belligerent states and between each of them and the subjects of the other, is not unregulated violence, but an institution of international law, not created but restrained and moulded by it, as much as the conquest to which war may lead. Private persons may be concerned in that institution before the king's courts, as the Dane, whom in the case of *Wolff v. Oxholm*, 6 M. & S. 92, 18 R. R. 313, Lord Ellenborough made to pay over again a debt due to British subjects, which he had paid to his own government under an ordinance confiscating the property and credits of such subjects, issued during war between the two countries. That judgment is at variance with others, especially United States ones, but whether confiscation is or is not lawful between belligerents, either way it was the international rule which had to be applied. If payment under the ordinance had been treated as a good discharge against the original creditors, that would have been international law interpreted in favour of the defendant; since it was not so treated, that was international law interpreted against him. And having regard to the growing mildness of practice and opinion, the question in any future case of the kind must be whether the confiscation is now allowable.

Another example, happily not likely to occur in England, of the liability of the international laws of war to come before a national court, may be furnished by the right generally allowed to an invader to collect the taxes due to the enemy government in the region which he occupies. Suppose that that government sues for them after the occupation has ceased. Will the payment of them to the invader be reckoned as a discharge? But it is needless further to multiply examples, since it may be hoped that those which have been given will be sufficient to indicate and illustrate the answer which I shall now attempt to make in general terms to the question whether international law is part of the law of England.

*The English courts must enforce rights given by international law as well as those given by the law of the land in its narrower sense, so far as they fall within their jurisdiction in respect of parties or places, subject to the rules that the king cannot divest or modify private rights by treaty (with the possible exception of treaties of peace or treaties equivalent to those of peace), and that the courts cannot question acts of state (or, in the present state of the authorities, draw consequences from them against the Crown).*

*The international law meant is that which at the time exists between states, without prejudice to the right and duty of the courts to assist in developing its acknowledged principles in the same manner in which they assist in developing the principles of the common law.*

## XI

### CONTRABAND OF WAR. 1907.

[A letter reprinted, with permission, from *The Times*, 20th July, 1907.]

To the Editor of *The Times*.

SIR,—The British proposal at the Peace Conference to abolish contraband and rely on blockade still hangs in the balance. It may well seem to many at home as startling as it did to your Special Correspondent at The Hague when he first mentioned it. They may confound it with the proposals sometimes dictated by a weak devotion to catchwords, and fear that an old and valuable right of belligerents is in danger of being thoughtlessly surrendered. It may reassure them if I mention that the suggestion was first made to me by the late Mr Hall, an international lawyer as conservative as he was eminent, who, however, did not publish it. That circumstance combined with my own reflection to support me in bringing the desirableness of the change before the Royal Commission on the Supply of Food and Raw Material in time of War. See in the Bluebooks, Appendix No. XXIX., p. 272, and my evidence, questions 6921–6924, and 6932–6934. Time was when England's superiority at sea was thought to depend largely on preventing our enemies from getting naval materials and stores, and when, since the main source of these was the Baltic, to declare them contraband and watch the outlet of that sea was an obvious policy. That state of things has disappeared with wooden ships, masts and sails, and a new difficulty has arisen to hamper our employment of the doctrine of contraband as belligerents. As belligerents we always had trouble with neutrals, or were on the verge of having it, in consequence of the want of any definition or enumeration of contraband universally agreed on, and of the grave question of convoy, which would fall of itself if contraband fell. Now, in addition, neutrals have begun to show themselves restive about the distance from its destination at which we claim the right to search ships for contraband. I need only remind your readers of the strong feeling aroused in Germany, early in the South African war, by our searching at Aden for contraband destined to the Transvaal through Delagoa Bay. The result was seriously to reduce the advantage derivable under the law of contraband from the principle of continuous voyage, and the same objection must in future bring down the efficacy of the law of contraband almost to a level with that of blockade, as practised under the French rule which allows the blockading squadron to be approached for enquiry.

I did not, before the Royal Commission referred to, insist with any pressure on the desirableness of abolishing contraband, because it then seemed impracticable. Now, however, it may not be impossible to facilitate the adoption of the proposal by connecting it with another change which may appeal to a great assemblage, predisposed to consider the amendment of international law in a broad spirit. The objection to search at a distance, with which as belligerents we shall have to reckon in future, must equally tell against the British system of blockade, which allows an intending blockade-runner to be captured as soon as she sets out on her voyage. It will be difficult on that account for blockade to be practised again in any manner very different from the French system already mentioned, only, if blockade is to be possible at all, that system must undergo some modification. A blockading squadron must be allowed sufficient mobility to avoid the necessity of lying in the dark within reach of torpedoes and submarines from the shore. What then if, along with the abolition of contraband, reasonable rules for blockade should be adopted which, while leaving it possible, should exclude the extreme claim to make captures at any distance from the blockaded coast? There would then be for the first time a system of maritime prize law in which there would be no difference between British and Continental views, which might be an inducement for acceding to a British proposal, and it would probably be a system that would meet the conflicting claims of belligerents and neutrals as far as it is possible to reconcile them.

I trust that the preceding observations have shown that in such a system belligerents would lose nothing of great value which they can hope to retain in practice. To neutrals it would be a great gain to be free from the arbitrary extensions which belligerents give to their lists of contraband, and against which recent experience shows that no previously declared policy of any Power is a safeguard. France had for more than three centuries been the leader in denying the contraband character of provisions, when in 1885 she prohibited the transport to northern China of rice intended for the food of the people as well as of that intended for military use. Russia had at the West African Conference of Berlin refused to sanction coal being enumerated as contraband, when in 1904 she placed it as such on her own list. There is no great nation that can afford to neglect the neutral side of the question, and least of all England, which, when not herself neutral, must depend so largely on neutral commerce for her supplies of food and raw material. Perhaps it is not too much to hope that the suggestion here made may be found to unite the permanent interests of all.

I am, Sir, yours obediently,

J. WESTLAKE.

CHELSEA.

# XII

## THE MUSCAT DHOWS. 1907.

[Reprinted, with permission, from the *Law Quarterly Review*, vol. XXIII. (1907), pp. 83–87.]

ON August 8, 1905, the international Hague Court of Arbitration pronounced a sentence in a cause between Great Britain and France which is of great importance in relation to the right of European powers to grant their protection in Eastern countries to persons who are not their subjects, and which should be especially interesting to all jurists on account of the reasons given for it. Those reasons amounted to the affirmation that international law is a progressive science, and to an avowed development of it in the matter of the protection mentioned.

Dhows, in French *boutres,* are ships of Arab build, ranging from 200 or 300 to 500 tons, which trade in the Indian Ocean, the Red Sea and the Persian Gulf. They are owned and manned by a class of men mostly subjects by birth of the Sultan of Muscat, largely indeed hailing from Sur in the southern part of his dominions. But, like sailors of other countries and religions, they are much addicted to having families and a *pied-à-terre* in the different places to which their calling takes them, and thus many of them have a connexion with one or other of the French colonies, such as the Comoro Islands, Mayotte, Nossi-Bé or Jibutil. Now the French law of May 5, 1866, is very strict as to the grant of the French flag, for which it requires that the ship must be owned to the extent of at least one-half by persons established in France, and that the captain, the officers and three-fourths of the crew must be of French nationality. But that law does not extend to the colonies. In them the *francisation* necessary for the grant of the flag depends on ministerial decisions, especially on a ministerial dispatch of October 15, 1880, and in conformity with these the French flag has been granted to a large number of dhows belonging to subjects of Muscat. This being done, those dhows have been considered, as between France and Muscat, to enjoy, even in the waters of the latter state, the inviolability which Art. 3 of the Franco-Muscat treaty of November 17, 1844, stipulates for properties possessed or occupied by Frenchmen.

This state of things was regarded by Great Britain as opposing a serious obstacle to the suppression of the East African slave trade, for it shielded the dhows from being visited by British cruisers, as they might have been under the Anglo-Muscat treaty of April 14, 1873, if they had belonged to Muscat, while France has not acceded to that part of the General Act of the Brussels Conference of 1890 which authorized the application of exceptional measures. In 1895 and 1897 the Sultan of Muscat, under British instigation applied in vain to France to withdraw her protection from the Gallicized dhow-owners (*boutriers francisés*). And at last the British Government brought forward the plea that the protection which France persisted in granting was a violation of the declaration of March 10, 1862, by which the two powers reciprocally promised to respect the independence of the Sultan of Muscat. That plea Great Britain and France referred to the arbitration of the Hague Court, by an agreement of October 13, 1904, in which the questions to be decided were determined by reference to a recital couched in the following terms :

"Whereas the Government of His Britannic Majesty and that of the French republic have thought it right, by the declaration of March 10, 1862, 'to engage reciprocally to respect the independence' of His Highness the Sultan of Muscat;

"And whereas difficulties as to the scope of that declaration have arisen in relation to the issue by the French republic, to certain subjects of His Highness the Sultan of Muscat, of papers authorizing them to fly the French flag,

"And also as to the nature of the privileges and immunities claimed by subjects of His Highness who are owners or masters of dhows and in possession of such papers, or are members of the crew of such dhows and their families, especially as to the manner in which such privileges and immunities affect the jurisdiction of His Highness the Sultan over his said subjects."

Thus two distinct questions were put to the Court, the first as to the lawfulness of the grant of the flag, the second as to the rights to be enjoyed under such grant if lawful.

The members of the Court chosen as arbitrators were, by Great Britain, Mr Melville W. Fuller, Chief Justice of the United States ; by France, the Jonkheer A. F. de Savornin Lohman, former Minister of the Interior of the Netherlands, former professor in the Free University of Amsterdam, member of the Second Chamber of the States-General. These not having agreed within a month on the choice of a third arbitrator, the king of Italy, named for the purpose in the agreement of reference, appointed as such Dr Henry Lammasch, Professor of International Law in the University of Vienna, member of the House of Lords in the Austrian Parliament.

The sentence, which is signed by all three arbitrators, deals as follows with the first question. They refer to Art. 32 of the General Act of the Brussels Conference of 1890, which on January 2, 1892, became binding on France in relation to Great Britain by her accession to that part of the Act. By it, for the purpose of suppressing the slave trade and in the general interests of humanity, it was agreed that the authority to use the flag of one of the signatory powers should in future only be granted to native vessels satisfying three conditions, of which the first was that " their fitters-out or owners must be either subjects of or persons protected by the power whose flag they claim to fly." Consequently, although " before January 2, 1892, France was entitled to authorize vessels belonging to subjects of His Highness the Sultan of Muscat to fly the French flag, being only bound by her own legislation and administrative rules"— first paragraph of formal award on first question— and although " dhow-owners who before 1892 were authorized to use the French flag retain that authority as long as France renews it to the grantee "— second paragraph of same award—after that date she could no longer grant her flag to subjects of Muscat not falling under the description of persons protected by her (*ses protégés*) as employed in the Brussels Act. What, then, is the sense to be given to that expression in the interpretation of the Act ? On the one hand there was to be considered the very widely extended right, sanctioned by long-standing custom, of granting European or American protection, in Turkey and other Eastern countries, to persons " whose religion and social manners do not assimilate with the religion and manners of those countries "—the words are Mr Secretary Marcy's of the United States—or who, notwithstanding the absence of any such dissimilarity, are connected by service or some other substantial tie with the power granting the protection. Viewed in this light, there could be no objection to the grant of French protection to Muscat Arabs having some kind of establishment or home in a French colony or protectorate.

On the other hand there was a consideration which prevailed with the Court, thereby constituting that testimony to international law as a progressive science, and that avowed development of it, which have been referred to above as making the sentence remarkable. Certain dealings with Turkey and Morocco, of no very old date, were held to have undermined the system of protection in the East, and introduced a new law of the widest application. This is so important that it shall be given in the words of the official translation of the sentence :

" Whereas, in default of a definition of the term *protégé* in the General Act of the Brussels Conference, this term must be understood in the sense which corresponds best as well to the elevated aims of the Conference and its Final Act as to the principles of the law of nations, as they have been expressed in treaties existing at that time, in internationally recognized legislation, and in international practice :

" Whereas the aim of the said Art. 32 is to admit to navigation in the seas infested by the slave trade only those native vessels which are under the strictest surveillance of the signatory powers, a condition which can only be secured if the owners, fitters-out and crew of such vessels are exclusively subjected to the authority and jurisdiction of the state under whose flag they are sailing :

"Whereas, since the restriction which the term *protégé* underwent in virtue of the legislation of the Ottoman Porte of 1863, 1865 and 1869, especially of the Ottoman law of Sefer 23, 1280 (August, 1863), implicitly accepted by the powers which enjoy the rights of capitulations—and since the treaty concluded between France and Morocco in 1863, to which a great number of other powers have acceded, and which received the sanction of the Convention of Madrid of July 30, 1880—the term *protégé* embraces, in relation to states of capitulations, only the following classes : 1st, persons being subjects of a country which is under the protectorate of a power whose protection they claim ; 2nd, individuals corresponding to the classes enumerated in the treaties with Morocco of 1863 and 1880, and in the Ottoman law of 1863 ; 3rd, persons who under a special treaty have been recognized as *protégés*, like those enumerated by Art. 4 of the French-Muscat Convention of 1844 ; and 4th, those individuals who can establish that they had been considered and treated as *protégés* by the power in question before the year in which the creation of new *protégés* was regulated and limited, that is to say before the year 1863, those individuals not having lost the status they had once legitimately acquired :

"Whereas, although the powers have *expressis verbis* resigned the exercise of the right to create *protégés* in unlimited number only in relation to Turkey and Morocco, nevertheless the exercise of this pretended right has been abandoned also in relation to other Oriental states, analogy having always been recognized as a means to complete the very deficient written regulations of the capitulations as far as circumstances are analogous :

"Whereas on the other hand the concession *de facto* made by Turkey, that the status of *protégés* [should] be transmitted to the descendants of persons who in 1863 had enjoyed the protection of a Christian power, cannot be extended by analogy to Muscat, where the circumstances are entirely dissimilar, the *protégés* of the Christian powers in Turkey being of race, nationality and religion different from their Ottoman rulers, whilst the inhabitants of Sur and other Muscat people who might apply for French flags are in all these respects entirely in the same condition as the other subjects of the Sultan of Muscat."

For these reasons the Court held—third paragraph of formal award on first question—that "after January 2, 1892, France was not entitled to authorize vessels belonging to subjects of His Highness the Sultan of Muscat to fly the French flag, except on condition that their owners or fitters-out had established or should establish that they had been considered and treated by France as her *protégés* before the year 1863." On comparing this with the first and second paragraphs of the same award, which have been given above, it appears that the change in the law as to the protection of persons is dated from 1863, but that it is not applied to the grant of the flag till 1892, when an express stipulation made that grant depend on the status of the recipient. The change made in 1863 would seem not to have been thought to limit the grant of the flag to the dhow, so far as that can have any effect independent of the status of the persons sailing the dhow under the flag.

The formal award on the second question needs only to be stated, as in the official translation:

" 1st. Dhows of Muscat authorized as aforesaid to fly the French flag are entitled in the territorial waters of Muscat to the inviolability provided by the French-Muscat treaty of November 17, 1844 :

" 2nd. The authorization to fly the French flag cannot be transmitted or transferred to any other person or to any other dhow, even if belonging to the same owner :

" 3rd. Subjects of the Sultan of Muscat who are owners or masters of dhows authorized to fly the French flag, or who are members of the crews of such vessels or who belong to their families, do not enjoy in consequence of that fact any right of exterritoriality which could exempt them from the sovereignty, especially from the jurisdiction, of His Highness the Sultan of Muscat."

It might have been foreseen that in the hands of an international court of arbitration, international law, like the English common law in the hands of the judges, would enter on a freer course of development than could be given it by jurists not writing with authority. The sentence now under consideration is an instructive example of that process, and it further illustrates the liberty of the Court in the fact that its conclusions are reached without any notice of the Anglo-French engagement to respect reciprocally the independence of Muscat, which figures at the head of the agreement of reference. The Court quotes Art. 48 of the Hague Convention under which it sits, as empowering it " to declare its competence in interpreting the agreement of reference as well as the other treaties which may be invoked in the case, and in applying the principles of international law."

# XIII

## THE HAGUE CONFERENCES. 1908.

[Reprinted, with permission, from the *Quarterly Review*, No. 414, January 1908, pp. 224-251.]

1. *Courrier de la Conférence de la Paix.* Rédigé par William T. Stead, nos 1–109. The Hague: June–October, 1907.
2. *Revue de Droit International et de Législation Comparée.* $2^{me}$ série, tome 9, no. 6 ($1^{er}$ fascicule), 1907. (This contains the complete Final Act of the Second Peace Conference.)
3. *The Arbiter in Council.* London: Macmillan, 1906.
4. *Problems of International Practice and Diplomacy*, with special reference to the Hague Conferences and Conventions and other general International agreements. By Sir Thomas Barclay. London: Sweet and Maxwell, 1907.
5. *International Law.* By L. Oppenheim. Vol. I: Peace, 1905; Vol. II: War and Neutrality, 1906. London: Longmans.
6. *International Law.* By J. Westlake, LL.D. Part I: Peace, 1904; Part II: War, 1907. Cambridge: University Press.
7. *Traité de Droit Public International.* $1^{re}$ partie: Les Prolégomènes et les Théories Générales. Par A. Mérignhac. Paris: Libraire Générale de Droit et de Jurisprudence, 1905.
8. *Commerce in War.* By L. A. Atherley-Jones, K.C., M.P., assisted by Hugh H. L. Bellot. London: Methuen, 1907.
9. *International Law as interpreted during the Russo-Japanese War.* By F. E. Smith and N. W. Sibley. London: Fisher Unwin, and Clowes, 1905.
10. *Neutral Duties in a Maritime War, as illustrated by recent events.* By T. E. Holland, K.C., D.C.L. From the Proceedings of the British Academy, vol. II. Oxford: University Press, 1905.
11. *War and Neutrality in the Far East.* By the Rev. T. J. Lawrence, LL.D. Second edition, enlarged. London: Macmillan, 1904.
12. *The Law of Private Property in War*, with a chapter on Conquest, being the Yorke Prize Essay for 1906. By Norman Bentwich. London: Sweet and Maxwell, 1907.

13. *A Digest of International Law, as embodied in diplomatic discussions, treaties,...international awards,...and the writings of jurists*. By John Bassett Moore, LL.D. Eight vols. Washington: Government Printing Office, 1906.

THE changes in men's point of view towards the problems of their nature and destiny, which have powerfully moulded their social and political relations to one another, so far as those relations have been confined within the city or the State, seem to have done nothing for the improvement of their international relations. It may be that those mental changes have exhausted, in the nearer and more necessary fields, the moving force which they were capable of exercising; or it may be that the help of the sword, in conquering and defending the new mental positions, has had to be paid for. Certainly the troubled times of the Renaissance and the Reformation had for one of their net results to exalt the irresponsibility of international action. To bring that action under some responsibility is the object of a great cry which goes up from modern Europe, a cry based on no new spiritual vision, but wrung from suffering and fear. During more than a generation no two Christian European States have been at war with one another; but the spectre of war has become more terrible. The burden of taxation caused by vast armaments and the cost of keeping them abreast of invention; the fear of the still greater losses which would attend even a short war; armies increasing automatically by the general liability of increasing populations to military service; the dread of bloody battles and devastating invasion on a scale increasing with the increase of armies—all this has been more acutely felt as manners have become milder and life easier, and therefore more valued. To the rational objections against all that tends to war there has been added a nervous tension. All history has known the electric tension of a mistaken patriotism, uniting for war a country divided yesterday within itself. We have now learnt the passionate tension which unites people in different countries in a cry for peace, while as yet few have considered whether they are prepared to renounce for themselves the desires which make for war.

The Peace Conference of 1899, which represented the first attempt of official agencies to lead the popular cry, was essentially a diplomatic one. It did not pretend to be a legislature, nor did it ape the ways of one, or aim at any results which it was plainly impossible to reach by agreement. Even " putting an end to the progressive increase of armaments by sea and land," which figured in the Tsar's invitation to it, could not, when first broached, be considered as entirely impracticable, although the Powers, when met together, found it to be such, at least for the time. Pursuing the diplomatic path of agreement, the Conference arrived at a codification of the laws of land war, for which the way had been prepared by official discussion at Brussels in 1874. Pursuing the same path, but venturing beyond the limits of previous official discussion, it made an important first step in facilitating the practice of international arbitration by establishing, with the name of a court, a list of judges to choose from, and some broad outlines of procedure.

The Peace Conference of 1907, proposed by President Roosevelt, but convoked by the Queen of the Netherlands on the invitation of the Emperor Nicholas, in whose favour the President gracefully retired, spread its sails more widely to the popular gale. It launched into a great variety of topics, almost wholly unprepared by official discussion, and of which some, as the British proposal for the abolition of contraband of war, had not been mooted even in scientific assemblages, though not quite unknown to scientific literature. And, most of all, it marked its popular affinity, if not its popular origin, by adopting the forms of a legislature, indeed of a democratic legislature, short only of the point at which those forms usually bear the fruit for the sake of which they have been devised. Speeches and votes gave a parliamentary air, not only to committees, sub-committees, and drafting committees, but even to full sittings. For the purpose of announcing the result of a division the votes of all States were treated as equal. For the purpose of carrying any matter a stage further they were treated as unequal. Sometimes a resolution approving the proposal of one delegation did not prevent an inconsistent approval being given to the proposal of another delegation, and the two resolutions would then go together to a drafting committee, there to be voted on again. Sometimes a majority was so frightened by its victory over an important minority that any further proceeding on the matter in question was dropped. If a real similarity can be traced between the Conference and a legislature, the comparison, for all the proceedings below the full sittings, must be made with the old Hungarian diet, in which the Palatine, represented at the Conference by the common-sense of the body, quashed a resolution which he disliked with the formula *suffragia non numeranda sed ponderanda*. For the full sittings the comparison may be made with the Polish diet, in which each individual enjoyed a *liberum veto*, since even the final vote did not bind any State without its own consent.

The most curious thing about this parody of a parliament is that, to some extent, it would seem to have imposed on those concerned in it. When the proceedings on the British proposal for the abolition of contraband of war had been dropped because France, Germany, Russia, and the United States opposed it, while twenty-six States voted for it, Sir Edward Fry attempted to unite the twenty-six in a treaty to that effect, which, of course, would have been outside the Conference. All but Haiti refused. The phantom of a legislature, powerless to enable the majority to carry their resolution as one of the Conference, revived with sufficient strength to prevent their carrying it into effect among themselves by a diplomatic step at the time and place of the Conference. M. Mérey de Kapos-Mére for Austria and Count Tornielli for Italy took the lead in saying that their votes in favour of the British proposal had been given as a part of the proceedings of the Conference, of which the principle was that unanimity, or an approach to it, was necessary for a result (*qu'on ne saurait agir qu'à l'unanimité ou à la presqu'unanimité*). To sign at it a convention outside it would damage the Conference, and might prevent the Powers from agreeing to hold another[1]. Perhaps we may

---
[1] *Courrier de la Conférence*, No. 89, September 26.

say that, in the general opinion of the Powers, the Conference combined diplomacy with an appeal to public opinion, which was encouraged to form itself by debate, and to some extent to triumph over opposition. " Let me be permitted," said M. Renault, as reporter on the scheme for an International Prize Court, " to draw attention to the beneficent influence of the atmosphere (*milieu*). How many years of diplomatic negotiations would it have needed to bring about an agreement on so difficult a subject, starting as we did from such opposite points ! The Conference has changed years into weeks, thanks to the approximation between men and ideas which it causes, and to the sentiment of justice to which it tends to give the victory over particular interests[1]." It will be well for Great Britain and the other Powers to bear this in mind, and on future occasions to guard against the possible surprises of an " atmosphere " by carefully preparing the ground through diplomatic conversations of the ordinary kind.

In any case it appears to us that in future all voting had better be avoided. No doubt, if agreement was not to be made a rigid condition, voting seemed inevitable to all who were unable to think except in the forms of democratic government, but with it, on the same democratic principles, there was bound to come the equality of votes for the purpose of display, and with that again, as we have seen, the worthlessness of votes for any purpose but that of display. The equality may have given a temporary satisfaction to the political feelings of many who joined in the cry of distress

---

[1] *Courrier de la Conférence*, No. 75, September 10.

for which they hoped the Conference would find a remedy, but the worthlessness must have taught them that votes were not helping them in the noble effort to bring international action under responsibility. The equality of votes flattered the small States, of which, not to mention that strength must always tell, the opinion on international doctrines is diminished in value by their inexperience of the situations to which they have to be applied. But that pleasure must have vanished when they found that the delegations of the larger States were prevented by the force of things from admitting them to a real equality. " The last speech of the most industrious and eloquent first Brazilian delegate, M. Ruy de Barbosa, was described by one of the leading continental members of the Conference as a fierce (*farouche*) exposition of the extreme conception of the equality of all States and Governments[1]." Perhaps it might have been less fierce if the conception had not been pampered. In a word, the voting was a sham, and of shams we ought to have no more.

Passing from the methods of the Conference to its work, we claim to be not among those who belittle the mark which it will have left in history. But the logical order of treatment obliges us, after noticing the popular aspect of its origin and ways, to take first the questions on which the popular cry had mainly fixed. It was not likely that those questions should prove the greatest successes of the gathering. It is a familiar character of popular movements to aim at their end by the most direct road, ignoring obstacles instead of seeking a way

[1] Special correspondent in *Times* of October 21.

round them. "The armaments are oppressive; let them be immediately limited." One could have better understood a demand for their immediate abolition. Any armament beyond the measure of an internal police force implies the conviction that an attack from the outside is possible and must be guarded against. To invite Governments, while still possessed by that conviction, to calculate the smallest armaments which it is necessary for their defence to maintain, is to invite each to pass in review its whole geographical and political situation, the quarters from which danger may arise and the friends whose aid may be hoped for. This is what we have done for ourselves in fixing the two-Power standard for the British navy, but the frame of mind in which it is done is not that which is most suited to a Peace Conference, not to mention the friction which would arise in the necessary comparison by the different Powers of the estimates respectively formed. Had anything happened between 1899 and 1907 to increase the probability of a satisfactory result from such investigations? There had been two great wars, the South African and the Russo-Japanese, and a third not inconsiderable one in China. Whichever side one may blame for any of them, this was a fact not of a nature to increase the feeling of security. We ourselves had concluded a friendly agreement with France, and were concluding one with Russia, and their principal effect on outsiders seemed to be to elicit the question against whom they were directed. Then, again, the Morocco question was thought, rightly or wrongly, to have endangered peace. And the unwholesome atmosphere of which these things were signs was displayed in a concrete shape by an enormous increase of armaments. It is, then, no wonder that a matter which in 1899 it was felt to be safest to avoid, notwithstanding its express mention by the august initiator of the Conference of that year, was not differently regarded in 1907. For a moment England seemed disposed to take it up with a magnificent if ill-directed courage. But it was dismissed with the declaration " that it is highly desirable that the Governments should resume the serious study of the question," from which it would be satisfactory to learn, could we believe it, that they had ever seriously studied it.

We would not, however, be understood to imply that Europe must always groan under the crushing weight of armaments. International problems will always arise so long as any part of the earth remains for which the existing political arrangements are not generally accepted as final. But in proportion as European States are grouped together in alliances and friendly understandings, those problems as they arise will have to be dealt with by the action of the groups, each of which, it may be hoped, will be less under the domination of some sinister interest than even the great Powers, taken singly, have hitherto been. Diplomatic solutions will more and more impose themselves on masses of such magnitude in place of violent ones, and as peace is felt to rest on a firmer basis our need for excessive armaments will be diminished. In this sense the Triple Alliance and the Anglo-French *entente cordiale* have been welcomed as making for peace, an opinion which we believe to be just, and to carry with it the best hope of an alleviation of military and naval expenditure.

After the limitation of armaments the most loudly voiced popular demand was for some notice of the outbreak of war. If this could be secured the cost of that large part of preparation might be spared which consists in not merely being provided with all necessary men and things, but in having them all so arranged that they may be capable of instant employment. Even here, however, the Conference was unable to give satisfaction. By the convention which it adopted " the contracting Powers recognize that hostilities between them ought not to commence without a preceding and unequivocal notice, which shall have the form either of a declaration of war expressing its motives, or of an ultimatum with a conditional declaration of war." But this did not go beyond the most general practice of the last half-century; and, so far from insisting on a substantial interval of notice between a declaration of war and the commencement of hostilities under it, the Conference did not even accept the very moderate proposal of a twenty-four hours' interval made by the delegation of the Netherlands. Nor is that result at all surprising. As a given negotiation becomes more acrimonious it is usually accompanied by advancing the last stages of preparation for a warlike issue, and the declaration of war by either party is deferred until the preparation of the other party has reached a point at which it is felt to be no longer safe to tolerate it. If a further lapse of time were then required before active steps could be taken to meet the danger, the definite pronouncement would have to be accelerated, and negotiations might be cut short of which the pacific issue was not quite hopeless. Even since the vote of the Conference a preliminary declaration without an interval of notice cannot be relied on. Each party will hold that the case of danger which can no longer be safely endured is reserved, and will throw the blame on its adversary, whom it will accuse of causing the danger. The moral to be drawn for England is that the necessity that, in order not to be taken unprepared, every nation must rely on its own vigilance and on no formal rule, has been rather emphasized than removed.

We now arrive at another topic of great popular interest, that of international arbitration, on which we are able to say that the Conference appears to us to have taken a valuable step in advance. But we must caution our readers against expecting too much. If any one dreams that even among men of good will—*homines bonæ voluntatis*—arbitration might be a means of finally extinguishing war, let him consider what figure arbitration would have made in 1857 between Sardinia, championing the resurrection of Italy, and France as her ally, on the one hand, and Austria on the other hand, with her legal title and her political convictions, with which even our good Queen Victoria sympathised; or again, of what use arbitration could have been in 1877 for averting a war between Turkish misrule and Russia as liberator. In other wars of no distant date quarrels centuries old have come to a head between populations so great that you cannot anathematise them without doing what Burke said he could not do, drawing an indictment against a nation. The kingdom of heaven, from which such causes of war shall have been eliminated, will come, not by observation, not by setting up any ambitious machinery, but by scarcely perceptible steps. The exception of vital interests and honour, or some other equivalent formula, will long have to stand as it does in the treaties which States conclude with one another for obligatory arbitration, barring the rare cases of those States between which, from their geographical and political situations, it is inconceivable that an important difference should arise. It expresses intelligibly enough the bed-rock against which all arrangements must be brought up until the international society is provided with a government. Meantime the essential is to bring the practice of international arbitration as close as possible to the line which limits it.

Let us see what was done for that end by the Conference of 1899. It established a rudimentary court consisting of a list of judges from which the parties on each occasion were to choose, but all the steps by which they were to come before that court were left to themselves. They had to draw up their own " agreement of reference (*compromis*), in which the subject of the difference is clearly defined as well as the extent of the arbitrators' powers"; and this, as every lawyer knows, is not always an easy task for litigants. Now, by Art. 53 of the improved rules adopted for the Hague Court at the Conference of 1907, that Court is not only competent to settle the agreement of reference if both the parties request it to do so, but it is competent to settle it on the demand of one alone of the parties, after they have tried in vain to come to an agreement by the way of diplomacy, (1) when the difference falls within a general treaty of arbitration, and the other party does not declare that in its opinion it is one of those to which obligatory arbitration does not apply ; (2) when the difference arises from debts claimed by one Power as due by contract to its subjects from another Power, and the offer of arbitration on them has been accepted. This is a distinct step towards establishing a court before which one State can summon another. It is true that it does not go that whole length, for the refusal of an offer of arbitration on contractual debts, and a declaration that the claim is non-arbitrable in the case of other claims, are left as means of escape. But let a State have concluded a treaty stipulating arbitration prospectively, or let it be exposed to contractual claims even without such a treaty, then, if it does not avail itself of those means of escape, it may find the agreement of reference settled for it on the demand of its antagonist, and the Hague Court will be seised of the case.

But this is not all. It was thought by many that, in order to attract more cases to an arbitral jurisdiction, it was necessary, not only to make the access to that jurisdiction easier, but to give it a reputation such as can only be acquired by a real permanence and embodiment. The value of names appearing in a list to choose from must be diminished by the uncertainty of their being chosen, and a good judgment given by persons who are immediately again dispersed, leaving no bench behind them to enjoy its credit, can but ill uphold the majesty of the law. To this view, which was more especially that of the United States delegation, it was not sought to give effect by a transformation of the existing Hague Court. The difficulties in the way of realising it were too great for that. It was determined to found a new court, working side by side with the existing one, to either of which States in difference may address themselves, leaving the superior vitality of either to the practical test of its popularity and efficiency. This project failed to be embodied in a general convention by reason of the impossibility of satisfying the desire of the smaller States for equality in the composition of the bench. The number of judges could not well exceed fifteen, and to apportion that number among all the States of the world it would have been necessary to group them, and even to allow to some only occasional turns. In the end the Conference, by what was called a *vœu*, recommended the adoption of an amended plan of convention for the establishment of a court of arbitral justice, and its effectuation as soon as an agreement should be come to on the choice of judges and the constitution of the court. The first article of the plan ran thus :

"With the object of promoting the cause of arbitration the contracting Powers agree to organise, without interfering with the Permanent Court of Arbitration [the existing Hague Court], a Court of Arbitral Justice of free and easy access, uniting judges representing the different juridical systems of the world, and capable of ensuring the continuity of arbitral justice."

This short paragraph contains more than one trace of United States authorship. By uniting the different juridical systems of the world it was meant to claim for the Anglo-American " common law " an equal place by the side of the Roman law, a very proper idea, which, however, would not have suggested itself to the Roman lawyers of Europe or America, though we are glad that they accepted it. And the design of ensuring the continuity of arbitral justice points to the hope, natural to an Anglo-American lawyer, but less so to one trained in the juridical systems in which precedent is of less value, of a stable body of international law being built up by the decisions of a permanent bench. The name "Court of Arbitral Justice" is, we fear, likely to cause some confusion with the existing Hague Court, which is called the Permanent Court of Arbitration; the more so since, if the two ever came to work side by side, the character of permanence could be predicated of the former much more appositely than of the latter. In what does not concern the constitution of the court, the plan for the one and the amended regulations for the other were conceived on the same lines. The Court of Arbitral Justice, by Art. 19 of the plan, is to have, through a delegation of three judges, the same power to settle the reference to it on a unilateral demand which we have quoted from Art. 53 of the amended regulations of the Hague Court. There is reason to believe that the Government of the United States is disposed to press on the Spanish American States and Brazil the institution of a Court of Arbitral Justice for America in accordance with the plan annexed to the *vœu* of the Conference. It is obvious that that can only be done if the smaller American republics will consent to waive their cherished equality in the nomination of the judges; but such a result is not unlikely, the influence of the United States being great, and common-sense having a better chance to prevail in pure diplomacy than under the incentive to self-assertion supplied by a worldwide assemblage with nominally equal voting.

It must be mentioned that an attempt was made, on a British proposal, to frame a list of subjects on which arbitration should be obligatory. Only eight subjects obtained in committee a majority in favour of their inclusion in such a list, and among these were such as weights and measures and the tonnage of ships. The attempt consequently failed, amid some public hilarity. The Conference did not expand the recommendation made in 1899 of juridical questions, and especially of those relating to the interpretation or application of international conventions, as suitable for arbitration. But it made a real step in advance by not allowing, as we have seen, pecuniary contractual claims to be exempted, by an allegation of their non-arbitrable character, from the competence of the Hague Court to settle an agreement of reference on the demand of a single party.

The pecuniary contractual claims urged on a Government by another Government on behalf of its nationals form a subject of great practical importance, independently of the general question of arbitration, especially having regard to the protection incidental to the Monroe doctrine which the United States extend to the weaker Spanish-American republics against which such claims are oftenest made. The Conference dealt with it in a manner in our view quite satisfactory. The coercive measures which Great Britain, Germany, and Italy employed against Venezuela for the enforcement of demands of that character were the occasion of a despatch which M. Drago, Minister of Foreign Affairs of Argentina, addressed to the United States through the Argentine Minister at Washington, of date December 29, 1902. He maintained the proposition, since much discussed under the name of the Drago doctrine, that coercive measures ought never to be employed for the redress of default in the service of a public loan, whether of interest, sinking fund, or principal; and he dwelt on the danger that such financial intervention might lead to the establishment, contrary to the principle of President Monroe, of European control, perhaps even of European territorial possession, on the American continent. On the question of equity there is no doubt that a public loan presents a very special case among contractual debts. The subscribers to it, or those who purchase its bonds in the market, trust the debtor State for a long period, during which many things, specifically unforeseen, may happen to impair its power of due payment without its good faith being necessarily impeachable; and for the risk thus foreseen in a general way a high rate of interest is exacted. On the other hand, a contractor for public works or a furnisher of supplies looks for speedy payment, and bases his prices on the market of the day, without reference to remote contingencies. An honest insolvency, such as the laws of all countries make some allowance for when it happens to a private person, is by no means improbable in the former case, but is scarcely to be thought of in the latter. The arguments urged in M. Drago's despatch did not, however, stop at these considerations of equity. He asserted that " one of the conditions proper to every sovereignty is that no executory proceeding can be commenced or completed against it, because that mode of recovery would compromise its very existence and cause the independence and action of the Government to disappear." Since this argument would not be limited to the case of public loans, it threw some doubt over the scope of the Drago doctrine, although it was only for them that it was enunciated. But the learned Argentine Minister has since presented his doctrine in 'a fully developed form. In cases of public loans it should be sufficient internationally if the foreign and internal holders receive equal treatment. Other pecuniary claims against a Government should first be brought before its courts of law, and the time to be allowed for payment of the sum adjudged by them should be submitted to an international arbitration, in which the debtor State's financial situation should be examined. The award would have the force of a treaty, and M. Drago does not absolutely exclude the employment of force for its vindication.

The United States delegate, General Porter, introduced the subject at the Conference by a proposal in which no distinction was made between public loans and other contractual debts. No such distinction has indeed been drawn by any Government. Lord Palmerston, whose doctrine on the subject was reaffirmed by Lord Salisbury, reserved in principle the right to demand redress in the case of public loans, though insisting on the differences which, as a matter of " British and domestic considerations," made it generally unwise to tempt British subjects into risky investments by demanding such redress on their behalf. The United States usually refrain from intervention in the case of all claims based on contract, and the continental Governments of Europe usually intervene in support of all, regarding them as an element of the national fortune. But the rule which General Porter sought to apply to all contractual debts was substantially that which the Drago doctrine in its perfected form sought to apply to those not arising from public loans. There must first be the offer of an arbitration in the Hague Court, the award of which shall determine not only the validity of the claim and the amount of the debt, but also the time and mode of payment. Only if such offer is refused, or if the debtor State fails to perform the award, may the recovery of the debt be prosecuted by armed force[1]. The proposal was adopted by the Conference, M. Drago making for Argentina the reservations (1) that for common contract debts arbitration must be preceded by the remedies in the courts of the debtor State being exhausted and justice denied; (2) that for redress in the case of public loans military aggression and the physical occupation of American soil shall in no case be permissible. We hope that nothing may prevent the ratification of the convention which embodies this resolution of the Conference. In order to determine the time and mode of payment the Hague Court must examine the financial situation of the debtor State and the honesty of the excuses made for its failure to perform its engagements. Thus,

[1] The text of this convention adds another case, that of the debtor State making the settlement of an agreement of reference impossible. But the convention for the improvement of the Hague Court, as we have already seen, gives that Court in such a case the power to settle the agreement of reference.

in a matter by no means inconsiderable, the court will be elevated into one of justice transcending the letter of the law, and will receive an accession of importance equal to that which we have pointed it out as receiving by being empowered in certain cases to settle an agreement of reference on a unilateral application. These steps in the progress of arbitration ought to satisfy its friends that it makes real way. Before they were thought of we had advocated the prohibition of force in support of claims arising from public loans as cutting off a class of interventions which are rarely justified and by which crying injustice has been done. But we are well content with the turn which the matter has taken, since it bids fair to remedy effectually an ignoble and dangerous branch of international practice, at the same time that it marks a stage of advance in another important direction.

We cannot express the same approval of the work of the Conference relating to the proposal of an international prize court. We have no doubt of the desirableness of such a court if a proper arrangement for one can be made. The prize jurisdiction of the captor's country, bound as it is by the prize law favoured by the supreme authorities of that country, has never been considered binding on foreigners, except so far as this, that the individual losing party is left helpless by a decision against him in its highest court. But his Government can espouse his cause; and on many occasions that Government and the Government of the prize court have entered into conventions under which the judgments complained of have been reviewed by mixed commissions, and damages have been paid by the State of which the court has been found by them to have pronounced erroneous judgments. But the tardy justice done by mixed commissions, instituted after the close of a war with much diplomatic toil and as the result of much international friction, and then only when the grievances complained of by individuals amount to a sum sufficient to induce their Government to seek an extraordinary remedy, has rather made apparent than effectually supplemented the inadequacy of a national jurisdiction in prize cases. It is anomalous that the lawfulness of a capture should, so far as jurisdiction is concerned, be finally determined by the captor's State. The question has often been mooted, both by individual thinkers and by private bodies like the Institute of International Law, and in 1907 Great Britain and Germany did well in laying before the Conference respective schemes for establishing an international prize court. They would have done better had they tried to meet the difficulties of the question by a joint scheme.

The greatest difficulty arises from the very fact which is the greatest source of the necessity, namely, the divergent views of prize law entertained in different countries. What is the law which the international court shall administer? For example, is the notice of blockade, to which a ship desiring to enter a blockaded port is entitled, to be measured by the British or the French rules? Is conditional contraband to be allowed? If not, can coal and provisions ever be absolute contraband? Does the declaration of the commander of a neutral convoy exclude the right of search? And so forth. One way of meeting the difficulty would be to withhold consent to the establishment of an international prize court until it can be combined with a settlement of all the major points of difference, in other words, with a codification of prize law.  It is possible, so far as we at present know the dates, that such may have been the original intention of the British Government ; in other words, that when its prize-court scheme was presented by its delegation it may have expected that such a codification would be achieved by the Conference.  But the delegation certainly took an active part in the elaboration and adoption of the scheme after it was clear that no codification would be attained.  The drafting committee (*comité d'examen*) on blockade reported to the fourth committee (*commission*) of the Conference that, at its first meeting, the British delegation proposed to suspend the discussion of that question, " on account of the profound divergence between the continental and Anglo-American systems, both long practised, the absence of instructions, and the want of time for arriving at a compromise acceptable to the Governments interested in so delicate and complicated a matter."  It must also have been apparent, from the early days of the Conference, that an agreement as to contraband of war was as little likely to be arrived at.  Therefore the proceedings as to an international prize court must have been conducted with the knowledge that the great difficulty of the case could only be met by a satisfactory declaration of the line which such a court should take in face of conflicting claims of law.

On that point the scheme adopted by the Conference laid down that the international court, which, it must be carefully borne in mind, was to be one of appeal from the national prize court, should apply in the first place any rule " provided for by a convention in force between the capturing belligerent and the Power which, or a subject of which, is a party to the suit, and, in default of such, the rules of international law. If there are no rules generally recognized, the court decides according to the general principles of justice and equity." Now the court appealed from will have decided according to the view of international law entertained by its own, the captor, State, and it would be utterly unjuridical to reverse a judgment which it was right in giving. And this was admitted by the eminent French jurist, M. Renault, who wrote, as reporter of the drafting committee :

"What will happen if positive law, written or customary, is silent? The solution dictated by the strict principles of judicial reasoning does not appear doubtful. In default of an international rule firmly established the international jurisdiction will apply the law of the captor. No doubt it is easy to object that we shall so have a very variable law, often very arbitrary and even such as to shock us, certain belligerents using to an excess the latitude left by positive law. That sould be a reason for hastening the codification of the latter in order to efface the gaps and uncertainties which are complained of, and which cause the difficult situation that has been pointed out."

Yet this cogent statement did not prevent the reporter from affecting the character of the statesman instead of his own proper character of the jurist, and proposing " the general principles of justice and equity " as the ultimate rule for the international court—a solution which he himself called bold, as inviting that court to make the law (*faire le droit*). Nor did he attempt to minimise the effect of the proposal, describing it as " of such a nature as seriously to ameliorate the practice of international law." We do not understand how such a solution was accepted on the part of Great Britain, when the true line to take was so forcibly pointed out by the very authority who advised the departure from it. Nor is it easy to reconcile its acceptance with the British withdrawal of blockade from the purview of the Conference. If, on that subject, " the profound divergence between the continental and the Anglo-American systems " was demanded more time than the Conference could command for its settlement, and if it was expected that that settlement must take the form of " a compromise acceptable to those Governments interested," one can only be surprised at finding such divergences, on that and on other subjects, remitted to the decision of judges of whom there might probably be a majority representing the system adverse to that of which it was thought necessary to make the defence a matter between Governments.

There has been in this country such a general expression of opinion against the ratification of a convention containing the objectionable clause that we have no fear on that score. But we must notice that Sir Henry Campbell-Bannerman, in a speech in which he joined in that opinion, contemplated the previous or concurrent codification of prize law as a condition for the establishment of an international prize court. Now, of the two ways in which the difficulty about the law of such a court can be surmounted, we decidedly prefer the other, namely, a satisfactory declaration of the line to be taken by the court in the face of conflicting claims of law. To put off the court itself till codification can be carried through would not only, as we have shown, be inconsistent with the course taken by us at the Hague, it would put it off to the Greek Kalends, ignoring the advantage which may be expected from it. The court would be a shield against the accusations of partiality which are made against national prize courts—though happily there is seldom a foundation for them in any country—and it would get rid of those better founded complaints which arise from undeniable personal or national tendencies, sometimes traceable in matters not falling under rules of law, such as the strong leaning in favour of captors which so great an authority as Chief Justice Marshall pointed out in Lord Stowell, at the same time acknowledging that he showed no disposition to press his principles with peculiar severity against neutrals. But, more than this, Governments are increasingly disposed to champion the commercial interests of their subjects, and differences between them thereby tend to arise about matters which, from their nature, belong less to law than to discretion, and as to which, therefore, an international jurisdiction is most desirable. For instance, after what happened during the South African war, a claim to search for contraband at any distance from the ship's destination cannot be said to be generally recognized, but to define the limiting distance for such a search by any general rule seems impossible. It would therefore be especially appropriate to an international court to decide whether any particular search was too remote. Whether therefore, the question of an international prize court be deferred till the next Peace Conference, or whether, as we should prefer, it should not be allowed by the Foreign Offices to sleep so long, we would take it up from the Conference draft. We would claim that Art. 7 of that draft be amended by naming the principles maintained by the captor's State as the law to be applied on the international appeal, failing relevant conventions and generally recognized rules. And we think that, after the frank recognition of the legal justice of that claim which was made at the Hague, it would be admitted if a firm stand were made on it. The scheme is, in general, a good one, and need not be further unripped. It would only remain to deal with the objections to the nomination and rotation of judges which were urged by China, Persia, Brazil, and eight Spanish-American republics.

The laws of war command less popular attention than the topics which have thus far occupied us, and there is danger lest the good work done on them by the Conference should pass unnoticed by its critics. Much of that work must always be known only to those professionally concerned with the subject, but we will cite some portions which ought to convince every one of its aggregate importance. The law of naval bombardments has been laid down for the first time. Undefended places on the coast are to be bombarded only for a refusal to furnish requisitions of victuals or other supplies, necessary for the actual wants of the naval force before the locality, and in proportion to the resources of the latter, never for the non-payment of contributions in money. On the proposal of Germany, for which great credit must be given her, the inviolability of postal correspondence has been proclaimed as a rule of naval war, whether its character is official or private, and whether the bags containing it or the ships carrying them are neutral or belligerent. If the ship is seized, her mail-bags must be forwarded by the captor with the least possible delay, except in the case of their coming from or being destined to a blockaded port by means of a breach of blockade. Among the amendments made to the laws of land war voted in 1899, one prohibits any compulsion of the population of an occupied territory to give information concerning their own army or the means of defence of their country; and that this must be interpreted to include a prohibition of their forced employment as guides is confirmed by the discussion. A regulation establishes the liberal practice which has grown up of sparing merchantmen which are found in an enemy's port at the outbreak of a war, or enter it or are met at sea by an enemy's cruiser while ignorant of the commencement of hostilities. One utterance of the Conference, not expressed as a rule, but as an earnest desire (*vœu*), would, if carried out in practice, work so great a change in war, both by land and sea, that we can scarcely criticise it till we know better what it means. It is "that in case of war the competent authorities, civil and military, shall make it a special duty to assist and protect the maintenance of peaceful relations, and in particular of commercial and industrial relations, between the inhabitants of the belligerent States and neutral countries." Does this mean, among other things, that an invader occupying a seaport in his enemy's country shall make it his special duty to promote the export thence to neutral countries of goods the payments for which may find their way to his enemy's war-chest? We imagine that at present the export trade of the occupied port, at least in belligerent ships, is as effectually stopped as if those ships were captured at sea by the occupier's cruisers.

There may, however, be some whom no record of progress in the other laws of war can console for the non-adoption of their cherished project of the immunity at sea of the enemy's property as such. This, proposed by the United States, was practically defeated, in spite of an illusory majority in its favour, by the solid opposition of Great Britain, France, Russia, Japan, Spain, Portugal and Mexico; besides which the delegations of Argentina and Colombia must be mentioned as deeming the right of capture necessary for the defence of Powers weaker at sea. Space forbids our entering here on the controversy; only, since the Conference expressed the desire (*vœu*) that the Powers should apply, as far as possible, to naval war the principles of the laws of land war, we will recommend the advocates of the change to prepare for the renewal of the controversy at the next Peace Conference by a careful study of the true analogies between naval and land war. Besides this, and the questions of contraband and blockade which have been already mentioned, there were other important questions of naval war on which the Conference arrived at no conclusive decision. Such were the questions whether the conversion of a merchantman into a ship of war may take place in the open sea; that whether neutral prizes may in any case be destroyed at sea; that whether unanchored contact mines, or any contact mines which do not become innocuous as soon as they get loose, may ever be employed; and those which concern the duties of neutral States. On the first and second of these no final vote took place; on the third there was a final vote which the British delegation declared " could not be regarded as a complete exposition of international law on the subject "; and on the questions mentioned in the fourth place there was a final vote in which the British delegate declined to take any part. Indeed it would seem that the Conference succeeded in nearly reaching the limits of possible agreement in the present state of opinion and of real or fancied interests, and that the condition of further progress is that the way shall be prepared by larger and more thorough study on the part of Governments, and that in that study each Government shall not maintain a proud aloofness, but seek by private conference with its neighbours to lay a foundation for a general agreement.

For the purpose of such preliminary study the recent Conference has prepared the way by making better known than before the sentiments with which different Governments approach the questions remaining to be decided. Previously those sentiments had to be inferred from the actions of the Governments, in which the occasion might count for more than any general attitude, or from the opinions of private thinkers, which might not always coincide with the official opinions of their respective States, and would, in any case, be opinions of what is just or desirable without authority to arrange a necessary compromise. Now the Governments have descended into the arena of public discussion, and with an illuminating effect, which has disclosed some features that might be regarded as discouraging if we forgot that a Conference so ill-prepared and so conducted as the late one has been is only a first experiment. In the works of many writers on international law, chiefly German, we have been familiar with the assertion of a necessity overriding the laws of war; but this was between belligerents. The action of the Conference about contact mines has been based on the right to plead necessity against neutrals. A drifting contact mine which has not become innocuous is a source of danger to neutral life and property in parts of the sea where neutrals have a perfect right to be, a danger the reality of which is testified by the disasters that continue to occur in the seas of the Far East long after the close of the Russo-Japanese war, and it has not yet been found possible to prevent anchored contact mines from getting loose even in moderately bad weather. Yet the Conference, while nominally prohibiting the employment of unanchored contact mines not becoming innocuous an hour after the control over them has been lost, and of anchored ones not becoming innocuous as soon as they have broken from their moorings, excused from the prohibition Powers not possessing such mines as contemplated, but undertaking to transform their mines as quickly as possible. This was what, as we have mentioned, the British delegation refused to consider as a complete exposition of international law on the subject. Baron Marschall von Bieberstein replied that

"a belligerent who lays mines assumes a very heavy responsibility towards neutrals and towards peaceful shipping. No one will resort to this instrument of warfare unless for military reasons of an absolutely urgent character.... But it would be a great mistake to issue rules the strict observation of which might be rendered impossible by the law of facts."

The plea of necessity thus flung in the face of neutrals was not allowed to shake the firm stand which the declaration read by Sir Ernest Satow had taken.

"By acceptance (it ran) of the proposal made by us at the beginning of the discussion, dangers would have been obviated which in every maritime war of the future will threaten to disturb friendly relations between neutrals and belligerents.... It remains for us to declare in the most formal manner that these dangers exist, and that the certainty that they will make themselves felt in the future is due to the incomplete character of the present convention."

Observe the words "will" and "certainty." The avowal that Germany will not scruple to sink British ships and sailors by drifting contact mines, if necessary for her victory over a third Power, stands opposed to the declaration that Great Britain will resent any such conduct. Nothing less would have been sufficient on the British side. But we are not pessimists. What the frank exchange of declarations will kill is not peace but the wrongful use of contact mines. All the same, the incident may cause any who believe in public conferences without preparation to reflect.

Another grave difference between Governments disclosed at the recent Conference relates to the duties of neutral States in naval war, in the final vote on which the British delegation, as we have said, declined to take any part. Great Britain, as a neutral, has limited the hospitality which she will extend to belligerent men-of-war by the closest analogy of which the case admits, to the acknowledged law in the case of a belligerent force crossing the land frontier of a neutral State. That force must be interned; but the exigencies of navigation require some allowance to be made for a man-of-war crossing the water boundary of a neutral State. The British regulation, in its latest form, allows her to stay only twenty-four hours, or twenty-four hours after her necessary repairs have been completed. She may receive only such repair as will enable her to keep the sea, and so much coal as may be sufficient to carry her to the nearest port of her own country, or to some nearer named neutral destination; and she may not receive even that quantity within three months from her last coaling in British waters. She may receive no coal when proceeding to the seat of war, or to any position on the line of route with the object of intercepting neutral ships carrying contraband of war; and she may not bring a prize into a British port except in case of distress. Rules more or less similar have been adopted by numerous States as the standard of their conduct, and have been recommended by the Institute of International Law. Nor are we aware that any difference of principle between the duties of neutrality in land and in naval war has been suggested before 1907 by international jurists. But the Conference has voted it open to neutral States to permit belligerent ships to remain in their ports and territorial waters without limit of time; to fill their bunkers there with coal even when on their way to the seat of hostilities; and to bring prizes into their ports and leave them there under sequestration pending the judgment of the prize court. It has also voted that, when a prize has been captured in the territorial waters of a neutral State and has been carried out of them, that State may refrain from applying to the belligerent Government for the redress of the violation of its neutrality. Such a negation of all recognized principle is, of course, only to be explained by jealousy of the advantage which recognized principle gives to a great naval Power having coaling stations of her own all over the world. It is a reservation of the right to favour the enemies of such a Power, and to receive favour when an enemy of it. It is as though a rule should be laid down that when two Powers are at war the army of one of which, on a war footing, exceeds that of the other in a certain proportion, a neutral State should be free to allow a passage across its territory to the forces of the latter but not to those of the former.

It was not to be supposed that such votes would be registered without some attempt to give them a legal colour. Accordingly it was argued that, because in time of peace ships of war are usually allowed to enter neutral ports and to choose their time of departure freely, that permission cannot be suddenly withdrawn in time of war—an argument formerly used for the traffic in contraband being as free in time of war as in time of peace, but long since decisively condemned in that application. It was also said that "the essential thing is that all shall know what to expect, and that there shall be no surprise," and that the abstention from rendering aid to a belligerent, which from the time of Vattel has been regarded as the essential thing in neutrality, is merely a duty to be reconciled with the duty of hospitality. Finally, that "the starting-point of a regulation must be the sovereignty of the neutral State, which cannot be affected by the sole fact of a war to which it intends to remain a stranger[1]." The only possible meaning of sovereignty in such a connexion is freedom of choice not seriously restricted by rules, a sense which, if it were admitted, would make all international law an infringement of sovereignty. These principles are familiar to us in international action, and are by no means unknown to the twilight of diplomatic expression. They are the relics of the time before the theory of neutrality had begun to be elaborated. Now that they have come out into quasi-scientific daylight we may hope that the voice of the British people will be as clearly expressed against them as we are sure that it will be against floating mines not rendered innocuous. It may be assumed that the British Government, by its withdrawal from the final vote, intended to indicate as firm a stand against them as in the case of floating mines it announced by its protest. Great Britain, as a belligerent, will no more tolerate a violation of the principles of neutrality because what those principles forbid has not been laid down in precise and agreed rules than, as a neutral, she will tolerate a violation of the same principles for the same insufficient reason.

Such was the Second Peace Conference. Its reputation has suffered because too much was expected from it by those whose influence was most concerned in calling it into being. But it was a great event. The procedure which it initiated,

---

[1] These quotations are from M. Renault, reporting the scheme adopted in the "Convention concerning the Rights and Duties of Neutral Powers in the case of Maritime War." The report is given in the *Courrier de la Conférence*, nos. 94–96.

and which, with modifications, will probably long play an important part ; the real though unassuming good work which it did ; the light which it has thrown on the disposition of certain Governments towards the principles of neutrality in naval war, and the attitude of the British Government in defence of those principles ; and the British proposal to abolish contraband of war—all these ensure to the Conference of 1907 that it will not be forgotten either in international law or in international politics.

At the head of this article I have placed the two sources which have made so early an appreciation of the Second Peace Conference possible. Mr Stead deserves the warmest thanks of all persons interested in international law and its progress for the zeal with which he conducted a daily journal during the four months of the session, and succeeded in publishing in its pages, in full or in abstract, most of the important documents submitted to or issuing from the Conference or its committees. In this he triumphed over the unwise and somewhat inconsistent officialism of the body, which, while admitting public discussion and voting, was at first unwilling to admit outsiders to a sufficient knowledge of what was being discussed and voted on. The result was probably due to the superior common-sense of the members as individuals to that displayed by the body, or by the diplomatic influences under which it began to act.

Next I have placed two works which belong, the former entirely and the latter in some degree, to the movement which brought about the Peace

Conferences. *The Arbiter in Council* shows wide reading and high purpose. It is put in the form of conversations between men of different professions, but its dominant point of view is that of the preacher, and the motives and restraints which it discusses are those which are felt by private persons in their affairs. It takes little note of the moral agencies by which nations are impelled, weak as they are in most individuals, but integrated in the action of masses, and made more intense by the sympathy which attends such integration. Sir Thomas Barclay attacks the subject from the technical side, but has great faith in the possibility of effecting much in a short time by skilful arrangements.

Then come three general treatises on international law, of which Dr Oppenheim's is a work of great merit, on the scale of Hall or of the English editions of Wheaton. We commend it highly to students, who will find in it abundant references to the latest continental literature on the subject. M. Mérignhac is one of the best of the younger men who are coming forward in France. The part of his work as yet published deals with the fundamental ideas of international law with a patient detail to which we are unaccustomed in this country in the treatment of the philosophical part of the subject. English students will do well to read it and reflect on it. Of my own work I can of course say nothing, except that it contains the compressed outcome of many years of study, and that the editor has kindly placed it among the books which are to head this article. With these I have named the book by Mr Atherley-Jones and Mr Bellot on *Commerce in War* as being, like them, no offspring of any present movement or recent incidents. Its " purpose is to provide a full exposition of the rules of international law which govern the commercial relations of the subjects of neutral and belligerent States." This its limited scope has enabled it to do, with fuller quotations from treaties, ordinances, judgments, and the opinions of great jurists than could be found room for in a general treatise on international law.

Messieurs Smith and Sibley, Professor Holland and Dr Lawrence have all written with special reference to the Russo-Japanese war or to the Second Peace Conference when it was in prospect; and the choice of a subject for the Yorke prize, won by Mr Bentwich, may well have been made under similar impressions. The list is closed by the monumental *Digest* with which the enlightened liberality of the United States Government and the well-known learning and accuracy of Mr Bassett Moore have enriched this department of literature. It would be a great gain if other countries would similarly open their records and make their contents accessible.

# XIV

## HOLLAND AND VENEZUELA. 1908.

[A letter reprinted, with permission, from *The Times*, 24th December, 1908.]

To the Editor of *The Times*.

SIR,—The news that the Dutch authorities have seized two Venezuelan gunboats has now remained long enough unaccompanied by any news of a declaration either of war or of a pacific blockade to create the reasonable belief that there has been no such declaration.

Consequently the question begins to be put whether there has not been a breach by the Government of the Netherlands of the rule voted at The Hague Conference of 1907, and now embodied in a Convention, that " hostilities must not commence without previous and explicit warning, in the form either of a declaration of war with the reasons assigned for it, or of an ultimatum with conditional declaration of war." That rule can have no meaning unless the hostilities mentioned in it include all acts of force, other than those of the most necessary self-defence against acts of force by the opposite party, which are not made exceptions to it by some other rule or recognized practice. Such other rule or practice exists in the case of pacific blockade, not indeed by any resolution of a conference but by a sufficient consent both of opinion and of tolerated examples. If, therefore, the Dutch had seized the gunboats for breach of a declared pacific blockade, they would not have been chargeable with violating the new law as to the commencement of hostilities. But it does not follow that they are in fault because they do not seem to have taken that course. There is another practice equally capable of operating in the interpretation of the new law—namely, that as to reprisals; and it is under this that we must suppose the Dutch to be acting. Reprisals as a mode of seeking redress or exerting pressure without war were a firmly established institution of the law of nations, and were very often resorted to in former days. They have now fallen much into disuse, mainly because their place has to a large extent been taken by pacific blockade, which is in truth a new form of reprisals, elaborated during the last three-quarters of a century. But the old forms have neither been entirely dropped in practice nor condemned by jurists, and, in view of present circumstances, it is worth while to recall what they were.

Vattel describes reprisals as the seizure of something to be held as a pledge for a pecuniary claim, whether in the nature of debt or of compensation for injury. If there is no longer hope of justice being obtained the pledge may be confiscated in satisfaction, and then the proceeding is ended without there having been war unless it is declared by either party (Liv. 2, ch. 101, section 342). And he goes on to say that when the claim is not of that nature but "in that of a contested right, after conciliation or the pacific means of obtaining justice have been tried in vain, it is a declaration of war which ought to follow and not pretended reprisals, which in such a case would be real acts of hostility without declaration of war, and would be contrary both to public faith and to the mutual duties of nations " (section 354). But more recent writers, and international practice as it must be confessed, have been less strict. Claims not or not wholly pecuniary have been asserted by the seizure of things not capable of being sold or applied in compensation, the term " material guarantee " has supplanted the narrower one of " pledge," and still the proceeding has been called one of " reprisal," as if a proceeding could be brought within the old law by the name used in that law being given to it. Indeed, the latter cases, few as they are, have rather been of that character, the kind of cases contemplated by Vattel being now dealt with by pacific blockade. Thus Mr John Bassett Moore, in his great *Digest of International Law*, gives the following as an " example " under the head of " reprisals " : " In November, 1901, France seized the Custom-house at Mytilene in order to enforce compliance by the Turkish Government with demands for the settlement of the Lorando claim, the rebuilding of French schools and institutions destroyed in 1895-6, the official recognition of existing schools and institutions, and the recognition of the Chaldean Patriarch" (vol. VII. p. 135).

It will be seen from the above that there is a practice of reprisals which The Hague Conference of 1907 can no more be imagined to have intended abolishing than it can be imagined to have intended abolishing pacific blockade, and yet that it is of the loosest kind. So far from advancing towards precision, as the doctrine of pacific blockade did until it culminated in the rules laid down for it by the Institute of International Law, it has receded from the precision which it once had. Far, then, from blaming a friendly nation for illegality, my object is to point out the danger that the vaunted new law may be undermined in such a way that no nation can ever be blamed for illegality in commencing hostilities without a declaration of war. Not only from the scientific point of view—which it would be idle to expect should have been much thought of for its own sake in a great official conference—but even from the practical point of view, a definition and regulation of reprisals were as necessary to a valuable rule requiring declarations of war as a proper definition of the law to be applied by an international Prize Court has been found to be to the establishment of such a Court. The filling the lacuna thus left may be commended to The Hague Conference of 1913, and in the meantime to friendly and thorough discussion by international lawyers. We may be sure that all Governments, including our own, will strive to retain as much as possible of their powers of action. They desire to exercise those powers for the good of their respective nations, and there is little use in appealing to altruistic sentiment in those nations. If there is to be much improvement in international law, and especially in so much of that law as tends to restrict the powers of Governments, each nation must be convinced that, even for its own good, it is better to rely on well-considered general law than on particular measures taken to meet particular occasions.

I am, Sir, &c.,

J. WESTLAKE.

CHELSEA, *Dec.* 19.

## XV

### PACIFIC BLOCKADE[1]. 1909.

[Reprinted, with permission, from the *Law Quarterly Review*, vol. xxv. (1909), pp. 13–23.]

MY attention has been recalled to pacific blockade by the treatise named below.  That subject is one in which it is especially necessary to attach a precise meaning to terms, and to adhere to it in employing them.  Any blockade established in time of peace is a pacific blockade in the etymological sense of the words, but in the technical sense the term signifies an institution of international law permitting certain acts of force to be done without a declaration or the intent of war, and denying to any state affected by them the right to regard them as acts of war, although of course no state can be prevented from declaring war because of them if it regards them as politically unjustifiable.  When it is asked whether a given incident was a pacific blockade, the question has in the etymological sense a bare historical meaning, namely, whether the blockade under consideration was established without a declaration or the intent of war, and whether any state affected by it treated it as war or declared war upon it. In other words, did the blockade exist in time of peace ?  But when the same question is put

[1] *Pacific Blockade.* By Albert E. Hogan, LL.D. Oxford: Clarendon Press. 1908. pp. 183.

in the technical sense it has a meaning which, if still historical, is not limited to the externals of history. It is asked whether, on the one hand, the given blockade was established in what may be called the random way in which acts of force have been and are still sometimes employed against diplomatic antagonists, leaving it to the development of events to determine their outcome and nature, as when between Great Britain and France there was fighting in America and India, and prizes were taken at sea as early as 1754, though there was no declared war till 1756—or whether, on the other hand, the blockading government intended to avail itself of an institution of international law, and restricted its action to what it conceived to be the limits of that institution. Only in the latter case can the blockade be quoted as contributing the testimony of the blockading government to the existence and limits of the institution, and even then, if the comparative weakness of the blockaded state caused it to endure the blockade without turning it into war, it will be impossible to quote that fact as a testimony on its side to the institution. If, however, it should be possible to quote a series of blockades established by important powers and permitted to exist in time of peace, restricted also to the limits recognized by the general assent of accredited writers, this would not only be weighty evidence in favour of the interpretation that the several blockading powers intended to adopt the institution and act on it, but would go far to give it a place in international law.

There are two rules of international law that are infringed by pacific blockade in its etymological, which may also be called its objective sense, and which, or at least one of them, will therefore have to be modified if pacific blockade is accepted in its technical sense as an institution. One of these is expressed as follows in the convention based on the votes of the Hague Conference of 1907: " The contracting powers recognize that hostilities between themselves must not commence without previous and explicit warning, in the form either of a declaration of war with the reasons assigned for it, or of an ultimatum with conditional declaration of war." This rule was taught by Grotius, but down to the middle of the nineteenth century practice stood in opposition to it, nor can more be said of its theoretical existence during that period than that the conscience of the civilized world has been gradually working up to it. It can have no meaning unless the hostilities mentioned in it include all acts of force, other at least than those of the most necessary self-defence against acts of force by the opposite party, which are not made exceptions to it by some other rule. To prevent the shipping of your diplomatic antagonist from leaving or entering his ports before he is converted into an enemy, even if you only sequester them and do not condemn them as prizes, is an act of force which can now only be deemed lawful if pacific blockade is accepted as an institution modifying the Hague rule quoted.

The other rule of international law with which our subject is concerned is that, as against third states, a right to employ force exists only under the laws relating to neutrality, and that these begin to operate only from the date when the existence of a war has either been notified to the third state or is generally notorious. It follows that to prevent the shipping of third states from leaving or entering the ports of your diplomatic enemy while no war exists between you and him—again, even if you only sequester them and do not condemn them as prizes—is a wrong to those states. It also follows that the wrong is not avoided by your notifying him of the blockade, unless such notification can be considered as carrying with it an implied notification of the existence of war. But in that case the incident is taken out of pacific blockade, whether in the etymological or in the technical sense, and the blockading state loses the hoped-for advantage of throwing a pacific veil over the employment of force. If, therefore, pacific blockade should be recognized as an institution permitting any interference with the shipping of third states, that will be a modification of international law, and those states will lose any right of treating the notification of the blockade as implying notification of the existence of a war. If pacific blockade is recognized as an institution permitting no interference with any shipping but that of the antagonist, such a modification of existing international law will not result. Then, however, it may be and has been asked, why the name and rules of blockade should be used at all, since all that would be done under them against the shipping of the antagonist might equally be done under the old names and rules of reprisal and embargo. Probably one reason why that course has not been taken is, that those rather obsolete modes of seeking redress or applying pressure offend modern sentiment by their too casual incidence. It may have been thought that in time of peace the subjects even of a diplomatic antagonist ought to have so much security for fair and equal treatment as is given by the notification and effective maintenance required for a blockade. But this as an historical supposition is not necessary. We shall see that pacific blockade was first discussed on the footing of its effects extending to third states, so the force of habit will sufficiently account for the name and rules being retained by those who have preferred a more limited form of the institution, though the consideration which has been suggested will warrant that retention.

Blockade was not, like reprisals, embargo, and material guarantees, one of what I have called the random ways in which, during the ages of misrule, hostilities were begun without declaration of war, by governments which did not trouble themselves about the legal character which their actions possessed or in the course of events might acquire. Possibly they saw that to notify a blockade to the world, and with it by implication to notify the existence of a war, would throw away the diplomatic advantage of leaving it open whether war should follow, while giving them no more against their antagonists than reprisals would give them. Perhaps the first recorded instance, and even that not of a power nominally at peace with the blockaded state being the principal in a blockade, but of such a power aiding in one, is to be found in *The Staadt Embden* (1798) 1 C. Rob. 26. England was in a state of declared war against both France and Holland, Russia against France alone, but the Russian fleet assisted the British in blockading Amsterdam. Sir W. Scott observed that " an auxiliary fleet is not of itself sufficient to make its government a principal in a war," but that since " in those Dutch hostilities " the Russians had repeatedly made captures and detained prizes " as taken from a common enemy," it was " not easy to discover the grounds on which the government to which the auxiliary fleet belonged could be considered as entirely neutral." In these words Messieurs Smith and Sibley find " the doctrine of pacific blockade[1]." What doctrine? The case rather shows how difficult Sir W. Scott found it to treat a power which joined in a blockade even as an auxiliary as being other than a belligerent.

Blockade not joined in by a nominally neutral auxiliary, but established by powers not nominally at war with the blockaded state, makes its first appearance in 1827, and then not as a means of enforcing a claim to redress but in support of a specific military purpose, for the attainment of which it was foreseen that the interception of supplies from any quarter might be necessary. England, France, and Russia, having determined to put an end to the operations of the Turkish forces in Greece, established what they expressly called a blockade of the Greek coast, applicable to what they expressly called neutral vessels, but limited to preventing the introduction into Greece of succours intended for the Turks[2]. History does not tell us whether ships of the so-called neutral states were in fact interfered with, and it is possible that the opportunity for such interference did not arise, considering the interruption which the long struggle

[1] *International Law as interpreted during the Russo-Japanese War*, p. 216.
[2] See Holland's *Studies in International Law*, p. 137.

in Greece must have caused to the commerce between the blockaded coast and its nearest neighbours, Austria and Italy. The equal silence of history as to any questions such as the condemnation of quasi-neutral prizes must have occasioned may warrant us in believing that at least nothing beyond sequestration was attempted. The mental attitude of the blockading powers with regard to their legal position was unquestionably that vague and expectant one which belonged to the time when a declaration of war was not deemed necessary to the commencement of hostilities. They said that they were not at war with Turkey. It was not likely, having regard to the political circumstances, that the quasi-neutrals should force them into a state of avowed war by refusing to endure an interference with their commerce on any other terms. But it would be an anachronism to impute to them any denial of the right of the quasi-neutrals to do so, or therefore to connect the incident in any way with pacific blockade as an institution.

During the next ten years a few instances occurred of operations in the nature of blockade being undertaken against states without declaration of war. In 1831 France, in the pursuit of the redress of grievances, blockaded several points on the coast of Portugal, without interfering with the ships of third states. The French admiral, with sailorly but illogical bluntness, wrote of war being declared *de facto*. A treaty was concluded, and the Portuguese merchant-ships which had been taken were restored; but not the ships of war, which implies that there had been war. In 1832–3 England and France blockaded the ports of the Netherlands in the pursuit of a political object, also without interfering with quasi-neutral ships. War did not follow. In 1837 England blockaded the ports of New Granada for the redress of a grievance, and a French barque was among the vessels stopped. No protest was made, but this may have been because the blockaded government gave in after twelve days. With regard to these cases the term " blockade " was creeping into general use, and it was officially used at least in the last of them. But really, with the exception of stopping that French barque, nothing was done under the term that had not been habitual for centuries under the name of reprisals[1].

We now come to the cases which effectually raised the question of pacific blockade as an institution. In 1838 France declared a blockade of the ports of Mexico, connecting the political demand for reciprocal treatment between the two nations in commerce and navigation with a demand for the redress of grievances, and applied it to quasi-neutral shipping. Lord Palmerston refused to make any formal protest to the French Government on behalf of the British vessels affected, and when pressed by Sir Robert Peel in the House of Commons he used language which seems to imply that he thought blockade to be one of the time-honoured methods by which war had been begun without declaration[2]. But the Hanse Towns—Bremen, Hamburg and Lübeck—protested, and in the end Mexico declared war. France then confiscated the Mexican and other ships which she had only held under

[1] See these three cases in Hogan, *Pacific Blockade*, pp. 77–84.
[2] *Annual Register*, 1839, p. 264.

sequestration, and, under the treaty of peace which followed, the legality of that confiscation of the Mexican ships and their cargoes was referred to the award of Queen Victoria. She, on August 1, 1844, pronounced it lawful, expressly on the ground of the declaration of war[1]. Thus the British position was taken up, that blockade without war gives no right against the ships of the quasi-enemy beyond sequestration. As to them, it was assimilated to embargo, which Sir W. Scott held to give the right of sequestration, to be followed by condemnation on the outbreak of war: *The Boedes Lust*, 5 C. Rob. 245. With the ships of quasi-neutrals the award was not concerned; but its spirit is opposed to their being even sequestrated, for if the name of blockade confers no right against the quasi-enemy which would not have existed against him without it, it seems impossible that it should confer any right at all against others.

In the same year, 1838, France declared a blockade of Buenos Ayres which she maintained till 1840, and in 1845 she renewed it in conjunction with England, the latter raising it in 1847 but France not until 1848; indeed it was not till 1850 that France raised her blockade of the port of Buceo, which an ally of Rosas, the Argentine dictator, held in the Republic of Uruguay. These blockades were applied to the ships of third states. France established a prize court in Uruguay, with which republic she concluded a convention recognizing the blockades and regulating the navigation of the River Plate during them, and an appeal lay to the council

---

[1] Hogan, *Pacific Blockade*, p. 88.

of state in France. That body sustained condemnations for breach of blockade, but doubted whether there was war until the Minister of Foreign Affairs stated in a letter that there was not, whereupon it reversed the condemnation of a cargo as contraband[1]. Among the ships thus condemned there were Uruguayan ones, which were bound by their own government's recognition of the blockade, and British ones, which were bound by their own government being a co-blockader. But there were also Brazilian and Argentine ones, and, besides the Hanse Towns, " three nations at least—Portugal, Bolivia, and the United States—protested against the blockade[2]." Thus France became committed to the view that blockade without war gives rights against third states even to the extent of condemning their shipping, while at the same time Palmerston, strangely enough for the Foreign Minister in a co-blockading government, adopted in theory the British view, as to which the Foreign Office had probably been fully instructed by the advice of the law officers which must have been given to the Queen for her award of 1844. He wrote as follows, in 1846, to Lord Normanby, the British Ambassador at Paris :

"The real truth is, though we had better keep the fact to ourselves, that the French and English blockade has been from first to last illegal. Peel and Aberdeen have always declared that we have not been at war with Rosas ; but blockade is a belligerent right, and unless you are at war with a state you have no right to prevent the ships of other states from communicating with the ports of that state, nay, you cannot prevent your own merchant ships from doing so. I think it important, therefore, in order to

[1] *Le Comte de Thomar*, sentence of 25 March, 1848, 1 Pistoye et Duverdy, 390.
[2] Hogan, *Pacific Blockade*, p. 103, quoting Falcke.

legalize retrospectively the operations of the blockade, to close the matter by a formal convention of peace between the two powers and Rosas[1]."

In this Palmerston did not take account of the constitutional authority of the British Crown over the commerce of its subjects abroad, and even as to the international aspect of the case he forgot that against third powers a subsequent notification or recognition of a war which was not notorious when they were interfered with can have no retrospective effect. But as to the main point of the right of interference with third powers the respective attitudes of France and England were now defined, and were maintained in 1884, when France announced a blockade of a part of the island of Formosa without declaring war against China. Lord Granville put her to the choice of abstaining from condemning British ships or of accepting a state of war with China. France chose the latter branch of the alternative, and England then forbade French ships of war coaling in her ports.

The Mexican and Argentine instances, having at least in French opinion introduced blockade without war as an institution, it was called simple blockade, for which term Hautefeuille in 1849, while severely condemning it, substituted "pacific blockade[2]." From that time to this the subject has been abundantly discussed by theoretical writers, and the prevailing opinion among them is that the ships of quasi-neutral states ought not to be interfered with at all in time of peace, thus rejecting

[1] Dalling, *Life of Lord Palmerston*, III. 327.
[2] *Droits et Devoirs des Nations Neutres en temps de Guerre Maritime*, 2ᵉ édition, 1858, II. 287. Holland cites to the same effect the first edition in 1849: *Studies in International Law*, p. 131.

the French institution. The two most important exceptions are furnished by the great German names of Heffter and Perels, of whom the latter limited the interference with quasi-neutral ships in time of peace to preventing their crossing the line of blockade, while the former allowed their sequestration but not their condemnation. There has thus arisen, so far as the matured opinion of thinkers is capable of creating one, a more limited institution of international law under the name of Pacific Blockade, by which the rule requiring hostilities to be preceded by a declaration of war is modified or interpreted, while the rule remains intact which requires the notification or notoriety of war as a condition of claiming against third states any rights but those of peace. The most approved regulations for the purpose are those laid down by the Institute of International Law in 1887 :

"(1) Ships under a foreign flag can enter freely notwithstanding the blockade :

"(2) The pacific blockade must be officially declared and notified, and maintained by a sufficient force :

"(3) The ships of the blockaded power which do not respect such a blockade can be sequestrated. When the blockade is raised, they must be restored with their cargoes to the owners, but without indemnity on any account[1]."

Mr Hogan reads No. (2) of these regulations as requiring notification to third states, and accordingly charges the Institute with inconsistency in imposing such a duty towards states which are not to be affected[2]. Surely it is more reasonable to consider the Institute as requiring notification only

[1] *Annuaire de l'Institut de Droit International*, 9<sup>me</sup> année, p. 301 Tableau Général, 1893, p. 133.
[2] *Pacific Blockade*, p. 34.

to the party which is to be affected. The solid reason which there may be for protecting that party against unequal and unfair pressure on individuals, by notification and the necessity for efficient maintenance of the blockade, has been already mentioned.

Coming now to the recognition which pacific blockade has received in international practice since the question was fairly launched, we find England thoroughly committed to it in its milder form. She did not interfere with any shipping but that of her antagonists in her blockades of Greece in 1850 and of Brazil in 1862–3, and only Greek shipping was interfered with by the blockade of Greece in 1886, in which she was joined with the other great powers except France, but in all these cases the antagonist was blockaded without declaration of war or what was considered to be war. In her opposition to what may be called the French institution she has been inflexible. The blockade of Siam by France in 1893 reproduced the essential features of the affair of 1884. There was no declaration of war; in French official opinion there was no war; British shipping was interfered with; the British governor of Singapore was ordered provisionally not to allow French coaling, but the resistance of Siam was brief and the blockade was soon raised.

With regard to the conduct of other powers, we may dismiss from consideration the blockade of Zanzibar in 1888–9, to which the native sovereign proclaimed his consent, and that of Crete in 1897, which was peculiar in that the coast blockaded was not Greek but belonged to the Sultan, who consented to it[1], although Greece was the antagonist whom it was intended to reduce to submission. As little is it necessary to dwell on the blockade of Gaeta and Messina in 1860-1 by Sardinia, which was really hostile though war was not declared, and occurred at the time when the old irregular commencements of hostilities were gradually giving way to the recognition of a necessity for declarations of war, so that it is difficult to say what standard should be applied to it. The case which it is important to examine is that of the blockade of Venezuela in 1902-3 by England and Germany, which was applied to neutrals. The action of England on that occasion appeared to Professor Holland to be "war *sub modo*," and to me to be war, and I deemed it to be no less difficult to regard the operations of Germany in any other light[2]. It now appears that the German government informed the ambassador of the United States at Berlin "that it was at first inclined to a pacific blockade, but that, yielding to the wishes of Great Britain, which had insisted on establishing a war-like blockade, it would join with that government in announcing such a blockade in a few days[3]." In response to a further inquiry by Mr Hay, "The German government stated that although it was not intended to make a formal declaration of war a state of war would actually exist, and that the warlike blockade would be attended with all the conditions of such a measure, just as if war had been formally declared[3]."

[1] Neither promptly nor willingly, but consent was ultimately given.
[2] Holland in *L. Q. R.* 133; Westlake, *International Law* (War), pp. 15, 16.
[3] Moore's *Digest of International Law*, vol. VII. pp. 140, 141.

By " pacific blockade " in the German statement the institution of the Institute was of course meant. By a " warlike blockade " we cannot say that the French institution was meant, for that was to be a blockade without a state of war, while this was to be a blockade with a state of war only without a declaration of war. It is therefore confessed that what was intended was just what I, and substantially Professor Holland, had perceived to be done. A few years later such a proceeding would have violated the new rule that war must be preceded by declaration, unless " warlike blockade " can be shown to be an accepted institution forming an exception to that rule, which it is plain is not the case.

The occasion just referred to brought out clearly the attitude of the United States towards the question.

"Mr Hay, on December 12, 1902, directed Mr Tower, the American ambassador at Berlin, to say that the United States adhered to its position in the case of the Cretan blockade in 1897, and therefore did 'not acquiesce in any extension of the doctrine of pacific blockade which may adversely affect the rights of states not parties to the controversy, or discriminate against the commerce of neutral nations'; and that the United States reserved all its rights in the premises[1]."

Having now before us the declared policies of the four greatest naval powers of Europe and America, we can sum up. Blockade interfering with third parties, and unaccompanied by a state of war, is admitted by France alone, and is not a part of the law of nations. Blockade not interfering with third parties, and unaccompanied by a state of war, is admitted by all four—for its admission by France is included in her assertion of her own

[1] Moore, u.s.

institution, as the less in the greater—and is a part of the law of nations. For this alone the name of Pacific Blockade should henceforth be reserved. Lastly, blockade interfering with third parties, accompanied by a state of war but unaccompanied by a declaration of war, has emerged once from the Land of Shadows, we may hope never to reappear ; but one can never feel sure. Discussion on the expediency of admitting pacific blockade has become out of date; discussion on the expediency of admitting blockade against third parties without war may perhaps be postponed until, if ever, another attempt shall be made to establish such a blockade in the teeth of the forces now arrayed against it.

Mr Hogan has made his work very useful by the information brought together in it. There is a good bibliography, and Part II consists of " Historical Accounts of the Various Blockades," which contain some matter previously unpublished, and correct some current errors, while the Appendix gives a large number of British, French and other official notices of blockade. We have Mr Hogan's authority for saying that at p. 94, l. 20, the words " The Vice-Admiralty Court in Jamaica " ought to have been preceded by the words " I think it right to add that Sir Charles Adam is incorrect in supposing that." This casual omission has affected the sense.

Mr Hogan's conclusions are generally in harmony with those of the Institute of International Law, except that he treats notice to the blockaded state merely as being usual, and the effectiveness of the blockade as desirable, instead of both being necessary. He also allows interference with the ships of third states, to the extent of their detention in two cases. One is "where the blockade has been instituted by the Concert of Europe," in which case there is little chance that the interference would be resisted; but the difficulty of defining the Concert and its powers stands in the way of formulating an exception. Did the abstention of France prevent the blockade of Greece in 1886 from being one by the Concert? Mr Hogan answers in the negative, p. 60. But a concert which survives abstentions is an intangible entity. His other case is where ships are detained "with the consent of the state whose flag they fly, such consent to be implied in the absence of any protest from such state," p. 71. It scarcely seems that the interests of peace and good order are served by encouraging the doing of things which are to become lawful only by not being opposed.

One other point is of some importance. Mr Hogan, while adopting the rule of the Institute that ships of the blockaded state must be restored when the blockade is raised, adds, by way of exception, that " where the demands made on the state blockaded, being of a pecuniary character, have not been satisfied, such vessels may be retained to satisfy them," p. 71. It is not clear that this is opposed to the real sense of the Institute, for in 1898 that body voted that when an embargo is laid on a foreign ship in a port by way of retorsion or reprisal, and satisfaction is not made, she may be sold and the price taken by the embargoing state (17 *Annuaire*, 284). And Hall says that

" vessels or other property seized otherwise than by way of embargo ...may be confiscated so soon as it appears that their mere seizure will not constrain the wrong-doing state to give proper redress. In recent times, however, instances of confiscation do not seem to have occurred, and probably no property seized by way of reprisal would now be condemned till after the outbreak of actual war" (§ 120).

It would therefore seem that in the resolution of the Institute on pacific blockade the case in question must be deemed not to have been contemplated, the more so as the case of the pacific blockade ending in war is also not mentioned. What was really meant, apparently, was only that breach of the blockade should not be an offence entailing confiscation. In all other respects the blockading state must be free to demand its own terms for raising the blockade, just as it might have demanded its own terms of peace if it had made war. The same remark will explain another of Mr Hogan's conclusions, namely that " in exceptional cases, where the blockade is directed against some practice, such as slavery, which is contrary to international morality, any vessels which are engaged in such practice may be condemned."

# XVI

### REPRISALS AND WAR. 1909.

[Reprinted, with permission, from the *Law Quarterly Review*, vol. xxv. (1909), pp. 127–137.]

IN an article [1] in the last number of this *Review* I described pacific blockade in the technical sense as "an institution of international law permitting certain acts of force to be done without a declaration or the intent of war, and denying to any state affected by them the right to regard them as acts of war, although of course no state can be prevented from declaring war because of them if it regards them as politically unjustifiable."

It will be well at once to state that in the foregoing and throughout this article the term "declaration of war" is not used in the limited sense of a declaration specially communicated to the enemy, but includes all manifestoes addressed to the public. Reprisals are another institution of international law to which the same description applies as to pacific blockade, and by a curious coincidence, while the article referred to was in the printer's hands, the Dutch government seized two Venezuelan gunboats in time of peace by way of reprisals.

In *The Times* [2] of December 24 I answered a question, which I found was being asked, namely whether that step was not a violation of the rule laid down by the Second Hague Peace Conference,

[1] [See above, pp. 572—589. L. O.]
[2] [See above, p. 568. L. O.]

that hostilities must be preceded by a declaration of war. The answer was of course in the negative, for the Conference and the consequent convention certainly did not intend to abolish either reprisals in time of peace or pacific blockade. But there are the further questions, pointed out in the letter which *The Times* did me the honour of inserting, namely whether the continuance of reprisals in time of peace as a legitimate measure does not endanger the security aimed at by the new rule as to declarations of war, and, if it does so, what further security can be taken. The whole matter demands a fuller investigation than can be given it in the daily press.

The terms of the new rule are that

"hostilities must not commence without previous and explicit warning, in the form either of a declaration of war with the reasons assigned for it, or of an ultimatum with conditional declaration of war."

In the article on pacific blockade I said that this

"can have no meaning unless the hostilities mentioned include all acts of force, other at least than those of the most necessary self-defence against acts of force by the opposite party, which are not made exceptions by some other rule."

That is to say, the word "hostilities" was taken in the most objective or external sense, and a tacit reservation of other rules, namely those on pacific blockade and reprisals, was assumed in order to limit the application of the new rule as its framers no doubt intended. But another interpretation was possible. Before the adoption of the new rule it was treated as legitimate to set up the state of war by acts of force, done with the intent of war without a declaration of that intent. It is not impossible to suppose that the word "hostilities" in the new rule refers to that practice, and means " acts of force done with the intent of war," in which case the sense will merely be that such acts are not to be done without preceding declaration, and pacific blockade and reprisals in time of peace will need no tacit reservation to take them out of the rule, because, not being entered on with intent of war, they will not be within it. But then the necessity for any accuracy in speaking either of pacific blockade or of reprisals in time of peace will also vanish, because no kind of violence exercised on any kind of occasion, while waiting to see whether the party on whom it is exercised will have the spirit to treat it as war, will be shut out by the rule. Add to this the general consideration that legal accuracy is better served by using words in objective senses, leaving motives and intentions to be distinctly mentioned, than by implying the latter in the terminology. I therefore maintain the opinion that in the new rule " hostilities " must be read as meaning all objective acts of force not called for by way of defence against equally objective acts of force by the opposite party, and that a tacit reservation is implied of pacific blockade and reprisals in time of peace as known cases. That pacific blockade has become such a known and even delimited case I undertook to show in the article on it. It now has to be seen whether the same can be said of reprisals in time of peace.

Originally reprisals were used in order to obtain the satisfaction of contracts or the redress of injuries, the sum claimed being in either case capable of pecuniary statement. And such mode of enforcement was allowed in time of peace to subjects with the sanction of their state, or to the state as making the claims of its subjects its own, or to the state for claims of its own, on the principle of self-help which even in internal procedure was by no means unknown to early systems of law. For these purposes the practice is now scarcely known except in that differentiated form of reprisals which has been developed under the name of pacific blockade. But the undifferentiated residue of the old practice has acquired a new scope under the old name by being used for the enforcement of state claims not of a pecuniary nature, of any claims therefore which might have been prosecuted by war if the state which makes them had chosen to take that course[1]. At least, if we sometimes find in books language which points more or less consciously to a distinction between legal and political claims, the latter not furnishing a proper occasion for using force while professing to be at peace, the distinction, though sound in principle, is often difficult in the present state of international law to be made in specific cases, and is certainly not observed in practice. Vattel wrote at the very time when these "modern reprisals," as they have been called, were coming into use, and he has let us know plainly what he thought of them. He described reprisals as the seizure of something to be held as a pledge for a pecuniary claim, whether in the nature of debt or of compensation for injury, and how, if there is no longer hope of justice being

---

[1] See s. 23 of Bulmerincq's treatise on "Die Staatsstreitigkeiten und ihre Entscheidung," in Holtzendorff's *Handbuch des Völkerrechts*, vol. IV., which is entitled *Unterschied der älteren und modernen Repressalien*.

obtained, the pledge may be confiscated in satisfaction, and then the proceeding is ended without there having been war unless it is declared by one of the parties. And he goes on to say that

"when the difference is not about an act of violence or a civil tort but about a contested right, after conciliation or the pacific means of obtaining justice have been tried in vain, it is a declaration of war which ought to follow and not pretended reprisals, which in such a case would be real acts of hostility without declaration of war, and would be contrary both to public faith and to the mutual duties of nations[1]."

But when an institution has become established without definite regulations having been made for it, as is the case with modern reprisals, it is important to inquire whether its spirit can be ascertained as furnishing some substitute for regulations; and in that inquiry it is not the critics of the institution, even though contemporary with its origin and as eminent as Vattel, that are most helpful, but such utterances as can be gleaned from its founders. Now it is certainly to the British practice of the second half of the eighteenth century that modern reprisals are due. The Seven Years' War between Great Britain and France was not declared till 1756, nor till then had there been any order for "general reprisals," that is for the generalization of such captures as were made by way of reprisal in time of peace for the recovery of specific pecuniary claims. But French vessels had been captured by the British navy as early as in 1754, and there can be no doubt that Vattel, whose work appeared in 1758, meant to refer to this recent and important

[1] Liv. 2, ch. 18, ss. 342, 354. As bearing on the interpretation of the new rule requiring declarations of war, observe that Vattel calls reprisals for other than pecuniary claims *de vrais actes d'hostilité*.

instance when he wrote of "pretended reprisals." All the indications of British opinion during the eighteenth century lead to the conclusion that the difference between the captures of 1754 and the old kind of reprisal was distinctly apprehended. The latter were familiar in England by the captures of French vessels which Cromwell made, and realized by sale, in order to indemnify an English Quaker merchant, without either the intention or the effect of breaking the peace with France; and by the letters of marque and reprisal which George II granted against Spain in 1739 for failure to pay a sum of money due by treaty, equally without the intention of thereby breaking the peace, though war was declared against Spain on her laying a counter embargo on British ships in Spanish harbours. But in 1754 the difference between the Governments concerned was not a pecuniary one but political, and the captures were made in the same spirit as that in which continental powers marched their armies across their frontiers during the pendency of negotiations. The object of such acts was clear, namely to enforce the negotiations by the advantage gained and by the show of determination. Their character was not clear or intended to be so, but would be hostile or not as the negotiations turned out. Accordingly, in 1761, in the course of the diplomatic overtures for peace, England refused to restore the captures made at sea before the declaration of 1756, on the ground that belligerent rights did not result from a formal declaration of war but from the hostilities which the aggressor first offered[1]. Those the British negotiators charged to

[1] *Annual Register* for 1761, p. 262.

France in respect of the acts of force which had taken place in America and India, but the legal argument would have been the same if the captures themselves had been the first links in a chain of hostilities, although the moral appreciation of them would have been different. The legal theory was explained by Sir W. Scott (Lord Stowell) in the case of *The Boedes Lust*, 5 Ch. Rob. 245, which arose out of an embargo laid by Great Britain on Dutch property in 1803. It must be premised that embargo is merely a form of reprisal, and that seizing ships in port or at sea was not distinguished until, later than that case, there grew up that milder treatment of enemy merchantmen in port at the outbreak of hostilities which has culminated in the convention on the subject resulting from the Second Peace Conference.

"The seizure," Sir W. Scott said, "was at first equivocal, and if the matter in dispute had terminated in reconciliation the seizure would have been converted into a mere civil embargo and so terminated. Such would have been the retroactive effect of that course of circumstances. On the contrary, if the transaction end in hostility the retroactive effect is exactly the other way. It impresses the direct hostile character upon the original seizure; it is declared to be no embargo; it is no longer an equivocal act subject to two interpretations; there is a declaration of the animus by which it is done; that it was done *hostili animo*, and is to be considered as a hostile measure *ab initio* against persons guilty of injuries which they refuse to redeem by any amicable alteration in their measures. This is the necessary course, if no particular compact intervenes for the restoration of such property taken before a formal declaration of hostilities."

Thus the learned judge draws a distinction between civil and hostile embargoes, each having its character latent in it from the beginning, though only the event could show in any case which that character was. The hostile embargoes are the modern ones, established at the date of the decision by a half-century of use, during which, however, the doctrine so formulated had been applied to them, for the British captures introductory of the Seven Years' War had not been condemned till that war was declared[1]. The civil embargoes are primarily the old ones, intended to enforce or to realize pecuniary claims, though the modern ones fall back into the class if the political claims in support of which they are employed are settled without war[2]. The mental attitude attributed by Sir W. Scott to a power laying an embargo for a

[1] This is stated in a letter of Lord Chancellor Thurlow, quoted from a MS. by Sir Travers Twiss in his *Law of Nations* (War), s. 35.

[2] Hall, s. 120, understands the judgment in *The Boedes Lust* differently. He appears to have been struck by the fact that Sir W. Scott, in speaking of the termination of the transaction if converted into a civil embargo, does not mention the confiscation of the property in order to realize a pecuniary claim. He draws the conclusion that embargo not followed by war can never pass beyond the stage of sequestration, and adds: "It is not necessary that vessels or other property, seized otherwise than by way of embargo, should be treated in a similar manner. They may be confiscated so soon as it appears that their mere seizure will not constrain the wrong-doing State to give proper redress. In recent times, however, instances of confiscation do not seem to have occurred, and probably no property seized by way of reprisal would now be condemned until after the outbreak of actual war." But since Sir W. Scott was not speaking at all of what he calls civil embargo except so far as a hostile embargo might fall into that class through a reconciliation which would exclude confiscation, he cannot be understood as excluding confiscation in every case of his civil embargo. That instances of confiscation under reprisals without war do not seem to have occurred in recent times is due to the discontinuance of the old reprisals except in the form of pacific blockade. In theory the Institute of International Law has admitted the right under the old reprisals, and, as it happens, in the case of an embargo, 17 *Annuaire* (1898), p. 284. As to whether the Institute admits the same right under pacific blockade, see my article on that institution, p. 23.

political object, at the time of laying it, is that which in the article on Pacific Blockade I have described as vague and expectant, and is the same which exists in the commencement of hostilities without declaration of war in almost any other case. The only case of the latter kind in which it would be otherwise would be that of a government deliberately intending war while commencing the employment of force, but that would involve a calculated surprise in time of peace, the behaviour of an enemy under the garb of a friend, which, for the credit of human nature, it may be believed has always been rare. It is not unfair to suppose that war without declaration, however bitterly it may have been complained of, has generally, in the minds of those to whom it was justly imputable, been, like reprisals, an incident belonging to the more acrimonious stage of negotiation.

Such, we may be sure, was the occupation by Russia of the Danubian principalities, Turkish territory, in 1853, under the name of "material guarantee." But any distinction between war and reprisals, for the purpose of the new rule as to the former, must be clear at the time of the occurrence to be classified as the one or the other; and it follows that it cannot be found in the intention of the government of which the action is in question, unless the rule is to be made nugatory by the scantiness of the cases for its application, cases, too, in which the intention condemned by the rule can always be denied by the party to which it is imputed.

Nor, if the distinction of which we are in search cannot be found in intention, is it more possible to find it in the objective character of the acts done.

Eminent writers have classified acts of reprisal as negative or positive, the former consisting in withholding something which the state is legally obliged to give, and the latter in taking something which legally belongs to the other state or its subjects[1]. But this classification does not help us, for the only acts of reprisal which there is any danger of confounding with war are such as include the employment of force, and these are necessarily all positive. We should be aided if any acts of war were excluded from the list of possible positive acts of reprisal, but the writers are so far from aiding us in this respect that some of the most accredited among them, when attempting to enumerate permitted acts of reprisal, mention only negative ones[2]. In contrast with such a naive extremity of peacefulness we may place the conduct of France in 1884, when put by Lord Granville to the choice of not condemning British ships for breach of a blockade of Formosa or of accepting a state of war with China. She chose in substance the latter branch of the alternative, as has been said in the article on Pacific Blockade, and England then exercised the right of a neutral by forbidding French ships of war to coal in her ports. But France gave to her choice the name of "the state of reprisals existing between her and China," and under this name, to borrow the summary given by F. de Martens, "she bombarded Chinese towns, stormed them,

[1] Calvo, s. 1570 of the 3rd edition, 1880; Bulmerincq in 4 Holtzendorff's *Handbuch*, s. 27; F. de Martens' *Traité de Droit International*, Léo's French translation, t. 3, p. 160, justly saying that *cette division n'a aucune signification pratique*.

[2] Thus Bluntschli, *Droit International Codifié*, s. 500. He does not expressly say that his enumeration is meant to be exhaustive.

fought regular battles in the open country, blockaded ports and coasts, and exacted from neutrals respect for the rules of international law relating to contraband of war, all without any declaration of war[1]."

There is, however, one circumstance which may put us on the track of the required distinction. No government dealing with another of strength even approximately equal to its own, certainly no Great Power dealing with another Great Power, would use force with the intention of its being only by way of reprisal, whether of the old or of the modern kind, either with a view to pecuniary satisfaction or in pursuance of a political claim, and whether by way of pacific blockade or of bare reprisal. It would know that war would follow if the force was not immediately withdrawn and apologized for, and it would therefore not be worth its while to use force without declaration of war unless with the intention of beginning war by surprise. On the other hand a government dealing with another which it does not regard as an equal makes no scruple about using force without declaration of war, and may in general be fairly credited with the intention of its being only by way of reprisal, because it would not regard its being met by a declaration of war as being a contingency to be seriously taken into account. The new rule was certainly intended to preclude force without declaration of war on the former class of occasions. We may be equally sure that it was not intended to do so in the latter class, and thereby to abolish the policy of material guarantees (*la politique des gages*), of which there have been such instances within the last three-quarters

[1] U. S.

of a century as the conduct of Great Britain towards the Two Sicilies in 1840, that of Russia towards Turkey in 1853, and that of France towards China in 1884 and towards Turkey in 1901. It is therefore possible to form a conception of reprisals which in most cases will be clear enough for practical purposes, but not a definition of them; and there can be no doubt, that, so far as the framers of the new rule had thought out their subject at all, that conception, together with the defined institution of pacific blockade, constituted in their minds exceptions to the prohibition of force without declaration of war. But the rule so conceived may fail of its effect, especially when the apparent inequality of strength between the powers immediately concerned may allow acts of force to pass for a time as reprisals, although it may turn out that nothing but aggression was intended from the beginning. A strong power may desire to surprise a weak one, not from any fear of the strength of the latter, but in order to prevent other powers from coming to its defence in time. The continuance of reprisals in time of peace as a legitimate measure does, then, endanger the security aimed at by the new rule as to declarations of war, and we must inquire what further security can be taken.

When entering on that inquiry it will be well to form a clear idea of what is wanted. The field for the exercise of that authority of the strong over the weak, which is manifested in pacific blockade or any other kind of reprisals, is contracting. If the Turkish revolution should realize the expectations which have generally been formed of it, we shall not again see a Turkish custom-house seized in time of peace, as France seized that of Mitylene in 1901. The strength of China seems to be increasing, and may before long be great. Mexico, Brazil, Argentina and Chile have become so important that none of them would now be likely to fail in responding by a declaration of war to any employment of force, as indeed Mexico responded to the blockade of 1838, though not till force had been carried further by the attack and capture of the fort of San Juan de Ulloa. Still there are some states, chiefly Spanish American, over which the authority in question may be exercised by single stronger ones, as by the Netherlands over Venezuela in 1908; and it is possible that the Great Powers or some of them, acting in concert, may use it as a means of coercing some state with which no single power would venture to deal in that manner. It cannot be said that in such cases it would be better either for the world at large, or for the parties immediately concerned, that reprisals should be replaced by war. The question of delimiting them must therefore be approached with no secret desire of putting an end to them faster than the progress of different states may do so in the nature of things. It may even be approached with the belief that, as the government of the world by great combinations makes progress, the weapon which bears the no longer appropriate name of reprisals may be one of its instruments, as a hybrid blockade of Crete was used by the Great Powers for the purpose of coercing Greece in 1897. Our only legitimate object will be to seek for security against abuse of the weapon.

The Second Peace Conference has provided the rule that " the recovery of contract debts, claimed from the government of one country by that of another country as being due to its nationals," shall not be pursued by " armed force " unless

" the debtor state refuses or neglects to reply to an offer of arbitration, or, after accepting the offer, prevents any agreement of reference from being concluded, or, after the arbitration, fails to submit to the award."

Some of the signatory states have made reservations limiting still further the employment of armed force, but this is the minimum of its limitation in the cases specified, which form a large part of those for which reprisals were originally permitted. If we extend them to the recovery of contract debts claimed from the government of one country by that of another as being due to itself, then, since all such debts must result from international conventional stipulations, we shall be within the Final Act of the same Conference, by which it was unanimously declared that

" certain differences, and notably those relating to the interpretation and application of international conventional stipulations, are susceptible of being submitted to compulsory arbitration without any restriction."

So far then as contract debts are concerned, there seems to be no objection to requiring an offer of arbitration in all cases before the employment of force, whether in the shape of war or in that of reprisals.

But what of claims not contractual, made on the government of one country by that of another, whether on its own behalf or on that of its nationals ? At the Second Peace Conference thirty-two states voted for compulsory arbitration in all cases not affecting vital national interests or national honour, a principle which is also embodied in a large number of treaties, some of them concluded between states of the first class in importance. In most cases in which damages or even an apology and the punishment of some one are sought, it would be impossible to say that vital interests or any question of national honour are affected. The blundering or negligence of some official is alleged, perhaps even his want of good will or of good faith. Such allegations, coupled with that of a serious defect in our laws, were made against England in the *Alabama* case, but probably no one now thinks that our national interests or honour would have been better served in that case by refusing an arbitration than they were by agreeing to one. Still, the question whether the conduct of an official, or even of some person not an official, was legitimate, does sometimes raise a really important issue concerning the rights of the state. It cannot, therefore, be recommended that arbitration on claims not contractual should be made compulsory without the reservation of vital interests and honour, but it does not follow that a state which in a particular case objects to arbitration ought to be allowed to enforce its claim by the easier proceeding of reprisals when the alternative of war is open to it. In proportion as the proceeding by war is the more serious, all the resources of diplomacy are the more likely to be exhausted before having recourse to it, and these may result in the difference being found less incapable of settlement, by other means than force, than it was at first thought to be. So true is this that we can hardly avoid agreeing with Vattel that for a disputed right the true remedy is in principle not reprisals but war, that is, the mode of force which experience shows is the less likely to be entered on with a light heart.

Suppose, then, it were agreed—and this is our proposal—that neither reprisals nor pacific blockade shall be used against any state unless it refuses or neglects to reply to an offer of arbitration, or, after accepting the offer, prevents any agreement of reference from being concluded, or, after an arbitration, refuses to submit to the award. Let us consider what would be the consequences, and in doing so I will for shortness mention only reprisals, it being understood that pacific blockade is always included in them. For the recovery of contract debts claimed on behalf of nationals, reprisals would not be otherwise restrained than they now are along with war. For the recovery of contract debts claimed by governments on behalf of themselves, reprisals, again along with war, would not be otherwise restrained than they now are, not indeed by any rule, but by unanimous and officially expressed opinion. For the enforcement of non-contractual claims which in the opinion of the complainant government did not affect the vital interests or honour of its nation, reprisals as well as war would be subjected to the condition of an offer of arbitration, for which an opinion little short of unanimous already considers that the case would be appropriate. The right of the defendant government to refuse the offer, if it deemed an arbitration dangerous to vital interests or honour on its side, would remain intact. For the enforcement of claims an arbitration on which, in the opinion of the complainant government, would seriously menace the vital interests or honour of its nation, that government would have to remain within diplomatic limits until it deemed war to be necessary. If, but for the rule proposed, it would have used reprisals, it must be the stronger of the two parties in difference, and will not suffer by substituting war for them. And when force is used without declaration of war by a government which has offered arbitration and been met by a refusal of it, or against a government which after nominally accepting arbitration has prevented an agreement of reference from being concluded, or which after an arbitration has refused to submit to the award, those circumstances will sufficiently indicate that the milder measure has been used against a weaker power without the intention of taking an unfair advantage by surprise.

I submit my proposal to the Peace Conference of 1915.

# XVII

## TRADE DOMICILE IN WAR. 1909.

[Reprinted, with permission, from the *Journal of the Society of Comparative Legislation*, New Series, vol. IX. pt 2, pp. 265–268.]

DR BATY's article on " Trade Domicile in War " in the last part of this Journal appears to call for some notice, as well of its doctrine as of its references to my writings. Both parts of the subject will be best elucidated by taking it under certain headings in which the doctrine shall have the priority :

(1) The received Anglo-American doctrine is that the condemnation of cargo depends on the enemy character either of its owner or of the house of business from which it emanates, one or the other being necessary and either being sufficient.

(2) It is further received that the enemy character of a cargo-owner depends on his domicile and that of a house of business on its situation, subject to a relaxation in favour of a cargo-owner who has taken steps to abandon his enemy domicile and any house of business connected with it, and in favour of the house of business of a cargo-owner who has taken such steps.

Here Dr Baty's dissent begins. He makes domicile in the enemy country " the secondary criterion of enemy character in war time, enemy nationality being a primary and conclusive criterion " (p. 157). And " the possession of a neutral domicile never saved an alien enemy's goods " (p. 163). He has against him Lord Lindley, who said: "The subject of a State at war with this country, but who is carrying on business here or in a foreign neutral country, is not treated as an alien enemy" (*Janson v. Driefontein Consolidated Mines*, [1902] A.C. 505). Nor would it be easy to show any Anglo-American practice, other than that founded on houses of business, contrary to the doctrine of Gronovius, who, commenting on the statement of Grotius that the persons subject by the law of nations to reprisals are those who are subjects of the offending state from a permanent cause, explains that the persons domiciled in the country are intended (see *Wheaton*, §§ 318, 319).

(3) From (1) and (2) it follows and is held that a person domiciled in the enemy's country loses his share in cargo emanating from a house of business in a neutral country.

(4) From (1) and (2) it also follows and is held that a person domiciled in a neutral country loses his share of cargo emanating from a house of business in the enemy's country.

Chief Justice Marshall and Wheaton thought the co-existence of (3) and (4) unfair. In other words, they would have liked to vary (1), so as to make the condemnation of cargo depend only on the enemy character of its owner, or only on the enemy character of the house of business from which it emanates. Lord Lindley, in the words immediately following those already quoted, said: "The validity of his contracts [those of the subject of a State at war with this country] does not depend on his nationality, nor even on what is his real domicile, but on the place or places in which he carries on his business or businesses." If it can be assumed that his lordship would like to apply to capture the rule which he lays down for contract, he will appear as sharing the opinion of Marshall and Wheaton, and as choosing (3) for the one of the two rules, (3) and (4), to be eliminated.

(5) The same tests for ascertaining domicile as in ecclesiastical and probate cases were long applied in Admiralty cases, except that in the latter, by the relaxation referred to under the head (2), the principle that native domicile easily reverts was more freely acted on, the new character being held to have been acquired as soon as the party took steps *animo removendi*. But when the civil courts found it necessary to assert the unity of domicile, they soon found it necessary to require stricter proof of its being changed, and their decisions have now entirely abandoned the view propounded by Lord Stowell in *The Harmony*, that "time is the grand ingredient in constituting domicile." It is not too much to say that in Stowell's time it was difficult to prove that a long residence in a country not that of origin did not amount to an adoption of its domicile, and that it is now difficult in the civil courts to prove that it does so. Dr Baty traces some perception of the change as far back as the case of *Stanley* v. *Bernes* in 1831, and he quotes Lushington as distinguishing in *The Baltica* a "mercantile national character" from ordinary domicile, and telling us that it " is governed by rules particularly applicable to it alone," and as warning us in *Hodgson* v. *De Beauchesne* that " decisions belonging to [domicile during war] must be applied with great caution to questions of domicile

independent of war." Yet he denies the distinction, and has not included Lushington in the list which he gives of Phillimore, Foote, Wharton, and Dicey as agreeing with me in asserting it. Only experience can instruct us whether the British prize jurisdiction will deal with domicile in a future war as Stowell dealt with it. In favour of its doing so there is the consideration which I have presented, that " the utility to a country of the industry or commerce carried on in it depends on the actual seat of the occupation, and not on its probable continuance" (*War*, p. 144).

(6) So long as the difference in the tests of a change of domicile shall continue, " commercial or trade domicile in war " will be a correct as well as convenient expression for the kind more easily attained. It appositely marks what is treated in Anglo-American prize law as the domicile of a person considered in a commercial capacity, that is as the owner of cargo or of a house of business from which cargo emanates. It denotes, not a domicile "established for commercial purposes" (Baty, p. 160), but one judicially appreciated for purposes connected with commerce in war. That Chief Justice Marshall used the expression is a strong testimony to its logical fitness. And it is vain to argue against it that a domicile in the enemy's country, complete for the ends of civil law, would also ensure condemnation of property, for where such existed it would include a commercial domicile. What is required is a term expressing the lowest grade of residence which in the Anglo-American system will be sufficient for condemnation, and this is given us by the term attacked.

(7) Dr Baty expresses his surprise at hearing that "domicile was a familiar conception in Admiralty when the idea of nationality was still in embryo," and says of Elizabeth's judges that they "had a pretty conclusive conception of what allegiance was, and would apply it to the determination of questions of belligerent right rather than their rudimentary notions of domicile" (p. 163). In this he is projecting backwards the error into which it has been shown above that he has fallen as to present Anglo-American law. In doing so he forgets that England was far in advance of other European countries in developing the consciousness of unity, and that Admiralty procedure aimed from the first at basing itself on the most widely accepted principle, and was indeed impelled in that direction by its being the procedure of a Roman Law court.

(8) Dr Baty says that I " restrict to merchants " a certain " plain statement of Wheaton's " (p. 159). The only passage to which this can refer is one in which I quote Wheaton as follows: "Residence in a neutral country will not protect [a merchant's] share in a house established in the enemy's country, though residence in the enemy's country will condemn his share in a house established in a neutral country" (*War*, pp. 141, 142). It will be seen that Wheaton speaks of cases in which houses of business are concerned, and that I complete the quotation by describing the owners of such houses as merchants. Either then the allegation that I have restricted Wheaton's statement is gratuitous, or Dr Baty regards "merchant" as a more restrictive term than "house of business."

(9) Dr Baty says that I am "obsessed by the

notion that trading is inseparably connected with war domicile," but admits that that notion " is common to most modern writers " (p. 159). I may venture to remark, on behalf of my fellow culprits as well as of myself, that the facility in asserting a change of domicile which is so referred to is displayed only in deciding questions about cargoes, and that we really are obsessed by the notion that where there are cargoes there is trading.

(10) Dr Baty concludes, or " would " conclude, that at one time I identified belligerent domicile with carrying on business in enemy territory, but that now I take the meaning of enemy or war domicile to be the carrying on of trade or business in a certain manner (pp. 157, 158). I trust that I have never spoken of trade domicile in war as being the carrying on of trade in any place or way, or as being anything else which a domiciled person may do. To pass from the impropriety of speech to the question of substance, what is intended under that name by the great body of authority against which Dr Baty contends, and indeed results under that name from a comparison of the Admiralty and other cases on domicile, has been sufficiently shown under the heads (5) and (6).

# XVIII

## BELLIGERENT RIGHTS AT SEA. 1909.

[Reprinted, with permission, from Latifi, *Effects of War on Property*, Macmillan & Co. 1909, pp. 145–152.]

THE immunity which is proposed for the enemy's mercantile flag would be a change in the laws of war so important that I willingly accede to my friend Mr Latifi's request that I should contribute a note on it to his valuable volume. In view of what Mr Latifi has himself written, it would be superfluous for me to discuss the practical results to which such a change would lead with reference to the safety or power of England. But although the British people and their representatives will have those results chiefly in their mind in deciding the question, its decision will involve the adoption or rejection of the dogma that the change is demanded by humanity, civilization, or justice. For those who hold that dogma the decision of the practical question will follow of itself, without any real examination of its probable results. Even for those who are not convinced of the dogma, the fact that it is widely assumed as a self-evident article in the creed of progress must tend to obscure the view, unless they have cleared their minds of all latent suspicion that it may be true. It will not therefore be superfluous to examine the philosophical and legal grounds on which the immunity of the enemy's mercantile flag is claimed, with as much insistence and repetition as are displayed in the assertion of those grounds.

The operations of war have for their object to compel the enemy State to accept such terms of peace as it is desired to impose on it, and as a means to that object to paralyse the enemy State—that is, to make all action impossible for it unless and until it accepts the terms desired. The impact of one State on another in war is intended to be like that of a torpedo-fish on its prey. The enemy's seat of Government is to be captured, and his Government pursued to any place to which it may be transferred. His resources are to be cut off by occupying as much as possible of the territory from which they are drawn, and by preventing as far as possible the creation of resources which might reach his Government. If industry is not interfered with in the part of his territory which is occupied, this is only because the occupying Power can prevent the resources created there from reaching him. And all this has hitherto been done by sea as well as on land, and by sea with the additional circumstance that, by the laws of blockade and contraband, so far as they respectively extend, the enemy's commerce under a neutral flag is prevented, as well as that under his own flag, from contributing to his resources. Wealth in any form, with the power of action which it gives, is not allowed to reach the enemy across his sea frontier any more than across the limit which separates his occupied from his unoccupied territory, so far at least as it can be prevented from doing so while preserving to neutrals the notice and equality of treatment which the rules of blockade are intended to secure to them. The proposal now under discussion is not that the enemy's sea-trade shall be exempted from attempts to paralyse him, but that such attempts on it shall be restricted to cases in which it is equally lawful to interfere with it under the neutral flag. Nothing but the blindness of habit prevents us from seeing that commercial blockades, as distinct from the investment of fortified ports, are a war waged against neutrals. But if only sentiment can be gratified by limiting the war against the enemy's commercial flag, the war against neutrals is to continue, with the certainty that commercial blockades, when they have become the sole means of paralysing the enemy's sea-trade, will be practically carried as far as audacity can venture to strain or to violate rules.

The name in which this topsy-turvy policy is advocated is that of the immunity at sea of private enemy property as such, and this is asserted to be the extension to the sea of a principle admitted on land. In truth, however, the immunity of private enemy property is not admitted anywhere as absolute.

It is only admitted so far as it does not interfere with any operations deemed to be useful for putting pressure on the enemy or for defence against him. Even on land no house or factory which stands in the way of a directly military operation is allowed to escape destruction, nor is compensation for its destruction ever paid by an invader unless he is compelled to do so at the peace. And, still on land, the habit of exacting requisitions and contributions, lawful within the limits set by The Hague rules, proves that it is not only when they are under fire that private property and means are not sacred. The things and money requisitioned are deemed useful for the purpose of the invasion, and the invader takes them without being obliged to pay for or restore them. Other cases show even more closely the identity of the principles applied on land and at sea. An invader would not allow the unoccupied part of his enemy's territory to be enriched and strengthened by railway traffic into it from the part which he has occupied, or that goods lying in the unoccupied part, unproductive for want of transport, should be brought to market by the railways which he controls. So far as he can he prevents trade which might create resources for the enemy Government, and he is not deterred from doing so by the knowledge that his measures cause damage to individuals. There is no difference of principle between this and the prohibition by a maritime Power of the appearance of its enemy's commercial flag on the sea, enforced by the condemnation of the ship and of her cargo being enemy property. That what is struck at is not primarily enemy's property but the trade is proved by the fact that, while the cargo is condemned, the captain and crew retain their personal effects if their conduct has been straightforward and open.

What it is really attempted to set up, under cover of a fallacious distinction between the practice on land and at sea, is the doctrine of Rousseau that individuals are foreign to a war. If that doctrine is sound, the interest of a State at war, however deeply involved, would not justify it in taking or interfering with the property of individuals. We may go further, and expose the absurdity of the premiss by pointing out the conclusion that it would equally forbid imposing war taxes on individuals. The assumption appears to rest on the truths that a State and an individual subject or citizen of it are distinct legal persons, and that a war is between States as legal persons. But the familiar example of a limited company and its shareholders shows that the latter, although distinct legal persons from it, are not, therefore, foreign to its operations, and may in certain circumstances be made liable for them. There may be a corporation for the operations of which its members are not liable, as a limited company of which the shares have been paid up in full, or a borough of which the mayor, aldermen, and burgesses are the corporators. But such cases can only exist under national law, the law of a superior power which sanctions the institution and is capable of preventing or remedying the evils which might arise from it. It cannot be too strongly stated that in natural justice there is no power for individuals to form themselves into a group and disclaim responsibility for the actions of that group. The individuals who form the groups called States are not authorized by natural justice to disclaim the responsibility attaching to the actions of those States, and there is no authority over them to impose the regulations which such a disclaimer would render necessary. Their own consent as States may take the place of legislation, but such consent has not been given to the assertion that individuals are foreign to a war.

The legal fallacy would not have deceived so many if there had not been a time when wars were often made by sovereigns from motives of personal or dynastic ambition, which found little echo in the subject populations. The memory of that time has helped to cause the notion that individuals are foreign to a war to become almost a democratic principle. But since 1815 there have been no wars in Europe which were merely those of ruling persons or families, and not those of the respective combatant nations. The wars have not necessarily been approved of by the numerical majority, though this has often been the case, but always they have been approved by such a part of the population in each combatant State as, by its numbers and influences combined, must for all practical purposes, external as well as internal, be regarded as representing the nation. The motives have been various—the aggrandisement or defence of the State—feelings of race, of nationality as contrasted with nation in the sense of State, of religion, even feelings of humanity excited by outrages in foreign countries—or the sympathy of political parties, Liberal or Conservative, with more or less similar struggles abroad. To these commercial and colonising rivalry may come to be added, as it has been in remoter periods, even if it has not in recent times, been a cause of European war. Such wars are as little foreign in international fact as in law to the individual whose desires or fears have made them, or who from loyalty or patriotism have fallen into line with the mass which made them. External as well as internal affairs are more and more directed by the popular will. This, it may be hoped, will become more pacific as enlightenment advances, but the popular will brooks resistance abroad as little as at home, and when it decides on war it will insist as much or more than any monarch on every means being employed to win success.

Lastly, if it cannot be maintained, either legally or as a question of political fact, that individual subjects or citizens are foreign to the wars of their State, there remains the plea urged on the ground of humanity—that they ought to be exempted as far as possible from the consequences of their solidarity. But they have to bear those consequences in land war, and in naval war the risk and loss are far more easily met and spread over the community by insurance, and by the increased price of the cargoes which escape the risk.

The conclusion is:

(1) That there is no principle, consistent with the existence and nature of war, on which a belligerent can be required to abstain from trying to suppress his enemy's commerce under his flag:

(2) That between trying by commercial blockades to suppress the enemy's commerce under the neutral flag and allowing it to pass free under his own flag there is a glaring inconsistency:

(3) And that the subject is therefore open to be dealt with on the ground of the probable effects of any change in the law.

# XIX

## THE NATIVE STATES OF INDIA. 1910.

[Reprinted, with permission, from the *Law Quarterly Review*, vol. XXVI. (1910), pp. 312–319.]

ALL who are interested in Indian politics will remember the flood of light which Sir William Lee-Warner, in his volume on *The Protected Princes of India*, threw on the relations between the British Government and those princes. They felt grateful to him for the frankness and clearness of his exposition, which for the first time made it possible, without such research as only special students of Indian affairs could undertake, to appreciate the principles and practice of our Indian Empire, and to assign to it and to its component parts their true places in a political classification. To the best of my ability I availed myself of the opportunity, in a work entitled *Chapters on the Principles of International Law*, which appeared in 1894. Sir William has now issued a second edition[1] under the altered title of *The Native States of India*, with a prefatory note in which an importance far beyond academic is attributed to questions of classification in relation to this matter. "The ruling chiefs," he says, "are sensitive and conservative; they take a deep interest in the controversies to which such phrases

---

[1] *The Native States of India*, by Sir William Lee-Warner, K.C.S.I. London: Macmillan & Co. 1910. xxi and 425 pp.

as suzerainty, subordinate alliance, independence and dependence have given rise ; and they realize that the general adoption of any title may give countenance to views which through the force of public opinion may direct the future conduct of the British authorities towards them." It is in deference to this consideration that Sir William has eliminated from his title-page the description of the princes as protected, although it still occurs abundantly in the body of the work, and has refrained from replacing it in his title-page by their description as semi-sovereign, to which nevertheless he attaches great importance. His view is that the tie which unites the British Government and the native states is not " strictly international," although those states may find " some shelter under the shadow of international law," as enjoying " a sovereignty which, if wanting completeness in every respect, may yet be a sure defence against annexation " (p. 398). He still more strongly disclaims for the tie the name of feudal (p. 393). And the name constitutional he regards, if I understand him rightly, as incompatible with the semi-sovereignty which he asserts, while I come under his friendly censure as being its " strongest advocate " (pp. 395–8). I am therefore called on to restate my position in the light of criticism from so eminent a quarter, and I trust that in doing so I shall feel a due sense of the responsibility arising from the audience before whose watchful ears we are told that such debates are carried on, at the same time not forgetting that accuracy of language can alone save us from the mischief, foreseen or unforeseen, which results from confused thought.

In the first place, then, since the applicability of international law to India is the subject of discussion, it is necessary that I should say what I mean by that term. As English law is the law of England and French law that of France, so international law is that of a certain part of the world, which comprises if it is not exclusively composed of Europe, all nations outside Europe but of European blood, and Japan. These are the peoples by whose consent it exists, and for the settlement of whose differences it is applied, or at least invoked. Whether the laxity with which it is enforced ought to deprive it of the name of law is a question beside the present mark, for I am now pointing out not what it is but whose it is. Whether we call it law, as I maintain that we have a right to do, or, with Austin, positive international morality, it is the law or the positive international morality of the part of the world which I have indicated. Outside that part of the world there are facts of the same nature as some of those which international law deals with, for example, governments and their dependence or independence, and to guide us in dealing with those facts there are the same principles of natural justice to which international law ought to conform and is supposed to conform. Even in discussions taking place outside the geographical limits of international law the doctrines of that legal system may be cited on account of the analogy of the case, and as expressing the considered judgment of the most enlightened part of mankind on certain combinations of circumstance. But all this no more recognizes international law as being in force beyond the geographical limits mentioned, than English law is recognized as being in force outside England because rules identical with those of English law may be found in the laws of other countries. A further testimony to my sense of the term being the received one is furnished by the fact that international law is admitted to exist by the consent of the world included in its domain, and to be capable of receiving modifications and additions by the same consent, as indeed it does. The necessary evidence of such consent is left rather vague, but no one whose eyes are open can doubt that in spite of such vagueness international law is a growing system. That Persia, Siam, and China have sought and been allowed admission to the Hague Conferences of 1899 and 1907 goes far to prove their acceptance of the system as it exists, but falls short of recognizing their voices as of equal importance with those of the European and American powers in its further development. Thus the haze which, much less for practical than for theoretical purposes, attends international law, and which has its root in the conflict between the existence of law at all, or of positive international morality if you will, and complete theoretical independence, hangs to some extent over the geographical limits of the system. But as long as no one dreams of any Indian state except Great Britain contributing to the consent by which international law exists, or being admitted to any conference for its development, it is at least clear that no such state is among those contemplated by that law.

Now when Sir William Lee-Warner says that the tie between the British Government and the native Indian states is not strictly international, it is fair to understand this as an admission that international law does not apply to their mutual relations. And when he says that the native states may still find some shelter under the shadow of international law, it is fair to understand what is meant as being that the same principles of natural justice which underlie international law must be applied to their relations so far as they are similar to the relations dealt with by that system, and will lead to rules similar to that extent. I therefore do not believe that Sir William's and my modes of stating the case would lead to any practical difference in the measures which the British Government ought to adopt in given circumstances, but they certainly, as he suggests, may produce different expectations in the minds of those concerned. Take, as an example, the maxim of British policy in India on which Sir William insists as strongly as any one, that the treaties and grants held by the protected princes, and the precedents of our dealings with them and with the protected princes who hold no treaties or grants, must be read as a whole, so that the principles most recently laid down are to be applied to all, and those relating to any department of conduct, as military affairs or the duties of humanity, are to be ascertained for all from the document in which that department is most fully worked out for any one. Imagine, if you can, such a doctrine being applied between nations of European blood, and Great Britain demanding from such a nation the extradition of criminals on a larger scale than her treaty with it provided for, or insisting on its submission to larger measures for preventing its flag from being used as a cover for the slave trade, on the ground that those departments of conduct had been most fully worked out in some treaty concluded with another power! It is plain that the maxim which I have cited could not stand if international law had anything to do with the relations between the British Government and the ruling princes of India, and to tell those princes frankly that it has nothing to do with them is surely a better way of preventing a feeling of unrest from arising than to tell them, first, that strictly it has nothing to do with them; secondly, with a "but" inclining to one side, that they nevertheless may hope for some protection from a shadow of it; thirdly, with a "but" inclining to the other side, that the maxim in question must be upheld after all. On what safeguard the princes may rely against abuse of the reserved authority of the British Government shall be considered when we come to the question of a constitutional tie.

The British Indian Government has spoken on the subject with no uncertain sound. In its official *Gazette*, No. 1700 E, 21 August, 1891, there appeared a notification that "the principles of international law have no bearing upon the relations between the government of India as representing the queen-empress on the one hand, and the native states under the suzerainty of Her Majesty on the other. The paramount supremacy of the former presupposes and implies the subordination of the latter." The only criticism to be made on that notification is that it would have been more accurate to speak in it of international law simply than of the principles of international law. If any distinction were intended between the two phrases, the former would suggest the body of rules and the latter the underlying considerations, among which are those of natural justice, which it was certainly not intended to exclude from the grounds of any policy to be pursued in India. The choice of phrase must therefore be referred to that wide use of the term " principles " which is characteristic of English writing, in proportion as our love of compromise makes us refer more rarely to principles properly so called.

I now come to the title of semi-sovereign which Sir William considers it important to vindicate for the ruling chiefs of India, in opposition, as he believes, to me. I am glad to be able to assure him that this is a misapprehension. I fully and willingly accept him as the highest authority on what may tend to smooth the position of the ruling chiefs, to soothe their feelings and remove any apprehension from their minds ; and in approving on that ground the title claimed by him for them I do not think that I have anything to retract. The sentence of mine which has occasioned the misapprehension is as follows : " To international law a state is sovereign which demeans itself as independent ; a state is semi-sovereign to the extent of the foreign relations which the degree of its practical dependence allows it ; and is non-existent if no foreign relations are allowed it " (*Chapters on the Principles of International Law*, p. 218). It will be seen that the passage deals expressly with international law, and that therefore the non-existence to which it condemns states to which no foreign relations are allowed is a non-existence to international law. Every branch of science must have its own classification and nomenclature for the subjects which fall within it. The Indian system is free to have its own nomenclature, and uses that freedom in employing the term suzerainty of a tie which is not feudal, although its employment in international law does not extend beyond feudalism, Western or Ottoman. Similarly, that system may include what it describes as states, and may attribute semi-sovereignty to them in its own sense; and if to do so can be of any help in India by all means let it be done there, on condition that the homonymy is not made a lever for introducing international conceptions.

As an aid in warding off the confusion of thought which might arise from the homonymy, it will be well to examine the comparison which has been made between the native Indian states and the United States of the Ionian Islands before the annexation of the islands to Greece, when their condition was one of undisputed international semi-sovereignty. After noticing that they were excluded from any higher or other form of separate diplomatic intercourse with the world than the reception of commercial agents or consuls, which he calls " a spark of diplomatic life," Sir William Lee-Warner says that " in all other respects, such as their deprivation of rights of war, their exclusive protection by Great Britain, and the particular solicitude over their administration with which the British power was entrusted, they presented a very marked parallel to the relations which in the present day subsist between the governments of India and the dependent protected states " (p. 401). It would seem as though the reception of consuls was regarded as all that stood between the Ionian Islands and that total absence of foreign relations which would have brought them under my condition for international non-existence. But what if they had wanted also that form of relation? During the Crimean war it was judicially held that the Ionian Islands were at peace with Russia, because Great Britain had not declared war for them as well as for herself, notwithstanding that as what may be called the trustee of their foreign relations she might have done so (*The Ionian Ships*, 1 Spinks 193). If their consular as well as their higher diplomatic business had been managed for them by the protector state, it would still have been impossible to say that the Islands had no separate foreign relations, when they held the relation of peace with Russia while their protector held the relation of war with that power. The test is not whether the state of which the condition is questioned has any foreign relations other than those determined for it by another state in the capacity of its protector, but whether its foreign relations, when determined in any way, are its own separate ones; in other words, whether it is not a part of the determining state, sharing the foreign relations of the latter because they are those of the whole of which it is a part.

If, in order to apply this test, we examine Sir William Lee-Warner's very instructive chapter on the Obligations affecting External Relations, we shall find that the official and the author's own language are not easily reconcilable with the possession by the native states of any foreign relations of their own, even managed for them, although it would not be proper to press too far words which were probably used without conscious reference to that point. The last remark applies especially to a statement by Sir William which, if literally pressed, contains my whole case. "For all international purposes, at any rate, the whole empire, including the protected states united to it, must be regarded as one nation represented by the British Government" (p. 259). On pp. 271, 272, there is a discussion of the obligations which arise under the Anglo-German extradition treaty of 1872, when a fugitive charged with crime finds his way into a native Indian state. And I think that Sir William's conclusion will not be misrepresented by saying that the only obligation under the treaty is that of the empire as a whole, that that obligation exists in the case, and that the duty of the native state is owed to Great Britain as the managing representative of the empire as a whole, and is that of aiding her in the performance of the international duty which is hers in that character. It is true that he says: "the source of obligation so devolving upon the native state is its connexion with the British Government, and its delegation to the government of all rights of negotiation." But I submit that the general tenour of his discussion would be better suited by speaking, not of delegation, but of the absence of any *persona standi* towards Germany which should make negotiation by or on behalf of the native state possible. I trust that no one will think that accuracy of diction is pushed too far in this. We have to deal in India with a people whose subtlety of thought is as much greater than that of the average Englishman as their ability for wise political action is smaller, and we must not be so confident of our position as to neglect strengthening it on every conceivable side. To make transitions easy has been a secret of empire for the noble series of statesmen who have developed our position in India from the time when the Company dealt with its leading rulers on equal terms as independent sovereigns. At present it is not too soon for us to take an accurate account of the situation which has resulted.

We now come to the existence of a constitutional tie between the king-emperor of India and the ruling princes within the peninsula. When a region must be regarded as one nation represented by a certain government, which we have seen to be Sir William's description of the whole peninsula, its parts and elements must be bound together by law, including treaty and custom having the force of law, and by usage of less force, or by one or more of these. This is equally true whether among the parts and elements there be or be not included principalities enjoying so much of internal autonomy that the title of semi-sovereign is not thought inappropriate to them. If there were no such ties the region would not be a political unit at all. When there are such ties there is no other description of them possible than that they are constitutional. No one hesitates to speak of the constitution of the Holy Roman Empire of the Germans, even with reference to a time when it included states that were internationally semi-sovereign, nor can it be doubted that India has its constitution no less than the United Kingdom. Sir William Lee-Warner's very instructive book embodies so much of the former as relates to the native states, in a manner which is a worthy parallel to Sir Erskine May's book on the latter and to other more recent ones on that subject. The same people has determined by its action the constitutions of the United Kingdom and of India, and as a consequence these are similar so far as that neither is an engine-turned structure, but the architecture of each includes history, theory, and modern fact, and the books which describe them are similarly varied in their composition. On the side of substance the principal difference between them is that, while in both the field covered by express definition leaves room for questions to arise, in the Indian constitution an acknowledged supreme will decides every question which arises, but in that of the United Kingdom a balance of power causes questions to be less easy of solution, as we are experiencing in this year of grace 1910. On the side of literary exposition, the principal difference is that the Indian constitution has passed and is passing through minds coloured by academical training, and is marked by classification and technical terms borrowed from sciences not always strictly in point. It is not indeed in this classification and academic technicality that the *ultima ratio* in the Indian constitution lies, but in practical necessity, of which we may take an example from the case, already referred to, of a German extraditable criminal finding his way into a native state. Sir William says that " the duty which the British Government has incurred of surrendering the accused to Germany is not discharged without the co-operation of the protected states " and that " if the hand of British law cannot directly reach the offender outside its own jurisdiction, the state which harbours the fugitive must produce him on British soil where he can be dealt with according to law" (p. 272). Who does not see that, by the "must" in the last clause, the internal sovereignty of a prince who is not allowed to shelter an alleged offender in his territory is as really invaded as if the British hand assumed to deal with the alleged offender in that territory?

The true security of the ruling chiefs lies in the facts that the categorical imperative of the royal-imperial government is acknowledged to belong to it only for the good of India, and that that government entertains no fantastic notion that it can do much to promote the good of India unless it carries a large body of Indian opinion with it. So long as the action of the government conforms to those standards, the native princes whose standards are similar may feel that in their respective spheres they are partners, and necessary partners, with it in a great and just undertaking. There is good reason to believe that both by them and by us a comradeship in difficulty and danger is indeed felt, such a comradeship as engages the strenuous and loyal exertions of a ship's crew under the categorical imperative of the captain. And this is perhaps the final word which sound analysis can furnish to us on the political condition of India.

## XX

### THE DECLARATION OF LONDON. 1910.

[Reprinted, with permission, from *The Nineteenth Century and After*, vol. LXVII. (1910), pp. 505-515.]

THAT the ten greatest naval Powers of the world should have met in conference on the laws of naval war as affecting neutrals, and that after careful consideration they should have agreed on a code so comprehensive as that contained in the Declaration of London, would alone suffice to make the year 1909 memorable to all who are interested in the improvement of international relations. It remains for the year 1910 to make that code binding on the parties by ratification, after which the natural course of events will speedily make it the binding code of the world. There are, however, some who object to it, and it does not seem to have aroused in its defence any great enthusiasm among those whose special aim is the promotion of peace. It is therefore important to invite public attention to it, now that the time approaches at which it must be submitted to Parliament with a view to its ratification by Great Britain.

To improve the conditions under which war is carried on, if that were all which the Declaration of London promises, would be a no less real service to humanity, though a less important one, than that which may reasonably be expected from international arbitrations in diminishing the frequency of war. But a Declaration which furnishes rules for deciding the questions arising between belligerents and neutrals tends to diminish the frequency of war no less than to humanise its conditions. The armed Neutralities of 1780 and 1800, the exasperation introduced into the politics of the world by the Continental policy of Napoleon and the measures taken by Great Britain to meet it, and the war of 1812 between Great Britain and the United States which arose out of that exasperation, are among the most salient, though they are far from being the only or the most recent, proofs of the menace which hangs over the stability of international relations from the uncertainty of the rights and duties of neutrals. The delegates to the Naval Conference of London laboured in the cause of peace as truly as the delegates to the Hague Conferences of 1899 and 1907, and they did so in spite of no lesser difficulties. Except in one or two instances where a serious quarrel between certain states is inconceivable, it has been found necessary, in all proposals for the prospective obligation of international arbitration, that the honour and vital interests of each party shall be excluded from them, and left to its exclusive appreciation. The Naval Conference of London, on the other hand, has succeeded in effecting an agreement on more than one rule which, on account of the consequences to national honour and vital interests supposed to be involved, has figured among the causes of war between the states represented. Old formulae have not been allowed to prevail against altered circumstances and more mature reflection. The Declaration has been weighed by its signatories as a whole, in which some give and take was necessary. The conclusion so arrived at, regarded both in itself and in view of the difficulties surmounted, may, when ratified, be not unfairly regarded as the greatest step yet made in the systematic improvement of international relations.

The novelty as well as the magnitude of the step is a reason for prefacing any detailed examination of it by a consideration of the attitude in which it ought to be approached. Down to the middle of the nineteenth century it was usual to regard the world as divided, in respect of the laws of naval war, into the two great classes of belligerents and neutrals, and to treat it as an axiom that the interests of Great Britain were those of the belligerent class. Such was the natural result of the immense preponderance of British naval power over that of any other state, and of the fact that the Scandinavian kingdoms, too weak to be willing participants in the wars of the greater states, were among the most important sources of what were then the chief necessaries of naval equipment—timber, tar with its allied products, and hemp. The scene has changed in both these respects. The naval power of Great Britain is not now out of comparison with that which possible combinations might unite against it, and her policy has become of a more pacific character. She was a neutral in most of the wars of the last half-century in the decision of which naval power played an important part, notably in the American Secession, Spanish-American, and Russo-Japanese wars. In her own South African war she felt the ominous dissatisfaction of neutrals at the exercise of her theretofore unquestioned belligerent rights. At the same time, iron and coal, which are found widely over the world, have taken the place of the special Baltic products as the most important of naval materials, while the density of modern populations has made commerce in the food of the people, and in the raw materials of the manufactures by which they live, of new importance even to belligerents, and particularly to Great Britain. It would now be a mistake to identify the interests of Great Britain, or of any other of the Great Powers, specially with those either of neutrals or of belligerents.

Another point in the proper attitude for approaching the Declaration of London is that its critics, as its signatories have done, should regard it as a whole, in which something less than they desire in one or another direction is compensated in other directions. More especially should they take into account the advantage of holding what it gives them under a written and signed agreement, therefore far more securely than what further they may have claimed was or could be held under appeals to reason or to precedent. One cause why the rules of naval war have hitherto been so much less settled than those of land war is probably to be found in the facts that on the one hand naval power has been less widely spread than military, and that on the other hand commerce so extensive as to be likely to suffer seriously from an abuse of naval power has also been less widely spread than that likely to be affected by the abuse of military power. Hence on both sides a practical appreciation of the exigencies of naval war, in comparison with those of world-wide commerce, has been less general than a corresponding appreciation of the exigencies of land war, with which the smallest populations having land frontiers can scarcely have failed to be early familiar. The world should now be wiser, and there is good reason to believe that it is ripe for an agreement on naval war as free from particular bias as the agreements arrived at by the Hague Conferences on land war, that the ten naval Powers of the London Conference met in that spirit, and that the result of their deliberations shows a satisfactory all-round fairness.

But the friendly attitude towards the Declaration which we claim cannot supersede, though it should accompany, its examination with special reference to the points in which it touches British interests, or may be thought to touch them. Its first chapter is on *Blockade in time of War*, a title which excludes its direct application to what is known as *Pacific Blockade*, although there can be no doubt that many of the rules which are laid down in it will have to be applied to that case by analogy. This chapter represents almost entirely the law as understood and administered in Great Britain. It rejects the rule that a blockade may only be maintained by stationary ships, which the Armed Neutralities of 1780 and 1800 attempted to set up, and which, if ever reasonable, would now be practically impossible on account of the danger which, under modern conditions of war, there would now be in lying very near an enemy's coast. It also rejects the rule on which some Admiralties have acted requiring that a ship to be seized shall in every case have received a special notification of the blockade, though she may have arrived at the spot from a port where it was notorious. On the other hand, Great Britain abandons her claim to capture a blockade-runner at any distance from the blockaded coast, and by the agency of any ship of war, whether belonging or not to the blockading squadron—a claim irritating to neutrals as exposing them to danger and to visit and search in any part of the globe, while not productive of condemnations on very distant captures, on account of the facility of representing the destination to the blockaded port as only contingent on finding the blockade to have ceased, on inquiry at a neighbouring unblockaded port. In future the capture can be lawfully made only by a ship of the blockading force (Art. 20), and either "within the area of operations of the warships detailed to render the blockade effective" (Art. 17), or on a chase begun within that area (necessary interpretation of Arts. 17 and 20). The area so described (*rayon d'action* in the French text) is necessarily rather vague, and may be found to extend to a greater or less distance from the blockaded port or coast, in proportion to the number of ships which the belligerent may be willing or able to assign to the particular service. Its introduction into the law must therefore tell least against the blockading efficiency of the Powers strongest at sea. On the whole it may safely be asserted that the law of blockade, as the Declaration of London settles it, leaves Great Britain in a more secure possession than before of all that is valuable to her in the matter.

The chapter on *Contraband of War*, where it decides adversely to the British rules, generally favours neutrals. The doctrine of Continuous Voyage[1], though admitted for absolute contraband (Art. 30), is excluded for conditional contraband (Art. 35), except when the enemy's territory does not touch the sea (Art. 36). The ship may in no case be captured for having carried contraband which she has delivered (Art. 38). She is not to be condemned on account of her owner, charterer, or captain knowing that she carried contraband, but only if the contraband is more than half her cargo, reckoned either by value, weight, volume, or freight (Art. 40). Lists are given of things which without further declaration are either absolute or conditional contraband, as well as of those which can never be declared either, in the last of which it is satisfactory to England to find raw cotton. By her proposal at the Hague Conference of 1907 to abolish the capture of contraband altogether, Great Britain showed that she deems her blockading power to be in general a sufficient security to her against the military resources of her enemies being notably increased by neutral maritime commerce. The opinion is probably correct for a State enjoying so great a naval supremacy, and the visit and search for contraband, having no geographical limits, is very irritating to neutrals, especially under the doctrine of continuous voyage. But that doctrine, as we have seen, she retains where her enemy's importation of contraband cannot be checked by blockade on account of his not having a coastline. And thus she may rest assured that in this chapter,

[1] That contraband goods destined to reach the enemy by transhipment, or overland carriage, are confiscable although the ship's destination is not to an enemy port.

as well as in that on blockade, she has sacrificed nothing essential to the great advantage of certainty reached through agreement.

The chapter on *Convoy*, though not following next in the Declaration, is essentially connected with that last noticed. The agreement on the lists of absolute and conditional contraband, and as to the conditions for adding to those lists, puts an end to the possible divergence of views between a belligerent and a convoying government as to the international character of a convoyed cargo. With it falls the chief reason for the former's mistrusting the assurance of its innocent character given by the officer of the latter, and the renunciation by Great Britain of the right of searching a convoyed ship (Arts. 61, 62) removes without appreciable loss what has been a serious cause of international contention.

In the chapter on *Unneutral Service* Great Britain concedes the claim of a belligerent to make prisoner and remove any individual, embodied in the armed forces of his enemy, who may be found on board a neutral merchant ship, even though she may not herself be liable to capture, and in that case without bringing her in for any adjudication (Art. 47). The British objection to the claim to make such persons prisoners has been the result of looking on the question as belonging to the law of contraband, when in truth it is a remnant of the right to search neutral merchant ships for enemy property and persons. In clauses stipulating the rule "free ships, free goods," it was commonly laid down that the freedom of the flag covers all persons on board except those in the enemy's military service. There was no solid ground for persisting in a singular view of international law, and to require the ship to be brought in would be a great hardship on passenger steamers and their passengers.

The chapter on the *Destruction of Neutral Prizes* does not contain anything contrary to established British doctrine, for that character certainly cannot be allowed to the claim of the British Government, during the Russo-Japanese war, that neutral prizes must under no circumstances be destroyed without being brought in for adjudication. That claim was opposed to the regulations of every other first-class Naval Power, and was founded on a strained interpretation of language used by Lord Stowell and Dr Lushington, which either expressed only a general rule or reserved the innocent neutral's right to full restitution in value, and on the directions given to commanders in the *Admiralty Manual* of 1888, which may have been dictated by caution without expressing a doctrine. The Declaration deals with the matter by Arts. 49 and 54. The former limits the destruction of a neutral prize to the case of her being liable to condemnation, and of an attempt to bring her in involving danger to the safety of the capturing ship or to the success of the operations in which she is engaged at the time, and even then a compensation must be paid for goods destroyed with her which were not liable to confiscation (Art. 53). Thus the definition of the cases for destruction is narrower than that given by the Institute of International Law, and would not have justified the Russian captain in sinking the *Knight Commander* for want of coal to proceed to Vladivostok. Art. 54 authorizes the captor of a neutral ship, which he must not destroy because she is not liable to condemnation, to take any goods liable to condemnation out of her before he allows her to continue her voyage. And it may be presumed that he would have the same right if the prize was liable to condemnation, but the circumstances did not warrant her destruction, or he did not choose to avail himself of them for that purpose. It may be expected that this right will save many a ship from destruction being resorted to by the cruiser where he is uncertain whether the proportion of contraband on board her would insure her condemnation, and yet does not feel justified in allowing the contraband to reach the enemy. These rules do not appear to err by any excess of favour to the captor's State. As an example of impartial opinion, the eminent American authority, Dr John Bassett Moore, may be quoted:

"Let us take [he says] the case of a neutral vessel laden with a cargo of arms and munitions of war, which is captured by a crew of one belligerent while approaching a port of the other. Soon afterwards a superior force of the latter belligerent appears, so that the only way to prevent the arms and munitions of war from being conducted to their hostile destination is to burn or sink the vessel in which they are borne. Is the captor bound in such circumstances practically to hand over the vessel and cargo to his enemy[1]?"

The chapter on *Transfer to a Neutral Flag*, which consists of Arts. 55 and 56, is perhaps the least clear of any in the Declaration. The English practice made no distinction between sales of merchant ships made by enemies to neutrals before or during a war. In each case the principle was that the transfer must be "out and out," reserving

[1] *Digest of International Law*, VII. 523.

no control or interest to the vendor; and as a consequence of that principle, since the practical control of a ship could not be changed while she was at sea. England did not recognize the transfer of a ship from the enemy's to a neutral flag made during her voyage. The French practice did not recognize the transfer of a merchant ship from her enemy to a neutral flag made during the war, and in other cases its principle was to ignore transfers made with the object of escaping capture, thus putting in the front place a slippery inquiry into motive instead of a reference to the objective character of the transaction. Although the Declaration has not maintained any sweeping condemnation of transfers made during the war, deference to the French mode of treating the subject is shown in its division into articles relating to the periods before and after the commencement of hostilities, with some difference in the presumptions in the two cases, and in taking the object of escaping capture as the leading character authorizing condemnation, though an "out and out" transfer made more than thirty days before the commencement of hostilities is to be absolutely presumed valid. These two circumstances have rendered the chapter less clear than it might have been, but a careful examination of its provisions will disclose their substantial accordance with the English practice, although, if in some cases there should be a difference, since it will arise from the introduction of the desire to escape capture as a ground of condemnation, it cannot be unfavourable to the capturing belligerent. The topic has excited interest in this country on account of the danger apprehended by some that, if Great Britain were a belligerent while the capture of enemy property as such is maintained, her merchant shipping would be transferred wholesale to neutral flags. They may be assured that the Declaration contains nothing to increase that danger.

The foregoing notice of the articles which their bearing on British interests marks out for consideration on the present occasion may be closed by the mention of one of incontestable equity. Art. 64 provides that

"if the capture of a ship or goods is not upheld by the prize court, or if the prize is released without its having been submitted to judgment, the parties interested are entitled to their damages unless there were good reasons for capturing the ship or the goods."

Where the prize is released without having been submitted to judgment, which, of course, will be where the impropriety of the capture is most manifest, the captor's government, or in some countries the law, will have to award the amount payable, and if the neutral is dissatisfied he will have only diplomatic means of redress.

Three questions of great importance remain untouched by the Declaration, since it was found impossible to arrive at an agreement about them. They are the doctrine known as the *Rule of the War of 1756*[1], the question whether the enemy character of cargoes is determined by the *Nationality or Domicile* of their owner, and that of the *Conversion of Merchantmen into Men-of-War on the High Sea*. As to these, therefore, British interests, and the validity of the British understanding of the law, are unaffected by the Declaration.

[1] That a ship loses her neutral character if she engages in a trade which, before the war, was closed by a belligerent to every flag but his own.

It remains to consider the position which the Declaration of London, when ratified, will occupy in international law. By the Hague Convention of 1907 relative to the establishment of an international prize court it is provided that, in the absence of treaty stipulations operative between the parties to a suit, " the court shall apply the rules of international law. If no generally recognized rule exists, the court shall give judgment in accordance with the general principles of justice and equity " (Art. 7). As a necessary preliminary to its ratification of that Convention, the British Government, as is recited in the Declaration, invited nine other Powers to meet it in the Naval Conference of London, "in order to determine in common what are the generally recognized rules of international law within the meaning of " that Art. 7. And the Declaration further connects itself with the prize-court Convention by providing (Art. 69) that any signatory Power may denounce it at periods corresponding with those fixed for the duration of the Convention—namely, twelve years at first and then from six years to six years. The Declaration therefore, so far as concerns the Powers signing or adhering to it, will be a part of the Convention, and all judges of the international prize court appointed by those Powers must abide by it in suits brought by or against subjects of the same Powers. Nevertheless, the Preliminary Provision of the Declaration is expressed in an absolute form, not limited by the contractual character of the document. " The signatory Powers," it says, " are agreed that the rules contained in the following chapters correspond in substance with the generally recognized principles of international law." There is, however, no real discrepancy, for if the rules contained in the Declaration were not deemed by the signatories to be those of international law, they could not be deemed by them to be a determination of what Art. 7 of the Convention requires. The Declaration, therefore, is a solemn expression of what the ten Powers understand in this year 1910 to be international law on the points comprised in it, and, as such, it will not be impaired or affected by any denunciation of it. A denunciation will *pro tanto* dissolve the contract, but the Declaration will remain as an historical fact, quotable even against the denunciant.

Nor can any inference diminishing the force of the work accomplished by the Naval Conference be drawn from the difference of wording between the generally " recognized rules of international law," which are adopted by the prize-court Convention as a standard of decision, and the " substantial conformity with the generally recognized principles of international law," which the Declaration predicates of its rules. International law does not exist in the shape of quotable statements of principle, from which a series of propositions can be worked out as the propositions of Euclid are worked out from his axioms. It has its very being in the rules which enjoy the express or tacit consent of States, the latter as shown by their practice, and its principles are those which can be deduced from the study of those rules. To say that any given rules are conformable to the generally recognized principles of international law is merely to claim for them that they do not run counter to any principles deducible from rules previously recognized, or, in other words, that they are not innovation but development. To this it may be added that if any judge of the future prize court, not appointed by one of the signatory or adhering Powers of the Declaration, should hesitate as to whether any of its rules is really international law, it will be his duty to reflect that the agreement of the ten greatest naval Powers of the world goes far in itself to settle that question. The weight of the States most conversant with a subject has always been allowed to tell in discussing it. The asserted rules between which it has been necessary to choose in framing the Declaration have had no other origin. What the prize court will have to do with the rules is to apply them, by the modes of interpretation known to legal science, to the cases which by those modes can be legitimately brought within them. When this process fails of a result, but the subject is within the scope of international law—a condition of which the force will presently be shown—recourse must be had to the justice and equity to which the prize-court Convention appeals in the last resort.

We have, lastly, to ask ourselves whether the prize-court Convention, linked with the Declaration of London such as we have seen the latter to be, presents such a danger to England, by its appeal to justice and equity in the failure of international law, as ought to prevent this country from ratifying it. The independence of States is prior to international law, both historically and logically, and fills the ground, subject to diplomatic action, at whatever point it is not limited by rules laid down by international consent. At any such point the national independence may assert itself in a policy the determination of which belongs to the higher orders of the State, with which therefore no court of law can interfere; other nations, if they think that they or their individual members suffer unjustly from it, being left to diplomatic methods of redress. An example is the *conversion of merchantmen into men-of-war on the high sea*, which is the policy of many nations, notably of Russia, and is objected to by Great Britain. Without in the least questioning the justice of that objection, it must be admitted that, since it has so far failed to obtain international consent to any prohibition or limitation of the conversion in question, the matter stands at present outside the scope of international law. In these circumstances, if a capture made by a merchantman converted at sea into a man-of-war were questioned before the future prize court, the question would probably be ruled out, without considering the plea of justice or equity, as belonging to a part of government with which the court could not meddle. The other matters which have been noticed as being untouched by the Declaration stand on a different footing. *The Rule of the War of* 1756 is defended by Great Britain on the ground of an asserted principle of international law. The determination of the enemy character of cargo by the owner's domicile is an old rule of international law which has ceased to command universal consent, and the newer determination of such character by the owner's nationality competes with it for adoption, some international rule on the subject being necessary. In all these cases, therefore, the rules contended for may be described as the modes in which international law is understood by the respective countries maintaining them, and it would be necessary to resort to justice and equity for the decision. The capture at sea of enemy property, as such, is sanctioned by an immemorial rule of international law to which objection is now widely made, but that objection has never reached the point of refusing acknowledgment to its continued existence, and it is repeatedly presumed in the Declaration. The future prize court will not, therefore, be able to bring it into question under the head of justice and equity.

We trust that the reader will accept the conclusion that the Declaration of London, and along with it the Convention for the establishment of an international prize court—which, in an elementary form, the present writer proposed in the Institute of International Law as far back as 1876—ought to be ratified by Great Britain on their merits as they stand. That being so, it would be permissible to appeal further to the impetus which their ratification must give to the accomplishment of yet more for the improvement of international relations, and the discouragement which would attend the refusal of it. But for the present it is enough to point out that the Naval Conference of London was remarkable not only for its achievement, but also for the fact that, notwithstanding the undeniably political character of much of the work entrusted to it, its members were not drawn from the higher ranks of diplomacy, but chiefly from the classes which, as jurists or naval men, are most conversant with the subject. It was deeply imbued by the atmosphere of scientific impartiality which belongs to discussions in such circles, with which, indeed, some of the members had been familiarised in non-official gatherings. Perhaps a wider combination of special, with diplomatic or political, competence than has hitherto been usual may be one of the means by which future improvement in international relations may be brought about.

# XXI

## THE DECLARATION OF LONDON. 1911.

[Letters reprinted, with permission, from *The Times*, 31st January; 6th, 9th, 25th February; 2nd, 13th, 16th, 18th March, 1911.]

To the Editor of *The Times*.

Sir,—In dealing with the Declaration of London the first necessity is to know what it is that we have before us. Is it merely the document in 71 articles which bears that name, or is it that document accompanied by an authoritative interpretation? The latter view was taken by the Foreign Office in the reply made by it on November 9 to the Edinburgh Chamber of Commerce:

"In view of the reference, under the first head of the conclusions summarized at the end of your letter, to the desirability of eliminating any elements of ambiguity from the rules as laid down, Sir E. Grey desires me to point out that this object is largely attained by the Report of the Drafting Committee of the London Naval Conference, 1908–9. Your directors are no doubt aware that it is the well-recognized practice of international conferences to entrust to a special committee the drafting of a General Act and of any Conventions to be adopted and signed by the plenipotentiaries. Where the report in which the Drafting Committee submits to the Conference the result of its labours contains a reasoned commentary elucidating the provisions of such Conventions, it becomes, if formally accepted by the Conference, an authoritative interpretation of the instruments, and the Conventions must thereafter be construed by the signatory Powers with reference to the commentary where necessary. The General Report of the Drafting Committee of the Naval Conference was adopted by the Conference at its eleventh plenary meeting on the 25th of February, 1909, and, accordingly, if the proposed International Prize Court is set up at The Hague, it will be bound, when applying the provisions of the Declaration of London as between the signatories, to construe the text in conformity with the terms of the Report." Parliamentary Paper Cd. 5418, p. 21.

It is perhaps natural that this statement, even when it has not passed unobserved, has not satisfied every one, and that it is repeatedly asked what is the evidence for the " well-recognized practice " asserted in it. The great importance of the question is shown by the following quotation from an article in the current number of the *Law Quarterly Review* by the Right Hon. Arthur Cohen :

> "It is, I think, to be regretted that the Declaration of London has not given its sanction to the Report by some kind of reference to it, or that some of the explanations given in the Report have not been inserted in the Declaration. For instance, the important Article 17 provides that neutral vessels may not be captured in breach of blockade except within the area of operations of the warships detailed in order to render the blockade effective, but it contains no definition whatever of the term area, whereas the Report, in its note to that article, gives a full explanation which is said to have been universally accepted. Indeed many of the arguments of Mr Thomas Gibson Bowles, in his vigorous onslaught on the Declaration of London in the May number of 1909 of the *Nineteenth Century*, would, I think, lose almost all their force if it were certain that Monsieur Renault's Report will be treated by the International Prize Court as being embodied in the Declaration."

It is scarcely necessary to mention that the report commonly referred to by the name of its eminent author, M. Renault, is that of the Drafting Committee. The question as to its authoritative character is mainly based on an analogy drawn from the rule of the English law courts, that the proceedings which have resulted in an Act of Parliament cannot be used for its interpretation. There is no analogy. Either House of Parliament decides as a unit, by a majority of votes given by members entirely independent one of another. The intentions of a member or of a group, could they be ascertained, would furnish no proof of those of the others ; and there is no common standard by which the general sense, whether real or assumed as a figment, can be ascertained except the words employed in the official conclusions. But an international conference does not decide, it agrees ; and no meaning can be attributed to its conclusions which it would have been inconsistent with good faith for an agreeing party to entertain. If the conclusions have been drafted by a committee in the form of articles along with which the committee presents a report expressing their meaning in more detail, good faith requires that a party who is not prepared to accept them in that meaning should then and there disclose his objection to it. Failing any such disclosure, to question that the report must be combined with the articles as the standard of the agreement arrived at, would be to question the sincerity of those concerned.

In the case of the Declaration of London the result to which we are led by this general view is confirmed and even strengthened by specific proof. The protocol of the eleventh plenary sitting of the Naval Conference, to which Sir Edward Grey referred, is to be found in the Blue-book, Cd. 4555, pp. 221–3. A discussion took place on the Articles and Report as presented on behalf of the Drafting Committee. Admiral Slade, one of the British representatives, made an observation on Article 16, to meet which M. Renault undertook to add some words to the Report. The context shows that the words *et de la connaissance présumée du blocus*, now appearing in the end of the explanation of

Article 16, were so added. Mr Wilson, one of the United States representatives, asked for an interpretation by the Conference of the words *navire de commerce*, which was given, and recorded by the words *il est entendu*. M. Renault himself proposed the addition, in the last paragraph of Article 67, of the words *qui les accompagnent*, which now appear there, and the president then declared that *le Rapport Général est accepté par la Conférence*. We have it, therefore, on the face of the documents that the full Conference took seriously the duty of putting the finishing touches to its work—that the report was not left by it precisely as it came from the committee, but was amended as became a State paper for which the full Conference was responsible—and that both the Report and the Articles were adopted, and are now accessible, only in the final form which they so assumed. There cannot be a more perfect demonstration of what Mr Cohen desires to be satisfied of, namely, " that M. Renault's Report will be treated by the International Prize Court as being embodied in the Declaration."

Having now laid the ground by showing what it is that we have to deal with, I hope, with your permission, to examine the Declaration itself in a further communication.

I am, Sir, yours faithfully,<br>J. WESTLAKE.

*January* 27.

To the Editor of *The Times*.

SIR,—If the International Prize Court shall be established, the law which it will have to apply is defined by the relevant Hague Convention of 1907—Article 7—as, first, any stipulations existing between the capturing belligerent and the Power which, or a subject of which, is a party to the suit; secondly, the generally-recognized rules of international law; and in the absence of such sources, the general principles of justice and equity. But what if the captor's country maintains some particular rule of international law not generally recognized? M. Renault, in the report which he presented on behalf of the sub-committee which prepared the Convention, admitted that on juridical principles the International Court, as one of appeal, could not reverse a decision given by the Court of First Instance in accordance with its own law. But he rejected that solution as involving the variable character of the law to be applied, and explained the article as entrusting the International Court with the duty of supplying the deficiency of positive law by its own conviction of justice and equity. The British Government has naturally withheld its ratification of the Convention until the enormous power thus conferred by it on the International Court shall have been limited by a sufficient agreement on the rules of prize law. The Naval Conference of London has framed an agreement which does not extend to three of the matters that were laid before it, and having ascertained in my last letter in what documents that agreement is to be found, the next question which arises is as to the sufficiency of its extent. Are the three excepted matters so important that the British Government ought not to allow the International Prize Court to come into being until they are settled? If that question should be answered in the affirmative, there would be little use in examining the agreement arrived at on the other points.

The point which among the three has aroused the widest interest is the conversion of a merchant vessel into a ship of war on the high seas. Such conversion, as well as the plans which have been adopted in different countries, Great Britain among the number, for giving the Government in time of war a claim on vessels which are merchantmen in time of peace, are often denounced as an indirect renewal of privateering. This is a confusion, since it is an essential mark of a privateer that she makes captures for the profit of her owners. But there is a grave objection on solid grounds to any change in the character of a ship taking place at sea. For example, a merchant vessel might enjoy in a neutral port a hospitality which could not have been extended to a ship of war, and immediately after leaving that port she might assume the character of a ship of war. Great Britain succeeded in getting Russia to agree to the restoration of the prizes captured in 1904 by vessels of her Volunteer Navy which had hoisted the flag of the Imperial Navy in the Red Sea, after they had passed through the Bosporus and Dardanelles as merchantmen. Still, there is no recognized rule to prevent a State from commissioning ships in waters in which, having no superior in them, it is free to exercise its sovereign power. Therefore, if a neutral who had suffered by a capture made after the obnoxious conversion, and who had failed to obtain redress in the captor's Court, as, of course, he would, should appeal to the International Prize Court, it would be quite impossible for that Court, as matters now stand, to do otherwise than reject his appeal. The International Judges will have been entrusted with the administration of the justice and equity of prize law, but the limitations which it may be wise to impose on the exercise of sovereignty belong to a deeper-lying juridical stratum than that of prize law.

This being so, a Court of Appeal certain to sustain the judgment of the captor's Court would never be resorted to by a British claimant, against whom a capture made by a merchantman converted on the high sea had been upheld. And, whether he resorted to it or not, its existence could do him no more harm than he is already subject to from the nature of the case. Neither would the British Government be prejudiced in any effort it may make to get the obnoxious conversion condemned by a new rule of international law, by its having consented to the establishment of an International Prize Court in the creation of which such a new rule, which, even if made, would not be one of prize law, was not laid down. But, to avoid any misunderstanding on that point, it would be wise to append to the exchange of ratifications, both of the International Prize Court Convention and of the Declaration of London, a note to the effect that " the British Government expressly reserves its liberty of objecting to the conversion of a merchant vessel into a ship of war on the high sea, and to any judgment of the International Prize Court maintaining a capture made by a merchant vessel so converted."

We will take next the question whether the nationality or the domicile of the owner should be adopted as the dominant factor in deciding whether property is enemy property. The latter is the older criterion and is still maintained by Great Britain, while the former has generally taken its place on the European Continent, although the Instructions of July 25, 1870, Article 10, informed the French naval commanders that the nationality of houses of business must be determined according to the place where they are established. I do not perceive that the choice between the two criteria is important to British interests, especially if that of nationality should only be adopted with the qualification just quoted from the French Instructions. And, on the other hand, the adoption by any agreement of the Anglo-American system in its entirety is almost inconceivable when we remember the censure passed on one part of it by no lesser authorities than Wheaton (*Elements of International Law*, § 335) and Chief Justice Marshall (in the *Venus*, 8 Cranch 299). Wheaton, repeating Marshall almost literally, writes:

> "Residence in a neutral country will not protect [a merchant's] share in a house established in the enemy's country, though residence in the enemy's country will condemn his share in a house established in a neutral country. It is impossible not to see in this want of reciprocity strong marks of the partiality towards the interests of captors, which is perhaps inseparable from a prize code framed by judicial legislation in a belligerent country, and adopted to encourage its naval exertions."

I am therefore prepared to find, in the judicial equity of the International Prize Court, as good a chance of a reasonable solution of this question as any which diplomacy can present. The British Delegates to the Naval Conference, in their report to Sir Edward Grey, say that " the adherents of the rival systems were evenly divided in the committee." That fact ought to reassure those who may fear that on the International Bench there would be a foregone conclusion against British arguments on the matter.

The third of the points on which the Naval Conference of London was unable to agree is what is known as the Rule of the War of 1756—namely, that a vessel loses her neutral character if she engages in a trade which, before the war, was closed by a belligerent to every flag but his own. The extent to which different Great Powers now have oversea possessions, or possessions which, although having an overland connexion, are so remote from their centres of empire as Vladivostok is from St Petersburg, and to which the trade between the centres and such possessions is now reserved to the national flag, certainly renders this rule an important adjunct to the capture of enemy ships and property. It cannot be said to be generally recognized, and there is a real danger that the International Prize Court might not recognize it on an appeal from a British captor. But the enforcement of its judgment would then belong to this country, and the case might be provided for by a further annex to the exchange of ratifications—namely, that " the British Government further reserves its liberty of objecting to any judgment of the International Prize Court maintaining the claim to a neutral character made by a ship engaging in a trade which, before the war, was closed by a belligerent to every flag but his own."

I conclude that the failure of agreement at the Naval Conference on the three matters above discussed need not prevent England's joining in the establishment of the International Prize Court, while guarding her interests by proper reservations, and that the agreements embodied in the Declaration of London must therefore be examined in order to determine whether they are acceptable in the aggregate. The method of reservations cannot be applied to them, because Article 65 provides that "the dispositions of the present Declaration form an indivisible whole." I hope to show in my next letter that they form an acceptable whole.

I am, Sir, yours faithfully,

J. WESTLAKE.

*January* 28.

To the Editor of *The Times*.

SIR,—Having discussed the topics on which the Naval Conference of London was unable to reach · an agreement, I come to the agreement comprised in the 71 Articles and the report. It will be well to take first a topic with which, if it was not to be another eliminated one, it was not possible to deal otherwise than as the Declaration does. This is the destruction of neutral prizes at sea. If the case of the *Knight Commander* and the others which occurred during the Russo-Japanese War have inflamed British opinion against such destruction, they have also proved our inability to prevent it without going to war whenever a British neutral prize is sunk, an heroic remedy when we consider that the practice is allowed by the regulations of France, the United States, and Japan, as well as of Russia, and that the Institute of International Law has declined to condemn it. The Declaration has done what was possible for the view claimed as the British one, by a reasonable limitation of the practice and the provision of indemnity in case the limits laid down are transgressed. No doubt Article 49 leaves it open that the inability to spare a prize crew may be held a justification; but the British Admiralty of 1888 expressly allowed that justification for sinking an enemy prize, even with neutral goods on board, between which case and that of sinking a neutral prize the distinction in principle is the very point in dispute.

Of the remaining questions, public opinion in this country has, not unjustly, fixed on that of contraband as the most important. It will be well to recognize at the outset that British feeling on that subject has undergone an important change since the Napoleonic Wars. Down to and including their period the British policy was to maintain the law of contraband at a level which should enable us to hinder the supply of naval and military stores and provisions to our enemies. Now our chief anxiety is that the law of contraband shall not stand at a level which should enable our enemies to hinder the supply of food and the raw materials of manufacture to ourselves. The change cannot be described as one from the disposition natural to a belligerent to the disposition natural to a neutral. The British people have not come to look with such confidence to their being able to maintain a position of neutrality in future wars that they should embrace the general interests of neutrals as being theirs. But a new and in some respects a conflicting interest, arising from the growth of our population and industry, has been added to our ancient concern for our power in war. The Declaration provides for this new interest by a free list of articles that in no case are to be declared contraband, either absolute or conditional, in which are included all the principal raw materials of our textile and iron industries. It needs only to mention raw cotton, wool, silk, jute, flax, and metallic ores, although many articles important for the same or other industries are enumerated. We are thus secured against such a proceeding as that of Russia in 1904 placing raw cotton on her list of contraband, entirely an absolute list, on the plea that it was impossible to distinguish whether that material was intended to be used in the manufacture of explosives or for textile purposes.

An equally complete satisfaction could not be given to British aspirations with regard to the supply of food, because it is impossible so to manipulate the law of contraband as to lessen difficulties in the way of victualling England without lessening them in the way of victualling hostile expeditions. But Article 33 adopts what is in effect our own rule—namely, that conditional contraband must be destined for the armed forces or Government departments of the enemy State. To this Article 34 adds certain presumptions of that destination, expressly not conclusive ones, two of which have caused much alarm. One is when the merchant in the enemy's country to whom the goods are addressed furnishes the enemy with goods of the kind, and here the fear is that furnishing to the enemy population may be within those words. It might appear sufficient to reply that use by the enemy population is not included in the destination of which the presumption is laid down. But a complete answer is given by the fact that in the general report this condition is expressed as notoriously furnishing to the enemy Government. The other presumption referred to is when the goods are going to a place serving as a base for the armed forces of the enemy, and here the fear is that any commercial part from which the enemy Government occasionally obtains supplies for its forces may be held to be such a base. The general report says that the base in question may be either one of operations or one of victualling (*ravitaillement*), which helps us towards the only reasonable conclusion, that magazines or at least some systematic tie with the military or naval administration is needed to make a commercial port a base. So far, then, as the contraband character is concerned, the Declaration leaves our means of food supply where they were under British doctrine: for it is idle to contend that by that doctrine the right to condemn conditional contraband depended on the special destinations found in the decided cases, as those to an army or dockyard. Reluctant as we are in England to admit generalities in questions of law, our doctrine had a principle, and we may be sure that no international conference will accept it in any narrow form; nor is it easy to see how its essence can be better expressed than is done in the Declaration.

But in another respect the Declaration makes

our food supply safer than it would be by our own rules; for, by abolishing the application to it of the doctrine of continuous voyage, it enables the American or other remote shipper to eliminate the risk of capture from the longer part of the transit of his goods. He can ship his grain or meat to a neutral port nearer England, from which it can be brought here with proportionally less danger. Of course our power to intercept conditional contraband really on its way to our enemy is similarly diminished. But, as already remarked, we cannot obtain more security for ourselves than we allow to our enemy. And it must not be forgotten that it is not with British rules alone that the Declaration must be compared. It prohibits for the future such attempts as that made by France in 1885, with German approval, to declare an important article of national food absolute contraband. Then it was rice, China being the enemy; but the principle of the attempt has not been disavowed, and next time it might be wheat.

The agreement on the lists of absolute and conditional contraband, and as to the conditions for adding to those lists, puts an end to the possible divergence of views between a belligerent and a convoying Government as to the character of a convoyed cargo. With it falls the chief reason for the former's mistrusting the assurance of its innocent character given by the officer of the latter, and the renunciation by England of the right of searching a convoyed ship—Articles 61, 62—removes without real sacrifice what has been a serious cause of international contention.

In the chapter on blockade there is give and take.

English doctrine is followed in rejecting the rule on which some Admiralties have acted, requiring that a ship to be seized shall in every case have received a special notification of the blockade, although she may have sailed from a port where it was notorious. At the same time England loses little or nothing by abandoning her claim to capture a blockade-runner at any distance from the blockaded coast, and by the agency of any ship of war, whether or not belonging to the blockading squadron. It was a claim peculiarly irritating to neutrals, and the captures made under it were always few, and the condemnations perhaps none. The precise meaning of " the area of operations " of the blockading squadron, only within which, or on a chase begun within it, a capture is henceforth to be made, is not clear to a landsman. But under the definition adopted in the Report it was admitted, both by Admiral Le Bois for France and by Admiral Slade for England, that it will extend to a distance of the blockaded coast proportionate to the number of ships which the belligerent will be able or willing to assign to the particular service. If so, its introduction into the law must tell least against the blockading efficiency of the Powers strongest at sea.

The remaining portions of the Declaration are scarcely important enough to weigh much with any one in favour of its rejection, and are highly technical. To what give and take may be found in them, or in the articles which have been selected for notice, there applies the general remark that not only is it fairly balanced, but that it has the great merit of securing to England the enjoyment of the rights in which the Declaration confirms her.

Those who would reject that benefit, or even, like Mr Bowles, return to an earlier state of things by undoing the Declaration of Paris, are usually ignorant how groundless was the claim to treat all British pretensions as recognized international law. Now, too, the multiplication of great sea Powers necessarily leads to the consequence that any flaw in our claims—whether arising from their never having been acknowledged law or from the change of circumstances to which all international law, however acknowledged at some time, is bound to adjust itself—will be pressed against us with a force very different from that which we had to meet when the neutrals were generally smaller Powers. A rare opportunity is offered us. On our belligerent rights against an enemy we must stand firm, and we are not asked to forgo them. In questions between belligerents and neutrals whatever can be described as vital has not been made the subject of compromise, but stands outside the Declaration of London, and, as I have shown, can be saved by the necessary reservations from prejudicing us either in an International Prize Court or in diplomacy. Regret that even on those points there has not been agreement must not prevent our accepting the agreement arrived at, which gives us the benefit of assured law on so wide a field, and of being relieved by an International Prize Court from the odium of being the final judges in our own case.

I am, Sir, yours faithfully,

J. WESTLAKE.

*February* 1.

## THE DECLARATION OF LONDON

To the Editor of *The Times*.

SIR,—Although the further general discussion of the Declaration of London may well be postponed till it will be revived by the Imperial Conference, I venture to ask for a little space in order to defend the authority of the General Report against the able attack made on it by my friend Professor Holland. It is an isolated point, and one which must influence our meditations on the subject during the interval in which Parliamentary proceedings will engross our utterances.

The outcome of an International Conference is an agreement, and if an International Prize Court shall come into being the essential question for it will be what the agreement was that the Conference of London arrived at. There are no technical rules to determine the answer, since the matter is outside the technical law of any country. There is only the rule of reason and of good faith—namely, that the best evidence must be sought, and obeyed when found. Now, in a passage which Professor Holland has quoted in French, the Drafting Committee presented its Report as

"a precise commentary, disentangled from all controversy, which, having become an official commentary by the approbation of the Conference, will be such as to guide the various authorities, administrative, military, or judicial, which may have to apply it."

The approbation thus sought was given (with a modification unimportant in itself, but important as being made by the full Conference) in the form of an " acceptance " ; a simple form but sufficient, because an offer simply accepted is accepted as made, and the Report had been offered, in the passage quoted from it, as guiding the application of the Declaration. My valued colleague, however, lays down that the acceptance

"amounted to nothing more than an expression of opinion on the part of the delegates to the Conference that the Report contained explanations which had satisfied themselves, and might satisfy their Governments, that the Convention which they were about to forward to those Governments might safely be accepted."

I must be allowed to say that this is a meaning attributed to acceptance in contradiction to the terms of the offer accepted, and that its attribution to the delegates singly, as matter of advice to be given to their respective Governments, is in contradiction to the fact that the acceptance was declared by the President on behalf of the Conference as a body. Whether the adoption of the Report by the Conference, as an authority guiding the application of the Declaration, can be treated by the Governments as *res inter alios acta* depends on whether it formed a part of the agreement come to by the Conference, for the preparation of an agreement was the very object of its sitting. And surely no Government, of which the delegate was present and kept silence at the adoption, can be heard to say that any agreement was there come to by which it was left open to interpret the Declaration otherwise than in accordance with the guiding authority adopted.

It is perhaps possible that those who ignore the authority of the Report may try to distinguish between the agreement come to by the Conference and the effect of the exchange of ratifications if such should take place. The answer is that what has to be ratified is not a piece of paper on which certain words are written, but an agreement expressed in certain words for the interpretation of which a certain authority has already been made a part of the agreement. A Sovereign Legislature may enact a form of words and leave it to its Courts to say what it means, but independent States must conclude an agreement with a meaning or nothing.

With the learned authorities quoted by Professor Holland there can only, as might be expected, be entire agreement by every one. Professor Ullman says that an authentic interpretation can only be made by the contracting parties in the form of a common document. My case is that in the present instance this has been done. Professor Fiore says that an authentic interpretation can only be made by " a declaration of what has already been agreed on, or a new treaty." Evidently he was only thinking of interpretations subsequent to the agreement, or perhaps he regarded a declaration of what is being agreed on as falling, too obviously for mention, within the principle of declarations of what has already been agreed on.

The General Report of the Conference of London is a part of the agreement of that Conference. That a Government or an International Prize Court should refuse to apply it in interpreting the 71 Articles is possible, but not more so than that there should be a refusal to apply one of the Articles, and in the case of the Court it is almost inconceivable. There can, however, be no objection to a reservation in the sense of the Report being appended to our ratification, as we are told it is intended to do in the case of Art. 34, to ensure that furnishing conditional contraband to the enemy shall not be interpreted as supplying the civil enemy population but only the enemy Government. By such means we shall gain an additional security.

I am, Sir, yours faithfully,<br>
J. WESTLAKE.

*February* 22.

To the Editor of *The Times*.

Sir,—I quite agree with Mr Arthur Cohen that it would be a good thing, as setting all doubts at rest, if the Naval Powers whose delegates met in the Naval Conference of London would sign a convention or declaration to the effect that the general report approved by that Conference is an official commentary on the articles intended to guide the various authorities, administrative, military, or judicial, which may have to apply them. I have taken the words of the report itself as being less likely than any new words to prevent a suspicion that something new is intended, but the same sense may, of course, be otherwise expressed. Failing such a conjoint document, and if in that case the British ratification should not be accompanied by a reservation of the sense of the word " enemy " in Article 34 in accordance with the report, I further agree that the Declaration of London had better not be ratified. The doubts about its meaning which have been raised in this country might be quoted against ourselves if any Government or Judge was inclined to be of bad faith.

I await with interest the consideration promised by Mr Cohen of the effect of reservations. At present I take the understanding and practice to be that when a ratification is offered with a reservation and this does not prevent the ratifications being exchanged, the reservation has been accepted and the Power which made it will have the benefit of it. Article 65 of the Declaration of London, by which the dispositions of that Declaration are made an indivisible whole, would render it unbecoming even to offer a ratification accompanied by a reservation eliminating any of those dispositions. But a reservation declaring the sense, either of the whole or of a particular disposition, to be what the Conference declared it to be by its report would be no severance of the indivisible whole; it would be a reservation only in name.

If I may be allowed one word of personal explanation, I have not striven " to prove that the report constitutes a convention " separate from, though equally binding with, " the Declaration itself." My point was, and is, that when parties exchange a document saying at the same time that it means *this* and not *that*, then the document does not exist for them in any other sense—barring the effect of any technical rules, of which in the law of nations there are none.

I am, Sir, yours faithfully,

J. WESTLAKE.

*March* 1.

To the Editor of *The Times*.

SIR,—The personal appeal made to me by Mr Wylie in your issue of the 18th inst. is my excuse for asking you to allow me once more a little space.

I had hoped that in your issue of February 9 I sufficiently indicated my opinion that I interpreted Article 34, even without the aid of the General Report, as Mr Wylie does. And I can assure him that I have no doubt but that any Court of real jurists would act in good faith and would give the Article the same meaning. But this persuasion ought not to prevent our taking all possible precautions, all the more because the opponents of the Declaration seem to have forgotten the handle which their insistence on a perverse interpretation, and on ignoring the General Report, might afford. Surely, when Sir Edward Grey himself has promised the desired reservation as to Article 34, to support him in this, and to suggest the extension of the reservation to the whole of the General Report, ought not to occasion any question as to one's fidelity to his own opinion.

I am, Sir, yours faithfully,

J. WESTLAKE.

*March* 9.

To the Editor of *The Times*.

SIR,—Will you allow me to point out that the writer on this subject, under the head of Political Notes in your issue of to-day, has fallen into an error in saying that " a much wider term of destination for conditional contraband is used in Article 35 " than in Article 34 ? On the contrary, Article 35 restricts the right of capturing conditional contraband which would otherwise exist under Article 34. The error has arisen from a failure to distinguish between the destination of contraband goods and that of the ship which carries them.

The destination of goods is that determined for them by the sender. It may be directly to a belligerent's country, or indirectly after unloading at a neutral port from which, by the sender's determination, they are forwarded to the belligerent's country, whether by reshipment or by land carriage. If at a neutral port they pass into the control of a purchaser, in pursuance of the destination given them by the sender, that destination of them was always only to the neutral port, and is now exhausted, although the hope of their being purchased by some one who would forward them to the belligerent's country may have been the motive of sending them. Articles 30, 33, and 34 deal with the destination of the goods thus ascertained. By Article 30 a destination to the territory of the enemy or to one occupied by his armed forces is conclusive against goods of the character of absolute contraband. By Article 33 a destination to the armed forces or to the administrations of the enemy State is conclusive against goods of the character of conditional contraband, and by Article 34 certain presumptions, in which the disputed terms "enemy" and "base" occur, are laid down for this case. If this were all, the hostile destination of the goods might be indirect for conditional as well as for absolute contraband, although Article 33 does not expressly say so. But Article 35 introduces the destination of the ship, which, in the case of conditional contraband, must be to the territory of the enemy or to one occupied by his armed forces, without unloading at an intermediate neutral port. It is the article, which, for conditional contraband, and subject to the exception made by Article 36, excludes the indirect though hostile destination of goods—in other words, excludes the doctrine of continuous voyage. Whether the destination of the ship, so far as her connexion with the particular goods is concerned, is neutral or hostile depends on whether she is to deposit them at a neutral port or to carry them on to an enemy one. The Declaration requires for the condemnation of conditional contraband, except in the case of Article 36, a hostile destination both of the goods and of the ship.

I am, Sir, yours faithfully,<br>J. WESTLAKE.

*March* 15.

To the Editor of *The Times.*

SIR,—With all deference to your excellent Parliamentary Correspondent, I must persist in correcting his statement that the combined effect of Articles 33, 34, and 35 " is to create a presumption of hostile destination, and therefore a liability to capture (unless the presumption is rebutted) in the case of all consignments of food to ports of this country in time of war." Suppose a ship having on board food not addressed either to any British authority or notorious Government contractor, or to any place in this country which is fortified or serves as a base for our armed forces, and that the ship herself is bound for some port in this country of no matter what the description. She may be brought in for adjudication under Article 33, if the captor hopes to prove at his own risk that the food was destined for the use of our armed forces or of our public administrations, but there will be no presumption under Article 34 to direct or aid him, nor does Article 35 supply that defect, even if the food is not to be unloaded at an intermediate neutral port. So far from adding any new presumption that Article forbids her being brought in, notwithstanding the presumptions of Article 34, if her British destination is only an ultimate one, to be prosecuted after discharging the food at a neutral port. The case is very clear, but *humanum est errare*.

I am, Sir, yours faithfully,

J. WESTLAKE.

*March* 17.

# XXII

## THE AEGEAN ISLANDS. 1913.

[A letter reprinted, with permission, from *The Times*, 9th January, 1913.]

To the Editor of *The Times*.

SIR,—With reference to the Aegean islands now in the occupation of Italy, may I direct attention to the bearing of their position on the conduct which the Great Powers, and England as one of them, ought to pursue as to their future?

The peace between Turkey and Italy arranged, to put its substance in plain language, for the islands being left by the former Power for a time on deposit with Italy, without any transfer or impairment of Turkish sovereignty over them. Practically this could only operate, in the events which have happened, as a defence of that sovereignty against both the inhabitants and Greece. If in the arrangements now to be made those islands should be handed back to Turkey, the Powers will have taken advantage of the peculiar position thus created by one of themselves to prevent the consequences which must have followed if they had been exposed, equally with the other Aegean islands, to the action of the Greek fleet. Is it possible, in these circumstances, that the Powers should not be held responsible for all the evils which restored Turkish domination may inflict on the miserable inhabitants?

I offer no criticism on the peace between Italy and Turkey, further than to point out the fact that, with whatever intention or justification, it has, to the extent of the islands in question, made Italy a practical party to the war between Turkey and Greece. As such, she cannot avoid a responsibility for the fate of the islanders, and I trust that England may refuse to share it with her by joining in handing them over to the savagery which even the latest events have proved to be the unvarying character of a Turkish Government.

I am, Sir, yours faithfully,

J. WESTLAKE.

CHELSEA.

# APPENDIX

## A LIST OF THE WRITINGS OF JOHN WESTLAKE

[Reprinted[1], with permission, from *Memories of John Westlake*, London, Smith, Elder & Co., 1914, pp. 147–154.]

"Treatise on Private International Law, or the Conflict of Laws, with principal reference to its practice in the English and other cognate systems of Jurisprudence."
 First edition. London : W. Maxwell, 1858.
 Second edition (with modified title) and largely rewritten :
  "Treatise on Private International Law, with principal reference to its practice in England." London: Maxwell & Son, 1880. (Translated into German by Von Holtzendorff. Berlin, 1884.)
 Third edition. London : Sweet and Maxwell, 1890.
 Fourth edition. London : Sweet and Maxwell, 1905.
 Fifth edition. London : Sweet and Maxwell, 1912. Translated into French by Paul Goulé—"Traité de Droit International Privé"—with a preface by de Lapradelle.

"International Law."
 Vol. I. "Peace." Cambridge University Press, 1904. (Second edition, 1910.)
 Vol. II. "War." Cambridge University Press, 1907. (Second edition, 1913.) A French translation, by de Lapradelle, of both volumes is in preparation.

"Ayala. De Jure et Officiis Bellicis et Disciplina Militari." Two volumes edited for Carnegie Institution of Washington with prefatory notice of Ayala, 1913. (In the "Classics of

---

[1] This list is based on one prepared by Westlake himself a few days before his death, as the last *item* on p. 686 shows.

International Law" under the general editorship of James Brown Scott.)

' Chapters on the Principles of International Law." Cambridge University Press, 1894. Translated into French (by Nys)— "Études sur les principes de droit international." Brussels and Paris, 1895—and Japanese.

" International Law (Private) " in the supplement to the fifth edition of the " Encyclopaedia Britannica."

"The Church in the Colonies." Contribution to "Essays on Church Policy," edited by the Rev. W. L. Clay, 1868.

" International Law." An Introductory lecture. London : Clay & Sons, 1888. (French translation by Ed. Rolin in *Revue de Droit International et de législation comparée*, vol. xxi. (1889), pp. 19–36.)

## SHORTER PAPERS

### (A) Read before the Social Science Association

" Is it desirable to prohibit the export of contraband of war ? " September 23, 1870. Transactions of that Association, 1870, pp. 109–125. (French translation in the *Revue de Droit International et de législation comparée*, vol. ii. (1870), pp. 614–635.)

" Domicile or Political Nationality ? " Transactions of that Association, and Spottiswoode & Co., 1880.

"Copyright Bill, 1881." Sessional proceedings of that Association, May 12, 1881, pp. 69–83.

" Copyright (Works of Fine Art, etc.) Bill." Sessional proceedings of that Association, May 1882, pp. 193–202.

" Addresses as President of Jurisprudence Department at Birmingham in 1884." Transactions of that Association.

### (B) Read before the Juridical Society

" Relations between Public and Private International Law." Transactions of that Society, 1855–8, pp. 173–192.

" Commercial Blockade." Transactions of that Society, 1858–63, pp. 681–721.

" Legal Reporting." Transactions of that Society, 1858–63, pp. 745–757.

(C) Contributed to the "Working Men's College Magazine"

"Study of Mathematics," April and August 1859. Reprinted 1879 for London Association of School-mistresses.
"American Constitution and the War." October 1861.
"On the Study of History," vol. xiii. no. 233. February 1913.

(D) Papers published in the "Revue de Droit International et de Législation Comparée"

### I. Articles.

"Est-il désirable de prohiber l'exportation de la contrebande de guerre?" Vol. ii. (1870), pp. 614–635.
"Exposé de lois anglaises récentes. Loi sur l'enseignement primaire, et loi pour le maintien de la paix en Irlande." By J. Westlake and Alice Westlake. Vol. iii. (1871), pp. 55–62.
"La loi anglaise de 1870 sur les biens des femmes mariées (Married Women's Property Act, 1870), 33 & 34 Vict. c. 93." Vol. iii. (1871), pp. 195–201.
"Exposé de lois anglaises récentes, Naturalisation Act, 1870, Foreign Enlistment Act, 1870, Landlord and Tenant (Ireland) Act, 1870." Vol. iii. (1871), pp. 601–615.
"Letter concerning Convention de Genève." M. Moynier's new project. Vol. iv. (1872), pp. 334–335.
"Cas de droit international, public ou privé, récemment jugés par les tribunaux anglais." Vol. vi. (1874), pp. 388–403, 612–629.
"Observations de Monsieur Westlake sur l'article de L. Gessner : ' De la Réforme du droit maritime de la guerre.' "
"Cas de droit international, public ou privé, récemment jugés par les tribunaux anglais." Vol. viii. (1876), pp. 478–482.
"Cas de droit international, public ou privé, récemment jugés par les tribunaux anglais." Vol. x. (1878), pp. 539–550.
"La Russie et l'Angleterre dans l'Asie centrale. Réponse à M. Martens." Vol. xi. (1879), pp. 401–410.
"Introduction au droit international privé." Vol. xii. (1880), pp. 23–46.

" Encore un mot sur la Russie et l'Angleterre dans l'Asie centrale. Note sur la réplique de M. Martens." Vol. xii. (1880), pp. 295-302.
" La doctrine anglaise en matière de droit international privé." Vol. xiii. (1881), pp. 435-446.
" La doctrine anglaise en matière de droit international privé." Vol. xiv. (1882), pp. 285-306.
" Introduction au cours de droit international professé à l'Université de Cambridge." Translation of Inaugural Lecture, by Ed. Rolin. Vol. xxi. (1889), pp. 19-36.
" Le Conflit anglo-portugais." Vol. xxiii. (1891), pp. 243-265 ; vol. xxiv. (1892), pp. 170-205 ; vol. xxv. (1893), pp. 58-71.
" L'Angleterre et la république Sud-Africaine." Translated into French by L. Devogel. Vol. xxviii. (1896), pp. 268-300.
" L'Angleterre et les républiques boers." Second series, vol. ii. (1900), pp. 515-554 ; vol. iii. (1901), pp. 140-187.
" Notes sur la neutralité permanente." Second series, vol. iii. (1901), pp. 389-397.
" A la mémoire de Gustave Rolin-Jaequemyns." Second series, vol. iv. (1902), pp. 120-122.
" Le Blocus pacifique." Translated from the *Law Quarterly Review* (1909) by Léon Devogel. Second series, vol. xi. (1909), pp. 203-216.
" La fortification de l'Escaut occidental." Second series, vol. xiii. (1911), pp. 105-112.

## II. *Reviews*.

" Commentaire sur les Éléments de droit international et sur l'Histoire des progrès du droit des gens de H. Wheaton," by W. B. Lawrence. Vol. i. (1869), pp. 637-643.
" The Law of Naturalisation, as amended by the Naturalisation Acts, 1870," by John Cutler. Vol. iii. (1871), p. 685.
" The Rights and Duties of Neutrals," by W. E. Hall. Vol. vi. (1874), pp. 703-4.
" Internationalism," by Don Arturo de Marcoartu, and " Prize Essays on International Law," by A. P. Sprague and Paul Lacombe. Vol. ix. (1877), pp. 145-147.
" A lecture on the Treaty Relations of Russia and Turkey from 1774 to 1853," by T. E. Holland. Vol. ix. (1877), p. 159.

"Nouveau traité de droit international privé, au double point de vue de la théorie et de la pratique," by Charles Brocher. Vol. ix. (1877), pp. 606–616.

"Éléments de droit civil anglais," by Ernest Lehr. Vol. xvii. (1885), pp. 95–96.

"Notices bibliographiques." Vol. xviii. (1886), pp. 543–544 and 632–633.

"Le droit de la guerre," by Emile Acollas. Vol. xx. (1888), pp. 94–95.

(E) Papers published in the "Law Quarterly Review," Vols. I–XVI.

### I. *Articles.*

"Note on *Sachs v. Sachs*." Vol. iv. (1888), pp. 108–109.

"Judicial Power in the United States." Vol. xi. (1895), pp. 81–85.

"Continuous Voyage in Relation to Contraband of War." Vol. xv. (1899), pp. 24–32.

"The Nature and Extent of the Title by Conquest." Vol. xvii. (1901), pp. 392–401.

"The South African Railway Case and International Law—a Reply." Vol. xxi. (1905), pp. 335–339.

"Is International Law a part of the Law of England?" Vol. xxii. (1906), pp. 14–26.

"The Muscat Dhows." Vol. xxiii. (1907), pp. 83–87.

"Pacific Blockade." Vol. xxv. (1909), pp. 13–23.

"Reprisals and War." Vol. xxv. (1909), pp. 127–137.

"The Native States of India." Vol. xxvi. (1910), pp. 312–319.

### II. *Reviews.*

"A Treatise on International Law," fourth edition, by W. E. Hall. Vol. xii. (1896), p. 185.

"The Principles of International Law" by T. J. Lawrence. Vol. xii. (1896), pp. 285–286.

"A Digest of the Law of England with reference to the Conflict of Laws," by A. V. Dicey. Vol. xii. (1896), pp. 397–401.

"A Treatise on the Subject of Collisions between Warships and Merchant Vessels according to English Law, etc.," by N. Matsunani. Vol. xvii. (1901), p. 319.

"A Treatise on International Public Law," by Hannis Taylor. Vol. xviii. (1902), pp. 310–313.

"Halbsouveränität : Administrative und politische Autonomie seit dem Pariser Vertrage," by M. Boghitchéwitch. Vol. xix. (1903), pp. 461–466.

"Elements of International Law," by Henry Wheaton. Vol. xx. (1904), p. 328.

"Recueil des arbitrages internationaux," vol. i., by A. de Lapradelle and N. Politis. Vol. xxi. (1905), p. 309.

"International Law," Vol. i., by L. Oppenheim. Vol. xxi. (1905), pp. 432–434.

"International Law," Vol. ii., by L. Oppenheim. Vol. xxii. (1906), p. 222.

"International Law," Vol. i., second edition, by L. Oppenheim. Vol. xxviii. (1912), p. 200.

"War and the Private Citizen," by A. Pearce Higgins. Vol. xxviii. (1912), pp. 316–317.

(F) MISCELLANEOUS

"The Kafir Revolt of 1873." *Fortnightly Review*, December 1874.

"Address at first annual meeting of Sunday Evening Association." "First annual report of that Association, 1881," pp. 6–11. *Sunday Review* for January 1882, pp. 91–96.

"England's Duty in Egypt." *Contemporary Review*, December 1882.

"On the Tenure of Fellowships." Cambridge : Macmillan, 1857.

"Bishop Colenso." An obituary notice. *Academy*, June 30, 1883.

"Proportional Representation." *Nineteenth Century*, February 1885.

"Compulsory Greek." *Nineteenth Century*, February 1895.

"International Arbitration." *International Journal of Ethics*, October 1896. (Reprinted in the Appendix of "International Law," vol. i., " Peace " ; first edition, pp. 332–350, second edition, pp. 350–368.)

"Appeals from England to Rome before the Reformation." Two letters signed Q.C. in *Westminster Gazette* of August 9 and 29, 1899.

"England and France in West Africa." *Contemporary Review*, April 1898.

"The Transvaal War." Lecture delivered at Cambridge, November 9, 1899, and second edition (Cambridge University Press, Clay & Sons, 1899).

"Hannibal's Pass." *Geographical Journal*, March and August, 1899.

"Introduction to Takahashi, Cases on International Law during the Chino-Japanese War." Cambridge, 1899, pp. xv–xxviii.

"L'Angleterre et les républiques boers." Brussels (Custaigne) and Paris (Fontemoing), 1901. This is apparently a reprint of two articles which appeared in the *Revue de Droit International et de législation comparée*, second series, vol. ii. (1900), pp. 515–554, and vol. iii. (1901), pp. 140–187.

"The Russo-Japanese Peace and the Anglo-Japanese Alliance." A lecture at Cambridge, reported *Cambridgeshire Weekly News* and *Cambridge Express*, October 20, 1905.

"Introduction to the International History of Europe in the Nineteenth Century" (in "Lectures on the History of the Nineteenth Century," 1907).

"A Letter on the Drago Circular" (in "La Doctrine de Monroe." Paris, 1903. See also " La Republica Argentina, etc.," por el Dr Luis M. Drago. Buenos Ayres, 1903).

"The Venezuelan Boundary Question." *Times*, January 6, 1896.

"Holland and Venezuela." *Times*, December 24, 1908.

"Note on Belligerent Rights at Sea," in Latifi's "Effects of war on property" (London, 1909), pp. 145–152.

"The Near East." *Times*, January 29, 1909.

"Capture of Private Property at Sea." *Times*, April 21, 1909.

"Commercial Blockade considered with reference to Law and Policy." London : Ridgway, 1862.

"Pacific Blockade." *Law Quarterly Review*. January 1909. (Translation by Léon Devogel in the *Revue de Droit International et de législation comparée*, second series, xi. (1909), pp. 203–216.)

"Reprisals and War." *Law Quarterly Review*. April 1909.

"Trade Domicile in War." *Journal of Society of Comparative Legislation*, N.S., vol. ix., pp. 265–8.

"Outlines of a Scheme of Redistribution." *Representation*—the journal of the Proportional Representation Society—No. 10, February 1909.

"Proportional Representation and Party." *Representation*, No. 13, July 1909.

"By-Elections." *Representation*, July 1912.

"Foreign Relations of U.S. during the Civil War." Supplementary to vol. vii. of "Cambridge Modern History," published as ch. ii. of vol. vii.

"The Violation of the Constitution of Finland." *National Review* (1900 to 1902).

[The *Review* was delivered in Russia with the article cut out and a page blackened which could not be cut out without damaging another article.]

"Russia and Finland." *Times*, August 18, 1909; November 1, 1910; January 20, 1911.

"The Hungarian Question" (in German). Pesther Lloyd. November 26, 1905. The English original appeared in the *Westminster Gazette*.

"The Norwegian Question." Christiania: *Aftenpost*, July 11, 1905.

"Scandinavian Affairs." *Aftenpost*, March 26, 1911.

"Contraband of War." *Times*, July 20, 1907. Approving the British proposal to abolish contraband and recommending regulation of blockade with reasonable mobility for blockading squadron but without liberty of capture at any distance.

"Declaration of London." *Nineteenth Century and After*, March 1910. *Times*, January 30, February 6, 9 and 25, March 2, 13, 16 and 18, 1911. *Spectator*, April 1, 1911.

"Fortification of Scheldt." *Handelsblad* (Amsterdam), January 26, 1911. Apparently translated into French under the title: "La fortification de l'Escaut occidental" in *Revue de Droit international et de législation comparée*, seconde série, Tome 13, pp. 105–112.

"Hague Conferences, 1907." *Quarterly Review*, January 1908.

"Our Naval Supremacy." *Westminster Gazette*, November 21, 1908.

"The House of Lords." *Westminster Gazette*, December 23, 1908.

"Duty of Unionist Free Traders." *Spectator*, December 25, 1909.

"The Referendum." *Times*, December 1, 1910.

"The Ægean Islands." *Times*, January 9, 1913.

"Anglo-American Arbitration." *Westminster Gazette*, March 28, 1911.

A Contribution to " British Citizenship : a discussion initiated by E. B. Sargant," 1912.
" J. M. Ludlow : Reminiscence." *Copartnership*, vol. xvii. No. 204.
A Contribution to " La Question Serbe et l'Opinion Européenne." En depôt 90, rue de Varenne, Paris, January 1913.
" On April 8, 1913, in the *Daily Mirror* of this date there is a reply of mine to a prepaid telegram asking my opinion on the coercion of Montenegro. I approved it." [John Westlake died on April 14, 1913.]

# INDEX

Abyssinia, 82
*Academy, The*, 35
acquisition, of territory, 171
   of protectorates, 188
Adam, Sir Charles, 587
Aden 520
Admiralty, Black Book of the, 61
   British, 61, 69, 332
   English Court of, 334
   *Manual* (1888), 641
   of Amsterdam, 326
Aegean Islands, 676
Aetolian council, the, 18
Afghanistan, 432
Africa, 141, 148, 152, 161, 166, 171, 220
African conference at Berlin, 140, 152, 162, 164, 166, 183
African tribes, 142, 152
Aix-la-Chapelle, 366
   Congress of (1818), 99
Alabama question, the, 368, 391, 604
Alatamaha river, 172
Alexander VI., Pope, 159
aliens and the South African Republic, 435, 437
alliance, European, against Napoleon, 97
Alphonso V. of Portugal, 159
Alsace-Lorraine, 496
Alverstone, Lord, 498
ambassador, arrest of Russian, 503
ambassadors:
   immunities of, 63
   representation by, general since Peace of Westphalia, 59
   sacred, 18, 21
   withdrawal of, 6
America, discovery of, 55
American-English War (1812), 634

American Indians, 37, 174
American revolution, the, 93, 257
American tribes, 142, 151, 157
   and property, 150
Amphictyonic oath, the, 17
Amphictyons, the, 274
Amsterdam, blockaded, 576
anarchism, 276
Ancona, March of, 33
Anglo-Dutch convention (1689), 330
Anglo-French *entente cordiale* 539
Anglo-German extradition treaty (1872), 629
Angra Pequeña, German flag hoisted at, 443
Anne, Queen, 91
annexation
   by England of the Dutch republics, 491
   of territory, 122
*Annuaire de l'Institut du Droit International*, 129, 469
*Annual Register*, 125
Anson, Lord, 176
Aragon, 53
*Arbiter in Council, The*, 531, 566
Arbitral Justice, proposed Court of, 544
arbitration:
   among the Hellenes, 17
   and contractual debts, 543, 547
   and mediation, 439
   compulsory, 603
   international, 541
   matters suitable for obligatory, 546, 603
   Permanent Court of, 545
archæology
   and international law, 138
Argaon, 199
Argentina, 602

# INDEX

Asiatic empires, 144, 206
  Europeans in, 144
Assaye, 199
Astor, J. J., 165, 174
Astoria (Columbia River), 165
Athens, 19
Atherley-Jones, L. A. and Bellot, H. H. L., *Commerce in War*, 531, 566
Austin, John, 11, 13, 223, 396, 481, 622
  his limitation of the term "law," 11
Australia, 376
Austria-Hungary, 87, 541
Austrian succession, war of the, 93
Ayala, Balthazar, 30-33
  *De Jure et Officis Bellicis et Disciplina Militari libri tres*, 28, 30, 35
Azores, the, 159

balance of power, 92, 121
Baltic, 52, 519
Baltic States, 341, 342
*Baltica*, case of the, 609
Balwant Singh, 210
Bar, Prof. von, 496
Barbeyrac, Jean, 504
Barcelona, 53, 319
Barclay, Sir Thomas, 490, 494, 566
  *Problems of International Practice and Diplomacy* 531
Barlow, Sir George, 205
Baroda, Gaekwar of, 221, 227
Bartolus, 293
Basle, treaty of (1795), 199
Bassein, treaty of (1802), 205, 206
Baty, Dr, "Trade Domicile in War," 607-612
Bavaria, 96, 198
Bayard, T. F., 104
Beaconsfield, Lord, 432
Bechuanaland, 444
Behar, 199
Belgium, 99, 365, 377
belligerent:
  rights at sea, 613-619
  states, rights of, 1
belligerents:
  and contraband of war, 8
  and neutral commerce, 323
  commerce of, 252

belligerents:
  commerce with, 379
  laws of war between, 238
  neutrals trade with, 365
  rights and duties of, 238
Bengal, 199
Bentham, J., 45, 403
  greatest happiness, doctrine of, 45, 46
  *Principles of Inter. Law*, 289, 298
Bentwich, Norman, 567
  *The Law of Private Property in War*, 531
Berlin, 365
  congress of, 56
  Final Act of, 146, 148
  treaty of (1878), 87, 88
Berlin decree (1806), 334, 366
*Bermuda*, case of the, 364
Bernard, Mountague, 14
  *Four Lectures on Subjects connected with Diplomacy*, 14
  on neutrality, 368
  on the law concerning the export of contraband, 363
Bernstorff, Count, 365, 369, 378, 387
beseiged areas (*see also* blockade), 325
Bezuidenhout, 427
Bhopal, 233
Bhurtpur state, 210
Bhutan, 215, 216
Bieberstein, Baron Marschall von, 560
Biscay Castile, 61
Bismarck, Prince, 267, 443
Black Book of the British Admiralty, 61
Black Sea, 345
Blenheim, battle of, 91
blockade,
  American system of, 552
  breach of, 253, 312, 465
  by powers not nominally at war, 577
  Cobden on commercial, 355
  commercial, 312-361, 615
  conditions of a lawful, 336
  conventions concerning, 383
  during American Civil War, 257
  effective, 334-337
  English system of, 552

blockade,
  etymology of, 337
  first rules of, 323
  French use of, 336, 520
  great extension of claim for, 329
  history of, 315–338
  inconsistency with regard to, 328, 329, 330, 332
  in time of war, 637
  invention of, by the Dutch, 62, 69, 325
  meaning of the word, 325, 334
  notice of, 551, 665
  pacific, 572–589, 591, 598, 637
  partial and inequitable, 334
  proposal to amend rules of, 520
  rules of, 338–342; considered on ground of justice, 342–352; on ground of general international policy, 352–355; on ground of British policy, 355–359
  use of, by England (1689), 332
  without declaration of war, 578
  without war, 582
blockade of
  Amsterdam, 576
  Brazil, 584
  British Isles, by Dutch (1652), 328
  Buceo, port of, 580
  Buenos Ayres, 580
  Crete, 584, 602
  Flanders, 325, 327
  Formosa, 582, 599
  Gaeta and Messina, 585
  Greek coast, 577, 584
  Mexican ports, 579
  Netherland ports, 578
  New Granada, 579
  Portugal, 328, 329, 332, 578
  Siam, 584
  Venezuela, 585
  Zanzibar, 584
blockade-runners, 1, 86, 521, 665
Bloemfontein Conference, 419, 423, 425, 452
  *Express*, 450
Bluntschli, *Droit International Codifié*, 599
Bodin, 36
*Boedes Lust, The*, 580, 596, 597

bombardment
  law of naval, 556
  of undefended places, 556
  of inhabited fortified cities, 242
  of unfortified places, 243, 280
Bombay, 214
  acquired by cession from Portugal, 197
Borneo, 177
Bosporus, the, 656
Bowles, T. G., 652, 666
Bracton and Glanville, 8
Brandenburg, 198
Brazil, 545, 556, 602
Bremen, 579
British Northwest Co., 165
  South Africa Co., 154
  system in India, 211
Bromberg, 365
Brussels Conference (1874), 247, 533; (1890), 186, 524, 526
  convention, 240, 251
Buchanan, James, 312
  Mr, H.M. Consul for Nyassa, 155
Buenos Ayres, 359
Bulgaria, 87, 90
bullets (*see also* projectiles)
  explosive, 241, 281
Bulmerincq, A. von, 599
  *Die Staatsstreitigkeiten und ihre Entscheidung*, 593
Burge, Mr, 310
Burlamaqui, J. J., 296
  *Droit de la Nature et des Gens*, 288
Burma, 201
Busch, Herr T. H. M., 141, 184
*Buvot* v. *Barbut*, 503
Buxar, victory of, 199
Bynkershoek, Cornelius van, 66–70, 322, 326, 334, 504
  *Dissertatio de Dominio maris*, 67
  *De foro Legatorum tam in causa civili quam criminali liber singularis*, 67
  *Quaestionum Juris Publici libri duo* (1737), 67
  general views, 67
  on the law respecting contraband, 68

Calcutta, 214, 217
California, 376

## INDEX

Calvo, Carlos, *Le Droit International Théorique et Practique*, 177, 599
Camden's Annals, 160
Campbell-Bannerman, Sir H., 554
*Campbell* v. *Hall*, 510
Canada, 174, 414
Canadian rebellion (1838), 117
Canning, Chas. John, 99, 125, 222
Cape of Good Hope, Dutch Colony founded, 426
Capetian kings, 52
Cape Town, 449
Cape Verde Islands, 159
capture of traders at sea, 257
Carnarvon, Lord, 431
Carnatic, Nawab of the, 199
Carolina, grant of, 172
*Caroline*, case of the, 117
Caroline Islands, 180
Carthage, 317
Carthaginians, 317
Cass, Lewis, 312, 339
Castile, 53
Castile and Leon, 159
Castlereagh, Lord, 125
Catharine of Braganza, 197
Catholic Church, 37, 48, 274
Catholics, 55, 275
cession :
    and private property, 132
    by uncivilised natives, 147
    of territory, 132
Cetewayo, 430
Chamberlain, Joseph, 422, 452
Charlemagne, 52
Charles V, 205
charter granted by James I. (1609), 172
    Georgia (1732), 172
Chase, Ch. Justice, U.S.A., 364
Chaudordy, Count de, 261
Chemnitz, Saxony, 63
*Cherokee Nation* v. *State of Georgia*, 157
Chile, 602
China, 82, 102, 522, 556, 582, 599, 623
Chino-Japanese War, 460
chivalry, the age of, 276
Christianity, 37, 274, 290
churches, 37, 48
civilisation, common, of Europe and America, 102

civilisation, government the international test of, 143
civilising influence, alleged international title by, 177
Civil War in U.S.A., 106, 368, 635
claims, legal and moral. 2
    of society, legal and moral, 2, 12
Clive, Lord, 199
coast fisheries, *see* fisheries
Cobden, Richard, on commercial blockade, 355
Cocceji, 483
Cockburn, Sir Alex., 501
Code Napoléon, 259
Cohen, A., 652, 654, 670
Coleridge, Lord, 112, 501
colony, title to land in a new, 137
Colquhoun (B.S.A. Co.), 154
Columbia river, 165, 174
Combermere, Lord, 210
Comfort, Cape, 172
commerce, neutral, 314
*Commerce in War*, 566
commercial blockade (1862), 312-361, 615
Commons, House of, 99
Commonwealth, English, 328
Comoro Islands, 524
companies, 176, 194
    are technical subjects of the state, 195
    Crown responsibility for acts of, 196
    nationality of, in Inter. Law, 494
    territorial sovereignty acquired by, belongs to the Crown, 196
    the relations of, are those of the parent state, 195
company
    British East Africa, 196
    British South Africa, 196
    Dutch East India, 196
    East India, *see* E. I. Co.
    French of St Malo, 176
    German, 176
*Comte de Thomar, Le*, 581
Congo state, 169, 192
conquest
    an institution of Inter. Law, 485

INDEX 691

conquest
   a succession of state to state, 476
   case of a state extinguished by, 491
   excludes cession, 476
   of capital of a state, 476, 489
consent, best evidence of, 83
   the immediate source of international law, 81
Consolat del Mar, 53, 61, 69, 516
consuls, jurisdiction of, 102
contagion of revolution, 123, 202
continuous voyage, doctrine of,
   as affecting goods, 463, 664, 674
   doctrine of, does not apply to breach of blockade, 464
   in relation to contraband of war, 461, 520, 639
   whether the doctrine of, affects persons, 470
contraband of war, 8, 62, 68, 314, 362, 371, 379, 519–522, 534, 535, 639
   absolute, 550, 662, 673
   a rule of, adopted by the Inst. of Inter. Law, 469
   conditional, 550, 662, 673
   continuous voyage in relation to, 461–474
   conventions concerning, 383
   difficulties of enforcing law against export of, 391
   raw cotton as, 662
contracts, set aside by legislative power, 234
contractual debts, 543, 546, 602
contributions in war time, 251, 556
Convention, French-Muscat (1844), 528
   of London, 434, 437, 440, 443
   of Madrid, 528
Convention, May 24th, 1881, 100
convoy, 640
*Cook* v. *Sprigg*, 478, 512
Cornwallis, Lord, 203, 208
*coutumiers*, 293, 294
Covarruvias, 139
Cranworth, Lord, 478
Crimean War, 56, 181, 365, 388, 628

Cromwell, Oliver, 595
Crusades, the, 424
Cuba, 496
custom,
   Bynkershoek on, 68
   introduces law, 27
Cuyuni basin, 416
Cyprus, 432

Dalhousie, Lord, 204
Dalling, Lord, *Life of Lord Palmerston*, 582
Danish fleet, seizure of the, 121
Danubian principalities, 598
Dardanelles, the, 345, 656
debts, *see* contractual debts *and* public loans
Deccan, Nizam of the, 198, 199
Declaration of London, *see* London
Decretal of Gratian, the, 65
Delagoa Bay, 447, 520
Delft, 36
Delhi, 199, 213
   emperor of, 198
Denman, Justice, 112
Denmark, 62
Derby, Lord, 512
devastation of tracts of country, 243, 280
   only allowed conditionally, 242
Dicey, A. V., 610
diplomacy, 377
diplomatic relations, forced on Eastern empires, 6
Discovery (as an International Title), 158
   duties of, 162
   inchoate title by, 163
domicile, Anglo-American prize law and, 610
*Domicile, Nationality or*, 644
   Sir R. Phillimore on the Law of, 505
   trade, 607
*dominium*, 135, 177, 286
   *eminens*, 135
Donellus, 34
*Doss* v. *Secretary of State*, 511
Douai, 32
Drago, Luis M., 546
Drago doctrine, the, 547
Drake, Francis, 160
*droit naturel, le*, 113
droit commun de l'humanité, 114

44—2

droit international, 254, 405
Dumont, 328
Dutch East India Co., 37
Dutch:
    law, 37
    'placards,' 327, 330
    Republic, 37
duties, non-fulfilment of, and title, 169
    of invaded population, 268
    of neutrality, 88
    of occupation and discovery, 162
    of states defined, 78
    perfect and imperfect, 73, 299
dynamite monopoly in the Transvaal, 436

Eastern empires, diplomatic relations with, 6
    Europeans in, 144
East India Company, 194, 195, 197, 510
    declared trustees for Crown of the U.K. (1833), 197
    trusteeship of, terminated (1858), 197
Ebro, 53
Edgar, Mr, 439
Edward I, 9
Edward III, 61, 319
Elbo, 96
Elizabeth, Queen, 160
Ellenborough, Lord, 201, 505, 516
eminent domain, 132, 135
    and the feudal system, 133
Empire of India, 194–236
*Enciclopedia Giuridica*, 135
enemy:
    character, 644
    merchant shipping, 253
    property, *see* property
England, 53, 94
English school of international law, 69
equality and independence of states, 86
Essequibo River, 417
ethics, 12, 13
Euripides, the *Phoenissae*, 37
Exeter Hall, 171
expedition, scientific, and acquisition of rights, 166
extradition, 74
    treaty, Anglo-German, 629

Falkland Islands, 176
Fashoda, 489
*feciales*, college of, 18
federal states, 90
federation of states, 90
Ferdinand and Isabella, 159
Ferrão, J. B. de Martens, 148, 177
    *L'Afrique, etc.*, 148
    on international law and savage tribes, 148
feudal:
    customs, 293
    system, the, 30, 133
    and eminent domain, 133, 222
Field, Dudley, 167
    *Outlines of an International Code*, 167
Finland, 423
Fiore, Pasquale, 669
    *Trattato di Diritto Internazionale Publico*, 135, 167
fisheries, coast, 250
Fitzmaurice, Lord Edward, 460
flag:
    French law concerning use of, 524
    German, hoisted at Angra Pequeña, 443
    transfer to neutral, 642
Flanders, ports of, blockaded, 325, 327
Flemings, 319
Florida, 514
Florida Blanca, Count de, 160
Foote, 610
foreigners, and state jurisdiction, 10
    subject to local courts, 103
    subject to two sovereignties, 128
foreign:
    bond-holder, position of with respect to public loans, 108
    Enlistment Act, 371, 390
    Jurisdiction Act (1890), 188
    state, right of intervention in a, 126
Forrester's *Cases*, 504
France, 36, 52, 54, 61, 86, 88, 224, 541
Francis II, 199
Franco-German War, 260, 369
*Franconia*, case of the, 501

INDEX 693

French Garde Mobile, 372
   law of May 5th, 1866, respecting grant of French flag, 524
French Revolution, 99, 424
   possessions in India, 215
Frere, Sir Bartle, 430
Fry, Sir Edward, 535
Fuller, Ch. Justice (U.S.A.), 525
Fusinato, Guido, 135

*Gaelic*, case of the, 461, 472
Gaius, 20, 22
Gallatin, Mr, 173
Geffcken, Dr, 169, 261
Geneva convention, 240, 278
Genoa, 319
Gentilis, Albericus, 33-36, 48
   *De Jure Belli libri tres*, 30, 33, 34
   *De Legationibus*, 33
   *De Jure Belli commentatio prima*, 34
George II, 595
Georgia Charter, the (1732), 172
"German committee" at Vienna Congress, 96
German flag hoisted at Angra Pequeña, 443
Germans, 291, 292
Germany, 53, 56, 88, 91, 180, 224
Gibraltar, 242, 459
*Gideon Henfield's* case, 505
Gladstone, W. E., 377, 432
Glanville and Bracton, 8
Golab Sing, Maharaja, 211
gold-diggings, new, 168
goods, destination of, 673
   hostile destination of, 674
Goshen, republic of, Land of, 445
government:
   and property, 10, 31
   the international test of civilisation, 143
Grant, Sir J. P., 204
Grant, Sir Wm., 465
grants to Indian native princes, form of, 222
Granville, Lord, 365, 369, 373, 378, 387, 582, 599
Gratian, Decretal of, 25
Gray, Captain, 165, 174
Great Mogul, the, 199
Greece, 17, 99, 100, 203, 290, 359, 676

Grey, Sir Edward, 651, 659, 672
Gronovius, 608
Grotius, Hugo, 27, 36-51, 60, 67, 133, 134, 277, 286, 321, 347, 504, 516, 608
   *De Jure Belli ac Pacis*, 28, 30, 36, 39 ff., 58, 76, 135, 324
   *De Jure prædæ*, 38, 42
   *Mare Liberum*, 38
   *Philosophorum sententiæ de fato*, 37
   against the interference of third parties, 45, 50
   legal distinctions, 41
   *lex loci contractus*, 294, 296
   numerous works, 37, 38
   on natural law, 44
   on contraband, 323
   "Proofs of the true religion," 37
   view of natural law, 50
Grove, Justice, 112
Guastalla, duchy of, 97
Guinea, 159
Gurkha government, 215
Gwalior, 199

*habeas corpus*, 106
Hague Conferences, 53
   Peace Conference, 570, 590, 597
Haiti (Hayti), 104, 535
Hall, W. E., 190, 519, 588
   *Foreign Powers and Jurisdiction of the British Crown*, 185, 186, 191
   *Treatise on International Law*, 107, 109, 117, 120, 129, 130
Halsbury, Lord, Chancellor, 512
Hamburg, 578
Hanover, 91, 96
Hanse towns, 61, 579
Hapsburgs, the, 54, 91
Harding, Lord; 211
*Harmony*, case of the, 609
Hastings, Lord, 209, 213, 233
   his administration, 209
Hautefeuille,
   on neutral rights, 345, 582
   *Droits et Devoirs des Nations Neutres en temps de Guerre Maritime*, 582
Hawaiian Islands, 82
*Heathfield* v. *Clinton*, 504

Heffter, A. W., 583
  *Das Europäisches Völkerrecht der Gegenwart*, 169, 261
Hellenes, the, 17
Hellenic race, the, 274
Henry II, 8
Henry III, 8
Henry VIII, 128
Hiero, 317
Himalaya Mts., 214
hinterland, claims regarding, 173
Hobbes, 48
  *De Cive*, 48, 64, 67
*Hodgson* v. *De Beauchesne*, 609
Hogan, A. E., 583, 587
  *Pacific Blockade*, 572
  "Historical Accounts of the Various Blockades," 587
Holland, Professor, 33, 34, 567, 585, 667
  *Neutral Duties in a Maritime War, as illustrated by recent events*, 531
  *Studies in International Law*, 577, 582
Holland, 36, 37, 38, 99
  and Venezuela, 568
Hollanders, 61
Holtzendorff, Franz von, 134, 165
  *Handbuch des Völkerrechts* 134, 166, 170, 177, 246, 251, 261, 268, 271, 593, 599
Holy Alliance, 59, 424
  Roman Empire, the, 31, 52, 57, 88, 197, 201, 224, 630
hostilities, commencement of, 591
Huber, Max, 310, 482, 510
  *Die Staatensuccession*, 483, 488
Huddleston, Baron, 112
Huguenots, 426
humanity and necessity in war, 273
  in war, 271
Hungarian Diet, 535
Hungary, 53, 92
*Hobbs* v. *Henning*, 468
Hong Kong, 472
Hyderabad, 207

*Imina*, case of the, 466
*Imperium*, 135, 177, 286
inchoate title, 161
  by discovery or occupation, 163

inchoate title,
  ripening of, into complete title, 166
  what geographical extent covered by an, 170
independence, identical with full sovereignty, 86
India:
  British government in, 210
  distinguished from British territory, 226
  infanticide in, 234
  native princes of, cannot unite, 218, 235
  native princes of, have no international existence, 220
  native states in, 621
  suttee in, 234
  *thana* circles in, 227
India, Empire of, 194
  importance of Cape of Good Hope with respect to, 427
  in relation to Constitutional Law, 224
  in relation to International Law, 216
  period of rise of, 213, 214
  "protectorate" in, 220
  rise of, from point of view of International Law, 197
Indian:
  Act, XXI of 1879, 230
  native state, constitutional position of, 228
  princes, subjects of, are British subjects, 228
  system of isolation and subordinate co-operation, 235
Indian Ocean, 523
Institute of International Law, 128, 248, 551, 583, 597, 661
insurgents, and regular war, 272
  and execution of prisoners, 272
insurrection:
  Greek, 203
  in Naples, 124
  in Spain, 126
international:
  arbitration, 541
  Prize Court Convention, 657
  Prize Court, proposed, 550, 554, 645

INDEX 695

international:
　rights of self-preservation, 111–130
　friction, causes of, 51
International law,
　allows rights of self-preservation, 115
　and abstract principles, 57
　and English courts, 518
　and English law, 498
　and international morality, 397
　and international right, 407
　and national law compared, 9, 10, 14
　and private persons, 1, 2
　and uncivilised natives, 138, 139, 146
　based on equal civilisation, 103
　changes in the substance of, 49
　consent the immediate source of, 81
　definition of, 67, 393
　difficulties in formulating and enacting, 280
　first fairly complete treatise on, 39
　foundation of, 27
　has no reference to the individual, 488
　Institute of, 128, 248, 551, 583, 597, 661
　nationality of companies in, 494
　not the same as the Roman *jus gentium*, 19
　of territory, 48
　philosophical part of, 395
　principles of, 78–85
　private, 9, 10, 285, 297
　relation between public and private, 285, 311
　relation of India to, 216, 622, 625
　Renaissance writers on, 25
　Roman law adopted into, 47
　temper needed for the study of, 410
　the body of rules between states, 1–16
　the great desideratum of, 66
　theory bearing on, down to the Renaissance, 17–29

'international morality,' 14
international organisation:
　and the right of intervention, 56
　imperfection of, 56
international relations and internal relations, 409
international rules (*and see* International law), 79
　and states of partial civilisation, 79
international society, 7
　emergence of, 55
　not for the mutual insurance of established governments, 124
　rules defining duties of members of, 60
international titles:
　alleged, by civilising influence, 177
　in uncivilised regions, 169
intervention, right of, 126
invaded countries, treatment of, 278
invaders, 268
Ionian Islands, 218, 627
　republic of the, 181
*Ionian ships, the*, case of, 628
Isidore of Seville, 23, 24, 65
Islands, near the coast, title to, 176
Italy, 52, 317, 541, 676

James I (VI of Scotland), 91
James, Vice-Chancellor (U.S.A.), 480, 482
Jameson Raid, the, 445, 446
*Janson* v. *Driefontein Consolidated Mines*, 608
Japan, 82, 102, 622
Jay, Ch. Justice (U.S.A.), 506
Jay treaty, the (1794), 500
Jibutil, 524
Johannesburg, 438
*Johnson* v. *McIntosh*, 149, 172
Jorissen, Dr, 441
Julius II, Pope, 159
jurisdiction, the limits of a state's, 10
　'delegated,' 231
　'residuary,' 231
　'substituted,' 231
*jus aequatorium*, 41
　*rectorium*, 41

696    INDEX

*jus voluntarium*, 42
   *voluntariun divinum*, 44
*jus Gentium*, 18, 22, 32, 42, 46
   Isidore of Seville's definition of, 25
   Saurez's definition of, 26
*jus militare*, 24
*jus Naturale*, 22, 113
   Saurez's definition of, 26
*justae aetas*, 33
   *nuptiae*, 33
justice, distributive, 40, 49
   expletive, 40
Justinian, 11, 22, 47, 294
   the laws of, 11
   *Institutes of*, 20
*justitia attributrix*, 40
   *expletrix*, 40
*justum bellum*, 33, 35

Kaffirs, 428
Kant, Emmanuel, 73
Kapos-Mére, Mérey de, 535
Karakoram Mts., 214
Kashmir, 211
Kasson, Mr (U.S.A.), 140, 152
Kathiawar, 227
Kennedy, Mr Justice, 498
Khalifa, the, 489
Kingsdown, Lord, 511
*King of the two Sicilies v. Willcox*, 478
*Knight-Commander*, case of the, 641, 660
Konigsberg, 365
Kriegsmanier (*les lois de la guerre*), 243
Kriegsraison (*raison de guerre*), 243, 255
   Lueder on, 244, 264
Kriegsrecht (*le droit de la guerre*), 244
Kruger, President, 419, 422, 431, 440, 444, 452, 459, 487

Laing's Nek, 432
Lake, Viscount, 199
Lambermont, Baron, 176
Lammasch, Dr Hy., 526
Lamu, island of, 176
Laswari, 199
Latifi, *Effects of War on Property*, 613
law, codified, is positive law, 114

law (*see also* International law *and* Natural law)
   introduced by custom, 27
   moral, 45
   necessary condition of the improvement of, 51
   of nations, not the same as the Roman *jus gentium*, 19
   Roman, 37, 159, 291
laws:
   and society, 2
   foreign, ground of reception of, 310
   Jural, 15, 399
   *Jural, and the Laws of Nature*, 4, 10, 11
   national and international, 10
   of England in the reigns of Henry II and Henry III, 8
   of Nature, never broken, 4
   of neutrality, 58
   of war, the improvement of the, 274
Lawrence, Rev. T. J., 567
   *War and Neutrality in the Far East*, 531
Le Bois, Admiral, 665
Lee-Warner, Sir W.
   *Native States of India, The*, 620
   *Protected Princes of India, The*, 203, 209, 212, 215, 221, 226, 233, 236, 620
legitimacy, principle of, 124, 203
Leibnitz, G. W. F. von, 74
Lewis XIII, 36
*lex loci contractus*, 294, 295, 300, 304
*lex non cogit ad impossibilia*, 303
Leyds, Dr, 454
Liberia, 82
Lincoln, President, 106
Lincoln's Inn, 171
Lindley, Lord, 608
Liviano, 36
loans, *see* public loans
Lobengula, accepts British protection, 153
Lohman, A. F. de Savornir, 525
London, Declaration of, 633–672, 651–676
   Naval Conference of, 634, 649, 651, 655, 659, 669
Lords, House of, 99
Lorimer, J., *Institutes of Law*, 73
Louis IX, of France, 222

## INDEX

Louis XIV, 205, 331
Louis XV, 176
Louis XVIII, 94, 97
Louisiana, 172, 174, 302, 310, 514
Low Countries, the, 52, 54
Lubbock, Sir J., 148
Lübeck, 579
Lucan, 37
Lueder, Prof., 244, 247, 251, 259, 261, 264, 267, 269
Lund, 63
Lunéville, 199
Lush, Mr Justice, 501
Lushington, Lord, 641
lynch law, 376

Madrid, Convention of, 528
Magdeburg, 365
    sack of, 39
Mahi Kanta, 227
mails, in time of war, 557
Maine, 414
Majuba Hill, 432
Makololo chiefs, 156
Malacca, straits of, 37
Malins, Vice-Chancellor, 512
Malouines (Falkland Islands), 176
Manipur, 223
Mansfield, Lord, 503, 510
*Manual of the Laws of Land War*, 248
Marcy, W. L. (U.S.A.), 312, 352, 527
Marhattas, the, 198, 199
*Maria*, case of the, 466
marriage, 292
    case of, with Frenchman, 309
    foreign, 304
    Mahometan and Hindoo laws of, 307
    when valid, 127
maritime cities, 53
Marshall, Chief Justice (U.S.A.), 149, 514, 555, 608, 658
Martens, Prof. F. de, *Traité de Droit International*, 136, 599
    on territorial sovereignty, 136
"material guarantee," 598
Mason (and Slidell), 471
Matamoras, 467
May, Sir Erskine, 630
Mayotte, 524
Mediterranean, maritime cities of the, 53, 61, 319

Melos, 17
Mendoza, 159
Mennonites, the, 37
merchantmen, and outbreak of war, 557
    conversion of, at sea, 558, 644, 648
merchant shipping, 253
merchants, neutral, 36
merger of crowns, 123
Mérignhac, A., 566
    *Traité de Droit Public International*, 531
Metcalfe, Sir Charles, 210
Metternich, Prince, 96
Mexico, 149, 353, 602
    declares war on France, 579
middle-distance, doctrine of, 175
military operations,
    particular, with whom responsibility for chiefly rests, 247
    principles relating to particular, 241
Mill, J. S., 73
Milner, Sir Alfred, 419, 425, 451
mines, contact, and neutrals, 560
    unanchored contact, 558
missionary enterprise, 179
    and international title, 180
Mississippi River, 173
Mitylene (Mytilene), 570, 602
Mlauli, treaty with, 156
Mogul empire, the, 198
Mir Kasim, of Bengal, 199
monarchical power, 47
Monomotapa, 152, 178
    "emperor" of, 153
Monroe policy, 416, 546, 547
Montenegro, 100
Montsioa, 444, 445
Moore, J. Bassett, *A Digest of International Law*, 532, 567, 585, 642
Morocco, 527
Mosaic law, 43
Moshette, 444
Mulhar Rao, Gaekwar of Baroda, 221
Munro, Major, 199
Muscat Arabs, 527
    Dhows, the, 1907, 523–530
    Sultan of, 219, 523, 524
Mutassa, *see* Umtasa

44—5

*Nabob of the Carnatic* v. *East India Co.*, 510
Nagasaki, 462
Nantes, edict of, 331
Naples, 53
  insurrection at, 124
Napoleon I, 94, 96, 121, 205, 267, 634
  European alliance against, 97
Napoleonic wars, 258, 278, 516, 661
Natal, 429
nationals of conquered state, position of, 445, 486
native states, 205, 207
  constitutional position of Indian, 228
  no official intercourse between Indian, 217
  of India, 226, 620–632
  political condition of Indian, 216
Natural law, 28, 32
  Grotius's view of, 50
Nature, Grotius on the law of, 44
*Nature, the Law of, as a Jural conception*, 10
Nature, the theory of a state of nature, 11
Naval Conference of London, see London
Navarre, 53
Nepal, 215, 216
Netherlands, 58, 602
neutrals
  and private war, 58
  duty of, towards belligerents, 381
  rights and duties of, 315
  rights of, 61, 322
  trade with belligerents, 365
neutral:
  commerce, 314, 319
  conduct and unneutral, 342, 343
  country, residence in a, 611
  flag, transfer to, 642
  merchants, 36
  property, 61
  prizes, destruction of, 641, 660
  ships and blockades, 1
  states, during American civil war, 257

neutrality:
  armed, 331, 358, 634, 637
  benevolent, 375
  duties of, 88
  first U.S. laws of, 506
  laws of, 58
  partial or unfair, 319
  rules of, are pre-eminently law, 238
  strict, 375
New Orleans, 302
New South Wales, 220, 228
New Testament, 37
Nicholas III, Czar, 533
Nicholas V, Pope, 159
Nootka Sound, 160
Normanby, Lord, 581
North German Confederation, 389
Norway, 97
Nossi-Bé, 524
*Nouvelle Biographie Générale*, 37
Nys, Ernest, *Le Droit de la Guerre et les Précurseurs de Grotius*, 24, 25, 27

occupation, 184
  alleged international title exerted beyond limits of, 177
  as an international title, 158
  duties of, 162
  inchoate title by, 163
*Ocean*, case of the, 467
Odessa, 340
  bombardment of, 280
Old Testament, 37
*Olivier* v. *Townes*, 302
Omdurman, 489
Oppenheim, Dr L., 566
  *International Law*, 531, 556
Orange Free State, 82, 429, 448, 458, 475
  declaration of war by the, 458
Orange River, 428, 443
Oregon dispute, 165, 172
Orissa, 199
*Orozembo*, case of the, 471
Ostend, 326
Ottoman Empire, 203
  Government, 87
  law of Sefer 23, 1280 (Aug. 1863), 528

INDEX 699

Oude, 203, 512
    Nawab Wazir of, 198, 199, 209
Oxford, 33

Pacific Blockade (1909), 572–589
Pakenham, Mr, 173
Palmerston, Lord, 109, 548, 579, 581
papacy, the, and temporal power, 52, 57
papal grants, 159
paramount power, 211
    British the, in India, 211
Paris, 258
    Declaration of, 257, 261, 262, 267, 516, 666
    treaty of (1856), secret articles in the, 94
Parma, duchy of, 97
Parthian empire, the, 25, 57
Paul of Russia, Emperor, 358
*pax Britannica*, 208
peace, an unfair, 65
    treaty of, 239
Peace Conference of 1899, the, 533, 542
Peace Conference of 1907, the, 533, 542
Peace of Westphalia, *see* Westphalia
Pennsylvania, grant of, 172
pentarchy of Europe, the, 99, 124
Peel, Sir Robert, 579
Perels, 583
Permanent Court of Arbitration (*and see* arbitration), 545
Persia, 102, 556, 623
Persian Gulf, 523
Peru, 149
Perugia, university of, 33
Peshwa, 209
petition of right, 509, 513
Peyresc, 38
Philip II, 159
Phillimore, Sir Robert, 505, 610,
    on the law of domicile, 505
philology and international law, 138
Pierce, Franklin, 312, 364, 367
pillage, 267, 278
Pillet, *Le Droit International Public*, 114
    on primary rights, 114

Pinheiro-Ferreira, 289
pirates, 1, 86
Placentia, duchy of, 97
Plataea, 17
poison, use of in war forbidden, 241, 281
Poland, 53, 423, 489
    suppression of, 202
Polish Diet, 535
Political Inequality of States, and the Great Powers of Europe, 92
Pollock, Baron, 112
Polybius, 317
Pomponius, 18, 21
Pondoland, 480, 512
population,
    of occupied territory, 557
    treatment of peaceable, in war time, 250
Portalis, M., 268
    on the French prize court, 266
Porter, Gen. (U.S.A.), 548
Portugal, 53, 61, 94, 139, 148, 153, 159
Portuguese, 37, 161
    possessions in India, 215
    treaties with African natives, 153
Posen, 365
Pragmatic Sanction, the, 92
Pretoria, 433
    Convention, 433, 440
    *Volksstem*, 450
principles of international law, the, 78
prisoners, killing of, prohibited, 272
private rights in foreign countries, 9
privateering, 278, 312, 506
prizes, captured, 656
    destruction of neutral, 558
prize court
    and blockades, 551
    English, 334
    French, 266
    proposed international, 550, 645, 651, 655, 667
    U.S.A., 334
Procopius, 37
prohibitions against killing prisoners, 272
    in war, 241, 247, 281

700                                INDEX

projectiles, explosive, 241, 281
    red hot, 242
property,
    and government, 11, 31
    and interests of citizens, 289
    and sovereignty, 131
    and territory, 10
    enemy, 61, 615
    enemy, at sea, 558, 649
    modes of, 301
    neutral, 61
    of a conquered state, 489
    private, treatment of, in war time, 250, 278, 312, 615
    Roman law of, 48
    the international question of, 302
    title to, 301
protected state,
    acquirement of imperial right over, 214
    falls under head of semi-sovereignty, 181
protection of persons not subjects, 523
protectorate,
    and acquisition of territory, 188
    classical passage respecting, in uncivilised regions, 183
    in India, 220
    in uncivilised regions, 181, 183, 220
*protégés*, 526
Protestant cause in Europe in the 15th century, 54
Protestants, 55, 275
Prussia, 94
public loans, 108, 547
    defaults on, 109
    European governments and, 549
    United States and, 548
Pufendorff, 48, 52, 63
    *De Jure Naturae et Gentium* (1672), 48, 63, 67
    his international principles, 64
    on an unfair peace, 65
Punic war, first, 317

quarter, not to be refused, when fight is over, 242
Queen v. *Dudley and Stephens*, 112
    v. *Keyn*, 190, 516

Rahming, case of, 106
*Rapid*, case of the, 466
Red Cross societies, 279
Red Sea, 523, 656
Reformation, the, 55, 275
*Reg* v. *Keyn*, 501
Reitz, S. W., 455
religion, wars of, 275, 277
Renaissance, the, 17, 25, 28, 31, 47, 49
Renault, M., 536, 553, 564, 652
reprisal, 569
    and war, 590–606
    "pretended," 595
requisitions, 251, 556, 616
retaliation, *see* retorsion
retorsion, 238, 259–264
    imprisonment of notables as an act of, 261, 263
    severities against persons in the power of the enemy in cases of, 271
revolution, 123, 407
    the suppression of, 124, 202
*Revue de Droit International et de législation comparée*, 531
*Revue Générale de Droit International Public*, 114
Rewa Kanta, 227
Richmond (U.S.A.), 258
right of intervention, 56
rights:
    and duties of states, 78
    and immunities of combatants and non-combatants, 273
    belligerent, at sea, 613–619
    grave difference between moral and legal, 114
    "imperfect," 76, 83
    international, of self-preservation, 111, 202
    jural and moral, 407
    primary, the foundation of law, 113
*Rights and Wrongs*, 16
rights, territorial, of states, 48
    of individuals, 48
rivers, international, 75
Rivier, Alphonse
    *Lehrbuch des Völkerrechts*, 244
    *Principes du Droit des Gens*, 481, 486
*robe d'ennemi confisque robe d'ami*, 61

# INDEX

Robinson, Sir Hercules (Lord Rosmead), 440
Roman Empire, the, 274
  dissolution of, 23, 48
  jurists, 287
Roman law, 11, 159, 291
  adopted into international law, 47
  and foreigners, 19
  and monarchical power, 47
  called written reason, 47
  of property, 48
  private 31, 321
Roman republic, 274, 290
Romans, 317
Rome, 17, 18, 22, 57, 317
  confusion in legal matters after the conquest of, 291
  courts of law at, 19
Roosevelt, Theodore, 533
Rosas, Juan Manuel de, 580
Roumania, 100
Rousseau, J. J., 616
  *Contrat Social*, 254, 262, 265
Royal Commission on the Supply of Food and Raw Material in time of war, 519
*rudimentary commerce*, 178
  *relations*, 177
*Rule of the War of* 1756, 644, 648, 659
Russell, Earl, 106
Russia, 56, 94, 203, 423, 656
  enters the European system, 56, 100
Russian Volunteer Navy, 656
Russo-Japanese War, 538, 560, 635, 641, 660
Russo-Turkish War, 279, 432, 541
*Rustonjee* v. *Reg*, 513
Ruy de Barbosa, 537

sack of places taken by storm prohibited, 241
Salic law, the, 91
Salisbury, Lord, 109, 460, 548
Sand River Convention, 440
San Ginesio, 33
San Juan de Ulloa, fort of, 602
San Marino, republic of, 182, 220
San Stefano, treaty of, 100
Sardinia, 56, 541
Sarje Arjengaon, treaty of, 199
Satow, Sir Ernest, 561
Sattara, 204
Savannah, 258
  river, 172
Savigny, *Gesch. des Römisches Rechts*, 292
Saxony, 96
  king of, deprived of portion of his dominion, 96
Scandinavia, 53
Schomburgk line, 415, 416
Schreiner, Mr, 447
Schurz, Mr, 414
Scotland, 53
Scott's *Cases on International Law*, 501
Scott, Sir W. (Lord Stowell), 163, 323, 463, 515, 555, 576, 597, 609, 641
seamen, detained as prisoners, 260
Sebastopol, siege of, 339
*Secretary of State* v. *Komachee*, 511
Sekokuni, 430
Selden, John, 38, 69, 262
  *Mare Clausum*, 38
self-defence, 5
  permissible to a state, 116
*self-preservation*:
  as an alleged Primary Right, 111
  International rights of, 111, 202
self-preservation, 129
  alleged right of, against contagion of revolution, 123
  cases illustrating rules governing right of, 116
  not always considered an absolute right, 113
  rights of, allowed by International law, 115
  Wolff on, 113
semi-sovereignty (*and see* sovereignty), 86, 89
  of protected state, 181
Servia, 87, 100
Seven Years' War, 93, 594, 597
Shah Alam, 200
Shanghai, 462
shareholders, company, 617
  in conquered territory, 494
Shepstone, Sir Theophilus, 430
shipwrecked crew, 112

# INDEX

Siam, 102, 201, 215, 623
Sicily, *see also* the Two Sicilies, 317
siege, 326, 327
Sigcan, 480, 512
Sikkim, 215
Sindhia, Marhatta, ruler of Gwalior, 199
Sivewright, Sir James, 449
Slade, Admiral, 653, 665
Slagter's Nek, 427
slavery, 32, 409
slaves in South Africa, 427
slave trade, 228, 527
    E. African, 524
Slidell (Mason &), 471
Smith, F. E. and Sibley, N. W., 567, 577
    *International Law as interpreted during the Russo-Japanese War*, 531, 577
socialism, 275
social life, similarity of, in Europe and America, 101
society,
    impossible without law, 3
    international and national, 7
    requires regulations, 50
    the growth of, 50, 407
Society of States, 78
    and private rights, 9
    a secular one, 56
    compared with other Societies, 6
    composition of about 1648, 57
Socinians, 37
Soto, 139
South African Railway case and International law, 490–497
South African Republic, 418–460, 474, 508
    a sovereign international state, 430
    aliens and the, 435, 437
    declaration of war by the, 422
South African War, 419–460, 520, 538, 555, 635
sovereignty (*see also* semi-sovereignty and territorial sovereignty), 86, 130
    and absent subjects, 299
    and property, 131

sovereignty
    exclusive local authority of, 298
    full, is independence, 87, 111
    right of, may be abandoned, 168
    territorial, *see* territorial sovereignty
Spain, 38, 54, 91, 94, 139, 159, 176, 180, 496, 595
Spaniards, 161
Spanish American States, 545, 546
Spanish-American War, 635
Spanish Armada, the, 33, 34
Spheres of Influence, 191
Sprigg, Sir J. Gordon, 449
*Staadt Embden, The*, case of, 576
State,
    a, defined, 127, 270
    Bhurtpur, 210
    case of a, extinguished by conquest, 491
    international idea of a, 394
    position of nationals of a conquered, 475
    property of conquered, 489
    recognition of a new, 485
    succession of state to, and succession in private law, 485
    succession of state to, nature of, 481
    ties, indispensable to the welfare of men, 113
states,
    American, 81
    and the right to punish foreigners, 128
    Catholic, 56
    duties of neutral, 559
    equality of, in civilisation, 101
    equality and independence of, 86–110
    European, in the 14th century, 53
    growth of mutual interest between, 55
    independence of, prior to International law, 647
    political inequality of, 92
    Protestant, 56
    rights and duties of, 78
    rules prevailing between, 2
    small, 93

INDEX 703

states
    sovereign and semi-sovereign, 86
    weak, 58
*Stanley* v. *Bernes*, 609
Stead, W. T., 565
    *Arbiter in Council, The*, 531, 566
    *Courrier de la Conférence de la Paix*, 531
Stellaland, Republic of, 445
*Stephen Hart*, case of the, 467
Steyn, M. T., 449
Stoics, 22
Stoic philosophy, 274, 279
Stowell, Lord, *see* Scott
St Petersburg convention, 240, 241, 278, 659
Suarez, 25, 48, 60, 64
    definition of *jus gentium* and *jus naturale*, 26
    *Tractatus de Legibus et Deo Legislatore*, 27
subjects,
    absent, and the authority of sovereigns, 299
    relation of, to a war, 264, 267
    right of interference on behalf of, 105
    rule of non-interference for the protection of, 101, 107
Sublime Porte (*see* Turkey), 81, 90
Suliman Mts., 214
Sulu Archipelago, 177
Suzerainty, 90
Sweden, 36, 54, 62, 94
Swiss cantons, 288
Switzerland, 58

Tacitus, 37
Takahashi, Professor, 461
Talbot, Lord, 504
Talleyrand, 95, 97
Tanjore, Raj of, 511
territorial sovereignty (*and see* sovereignty), 131, 183
    and private property, 136
    and uncivilised regions, 131–193
    distinguished from property, 131
    inchoate title to, 183
    non-fulfilment of duties of, 169, 187
    Prof. Martens on, 136

territorial sovereignty
    the title to, 136
territorial waters, right of fishery in, 507
Territorial Waters Jurisdiction Act (1878), 501
territory and property, 10
    international law of, 48
    title to national, 321
Texas, 475
Thirty Years War, the, 36, 39
Thomasius, Christian, 73
Thorn, 365
three-miles limit, the, 190
Thucydides, 17
Thurlow, Lord Chancellor, 597
Tiber, the, 52
Tibet, 215
Tilsit, treaty of, 121
title
    and non-fulfilment of duties, 169, 187
    by conquest, nature and extent of, 473–489
    inchoate, 161
    international, in uncivilised regions, 169
    to islands near the coast, 176
    to land, in a new colony, 137
    to national territory, 321
Tobago, Island of, 169
Tordesillas, treaty of, 159
Tornielli, Count, 535
Tournay, 32
trade domicile in war, 607–612
transfer to neutral flag, 642
Transvaal Concessions Commission, 478, 483, 484, 493
Transvaal, 433
    British suzerainty over the, 454, 455
    education in the, 437
    franchise in the, 453
    press law of the, 450
    ultimatum issued by government of the, 456
Transvaal Republic, 425, 429, 520
    a sovereign international state, 430
Transvaal War, the, 419–460
    causes of the, 457
treaties,
    with Indian princes, 211
    with uncivilised tribes, 145, 151, 153, 155

Treaty,
    Anglo-Dutch (1674), 330
    Anglo-French (1655), 328, 329
    Anglo-German extradition (1872), 629
    Anglo-Muscat (1873), 524
    Anglo-Swedish (1661), 329
    Dutch-Algerian, 329
    Dutch-Swedish (1667), 329, 338, (1679), 330
    Franco-Dutch (1646), 327, (1678), 330
    Franco-Muscat (1844), 524, 528
    Franco-Spanish, 328, 329
    Holland-Denmark (1701), 334
Treaty:
    between England and Baltic States (1801), 341
    between France and Morocco (1863), 528
    of Basle (1795), 199
    of Bassein (1802), 205, 206
    of Paris (1856), 56, 81, 312, 336, 340
    of Sarje Arjengaon, 199
    of Tilsit, 121
    of Tordesillas, 159
    of Umritsur (1846), 211
    with Lobengula, 153
    with Yarkand, 219
treaty, power of making law by, in U.S.A., 500
    Jay (1794), 500
treaty and private rights, 499, 507
Trek, the great, 427
*Trent*, the incident of the, 471
Tribur, council of, 292
Triple Alliance, the, 539
*Triquet* v. *Bath*, 503
Troppau, 124
Tunis, 178, 182
Tupper, C. L., *Our Indian Protectorate*, 200, 204, 205, 209
Turkey (*see* Sublime Porte), 56, 82, 95, 345, 527, 570, 601, 676
    enters the European system, 56, 102, 103, 203
Turkish revolution, 601
Tuscany, 97
Twiss, Sir Travers
    *Oregon Question*, 160, 161, 172
    *Law of Nations, Peace*, 173, 175, 597
Two Sicilies, the, 601

*ubi societas ibi jus est*, 2, 3, 16, 60
Uitlanders, 418–460
    in S. A. Republic, 438
Ulpian, 22
Umritsur, 211
Umtasa, or Mutassa, 154, 171
    treaty between, and the B.S.A. Co., 154
uncivilised natives
    and international law, 138, 139, 146
    treaties with, 145, 151
    United States and, 150
uncivilised regions, 169
    protectorates in, 181
undefended areas, declaration concerning, 247
United Kingdom, 88
United Netherlands, 58
United Provinces, the, 36
United States, the, 88, 89, 106, 117, 157, 165, 219, 224, 545
    Constitution of, 225
*United States* v. *Percheman*, 514
*U.S. of America* v. *Prioleau*, 478
*Unneutral Service*, 640
Uruguay, Republic of, blockade of a port of, 580
Ullman, Professor, 669

Vaal River, 428, 446
Van Bokkelen, case of, 104
*vassalage*, 177
Vattel, Emerich de, 76, 77, 89, 160, 165, 322, 505, 563, 569, 593, 604
    *Le Droit des Gens, ou principes de la loi naturelle appliqués à la conduite et aux affaires des nations et des souverains* (1758), 76, 86, 105, 288
Venetians, 294
Venezuela, 546, 568
    blockade of, by England and Germany, 585
    Boundary Question (1896), 414–418
    gunboats belonging to, seized by Holland, 590
Venice, 53, 294, 319
*Venus*, case of the, 658
Vespucci, Amerigo, 176
Victoria, Guadalupe, 139

INDEX 705

Victoria, Queen, 491, 541, 580
Vienna, Congress of, 56, 95, 124
Virginia, 172, 174
*Virginius*, case of the, 118
*Viveash* v. *Becker*, 505
Vladivostok, 642, 659
*Völkerrecht, das*, 67, 254
volunteer navy, Russian, 656

*Walker* v. *Baird*, 507
war:
  a relation of state to state, 269
  and private violence, 32
  considered by Ayala not incompatible with law, 32
  declaration of, 320, 540, 590
  destruction of private property during, 615
  improvement of the laws of, 274
  international military code of, 240
  laws of land, 557
  laws of, between belligerents, 238, 560
  mitigation of, 273, 274, 277
  not a relation of individual to individual, 270
  object of, 614
  of religion, 275
  outbreak of and merchantmen, 557
  principles relating to the conduct of, 243
  prisoners of, 17
  private, and neutrals, 58
  rates of insurance, 256
  relation of subjects to a, 264
  reprisals and, 590
  rule of the, of 1756, 644, 648, 659
  rules of, considered as laws, 237–282
Warren, Sir Charles, 445
wars, dynastic, 618
Waterloo, 98
Wellesley (Lord), 199, 200, 203, 208, 232
West African Conference of Berlin, 522
West Indian Islands, British, 368
Westlake, J.,
  *Chapters on the Principles of International Law*, 620, 626
  *International Law*, 531

Westphalia, Peace of, 37, 48, 49, 51, 55, 66, 77, 81, 122, 197
  and Pufendorff, 52–65
  magnitude of the questions intended to be settled by the, 55
*West Rand Central Gold Mining Co.* v. *Rex*, 498, 510, 513
Wharton, 610
  *Digest of the International Law of the United States*, 104, 120, 173
  *State Trials of the United States*, 505
Wheaton, H., 149, 608
  *Elements of International Law*, 658
  Supreme Court Reports, U.S.A., 149, 150, 151
*Whitney* v. *Robertson*, 501
Wicquefort, 504
Wilhelmina, Queen, 534
William I, 223
William III, 91
*William*, case of the, 466
Wills, Mr Justice, 498
Wilson, 654
Wolff, 70, 76–89
  *Jus Gentium methodo scientifica pertractatum, in quo jus gentium naturale ab eo quod voluntarii pactitii et consuetudinarii est accurate distinguitur* (1749), 71, 86, 289, 299
  his legacy to international law, 71
  and the "right of security," 73
  on "self-preservation," 113
*Wolff* v. *Oxholm*, 517
Wood, Sir E., 440
wounded and sick, care of, 278
  killing of, prohibited, 241
Wurtemberg, 96
Wylie, 671

Yarkand, 219
Yokohama, 461

Zanzibar, 178, 182
  Sultan of, 176
Zollverein, States of the, 365
Zouch, 69

For EU product safety concerns, contact us at Calle de José Abascal, 56–1°, 28003 Madrid, Spain or eugpsr@cambridge.org.

www.ingramcontent.com/pod-product-compliance
Ingram Content Group UK Ltd.
Pitfield, Milton Keynes, MK11 3LW, UK
UKHW010855060825
461487UK00012B/1133